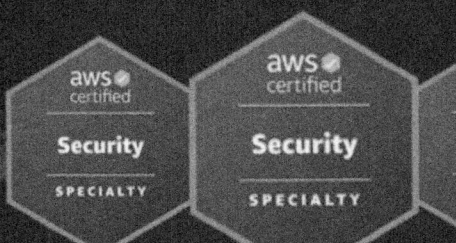

CW01338244

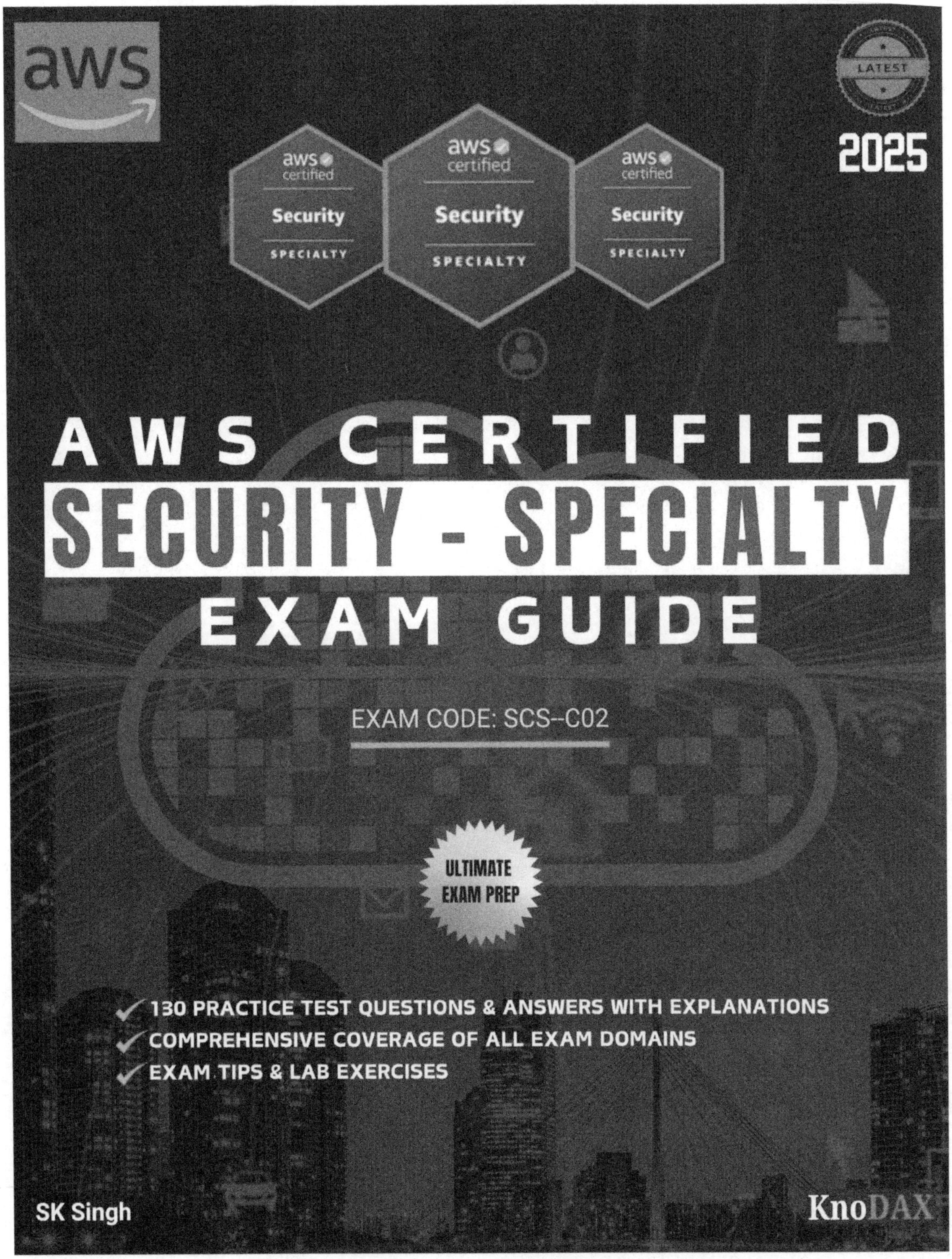
aws
aws certified
Security
SPECIALTY
aws certified
Security
SPECIALTY
aws certified
Security
SPECIALTY
LATEST
2025
AWS CERTIFIED
SECURITY - SPECIALTY
EXAM GUIDE
EXAM CODE: SCS--C02
ULTIMATE
EXAM PREP
130 PRACTICE TEST QUESTIONS & ANSWERS WITH EXPLANATIONS
COMPREHENSIVE COVERAGE OF ALL EXAM DOMAINS
EXAM TIPS & LAB EXERCISES
SK Singh
KnoDAX

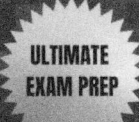

Copyright © 2024 KnoDAX All rights reserved.

The characters and events portrayed in this book are fictitious. Any similarity to real persons, living or dead, is coincidental and not intended by the author.

No part of this book may be reproduced, or stored in a retrieval system, or transmitted in any form or by any means, electronic, mechanical, photocopying, recording, or otherwise, without express written permission of the publisher.

**TABLE OF CONTENTS**

# BECOMING CERTIFIED IN AWS CERTIFIED SECURITY - SPECIALTY ...... 15

# INTRODUCTION ...... 17

# CHAPTER 1. INTRODUCTION TO AWS SECURITY ...... 19

## 1.1 Introduction to AWS Security Certification ...... 20
### 1.1.1 What Security is Not ...... 20
### 1.1.2 What Security is ...... 20

## 1.2 Basic Security Concepts ...... 22
### 1.2.1 Vulnerability, Threat, and Security Risk ...... 22
### 1.2.2 Security Controls or Security Countermeasures ...... 22
### 1.2.3 Confidentiality, Integrity, and Availability (CIA Triad) ...... 23
### 1.2.4 Accountability and Nonrepudiation ...... 23
### 1.2.5 Authentication, Authorization, and Accounting ...... 23

## 1.3 Networking Foundational Concepts ...... 24
### 1.3.1 The OSI Reference Model ...... 24
### 1.3.2 The TCP/IP Model ...... 26
#### 1.3.2.1 The Internet Protocol (IP) Layer ...... 26
#### 1.3.2.2 The Transport Layer ...... 27

## 1.4 Different Types of Cyber Attacks ...... 27
### 1.4.1 Reconnaissance ...... 28
### 1.4.2 Password Attacks ...... 28
### 1.4.3 Eavesdropping Attacks ...... 28
### 1.4.4 IP Spoofing Attacks ...... 29
### 1.4.5 Man-in-the-Middle (MITM) Attacks ...... 29
### 1.4.6 DDoS Attacks ...... 29
#### 1.4.6.1 Volumetric DDoS (Layer 3 DDoS) ...... 30
#### 1.4.6.2 Protocol DDoS (Layer 4 DDoS) ...... 30
#### 1.4.6.3 Application DDoS ...... 30
### 1.4.7 Malware Attacks ...... 30
### 1.4.8 Phishing Attacks ...... 31

## 1.5 Security Defense Management ...... 31

## 1.6 Key Security Solutions and Services ...... 31
### 1.6.1 Firewall ...... 31
### 1.6.2 Web Proxy ...... 32
### 1.6.3 Web Application Firewalls ...... 33
### 1.6.4 Intrusion Detection and Intrusion Prevention ...... 34
### 1.6.5 Virtual Private Networks ...... 34
#### 1.6.5.1 IPSec VPN ...... 35
#### 1.6.5.2 SSL VPN ...... 35

## 1.7 Tools for Vulnerability Analysis and Management ...... 35

## 1.8 Security Information and Event Management ...... 36

1.9 TLS/SSL Offload ........................................................................................... 37

1.10 Well-Known Security Frameworks and Models ...................................... 37

1.11 Security Controls ....................................................................................... 38

1.12 The Security Wheel ................................................................................... 38

1.13 The Attack Continuum Model .................................................................. 39

1.14 The Zero-Trust Model ............................................................................... 40

1.15 Chapter Review Questions ....................................................................... 41

1.16 Answers to Chapter Review Questions .................................................. 42

## CHAPTER 2. CLOUD SECURITY PRINCIPLES AND FRAMEWORKS ........................ 44

2.1 Cloud Security Principles ............................................................................ 45

2.2 Key Cloud Security Principles ..................................................................... 45

2.3 Overview of AWS Security Framework ...................................................... 46

2.4 AWS Shared Responsibility Model ............................................................. 48

2.5 Security Best Practices Documentation .................................................... 49

2.6 AWS Compliance Programs ........................................................................ 49

2.7 AWS Artifact Portal ..................................................................................... 52

2.8 AWS Marketplace ........................................................................................ 53

2.9 Lab Exercises ............................................................................................... 53
    2.9.1 Generating PCI DSS Report ................................................................. 53
    2.9.2 Check ISO 27001 .................................................................................. 54

2.10 Chapter Review Questions ....................................................................... 54

2.11 Answers to Chapter Review Questions ................................................... 56

## CHAPTER 3. AUTHENTICATION OF AWS RESOURCES ........................................ 57

3.1 Introduction to Authentication in AWS ..................................................... 58

3.2 Methods and Services for Creating and Managing Identities .................. 59
    3.2.1 AWS IAM (Identity and Access Management) ................................... 59
    3.2.2 AWS IAM Identity Center (AWS Single Sign-On) ............................... 59
    3.2.3 Amazon Cognito .................................................................................. 60

3.3 Identity Federation ..................................................................................... 61
    3.3.1 Identity Federation In AWS ................................................................. 61

    3.3.2 Federation and Identity Providers ..................................................................................62
    3.3.3 Integrating External Identity Providers .............................................................................63

3.4 Credential Mechanisms....................................................................................................... 63
    3.4.1 Long-term Credentials..............................................................................................63
    3.4.2 Temporary Credentials with AWS STS (Security Token Service) ........................................64
    3.4.3 Managing MFA Devices .............................................................................................65

3.5 Troubleshooting Authentication Issues ................................................................................ 65
    3.5.1 Using AWS CloudTrail for Troubleshooting ..................................................................65
    3.5.2 IAM Access Advisor ..................................................................................................66
    3.5.3 IAM Policy Simulator ................................................................................................66

3.6 Best Practices for Authentication......................................................................................... 67
    3.6.1 Implementing the Principle of Least Privilege...............................................................67
    3.6.2 Regularly Rotating Credentials...................................................................................68
    3.6.3 Auditing and Monitoring Authentication Activities........................................................69

3.7 Lab Exercises..................................................................................................................... 70
    3.7.1 Creating and Managing IAM Users and Groups .............................................................70
    3.7.2 Setting Up and Configuring MFA .................................................................................71
    3.7.3 Using AWS STS for Temporary Credentials ...................................................................72
    3.7.4 Troubleshooting Authentication Issues with CloudTrail and IAM Tools ............................73
        3.7.4.1 Setting Up AWS CloudTrail for Logging ................................................................73
        3.7.4.2 Using IAM Access Advisor to Review Permissions .................................................74
        3.7.4.3 Using IAM Policy Simulator to Test Permissions ...................................................74
        3.7.4.4 Troubleshooting Common Authentication Issues..................................................75

3.8 Key Exam Tips ................................................................................................................... 75

3.9 Chapter Review Questions ................................................................................................. 76

3.10 Answers to Chapter Review Questions ............................................................................... 78

## CHAPTER 4. AUTHORIZATION OF AWS RESOURCES ..................................................... 81

4.1 Introduction to Authorization in AWS.................................................................................. 82

4.2 IAM Policies....................................................................................................................... 83
    4.2.1 Managed Policies .....................................................................................................83
    4.2.2 Inline Policies..........................................................................................................83
    4.2.3 Identity-Based Policies .............................................................................................85
    4.2.4 Resource-Based Policies...........................................................................................86
    4.2.5 Session Control Policies ...........................................................................................87
    4.2.6 Session Policies with AWS STS...................................................................................87

4.3 IAM Policy Components and Impact.................................................................................... 89
    4.3.1 IAM Policy Structure ................................................................................................89
    4.3.2 Effect of Policies on Environments and Workloads .......................................................90
    4.3.3 Interpreting an IAM Policy's Effect .............................................................................90

4.4 Constructing Access Control Strategies ............................................................................... 92
    4.4.1 Attribute-Based Access Control (ABAC)......................................................................92
    4.4.2 Steps to Construct ABAC Policies ...............................................................................92

4.4.3 Role-Based Access Control (RBAC)..................................................................................93

**4.5 Applying the Principle of Least Privilege ............................................................................ 95**
4.5.1 Implementing Least Privilege ............................................................................................95
4.5.2 Enforcing Separation of Duties ..........................................................................................97

**4.6 Troubleshooting Authorization Issues .................................................................................. 99**
4.6.1 Using AWS CloudTrail for Authorization Troubleshooting...............................................99
4.6.2 IAM Access Advisor .........................................................................................................100
4.6.3 IAM Policy Simulator ......................................................................................................102
4.6.4 Analyzing Access Errors ..................................................................................................103

**4.7 Best Practices for Authorization ........................................................................................ 104**
4.7.1 Regular Policy Audits ......................................................................................................104
4.7.2 Monitoring and Logging...................................................................................................106

**4.8 Lab Exercises....................................................................................................................... 107**
4.8.1 Creating and Applying IAM Policies ...............................................................................107
4.8.2 Constructing ABAC and RBAC Policies..........................................................................109
4.8.3 Troubleshooting Authorization Issues ..............................................................................112

**4.9 Key Exam Tips .................................................................................................................... 114**

**4.10 Chapter Review Questions ............................................................................................... 115**

**4.11 Answers to Chapter Review Questions ........................................................................... 117**

# CHAPTER 5. DETECTIVE CONTROLS ..................................................................... 119

**5.1 AWS Security Detective Controls......................................................................................120**

**5.2 Detective Controls Process Flow Framework ...................................................................120**

**5.3 Stage 1: Resources State.....................................................................................................122**
5.3.1 AWS Config ......................................................................................................................122
5.3.2 Configuration Recorder ...................................................................................................123

**5.4 Stage 2: Events Collection ..................................................................................................123**
5.4.1 AWS CloudTrail ...............................................................................................................123
    5.4.1.1 CloudTrail Event Types .........................................................................................125
    5.4.1.2 CloudTrail Integration............................................................................................125
    5.4.1.3 How AWS CloudTrail Protects Records ................................................................126
    5.4.1.4 Regional Scoped Service ........................................................................................126
    5.4.1.5 AWS Organizations Scope .....................................................................................127
5.4.2 Amazon CloudWatch ........................................................................................................127
5.4.3 Amazon CloudWatch Logs ...............................................................................................128
5.4.4 Amazon Log Group, Log Steams, and Log Event............................................................129
5.4.5 AWS Health......................................................................................................................130

**5.5 Stage 3: Events Analysis ....................................................................................................131**
5.5.1 AWS Config Rules ............................................................................................................131
    5.5.1.1 Config Rules Notifications .....................................................................................131
5.5.2 Amazon Inspector ............................................................................................................132
    5.5.2.1 Amazon Inspector Assessment Template...............................................................132

  5.5.3 Amazon GuardDuty.................................................................................................. 133
  5.5.4 AWS Security Hub ................................................................................................... 135
  5.5.5 AWS Systems Manager ............................................................................................ 135

**5.6 Stage 4: Action..................................................................................................................141**
  5.6.1 AWS Systems Manager: SSM Automation............................................................. 142
  5.6.2 AWS Config Rules: Remediation............................................................................. 142
  5.6.3 Amazon EventBridge ............................................................................................... 142
    5.6.3.1 EventBridge Generic Workflow ................................................................ 143
    5.6.3.2 Integration of Amazon GuardDuty and AWS Security Hub ..................... 144

**5.7 Lab Exercises....................................................................................................................145**
  5.7.1 How to Enable Configuration Recorder ................................................................. 145
  5.7.2 How to Set Up a Trail in CloudTrail ......................................................................... 150
  5.7.3 Create Amazon CloudWatch Alarm ........................................................................ 151
  5.7.4 AWS CloudTrail and CloudWatch Logs integration ............................................... 151
  5.7.5 Enable Amazon GuardDuty in Your AWS Account ................................................ 152
  5.7.6 How to Enable AWS Security Hub in your AWS Account ...................................... 153
  5.7.7 AWS Config Rules Remediation............................................................................... 153
  5.7.8 AWS CloudTrail Integration with Amazon EventBridge ........................................ 154

**5.8 Key Exam Tips ..................................................................................................................155**

**5.9 Chapter Review Questions ..............................................................................................156**

**5.10 Answers to Chapter Review Questions ........................................................................158**

## CHAPTER 6. THREAT DETECTION AND INCIDENT RESPONSE .......................... 160

**6.1 Introduction to Threat Detection and Incident Response.............................................161**

**6.2 Designing an Incident Response Plan.............................................................................162**
  6.2.1 AWS Best Practices for Incident Response ............................................................ 162
  6.2.2 Understanding Cloud Incidents............................................................................... 162
  6.2.3 Roles and Responsibilities in Incident Response................................................... 163
  6.2.4 AWS Security Finding Format (ASFF) ..................................................................... 164

**6.3 Implementing Incident Response Strategies ................................................................165**
  6.3.1 Credential Invalidation and Rotation ..................................................................... 165
  6.3.2 Isolating AWS Resources......................................................................................... 166

**6.4 Playbooks and Runbooks .................................................................................................168**
  6.4.1 Playbook ................................................................................................................... 168
  6.4.2 Runbook ................................................................................................................... 168
  6.4.3 Example Scenario: Phishing Attack ........................................................................ 168
  6.4.4 Designing Playbooks and Runbooks ...................................................................... 169

**6.5 Deploying AWS Security Services ...................................................................................171**
  6.5.1 AWS Security Hub .................................................................................................... 171
  6.5.2 Amazon GuardDuty.................................................................................................. 173
  6.5.3 Amazon Macie ......................................................................................................... 174
  6.5.4 Amazon Inspector ................................................................................................... 175
  6.5.5 AWS Config .............................................................................................................. 176
  6.5.6 Amazon Detective.................................................................................................... 177

- 6.5.7 AWS IAM Access Analyzer .................................................................................. 179

## 6.6 Configuring Integrations with Native and Third-Party Services ........................... 180
- 6.6.1 Using Amazon EventBridge............................................................................... 180
- 6.6.2 Integrating AWS Services with Third-Party Tools.......................................... 182

## 6.7 Best Practices for Threat Detection and Incident Response................................... 184
- 6.7.1 Continuous Monitoring and Alerting ............................................................... 184
- 6.7.2 Regular Incident Response Drills..................................................................... 185
- 6.7.3 Post-Incident Analysis and Improvement ...................................................... 186

## 6.8 Lab Exercises.................................................................................................................. 188
- 6.8.1 Creating an Incident Response Plan ................................................................ 188
- 6.8.2 Deploying AWS Security Services .................................................................... 190
- 6.8.3 Configuring Event-Driven Security Automation ........................................... 192
- 6.8.4 Simulating and Responding to Security Incidents ........................................ 194

## 6.9 Key Exam Tips ................................................................................................................ 196

## 6.10 Chapter Review Questions ......................................................................................... 197

## 6.11 Answers to Chapter Review Questions ................................................................... 199

# CHAPTER 7. DETECTING SECURITY THREATS AND ANOMALIES ...................... 201

## 7.1 Introduction to Security Threat Detection ................................................................ 202

## 7.2 AWS Managed Security Services ................................................................................. 202
- 7.2.1 Amazon GuardDuty............................................................................................. 203
- 7.2.2 AWS Security Hub ............................................................................................... 203
- 7.2.3 Amazon Macie ..................................................................................................... 205
- 7.2.4 AWS Config .......................................................................................................... 206
- 7.2.5 IAM Access Analyzer .......................................................................................... 207

## 7.3 Anomaly and Correlation Techniques ........................................................................ 208
- 7.3.1 Anomaly Detection Techniques ....................................................................... 208
- 7.3.2 Using Amazon Detective ................................................................................... 210

## 7.4 Visualizing Security Threats ........................................................................................ 211
- 7.4.1 Creating Visualizations ...................................................................................... 211
- 7.4.2 Dashboards and Metric Filters ......................................................................... 213

## 7.5 Centralizing Security Findings..................................................................................... 214
- 7.5.1 Strategies for Centralization ............................................................................. 215
- 7.5.2 Integrating with AWS Security Hub ................................................................. 216

## 7.6 Validating Security Events ........................................................................................... 218
- 7.6.1 Performing Queries with Amazon Athena ..................................................... 218
- 7.6.2 Analysis and Investigation Techniques........................................................... 219

## 7.7 Best Practices for Threat Detection ............................................................................ 221
- 7.7.1 Continuous Monitoring and Real-Time Alerts ............................................... 221
- 7.7.2 Regular Audits and Reviews ............................................................................. 222

7.8 Lab Exercises ................................................................................................ 224
   7.8.1 Setting Up Amazon GuardDuty ........................................................... 224
   7.8.2 Creating Visualizations with CloudWatch ............................................ 225
   7.8.3 Using Amazon Athena for Log Analysis ............................................... 226
   7.8.4 Integrating AWS Security Services ...................................................... 229

7.9 Key Exam Tips ............................................................................................. 231

7.10 Chapter Review Questions ........................................................................ 232

7.11 Answers to Chapter Review Questions ..................................................... 234

## CHAPTER 8. RESPONDING TO COMPROMISED RESOURCES ............................ 236

8.1 Introduction to Incident Response ............................................................. 237

8.2 AWS Security Incident Response Guide ..................................................... 239
   8.2.1 Overview of the AWS Security Incident Response Guide ................... 239
   8.2.2 Incident Response Lifecycle ................................................................ 240

8.3 Resource Isolation Mechanisms ................................................................. 241
   8.3.1 Techniques for Isolating Compromised Resources ............................. 241
   8.3.2 Automating Resource Isolation .......................................................... 242

8.4 Root Cause Analysis ................................................................................... 243
   8.4.1 Conducting Root Cause Analysis ......................................................... 243
   8.4.2 Using Amazon Detective for Investigations ........................................ 244

8.5 Data Capture Mechanisms ......................................................................... 246
   8.5.1 Capturing Forensic Data ...................................................................... 246
   8.5.2 Preserving Forensic Artifacts .............................................................. 247

8.6 Log Analysis for Event Validation ............................................................... 248
   8.6.1 Techniques for Log Analysis ................................................................ 248
   8.6.2 Using Amazon Athena for Log Queries .............................................. 249

8.7 Automating Remediation .......................................................................... 250
   8.7.1 Using AWS Lambda for Remediation ................................................. 250
   8.7.2 Implementing AWS Step Functions .................................................... 252
   8.7.3 Event-Driven Remediation with EventBridge ..................................... 253

8.8 Preparing and Recovering Services ........................................................... 255
   8.8.1 Preparing Services for Incidents ......................................................... 255
   8.8.2 Recovering Services After Incidents ................................................... 256

8.9 Best Practices for Incident Response ......................................................... 257
   8.9.1 Continuous Monitoring and Improvement ........................................ 257
   8.9.2 Incident Response Drills ..................................................................... 257

8.10 Lab Exercises ............................................................................................ 258
   8.10.1 Simulating a Security Incident .......................................................... 258
   8.10.2 Automating Incident Response with AWS Lambda and EventBridge ............ 260
   8.10.3 Using Amazon Detective for Investigations ...................................... 261
   8.10.4 Capturing and Analyzing Forensic Data ............................................ 263

8.11 Key Exam Tips ..................................................................................................265

8.12 Chapter Review Questions ................................................................................266

8.13 Answers to Chapter Review Questions ............................................................268

# CHAPTER 9. SECURITY LOGGING AND MONITORING ........................ 270

## 9.1 Introduction to Security Logging and Monitoring ............................................272

## 9.2 Designing Monitoring and Alerting Solutions ..................................................273
9.2.1 AWS Services for Monitoring and Alarms ................................................. 273
9.2.2 Automated Alerting Services ...................................................................... 274
9.2.3 Monitoring Metrics and Baselines .............................................................. 275
9.2.4 Identifying Monitoring Requirements ........................................................ 275
9.2.5 Designing Monitoring Solutions ................................................................. 276
9.2.6 Setting Up Automated Audits ..................................................................... 277
9.2.7 Defining Metrics and Thresholds ............................................................... 278

## 9.3 Troubleshooting Monitoring and Alerting ........................................................280
9.3.1 Configuration of Monitoring Services ........................................................ 280
9.3.2 Analyzing Security Events .......................................................................... 281
9.3.3 Evaluating Service Functionality and Permissions .................................... 281
9.3.4 Troubleshooting Custom Applications ....................................................... 282
9.3.5 Aligning with Security Requirements ........................................................ 283

## 9.4 Designing and Implementing Logging Solutions ..............................................283
9.4.1 Logging Capabilities of AWS Services ...................................................... 284
9.4.2 Attributes of Logging .................................................................................. 284
9.4.3 Log Destinations and Lifecycle Management ............................................ 284
9.4.4 Configuring Logging for Services and Applications .................................. 285
9.4.5 Identifying Logging Requirements ............................................................. 286
9.4.6 Implementing Log Storage and Management ............................................ 287

## 9.5 Troubleshooting Logging Solutions ..................................................................288
9.5.1 Capabilities and Use Cases of Logging Services ....................................... 288
9.5.2 Access Permissions for Logging ................................................................. 288
9.5.3 Identifying and Remediating Misconfigurations ........................................ 289
9.5.4 Determining Causes of Missing Logs ........................................................ 290

## 9.6 Designing Log Analysis Solution ......................................................................292
9.6.1 Services and Tools for Log Analysis .......................................................... 292
9.6.2 Log Analysis Features of AWS Services .................................................... 293
9.6.3 Log Formats and Components ................................................................... 293
9.6.4 Identifying Patterns in Logs ....................................................................... 295
9.6.5 Normalizing, Parsing, and Correlating Logs ............................................. 296

## 9.7 Lab Exercises .....................................................................................................297
9.7.1 Setting Up CloudWatch Alarms ................................................................. 297
9.7.2 Configuring AWS Security Hub ................................................................. 298
9.7.3 Implementing VPC Flow Logs and Analyzing Data .................................. 299
9.7.4 Troubleshooting Logging and Monitoring Issues ...................................... 301
9.7.5 Creating Log Analysis Dashboards ............................................................ 302

9.8 Key Exam Tips ........................................................................................................... 305

9.9 Chapter Review Questions ....................................................................................... 306

9.10 Answers to Chapter Review Questions .................................................................. 309

## CHAPTER 10. AWS NETWORKING ESSENTIALS ............................................. 311

### 10.1 Understanding CIDR - IPv4 ................................................................................. 311
10.1.1 CIDR Components ........................................................................................... 312
10.1.2 Subnet Mask ................................................................................................... 313
10.1.3 CIDR - Review Exercise .................................................................................. 313

### 10.2 Public vs. Private IP Address ............................................................................... 313

### 10.3 AWS VPC ............................................................................................................. 314

### 10.4 VPC Subnets ....................................................................................................... 315

### 10.5 Internet Gateway (IGW) ...................................................................................... 316

### 10.6 Routing in VPC .................................................................................................... 317
10.6.1 What About VPC Resources Communicating to the Internet ....................... 318
10.6.2 Private Subnet ................................................................................................ 319

### 10.7 Bastion Hosts ...................................................................................................... 319

### 10.8 NAT Gateway ...................................................................................................... 320

### 10.9 AWS Network Security ....................................................................................... 322
10.9.1 Security Group ................................................................................................ 322
10.9.2 Default Inbound Rule ..................................................................................... 325
10.9.3 Default Outbound Rule .................................................................................. 325
10.9.4 Network Access Control List (NACLs) ........................................................... 326
10.9.5 Security Groups & NACLs Request Response Flow ..................................... 328
10.9.6 Ephemeral Ports ............................................................................................. 330
10.9.7 Ephemeral Ports with NACL Example Diagram ........................................... 330
10.9.8 Troubleshoot SG & NACL Related Issues ..................................................... 331
10.9.9 Security Groups vs. NACLs ........................................................................... 331

### 10.10 VPC Flow Logs .................................................................................................. 331
10.10.1 How to Create VPC Flow Logs ..................................................................... 332
10.10.2 How to Create Subnet Flow Logs ................................................................. 332
10.10.3 Analyzing Flow Log Record .......................................................................... 333

## CHAPTER 11. INFRASTRUCTURE SECURITY .................................................. 334

### 11.1 Introduction to Infrastructure Security ............................................................... 336

### 11.2 Security Controls for Edge Services .................................................................... 337
11.2.1 Overview of Edge Security Services .............................................................. 337
11.2.2 Understanding Common Attacks and Threats .............................................. 338
11.2.3 Layered Web Application Architecture .......................................................... 339

11.2.4 Defining Edge Security Strategies ..... 340
11.2.5 Selecting Appropriate Edge Services ..... 341
11.2.6 Defining Layers of Defense ..... 342
11.2.7 Applying Restrictions at the Edge ..... 343
11.2.8 Monitoring Edge Services ..... 345

## 11.3 Network Security Controls ..... 345
11.3.1 VPC Security Mechanisms ..... 346
11.3.2 Inter-VPC Connectivity ..... 346
11.3.3 Security Telemetry Sources ..... 347
11.3.4 VPN Technology and Usage ..... 348
11.3.5 On-Premises Connectivity Options ..... 348
11.3.6 Implementing Network Segmentation ..... 349
11.3.7 Designing Network Controls ..... 350
11.3.8 Designing Network Flows ..... 351
11.3.9 Monitoring Network Telemetry ..... 352
11.3.10 Redundancy and Security for On-Premises Communication ..... 353
11.3.11 Identifying and Removing Unnecessary Access ..... 354
11.3.12 Managing Network Configurations ..... 356

## 11.4 Security Controls for Compute Workloads ..... 357
11.4.1 Provisioning and Maintenance of EC2 Instances ..... 357
11.4.2 IAM Instance Roles and Service Roles ..... 358
11.4.3 Vulnerability Scanning for Compute Workloads ..... 360
11.4.4 Host-Based Security Mechanisms ..... 361
11.4.5 Creating Hardened EC2 AMIs ..... 362
11.4.6 Applying Patches Across EC2 Instances ..... 364
11.4.7 Analyzing Amazon Inspector Findings ..... 366
11.4.8 Passing Secrets and Credentials Securely ..... 367

## 11.5 Troubleshooting Network Security ..... 369
11.5.1 Analyzing Reachability ..... 369
11.5.2 Understanding TCP/IP Networking Concepts ..... 371
11.5.3 Reading Relevant Log Sources ..... 372
11.5.4 Identifying Network Connectivity Problems ..... 374
11.5.5 Determining Solutions for Desired Network Behavior ..... 375
11.5.6 Analyzing Log Sources ..... 377
11.5.7 Capturing Traffic Samples ..... 380

## 11.6 Lab Exercises ..... 381
11.6.1 Implementing Edge Security Controls ..... 381
11.6.2 Designing Network Security Configurations ..... 383
11.6.3 Hardening EC2 Instances ..... 385
11.6.4 Troubleshooting Network Issues ..... 387

## 11.7 Key Exam Tips ..... 389

## 11.8 Chapter Review Questions ..... 391

## 11.9 Answers to Chapter Review Questions ..... 393

# CHAPTER 12. DATA PROTECTION ..... 396

## 12.1 Introduction to Data Protection ..... 398

## 12.2 Designing and Implementing Controls for Data in Transit ........................................... 399
- 12.2.1 TLS Concepts ................................................................................................. 399
- 12.2.2 VPN Concepts ................................................................................................ 399
- 12.2.3 Secure Remote Access Methods .................................................................. 400
- 12.2.4 Systems Manager Session Manager Concepts ........................................... 401
- 12.2.5 TLS Certificates and Network Services ....................................................... 401

## 12.3 Implementing Secure Connectivity ................................................................................ 402
- 12.3.1 Secure Connectivity between AWS and On-Premises Networks ............... 402
- 12.3.2 Encryption for Connecting to AWS Resources ........................................... 402
- 12.3.3 Requiring TLS for AWS API Calls .................................................................. 403
- 12.3.4 Forwarding Traffic over Secure Connections ............................................. 404
- 12.3.5 Cross-Region Networking with Private and Public VIFs ............................. 405

## 12.4 Designing and Implementing Controls for Data at Rest .............................................. 405
- 12.4.1 Encryption Techniques .................................................................................. 406
- 12.4.2 Encryption for S3 Objects at Rest ................................................................. 406
- 12.4.3 Integrity-Checking Techniques ..................................................................... 408
- 12.4.4 Resource Policies for Data Protection ......................................................... 409
- 12.4.5 IAM Roles and Policies ................................................................................... 411

## 12.5 Implementing Encryption for Data at Rest .................................................................... 412
- 12.5.1 Activating Encryption for AWS Services ...................................................... 413
- 12.5.2 Protecting Data Integrity ............................................................................... 413
- 12.5.3 Using AWS CloudHSM .................................................................................... 415
- 12.5.4 Choosing Encryption Techniques ................................................................. 416

## 12.6 Managing the Lifecycle of Data at Rest .......................................................................... 416
- 12.6.1 Lifecycle Policies ............................................................................................. 416
- 12.6.2 S3 Lifecycle Mechanisms ............................................................................... 417
- 12.6.3 Automatic Lifecycle Management for AWS Services .................................. 419
- 12.6.4 Backup Scheduling and Retention ................................................................ 420

## 12.7 Protecting Credentials, Secrets, and Cryptographic Key Materials .......................... 422
- 12.7.1 AWS Secrets Manager .................................................................................... 422
- 12.7.2 Systems Manager Parameter Store .............................................................. 423
- 12.7.3 Symmetric and Asymmetric Key Management ........................................... 424
- 12.7.4 Managing and Rotating Secrets .................................................................... 426
- 12.7.5 KMS Key Policies ............................................................................................. 428
- 12.7.6 Importing and Removing Customer-Provided Key Material ..................... 430

## 12.8 Best Practices for Data Protection .................................................................................. 431
- 12.8.1 Encryption Best Practices .............................................................................. 431
- 12.8.2 Data Integrity Best Practices ......................................................................... 432
- 12.8.3 Managing Data Lifecycle Best Practices ...................................................... 434
- 12.8.4 Protecting Credentials and Secrets .............................................................. 435

## 12.9 Lab Exercises ....................................................................................................................... 437
- 12.9.1 Configuring TLS for AWS Services ................................................................ 437
- 12.9.2 Implementing Encryption for Data at Rest ................................................. 439
- 12.9.3 Managing Secrets with AWS Secrets Manager ........................................... 440
- 12.9.4 Designing S3 Lifecycle Policies ...................................................................... 442

## 12.10 Key Exam Tips .................................................................................................................. 444

12.11 Chapter Review Questions ......................................................................................446

12.12 Answers to Chapter Review Questions ...................................................................448

# CHAPTER 13. MANAGEMENT AND SECURITY GOVERNANCE..............................450

## 13.1 Introduction to Management and Security Governance ..........................................452

## 13.2 Multi-Account Management with AWS Organizations..............................................453
### 13.2.1 Organization Units (OU) Examples ....................................................................454

## 13.3 AWS Service Control Policy (SCP) .........................................................................457
### 13.3.1 Strategies for Using SCP ....................................................................................457

## 13.4 IAM Conditions........................................................................................................459

## 13.5 IAM Roles vs. Resource-Based Policies .................................................................461

## 13.6 IAM Permission Boundaries ....................................................................................462

## 13.7 IAM Policy Evaluation Logic ....................................................................................463

## 13.8 Developing a Strategy to Centrally Deploy and Manage AWS Accounts .................464
### 13.8.1 Multi-Account Strategies ....................................................................................464
### 13.8.2 Managed Services for Delegated Administration................................................465
### 13.8.3 Policy-Defined Guardrails ..................................................................................466
### 13.8.4 Root Account Best Practices ..............................................................................467
### 13.8.5 Cross-Account Roles ..........................................................................................469

## 13.9 Central Deployment and Management ...................................................................471
### 13.9.1 Deploying and Configuring AWS Organizations .................................................471
### 13.9.2 Deploying AWS Control Tower ...........................................................................472
### 13.9.3 Implementing Service Control Policies (SCPs)...................................................474
### 13.9.4 Central Management and Aggregation...............................................................476
### 13.9.5 Securing Root User Credentials..........................................................................478

## 13.10 Implementing Secure and Consistent Deployment Strategies...............................479
### 13.10.1 Infrastructure as Code (IaC) Best Practices .....................................................479
### 13.10.2 Tagging Best Practices......................................................................................482
### 13.10.3 Centralized Management and Deployment ......................................................484
### 13.10.4 Visibility and Control ........................................................................................485

## 13.11 Secure Deployment................................................................................................487
### 13.11.1 Using CloudFormation ......................................................................................487
### 13.11.2 Implementing Tagging Strategies .....................................................................489
### 13.11.3 Deploying Portfolios with AWS Service Catalog................................................491
### 13.11.4 Organizing AWS Resources ..............................................................................492
### 13.11.5 Using AWS Firewall Manager............................................................................494
### 13.11.6 Sharing Resources Securely .............................................................................495

## 13.12 Evaluating Compliance of AWS Resources...........................................................497
### 13.12.1 Data Classification with AWS Services .............................................................497
### 13.12.2 Assessing and Auditing Configurations ............................................................499

**13.13 Compliance Evaluation** .................................................................................................500
  13.13.1 Identifying Sensitive Data................................................................................. 500
  13.13.2 Creating AWS Config Rules ............................................................................... 502
  13.13.3 Collecting and Organizing Evidence .................................................................. 503

**13.14 Identifying Security Gaps through Reviews and Analysis** ............................................505
  13.14.1 Anomaly Identification Based on Cost and Usage .............................................. 505
  13.14.2 Anomaly Identification Based on Resource Util and Trends ............................... 507
  13.14.3 Reducing Attack Surfaces ................................................................................. 508
  13.14.4 Identifying Unused Resources .......................................................................... 510
  13.14.5 AWS Well-Architected Framework..................................................................... 512
  13.14.6 Using AWS Well-Architected Tool...................................................................... 514

**13.15 Lab Exercises** ..............................................................................................................515
  13.15.1 Deploying AWS Organizations........................................................................... 515
  13.15.2 Creating and Implementing SCPs ...................................................................... 517
  13.15.3 Using CloudFormation for Secure Deployment................................................... 518
  13.15.4 Evaluating Compliance with AWS Config ........................................................... 520
  13.15.5 Identifying and Addressing Security Gaps ......................................................... 523

**13.16 Key Exam Tips** ............................................................................................................525

**13.17 Chapter Review Questions** ..........................................................................................527

**13.18 Answers to Chapter Review Questions** .......................................................................530

# PRACTICE TEST SET 1 ........................................................................................... 532

Practice Test Set 1 - Answers........................................................................................545

# PRACTICE TEST SET 2 ........................................................................................... 553

Practice Test Set 2 - Answers........................................................................................566

# FINAL THOUGHTS ................................................................................................. 574

# REFERENCES ......................................................................................................... 575

# Becoming Certified in AWS Certified Security - Specialty

Achieving the AWS Certified Security - Specialty certification sets you apart as an expert in cloud security, capable of safeguarding critical data and infrastructure on the AWS platform. This certification not only validates your skills but also opens doors to advanced career opportunities and positions you as a trusted professional in the rapidly growing field of cloud security.

Obtaining the AWS Certified Security - Specialty certification offers several benefits. It validates your expertise in securing AWS environments, enhancing your credibility and marketability as a cloud security professional. This certification demonstrates your ability to design and implement robust security solutions, manage data protection, and adhere to best practices for compliance, making you a valuable asset to any organization leveraging AWS services. Additionally, it can open up advanced career opportunities and lead to higher earning potential in the cloud security domain.

## Exam overview

| Category | Specialty |
| --- | --- |
| Exam duration | 170 minutes |
| Exam format | 65 questions; either multiple choice or multiple response |
| Cost | 300 USD. Visit Exam pricing for additional cost information, including foreign exchange rates |
| Test in-person or online | Pearson VUE testing center or online proctored exam |
| Languages offered | English, French (France), Italian, Japanese, Korean, Portuguese (Brazil), Simplified Chinese, and Spanish (Latin America) |

Screenshot Reference: https://aws.amazon.com/certification/certified-security-specialty/

## Exam Domains

The following table lists the main content domains and their weightings.

| Domain | % of Exam |
| --- | --- |
| Domain 1: Threat Detection and Incident Response | 14% |
| Domain 2: Security Logging and Monitoring | 18% |
| Domain 3: Infrastructure Security | 20% |
| Domain 4: Identity and Access Management | 16% |
| Domain 5: Data Protection | 18% |
| Domain 6: Management and Security Governance | 14% |
| Total | 100% |

You can find detailed information about the exam at:
- https://d1.awsstatic.com/training-and-certification/docs-security-spec/AWS-Certified-Security-Specialty_Exam-Guide.pdf
- https://aws.amazon.com/certification/certified-security-specialty/

# Introduction

Welcome to "AWS Certified Security – Specialty Exam Guide," a comprehensive resource designed to equip you with the knowledge and skills required to pass the AWS Certified Security – Specialty exam and secure your AWS environment effectively. This book is structured to provide a thorough understanding of AWS security, starting with foundational concepts and progressing to advanced topics. Each chapter builds upon the previous one, ensuring a cohesive and comprehensive learning experience. You will find detailed explanations, best practices, hands-on exercises, and exam practice questions that will reinforce your knowledge and prepare you for real-world scenarios.

*For the lab exercises, in some cases, there are costs to execute, so please check the price and costs before you perform the exercise from this certification guide. Also, turn off or delete paid resources after you finish your exercises.*

Here's a brief overview of what each chapter covers:

**Chapter 1: Introduction to AWS Security**
This chapter introduces the basic concepts of AWS security, including what security is and isn't, key security principles, and foundational networking concepts. It covers various types of cyber-attacks and key security solutions and services such as firewalls, VPNs, and intrusion detection systems. You will also learn about well-known security frameworks and models.

**Chapter 2: Cloud Security Principles and Frameworks**
Dive into cloud security principles and frameworks specific to AWS. This chapter covers the AWS Security Framework, the Shared Responsibility Model, and best practices documentation. You will also explore AWS compliance programs and hands-on exercises to generate compliance reports.

**Chapter 3: Authentication of AWS Resources**
Learn about authentication methods and services for creating and managing identities in AWS. This chapter covers IAM, Single Sign-On, Amazon Cognito, and identity federation. It also discusses credential mechanisms, troubleshooting authentication issues, and best practices for authentication.

**Chapter 4: Authorization of AWS Resources**
Understand the principles of authorization in AWS, including IAM policies, policy structures, and access control strategies. This chapter covers the implementation of least privilege, separation of duties, and troubleshooting authorization issues. It also includes lab exercises to apply IAM policies and construct access control strategies.

### Chapter 5: Detective Controls
Explore AWS security detective controls and the process flow framework for detecting security events. This chapter covers AWS Config, CloudTrail, CloudWatch, and other tools for events collection and analysis. You will also learn about remediation actions and best practices for implementing detective controls.

### Chapter 6: Threat Detection and Incident Response
Learn how to design and implement an incident response plan, understand cloud incidents, and deploy AWS security services like Security Hub, GuardDuty, and Macie. This chapter covers playbooks, runbooks, and best practices for continuous monitoring and incident response.

### Chapter 7: Detecting Security Threats and Anomalies
This chapter focuses on detecting security threats and anomalies using AWS managed security services. It covers anomaly detection techniques, visualizing security threats, centralizing security findings, and validating security events. You will also learn best practices for threat detection.

### Chapter 8: Responding to Compromised Resources
Understand how to respond to compromised resources with techniques for resource isolation, root cause analysis, and data capture mechanisms. This chapter covers log analysis, automating remediation, and preparing and recovering services after incidents. Best practices for incident response are also discussed.

### Chapter 9: Security Logging and Monitoring
Learn how to design and implement logging and monitoring solutions. This chapter covers AWS services for monitoring and alerting, troubleshooting monitoring issues, and designing log analysis solutions. It also includes best practices for logging and monitoring.

### Chapter 10: AWS Networking Essentials
Get a deep understanding of AWS networking concepts, including VPCs, subnets, routing, bastion hosts, NAT gateways, and network security controls. This chapter covers VPC peering, endpoints, transit gateways, and DNS in VPCs. You will also learn about connecting on-premises networks to AWS.

### Chapter 11: Infrastructure Security
Explore security controls for edge services and network security. This chapter covers VPC security mechanisms, inter-VPC connectivity, VPN technology, and network segmentation. It also discusses security controls for compute workloads and troubleshooting network security issues.

### Chapter 12: Data Protection
Learn about designing and implementing controls for data in transit and at rest. This chapter covers encryption techniques, secure connectivity, integrity-checking techniques, and managing the lifecycle of data at rest. You will also explore best practices for data protection.

### Chapter 13: Management and Security Governance
Understand strategies for multi-account management, IAM conditions, and policy-defined guardrails. This chapter covers deploying and configuring AWS Organizations, Control Tower, and implementing service control policies. It also includes best practices for secure deployment and evaluating compliance of AWS resources.

**Practice Tests:** This section provides two full-length practice tests to help you prepare for the exam. Each test includes answers and explanations to enhance your understanding of key concepts. Use these tests to assess your readiness and improve your exam performance.

As you embark on this journey, you'll gain the expertise needed to secure your AWS environment and achieve AWS Security Certification. Let's get started!

# Chapter 1. Introduction to AWS Security

**This chapter addresses the following exam objectives:**
Provides foundational knowledge essential for the exam.

The landscape of cybersecurity is ever-evolving, with new threats and vulnerabilities emerging daily. To stay ahead in this dynamic environment, it is crucial to understand the foundational concepts of security, particularly within the context of Amazon Web Services (AWS). This chapter provides an essential introduction to AWS Security, laying the groundwork for more advanced topics covered later in this guide.

We begin by discussing the importance of AWS Security Certification and clarifying common misconceptions about what security entails. Understanding the distinctions between vulnerabilities, threats, and risks is crucial, as is familiarizing oneself with security controls and countermeasures that mitigate these risks. Concepts like accountability, nonrepudiation, authentication, authorization, and accounting form the bedrock of secure system design and are explored in detail.

Networking foundational concepts such as the OSI Reference Model and the TCP/IP Model are critical to comprehending how data travels across networks and the potential points of vulnerability. We then delve into various types of attacks, including reconnaissance, eavesdropping, IP spoofing, man-in-the-middle (MITM) attacks, DDoS attacks, malware, and phishing attacks. Each attack type is examined to understand the methods and impacts, providing a basis for developing effective defense strategies.

Security defense management and key security solutions and services, such as firewalls, web proxies, web application firewalls, intrusion detection and prevention systems, and virtual private networks, are discussed. The tools and techniques for vulnerability analysis and management, security information and event management (SIEM), and TLS/SSL offloading are covered to illustrate how organizations can safeguard their systems.

Finally, we explore well-known security frameworks and models, including the attack continuum model and the zero-trust model. These frameworks provide structured approaches to implementing comprehensive security measures, ensuring that AWS environments are protected against a wide array of threats. By the end of this chapter, readers will have a solid understanding of the foundational elements of AWS Security, preparing them for the more advanced concepts and practices necessary to secure AWS deployments effectively.

# 1.1 Introduction to AWS Security Certification

The AWS Certified Security – Specialty certification is a prestigious credential designed for professionals who want to demonstrate their advanced skills and expertise in securing AWS environments. This certification validates your ability to implement and manage security controls, protect data and applications, and maintain a robust security posture within the AWS cloud. It covers a wide range of security topics, including incident response, logging and monitoring, infrastructure security, identity and access management, data protection, and compliance. By earning this certification, you showcase your commitment to security excellence and your ability to effectively secure AWS workloads, making you a valuable asset to any organization leveraging AWS services.

## 1.1.1 What Security is Not

Sometimes some grey areas cause confusion and noise in understanding the subject well -- in security also; there are some. Let's see what security is not – what is outside our scope as security professionals.

Security is not a product or service; no single product can solve all security issues, though some features and services can help. It is not a static technology; network security technologies must evolve to counter new threats. Security requires continuous processes for planning, implementation, testing, and updating. It is absolute, not just a checklist; you need to know what you are securing, plan effectively, and update processes regularly. Finally, security is not just about a beautiful UI; understanding what happens behind the scenes is crucial to ensuring actual protection. This knowledge helps eliminate distractions and focus on real security needs in exams and practice.

The knowledge of "what security is not" would help you eliminate potential noise or distraction answer choice in the exam.

## 1.1.2 What Security is

To understand what security can be, we use the concept of general to specific, similar to object-oriented systems. This approach helps in understanding security requirements and implementing relevant policies, procedures, and tools. For instance, when tasked with securing an organization's digital assets, you start by understanding the organization's vision, objectives, and competitors. This information forms the basis of the security policy, which guides all initiatives and tasks related to securing the digital assets.

High-level information about the organization helps in creating a comprehensive security policy document, which establishes the foundation for implementing security measures effectively.

These documents are:
**Business Objectives**: This document is about why the company exists – what the company is trying to achieve.

**Regulatory Requirements**: These requirements broadly fall under the industry in business. For example, companies in the financial industry have similar types of regulatory requirements. Companies in the health sector will have similar types of regulatory requirements. These requirements give a clue about what type of data is important in a particular industry.

**Risk**: The risk document talks about risks of various categories, such as direct financial loss, improper disclosure of intellectual property, and public images of the organization.

**Cost/Benefits Analysis:** This document talks about what would be the cost of implementing various security tools, resources, processes, etc., and what the benefits would be. For example, if the company's annual profit is $1M, hiring ten security engineers with a 100K annual salary would be the right decision. Once we got the input documents that were needed to create security policy documents, the security policy document is written in a more general broader scope keeping in mind the organization's objectives, regulatory requirements, risks, and cost-benefit analysis.

The security policy documents should have practical applicability, general rules and principles to guide the overall security of the company as an umbrella, overarching document. The most common elements that these security policy documents include are:

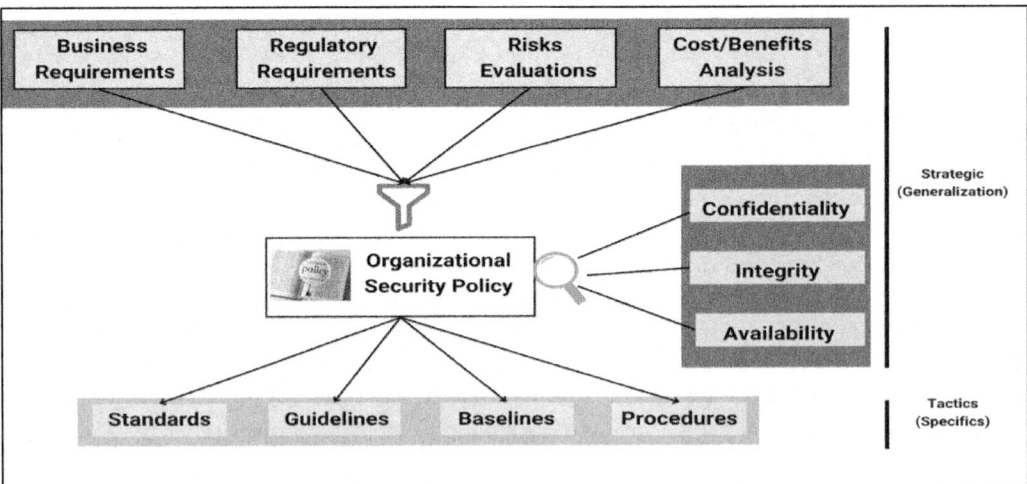

**Standards**: Standards specify mandatory rules, regulations, or activities.

**Guidelines**: These include sets of recommendations, actions, and operational guides that are to be considered under circumstances in which standards are not applicable, or standards are ambiguous.

**Baselines:** As the name says, these documents specify the minimum level of security that should be in place for a given system type.

**Procedures:** This document talks about step-by-step for performing specific tasks, such as how to implement security policies such as standards, guidelines, and baselines with the operating environment.

As you can see in the diagram that how the organizational policy is formed using top-level business-related requirements: business requirements, regulatory requirements, risk evaluations, and cost/benefits analysis. The organizational security policy document then defines standards, guidelines, baselines, and procedures for organization security and helps achieve key features of security: confidentiality, integrity, and availability.

## Attacks do happen

Security-related attacks are a reality, especially for web applications accessible worldwide. Observing attempts from various IP addresses, often bots, trying to access your system illegitimately is common. The absence of a successful attack doesn't guarantee future immunity.

It's essential to maintain an attack-and-defense culture, continually assessing potential exposures and mitigation techniques. Consider how often you back up data, how quickly you can recover from an attack, and the layers of security you have in place. Ensure your critical digital assets are secure and that you have sufficient logging and auditing beyond standard weblogs. Always remember that attacks do happen, and being prepared to mitigate risks is crucial.

**Any networked element is a potential attack target**
Every networked element is a potential attack target, including web servers, application servers, database servers, client devices, and infrastructure devices like routers and switches. Around 2002, I worked at an organization with critical data where database servers were not connected to the Internet. Only one port was open, allowing traffic only from the web server, while all other services were disabled.

Compared to today's complex security measures, this approach was basic but effective in minimizing attack exposure. In the cloud environment, security threats have intensified, emphasizing the importance of minimizing the attack surface. Ensuring only necessary ports are open and allowing traffic only from trusted sources significantly enhances system security.

**Hope is Not a Strategy**
As discussed, attacks are inevitable, so hoping for the best is not a strategy. A robust security strategy should include clear access policies, protocol types, and allowed input traffic sources. Documenting network topologies helps in understanding and managing network connections from source to destination, making them easier to control, troubleshoot, audit, and manage.

Layered security, like the layers of an onion, adds depth to defense by placing security measures at multiple levels. This approach ensures that if an attacker bypasses one layer, they can be stopped by subsequent layers. Additionally, delays in breaching layers can trigger alarms or notifications, allowing for additional security measures or network disconnection to protect digital assets.

## 1.2 Basic Security Concepts

Every domain has its own terminology that people use to easily communicate with others in the same domain. These terms form a dictionary of the domain. In this section, we will go through the terminologies in the IT security domain we will use in the rest of the book. While reading this book, you can revisit this section if you find a term that seems foreign to you.

I have grouped some terms together to make understanding much easier. The reason is that when reading them together with other terms in the same group, you can find their context and how they are related. This would help increase understanding and retention.

### 1.2.1 Vulnerability, Threat, and Security Risk

The terms vulnerability, threat, and security risk are interrelated but distinct. A vulnerability is a system weakness that can be exploited for unauthorized actions, such as allowing SQL payloads from a URL leading to SQL injection or using telnet, which sends login credentials as clear text.

A threat is an entity (person, software, tool) that can exploit a vulnerability, either intentionally or accidentally, and is known as a threat actor or agent.

Security risk is the probability that a vulnerability will be exploited by a threat actor. The value of the digital asset being exploited influences the risk. For example, a vulnerability in a test environment poses a lower security risk compared to the same vulnerability in a production system.

### 1.2.2 Security Controls or Security Countermeasures

Security controls (also called security countermeasures) are the mechanisms used for or aimed at security risk mitigation.

Many types of security controls can be leveraged for security risk mitigations.
- **Software patching** is used to eliminate the previously known vulnerability. It is very common nowadays to deliver and apply these patches on the Internet. Companies such as Microsoft, Apple, and

others that sell software for consumers continuously make software patches available if they find any security vulnerability.
- **Security tools or services** that are specifically designed as defensive tools to mitigate security risks.
- **Authentication and authorization** (user identity verification) before granting access to use critical digital assets.

## 1.2.3 Confidentiality, Integrity, and Availability (CIA Triad)

These three security attributes are usually used together to evaluate security effectiveness.

**Confidentiality** deals with preventing unauthorized access or disclosure of sensitive and private data and ensuring a suitable level of privacy. Encryption is a typical mechanism that is used to implement confidentiality. This mechanism has been used for quite a long time that pre-date.

**Integrity** deals with preventing unauthorized modification of data for data accuracy. Hash-based message authentication codes (HMAC) such as HMAC-MD5 and HMAC-SHA (mathematical functions) are used to check if data is compromised. This mechanism is largely used in the IPSec (Internet Protocol Security) framework to provide integrity for data transmitted in Internet Protocol (IP) packets.

**Availability** deals with ensuring the data are available at an expected level of performance, and provisions must be in place to manage availability in case of an eventual failure in the operating environment. Encryption reduces performance because of the extra computation involved in the process of encryption/decryption.

Confidentiality, Integrity, and Availability are sometimes mentioned as a CIA triad.

## 1.2.4 Accountability and Nonrepudiation

**Accountability** is used to hold an individual or organization responsible for their actions. The main concept behind this term is ensuring that all operations performed by systems or processes can be traced or identified to determine who (individual/organization) did that.

**Nonrepudiation** is the term used to ensure that individuals or organizations held accountable for their actions cannot avoid that they didn't do it. Digital signatures, authentication, and asking users to enter their names are typically used for nonrepudiation.

## 1.2.5 Authentication, Authorization, and Accounting

Authentication, authorization, and accounting are three access control functions related to security. Though they are very much related yet distinct in access control functions they deal with.

Authentication, authorization, and accounting are three crucial access control functions in security.

**Authentication:** This function verifies "Who is the user?" by checking against a database of registered users. It ensures accountability by allowing only authenticated users to access the system. Users can be individuals, systems, or services.

**Authorization:** This function determines "What is the user allowed to do?" by defining roles and permissions for authenticated users. For example, an admin user typically has access to more resources and features than a regular user.

**Accounting**: This function tracks user activities to monitor traffic volume and detect abnormal access patterns. It helps identify suspicious activities, frequently used APIs, service exceptions, and unauthorized access attempts. For instance, AWS CloudTrail logs API requests to provide insights into user actions and system access patterns.

These functions collectively enhance security by ensuring proper user verification, permission management, and activity monitoring.

# 1.3 Networking Foundational Concepts

Cloud systems are connected to the internet. This means it is easier to perform cloud security well with a good knowledge of network security. In this section, we will understand the basics of network communication by looking at two network communication models: OSI (Open Systems Interconnection) and the TCP/IP *protocol stack* (a more popular model for network-based communications). Understanding the networking model will help you determine which networking layer the attack is taking place. Thus, it makes it easier for you to figure out the appropriate protection mechanisms.

## 1.3.1 The OSI Reference Model

The OSI Model (a reference model) defines how two systems talk to each other over a network. It was developed by the International Organization for Standardization (ISO) in 1984.

The OSI model helps network device manufacturers, mainly networking software vendors, to create devices and software that can communicate with products from any other network vendor, allowing open interoperability. The OSI reference model defines which parts of the network their products should work with. The OSI model is based on the layered architecture where each layer has a defined function. Each OSI layer provides an abstraction and collaborates with its next layer to perform data transmission between two systems.

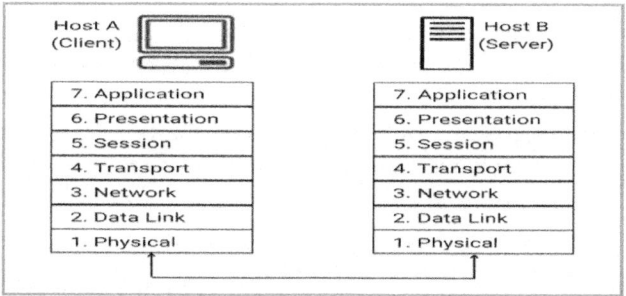

Let's look into some key features of the OSI model:
- The OSI reference model provides standardization, thus helping network device manufacturers and networking software vendors to build devices/solutions that could integrate well with the devices/solutions created by the other vendors. In other words, it helps create interoperability between diverse network devices/solutions, even those created by different vendors.
- The layered architecture provides modularity to the OSI model. That way, it helps allow build features for a particular layer – without having to know about the other layers (if you don't want to).
- The OSI model helps network device manufacturers and networking software vendors to build specialized devices for a particular OSI layer.

Let's look into each layer of the OSI reference model, as this will form a basic understanding of each layer's functionality.

**Physical Layer (Layer 1):** This layer ensures the successful transmission of raw data bits, handling mechanical, electrical, and optical interfaces.

**Data Link Layer (Layer 2):** Above the physical layer, this layer manages the reliable delivery of data frames between nodes using physical addressing like MAC addresses. It handles flow control, error detection, and access to shared media. Examples include Ethernet and PPP.

**Network Layer (Layer 3):** Using IP addresses, this layer routes data packets from the source to the destination host, even across different networks. The primary protocol here is IP, which routes packets across interconnected networks.

**Transport Layer (Layer 4):** Responsible for reliable data delivery from source to destination, this layer uses ports for data communication channels. It handles retransmissions and error detection, with TCP (connection-oriented) and UDP (connectionless) being the main protocols.

> **TCP vs. UDP**
> The key distinction between TCP and UDP is that TCP is connection-oriented, involving a three-way handshake (SYN, SYN-ACK, ACK) to establish a reliable connection. TCP ensures full duplex communication where both sides synchronize and acknowledge each other.
>
> In contrast, UDP is connectionless, meaning it does not require a handshake to start sending packets, making it faster and more efficient. UDP is popular for its speed and is used in applications like Voice over IP (VoIP), online games, media streaming, and query-response protocols such as DNS, where data packets are small and transactional.

**Session Layer (Layer 5):** Manages coordinated exchanges of requests and responses between application processes on different hosts. It handles session management tasks such as establishing, maintaining, terminating, and controlling dialogues (half-duplex and full-duplex) between communicating parties. It also inserts synchronization points to allow large transfers to resume from where they were interrupted.

**Presentation Layer (Layer 6):** Deals with the syntax and semantics of the data being transmitted, enabling devices with different data representations to communicate. Known as the translation layer, it handles encryption, decryption, data translation, and compression to ensure compatible, acceptable, and secure data communication.

**Application Layer (Layer 7):** The top layer of the OSI model, closest to the end user, facilitating user interaction. It provides protocols for software to send, receive, and present data to users. Well-known protocols at this layer include HTTP, FTP, and DNS, which resolve IP addresses for website names before connections are made.

# 1.3.2 The TCP/IP Model

**OSI Model vs. TCP/IP Stack**

| OSI Model | TCP/IP Stack |
|---|---|
| 7. Application | Application |
| 6. Presentation | Application |
| 5. Session | Application |
| 4. Transport | Transport |
| 3. Network | Internet |
| 2. Data Link | Network Access |
| 1. Physical | Network Access |

The OSI Model is a reference model explaining how two systems communicate over a network, but in real-life applications, the simpler TCP/IP model is used, forming the basis of the modern Internet. The OSI 7-layer model remains useful for visualizing and troubleshooting network operations.

The Internet's foundation lies in ARPANET, which introduced packet switching—a key aspect of the TCP/IP protocol suite. TCP/IP is used for communication over the Internet and in private networks like intranets. When a user requests a web page, the HTTP protocol relies on the TCP layer to establish a connection and send the HTML file.

**Circuit switching vs. Packet switching:** Circuit switching is connection-oriented and used for continuous, long-duration connections, like traditional telephone systems. Packet switching, used by TCP/IP, is connectionless and allows data to be routed through various transmission points, making networks decentralized and resilient to failures.

The TCP/IP model's lowest layer, the network access layer, combines the OSI model's physical and data link layers. The top application layer encompasses all processes using transport layer protocols to deliver data, supporting numerous application protocols and services. Understanding IP, TCP, and UDP within the TCP/IP stack is crucial for security professionals.

## 1.3.2.1 The Internet Protocol (IP) Layer

The Internet Protocol (IP) layer of the TCP/IP stack functionally is almost similar to the OSI model's network layer -- packet routing is its key functionality. Internet Protocol (IP) connects with hosts through interfaces-- it converts data into datagrams. Datagrams contain header information consisting of source/destination, metadata, and the payload, which is the data itself. IP routing deals with the choice of a path over which IP packets (or datagrams) destined for a particular host will be sent.

IP routing can be divided into four basic functions: getting routing information, building the routing table, searching for the longest bitwise match, and forwarding the packet to the outgoing interface.

**Getting Routing Information**
This can be done by finding static routes or by using dynamic routing protocols, such as *Open Shortest Path First (OSPF)*, *Routing Information Protocol (RIP)*, or *Border Gateway Protocol (BGP)*.

**Building the Routing Table**
To build the routing table, a router performs two comparisons: Among multiple equal-length network paths (prefixes) to the destination, it prefers the one with the lowest administrative distance, which measures the

trustworthiness of routes (static or dynamic). If paths have the same administrative distance, the router selects the one with the lowest cost according to the routing protocol.

**Searching for the longest bitwise match**
When a packet arrives at the incoming interface, its destination IP address is used to compare with the available entries in the routing table. Then, the comparison -- that results in the longest bitwise match for the network mask -- is selected. A default route (if configured) can always be used as the last resort.

**Forwarding the packet on the outgoing interface**
When a match is found in the previous step, the routing table entry's corresponding outgoing interface is used. And the packet is forwarded to the outgoing interface by building the appropriate header for this interface.

**Functions of the Internet layer**
The following are some main functions of the Internet (IP) layer:
- One of the main functions is sending data packets to their destination networks.
- Packet forwarding, path determination, and logical addressing.
- IP datagram routing is the responsibility of the Internet layer.
- Routers utilize routing protocols to learn about various networks they can access and deliver error messages.

**Internet Layer Protocols**
IP, RARP, ICMP, IGMP, and ARP are the primary protocols used at the Internet layer (Internet Group Management Protocol).

## 1.3.2.2 The Transport Layer

The TCP/IP model offers TCP and UDP as transport layer protocols, chosen based on application needs. TCP is reliable, connection-oriented, and includes flow control. UDP is connectionless, simpler, and provides best-effort delivery, making it suitable for real-time communication like voice and video where packet loss is acceptable.

UDP, being connectionless and lacking error control, discards packets with errors. Packet loss in UDP is minimal when links are functioning properly but can increase with network congestion. The key distinction is that TCP is connection-oriented, while UDP is connectionless. UDP is faster and more efficient, popular for its speed and efficiency as it doesn't require a connection setup to send packets.

Examples of UDP include Voice over IP (VoIP), online games, and media streaming.

Because of UDP's speed, it is very useful for query-response protocols such as DNS, in which data packets are small and transactional.

# 1.4 Different Types of Cyber Attacks

Attacks on security vulnerabilities began in the early stages of the Internet. For example, Java Applets, popular in the mid-90s, were later restricted due to security flaws. Comparing early Internet attacks to modern cyberattacks reveals significant differences, primarily in the attackers' intent. Initially, motivations included learning and notoriety, but now the focus is on personal profit, such as accessing digital items without payment, committing bank or credit card fraud, and stealing intellectual property.

Cyberattacks are also used as weapons in international tensions. A new challenge is the easy availability of hacking tools, complete with usage examples, automation scripts, and user interfaces, reducing the technical knowledge required to execute cyberattacks.

In this section, we will examine the main security threat classes. Because of the highly dynamic field, it can be hard to assume that I should have covered them entirely. Additionally, it is common to find that some security attacks may fall into multiple classes.

## 1.4.1 Reconnaissance

Reconnaissance (recon) is the initial phase of a cyberattack where attackers or security professionals gather information about a target system or network to identify weaknesses and potential entry points. This phase lays the groundwork for a successful attack by gaining insights into the target's infrastructure, systems, applications, and vulnerabilities.

There are three types of reconnaissance: social, public, and software. Common recon techniques include ICMP ping, port scanning (TCP & UDP), host behavior observation, and social engineering. Tools such as Google, Maltego, FireCompass, and nMap are often used for recon.

An important point is that reconnaissance is often overlooked. Noticing reconnaissance activities can indicate that an attack is imminent.

## 1.4.2 Password Attacks

A password attack is a cyberattack where an attacker tries to gain unauthorized access by guessing or cracking a user's password. Common methods include brute force and dictionary attacks.

**Brute Force:** Involves trying all possible combinations of characters until the correct password is found.
**Dictionary Attack:** Uses common words or phrases, assuming users often choose simple passwords.

Other types include:

**Password Spraying:** Uses a single common password against multiple accounts on the same application.
**Credential Stuffing:** Uses lists of compromised credentials to breach a system.

Passwords are prime targets for attackers due to their role in protecting sensitive information and resources.

## 1.4.3 Eavesdropping Attacks

Eavesdropping attacks, or snooping attacks, are cybersecurity threats where unauthorized parties intercept and monitor communications between two parties without their knowledge. These attacks aim to capture sensitive information like login credentials, personal data, financial information, or confidential business communications.

Eavesdropping is especially concerning over unsecured or poorly encrypted channels, allowing attackers to easily intercept and analyze data. Hackers "listen" to data transmitted between network devices, often targeting unsecured networks like public Wi-Fi. The goal is often to obtain valid username and password combinations.

There are two types of eavesdropping attacks:
- **Passive Eavesdropping:** The attacker listens to network traffic without altering it, using techniques like wiretapping or configuring switch port mirroring.
- **Active Eavesdropping:** The attacker actively manipulates the network to intercept data, exploiting weaknesses in protocols like DHCP or ARP.

Eavesdropping attacks are aimed at compromising data confidentiality, often through public networks.

## 1.4.4 IP Spoofing Attacks

IP Spoofing is a cyber-attack where an attacker disguises their source IP address in a network packet to make it appear as if it originates from a trusted source. The goal is to deceive the recipient or network devices into accepting the packet as genuine, bypassing security measures to gain unauthorized access or launch further attacks.

The attacker creates packets and alters the source IP address to impersonate a different system or host, disguising their identity. Motivations for IP spoofing include taking advantage of privileges associated with a trusted user or host and diverting attention away from the actual attack originator to remain undetected.

## 1.4.5 Man-in-the-Middle (MITM) Attacks

A Man-in-the-Middle (MITM) attack is a type of cyber attack where an attacker secretly intercepts and relays communication between two parties. The key point is that both parties believe they are directly communicating -- not knowing there is someone in the middle is intercepting their communication. In a MITM attack, the attacker positions themselves between the sender and the receiver, allowing them to eavesdrop on the communication, modify the contents of the messages, and even impersonate one or both parties.

For example, in a MITM attack, which can also be considered active eavesdropping, the attacker establishes independent connections with the victim's machines and relays the exchanged messages to make them believe they are talking directly to each other over a private connection. Thus, the attacker intercepts and controls the entire conversation, tricking both victim machines into believing they are directly communicating.

## 1.4.6 DDoS Attacks

DDoS (Distributed Denial of Service) is a cyber attack where numerous compromised computers (bots or zombies) flood a target system or network with excessive traffic or requests. The aim is to exhaust the target's resources, causing disruptions and denying access to legitimate users.

A DoS (Denial of Service) attack involves a single source, while a DDoS attack involves multiple source hosts attacking simultaneously in a coordinated manner. The frequency, volume, and sophistication of DDoS attacks are increasing every year.

**Types of DDoS Attacks**

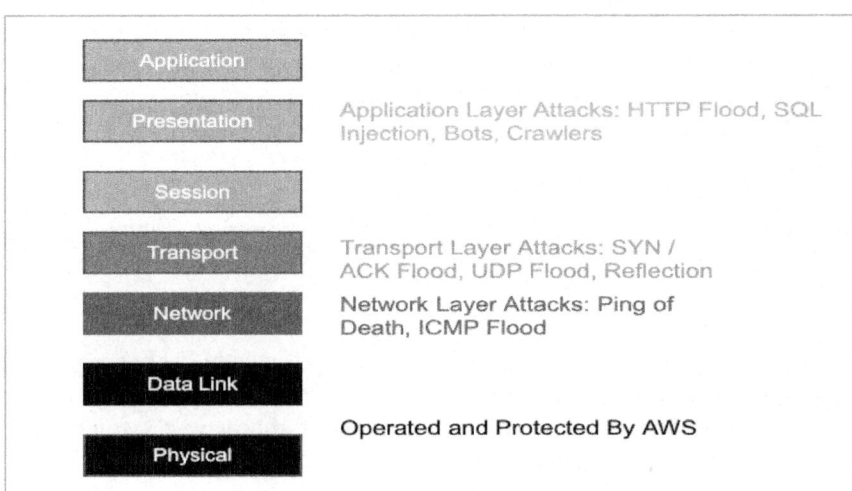

DDoS attacks are mainly of three types depending on what layer of OSI they attack.

### 1.4.6.1 Volumetric DDoS (Layer 3 DDoS)

Volumetric DDoS (Network Layer or Layer 3 DDoS) is the most common type of DDoS attack. It focuses on overwhelming the target system or network with an extremely high volume of traffic, such as Ping of Death and ICMP Flood.

A volumetric DDoS attack aims to saturate the target's bandwidth, network capacity, or computational resources, causing the service to become slow or entirely unavailable for legitimate users. For example, if the target computer is sent a million ping requests per second to test the network connection to the target computer. Network bandwidth may be flooded and unavailable for other legitimate requests to succeed.

### 1.4.6.2 Protocol DDoS (Layer 4 DDoS)

As you move to layer 4, in this layer, you will get Protocol DDoS (Transport Layer, or Layer 4 DDoS). Protocol DDoS attack targets the protocols and services used in network communication. Unlike volumetric DDoS attacks that focus on overwhelming the target's bandwidth with a massive amount of traffic, protocol DDoS attacks exploit vulnerabilities or weaknesses in network protocols and services to disrupt the target's normal operation.

In protocol DDoS attacks, the attackers target specific network protocols and services to exhaust system resources, cause service disruptions, or take advantage of protocol limitations.

For example, we can get SYN/ACK flood, UDP Flood, and Reflection attacks. In this layer, the transport will be flooded, so they will not be able to send the packet to the target computer because the connection tables within the firewalls or routers will be filled.

### 1.4.6.3 Application DDoS

Application-level DDoS attacks target web applications, online services, or APIs by overwhelming their resources, causing disruptions and denying access to legitimate users. Unlike network-level DDoS attacks, application DDoS exploits vulnerabilities in the application layer, consuming server resources with illegitimate requests.

Examples include HTTP flood, SQL injection, SSL abuse, malformed SSL, crawlers, and application exploits. DDoS attacks at various layers impact application availability, financial stability, and security. They can last hours or days, causing downtime and financial losses, especially for e-commerce sites, and can damage business reputation.

To mitigate these attacks, scaling resources increases costs. Additionally, application layer attacks can lead to data loss or theft, such as through SQL injection or content scraping.

## 1.4.7 Malware Attacks

A malware attack involves malicious software compromising a computer system, network, or device. Malware can steal sensitive information, disrupt operations, or cause irreversible damage. It enters networks through vulnerabilities and performs malicious actions, such as blocking access, installing hostile software, spreading to other hosts, and creating remote control channels.

Types of malware include:
- **Virus:** Replicates by inserting code into programs or files, spreading through devices and emails.
- **Trojan Horse:** Disguises as legitimate software, setting up backdoors for attackers.
- **Worm:** Replicates and spreads without human activation, infecting unprotected devices.
- **Adware:** Presents unwanted ads and may track online behavior.

- **Keylogger:** Records keystrokes, transmitting data to remote systems.
- **Ransomware:** Encrypts files and demands a ransom for decryption.

Each type of malware serves different malicious purposes, from data theft to system disruption.

## 1.4.8 Phishing Attacks

In Phishing, attackers use fraudulent communication, often disguised as legitimate messages, to trick people into falling for a scam, or to trick individuals into revealing sensitive information, such as login credentials, financial details, or personal information. The term "phishing" is a play on the word "fishing" because attackers are "fishing" for personal data from unsuspecting victims.

In Phishing, It is the common practice to send fraudulent emails that appear to have come from trusted sources to obtain personal information. The main idea behind Phishing is to induce the victim to perform some action, such as clicking on a hyperlink to install malware. Typically, Phishing intends to get users to reveal sensitive data such as financial information, system credentials, etc.

Phishing attacks can take various forms, including email phishing, SMS (text message) Phishing, voice phishing (vishing), and social media phishing.

To protect against phishing attacks, some guidelines: verify the source, hover the mouse pointer over them to see the actual URL, avoid sharing personal information, use Multi-Factor Authentication (MFA), use anti-phishing tools.

Spear phishing is a more advanced technique in which the attackers often will include information known to be of interest to the target, such as current events or financial documents.

## 1.5 Security Defense Management

Now that you have understood the standard attacks class, the intent of attacks, how they operate, etc., it is time to look into how we can set up defense-related activities.

The defense-related activities typically involve, but are not limited to, the following:
- Understanding what security technologies, you can leverage
- Knowing the key people in your organization when it comes to security.
- Knowing the level of security education, your organization has or needed
- Designing the security processes to be implemented
- Building the required security culture inside your organization

## 1.6 Key Security Solutions and Services

This section provides a quick overview of the main security solutions and services that are currently available. You can leverage them as a defense system to safeguard against cyber-attacks.

## 1.6.1 Firewall

A firewall is a security device or software that acts as a barrier between a trusted internal network and an untrusted external network, like the Internet. It monitors and controls incoming and outgoing network traffic based on predefined security rules, protecting the internal network from unauthorized access and cyber threats.

Firewalls inspect data packets and determine whether to allow or block them based on criteria such as IP addresses, ports, protocols, and application types. They typically operate at Layer 3 (Network Layer) and Layer

4 (Transport Layer) of the OSI model, with many modern firewalls also understanding Layer 7 (Application Layer).

Firewalls are essential for network security, blocking unauthorized access, protecting against threats, enforcing security policies, and monitoring traffic. They have evolved from simple packet filters in the 1980s to advanced security devices that proactively protect networks in various environments.

Here's a brief review of the various generations of firewalls:

- Packet Filtering Firewall
- Circuit-Level Proxy
- Application-Level Proxy (aka proxy firewall)
- Stateful Firewall
- Next-Generation Firewall (NGFW)

**Packet Filtering Firewall:** Examines packet headers (source/destination IPs, port numbers) and allows or blocks packets based on defined rules. It's efficient and cost-effective, focusing on static parameters at the network and transport layers.

**Circuit-Level Proxy:** Works at the session layer, providing TCP and UDP connection security by establishing sessions on behalf of source hosts. SOCKS5 is a classic example, using a tunneling method to support various traffic types.

**Application-Level Proxy:** Acts as a client proxy, requesting services on behalf of the client and understanding application protocol commands. It offers caching, detailed logging, and user authentication.

**Stateful Firewall:** Operates at the network and transport layers, maintaining a state table to track active connections. It monitors network traffic states and defends against unauthorized access, offering higher performance than dedicated proxies.

**Next-Generation Firewall (NGFW):** Combines traditional firewall capabilities with advanced security features like application-layer inspection, threat detection, antivirus, and role-based access control. It provides multi-layered protection and can inspect HTTPS-encrypted traffic and filter URLs.

## 1.6.2 Web Proxy

A web proxy (or web gateway) is a server or software that acts as an intermediary between a client and the internet. When a client requests a web resource, the request is sent to the web proxy, which forwards it to the destination server and returns the response to the client.

Web proxies serve as application-level firewalls, controlling internal corporate users' access to external web servers. They block malware, enforce use policies, filter URLs, and control content based on site reputation. The primary objectives are to enhance security, privacy, and performance for internet access, ensuring external content doesn't harm the organization. However, with the evolution of Next-Generation Firewalls (NGFWs), web proxies are becoming obsolete.

**Proxy vs. Firewall:** A firewall and a proxy server are used for network security. Firewalls can prevent unauthorized access to your systems by blocking applications and ports. However, proxy servers hide your internal (corporate) network from the Internet.

## 1.6.3 Web Application Firewalls

A Web Application Firewall (WAF) is a security solution that sits between a user's web browser and the web application server to protect web applications from various online threats and attacks. It acts as a full-reverse proxy, protecting applications accessed through the HTTP protocol.

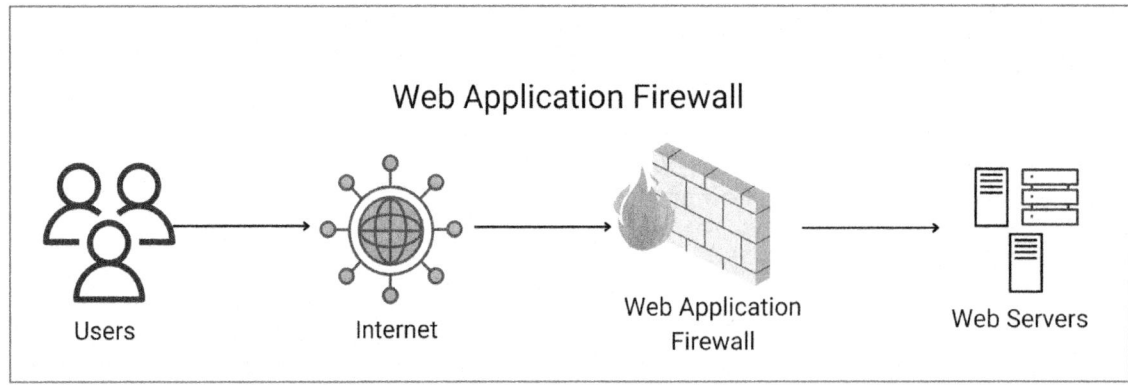

Unlike traditional network firewalls that operate at the network or transport layer, WAFs operate at the application layer (Layer 7) of the OSI model. They analyze the HTTP and HTTPS traffic to and from the web application, inspecting the content and parameters of each request and response. This deep inspection allows WAFs to understand the context of web application traffic and apply security rules accordingly.

It is specifically designed to target and mitigate threats that are specific to web applications, such as Cross-Site Scripting (XSS), SQL injection, and other application-layer attacks. Essentially WAF can be used to protect against the top vulnerabilities identified by Open Web Application Security Project (OWASP).

If you compare WAF with web proxies, web proxies protect the client side, and WAF devices protect the servers (back-ends) from application layer attacks. The primary objective of web proxies is to keep external access requested by internal clients from harming the organization.

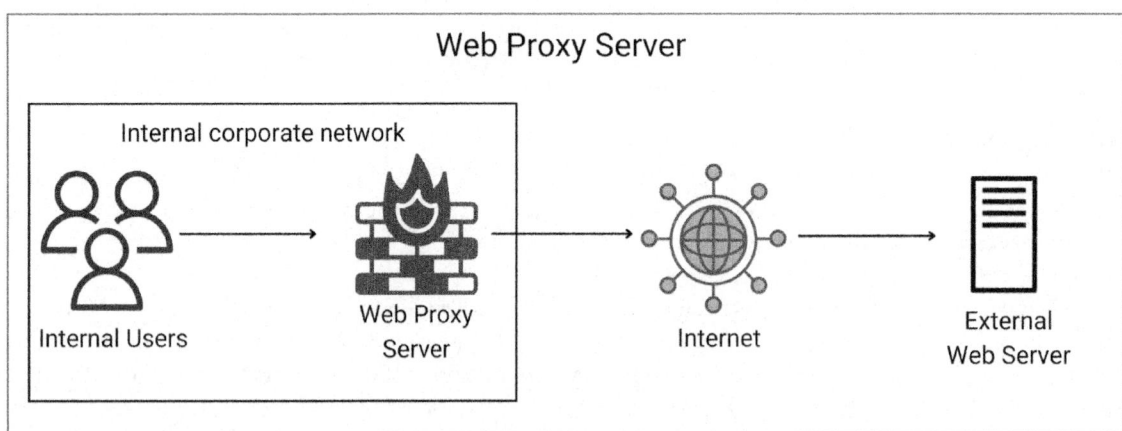

You should distinguish WAFs from the Application Visibility and Control (AVC) capabilities of NGFWs. The Application Visibility and Control (AVC) of NGFWs are focused on controlling outbound user access from the services provided by WAFs. They can work in tandem instead of replacing one with another.

## 1.6.4 Intrusion Detection and Intrusion Prevention

Intrusion Detection System (IDS) and Intrusion Prevention System (IPS) are two important components of network security that work together to detect and respond to potential security threats and attacks on a network.

These technologies are critical network security technology of any enterprise security system that continuously monitors network traffic for suspicious activities and takes steps to prevent it. In addition, it provides in-depth inspection capabilities so that the occurrence of malicious traffic can be discovered inside network packets.

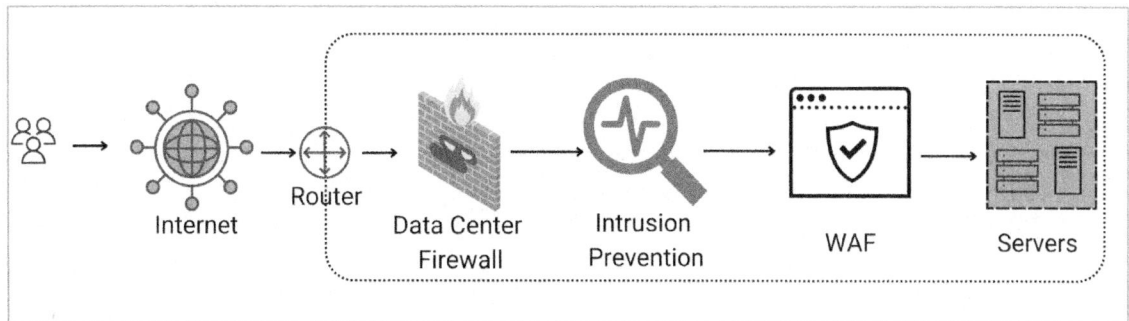

**Sample Inbound Topology With IP**

While both IDS and IPS are designed to enhance the overall security posture, they have distinct functionalities and purposes. Intrusion-detection system (IDS) devices are mainly concerned with monitoring and alerting tasks. However, intrusion-prevention system (IPS) solutions are deployed in line with the traffic flow and aim to avoid actual attack/damage to systems.

IDSs and IPSs can look within packets for well-known attack patterns and take action according to the configured rules. Some common activities are dropping the packet, blocking the connection, denying any further access to the source address that initiated the attack, and sending an alert when an attack indication signature is spotted.

IPSs can be combined with stateful firewalls for data center inbound traffic protection. In addition, they provide detailed analyses of the connections permitted by firewalls, complementing their work.

An IPS concentrates most of its packet analysis tasks at the Network, Transport, and Application OSI layers using stateful pattern matching and executing traffic anomaly detection.

IPS can be deployed in many possible formats, such as a dedicated appliance, a dedicated hardware (or software) module inside a stateful firewall, or a resource enabled on a rule basis on NGFWs.

## 1.6.5 Virtual Private Networks

A Virtual Private Network (VPN) is a secure and encrypted network connection that allows users to access the Internet or private networks over a public network, such as the Internet. The term virtual private network (VPN) refers to technologies that provide the characteristics of a private corporate network, even when traffic is sent outside the private corporate network over a shared network infrastructure.

VPNs were created to provide a secure extension to corporate networks without any need to set up a dedicated extended private network based on expensive WAN infrastructure. The primary purpose of a VPN is to enhance privacy, security, and anonymity for users while they browse the web or access resources on the internet or a private network.

Virtual Private Networks fall into several categories. We look at two common VPN types (IPSec and SSL) that will help your understanding about VPN further.

### 1.6.5.1 IPSec VPN

IPSec (Internet Protocol Security) VPN is a type of Virtual Private Network (VPN) that utilizes the IPSec protocol suite to establish secure and encrypted communication between two or more devices over the Internet or other networks. IPsec includes a group of protocols used together to set up encrypted connections between devices. IPsec works by encrypting IP packets and authenticating the source where the packets come from.

IPSec is widely used with VPN for creating secure site-to-site connections or remote access connections, providing a high level of data confidentiality, integrity, and authentication.

For example, the IPsec framework helps answer questions such as confidentiality, integrity, and authentication of VPN participants. It also includes the management of cryptographic keys. All of these tasks are accomplished by using standardized protocols and algorithms, which is why IPsec became ubiquitous.

### 1.6.5.2 SSL VPN

SSL VPN is another VPN technology that does not require a dedicated client. Instead, SSL VPNs rely on the TLS to secure remote access. SSL It uses the SSL/TLS (Transport Layer Security) protocol to establish a secure and encrypted connection between a client and a VPN server. SSL VPN allows users to securely access private networks or resources over the internet, providing a secure remote access solution.

Unlike traditional IPsec VPNs, which operate at the network layer (Layer 3) of the OSI model, SSL VPNs operate at the application layer (Layer 7). They leverage the security features of SSL/TLS, which are commonly used to secure web traffic, to create a secure communication channel for remote access.

VPNs enable authenticated users to establish secure connections to internal HTTP and HTTPS services via standard web browsers. This possibility of providing secure remote access over web browsers sounded appealing to administrators as they don't need to manage corporate machines for SSL VPN connections.

Endpoints are the main differentiator between IPsec and SSL VPNs. An IPsec VPN allows users to connect remotely to an entire network and all its applications. On the hand, SSL VPNs enable users to access a specific system or application on the network using remote tunneling.

# 1.7 Tools for Vulnerability Analysis and Management

Vulnerability is a system weakness that can be exploited. To find and manage these vulnerabilities, tools like Nessus, OpenVAS, Rapid7 Nexpose, and Burp Suite help organizations scan for security weaknesses and assist in remediation.

The vulnerability assessment and management process involves several key steps:

> **Inventory Compiling:** Identify and list all assets (hardware, software, systems) in the network, both on-premises and cloud-based, focusing on mission-critical assets.
> **Identification of Vulnerabilities:** Use scanning tools to detect vulnerabilities, such as software bugs and misconfigurations, regularly or in response to events.
> **Assigning Priorities:** Evaluate the criticality and business relevance of vulnerabilities to prioritize efforts.
> **Remediation:** Create a roadmap of actions to reduce exposure based on identified vulnerabilities and their priorities.

**Effective Exposure Level Measurement:** Measure progress by assessing how much exposure has been reduced and comparing with competitors.

Security is a continuous, repeatable process involving technology and people. These steps should be part of the routine for any security team.

## 1.8 Security Information and Event Management

Security Information and Event Management (SIEM) is a cybersecurity approach that collects, aggregates, analyzes, and correlates security event data from various sources within an organization's IT infrastructure. SIEM solutions provide real-time monitoring and analysis of events, helping to detect potential security incidents, minimize false positives, and prioritize response actions based on risk levels.

SIEM helps organizations identify security threats and vulnerabilities before they cause damage or disrupt business operations. It involves data aggregation, consolidation, and sorting tasks to identify threats and adhere to compliance requirements. SIEM solutions collect logs and flow information from systems, network devices, and security tools like firewalls and antivirus software.

Core functionalities of SIEM include log management, event correlation, analytics, incident monitoring, security alerts, and compliance management and reporting.

**Log Management:** Log management is essential for providing centralized visibility and real-time analysis of log data to detect security threats, monitor suspicious activities, and respond to incidents effectively. SIEM solutions capture event data from various sources across an organization's network, storing and analyzing logs and flow data from hosts, users, applications, and network devices in real-time. This centralization allows security teams to manage event logs and network flow data from one location.

**Event Correlation and Analytics:** Event correlation and analytics in SIEM involve analyzing data from multiple sources to identify patterns, relationships, and potential security threats. By using analytics to detect data patterns and event correlations, SIEM solutions help quickly identify and mitigate potential threats. This process improves the mean time to detect (MTTD) and mean time to respond (MTTR) for the SOC team, automating the manual workflows associated with in-depth security event analysis.

**Incident Monitoring and Security Alerts:** Incident monitoring and security alerts focus on real-time monitoring and proactive detection of potential security incidents. SIEM solutions provide centralized management of on-premise and cloud-based infrastructure, monitoring security incidents across the entire IT security boundary. By using customizable correlation rules, the security team can receive immediate alerts and take appropriate actions to mitigate threats before they cause damage.

**Compliance Management and Reporting:** Compliance management and reporting ensure that an organization adheres to regulatory standards, industry best practices, and internal security policies. SIEM solutions generate real-time compliance reports for standards such as PCI-DSS, GDPR, HIPAA, and SOX. These reports reduce the burden on the security management team and help detect potential violations early. Many SIEM solutions come with pre-built reports that can be automated to meet compliance requirements.

Modern SIEM solutions often include artificial intelligence (AI) and user behavior analytics (UBA) to quickly identify deviations from a user's normal network activity. Effective use of SIEM requires investment in training to understand its capabilities and detailed documentation about the environment being monitored.

## 1.9 TLS/SSL Offload

Secure Sockets Layer (SSL) Protocol: SSL provides data integrity, confidentiality, and peer authentication for applications communicating over TCP. Developed to create a generic layer of security, SSL was deprecated in 2015 and replaced by the Transport Layer Security (TLS) protocol.

An interesting challenge with SSL/TLS is that while they enhance security, they can obscure visibility, allowing malicious traffic to hide inside encrypted channels. To address this, many security solutions like NGFWs, WAFs, and IPSs now support TLS stream decryption before data analysis.

TLS/SSL Offload: TLS/SSL offload, also known as SSL termination or SSL acceleration, involves offloading the encryption and decryption tasks from the application server to a specialized device or software component. This improves the performance and scalability of web applications by relieving the application servers of the computational burden associated with cryptographic processing, especially during high traffic loads. This process is crucial for maintaining server efficiency while ensuring secure data transmission over HTTPS.

By deploying TLS-offload operations, these solutions can provide the following benefits:

- Web servers can be offloaded from encryption duties and leverage less-intensive encryption algorithms, allowing them to serve more concurrent clients with a better response time.
- The security solutions can centralize public certificates and allow the use of private certificates in the web servers, which are less expensive and easier to maintain.

## 1.10 Well-Known Security Frameworks and Models

The security risk is based on the possibility of a particular vulnerability being exploited and the potential impact due to the exploitation of the exposure.

Security frameworks are a series of documented processes defining policies and procedures for implementing and managing information security controls. They typically include standards, guidelines, sample policies, recommended security safeguards and tools, risk management approaches, relevant technologies, and recognized best practices for protecting specific computing environments. These security frameworks are a blueprint for managing risk and reducing vulnerabilities.

If you look at the tactical level, the contents inside the framework are security controls that can be mapped to the threats an organization may be exposed to.

Many security frameworks were developed with a particular goal in mind, such as providing security control related guidance for a given industry. On the other hand, many security frameworks are created for more general usage.

Let's have a brief overview of some of these security frameworks.

**Payment Card Industry Data Security Standard (PCI DSS):** Ensures merchants processing credit card transactions meet security standards for accepting, processing, storing, and transmitting cardholder data.

**Health Insurance Portability and Accountability Act (HIPAA):** A federal law protecting certain electronic health information from being disclosed without the patient's consent or knowledge.

**National Institute for Standards and Technology Cybersecurity Framework (NIST CSF):** A publication developed collaboratively among industry, academia, and the U.S. government. It guides cybersecurity activities within an organization, combining standards, guidelines, and proven practices.

**General Data Protection Regulation (GDPR):** A legal framework ensuring the protection of personal data of EU members, requiring companies to have robust processes for handling and storing personal information. It applies to transactions within the EU and to personal data transferred outside the EU. Compliance with GDPR is necessary for businesses conducting transactions with EU companies.

## 1.11 Security Controls

Security controls are implemented to reduce the level of risk to which an organization is exposed. Security controls are a type of safeguard or countermeasure used to detect, avoid, counteract, or minimize security risks to physical property, data, computer systems, or other assets.

There are three main types of IT security controls technical, administrative, and physical.

**Physical Controls:**
Physical security controls are measures and procedures designed to protect physical assets, resources, and personnel from unauthorized access, theft, damage, or harm. They ensure the security and safety of an organization's premises and complement other security measures like information security. Examples include locks, fencing, monitoring cameras, and security agents, commonly used in on-premises data centers and large cloud service providers.

**Logical Controls:**
Logical controls, also known as technical controls, protect systems, networks, and environments that process, transmit, and store data. They focus on securing digital information and technology resources from unauthorized access, data breaches, and cyber threats. Examples include anti-virus software, passwords, encryption, firewalls, and intrusion detection systems.

**Administrative Security Controls:**
Administrative security controls are policies, procedures, and practices implemented to manage, monitor, and enforce security across an organization's operations. These controls focus on the human aspect of security, including roles, responsibilities, training, and governance. They ensure adherence to security policies and procedures, reducing the risk of security breaches. Examples include risk management processes, security documentation, and security education training and awareness programs.

## 1.12 The Security Wheel

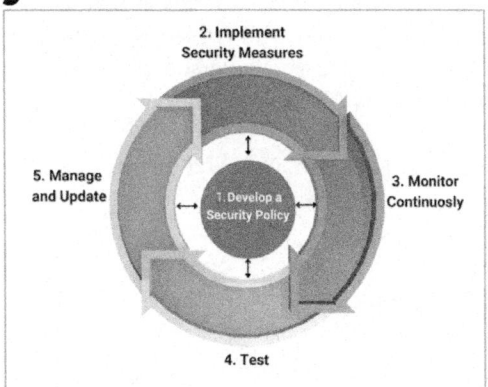

The security wheel, also known as the cybersecurity wheel or security wheel diagram, is a graphical representation of the various components and layers of an organization's cybersecurity framework. It provides a visual overview of the key areas of focus that contribute to a comprehensive and effective cybersecurity strategy. The security wheel typically includes different segments or sections, each representing a specific aspect of cybersecurity. The exact layout and contents of the security wheel may vary based on the organization's specific needs, industry, and regulatory requirements.

The security wheel symbolizes that security operations are an iterative process. It is a closed-loop model based on the foundational concept of security policy. The wheel identifies the four stages of developing a secure system. Everything you do in securing, monitoring, testing, and improving security occurs with reference to security policy. In other words, at the heart of the process is the security policy.

This model is structured in five basic stages: develop a security policy, implement security measures, monitor continuously, test, and last one is managed and update.

**Develop a Security Policy:** The first stage starts with a high-level policy that establishes and documents the strategic goals related to the organization's business objectives/goals or mission. The policy should outline the principles, appropriate standards, guidelines, procedures, and baselines to guide the implementation.

**Implement Security Measures:** Once you have recognized and defined the organization's assets that need to be protected and the appropriate protection level based on their business relevance, you next deploy the security controls. The security controls will help in managing risk mitigation. When implementing security measures, to help provide better security, you will need to have many layers of defense, as mentioned in the "Key Security Solutions and Services" section.

**Monitor Continuously**: In this stage, you can employ logging, security resources and tools such as intrusion detection, and security techniques such as SIEM to find out violations of the access policies.

**Test:** You should always pay attention to this phase -- means testing. You should not take for granted that all protection and monitoring capabilities you built and set up will work as you intended. There is always a possibility of hackers finding new ways to exploit weaknesses. Vulnerability analysis and management is the key objective of this phase.

**Manage and Update**: The feedback you get from the monitoring and testing phase, you apply as improvements in the form of new or updated controls. You may need to review the security policy depending on the specific findings. For example, if the security policy was too permissive or too simple, that led to exposure to high risk to the organization's assets.

## 1.13 The Attack Continuum Model

Security is a moving target, and it's unrealistic to think that any system is entirely impenetrable. Despite robust defenses, cyberattacks are inevitable. The key is to minimize their impact through a solid, layered defense system. The Attack Continuum Model by Cisco is a cybersecurity framework that divides the attack process into three phases: "Before," "During," and "After" the attack.

Before: This stage focuses on proactive prevention, reducing the attack surface through tools and methods like firewalls, VPNs, WAFs, anti-DDoS measures, and endpoint security.

During: This stage emphasizes real-time detection and monitoring, offering visibility and awareness of network activities through IPS/IDS, sandboxing, and TLS offload.

**The Attack Continuum Model**

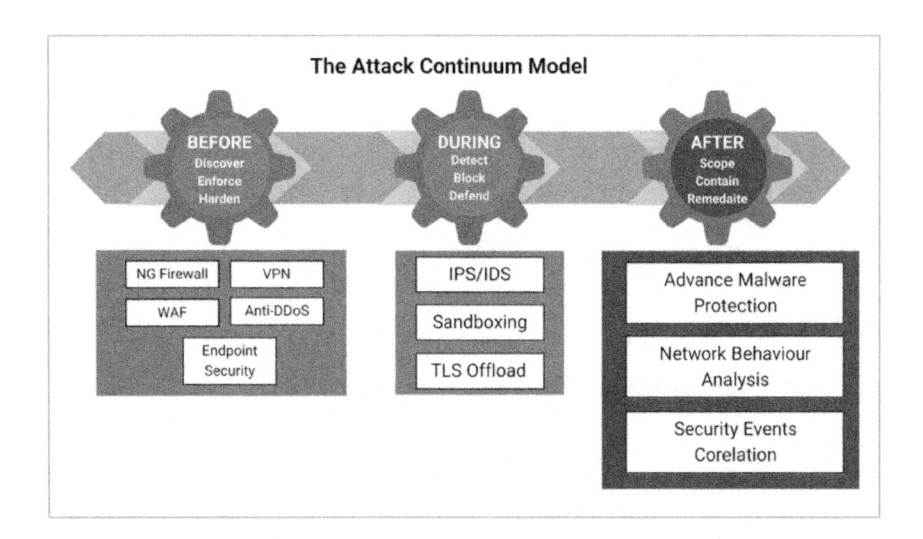

After: In this stage, the focus is on post-incident analysis and recovery, dealing with threats that may remain undetected initially. Tools for advanced malware protection, network behavior analysis, and security events correlation help identify entry points, understand the threat reach, contain propagation, and remediate damage. The model includes an implicit feedback loop to prevent future attacks of the same type, ensuring continuous improvement in the organization's security posture.

## 1.14 The Zero-Trust Model

In the early to mid-90s, corporate networks had clearly defined perimeters with central access points to the internet protected by classic firewalls and web proxies. All internal traffic was trusted, while external IP addresses were not. However, the modern landscape of ubiquitous internet access, multiple user devices, and direct internet connections from branch offices has complicated network security.

Companies are moving workloads to the cloud, requiring coordinated security efforts for both on-premises and cloud data. Extranet connections, while facilitating business transactions, can introduce shared vulnerabilities. Network administrators face these and other daily challenges.

To address these, the *Zero-Trust Model* has emerged, based on the principle of least privilege. Organizations should grant only minimal necessary permissions and should not implicitly trust any entity, inside or outside the network. The model adopts a "never trust, always verify" approach, continuously assessing and authorizing access to resources based on contextual factors.

The *Zero-Trust Model* mandates authentication and authorization for all entities before granting access to applications and data. Key practices include advanced authentication, micro-segmentation, and widespread use of encryption to ensure data confidentiality and integrity. This approach is well-suited for cloud environments, which are typically multitenant and do not inherently allow for trust within a shared network.

### Summary

In this chapter, we looked into general concepts and terminology that are foundations of understanding security. This is important for demonstrating a good level of general education on the security subject matter and for a better understanding of future chapters.

After getting an overview of basic networking and security definitions, we introduced some main classes of attacks and how to address and protect resources against them. Considering the fundamental principle that security is not a product, we reviewed some well-known security frameworks.

We discussed the security wheel, designed to remind you of the importance of building a security policy and having processes to deal with day-to-day organizations' security challenges. We next discussed the attack continuum model, which shows you how to position the available security controls according to their capability in a particular attack stage.

Finally, we introduced the zero-trust model based on the principle of least privilege. The zero-trust model provides the recommended mindset for creating controls on shared computing environments, which is the key characteristic of cloud computing.

## 1.15 Chapter Review Questions

**Question 1:**
What does the "CIA Triad" in security stand for?
A. Cyber Intelligence Agency
B. Confidentiality, Integrity, and Accountability
C. Confidentiality, Integrity, and Availability
D. Control, Integrity, and Assurance

**Question 2:**
Which of the following best describes a man-in-the-middle (MITM) attack?
A. An attacker sends a high volume of traffic to overwhelm a target system
B. An attacker intercepts and possibly alters the communication between two parties
C. An attacker gains unauthorized access by guessing a password
D. An attacker monitors network traffic to capture sensitive information

**Question 3:**
What is the purpose of a web application firewall (WAF)?
A. To filter and monitor HTTP requests
B. To block IP addresses based on a blacklist
C. To encrypt web traffic between servers
D. To detect and prevent phishing attempts

**Question 4:**
Which OSI layer does the Transport Layer in the TCP/IP model correspond to?
A. Layer 3
B. Layer 4
C. Layer 5
D. Layer 7

**Question 5:**
Which of the following is an example of a protocol-based DDoS attack?
A. Sending large amounts of data to overwhelm a system's network bandwidth
B. Exploiting server weaknesses to prevent legitimate access
C. Overwhelming resources by exhausting connection limits
D. Using phishing emails to compromise user credentials

**Question 6:**
What type of VPN is based on the IPSec protocol?
A. SSL VPN
B. IPSec VPN
C. Layer 7 VPN

D. MPLS VPN

**Question 7:**
Which of the following is a basic security concept that involves ensuring data is only accessible to authorized individuals?
A. Availability
B. Confidentiality
C. Integrity
D. Nonrepudiation

**Question 8:**
What is the primary focus of vulnerability analysis?
A. Finding and fixing software bugs
B. Identifying weaknesses that could be exploited in a system
C. Monitoring network traffic for anomalies
D. Conducting penetration testing on applications

**Question 9:**
Which of the following best describes the Zero-Trust Model?
A. Allowing access to all network users by default
B. Denying all access unless explicitly allowed
C. Implementing security only at the network perimeter
D. Trusting users after their first successful authentication

**Question 10:**
In the Security Wheel model, which phase follows prevention?
A. Monitoring
B. Detection
C. Response
D. Recovery

## 1.16 Answers to Chapter Review Questions

1. C. Confidentiality, Integrity, and Availability
Explanation: The CIA Triad is a fundamental security model focusing on Confidentiality (ensuring only authorized users can access data), Integrity (ensuring data is not tampered with), and Availability (ensuring data and systems are accessible when needed).

2. B. An attacker intercepts and possibly alters the communication between two parties
Explanation: In a man-in-the-middle (MITM) attack, the attacker secretly intercepts and possibly alters communications between two parties, making it seem as though the communication is still private.

3. A. To filter and monitor HTTP requests
Explanation: A Web Application Firewall (WAF) is used to monitor and filter HTTP requests to protect web applications from common exploits such as SQL injection and cross-site scripting (XSS).

4. B. Layer 4
Explanation: The Transport Layer in the TCP/IP model corresponds to Layer 4 in the OSI model, responsible for end-to-end communication and data transfer between systems.

5. C. Overwhelming resources by exhausting connection limits

Explanation: A protocol-based DDoS attack targets server resources by overwhelming them through the exhaustion of connection limits, such as SYN floods or ping of death attacks.

6. B. IPSec VPN
Explanation: An IPSec VPN uses the IPSec protocol for secure, encrypted communication over the internet between two or more networks.

7. B. Confidentiality
Explanation: Confidentiality ensures that sensitive information is only accessible to authorized individuals and not disclosed to unauthorized parties.

8. B. Identifying weaknesses that could be exploited in a system
Explanation: Vulnerability analysis focuses on identifying weaknesses in a system that could be exploited by attackers, with the goal of mitigating potential threats.

9. B. Denying all access unless explicitly allowed
Explanation: The Zero-Trust Model operates on the principle of "never trust, always verify," where no one is trusted by default, and access is denied unless explicitly permitted.

10. B. Detection
Explanation: In the Security Wheel, the phase following prevention is detection, where the system monitors for potential security threats and vulnerabilities to respond appropriately.

# Chapter 2. Cloud Security Principles and Frameworks

**This chapter addresses the following exam objectives:**
Provides foundational knowledge essential for the exam.

◆◆◆◆◆◆

Navigating the complexities of cloud security requires a deep understanding of fundamental principles and established frameworks. This chapter serves as a introduction to the key tenets of securing cloud environments, with a particular focus on Amazon Web Services (AWS). We begin by exploring the core principles that underpin cloud security, highlighting the essential practices and considerations that ensure robust protection in cloud-based systems.

Key cloud security principles form the foundation of this discussion, providing a structured approach to understanding the unique challenges and opportunities presented by cloud computing. We then delve into the AWS Security Framework, offering an overview of its components and how it integrates with broader security strategies. The AWS Shared Responsibility Model is a critical concept that delineates the security responsibilities between AWS and its customers, ensuring clarity and effective collaboration in maintaining a secure environment.

To further support your security strategy, we review the extensive documentation of security best practices provided by AWS. These resources guide implementing and maintaining security measures across various AWS services. Compliance programs are another pivotal aspect, and we explore AWS's commitment to meeting rigorous compliance standards, facilitated by the AWS Artifact Portal, which provides on-demand access to security and compliance reports.

The chapter also examines the AWS Marketplace, an online store where customers can find, buy, and deploy software that runs on AWS, including a variety of security solutions. Practical application of these concepts is reinforced through lab exercises, such as generating PCI DSS reports and checking compliance with ISO 27001 standards. These hands-on activities help solidify understanding and provide actionable skills for managing cloud security in real-world scenarios.

By the end of this chapter, readers will have a solid grounding in cloud security principles and frameworks, equipped with the knowledge to implement effective security strategies within the AWS ecosystem.

## 2.1 Cloud Security Principles

In the previous chapter, we went through security fundamentals. In general, these security fundamentals apply to both on-premises and cloud environments. However, before moving to the Cloud, it is essential to determine which part of your total workload you plan to move to the Cloud and which part stays on the on-premises.

One obvious challenge in cloud security is the inherent perception of loss of control. This initial suspicion could emanate from the lack of visibility into the provider's environment or the incompatibility of security rules or tools used on the Cloud that is different from what you use in your on-prem environment.

You should not move your workload to a cloud provider you do not trust. Trust means not only if the provider has displayed some famous certification or accreditation on its website. Trust means you understand security practices and controls available on the provider's infrastructure and, more importantly, how to enable and disable those controls.

As a clear leader in the cloud service provider market, AWS has focused its development efforts on each cloud service. In addition, AWS has developed many services related services such as AWS IAM, AWS Security Hub, Amazon GaurdDuty, AWS Shield, AWS Web Application Firewall (WAF), AWS Key Management Service (KMS), Amazon Macie, AWS Artifact, Amazon Detective, and AWS Secrets Manager, Amazon Detective, and AWS Secrets Manager and many more.

With that being said, it is important to familiarize yourself with the AWS security and compliance services, tools, security best practices, and responsibilities, as well as a good understanding of your own responsibilities during your cloud adoption journey.

With this background, you should be able to build and maintain and steadily improve your security posture using the AWS Cloud, create a better security plan, and implement security controls based on the industry security best practices, frameworks, and regulations your organization needs to be compliant with.

## 2.2 Key Cloud Security Principles

The NCSC (National Cyber Security Centre) has published 14 cloud security principles. These principles are designed to give guidance to cloud service providers to protect their customers.

- **Data in-transit protection**: User data that is transitioning between networks should be protected against any interference.

- **Asset Protection and Resilience**: User data and assets should be protected against physical tampering, loss, damage, or seizure.

- **Separation between customers**: If a service user is compromised by malicious software, this should not affect another user's data or service.

- **Governance framework**: The service provider should follow a Security Governance Framework to coordinate its management of the service internally.

- **Operational security**: The service must be operated securely to prevent and detect attacks. Adequate security should be simple and inexpensive.

- **Personnel security**: Service provider personnel should be thoroughly screened and need to have in-depth training to reduce the likelihood of accidental or malicious compromise.

- **Secure development**: Cloud services should be designed with security in mind.

- **Supply chain security**: The cloud service provider (CSP) should ensure that their supply chain follows the same security principles.

- **Secure user management**: Your service provider should ensure that you have the relevant tools to manage the use of their services securely. Management interfaces prevent unauthorized access to your data, making them a vital part of the security barrier.

- **Identity and authentication**: Access to the service interfaces should only be granted to specific individuals and should all be guarded by adequate authentication measures – two-party authentication if possible.

- **External interface protection**: Any external or less trustworthy service interfaces must be identified and defended appropriately.

- **Secure service administration:** Important company data could be stolen or manipulated if a cloud service is compromised through its administration system. It is vital that these services are secure.

- **Audit information for users**: A service provider should supply their customers with the audit record needed to monitor the service and who can access your data. This is vital as it allows you to identify inappropriate or malicious activity.

- **Secure use of service**: You are responsible for ensuring the service is used properly, and your data is protected. While these 14 principles are mainly guidelines for cloud service providers, they still need to consider the user's role. Indeed, this last principle reminds us that a fully secure system requires its users' and providers' active efforts.

Reference: https://www.ncsc.gov.uk/collection/cloud/the-cloud-security-principles

## 2.3 Overview of AWS Security Framework

The AWS Security Framework is designed to help customers build secure, high-performing, resilient, and efficient application infrastructure. This framework incorporates best practices and guidelines that AWS has developed based on its experiences with numerous customers.

The following are the key components of AWS Security Framework:

### Security Pillar of AWS Well-Architected Framework
The Security Pillar guides protecting data, systems, and assets in the cloud. It focuses on five key areas: Identity and Access Management, Detective Controls, Infrastructure Protection, Data Protection, and Incident Response. For example, implementing the principle of least privilege using AWS IAM to ensure users have only the permissions they need.

### Shared Responsibility Model
This model delineates the security responsibilities of AWS (security of the cloud) and the customer (security in the cloud). AWS is responsible for protecting the infrastructure that runs all of the services offered in the AWS Cloud, while customers are responsible for securing their data, identities, and applications. For example, AWS is responsible for the physical security of data centers, while customers are responsible for managing user access to their AWS resources.

### AWS Security Services
AWS provides a wide range of security services to help customers enhance their security posture. These services include AWS Identity and Access Management (IAM), Amazon GuardDuty, AWS Security Hub, AWS Shield, AWS WAF, and many more. For example, Amazon GuardDuty can detect and respond to potential threats by continuously monitoring and analyzing AWS account activity.

### Compliance Programs
AWS supports various compliance programs, helping customers meet various regulatory and industry requirements. These programs include certifications and attestations such as ISO 27001, SOC 1/2/3, PCI DSS, and others. For example, a healthcare provider using AWS to store patient data can leverage AWS's HIPAA-compliant services to ensure that they meet regulatory requirements.

### Encryption and Key Management
AWS offers robust encryption and key management services, such as AWS Key Management Service (KMS), AWS CloudHSM, and server-side encryption options for S3, EBS, and other services. For example, encrypting data stored in Amazon S3 using AWS KMS keys to ensure data confidentiality and integrity.

### Network Security
AWS provides multiple layers of network security, including VPCs, security groups, network ACLs, AWS Network Firewall, and more, to protect resources and data. For example, using VPC peering to securely connect multiple VPCs and applying security groups to control inbound and outbound traffic at the instance level.

### Monitoring and Logging
AWS offers comprehensive monitoring and logging services, such as Amazon CloudWatch, AWS CloudTrail, and AWS Config, to provide visibility into AWS resource usage and security. For example, AWS CloudTrail can log all API calls made within an AWS account for audit purposes and forensic analysis.

### Incident Response
AWS helps customers develop and implement incident response plans by providing tools and services such as AWS Lambda, AWS Systems Manager, and Amazon SNS for automation and communication during incidents. For example, you can automate the isolation of compromised instances using AWS Lambda and Systems Manager Automation documents.

By integrating these components, customers can create a secure environment that protects their applications and data, maintains compliance, and ensures that they can effectively respond to security incidents.

## Example Scenario
A company wants to build a secure web application on AWS.

**Identity and Access Management:** The company uses AWS IAM to create roles and policies that grant specific permissions to developers, ensuring that they have access only to the resources they need.
**Network Security:** The application is hosted within a VPC, with public subnets for web servers and private subnets for databases. Security groups are configured to allow only necessary traffic.
**Data Protection:** Data stored in Amazon S3 is encrypted using AWS KMS keys. Database instances in Amazon RDS are encrypted and use SSL/TLS for data in transit.
**Monitoring and Logging:** Amazon CloudWatch is used to monitor application performance, while AWS CloudTrail logs API activity for auditing purposes.
**Incident Response:** The company sets up Amazon GuardDuty to monitor for unusual activity and uses AWS Lambda to automate responses to potential security incidents, such as isolating compromised instances.

By following AWS security best practices and leveraging AWS security services, the company can ensure that their web application is secure and compliant with industry standards.

# 2.4 AWS Shared Responsibility Model

Security and Compliance are a shared responsibility between AWS and the customer. This shared responsibility model can reduce the customer's responsibility on the AWS Cloud, as AWS operates, manages, and controls components in the host operating system, the virtualization layer, and the physical security of data centers. The customer assumes management responsibility for the guest operating system, including updates, security patches, and other associated application software; however, AWS provides a security group firewall. Therefore, AWS customers must carefully consider the services they choose, as their responsibilities vary depending on the services used and applicable laws and regulations. This differentiation of responsibility between AWS and AWS Customers is commonly referred to as Security "of" the Cloud versus Security "in" the Cloud.

AWS is responsible for the "Security of the cloud," meaning the infrastructure that runs the Cloud, including physical hardware, software, network, and physical facilities that host infrastructure and run Cloud services. Based on the AWS Responsibility Model, AWS is responsible for AWS's global infrastructure, which includes the hardware and software of AWS Regions, AWS Availability Zones, and Edge Locations. Additionally, AWS is responsible for computing, storage, databases, and networking infrastructure along with physical facilities hosting data centers for the AWS global infrastructure.

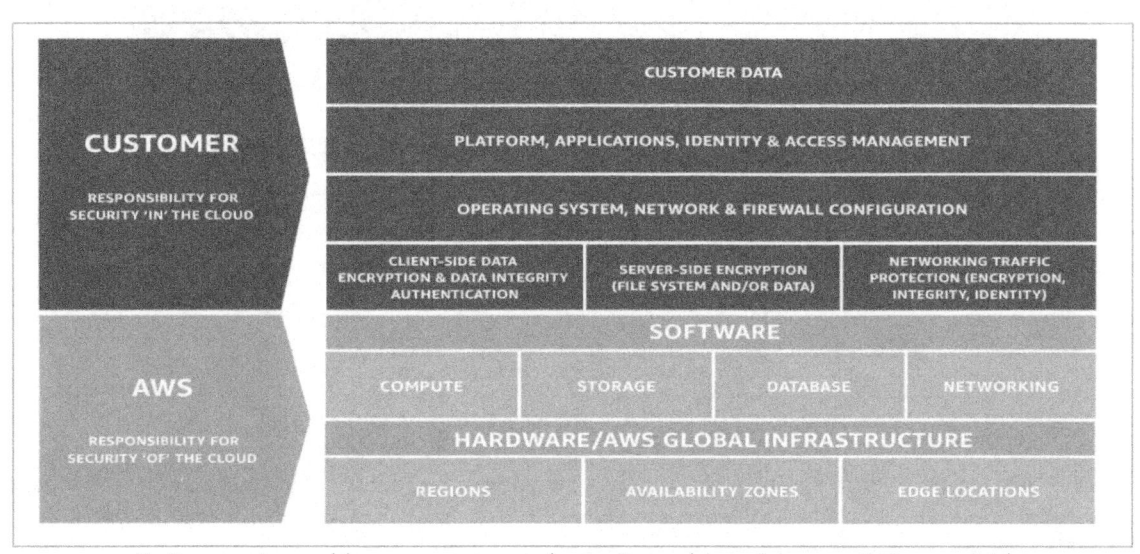

Reference: https://aws.amazon.com/compliance/shared-responsibility-model/

"Security in the Cloud" is the responsibility of the customer. AWS Customer responsibilities depend on the AWS services they use. For example, customers have more responsibility and control when using EC2, where they are responsible for securing the instance by configuring Security Groups and Network ACLs, along with applying updates and security patches. For abstracted services, such as Amazon S3 and Amazon DynamoDB, AWS operates the infrastructure layer, the operating system, and platforms, while customers access the endpoints to store and retrieve data. This includes the disposal and replacement of disk drives and data center security.

Inherited controls, such as physical and environmental controls, are AWS's responsibility. For example, replacing faulty hardware of Amazon EC2 instances falls under infrastructure maintenance, which is AWS's responsibility. Shared controls between AWS and customers include patch management, configuration management, training employees, OS configuration, and data security and encryption. AWS provides the underlying infrastructure, but customers are responsible for managing their guest operating systems, application software, and data.

Customers must manage their data, including encryption, and use AWS tools like IAM to implement appropriate permissions. AWS is responsible for maintaining the infrastructure's security, availability, and durability, while customers must enable MFA on accounts, analyze access patterns, and review permissions.

The shared responsibility model varies depending on the type of AWS service. For infrastructure services like Amazon EC2, customers handle most security configurations. For container services, AWS manages the underlying platform, while customers handle data protection and IAM. Abstracted services like Amazon S3 and DynamoDB have AWS managing most components, with customers responsible for data protection and access management.

In conclusion, the AWS Shared Responsibility Model ensures that both AWS and its customers understand their roles in securing the cloud environment, providing a clear framework for managing and securing cloud resources based on the type of service being used.

## 2.5 Security Best Practices Documentation

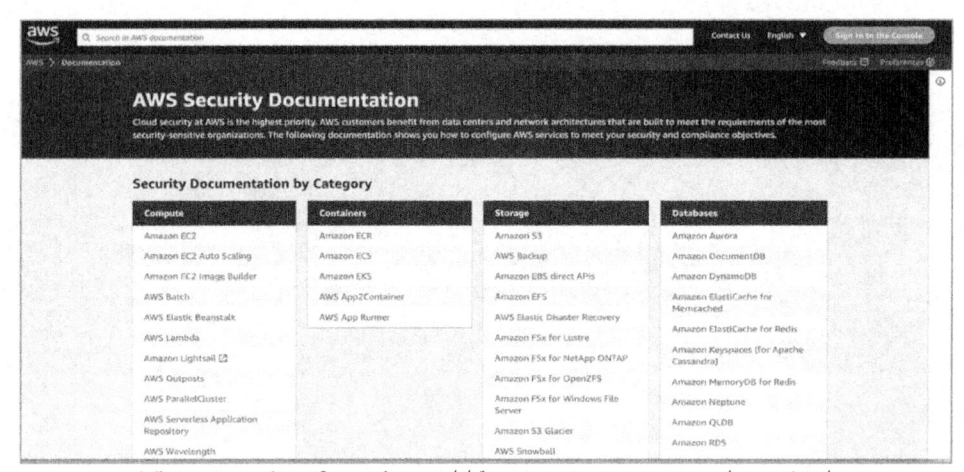

The screenshot from: https://docs.aws.amazon.com/security/

AWS provides a set of documents (https://docs.aws.amazon.com/security/) with security best practices for each one of its cloud services. These documents' main goal is to help you implement your own controls in AWS Cloud environments.

## 2.6 AWS Compliance Programs

Another essential foundational security concept to understand is how AWS approaches Compliance. AWS helps organizations when it comes to Compliance with applications deployed on its platform.

When running your workloads in the AWS Cloud, you inherit all the security controls and compliance best practices that AWS has developed for its most security-demanding customers. Compliance requirements vary country or region-wise due to its global presence. AWS must comply with various regulations and best practices worldwide for security, Compliance, and data protection.

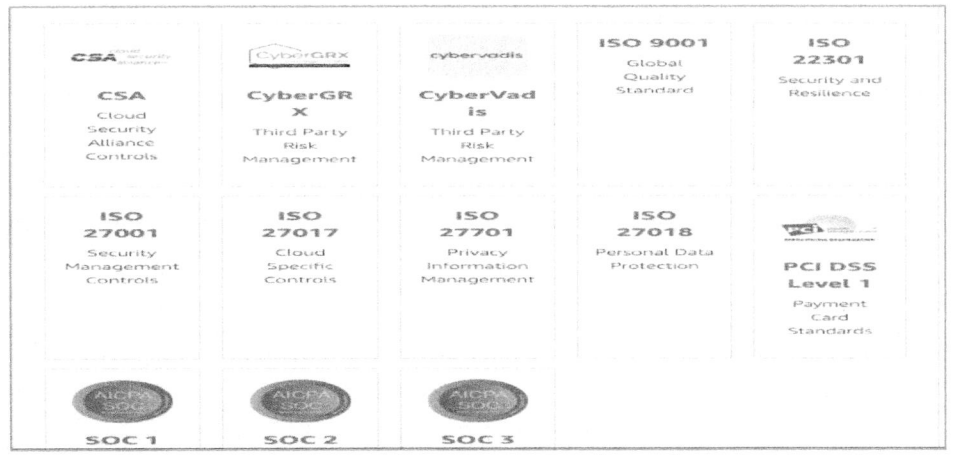

Screenshot from: https://aws.amazon.com/compliance/programs/

All certifications and compliance programs that AWS supports can be found on the AWS Compliance Programs site (aws.amazon.com/compliance/programs), as you can see in the screenshot.

When deciding on choosing the cloud service provider to run your workloads, the evaluation should include the provider's security controls, best practices, and certifications relevant to your industry and organization. This section will give us an overview of some of the main security best practices and standards you must consider as part of your evaluation process.

## ISO 27001
ISO 27001: A standard from the International Organization for Standardization, ISO 27001 is part of the ISO 27000 information security standards family. It is used to define and implement an information security management system (ISMS) -- a global standard for effective information management.

It helps organizations avoid potentially costly security breaches by assisting the companies in managing information assets that include sensitive data. Additionally, ISO 27001-certified organizations can show customers, partners, and shareholders that they have taken steps to protect data in case of a breach.

This standard also leverages ISO 27002 as the basis for security control best practices.

## ISO 27017
ISO 27017: ISO 27017 (part of the ISO 27000 family) is an information security framework for organizations using (or considering) cloud services -- it is focused on the information security practices for cloud computing. It provides a consistent and comprehensive approach to information security. It extends the guidance explained in ISO 27002.

## ISO 27018
ISO 27018 focuses on protecting personal data in the Cloud it defines standards, controls, and guidelines to protect personally identifiable information (PII) in public cloud computing environments.

## PCI DSS
The Payment Card Industry Data Security Standard (PCI DSS) is an information security standard for organizations that process and store credit card information.

## CSA STAR
The Cloud Security Alliance (CSA) (a not-for-profit organization) aims to promote best practices for security assurance within cloud computing environments. The Security, Trust, Assurance, and Risk (STAR) registry is

a publicly accessible registry that documents popular cloud computing offerings' security and privacy controls. The CSA STAR helps cloud service providers, customers, auditors, and consultants verify that available cloud security controls meet the adequate assurance required to protect data.

### SOC 1, SOC 2, and SOC 3

The System and Organization Controls (SOC) reports are independent third-party examination reports demonstrating how AWS achieves compliance and control objectives. Thus, these reports help your auditors understand the AWS security control models. There are four critical reports. You can access three of them using the AWS Artifact portal, and the other is publicly available.

The AWS SOC 1 Type 2 Report provides the effectiveness of AWS controls that might affect internal controls over financial reporting (ICFR). The auditing process is based on the SSAE 18 and ISAE 3402 standards.

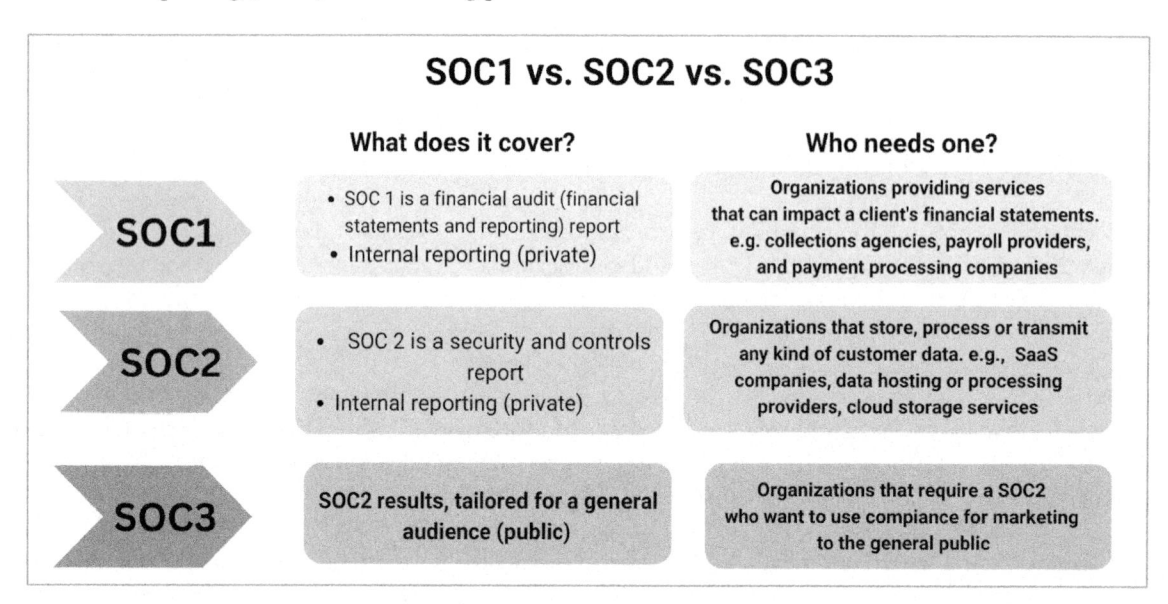

## SOC1 vs. SOC2 vs. SOC3

| | What does it cover? | Who needs one? |
|---|---|---|
| **SOC1** | • SOC 1 is a financial audit (financial statements and reporting) report<br>• Internal reporting (private) | Organizations providing services that can impact a client's financial statements. e.g. collections agencies, payroll providers, and payment processing companies |
| **SOC2** | • SOC 2 is a security and controls report<br>• Internal reporting (private) | Organizations that store, process or transmit any kind of customer data. e.g., SaaS companies, data hosting or processing providers, cloud storage services |
| **SOC3** | SOC2 results, tailored for a general audience (public) | Organizations that require a SOC2 who want to use compiance for marketing to the general public |

The AWS SOC 2 Privacy Type I Report assesses the AWS controls that meet the American Institute of Certified Public Accountants (AICPA) criteria for privacy. The AWS SOC 2 Security, Availability, & Confidentiality Report assesses the AWS controls that meet the American Institute of Certified Public Accountants (AICPA) criteria for security, availability, and confidentiality.

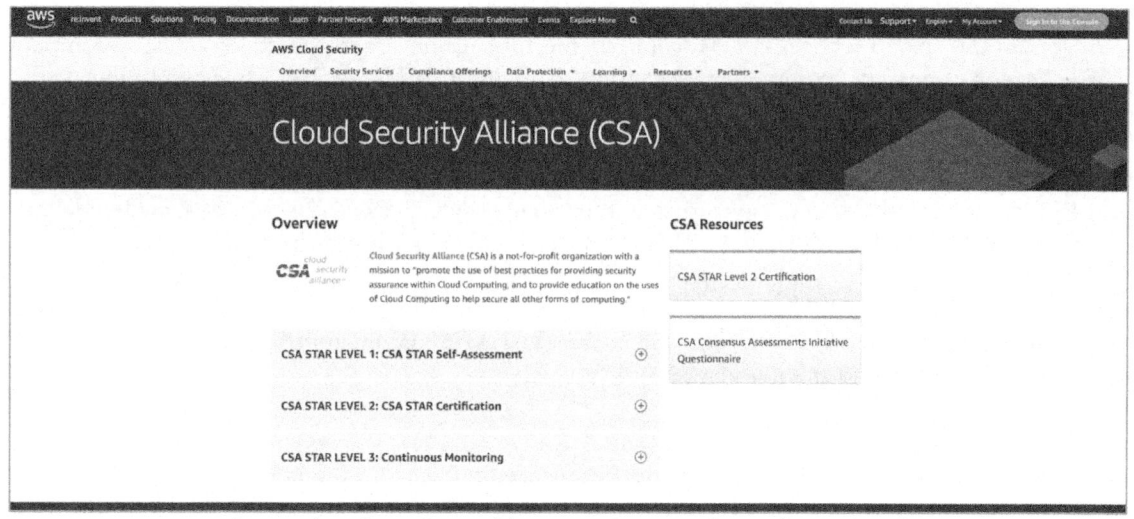

Screenshot from: https://aws.amazon.com/compliance/csa/

The AWS SOC 3 Security, Availability, & Confidentiality Report summarizes what is in AWS SOC 2 report. If you are looking for PCI DSS standards, AWS has published a very interesting report that you can refer to when implementing security controls based on the Shared Responsibility Model. The URL: https://d1.awsstatic.com/whitepapers/compliance/AWS_Anitian_Workbook_PCI_Cloud_Compliance.pdf

There is another URL related to this: https://www.anitian.com/pci-compliance-for-the-aws-cloud/.

The Cloud Security Alliance (CSA) is a not-for-profit organization dedicated to defining and raising awareness of best practices to help ensure a secure cloud computing environment. CSA's mission is to "promote the use of best practices for providing security assurance within Cloud Computing and to provide education on the uses of Cloud Computing to help secure all other forms of computing."

You can use the ISO 27000 certifications, SOC Reports, and other necessary regulations and accreditation models to evaluate how the security controls are implemented in the AWS data centers and services. This will help you determine whether the level of Compliance will achieve the protection you desire for your business.

## 2.7 AWS Artifact Portal

Once you have defined the controls, certifications, and regulations necessary to meet your business protection requirements, you will need to perform periodic assessments and audits of those controls in AWS. AWS Artifact is a central place for compliance-related information that matters to you. It provides on-demand access to AWS' security and compliance reports. AWS Artifact is a portal using which an enterprise can access security and compliance reports related to the AWS public cloud. You can access the Artifact portal using the AWS Console directly, and there are no costs to use it.

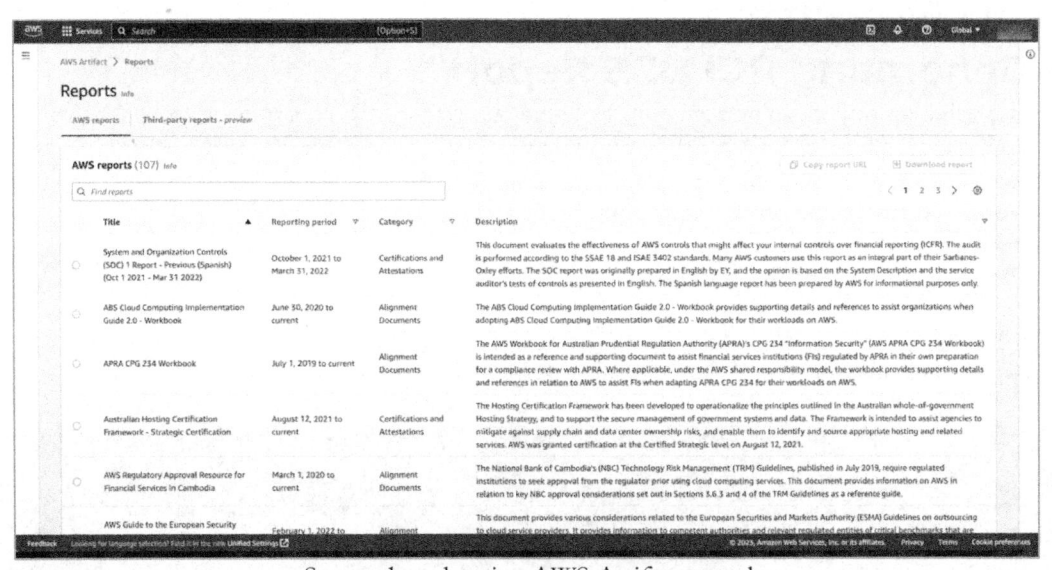

*Screenshot showing AWS Artifact portal*

The following reports are available in AWS Artifact:
- SOC (Service Organization Control) reports.
- PCI (Payment Card Industry) reports.
- Certifications from accreditation bodies across geographies and compliance verticals that validate the implementation and operating effectiveness of AWS security controls.

Agreements available in AWS Artifact include the Business Associate Addendum (BAA) and the Nondisclosure Agreement (NDA). These reports can also guide team members, such as developers, to ensure that they adhere to these standards. Additionally, a user can download reports and other internal AWS documents via Artifact to ensure and demonstrate to auditors or regulators that the AWS offerings meet security and compliance standards.

## 2.8 AWS Marketplace

AWS Marketplace, an online software store, helps customers find, buy, and immediately start using software and services that run on AWS. In addition, the AWS Marketplace enables qualified AWS partners to market and sells their software to AWS Customers.

AWS Marketplace consists of thousands of software listings from popular categories such as security, networking, storage, machine learning, IoT, business intelligence, database, and DevOps. AWS Marketplace is designed for ISVs (Independent Software Vendors), Value-Added Resellers, and Systems Integrators who have software products they want to provide to customers in the AWS Cloud. You can use AWS Marketplace as a buyer, a seller, or both. In addition, anyone with an AWS account can use AWS Marketplace as a consumer and register to become a seller.

The screenshot shows the first search results using the keyword "Security" in AWS Marketplace.

The solutions are available from the marketplace are divided into different categories and are available from several strategic partners. Thus, enabling you to easily replicate and migrate security solutions from your on-premises environment to the AWS Cloud. Moreover, many solutions allow you to use your previously available licenses as Bring Your Own License (BYOL) model. Be sure to regularly visit the AWS Marketplace -- to keep up to date with the latest releases.

## 2.9 Lab Exercises
### 2.9.1 Generating PCI DSS Report

This exercise will help you get an understanding of generating PCI DSS report using the AWS Artifact Portal. In this exercise, you will use the AWS Artifact portal available to generate a PCI DSS report and evaluate your and AWS's responsibilities for each requirement. To complete this exercise, please refer to the AWS Artifact documentation at https://docs.aws.amazon.com/artifact.

1. Login to AWS Console.
2. Search the "AWS Artifact" service.
3. Click the Artifact service.
4. If you have not generated the report, generate the report and click on "View reports." If you have already generated reports, click on "View reports."

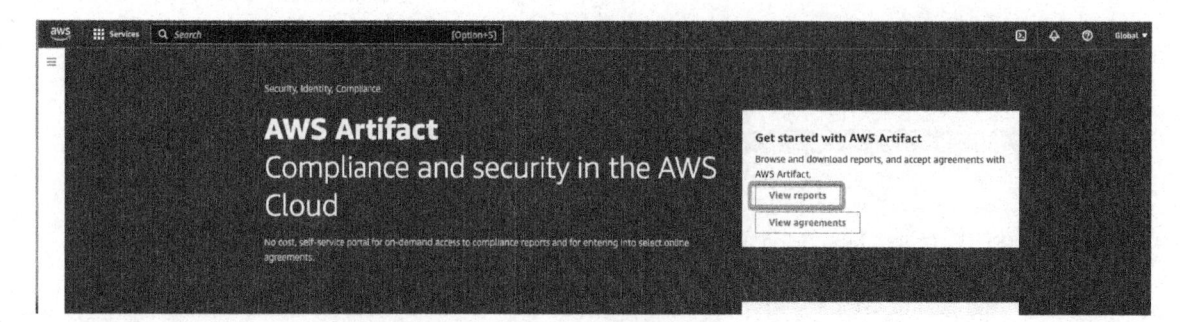

5. Search for the report "PCI DSS Attestation of Compliance (AOC) and Responsibility Summary" and click the link to get the current report. You can also get the previous report.
6. Click on the download report; you can also copy the URL
7. Open the generated PDF using Adobe Acrobat Reader.
8. In the PDF, follow the instructions to open the Artifact.

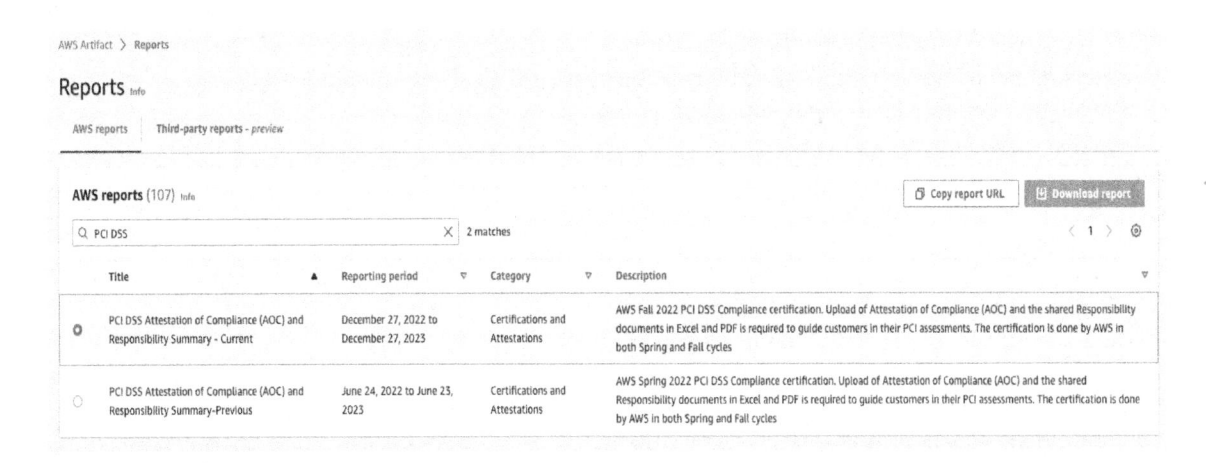

## 2.9.2 Check ISO 27001

This exercise will help you learn how to use the AWS Artifact portal to check ISO 27001. In this exercise, you will use the AWS Artifact portal available to check the ISO 27001 report. To complete this exercise, please refer to the AWS Artifact documentation at https://docs.aws.amazon.com/artifact.

1. Login to AWS Console.
2. Search for the "AWS Artifact" service.
3. Click the Artifact service.
4. If you have not generated the report, generate the report and click on "View reports." If you have already generated reports, click on "View reports."
5. Search for the report "ISO 27001:2022" and click to get the Artifact.

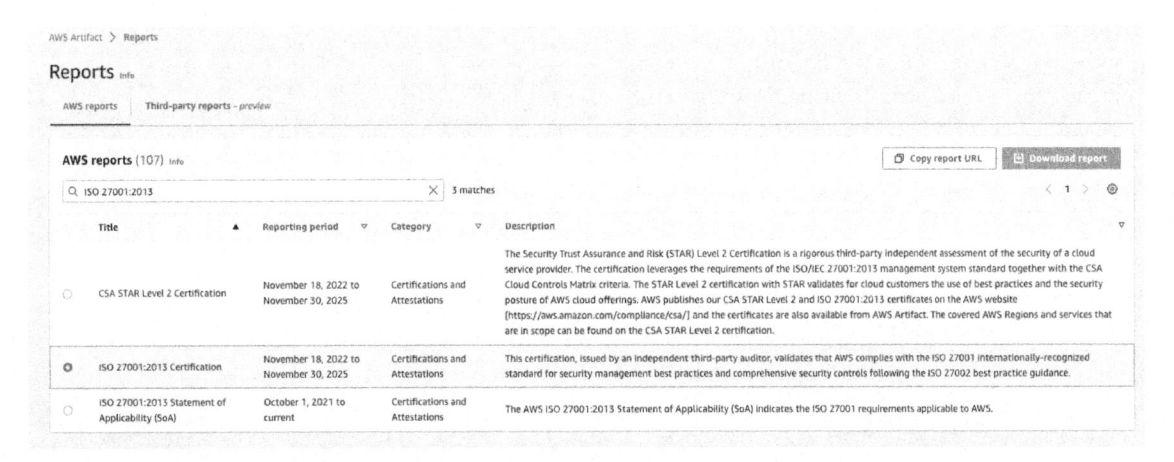

6. Click on the download report; you can also copy the URL
7. Open the generated PDF using Adobe Acrobat Reader. (Be sure to use Adobe Acrobat or Adobe Reader to view the files in the download reliably.)

*In some cases, there are costs to execute the labs, so please check the price and costs before you perform any exercise from this certification guide. Also, turn off or delete paid resources after you finish your exercises.*

## 2.10 Chapter Review Questions

**Question 1:**
What is a core principle of the AWS Shared Responsibility Model?

A. AWS manages security of the cloud, and customers manage security in the cloud
B. AWS is responsible for all aspects of cloud security
C. Customers manage both the physical and virtual security of their data
D. AWS manages customer encryption keys automatically

**Question 2:**
Which of the following best describes AWS compliance programs?
A. They automatically enforce compliance for all AWS services
B. They provide certifications and assurances to meet various industry and regulatory requirements
C. They focus exclusively on GDPR compliance
D. They manage third-party access to AWS resources

**Question 3:**
What is the primary function of the AWS Artifact Portal?
A. To provide access to AWS's compliance reports and documentation
B. To manage user access to AWS resources
C. To automate security audits and assessments
D. To encrypt data at rest automatically

**Question 4:**
In the AWS Shared Responsibility Model, which of the following is an example of a customer responsibility?
A. Managing physical security of AWS data centers
B. Configuring IAM roles and permissions
C. Patching the underlying hardware infrastructure
D. Implementing AWS Shield

**Question 5:**
What is the purpose of the AWS Security Framework?
A. To create custom security policies for each AWS service
B. To provide a comprehensive guide for securing workloads on AWS
C. To manage third-party security tools
D. To ensure application performance optimization

**Question 6:**
Which document should you refer to for AWS security best practices?
A. AWS Security Whitepaper
B. AWS Artifact Portal
C. AWS Well-Architected Framework
D. AWS Compliance Program

**Question 7:**
What is the role of AWS Marketplace in cloud security?
A. It provides a marketplace for AWS security tools and third-party security solutions
B. It is the central repository for compliance reports
C. It manages the encryption keys for AWS services
D. It automates identity and access management

**Question 8:**
Which of the following is NOT a key principle of cloud security?
A. Least privilege access
B. Data residency
C. End-to-end encryption

D. Default public access

## 2.11 Answers to Chapter Review Questions

1. A. AWS manages security of the cloud, and customers manage security in the cloud
Explanation: The AWS Shared Responsibility Model defines that AWS is responsible for protecting the infrastructure that runs all the services offered, while customers are responsible for securing their data and workloads in the cloud, including access management and data encryption.

2. B. They provide certifications and assurances to meet various industry and regulatory requirements
Explanation: AWS compliance programs help organizations meet regulatory requirements through various certifications, frameworks, and industry standards such as HIPAA, SOC, GDPR, and ISO certifications.

3. A. To provide access to AWS's compliance reports and documentation
Explanation: The AWS Artifact Portal is a self-service portal that provides on-demand access to AWS compliance reports, including security certifications and attestations.

4. B. Configuring IAM roles and permissions
Explanation: Customers are responsible for managing their access controls in AWS by configuring IAM roles, policies, and permissions to ensure proper security for their cloud workloads.

5. B. To provide a comprehensive guide for securing workloads on AWS
Explanation: The AWS Security Framework provides guidelines and recommendations for securing workloads running in AWS, addressing both customer and AWS responsibilities in the shared model.

6. A. AWS Security Whitepaper
Explanation: The AWS Security Whitepaper provides best practice guidance on securing data and workloads in AWS, covering topics such as encryption, identity management, and compliance.

7. A. It provides a marketplace for AWS security tools and third-party security solutions
Explanation: The AWS Marketplace offers a range of security tools, both from AWS and third-party vendors, to help organizations secure their cloud environments.

8. D. Default public access
Explanation: Default public access is not a security principle; in fact, the opposite is true: security best practices advocate restricting access by default and granting the least privilege necessary to meet business needs.

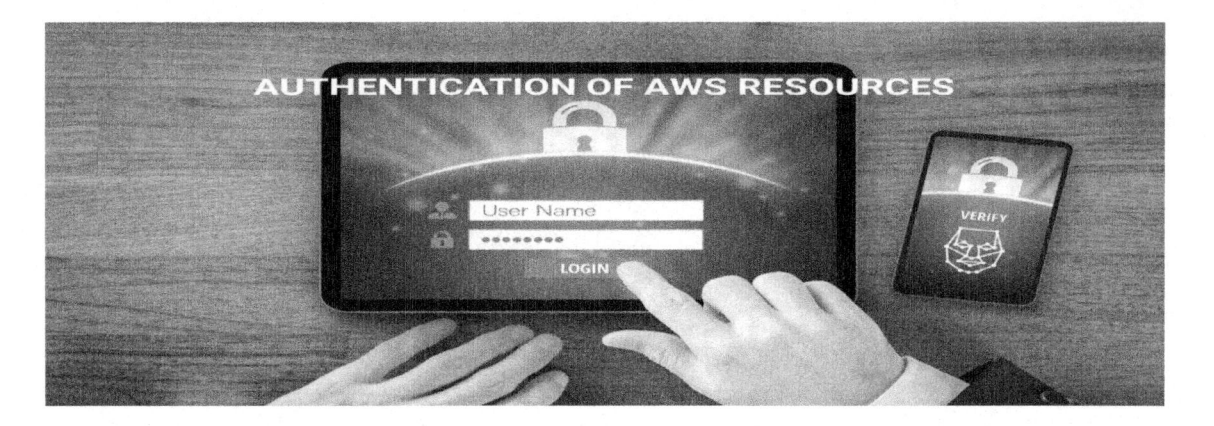

# Chapter 3. Authentication of AWS Resources

**This chapter addresses the following exam objectives:**
Domain 4: Identity and Access Management
Task Statement 4.1: Design, implement, and troubleshoot authentication for AWS resources.
Knowledge of:
- Methods and services for creating and managing identities (for example, federation, identity providers, AWS IAM Identity Center [AWS Single Sign-On], Amazon Cognito)
- Long-term and temporary credentialing mechanisms
- How to troubleshoot authentication issues (for example, by using CloudTrail, IAM Access Advisor, and IAM policy simulator)

Skills in:
- Establishing identity through an authentication system, based on requirements
- Setting up multi-factor authentication (MFA)
- Determining when to use AWS Security Token Service (AWS STS) to issue temporary credentials

◆◆◆◆◆◆

In the realm of cloud computing, robust authentication mechanisms are crucial for ensuring that only authorized individuals and systems can access resources. Chapter 4, "Authentication of AWS Resources," delves into the various methods and services that AWS offers to create and manage identities, providing a comprehensive guide to securing your AWS environment through effective authentication practices.

We start with an introduction to authentication in AWS, setting the stage for understanding the critical role authentication plays in cloud security. The chapter then explores the methods and services available for creating and managing identities, including AWS IAM Identity Center (formerly AWS Single Sign-On) and Amazon Cognito, both of which offer powerful solutions for managing user access.

Identity federation is a key concept that allows for the integration of external identity providers with AWS, enabling seamless and secure access across different platforms. We discuss the principles of identity federation in AWS, the role of federation and identity providers, and how to integrate external identity providers effectively.

Credential mechanisms are another focal point, with detailed coverage of long-term credentials, temporary credentials provided by AWS Security Token Service (STS), and the management of Multi-Factor Authentication (MFA) devices. These mechanisms are essential for ensuring secure and flexible access to AWS resources.

Troubleshooting authentication issues is vital for maintaining a secure environment. The chapter provides insights into using AWS CloudTrail for tracking and diagnosing authentication problems, leveraging IAM Access Advisor, and utilizing the IAM Policy Simulator to test and troubleshoot policies.

Best practices for authentication are emphasized throughout, including the implementation of the principle of least privilege, regular rotation of credentials, and the auditing and monitoring of authentication activities. These practices help maintain a secure and compliant AWS environment.

To reinforce the theoretical knowledge, the chapter concludes with lab exercises that provide hands-on experience in creating and managing IAM users and groups, setting up and configuring MFA, using AWS STS for temporary credentials, and troubleshooting authentication issues with CloudTrail and IAM tools. These exercises are designed to solidify your understanding and skills in AWS authentication.

By the end of this chapter, readers will have a thorough understanding of AWS authentication mechanisms, best practices, and troubleshooting techniques, equipping them to manage and secure access to AWS resources effectively.

## 3.1 Introduction to Authentication in AWS

Authentication within AWS is fundamental to cloud security, ensuring that only authorized users and services can access AWS resources. At its core, authentication is verifying the identity of a user or service attempting to access AWS. This verification is essential because it is the first line of defense against unauthorized access, protecting sensitive data and critical resources from potential threats.

AWS Identity and Access Management (IAM) is the primary service responsible for managing authentication. IAM allows administrators to create and manage AWS users and groups and assign permissions to allow or deny access to AWS resources. Each user is given a unique set of security credentials, typically including an access key ID and a secret access key. These credentials are used to sign requests made to AWS services, ensuring that the requests are coming from an authenticated source.

Multi-factor authentication (MFA) enhances this security by requiring users to provide a second form of identification, such as a code from an MFA device and their password. This additional layer of security significantly reduces the risk of unauthorized access due to compromised credentials.

In addition to managing user authentication, IAM facilitates service-to-service authentication, enabling AWS services to communicate securely. Roles can be assigned to AWS services, providing them the necessary permissions to perform specific actions without embedding long-term credentials in the code. This is particularly useful for temporary access scenarios, where AWS Security Token Service (STS) can be used to issue short-lived credentials.

The importance of authentication in AWS cannot be overstated. It ensures that only authenticated users and services can access and interact with AWS resources, thereby maintaining data integrity, confidentiality, and availability. By implementing robust authentication mechanisms, organizations can protect their AWS environments from unauthorized access, prevent data breaches, and comply with regulatory requirements. Effective authentication practices are the foundation of a secure AWS infrastructure, supporting the organization's overall security posture.

# 3.2 Methods and Services for Creating and Managing Identities

## 3.2.1 AWS IAM (Identity and Access Management)

Identity and Access Management (IAM) is a critical component of AWS that enables secure control over access to AWS services and resources. IAM allows you to manage permissions and define who can access what in your AWS environment. At its core, IAM involves users, groups, roles, policies, and authentication methods.

**Users** are individual identities with long-term credentials used to access AWS resources. Groups are collections of users, allowing for easier permissions management. Roles are similar to users but intended to be assumed by trusted entities, such as an IAM user, an AWS service, or an external identity provider, which allows for temporary security credentials. Policies define permissions and can be attached to users, groups, or roles to specify allowed or denied actions.

```
IAM Policy is a set of permissions
{
"Action" : "ec2:*",
"Effect": "Allow",
"Resource": "*"
}
```

**IAM policies** can be managed policies created and managed by AWS or custom policies created by you to meet specific needs. Policies are written in JSON and detail the allowed actions (such as S3), resources (such as an S3 bucket), and conditions under which the actions are allowed.

IAM also supports **multi-factor authentication (MFA)**, enhancing security by requiring a second form of authentication in addition to the password. You can set up MFA for individual users, adding an extra layer of security.

**IAM roles** and policies are pivotal in enabling the principle of least privilege, ensuring users and services only have the permissions necessary to perform their tasks, thus minimizing potential security risks.

By utilizing IAM effectively, organizations can manage and secure their AWS environments, ensuring proper governance and compliance.

In summary, IAM in AWS provides a comprehensive and flexible framework for managing access and ensuring that the right individuals and services have appropriate permissions. IAM supports fine-grained control through its various components and enhances security across AWS environments.

## 3.2.2 AWS IAM Identity Center (AWS Single Sign-On)

AWS IAM Identity Center, previously known as AWS Single Sign-On (SSO), is a cloud-based service designed to streamline and simplify access management across multiple AWS accounts and business applications. One of its primary features is providing a centralized interface where administrators can manage user access and permissions for various AWS environments and supported applications, reducing the complexity of handling access control across different platforms.

A key benefit of AWS IAM Identity Center is its support for Single Sign-On (SSO). SSO allows users to log in once and gain access to all their assigned AWS accounts and applications without needing to sign in multiple times. This feature significantly enhances user productivity by offering a seamless access experience.

Additionally, AWS IAM Identity Center integrates with existing identity providers (IdPs) such as Microsoft Active Directory, Okta, and others that support the Security Assertion Markup Language (SAML) 2.0 standard. This integration enables organizations to leverage their current authentication systems, ensuring a consistent and secure user authentication process.

AWS IAM Identity Center also supports automated user provisioning and management, allowing administrators to synchronize user data with identity sources automatically. This feature ensures that user access is always up-to-date with the changes made in the corporate directory, reducing the administrative overhead associated with manual updates. Moreover, IAM Identity Center provides:
- Fine-grained access control.
- Enabling administrators to assign specific permissions to users based on their roles and responsibilities.
- Ensuring that users have the necessary access to perform their tasks without over-provisioning permissions.

In summary, AWS IAM Identity Center simplifies access management by offering a centralized platform for managing user permissions, supporting single sign-on for seamless access, integrating with existing identity providers, automating user provisioning, and providing fine-grained access control. These features collectively enhance security and efficiency in managing access across AWS accounts and applications.

## 3.2.3 Amazon Cognito

Amazon Cognito is a powerful AWS service that facilitates user authentication, authorization, and user management for mobile and web applications. It offers two primary components: user pools and identity pools, each serving distinct purposes in the authentication process.

**User pools** in Amazon Cognito are managed user directories that enable developers to handle user registration, authentication, and account recovery. With user pools, developers can create and maintain a user directory, allowing users to sign up, sign in, and manage their profiles. User pools provide customizable sign-up and sign-in processes, including multi-factor authentication (MFA) support to enhance security. Additionally, user pools offer features like email and phone number verification, password policies, and account recovery options. They also support federation through social identity providers like Google, Facebook, and Amazon, as well as enterprise identity providers via SAML.

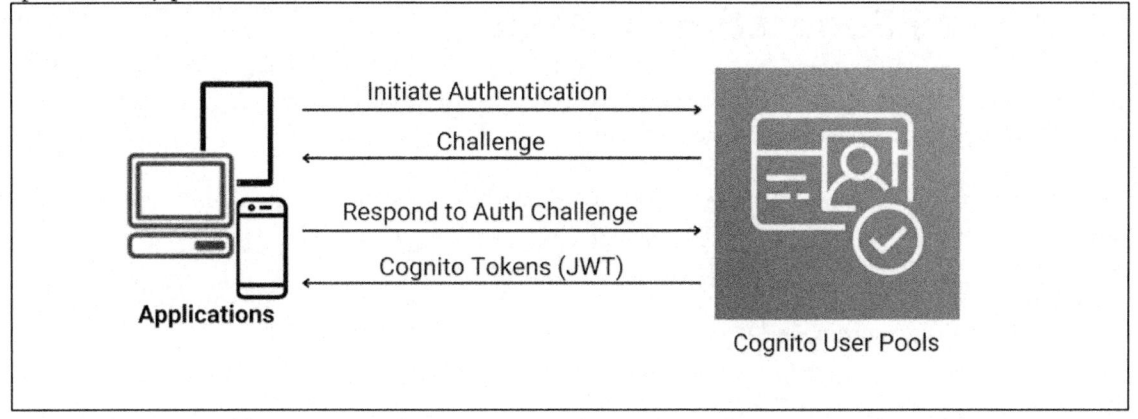

**Identity pools** in Amazon Cognito are the key to flexibility in user authentication. They provide temporary AWS credentials to users authenticated through a variety of identity providers, allowing these users to access AWS resources directly. Identity pools support authentication through user pools, social identity providers, and enterprise identity providers, making them a versatile solution for a wide range of user authentication scenarios. With identity pools, developers can create unique identities for users, assign fine-grained permissions to these identities, and securely access AWS services like S3, DynamoDB, and more. Identity pools enable authenticated users to obtain temporary, limited-privilege AWS credentials, facilitating secure and scalable access to AWS resources.

Amazon Cognito is a time-saving tool for developers. By leveraging Cognito, developers can offload the heavy lifting of authentication and user management, allowing them to focus more on building the core functionality of their applications. Cognito integrates seamlessly with other AWS services, providing a robust and scalable solution for managing user identities and access. It simplifies the process of adding authentication to mobile and web applications, ensuring that users can securely sign in and access their personalized content and resources.

In summary, Amazon Cognito is a comprehensive service that simplifies authentication for mobile and web applications through its user pools and identity pools. User pools manage user directories and authentication processes, while identity pools provide temporary AWS credentials for accessing AWS resources. This dual-component system ensures secure, scalable, and flexible user authentication and authorization, enabling developers to build secure applications easily.

## 3.3 Identity Federation

Identity federation is a mechanism to allow users to access multiple systems or applications using a single set of login credentials. That way, they don't need to create and remember separate usernames and passwords for each system or application.

In identity federation, a trusted third-party identity provider (IDP) is used to authenticate the user's identity. After successful authentication, this IDP issues security tokens that are used to access different systems or applications. That being the case, when a user attempts to access a system or application, the system sends a request to the identity provider for authentication. If the user is authenticated, the identity provider provides a security token that the user can use to access the system or application.

Identity federation has several benefits, such as reduced password fatigue, improved security, and simplified user management. As a result, it is widely used in enterprise environments where users need access to multiple systems and applications across different domains or organizations. Popular identity federation standards include SAML (Security Assertion Markup Language) and OAuth (Open Authorization).

### 3.3.1 Identity Federation In AWS

Identity Federation in AWS allows you to exchange valid credentials from external IdPs, such as Microsoft Active Directory, through open standards, such as Security Assertion Markup Language 2.0 (SAML), for temporary AWS credentials provided by the Amazon Security Token Service (STS).

Let's go through some essential key terms to have a good handle on understanding identity federation in AWS Cloud.

- **Identity:** It is a user in your corporate or web identity store, such as Microsoft Active Directory, Google, Apple, Amazon, and Facebook.

- **Identity Store:** This is a central location where identities are stored, for example, Microsoft Active Directory, Amazon, Apple, Facebook, and Google.

- **Identity Broker**: It is a client application that performs the authentication of the users against the IdPs, then gets AWS temporary security credentials, and finally provides the users with access to the AWS resources.

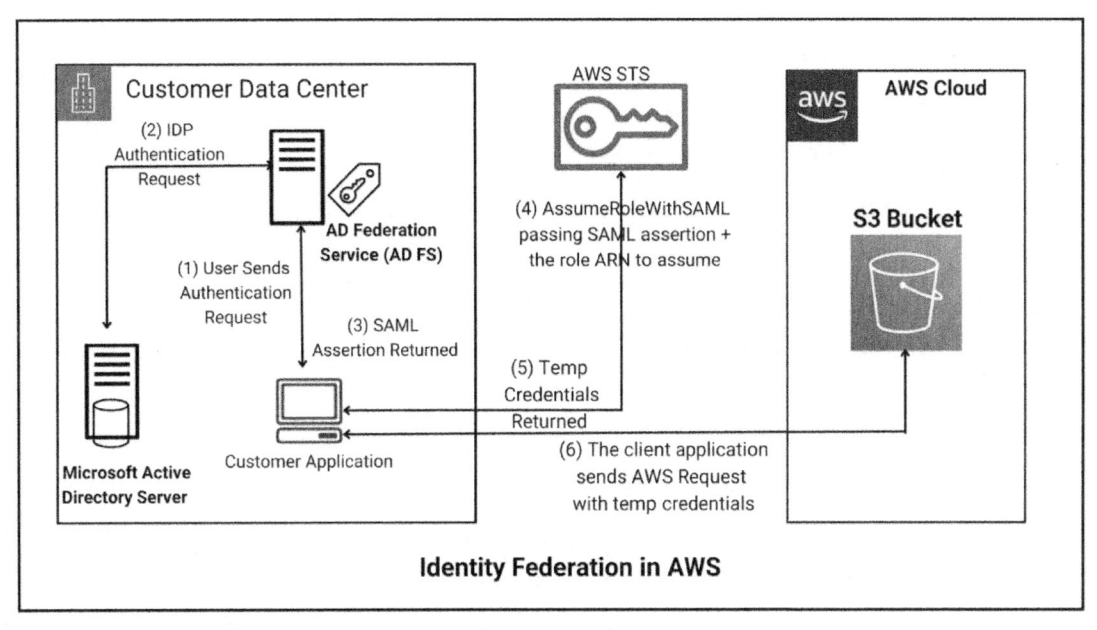

**Identity Federation in AWS**

The picture above explains the identity federation in the AWS, where Microsoft Active Directory is used to allow login into the AWS Console.

The identity federation process shown in the picture above follows these steps:

- The application sends the identity broker [in this example, to ADFS that provides client applications SSO access] the user's corporate credentials.
- The ADFS then sends to the LDAP-based identity store, which then the IdP authenticates the user against the LDAP-based identity store.
- The IdP generates a SAML assertion with all the required user information and submits the assertion to the identity broker.
- The identity broker calls the AssumeRoleWithSAML STS API, in which it passes the SAML assertion and the role ARN to assume.
- The API response, if successful, includes AWS temporary security credentials with their associated permissions.
- With the temporary credentials received by STS service, the client application can perform operations on AWS resources.

## 3.3.2 Federation and Identity Providers

Federation and integration with external identity providers are essential features in modern authentication systems. They enable users to access resources across different domains and services using a single set of credentials, providing a seamless and convenient single sign-on experience. This not only enhances user convenience and security but also simplifies the authentication process by leveraging existing identity frameworks.

Federation refers to the practice of linking and using identities from multiple identity management systems. This allows users to authenticate with one system and gain access to resources in another without maintaining separate credentials for each system. Federation is often achieved through the use of industry-standard and trusted protocols such as Security Assertion Markup Language (SAML) and OpenID Connect (OIDC).

## 3.3.3 Integrating External Identity Providers

**Active Directory:** Many organizations use Microsoft Active Directory (AD) as their primary identity provider for managing user credentials and access within corporate environments. AWS services, such as AWS IAM Identity Center and Amazon Cognito, support integration with AD through SAML-based federation. This allows users to sign in to AWS services using their AD credentials, enabling seamless access to AWS resources while maintaining centralized identity management within the organization.

**Google:** Google provides identity services through its Google Identity platform, supporting both OAuth 2.0 and OpenID Connect protocols. By integrating with Google as an identity provider, applications can allow users to authenticate using their Google credentials. This is particularly useful for applications targeting a broad user base, as many people already have Google accounts. Integration is facilitated through services like Amazon Cognito, which can federate identities from Google and other providers, allowing users to sign in to your applications with their Google accounts.

**Facebook:** Like Google, Facebook offers identity services supporting OAuth 2.0 and OpenID Connect. By integrating with Facebook as an identity provider, applications can leverage Facebook's widespread user base for authentication. This integration allows users to sign in using their Facebook credentials, simplifying the login process and potentially increasing user engagement. Amazon Cognito provides built-in support for Facebook federation, making incorporating Facebook login into your applications easy.

In practice, integrating external identity providers involves configuring your application to trust and accept authentication tokens from these providers. This typically includes setting up the identity provider's configuration in your authentication service (e.g., Amazon Cognito), obtaining client IDs and secrets from the identity provider, and defining the scopes and claims required for your application.

Overall, federation and integration with external identity providers streamline the authentication process, enhance user experience, and improve security by centralizing identity management. By leveraging trusted external identity providers like Active Directory, Google, and Facebook, organizations can provide seamless and secure access to their applications and resources.

## 3.4 Credential Mechanisms

Credential mechanisms are fundamental to ensuring secure access and authentication in any IT environment. They encompass a variety of methods used to verify and manage identities, such as passwords, multi-factor authentication (MFA), digital certificates, and biometric verification. These credential mechanisms play a crucial role in protecting sensitive information and ensuring that only authorized users can access specific resources.

## 3.4.1 Long-term Credentials

Long-term credentials, such as IAM user passwords and access keys, are fundamental components for authenticating and authorizing access to AWS resources. IAM user passwords are used for console access, allowing users to log in to the AWS Management Console and manage AWS resources. These passwords are typically managed through IAM policies, which enforce password complexity, rotation policies, and multi-factor authentication (MFA) to enhance security. Regularly rotating passwords and enforcing strong password policies are critical practices to mitigate the risk of compromised credentials.

**Access keys**, that includes an access key ID and a secret access key, provide programmatic access to AWS resources. These keys enable applications, scripts, and other automated processes to interact with AWS services. However, long-term access keys pose significant security risks if not managed properly. To minimize these risks, following best practices such as regularly rotating access keys, using IAM roles instead of long-term access keys where possible, and never embedding access keys directly in code or configuration files is essential.

The management of long-term credentials involves:
- Monitoring and auditing their usage.
- Ensuring that only authorized individuals and processes have access.
- Immediately revoking credentials that are no longer needed or are suspected to be compromised.

AWS provides tools such as **AWS IAM Access Analyzer** and **AWS CloudTrail** to help administrators track the usage of access keys and identify any unusual activity.

In conclusion, while long-term credentials like IAM user passwords and access keys are necessary for accessing AWS resources, their management requires diligent practices to maintain security. Regular rotation, strict access controls, and vigilant monitoring are essential to prevent unauthorized access and protect sensitive data.

## 3.4.2 Temporary Credentials with AWS STS (Security Token Service)

AWS Security Token Service (STS) allows to request temporary, limited-privilege credentials for AWS Identity and Access Management (IAM) users or federated users. These temporary security credentials provide a secure way to grant limited-time access to AWS resources without having to create long-term IAM credentials. AWS STS issues temporary security credentials, which consist of an access key ID, a secret access key, and a security token.

These credentials are typically valid for a duration ranging from a few minutes to several hours, depending on the specific requirements and configurations. Temporary security credentials are generated dynamically and are automatically invalidated when they expire, reducing the risk of credential exposure and unauthorized access.

There are several scenarios where using AWS STS and temporary security credentials is advantageous:

- **Federated Access:** STS allows users to authenticate through external identity providers, such as Active Directory, Google, or other SAML-compliant identity providers. Once authenticated, users receive temporary credentials to access AWS resources, facilitating seamless and secure access without managing separate AWS credentials.

- **Cross-Account Access:** When users or services in one AWS account need to access resources in another account, STS can issue temporary credentials, enabling cross-account access while maintaining security boundaries. This is particularly useful in multi-account AWS environments.

- **Mobile and Web Applications:** Temporary security credentials are ideal for mobile and web applications where embedding long-term credentials in the application code would pose a security risk. Using STS, applications can request temporary credentials dynamically, ensuring that the credentials are short-lived and reducing the risk of exposure.

- **Delegation and Limited-Privilege Access:** AWS STS is useful for delegating access to AWS resources with specific permissions for a limited duration. This is often used in scenarios where a user or service needs temporary elevated privileges to perform a particular task.

In conclusion, AWS STS is a secure and flexible solution for managing access to AWS resources. It provides a secure way to issue temporary security credentials, enhancing security and flexibility in various use cases. By leveraging STS, organizations can manage access dynamically, reduce the risk of credential exposure, and ensure that users and services have the appropriate level of access for a limited time.

### 3.4.3 Managing MFA Devices

Managing Multi-Factor Authentication (MFA) devices in AWS involves several key processes, including provisioning, deprovisioning, and troubleshooting.

**Provisioning MFA devices** is the initial setup process where devices such as virtual MFA apps (like Google Authenticator), U2F security keys, or hardware MFA devices are configured. For virtual MFA devices, users scan a QR code or enter a secret key from the AWS Management Console into their MFA application, confirming the setup by entering two consecutive codes generated by the app. Hardware devices require entering the device's serial number into the AWS Management Console and confirming with two consecutive codes displayed by the device.

**Deprovisioning, or removing MFA devices,** is necessary when devices are no longer needed or being replaced. This involves navigating to the IAM dashboard in the AWS Management Console, selecting the user, and removing the existing MFA device under the Security credentials tab. If a new device is to be assigned, the provisioning steps are followed again. Additionally, it's crucial to revoke any temporary credentials issued via STS to ensure no unauthorized access occurs.

**Troubleshooting MFA devices** is essential for maintaining secure access. Common issues include lost or damaged devices, synchronization problems, incorrect MFA codes, and user lockouts. For lost or damaged devices, administrators must deactivate the old device and provision a new one. Synchronization issues can be resolved by re-syncing the time on the MFA app. Incorrect MFA codes require verifying that the correct 6-digit code is entered, and may necessitate resetting the MFA device. User lockouts can be addressed by temporarily disabling MFA requirements to allow access and further troubleshooting.

Overall, effective management of MFA devices involves regular reviews of MFA configurations, educating users on proper usage, implementing policies to enforce MFA across all accounts, and monitoring activities with AWS CloudTrail and AWS Config. By diligently provisioning, deprovisioning, and troubleshooting MFA devices, organizations can enhance the security of their AWS environments, ensuring that only authorized users access critical resources.

## 3.5 Troubleshooting Authentication Issues

Troubleshooting authentication issues is critical to maintaining secure and reliable access to systems and applications. This process involves diagnosing and resolving problems that prevent users from successfully authenticating and accessing resources. Common authentication issues can stem from various sources, including incorrect credentials, synchronization problems, misconfigured settings, and network-related issues. Effective troubleshooting requires a systematic approach to identify the root cause, whether it be a user error, system misconfiguration, or external factor impacting authentication.

### 3.5.1 Using AWS CloudTrail for Troubleshooting

AWS CloudTrail logs are an invaluable resource for troubleshooting authentication issues in AWS environments. CloudTrail records all API calls made within an AWS account, providing a comprehensive audit trail of user activities and changes to your AWS resources.

To utilize CloudTrail logs for troubleshooting authentication issues, start by accessing the CloudTrail console and locating the relevant log files. These logs contain detailed information about every API call, including the caller's identity, the time of the call, the source IP address, and the request parameters.

When troubleshooting, filter the logs to focus on authentication-related events, such as AssumeRole, Login, GetSessionToken, and STS operations. Analyze the entries to identify any failed attempts, noting the specific error codes and messages provided. Common issues may include incorrect credentials, insufficient permissions, or MFA-related problems. By examining the context of these failures, such as the source IP and the user or role involved, you can pinpoint the underlying cause.

CloudTrail logs also help verify if the appropriate IAM policies and permissions are in place. You can cross-reference the logs with your IAM policies to ensure that users have the correct permissions for the actions they are attempting. Additionally, by checking the timeline of events, you can determine if there were any recent changes to policies or roles that might have triggered the authentication issues.

In summary, AWS CloudTrail logs provide detailed insights into API calls and user activities, enabling you to effectively troubleshoot authentication issues by analyzing event details, identifying patterns of failure, and verifying IAM configurations. This systematic approach ensures that authentication problems are resolved quickly and accurately, maintaining the security and functionality of your AWS environment.

## 3.5.2 IAM Access Advisor

IAM Access Advisor is a feature within AWS Identity and Access Management (IAM) that provides insights into the permissions and access patterns of IAM users and roles. Access Advisor helps administrators understand which services are being used and how frequently by analyzing the last-accessed information for various AWS services. This visibility is crucial for ensuring that permissions are appropriately assigned and not overly permissive, thereby enhancing security and compliance.

IAM Access Advisor plays a vital role when troubleshooting permissions and access issues. It allows administrators to view the last time a user or role accessed a particular service, which can help identify unused permissions. For example, suppose a user has permissions for several AWS services but has only accessed a subset of them. Administrators can consider refining the user's permissions to follow the principle of least privilege. This reduces the risk associated with excessive permissions and potential misuse.

The IAM Access Advisor can also help identify stale roles and users that no longer require certain permissions. Administrators can make informed decisions about modifying or revoking permissions by reviewing the access patterns. This not only tightens security but also simplifies the management of IAM policies.

To start using IAM Access Advisor, simply navigate to the IAM dashboard in the AWS Management Console, select a user or role, and view the Access Advisor tab. Here, you can see a detailed list of AWS services along with the last accessed information. This data is invaluable in assessing whether the permissions granted are necessary for the user's or role's current activities, and it's just a few clicks away.

In summary, IAM Access Advisor is a powerful tool for understanding and troubleshooting permissions and access in AWS. It provides actionable insights into usage patterns, helping administrators refine permissions, enhance security, and ensure compliance with best practices for access management.

## 3.5.3 IAM Policy Simulator

The IAM Policy Simulator, a crucial tool provided by AWS, empowers administrators to test and troubleshoot IAM policies and permissions without the risk of deploying them in a live environment. This tool is instrumental in ensuring that the policies function as intended, thereby preventing potential security risks or access issues.

Let look into how to effectively use the IAM Policy Simulator:

To begin, access the IAM Policy Simulator through the AWS Management Console. Navigate to the IAM dashboard, select **Policies** from the left-hand navigation pane, and click on **Policy Simulator**. Alternatively, you can directly go to the Policy Simulator web page.

In the Policy Simulator interface, you can choose the user, group, or role whose policies you want to test. You can also input specific policies directly if you are testing a new policy that has yet to be attached to any IAM entities.

Once you have selected the target entity or policy, specify the AWS services and actions you want to test. The simulator allows you to choose from a comprehensive list of AWS services and their associated actions. This step is crucial to understanding how the policy affects access to services and operations.

After setting up the services and actions, run the simulation by clicking the **Simulate** button. The simulator will evaluate the policies and provide a detailed report showing whether the actions are allowed or denied. This report includes the specific statements in the policies that grant or deny permissions, helping you pinpoint any issues.

The IAM Policy Simulator also supports advanced testing scenarios. To test policies with conditions, you can simulate context keys, such as IP addresses or AWS regions. This feature is particularly useful for complex policies that include conditional statements.

By leveraging the IAM Policy Simulator, administrators can proactively identify and resolve potential issues in IAM policies. This tool plays a key role in ensuring that policies enforce the principle of least privilege, thereby reducing the risk of inadvertently granting excessive permissions or causing access disruptions. It also aids in verifying policy changes before deployment, further enhancing security.

In conclusion, the IAM Policy Simulator is an indispensable tool for testing and troubleshooting IAM policies and permissions. It provides a secure environment to evaluate the effects of policies, ensuring they are correctly configured to secure AWS resources while allowing necessary access for users and applications.

## 3.6 Best Practices for Authentication

Best practices for authentication are essential to ensure the security and integrity of user accounts and sensitive information. Implementing robust authentication mechanisms helps protect against unauthorized access and potential breaches. By adhering to these best practices, organizations can enhance their security posture, minimize risks, and maintain user trust.

### 3.6.1 Implementing the Principle of Least Privilege

Implementing the principle of least privilege (PoLP) is a fundamental best practice for minimizing security risks in any environment. The principle dictates that users, systems, and processes should only be provided the minimum level of access (least access) necessary to perform their functions. Thus, implementing the principle of least privilege (PoLP) reduces the attack surface and limits the potential damage that accidental or malicious actions could cause.

To effectively implement PoLP, start by thoroughly assessing the roles and responsibilities within your organization. Clearly define the access requirements for each role, ensuring that permissions are tightly scoped to what is essential. Use role-based access control (RBAC) to manage permissions at a granular level, grouping users by their roles and assigning permissions accordingly. Regularly review and update these roles to adapt to job functions or organizational structure changes.

Another critical practice is the use of temporary credentials and just-in-time access. Instead of providing long-term credentials, issue time-limited, temporary access tokens that expire after a short period. This approach minimizes the risk of credential compromise. Tools like AWS Security Token Service (STS) and Azure Active Directory Privileged Identity Management (PIM) can help automate the issuance and management of temporary credentials.

Continuous monitoring and auditing are also essential components of PoLP. Implement logging and monitoring to track access patterns and detect anomalies. Regularly audit permissions and access logs to ensure compliance with the least privilege principle. Tools like AWS CloudTrail, Azure Monitor, and Google Cloud Audit Logs can facilitate these activities.

Furthermore, strong authentication mechanisms, such as multi-factor authentication (MFA), should be enforced to add an extra layer of security. Even if credentials are compromised, MFA ensures that unauthorized access is still mitigated.

In summary, implementing the principle of least privilege involves:
- Defining precise access needs.
- Using role-based access control.
- Employing temporary credentials.
- Continuously monitoring access.
- Enforcing strong authentication.

Adhering to these best practices can significantly reduce organizations' security risks and protect their critical assets from unauthorized access and potential breaches.

## 3.6.2 Regularly Rotating Credentials

Rotating credentials regularly is crucial for maintaining security in any IT environment. Over time, credentials can become compromised for various reasons, such as phishing attacks, accidental sharing, or exposure to data breaches. Regularly rotating credentials reduces the risk associated with these potential compromises by ensuring that their validity is limited even if credentials are exposed.

Automating the process of credential rotation enhances security by ensuring that it happens consistently and without human error. Automation minimizes the risk of forgetting to rotate credentials or delaying the rotation, which can create security vulnerabilities.

To automate credential rotation, you can leverage several tools and practices:

**AWS Secrets Manager:** AWS Secrets Manager is a service designed to manage and automatically rotate credentials for AWS resources such as databases and API keys. By integrating Secrets Manager with your applications, you can ensure that credentials are rotated automatically according to a predefined schedule. The service provides built-in support for common databases and can be extended to rotate other types of secrets using Lambda functions.

**AWS IAM Access Keys:** To rotate IAM access keys, you can use AWS CLI or SDKs to automate the creation of new access keys and the deletion of old ones. Implement a script or Lambda function that periodically generates new keys, updates your applications with the new ones, and deactivates and deletes the old ones after a certain period.

**HashiCorp Vault:** HashiCorp Vault is a tool designed to securely store and access secrets. It supports dynamic secrets, which are generated on demand and automatically revoked after their lease expires. This ensures that credentials are rotated frequently and are only valid for a short period.

**Periodic Scripts:** For simpler use cases, periodic scripts can be used to rotate credentials. These scripts can be scheduled using cron jobs or similar scheduling tools to generate new credentials, update the necessary configurations, and invalidate old credentials. Ensure that these scripts are secure and that access to them is tightly controlled.

Implementing automated credential rotation involves several steps, including identifying all the credentials that need rotation, integrating with the appropriate tools, and ensuring that applications and services can dynamically retrieve updated credentials. Testing the automation thoroughly is essential to ensure that there are no disruptions to services during the rotation process.

In summary, rotating credentials regularly is a vital security practice that mitigates the risk of credential compromise. Automating this process using tools like AWS Secrets Manager, Azure Key Vault, and HashiCorp Vault, or through custom scripts, ensures that credential rotation happens consistently and securely, reducing human error and enhancing overall security.

## 3.6.3 Auditing and Monitoring Authentication Activities

Auditing and monitoring authentication activities are essential for detecting and responding to potential security issues within an IT environment. These processes involve:
- Continuously tracking user access patterns.
- Identifying anomalies.
- Taking swift action to mitigate risks.

Effective auditing and monitoring help prevent unauthorized access, detect breaches early, and ensure compliance with security policies.

To start, leverage AWS CloudTrail to log all API calls made within your AWS account. CloudTrail provides detailed records of all authentication-related activities, such as login attempts, session starts, and changes to IAM policies. Regularly reviewing these logs helps identify unusual access patterns or unauthorized attempts to access resources. Integrating CloudTrail with Amazon CloudWatch allows for real-time monitoring and alerting. Set up CloudWatch Alarms to notify you of suspicious activities, such as multiple failed login attempts or access from unfamiliar IP addresses.

AWS Config is another useful tool for auditing and monitoring. It continuously evaluates your AWS resources against desired configurations, helping you ensure that IAM policies and security groups comply with best practices. Config Rules can be set to trigger alerts or remediation actions when deviations are detected, providing an additional layer of security oversight.

Implementing centralized logging with AWS Security Hub consolidates findings from multiple AWS services, offering a unified view of security alerts and compliance status. Security Hub integrates with CloudTrail, GuardDuty, and other security services to provide comprehensive insights into your security posture. It helps prioritize security findings and streamline the response process.

Conduct security audits and reviews of IAM policies, user permissions, and access logs regularly. Use the IAM Access Analyzer to identify resources shared with external entities and verify that only authorized access is granted. Periodic reviews help ensure that permissions adhere to the principle of least privilege and that any unnecessary access rights are revoked.

For real-time threat detection, enable Amazon GuardDuty, which uses machine learning to analyze logs and identify potential security threats. GuardDuty monitors CloudTrail logs, VPC flow logs, and DNS logs for signs of malicious activity, providing actionable insights and recommendations for mitigation.

Finally, multi-factor authentication (MFA) should be implemented as an additional layer of security. MFA significantly reduces the risk of unauthorized access by requiring users to provide two forms of authentication. Monitor MFA usage and ensure that all privileged accounts are protected with MFA.

Auditing and monitoring authentication activities involve using tools like AWS CloudTrail, CloudWatch, AWS Config, Security Hub, IAM Access Analyzer, and GuardDuty to continuously track access patterns, identify anomalies, and respond to potential security issues. Regular audits, real-time monitoring, and the implementation of strong authentication measures are crucial for maintaining a secure and compliant AWS environment.

## 3.7 Lab Exercises
### 3.7.1 Creating and Managing IAM Users and Groups

Here are the step-by-step instructions for a hands-on lab to create IAM users, groups, and assign policies in AWS:

**1. Sign In to the AWS Management Console:** Open your web browser and go to the AWS Management Console. Log in with your AWS credentials.

**2. Navigate to the IAM Dashboard:** In the AWS Management Console, click on Services in the top-left corner. Under Security, Identity, & Compliance, select IAM to open the IAM dashboard.

**3. Create an IAM Group:** In the left-hand navigation pane, click on User groups. Click on the Create group button. Enter a group name (e.g., Developers.

**4. Attach a Policy to the Group:** Search for and select the policies you want to attach to the group. For example, search for AdministratorAccess for full access. Check the box next to the policy name and click Create user group. This will create the IAM group.

**5. Create an IAM User:** In the left-hand navigation pane, click on Users. Click on the Create User button. Enter a username (e.g., john_doe).
Select the type of access this user will have:
- Programmatic access: Grants access to AWS API, CLI, SDK, and other development tools.
- AWS Management Console access: Grants access to the AWS Management Console.

If you select AWS Management Console access, set a custom password or let AWS generate one. Click Next.

**6. Assign User to the Group:** On the Set Permissions page, choose Add user to group. Check the box next to the group you created earlier (e.g., Developers). Click Next.

**7. Add Tags (Optional):** You can add metadata to the user by attaching tags (key-value pairs). For example, "Cost-Center" as key and "Product Development" as a Value.

**8. Review and Create User:** Review the user details. Click Create user.

**9. Download Credentials:** On the confirmation page, download the .csv file containing the user's credentials (Access key ID and Secret access key). This is crucial for programmatic access. Click "Returns to users list".

**10. Verify the User and Group:** In the IAM dashboard, click on Users to see the list of users. Click on the username you created to view details. In the Permissions tab, ensure the user has the policies attached through the group.

**11. Test the IAM User:** Log out of the AWS Management Console. Log in using the new user's credentials to ensure that the permissions and access settings are correctly applied.

This hands-on lab guides you through creating IAM users and groups and assigning policies in AWS. By following these steps, you can manage user access effectively and securely within your AWS environment. This process helps enforce the principle of least privilege by ensuring users have only the necessary permissions for their roles.

## 3.7.2 Setting Up and Configuring MFA

Enabling and configuring Multi-Factor Authentication (MFA) for an AWS account enhances security by requiring a second form of authentication in addition to your password. Here are step-by-step instructions to set up MFA for an AWS account:

**1. Sign In to the AWS Management Console:** Open your web browser and navigate to the AWS Management Console. Log in with your AWS account credentials.

**2. Navigate to the IAM Dashboard:** In the AWS Management Console, click on Services in the top-left corner. Under Security, Identity, & Compliance, select IAM to open the IAM dashboard.

**3. Access the Security Credentials Section:** In the IAM dashboard, click on Users in the left-hand navigation pane. Click on the name of the IAM user for whom you want to enable MFA. Click on the Security credentials tab.

**4. Manage MFA Device:** Scroll down to the Multi-factor authentication (MFA) section. Click on Manage MFA device.

**5. Choose MFA Device Type:** Click on the Assign MFA device button. Select the type of MFA device you want to use:
- Virtual MFA device: Use a mobile app like Google Authenticator or Authy.
- U2F security key: Use a hardware security key.

**Other hardware MFA device:** Use a hardware MFA device compatible with AWS.

**6. Configure Virtual MFA Device (Using Google Authenticator):** Select Virtual MFA device and click Continue. Open the Google Authenticator app on your mobile device. If you don't have it, download and install it from the Google Play Store (Android) or the Apple App Store (iOS). In the Google Authenticator app, tap the plus sign (+) to add a new account and select Scan a QR code. In the AWS Management Console, a QR code will be displayed. Scan this QR code with the Google Authenticator app. Alternatively, you can click on Show secret key and manually enter the key into the Google Authenticator app if scanning the QR code is not possible.

**7. Enter MFA Codes:** After scanning the QR code, the Google Authenticator app will start generating 6-digit MFA codes. In the AWS Management Console, enter two consecutive MFA codes from the Google Authenticator app to verify the configuration. Click on Assign MFA.

**8. Confirmation:** Once the MFA device is successfully assigned, you will see a confirmation message in the AWS Management Console. Your IAM user now has MFA enabled.

**9. Test the MFA Setup:** Sign out of the AWS Management Console. Sign back in using the IAM user credentials. After entering your username and password, you will be prompted to enter an MFA code. Open the Google Authenticator app, enter the current 6-digit code displayed, and sign in.

By following these steps, you have successfully enabled and configured Multi-Factor Authentication for an AWS account using a virtual MFA device like Google Authenticator. This additional security layer helps protect your AWS account from unauthorized access, ensuring that only authenticated users can perform actions within your AWS environment.

## 3.7.3 Using AWS STS for Temporary Credentials

AWS Security Token Service (STS) allows you to create and use temporary security credentials to access AWS resources. These credentials are ideal for short-term access and provide enhanced security by reducing the lifespan of credentials. In this hands-on exercise, we'll explore how to enable cross-account access using the AWS Management Console by leveraging the 'Switch Role' feature. Extending this exercise further, you will also learn how to enable cross-account access by using AWS Security Token Service (STS) to generate temporary security credentials, enabling access to resources in another account.

We'll use the terms 'source account' and 'target account.' The source account refers to the account that the user will use to access the resource on the target account. You may also find the terms 'trusting account' for the target account and 'trusted account' for the source account.

### Part 1: AWS Management Console - Switch Role
### Create IAM Role in Target Account
- Login to the target account (trusting account).
- Navigate to the IAM console.
- Click on "Roles" on the left navigation panel.
- Click on "Create Role."
- Select "AWS Account" and choose "Another account."
- Enter the account ID of the source account.
- Click "Next" and search for "AmazonS3ReadOnlyAccess."
- Select "AmazonS3ReadOnlyAccess" and click "Next."
- Enter the role name "DevS3Role."
- Optionally add a tag, e.g., Key: "Used By," Value: "Dev Team."
- Click on "Create Role."

### Create IAM User in Source Account
- Login to the source account (trusted account).
- Navigate to the IAM console.
- Click on "Users" on the left navigation panel.
- Click on "Create User."
- Enter username "Alice."
- Provide AWS Management Console access and set a custom password.
- Uncheck "User must create a new password at next sign-in" for the exercise.

### Create IAM Group and Policy in Source Account
- Create a group named "Assume STS Role."
- Create a policy that allows assuming the role created in the target account.
- Click on "Create Policy."
- Search for STS service and select "AssumeRole."
- Add ARN of the target account role (e.g., "arn:aws:iam::<target-account-id>
- /DevS3Role").

- Name the policy "AWSAssumeSTSPolicy."
- Attach this policy to the "Assume STS Role" group.
- Add user Alice to this group.

### Test Cross-Account Access via Switch Role
- Sign out from the source account.
- Login as user Alice in the source account.
- Click on the top-right corner and select "Switch Role."
- Enter the target account ID and role name "DevS3Role."
- Click "Enable Role" to switch to the target account.
- Access the S3 buckets in the target account.

## Part 2: AWS CLI - STS Token
### Download Security Credentials
- Download the access keys for user Alice.
- Configure the AWS CLI environment with Alice's access keys.

### Generate STS Token
Run the CLI command to generate the STS token:
```
aws sts assume-role --role-arn arn:aws:iam::<target-account-id>:role/DevS3Role --role-session-name AliceSession
```
Note the expiration time of the STS token.

### Access S3 Buckets Using STS Token
Export access keys and session token as environment variables:
```
1. export AWS_ACCESS_KEY_ID=<AccessKeyID>
2. export AWS_SECRET_ACCESS_KEY=<SecretAccessKey>
3. export AWS_SESSION_TOKEN=<SessionToken>
```

Run the command to list S3 buckets in the target account:
```
aws s3 ls
```

That's how you can enable cross-account access using both the AWS Management Console and AWS CLI. This exercise demonstrates the flexibility and security provided by AWS when managing resources across multiple accounts.

# 3.7.4 Troubleshooting Authentication Issues with CloudTrail and IAM Tools

This lab will guide you through troubleshooting common authentication issues in AWS using three essential tools: AWS CloudTrail, IAM Access Advisor, and IAM Policy Simulator. These tools help identify and resolve access problems, ensuring secure and effective management of IAM policies.

## 3.7.4.1 Setting Up AWS CloudTrail for Logging

Though CloudTrail event history logs events in provides a comprehensive record of activities and actions taken by users, roles, and AWS services within your AWS account. However, Event history feature retains data for only the last 90 days. For long-term storage and more extensive historical analysis, you'll need to create a trail that delivers logs to an S3 bucket.

**Create Trail for logging events**
- Sign in to the AWS Management Console.
- Navigate to the CloudTrail console by selecting Services and then CloudTrail.
- Click on Trails in the left navigation pane.
- If you don't have a trail created, click on Create trail.
- Provide a name for your trail (for example, management-events-trail)
- For storage location. where logs are stored, you can create a new S3 bucket or use an existing S3 bucket. The default option is ok which is to create a new bucket.
- The default bucket is also populated. you can change it if you want. but there is naming standard in your organization.
- Uncheck the "Log file SSE-KMS encryption" as this is just for the learning exercise.
- Rest all default is fine. Click on Next.
- This will take you to the "Choose log events" page. On this page, all default options are ok. "Management events" is checked. And Read and Write API activity are checked
- Click on Next.
- This will take you to the "Review and create" page. Here review all the information and if it looks ok, click on Create trail.
- You will notice that the trail is created. And logging is started by default.
- To test the trail that you created, create an S3 bucket in your account. and check the trail log file on S3 if the bucket creation event is logged.

- You can stop the trail logging by edited the trail on the management console. You can also use AWS CLI to start logging.

```
aws cloudtrail get-trail-status --name <trail -name>
```

- To get trail status from CLI. Use the command

```
aws cloudtrail get-trail-status --name <trail name>
```

## 3.7.4.2 Using IAM Access Advisor to Review Permissions
**Navigate to IAM Access Advisor:**
- In the AWS Management Console, go to Services and select IAM.
- Click on Users and select the user you want to troubleshoot.
- Go to the Access Advisor tab.

**Review Service Access:**
- The Access Advisor shows the last accessed time for each AWS service the user has permissions for.
- Identify services that the user has never accessed or hasn't accessed recently. This information helps refine policies and remove unnecessary permissions.

## 3.7.4.3 Using IAM Policy Simulator to Test Permissions
**Open IAM Policy Simulator:**
- In the IAM console, click on Policy Simulator under Access Management.

**Simulate User Permissions:**

- Select the IAM entity (user, group, or role) you want to test.
- Choose the policies attached to the entity.
- Select the service and actions you want to test.
- Click Run Simulation to see if the actions are allowed or denied based on the current policies.

**Analyze Simulation Results:**
- The results will show whether the selected actions are permitted or blocked.
- Identify which policies and specific statements are granting or denying permissions.
- Adjust the policies as necessary to fix the issues.

## 3.7.4.4 Troubleshooting Common Authentication Issues
**Identify Login Failures Using CloudTrail:**
- In CloudTrail logs, look for ConsoleLogin events with a status of Failure.
- Review the error messages and source IP addresses to understand why the login failed (e.g., incorrect password, MFA issues).

**Check Access Denials with IAM Access Advisor:**
- Use Access Advisor to check if the user has permissions for the services they are trying to access.
- Ensure that the required permissions are granted and that there are no unintended denials.

**Validate and Adjust Policies with Policy Simulator:**
- Use the Policy Simulator to test scenarios where users are experiencing access issues.
- Validate if the policies grant the required permissions for the user's tasks.
- Adjust the policies based on the simulation results to fix any misconfigurations.

By using AWS CloudTrail, IAM Access Advisor, and IAM Policy Simulator, you can effectively troubleshoot and resolve common authentication issues. CloudTrail provides detailed logs of authentication events, Access Advisor helps review service usage, and Policy Simulator allows testing and validating IAM policies. Together, these tools ensure secure and efficient management of user access and permissions in AWS.

# 3.8 Key Exam Tips
**AWS IAM Fundamentals:**
IAM (Identity and Access Management) is central to authentication and authorization in AWS. Understand how to create and manage IAM users, groups, roles, and policies. Be comfortable with the concept of managed vs. inline policies and the principle of least privilege.

**AWS IAM Identity Center (AWS Single Sign-On):**
Learn how AWS IAM Identity Center (formerly known as AWS Single Sign-On) allows centralized management of access to AWS accounts and applications. Understand how SSO can simplify user access with integration into identity providers like Active Directory and other SAML-based systems.

**Amazon Cognito:**
Amazon Cognito is a service primarily used for authentication in mobile and web apps. Be sure to grasp the difference between User Pools (for authentication) and Identity Pools (for temporary AWS credentials), and how to integrate these services with third-party identity providers.

**Identity Federation:**

Understand how Identity Federation works in AWS, allowing external identities from SAML, OIDC, or social identity providers to access AWS resources. Be familiar with integrating external providers into your AWS environment.

**Credential Mechanisms:**
Master the difference between long-term credentials (permanent IAM user credentials) and temporary credentials (provided by AWS STS). Know when to use temporary credentials and how they enhance security. Be aware of the use cases for AWS STS.

**Multi-Factor Authentication (MFA):**
MFA is an essential security feature to add an extra layer of protection. Be prepared to configure and manage MFA devices for both root and IAM users. Understand how MFA works alongside temporary credentials.

**Troubleshooting with AWS CloudTrail:**
CloudTrail plays a key role in tracking and logging all API calls in AWS. Familiarize yourself with how to use CloudTrail for troubleshooting authentication issues and monitoring changes in IAM policies and credentials.

**IAM Access Advisor and Policy Simulator:**
IAM Access Advisor helps identify unused permissions, while IAM Policy Simulator is useful for testing policy configurations. Be comfortable using these tools to troubleshoot permission issues and simulate policy effects.

**Best Practices:**
Implement the Principle of Least Privilege: Always grant the minimum permissions necessary. Regularly rotate credentials, audit IAM policies, and monitor authentication activity through CloudTrail.

# 3.9 Chapter Review Questions

**Question 1:**
What is the primary function of AWS IAM (Identity and Access Management)?
A. To manage AWS billing and subscription services
B. To encrypt data stored in AWS services
C. To manage and control access to AWS resources
D. To monitor the health of AWS services

**Question 2:**
Which of the following is a key feature of AWS IAM Identity Center (AWS Single Sign-On)?
A. Provides automated access to external applications without credentials
B. Enables centralized management of access for multiple AWS accounts and applications
C. Generates temporary security credentials
D. Facilitates multi-region application deployment

**Question 3:**
What is the primary purpose of Amazon Cognito?
A. To manage server infrastructure for web applications
B. To provide user authentication, authorization, and user pools
C. To monitor API activity in AWS
D. To manage multi-region failover

**Question 4:**
What does identity federation in AWS allow?
A. Creation of new AWS IAM users
B. Authentication for AWS services using third-party identity providers

C. Encryption of data at rest
D. Real-time monitoring of user activities

**Question 5:**
Which AWS service provides temporary security credentials for users who need temporary access to resources?
A. AWS Identity Center
B. Amazon Cognito
C. AWS STS (Security Token Service)
D. AWS Organizations

**Question 6:**
Which tool in AWS helps simulate and test the impact of IAM policies on resource access?
A. AWS CloudTrail
B. IAM Policy Simulator
C. AWS IAM Access Advisor
D. Amazon Macie

**Question 7:**
What is a recommended best practice for managing long-term credentials in AWS?
A. Storing them in publicly accessible S3 buckets
B. Regularly rotating credentials to reduce the risk of unauthorized access
C. Using a single set of credentials for all users
D. Disabling MFA for quicker access

**Question 8:**
How does AWS CloudTrail assist with troubleshooting authentication issues?
A. By providing encryption keys for troubleshooting
B. By logging API calls and tracking all actions taken by users and roles
C. By automatically resolving access issues in IAM
D. By generating compliance reports

**Question 9:**
Which authentication mechanism allows integrating external identity providers like Google and Facebook with AWS resources?
A. AWS STS
B. Amazon Cognito
C. AWS Key Management Service (KMS)
D. AWS Organizations

**Question 10:**
What is the purpose of multi-factor authentication (MFA) in AWS?
A. To allow users to log in using social media accounts
B. To require users to authenticate using more than one method, improving security
C. To encrypt user data across regions
D. To generate temporary credentials for IAM users

**Question 11:**
Your company is using AWS to host a web application that handles sensitive customer data. You need to ensure that only authenticated users can access specific resources within the application. Which AWS service would be the best fit to authenticate users and manage their identities?
A. AWS IAM Identity Center
B. AWS IAM Roles

C. Amazon Cognito
D. AWS STS

**Question 12:**
A developer in your organization accidentally configured an overly permissive IAM role, granting access to more services than required. You need to identify which AWS resources were accessed using this role. Which AWS tool would you use to troubleshoot and analyze this issue?
A. IAM Policy Simulator
B. AWS CloudTrail
C. AWS Trusted Advisor
D. IAM Access Advisor

**Question 13:**
Your organization has a requirement to integrate external identity providers such as Google and Facebook for user authentication in a mobile application. The app must allow users to log in using their existing social media accounts. Which AWS service should you implement?
A. AWS IAM
B. Amazon Cognito
C. AWS SSO
D. AWS STS

**Question 14:**
Your team is using temporary security credentials to grant external users access to certain AWS resources. However, there have been some reports of unauthorized access attempts. You need to monitor and audit all API calls to ensure the security of these temporary credentials. Which service would help you with this task?
A. AWS CloudTrail
B. AWS Config
C. Amazon Inspector
D. AWS Artifact

**Question 15:**
You need to configure multi-factor authentication (MFA) for users in your AWS account to enhance security. However, after enabling MFA for some users, they are still able to access certain services without MFA. What is the most likely cause of this issue, and what would you use to simulate and test the policy?
A. The MFA device is not activated correctly; use AWS CloudTrail to simulate
B. The IAM policies are not properly configured; use IAM Policy Simulator to test
C. The users need additional permissions; use IAM Access Advisor
D. The IAM roles are expired; regenerate long-term credentials

# 3.10 Answers to Chapter Review Questions

1. C. To manage and control access to AWS resources
Explanation: AWS IAM allows you to manage permissions and control access to AWS resources securely, ensuring that only authorized users and applications have access.

2. B. Enables centralized management of access for multiple AWS accounts and applications
Explanation: AWS IAM Identity Center (AWS SSO) provides centralized access management across AWS accounts and applications, enabling seamless user access control.

3. B. To provide user authentication, authorization, and user pools

Explanation: Amazon Cognito enables secure user authentication and authorization, with user pools that allow you to manage user identities and access for web and mobile apps.

4. B. Authentication for AWS services using third-party identity providers
Explanation: Identity Federation allows users to authenticate with AWS resources using external identity providers (e.g., Google, Facebook, or enterprise SSO), streamlining user access.

5. C. AWS STS (Security Token Service)
Explanation: AWS STS issues temporary security credentials to grant users or services short-term access to AWS resources, minimizing the need for long-term credentials.

6. B. IAM Policy Simulator
Explanation: The IAM Policy Simulator is a tool that allows you to test the effects of IAM policies on access to AWS resources before implementing them, helping prevent misconfigurations.

7. B. Regularly rotating credentials to reduce the risk of unauthorized access
Explanation: Regularly rotating long-term credentials (e.g., access keys) reduces the risk of compromised credentials being used by unauthorized users.

8. B. By logging API calls and tracking all actions taken by users and roles
Explanation: AWS CloudTrail records API activity and tracks user and role actions, which can be used to troubleshoot authentication and access issues.

9. B. Amazon Cognito
Explanation: Amazon Cognito supports integrating external identity providers (e.g., Google, Facebook) for user authentication, allowing users to sign in to AWS resources using existing credentials.

10. B. To require users to authenticate using more than one method, improving security
Explanation: Multi-factor authentication (MFA) adds an extra layer of security by requiring users to authenticate using both their password and a secondary method, such as a mobile device or security token.

11. C. Amazon Cognito
Explanation: Amazon Cognito is the best service for authenticating users and managing identities for web and mobile applications. It allows you to create user pools for managing user sign-up and sign-in, as well as integrate with external identity providers such as Google and Facebook.

12. B. AWS CloudTrail
Explanation: AWS CloudTrail logs all API calls made in your AWS environment. This will allow you to track and audit which AWS resources were accessed using the overly permissive IAM role, helping you troubleshoot and identify any unauthorized access.

13. B. Amazon Cognito
Explanation: Amazon Cognito supports identity federation by integrating with external identity providers like Google and Facebook. It allows users to log in using their social media credentials, making it an ideal solution for mobile applications requiring this capability.

14. A. AWS CloudTrail
Explanation: AWS CloudTrail logs API calls made in your AWS environment, including actions taken with temporary credentials from services like AWS STS. CloudTrail will help you monitor and audit all activities related to temporary credentials to ensure there are no security breaches.

15. B. The IAM policies are not properly configured; use IAM Policy Simulator to test

Explanation: The issue likely arises from the IAM policies not being configured correctly to enforce MFA. The IAM Policy Simulator allows you to simulate and test the impact of policies and ensure that MFA is required for all specified resources and actions.

# Chapter 4. Authorization of AWS Resources

**This chapter addresses the following exam objectives:**
Domain 4: Identity and Access Management
Task Statement 4.2: Design, implement, and troubleshoot authorization for AWS resources.
Knowledge of:
- Different IAM policies (for example, managed policies, inline policies, identity-based policies, resource-based policies, session control policies)
- Components and impact of a policy (for example, Principal, Action, Resource, Condition)
- How to troubleshoot authorization issues (for example, by using CloudTrail, IAM Access Advisor, and IAM policy simulator)

Skills in:
- Constructing attribute-based access control (ABAC) and role-based access control (RBAC) strategies
- Evaluating IAM policy types for given requirements and workloads
- Interpreting an IAM policy's effect on environments and workloads
- Applying the principle of least privilege across an environment
- Enforcing proper separation of duties
- Analyzing access or authorization errors to determine cause or effect

♦♦♦♦♦♦

Securing access to AWS resources is a multi-faceted process that goes beyond authentication to include robust authorization mechanisms. This chapter provides an in-depth exploration of how AWS controls access to resources through various policies and strategies, ensuring that users and applications have the appropriate permissions necessary to perform their tasks without overstepping boundaries.

We begin with an introduction to authorization in AWS, laying the groundwork for understanding how permissions are granted and enforced. The chapter then delves into IAM policies, including managed policies, inline policies, identity-based policies, resource-based policies, and session control policies. Each type of policy serves a specific purpose and offers different levels of control and flexibility.

Understanding the components and impact of IAM policies is crucial. We explore the structure of IAM policies, the effects they have on environments and workloads, and how to interpret their impact accurately. This knowledge is essential for constructing effective access control strategies.

The chapter examines the construction of access control strategies, focusing on Attribute-Based Access Control (ABAC) and Role-Based Access Control (RBAC). We provide step-by-step guidance on constructing ABAC policies and discuss the principles of RBAC, both of which are critical for implementing fine-grained access control.

Applying the principle of least privilege and enforcing separation of duties are best practices that help minimize the risk of unauthorized access. We discuss these principles in detail, offering practical advice on how to implement them effectively within your AWS environment.

Troubleshooting authorization issues is an essential skill for maintaining secure access control. The chapter covers tools such as the IAM Policy Simulator and techniques for analyzing access errors, providing the knowledge needed to resolve authorization problems efficiently.

Best practices for authorization include monitoring and logging activities to detect and respond to unauthorized access attempts. These practices are crucial for maintaining a secure and compliant AWS environment.

To reinforce the concepts discussed, the chapter concludes with lab exercises that provide hands-on experience in creating and applying IAM policies, constructing ABAC and RBAC policies, and troubleshooting authorization issues. These exercises are designed to deepen your understanding and practical skills in managing authorization in AWS.

By the end of this chapter, readers will have a comprehensive understanding of AWS authorization mechanisms, best practices, and troubleshooting techniques, enabling them to effectively control access to AWS resources.

## 4.1 Introduction to Authorization in AWS

Authorization within AWS is a critical security mechanism that ensures only authenticated users or services can perform specific actions on AWS resources. This concept is implemented using Identity and Access Management (IAM) policies, roles, and permissions that control access at a granular level. Once a user or service is authenticated, AWS determines what actions they are authorized to perform by evaluating the associated policies.

IAM policies are JSON documents that define permissions for users, groups, and roles. They specify which AWS resources can be accessed and the actions that can be performed on those resources. There are several types of policies, including managed policies (provided by AWS), inline policies (attached directly to a user, group, or role), and resource-based policies (attached to AWS resources like S3 buckets).

Roles in IAM are designed to delegate access to users or services without sharing long-term credentials. They are particularly useful for granting permissions to applications running on EC2 instances or to services in different AWS accounts. When an entity assumes a role, temporary security credentials are issued, allowing it to perform actions defined by the role's policies.

Authorization decisions in AWS are made by evaluating the effect (allow or deny) of all applicable policies. The default behavior is to deny all actions, and explicit allow permissions must be granted through policies. If there is an explicit deny in any policy, it overrides any allows. This ensures that permissions are only granted intentionally and securely.

For example, an IAM policy can allow a specific user to read objects from an S3 bucket but not delete or upload objects. Another policy might grant an EC2 instance role permission to access a specific DynamoDB table. By carefully crafting these policies, AWS ensures that users and services have the minimum necessary permissions to perform their tasks, adhering to the principle of least privilege.

In summary, authorization in AWS is about controlling access to resources through finely tuned policies and roles. By evaluating these policies, AWS ensures that only authenticated entities can perform specific actions on AWS resources, thereby maintaining security and preventing unauthorized access.

## 4.2 IAM Policies
### 4.2.1 Managed Policies
AWS managed policies are pre-defined policies created and maintained by AWS to provide permissions for common use cases. These policies are designed to simplify the management of access controls by offering ready-made, best-practice policies that can be attached directly to users, groups, and roles within an AWS account. AWS managed policies help ensure that permissions are granted securely and efficiently without requiring administrators to write policies from scratch.

One of the primary advantages of using AWS managed policies is that they are automatically updated and maintained by AWS. When new services or features are introduced, AWS ensures that the managed policies are updated to reflect these changes. This reduces the administrative overhead of keeping policies up-to-date and helps maintain a secure environment.

AWS managed policies cover a wide range of use cases, from basic read-only access to full administrative access. For example:
- **AdministratorAccess:** This policy grants full access to all AWS services and resources. It is typically used for administrators who need complete control over the AWS account. The policy allows all actions (`"Action": "*"`) on all resources (`"Resource": "*"`) with an effect of `"Allow"`.
- **ReadOnlyAccess:** This policy grants read-only access to all AWS services and resources. It is useful for users who need to view resources and their configurations but should keep the same. The policy allows all read-only actions across AWS services (`"Action": "list"`, `"describe"`, `"get"`) on all resources with an effect of `"Allow"`.
- **AmazonS3ReadOnlyAccess:** This policy provides read-only access to Amazon S3 buckets and objects. It is ideal for users who need to retrieve or list objects but should not modify or delete them. The policy allows `s3:Get*` and `s3:List*` actions on all S3 resources with an effect of `"Allow"`.
- **AmazonEC2FullAccess:** This policy grants full access to Amazon EC2 services, allowing users to create, modify, and delete EC2 instances, security groups, and related resources. It includes actions like `ec2:RunInstances`, `ec2:TerminateInstances`, `ec2:CreateSecurityGroup`, and more.

Using AWS managed policies helps enforce the principle of least privilege by providing specific access controls tailored to common tasks. Administrators can quickly assign appropriate permissions to users without the risk of over-permissioning. Additionally, these policies are continuously reviewed and updated by AWS security experts, ensuring they adhere to best security practices.

In summary, AWS managed policies are pre-defined, AWS-maintained policies that simplify access management by providing secure and up-to-date permissions for common use cases. Examples include policies for full administrative access, read-only access, and specific service permissions, like S3 read-only or EC2 full access. These managed policies help streamline permission management while ensuring security best practices are followed.

### 4.2.2 Inline Policies
Inline policies in AWS Identity and Access Management (IAM) are policies that are directly embedded into a single user, group, or role. Unlike managed policies, which can be reused across multiple IAM entities, inline policies are unique to the specific entity to which they are attached. This provides a high level of granularity and control over the permissions granted to that particular entity.

Inline policies are tightly coupled with the IAM entity they are attached to, meaning that if the user, group, or role is deleted, the inline policies are also deleted. This can be advantageous when you need to grant permissions that are highly specific to a particular user or role, and you do not intend to reuse these permissions across multiple entities.

## Key Characteristics of Inline Policies:
**Specificity:** Inline policies are designed to provide specific permissions to a single IAM entity, ensuring that the permissions are tailored to the precise needs of that entity.
**Management:** Since inline policies are directly associated with an entity, managing them is straightforward in scenarios where permissions need to be closely monitored and controlled for individual users or roles.
**Unique Application:** Inline policies are not shared across multiple entities, which can be beneficial for maintaining strict access control and minimizing the risk of unintended permission propagation.

## Example of Inline Policy:
Imagine you have a specific IAM user, John_Doe, who needs permission to read and write objects in a particular S3 bucket named example-bucket. You can create an inline policy for John_Doe that grants these specific permissions.

## Steps to Create an Inline Policy for a User
**Navigate to the IAM Console:**
- Open the AWS Management Console and navigate to the IAM service.
- Click on Users in the left-hand navigation pane and select the user 'John_Doe.'

**Attach Inline Policy:**
- In the user details page, click on the Permissions tab.
- Click on Add inline policy.

**Create Policy:**
- Use the visual editor or JSON editor to define the policy.
- Example JSON policy to grant read and write access to example-bucket:

```
1.  {
2.      "Version": "2012-10-17",
3.      "Statement": [
4.          {
5.              "Effect": "Allow",
6.              "Action": [
7.                  "s3:GetObject",
8.                  "s3:PutObject"
9.              ],
10.             "Resource": "arn:aws:s3:::example-bucket/*"
11.         }
12.     ]
13. }
```

**Review and Apply:**
Review the policy summary.
Click Create policy to attach it to the user.

This inline policy allows the John_Doe user to read and write objects within the example-bucket S3 bucket but does not grant any other permissions. This ensures that John_Doe has the necessary access to perform his job without over-permissioning.

**Benefits of Inline Policies:**
- Fine-Grained Control: They allow for very specific access controls tailored to a single entity's needs.
- Simplified Management: Inline policies can be easier to manage when you have distinct permissions for individual entities rather than shared permissions.
- Direct Association: The direct association between the policy and the IAM entity simplifies auditing and ensures that permissions are closely monitored.

Inline policies in AWS IAM provide a method for granting highly specific permissions to individual users, groups, or roles. They are directly attached to the entity, offering fine-grained control over access. While managed policies are ideal for reuse and broader application, inline policies are useful for scenarios where permissions need to be tightly controlled and unique to a particular entity.

## 4.2.3 Identity-Based Policies

Policies in AWS Identity and Access Management (IAM) are critical components that define the permissions for IAM identities, such as users, groups, and roles. These policies determine what actions the identities can perform on AWS resources and are crucial for enforcing security and access control within an AWS environment. Several types of policies can be attached to IAM identities, including managed policies and inline policies.

Managed policies are standalone policies created and maintained by AWS (AWS managed policies) or the user (customer-managed policies). These policies can be attached to multiple IAM identities, making them reusable and easier to manage. For instance, the AWS managed policy `AdministratorAccess` grants full access to all AWS resources and services. This policy can be attached to an administrative user or role to ensure they have the necessary permissions to manage the entire AWS account.

Inline policies, on the other hand, are embedded directly within a specific user, group, or role. They are unique to the entity they are attached to and provide a more granular level of control. For example, suppose there is a specific IAM user named `John_Doe` who requires permissions to only read and write objects in a particular S3 bucket called example-bucket. An inline policy can be created and attached directly to `John_Doe` to grant these specific permissions:

```
1.  {
2.    "Version": "2012-10-17",
3.    "Statement": [
4.      {
5.        "Effect": "Allow",
6.        "Action": [
7.          "s3:GetObject",
8.          "s3:PutObject"
9.        ],
10.       "Resource": "arn:aws:s3:::example-bucket/*"
11.     }
12.   ]
13. }
```

This inline policy ensures that `John_Doe` can only perform the `s3:GetObject` and `s3:PutObject` actions within the example-bucket S3 bucket and does not have permissions for other actions or resources.

Groups in IAM are collections of users that make managing permissions for multiple users easier. By attaching policies to a group, all users within the group inherit the permissions defined in those policies. For example, a group named Developers might have a managed policy attached that grants permissions to use AWS CodeCommit, AWS CodeBuild, and other development-related services. All users added to the Developers group will automatically have the permissions defined by the attached policy.

Roles in IAM are intended to be assumed by trusted entities, such as IAM users, applications, or AWS services. Roles are commonly used to delegate access between different AWS accounts or to grant permissions to AWS services running on EC2 instances. For example, `EC2AccessRole` could be created with a policy allowing the role to read and write to a specific DynamoDB table. An EC2 instance can then assume this role to access the DynamoDB table without needing to store long-term credentials on the instance.

In summary, policies in IAM play a fundamental role in managing access to AWS resources by defining permissions for users, groups, and roles. Managed policies offer reusability and easier management, while inline policies provide fine-grained control specific to individual identities. By attaching appropriate policies to IAM identities, organizations can enforce the principle of least privilege and enhance security within their AWS environments.

## 4.2.4 Resource-Based Policies

Policies attached to AWS resources, such as S3 buckets and SNS topics, are known as resource-based policies. These policies are crucial for defining who can access the resource and what actions they can perform. Unlike identity-based policies, which are attached to IAM identities, resource-based policies are directly attached to the resources they govern. This allows for more granular control and the ability to grant cross-account access.

### S3 Bucket Policies

S3 bucket policies are JSON documents that specify what actions are allowed or denied for which principals (users or roles) on the specified bucket and its objects. These policies can grant permissions to other AWS accounts, IAM users, or roles.

For example, consider an S3 bucket named `example-bucket` that needs to be accessed by users from another AWS account (with Account ID 123456789012). The following bucket policy grants read (list and get) permissions to all users in that account:

```
1.  {
2.    "Version": "2012-10-17",
3.    "Statement": [
4.      {
5.        "Effect": "Allow",
6.        "Principal": {
7.          "AWS": "arn:aws:iam::123456789012:root"
8.        },
9.        "Action": [
10.         "s3:ListBucket"
11.       ],
12.       "Resource": "arn:aws:s3:::example-bucket"
13.     },
14.     {
15.       "Effect": "Allow",
16.       "Principal": {
17.         "AWS": "arn:aws:iam::123456789012:root"
18.       },
19.       "Action": [
20.         "s3:GetObject"
21.       ],
22.       "Resource": "arn:aws:s3:::example-bucket/*"
23.     }
24.   ]
25. }
26.
```

In this policy, the `Principal` element specifies the AWS account that is granted access. The Action element specifies the S3 actions that are allowed (`s3:ListBucket` for listing the bucket and `s3:GetObject` for getting objects). The `Resource` element specifies the S3 bucket and objects the policy applies to.

### SNS Topic Policies

SNS topic policies are also JSON documents that define who can publish to or subscribe to an SNS topic. These policies can grant permissions to other AWS accounts, IAM users, or roles.

For example, consider an SNS topic named `example-topic` that allows a specific IAM user (with ARN `arn:aws:iam::123456789012/ExampleUser`) to publish messages to the topic:

```
1.  {
2.    "Version": "2012-10-17",
3.    "Statement": [
4.      {
5.        "Effect": "Allow",
6.        "Principal": {
7.          "AWS": "arn:aws:iam::123456789012:user/ExampleUser"
8.        },
9.        "Action": "sns:Publish",
10.       "Resource": "arn:aws:sns:us-east-1:123456789012:example-topic"
11.     }
12.   ]
13. }
14.
```

In this policy, the `Principal` element specifies the IAM user who is granted permission to publish messages. The `Action` element specifies the `sns:Publish` action, and the `Resource` element specifies the ARN of the SNS topic.

Resource-based policies for S3 buckets and SNS topics enable detailed control over who can access these resources and what actions they can perform. S3 bucket policies allow for actions like listing and retrieving objects, while SNS topic policies control who can publish to or subscribe to topics. By carefully crafting these policies, AWS users can ensure secure and appropriate access to their resources, maintaining the principle of least privilege and enhancing overall security.

## 4.2.5 Session Control Policies

Policies that control session permissions are crucial for managing access when using temporary security credentials in AWS. These policies are often used with AWS Security Token Service (STS) to define the permissions for temporary sessions assumed by users, applications, or services. Session policies provide an additional layer of security by further restricting what actions can be performed during the temporary session.

## 4.2.6 Session Policies with AWS STS

When using AWS STS to assume a role or obtain temporary credentials, you can specify a session policy that limits the permissions of the session. This session policy can be used to reduce the permissions granted by the role's permissions policies, ensuring that the temporary credentials only have the minimum necessary permissions for the duration of the session.

### Example: Assuming a Role with a Session Policy

Suppose you have a role named `DataProcessingRole` with broad permissions, including full access to an S3 bucket named `data-bucket`. However, you want to create a temporary session with limited permissions, allowing only read access to a specific folder within the bucket. You can achieve this using a session policy.

**Create the Role with Broad Permissions:**

```
{
  "Version": "2012-10-17",
  "Statement": [
    {
      "Effect": "Allow",
      "Action": "s3:*",
      "Resource": "arn:aws:s3:::data-bucket/*"
    }
  ]
}
```

**Assume the Role with a Session Policy:**

When assuming the role, specify a session policy to limit the session's permissions. Use the AWS CLI or AWS SDK to assume the role with the session policy.

**Using AWS CLI:**

```
aws sts assume-role \
  --role-arn "arn:aws:iam::123456789012:role/DataProcessingRole" \
  --role-session-name "LimitedAccessSession" \
  --policy '{
    "Version": "2012-10-17",
    "Statement": [
      {
        "Effect": "Allow",
        "Action": "s3:GetObject",
        "Resource": "arn:aws:s3:::data-bucket/specific-folder/*"
      }
    ]
  }'
```

In this command, the `--policy` parameter specifies the session policy. The policy grants only `s3:GetObject` permissions to the `specific-folder` within the `data-bucket`.

## Benefits of Session Policies

- **Least Privilege**: Session policies enforce the principle of least privilege by ensuring that temporary credentials have only the necessary permissions for a specific task.
- **Enhanced Security**: Limiting permissions during a session reduces the risk of misuse or accidental actions that could compromise security.
- **Flexibility**: Session policies allow for dynamic permission adjustments based on the context of the session, providing more control over temporary credentials.

Session policies are an essential tool for controlling permissions when using temporary credentials in AWS. They provide an additional security layer by allowing you to specify the exact permissions required for a temporary session, reducing the risk of over-permissioning and enhancing overall security. By carefully crafting and applying session policies, organizations can ensure that temporary credentials adhere to the principle of least privilege, ensuring secure and efficient access to AWS resources.

## 4.3 IAM Policy Components and Impact
### 4.3.1 IAM Policy Structure

IAM policies in AWS are structured documents that define permissions and are composed of several key components: Principal, Action, Resource, and Condition. Understanding these components is essential for creating precise and secure policies.

### Principal

The `Principal` element specifies the user, group, role, or service to which the policy applies. It identifies who is allowed or denied access. In a resource-based policy, the principal is the entity that is being granted permissions. For example, the principal in an S3 bucket policy might be an IAM user or an AWS account.

Example:
```
1. "Principal": {
2.   "AWS": "arn:aws:iam::123456789012:user/JohnDoe"
3. }
```
This specifies that the IAM user `JohnDoe` from account `123456789012` is the principal.

### Action

The `Action` element specifies the actions that are allowed or denied. AWS service APIs, such as `s3:PutObject` or `ec2:StartInstances` define actions. Each action corresponds to a specific API operation that can be performed on AWS resources.

Example:
```
1. "Action": [
2.   "s3:ListBucket",
3.   "s3:GetObject"
4. ]
```
This allows for listing the contents of an S3 bucket and acquiring objects from the bucket.

### Resource

The `Resource` element specifies the AWS resources to which the actions apply. Resources are identified using Amazon Resource Names (ARNs). This component helps to restrict the policy to specific resources.

Example:
```
1. "Resource": [
2.   "arn:aws:s3:::example-bucket",
3.   "arn:aws:s3:::example-bucket/*"
4. ]
```
This specifies that the policy applies to the S3 bucket named `example-bucket` and all objects within that bucket.

### Condition

The `Condition` element allows you to specify conditions that must be met for the policy to take effect. Conditions are expressed as key-value pairs, where the key is a condition operator (such as `StringEquals` or `IpAddress`) and the value is the condition value (such as an IP address or date).

Example:
```
1. "Condition": {
2.   "IpAddress": {
3.     "aws:SourceIp": "203.0.113.0/24"
4.   }
```

```
5. }
```

This condition restricts access to the specified actions and resources to requests from IP range `203.0.113.0/24`.

**Putting It All Together**

Here is an example of a complete IAM policy that incorporates all these components:

```
1.  {
2.    "Version": "2012-10-17",
3.    "Statement": [
4.      {
5.        "Effect": "Allow",
6.        "Principal": {
7.          "AWS": "arn:aws:iam::123456789012:user/JohnDoe"
8.        },
9.        "Action": [
10.         "s3:ListBucket",
11.         "s3:GetObject"
12.       ],
13.       "Resource": [
14.         "arn:aws:s3:::example-bucket",
15.         "arn:aws:s3:::example-bucket/*"
16.       ],
17.       "Condition": {
18.         "IpAddress": {
19.           "aws:SourceIp": "203.0.113.0/24"
20.         }
21.       }
22.     }
23.   ]
24. }
```

In this policy:
- The `Principal` is `JohnDoe`, specifying who can perform the actions.
- The `Action` elements `s3:ListBucket` and `s3:GetObject` define what actions are allowed.
- The `Resource` elements specify the `example-bucket` and its contents as the resources on which these actions can be performed.
- The `Condition` restricts access to the specified actions and resources to requests originating from the IP range `203.0.113.0/24`.

Breaking down IAM policy components into Principal, Action, Resource, and Condition allows for precise control over permissions. Principals specify who the policy applies to, Actions define what operations can be performed, Resources determine what objects those actions can target, and Conditions add an extra layer of control by stipulating specific requirements that must be met for the policy to apply. This granular control is essential for implementing the principle of least privilege and ensuring secure access management in AWS.

## 4.3.2 Effect of Policies on Environments and Workloads

IAM policies in AWS define permissions through a combination of Principal, Action, Resource, and Condition components. These components interact to control access and affect AWS environments and workloads by determining who can do what, to which resources, and under what conditions. Understanding how these components interact is crucial for interpreting the policy's effect on environments and workloads.

## 4.3.3 Interpreting an IAM Policy's Effect

When an IAM policy is evaluated, AWS considers the interaction of all policy components to decide whether to allow or deny a request. The process starts by identifying the Principal making the request, followed by checking the Action they are attempting to perform. Next, the policy evaluates the Resource specified in the request and any Conditions that must be met for the action to be allowed.

## Example Policy Interaction

Consider an IAM policy that controls access to an S3 bucket. The policy might look like this:

```
{
  "Version": "2012-10-17",
  "Statement": [
    {
      "Effect": "Allow",
      "Principal": {
        "AWS": "arn:aws:iam::123456789012:user/JohnDoe"
      },
      "Action": [
        "s3:ListBucket",
        "s3:GetObject",
        "s3:PutObject"
      ],
      "Resource": [
        "arn:aws:s3:::example-bucket",
        "arn:aws:s3:::example-bucket/*"
      ],
      "Condition": {
        "IpAddress": {
          "aws:SourceIp": "203.0.113.0/24"
        }
      }
    },
    {
      "Effect": "Deny",
      "Principal": {
        "AWS": "*"
      },
      "Action": [
        "s3:DeleteObject"
      ],
      "Resource": [
        "arn:aws:s3:::example-bucket",
        "arn:aws:s3:::example-bucket/*"
      ]
    }
  ]
}
```

## How Components Interact:

**Principal:** The Principal in the first statement is `JohnDoe`, which means the permissions in this statement apply specifically to this user. The second statement's Principal is **"*" (all users),** applying the deny rule globally.

**Action:** The policy allows `JohnDoe` to perform `s3:ListBucket`, `s3:GetObject`, and `s3:PutObject` actions. However, the policy explicitly denies all users from performing `s3:DeleteObject` actions on the bucket and its contents.

**Resource:** The actions allowed or denied are specifically tied to the S3 bucket example-bucket and all objects within it. This ensures that the permissions are only applicable to this bucket and not any other resources.

**Condition:** The first statement includes a condition that restricts the allowed actions to requests coming from the IP range `203.0.113.0/24`. This means `JohnDoe` can only list, get, or put objects in the `example-bucket` if the request originates from within this IP range.

### Effect on Environments and Workloads
**Controlled Access:** By specifying the Principal, the policy ensures that only `JohnDoe` has the permissions to list, get, and put objects in the `example-bucket`, while no one can delete objects.

**Security:** The use of Conditions adds an extra layer of security by restricting access based on IP address, ensuring that even `JohnDoe` cannot perform actions outside the specified IP range.

**Granular Permissions:** The interaction of these components ensures that permissions are tightly controlled, preventing unauthorized actions that could disrupt environments or workloads. The explicit deny for `s3:DeleteObject` ensures that objects in the bucket cannot be deleted by anyone, protecting critical data.

**Interpreting Policy Effect:**
By analyzing each component, administrators can understand how a policy will affect access to AWS resources. This comprehensive view allows for better security management and ensures that workloads operate smoothly without unexpected interruptions or security breaches. The detailed control over who can access what resources and under what conditions helps maintain a secure and efficient AWS environment.

The interaction of Principal, Action, Resource, and Condition components in an IAM policy determines the specific permissions and restrictions applied to AWS environments and workloads. By carefully crafting these policies, AWS users can enforce precise access controls that enhance security and operational efficiency.

# 4.4 Constructing Access Control Strategies
## 4.4.1 Attribute-Based Access Control (ABAC)
Attribute-Based Access Control (ABAC) is an advanced access control strategy in AWS that uses user attributes, such as department, job role, or project assignment, to define permissions. ABAC enables more dynamic and granular access controls compared to traditional role-based access control (RBAC), where permissions are static and tied to predefined roles.

### Explanation of ABAC
ABAC allows policies to evaluate attributes from AWS IAM users and other resources to make access decisions. This approach is particularly useful in large, dynamic environments where managing roles and permissions manually would be cumbersome. Attributes can include information such as user names, tags, department names, or any other metadata that can describe a user's identity or context.

### Constructing ABAC Policies
To construct ABAC policies, you need to define policies that include conditions evaluating user attributes. AWS supports this through the use of tags and policy variables. Tags are key-value pairs that you can attach to IAM users and resources, while policy variables can reference these tags.

## 4.4.2 Steps to Construct ABAC Policies
**Tagging IAM Users and Resources**
- First, tag IAM users with relevant attributes. For example, you might tag users with their department and project.
- Similarly, tag AWS resources with attributes that match user attributes. For instance, tag S3 buckets with project identifiers.

**Defining ABAC Policies**
- Create IAM policies that include conditions evaluating these tags. Use policy variables to dynamically reference user attributes.

**Example ABAC Policy**

Suppose you have an IAM user tagged with Department=Finance and you want to grant access to S3 buckets tagged with Department=Finance. Here's how you can construct the policy:

**Tagging Users and Resources**

IAM User `JohnDoe` tagged with Department=Finance.
S3 Bucket `finance-reports` tagged with Department=Finance.

**ABAC Policy**

```
{
  "Version": "2012-10-17",
  "Statement": [
    {
      "Effect": "Allow",
      "Action": "s3:*",
      "Resource": "arn:aws:s3:::${aws:username}-*",
      "Condition": {
        "StringEquals": {
          "aws:RequestTag/Department": "${aws:PrincipalTag/Department}"
        }
      }
    }
  ]
}
```

**Explanation**
- Action: The policy allows all S3 actions (`s3:*`).
- Resource: The resource ARN uses a variable `${aws:username}-*` to dynamically reference S3 buckets named after the username.
- Condition: The condition uses `StringEquals` to ensure that the Department tag on the request matches the Department tag on the principal (user). This ensures that users can only access resources tagged with the same department they belong to.

ABAC in AWS provides a powerful and flexible way to manage access control using user attributes and tags. By constructing policies that evaluate attributes dynamically, organizations can achieve fine-grained access control that scales with their environment. Understanding how to tag users and resources, use policy variables, and define conditions are key skills for implementing effective ABAC strategies. This approach ensures that users have the right access based on their attributes, enhancing both security and operational efficiency.

## 4.4.3 Role-Based Access Control (RBAC)

Role-Based Access Control (RBAC) is a widely used approach in AWS for managing permissions by assigning them to roles rather than individual users. This method simplifies the administration of permissions, ensuring that users have the needed access to perform their job functions while adhering to the principle of least privilege.

## Overview of RBAC

In RBAC, roles are created to represent job functions within an organization. Each role is assigned a set of permissions that specifies what actions can be performed and on which resources. Users are then assigned to these roles based on their job responsibilities. This approach allows for easier management of permissions, as changes can be made at the role level rather than individually for each user.

## Constructing RBAC Strategies

Constructing effective RBAC strategies involves several key steps:
- **Identify Job Functions:** Determine the various job functions within your organization. Common roles might include Developer, Administrator, and Auditor.
- **Define Roles:** Create roles in AWS IAM that correspond to these job functions. For each role, identify the necessary permissions required to perform the associated tasks.
- **Assign Permissions to Roles:** Attach the appropriate policies to each role. These policies define the actions the role can perform and the resources it can access.
- **Assign Users to Roles:** Add users to the roles based on their job functions. This can be done directly or by adding users to groups that are then assigned to roles.

## Example of RBAC

Suppose an organization has three primary job functions: Developers, Administrators, and Auditors. Here's how you might construct an RBAC strategy for these roles.

**Define Roles**
- DeveloperRole: Responsible for developing and deploying applications.
- AdminRole: Responsible for managing AWS resources and configurations.
- AuditorRole: Responsible for reviewing and auditing activities in the AWS account.

**Assign Permissions to Roles**

DeveloperRole:

```
{
  "Version": "2012-10-17",
  "Statement": [
    {
      "Effect": "Allow",
      "Action": [
        "ec2:DescribeInstances",
        "s3:ListBucket",
        "s3:GetObject",
        "s3:PutObject"
      ],
      "Resource": "*"
    }
  ]
}
```

AdminRole:

```
{
  "Version": "2012-10-17",
  "Statement": [
    {
      "Effect": "Allow",
      "Action": "*",
      "Resource": "*"
    }
  ]
}
```

AuditorRole:

```
1.  {
2.    "Version": "2012-10-17",
3.    "Statement": [
4.      {
5.        "Effect": "Allow",
6.        "Action": [
7.          "cloudtrail:DescribeTrails",
8.          "cloudtrail:GetTrailStatus",
9.          "cloudtrail:LookupEvents",
10.         "s3:ListBucket",
11.         "s3:GetObject"
12.       ],
13.       "Resource": "*"
14.     }
15.   ]
16. }
```

**Assign Users to Roles**
- Add `UserA` and `UserB` to the `DeveloperRole`.
- Add `AdminUser` to the `AdminRole`.
- Add `AuditUser` to the `AuditorRole`.

By following these steps, permissions are managed at the role level. When a new engineer joins the team, they can simply be added to the `DeveloperRole` without needing to individually assign all the necessary permissions. Similarly, if a developer leaves, removing them from the role immediately revokes their access.

**Benefits of RBAC**
- Simplified Management: Permissions are managed centrally at the role level, making it easier to administer and audit.
- Consistency: Ensures that users with the same job function have consistent access rights.
- Scalability: Roles can be easily adjusted as the organization grows, reducing the administrative overhead.
- Security: Commits to the principle of least privilege by ensuring users only have the permissions necessary for their roles.

To summarize, RBAC in AWS simplifies access management by assigning permissions to roles rather than individual users. Constructing an effective RBAC strategy involves defining roles based on job functions, assigning appropriate permissions to these roles, and then associating users with the roles. This approach enhances security, simplifies administration, and ensures consistent and scalable access control within an organization.

# 4.5 Applying the Principle of Least Privilege

Applying the principle of least privilege involves granting users and systems the minimum level of access necessary to perform their required tasks. This security practice minimizes the potential for unauthorized access or malicious activity by ensuring that permissions are tightly controlled and only expanded when absolutely necessary. Implementing this principle helps to protect sensitive data and maintain the integrity of the system.

## 4.5.1 Implementing Least Privilege

Applying the principle of least privilege (PoLP) in AWS environments involves several key techniques to ensure that users, applications, and services have only the permissions necessary to perform their tasks. This approach significantly reduces security risks by limiting the potential impact of compromised credentials or malicious activities.

## Techniques for Applying PoLP in AWS
### Role-Based Access Control (RBAC)
- Use IAM roles to define permissions based on job functions rather than assigning permissions directly to individual users. For example, create roles such as `Developer`, `Administrator`, and `Auditor`, and attach appropriate policies to these roles. Assign users to these roles based on their responsibilities.
- Example: An `Administrator` role might have full access to all AWS services (`"Action": "*"`, `"Resource": "*"`), whereas a `Developer` role might have limited permissions to access EC2 instances and S3 buckets necessary for development tasks.

### Fine-Grained Policies
- Create and attach fine-grained IAM policies that specify exact permissions required for each role or user. Avoid using overly permissive policies like `AdministratorAccess` for non-admin users.
- Example: A policy for a developer role might look like this:

```
1.  {
2.    "Version": "2012-10-17",
3.    "Statement": [
4.      {
5.        "Effect": "Allow",
6.        "Action": [
7.          "ec2:DescribeInstances",
8.          "s3:ListBucket",
9.          "s3:GetObject",
10.         "s3:PutObject"
11.       ],
12.       "Resource": "*"
13.     }
14.   ]
15. }
```

### Use of IAM Policies with Conditions
- Leverage policy conditions to add context to permissions. Conditions can include specific IP addresses, times of day, or use of multi-factor authentication (MFA).
- Example: Restricting access to an S3 bucket based on IP address:

```
1.  {
2.    "Version": "2012-10-17",
3.    "Statement": [
4.      {
5.        "Effect": "Allow",
6.        "Action": "s3:GetObject",
7.        "Resource": "arn:aws:s3:::example-bucket/*",
8.        "Condition": {
9.          "IpAddress": {
10.           "aws:SourceIp": "203.0.113.0/24"
11.         }
12.       }
13.     }
14.   ]
15. }
16.
```

**Temporary Credentials with AWS STS**
- Use AWS Security Token Service (STS) to issue temporary security credentials for accessing AWS resources. Temporary credentials have a limited lifetime and automatically expire, reducing the risk of long-term exposure.
- Example: Assume a role to get temporary credentials with limited permissions:

```
1. aws sts assume-role \
2.   --role-arn "arn:aws:iam::123456789012:role/ReadOnlyRole" \
3.   --role-session-name "ExampleSession"
4.
```

**Regular Audits and Monitoring**
- Regularly review IAM policies, roles, and user permissions to ensure they follow the least privilege principle. Use AWS IAM Access Analyzer to identify any overly permissive policies and make adjustments.
- Example: Use AWS Config rules to monitor compliance with PoLP and generate alerts for any deviations.

**Use of Service Control Policies (SCPs)**
- In AWS Organizations, use SCPs to define the maximum available permissions for accounts within the organization. SCPs help enforce PoLP across all accounts, preventing users from exceeding their designated permissions.
- Example: An SCP to restrict all accounts from using certain high-risk actions:

```
1.  {
2.    "Version": "2012-10-17",
3.    "Statement": [
4.      {
5.        "Effect": "Deny",
6.        "Action": [
7.          "s3:DeleteBucket",
8.          "ec2:TerminateInstances"
9.        ],
10.       "Resource": "*"
11.     }
12.   ]
13. }
14.
```

By applying these techniques, organizations can effectively enforce the principle of least privilege in their AWS environments. This ensures that users and services have only the necessary permissions to perform their tasks, thereby minimizing security risks and enhancing the overall security posture. Regular audits, fine-grained policies, temporary credentials, and conditions are essential components of a robust PoLP strategy.

## 4.5.2 Enforcing Separation of Duties

Ensuring proper separation of duties (SoD) is a critical security principle that involves assigning different permissions to different roles and users to minimize the risk of fraud, errors, and unauthorized access. By implementing SoD, organizations can ensure that no single individual has control over all aspects of a critical task, thereby reducing the potential for abuse or mistakes.

## Implementing Separation of Duties in AWS

To achieve SoD in AWS, you need to carefully define roles and assign permissions in a way that divides responsibilities among multiple users. This can be done by creating IAM roles with specific permissions and then assigning users to these roles based on their job functions.

## Example of Separation of Duties

Consider an organization that needs to manage financial transactions in AWS. The organization might define three key roles: Initiator, Approver, and Auditor. Each role has distinct permissions and responsibilities, ensuring that no single user can initiate, approve, and audit a financial transaction.

**Initiator Role:** The Initiator is responsible for creating financial transactions but cannot approve or audit them.

Permissions:

```
1.  {
2.    "Version": "2012-10-17",
3.    "Statement": [
4.      {
5.        "Effect": "Allow",
6.        "Action": [
7.          "dynamodb:PutItem",
8.          "dynamodb:UpdateItem"
9.        ],
10.       "Resource": "arn:aws:dynamodb:us-east-1:123456789012:table/FinancialTransactions"
11.     }
12.   ]
13. }
14.
```

**Approver Role:** The Approver can review and approve transactions initiated by the Initiator but cannot create or audit transactions.

Permissions:

```
1.  {
2.    "Version": "2012-10-17",
3.    "Statement": [
4.      {
5.        "Effect": "Allow",
6.        "Action": [
7.          "dynamodb:UpdateItem"
8.        ],
9.        "Resource": "arn:aws:dynamodb:us-east-1:123456789012:table/FinancialTransactions",
10.       "Condition": {
11.         "StringEquals": {
12.           "dynamodb:NewImage/Status": "Pending"
13.         }
14.       }
15.     }
16.   ]
17. }
18.
```

**Auditor Role:** The Auditor has read-only access to review all transactions and audit logs but cannot create or approve transactions.

Permissions:

```
1.  {
2.    "Version": "2012-10-17",
```

```
3.    "Statement": [
4.      {
5.        "Effect": "Allow",
6.        "Action": [
7.          "dynamodb:Scan",
8.          "dynamodb:Query",
9.          "cloudtrail:LookupEvents"
10.       ],
11.       "Resource": [
12.         "arn:aws:dynamodb:us-east-1:123456789012:table/FinancialTransactions",
13.         "arn:aws:cloudtrail:us-east-1:123456789012:trail/*"
14.       ]
15.     }
16.   ]
17. }
18.
```

**Assigning Users to Roles**
- `UserA` is assigned the `InitiatorRole`.
- `UserB` is assigned the `ApproverRole`.
- `UserC` is assigned the `AuditorRole`.

By assigning users to these distinct roles, the organization ensures that financial transactions require collaboration among multiple users, thus enforcing separation of duties.

**Benefits of Separation of Duties**
- **Enhanced Security:** No single user has excessive control over critical processes, reducing the risk of fraud or malicious activity.
- **Error Prevention:** Dividing responsibilities helps catch errors early, as different users review and approve actions.
- **Compliance:** Many regulatory frameworks require SoD to prevent conflicts of interest and ensure proper governance.
- **Auditability:** Clear role assignments and distinct permissions make it easier to track actions and identify responsibility during audits.

To summarize, implementing separation of duties in AWS involves creating specific roles with distinct permissions and assigning users to these roles based on their job functions. By ensuring that no single user can control all aspects of a critical process, organizations can enhance security, prevent errors, comply with regulations, and maintain clear audit trails. This approach is fundamental to effective access management and risk mitigation in AWS environments.

# 4.6 Troubleshooting Authorization Issues

Troubleshooting authorization issues in AWS involves identifying and resolving problems related to permissions and access controls. This process requires a systematic approach to diagnose why certain users or roles cannot perform specific actions on AWS resources. By utilizing tools like IAM Access Analyzer, AWS CloudTrail, and the IAM Policy Simulator, administrators can effectively pinpoint and correct these issues to ensure secure and proper access management.

## 4.6.1 Using AWS CloudTrail for Authorization Troubleshooting

AWS CloudTrail logs are a powerful tool for troubleshooting authorization issues by providing detailed records of all API calls made within an AWS account. When a user or service attempts to perform an action and encounters a permissions error, CloudTrail logs can help administrators identify the root cause of the issue. To utilize CloudTrail logs for troubleshooting, follow these steps:

First, access the CloudTrail console in the AWS Management Console and navigate to the 'Event history' section. Here, you can filter the logs to focus on events related to the authorization issue. Use filters such as event name, user name, resource type, and event time to narrow down the relevant entries. For example, if a user cannot access an S3 bucket, filter the logs for `s3:*` actions and the specific user in question.

Next, examine the details of the relevant log entries. Each log entry includes critical information such as the event name, event source, AWS account involved, IAM user or role, and error messages. Pay close attention to the `errorCode` and `errorMessage` fields, which provide specific details about why the request was denied. Common errors like AccessDenied indicate that the user or role lacks the necessary permissions.

Additionally, review the `requestParameters` and `responseElements` fields to understand the context of the request. These fields show the exact parameters passed in the API call and the response returned by AWS. This information can help determine if the request was correctly formed and if any conditions or resource-specific restrictions might have caused the denial.

To further diagnose the issue, use the `sourceIPAddress` and `userAgent` fields to verify the origin of the request. This can help identify if the request was made from an expected location or application, which is particularly useful for detecting unauthorized access attempts.

After identifying the cause of the authorization issue, update the relevant IAM policies to grant the necessary permissions. Use the IAM Policy Simulator to test the updated policies before applying them, ensuring that they provide the required access without granting excessive permissions. Finally, monitor CloudTrail logs continuously to detect and resolve future authorization issues promptly.

In summary, AWS CloudTrail logs are invaluable for troubleshooting authorization issues by providing detailed insights into API calls and permissions errors. By filtering and analyzing these logs, administrators can identify the root cause of access denials and take corrective actions to ensure proper and secure access to AWS resources.

## 4.6.2 IAM Access Advisor

IAM Access Advisor is a feature within AWS Identity and Access Management (IAM) that provides insights into the permissions and access patterns of IAM users and roles. It helps administrators understand which services are being accessed and how frequently, making it easier to troubleshoot permissions and optimize access policies. By showing the last accessed information for various AWS services, Access Advisor allows administrators to identify unused or rarely used permissions, which can then be removed or adjusted to adhere to the principle of least privilege.

### How IAM Access Advisor Helps

When troubleshooting permissions, IAM Access Advisor provides a detailed view of the services that an IAM user or role has accessed, along with the timestamp of the last access. This visibility is crucial for ensuring that permissions are appropriately assigned and not overly permissive. For instance, if a user has permissions for several AWS services but only uses a subset of them, administrators can refine the user's permissions to reduce security risks.

Additionally, Access Advisor is helpful in identifying and cleaning up stale permissions. For example, if a user or role has not accessed a particular service for a prolonged period, it may indicate that the permission is unnecessary and can be safely removed. This practice not only tightens security but also simplifies policy management by reducing clutter.

### Example
Consider an IAM role named `DataAnalystRole` that has broad permissions to access multiple AWS services, including Amazon S3, Amazon Redshift, and AWS Glue. To ensure that the role only has necessary permissions, an administrator can use IAM Access Advisor to review the access patterns.

### Steps to Use IAM Access Advisor

#### Navigate to IAM Access Advisor
- Open the AWS Management Console.
- Navigate to the IAM service and select the `Roles` tab.
- Click on `DataAnalystRole` to view its details.
- Go to the `Access Advisor` tab.

#### Review Access Patterns
- In the `Access Advisor` tab, a list of AWS services with associated permissions will be displayed.
- The `Last Accessed` column shows the date and time when the role last accessed each service.

#### Analyze and Adjust Permissions
- If the `DataAnalystRole` has not accessed AWS Glue for several months, the administrator might decide to remove or restrict the permissions related to AWS Glue.
- The policy attached to `DataAnalystRole` can be updated to reflect the refined permissions, ensuring that the role only has access to Amazon S3 and Amazon Redshift, which are frequently used.

### Updated Policy Example:

```
1.  {
2.    "Version": "2012-10-17",
3.    "Statement": [
4.      {
5.        "Effect": "Allow",
6.        "Action": [
7.          "s3:*",
8.          "redshift:*"
9.        ],
10.       "Resource": "*"
11.     }
12.   ]
13. }
14.
```

### Benefits of Using IAM Access Advisor
- Enhanced Security: By removing unused permissions, the risk of unauthorized access or exploitation is minimized.
- Cost Efficiency: Reducing unnecessary access can potentially lower costs by preventing accidental usage of AWS services.
- Simplified Management: Streamlining permissions makes it easier to manage and audit IAM policies.
- Compliance: Ensuring that only necessary permissions are granted helps maintain compliance with security best practices and regulatory requirements.

To summarize, IAM Access Advisor is a powerful tool for understanding and troubleshooting permissions in AWS. By providing insights into access patterns and last accessed information, it helps administrators refine permissions to enforce the principle of least privilege. This practice enhances security, simplifies policy management, and ensures that users and roles only have the permissions they need.

## 4.6.3 IAM Policy Simulator

The IAM Policy Simulator is a powerful tool provided by AWS to test and troubleshoot IAM policies and permissions before deploying them in a live environment. It allows administrators to simulate and evaluate how policies affect access to AWS resources, ensuring that the policies grant the intended permissions and do not inadvertently restrict necessary access or allow excessive permissions.

### How to Use the IAM Policy Simulator

To begin, access the IAM Policy Simulator by opening the AWS Management Console, navigating to the IAM service, and selecting the **Policy Simulator** from the left-hand navigation pane. Once there, choose the type of IAM entity you want to test, such as a user, group, or role. For example, if you want to test permissions for a user named `JohnDoe`, select the user and choose the policies attached to them. These can include managed policies, inline policies, or both.

Next, define the simulation settings by selecting the AWS services and actions you want to test. Specify the resources by entering the ARNs of the resources you want to test against. For instance, you might want to verify whether `JohnDoe` can perform `s3:ListBucket` and `s3:GetObject` actions on an S3 bucket named `example-bucket`.

After setting up the simulation parameters, click the **Simulate** button to run the test. The Policy Simulator will evaluate the selected policies and display the results, showing whether the specified actions are allowed or denied based on the current policies. Each action will have a status indicating if it is permitted (Allow) or blocked (Deny).

Analyze the results by reviewing the policy details provided for each action. This information will include which policy (or policies) affected the decision and specific statements within the policies that granted or restricted access. This detailed view helps identify missing permissions if an action is incorrectly denied, or it can highlight areas where conditions or restrictions need to be tightened if an action is incorrectly allowed.

For example, if `JohnDoe` needs permission to list and retrieve objects from the `example-bucket` but not to delete objects, the inline policy might look like this:

```
1.  {
2.    "Version": "2012-10-17",
3.    "Statement": [
4.      {
5.        "Effect": "Allow",
6.        "Action": [
7.          "s3:ListBucket",
8.          "s3:GetObject"
9.        ],
10.       "Resource": [
11.         "arn:aws:s3:::example-bucket",
12.         "arn:aws:s3:::example-bucket/*"
13.       ]
14.     },
15.     {
16.       "Effect": "Deny",
17.       "Action": "s3:DeleteObject",
18.       "Resource": "arn:aws:s3:::example-bucket/*"
19.     }
20.   ]
21. }
```

By simulating these actions, the results should show `Allow` for `s3:ListBucket` and `s3:GetObject`, and `Deny` for `s3:DeleteObject`. If the results are as expected, the policy configuration is correct. If not, adjust the policy statements and rerun the simulation until the desired permissions are achieved.

The IAM Policy Simulator is essential for proactively verifying and fine-tuning IAM policies. By simulating access scenarios and analyzing the results, administrators can ensure that policies enforce the principle of least privilege, granting only the necessary permissions while maintaining a secure AWS environment. This proactive approach helps prevent access issues and security vulnerabilities, ensuring a secure and well-managed AWS environment.

## 4.6.4 Analyzing Access Errors

Analyzing access or authorization errors in AWS to determine their cause or effect involves a systematic approach using various tools and techniques. By following these steps, administrators can identify and resolve permission-related issues, ensuring that users and services have the appropriate access levels without compromising security.

### Techniques for Analyzing Access or Authorization Errors

**Reviewing CloudTrail Logs**
- AWS CloudTrail logs provide a comprehensive record of all API calls made within an AWS account. When an authorization error occurs, start by reviewing the CloudTrail logs to trace the specific API call that was denied. Look for entries with `errorCode` and `errorMessage` fields that indicate why the request was denied. For example, an `AccessDenied` error can highlight a missing permission.
- By filtering logs based on the event name, user, or resource, administrators can quickly pinpoint the exact action that failed and analyze the context in which it was attempted.

**Using IAM Access Advisor**
- IAM Access Advisor helps determine which services an IAM user or role has accessed recently. If a user reports an access issue, check the Access Advisor to see if the required permissions are in place and if the services in question have been accessed before. This can reveal whether the user has the necessary permissions but hasn't used them, or if permissions are missing or outdated.
- For example, if a user should have access to Amazon S3 but reports issues, Access Advisor can show if they have ever successfully accessed S3, helping narrow down the problem.

**IAM Policy Simulator**
- The IAM Policy Simulator is a tool for testing and troubleshooting IAM policies. Use it to simulate the actions the user is attempting to perform and see whether the policies allow or deny these actions. This helps identify specific policy statements that might be causing the issue.
- For instance, if a user is denied access to list objects in an S3 bucket, use the Policy Simulator to test the `s3:ListBucket` action and examine the results. This can reveal if an explicit deny statement is in place or if necessary allow statements are missing.

**Analyzing Resource-Based Policies**
- AWS resources like S3 buckets, SNS topics, and SQS queues can have their own resource-based policies. These policies might conflict with identity-based policies attached to IAM users or roles. Review the resource-based policies to ensure they grant the required permissions and do not contain overly restrictive conditions.
- For example, an S3 bucket policy might inadvertently deny access to all users except a specific subset, causing unexpected access issues.

**Evaluating Policy Conditions**
- Conditions in IAM policies add another layer of control by specifying when and how policies apply. Incorrect conditions can lead to access issues. Review the conditions in policies to ensure they are correctly configured and relevant to the intended use case.
- For example, a policy with a condition that restricts access based on IP address might deny access to users working remotely if their IP addresses are not whitelisted.

**Checking Service Control Policies (SCPs)**
- In AWS Organizations, SCPs can restrict permissions for accounts within the organization. If a user or service in a member account encounters access issues, verify the SCPs applied to their account to ensure they do not override necessary permissions.
- For example, an SCP might deny the `s3:DeleteObject` action across all accounts, which could prevent users from deleting objects in S3 even if their individual IAM policies allow it.

## Example Scenario

Suppose an IAM user named `JaneDoe` reports that she cannot upload objects to a specific S3 bucket (`example-bucket`). Here's how to analyze and troubleshoot the issue:

**Check CloudTrail Logs**
- Filter CloudTrail logs for `PutObject` actions by `JaneDoe` on `example-bucket`.
- Look for any `AccessDenied` errors and review the details.

**Use IAM Access Advisor:** Check if `JaneDoe` has accessed S3 recently and if there are any indications of missing permissions.

**Simulate Policies:**
- Use the IAM Policy Simulator to test the `s3:PutObject` action for `JaneDoe` on `example-bucket`.
- Analyze the results to identify which policies allow or deny the action.

**Review Resource-Based Policies:** Examine the bucket policy for `example-bucket` to ensure it allows `JaneDoe` to perform `PutObject`.

**Evaluate Conditions:** Check if any conditions in the policies are restricting access, such as IP restrictions or time-based conditions.

**Verify SCPs:** Ensure there are no SCPs in place that deny the `s3:PutObject` action for the account `JaneDoe` belongs to.

By following these steps, you can systematically identify and resolve the authorization issue, ensuring that `JaneDoe` has the necessary permissions to upload objects to the S3 bucket.

To summarize, analyzing access or authorization errors in AWS requires a combination of reviewing logs, using simulation tools, examining policies, and understanding conditions and restrictions. By systematically applying these techniques, administrators can identify the root causes of permission issues and take corrective actions to ensure secure and appropriate access to AWS resources.

# 4.7 Best Practices for Authorization
## 4.7.1 Regular Policy Audits
Regularly auditing IAM policies is crucial to ensure that they remain up-to-date and aligned with current security requirements. Over time, an organization's security landscape can change due to new threats, evolving business

needs, or updates to regulatory requirements. Without regular audits, IAM policies may become outdated, potentially leading to security vulnerabilities or compliance issues.

## Importance of Regular IAM Policy Audits

### Identify and Mitigate Risks
Regular audits help identify permissions that are no longer necessary or that are overly permissive. By reviewing and adjusting these policies, organizations can reduce the risk of unauthorized access and data breaches. For instance, removing permissions for users who have changed roles or no longer require access minimizes the attack surface.

### Ensure Compliance
Many industries have strict regulatory requirements regarding data access and security. Regularly auditing IAM policies ensures that access controls meet these regulatory standards, helping to avoid penalties and legal issues. Compliance with standards such as GDPR, HIPAA, and PCI-DSS often necessitates stringent access controls and regular reviews.

### Adapt to Organizational Changes
Organizations frequently undergo changes, such as restructuring, mergers, or new projects. These changes can affect who needs access to what resources. Regular IAM policy audits ensure that access permissions reflect the current organizational structure and needs, preventing former employees or shifted roles from retaining unnecessary access.

### Optimize Access Management
Auditing IAM policies helps streamline and optimize access management. By regularly reviewing and updating policies, administrators can ensure that the principle of least privilege is enforced. This means users only have the minimum necessary permissions to perform their tasks, reducing the risk of accidental or intentional misuse of access.

### Improve Security Posture
Continuous improvement of security policies is a cornerstone of a robust security posture. Regular audits provide insights into potential weaknesses and areas for improvement in IAM policies. Addressing these issues promptly helps maintain a strong defense against evolving security threats.

## Example Scenario
Consider an organization that has not audited its IAM policies in a year. During the audit, administrators might discover that several users still have administrative access even though they have moved to different roles that do not require such privileges. Additionally, they may find that some S3 buckets have open access permissions, posing a significant security risk. By auditing and updating these policies, the organization can ensure that only authorized personnel have access to sensitive resources, and that the access controls align with best security practices.

## Best Practices for IAM Policy Audits
- **Schedule Regular Audits:** Establish a regular schedule for auditing IAM policies, such as quarterly or biannually.
- **Use Automated Tools:** Leverage AWS tools like IAM Access Analyzer and AWS Config to automate parts of the auditing process and provide continuous monitoring.
- **Review Access Patterns:** Analyze access patterns to identify unused or rarely used permissions and adjust policies accordingly.
- **Engage Stakeholders:** Involve relevant stakeholders, such as security teams and department heads, to ensure that access requirements and security policies are accurately aligned with business needs.

- **Document Changes:** Maintain a record of changes made during audits to track the evolution of access policies and support compliance efforts.

To summarize, regularly auditing IAM policies is essential for maintaining a secure and compliant AWS environment. It helps identify and mitigate risks, ensures compliance with regulatory requirements, adapts to organizational changes, optimizes access management, and improves the overall security posture. By following best practices and leveraging automated tools, organizations can effectively manage and secure their AWS resources through proactive and ongoing policy reviews.

## 4.7.2 Monitoring and Logging

Setting up monitoring and logging for authorization activities is essential for detecting and responding to potential security issues in AWS environments. By implementing robust monitoring and logging mechanisms, organizations can gain visibility into access patterns, detect anomalies, and respond promptly to unauthorized access attempts or policy violations.

### Setting Up Monitoring and Logging for Authorization Activities
**Enable AWS CloudTrail**
- AWS CloudTrail is a service that logs all API calls made within an AWS account. Enabling CloudTrail ensures that all authorization activities, such as login attempts, permission changes, and access to resources, are recorded. This comprehensive logging is critical for auditing and forensic analysis.
- To set up CloudTrail, navigate to the CloudTrail console, create a trail, and configure it to log all management and data events. Store the logs in an S3 bucket with appropriate access controls.

**Configure Amazon CloudWatch**
- Amazon CloudWatch provides monitoring and alerting capabilities for AWS resources. By integrating CloudTrail with CloudWatch Logs, you can create log groups and metric filters to monitor specific authorization activities and set up alarms for unusual patterns or unauthorized access attempts.
- For example, create a CloudWatch log group for CloudTrail logs, set up a metric filter to detect `AccessDenied` errors, and configure a CloudWatch alarm to notify the security team when such errors exceed a threshold.

**Use AWS Config for Continuous Compliance**
- AWS Config continuously monitors and records AWS resource configurations and changes. By setting up AWS Config rules, you can ensure that IAM policies and roles comply with security best practices and detect any deviations in real-time.
- For instance, create a custom AWS Config rule to check that IAM users do not have overly permissive policies attached, and trigger an alert if a policy violates the least privilege principle.

**Leverage AWS Security Hub**
- AWS Security Hub aggregates and prioritizes security findings from various AWS services, including CloudTrail, GuardDuty, and Config. By enabling Security Hub, you can gain a centralized view of your security posture and receive actionable insights into potential security issues related to authorization activities.
- Enable Security Hub and configure it to receive findings from CloudTrail and Config. Review and act on high-priority findings, such as unauthorized API calls or misconfigured IAM policies.

**Set Up Amazon GuardDuty**
- Amazon GuardDuty is a threat detection service that continuously monitors for malicious activity and unauthorized behavior. GuardDuty analyzes CloudTrail logs, VPC Flow Logs, and DNS logs to identify potential threats, such as compromised IAM credentials or anomalous access patterns.

- Enable GuardDuty in your AWS account, and configure it to monitor all supported data sources. Review GuardDuty findings regularly and investigate any flagged authorization activities.

**Implement Fine-Grained Access Controls**
- Use IAM policies with fine-grained permissions and conditions to restrict access based on specific criteria, such as source IP address, time of day, or use of multi-factor authentication (MFA). These controls help prevent unauthorized access and make it easier to detect deviations from expected access patterns.
- For example, create an IAM policy that requires MFA for administrative actions and logs any attempts to bypass this requirement.

**Example Scenario**

Consider an organization that wants to monitor and respond to unauthorized access attempts to its S3 buckets. By setting up CloudTrail, CloudWatch, and GuardDuty, the organization can achieve this:

- Enable CloudTrail to log all S3 access activities.
- Integrate CloudTrail with CloudWatch Logs and create a metric filter to detect `AccessDenied` errors for S3 actions.
- Set up a CloudWatch alarm to notify the security team when the number of `AccessDenied` errors exceeds a threshold within a specific timeframe.
- Enable GuardDuty to detect anomalous access patterns to the S3 buckets, such as access from unusual IP addresses or geolocations.
- Review findings in Security Hub to prioritize and respond to potential security issues.

Setting up monitoring and logging for authorization activities in AWS involves enabling services like CloudTrail, CloudWatch, Config, Security Hub, and GuardDuty. These tools provide comprehensive visibility into access patterns, detect unauthorized activities, and enable prompt responses to potential security issues. By implementing fine-grained access controls and continuously monitoring authorization events, organizations can enhance their security posture and protect their AWS environments from threats.

# 4.8 Lab Exercises
## 4.8.1 Creating and Applying IAM Policies

Creating and applying different types of IAM policies in AWS involves several steps. Below is a step-by-step hands-on lab that guides you through creating and applying inline policies, managed policies, and resource-based policies.

**Prerequisites**
- AWS Management Console access
- Basic understanding of IAM concepts

### Step 1: Creating an Inline Policy

**Navigate to IAM Console:** Open the AWS Management Console and go to the IAM service.

**Select a User:**
- In the IAM dashboard, click on Users from the left-hand navigation pane.
- Select a user (e.g., `JohnDoe`) to whom you want to attach the inline policy.

**Add Inline Policy:**
- In the user details page, click on the Permissions tab.

- Click on Add inline policy.

**Create Policy:**
- Use the Visual editor or JSON tab to create the policy. Here is an example policy to allow `JohnDoe` to list and get objects from an S3 bucket named `example-bucket`:

```
{
  "Version": "2012-10-17",
  "Statement": [
    {
      "Effect": "Allow",
      "Action": [
        "s3:ListBucket",
        "s3:GetObject"
      ],
      "Resource": [
        "arn:aws:s3:::example-bucket",
        "arn:aws:s3:::example-bucket/*"
      ]
    }
  ]
}
```

**Review and Create Policy:** Click Review policy, enter a policy name (e.g., `S3ReadAccess`), and then click Create policy.

## Step 2: Creating a Managed Policy

**Navigate to IAM Policies:** In the IAM dashboard, click on Policies from the left-hand navigation pane.

**Create Policy:** Click on Create policy.

**Define Policy:** Use the Visual editor or JSON tab to define the policy. Here is an example policy to allow EC2 start and stop actions:

```
{
  "Version": "2012-10-17",
  "Statement": [
    {
      "Effect": "Allow",
      "Action": [
        "ec2:StartInstances",
        "ec2:StopInstances"
      ],
      "Resource": "arn:aws:ec2:*:*:instance/*"
    }
  ]
}
```

**Review and Create Policy:**
- Click Next: Tags to add tags if needed, then click Next: Review.
- Enter a name for the policy (e.g., `EC2StartStopPolicy`) and click Create policy.

**Attach Policy to User/Role/Group:**
- Go to the Users, Groups, or Roles section in the IAM dashboard.
- Select the user, group, or role to which you want to attach the policy.
- In the Permissions tab, click Add permissions, then Attach policies.

- Search for your newly created policy (`EC2StartStopPolicy`), select it, and click Add permissions.

### Step 3: Creating a Resource-Based Policy (S3 Bucket Policy)

**Navigate to S3 Console:** Open the AWS Management Console and go to the S3 service.

**Select a Bucket:** Select the bucket to which you want to attach the policy (e.g., `example-bucket`).

**Open Permissions Tab:** Click on the Permissions tab of the bucket.

**Edit Bucket Policy:** Scroll down to the Bucket policy section and click Edit.

**Create Policy:** Enter the following bucket policy to allow a specific IAM user to list and get objects from the bucket:

```
1.  {
2.    "Version": "2012-10-17",
3.    "Statement": [
4.      {
5.        "Effect": "Allow",
6.        "Principal": {
7.          "AWS": "arn:aws:iam::123456789012:user/JohnDoe"
8.        },
9.        "Action": [
10.         "s3:ListBucket",
11.         "s3:GetObject"
12.       ],
13.       "Resource": [
14.         "arn:aws:s3:::example-bucket",
15.         "arn:aws:s3:::example-bucket/*"
16.       ]
17.     }
18.   ]
19. }
20.
```

**Save Policy:** Click Save changes.

By following these steps, you can create and apply different types of IAM policies, including inline policies, managed policies, and resource-based policies. This hands-on lab helps ensure that you understand how to manage permissions and enforce security best practices in AWS. Regularly review and update these policies to adapt to changing security requirements and organizational needs.

## 4.8.2 Constructing ABAC and RBAC Policies

This hands-on lab provides a step-by-step guide to creating Attribute-Based Access Control (ABAC) and Role-Based Access Control (RBAC) policies in AWS.

**Prerequisites**
- Access to AWS Management Console
- Basic understanding of IAM concepts

### Part 1: Constructing Attribute-Based Access Control (ABAC) Policies

ABAC uses tags to dynamically manage access permissions based on user attributes.

## Step 1: Tagging IAM Users and Resources

**Tag IAM Users:**
- Navigate to the IAM console.
- Select Users from the left-hand navigation pane.
- Click on a user (e.g., `JohnDoe`) to add tags.
- In the user details page, go to the Tags tab and click Add tag.
- Add a tag with Key as `Department` and Value as `Finance`.

**Tag Resources:**
- Navigate to the S3 console.
- Select the bucket to tag (e.g., `example-bucket`).
- Click on the Properties tab.
- Scroll down to Tags and click Edit.
- Add a tag with Key as `Department` and Value as `Finance`.
- Save changes.

## Step 2: Create an ABAC Policy

**Navigate to IAM Policies:**
- In the IAM console, click on Policies from the left-hand navigation pane.
- Click Create policy.

**Define Policy Using JSON:**
Switch to the JSON tab and enter the following policy:

```
{
  "Version": "2012-10-17",
  "Statement": [
    {
      "Effect": "Allow",
      "Action": "s3:*",
      "Resource": "arn:aws:s3:::example-bucket/*",
      "Condition": {
        "StringEquals": {
          "aws:RequestTag/Department": "${aws:PrincipalTag/Department}"
        }
      }
    }
  ]
}
```

**Review and Create Policy:**
- Click Next: Tags, add any tags if necessary, then click Next: Review.
- Enter a name for the policy (e.g., `ABACFinancePolicy`) and click Create policy.

## Step 3: Attach ABAC Policy to a Role

**Create a Role:**
- In the IAM console, click on Roles from the left-hand navigation pane.
- Click Create role.
- Select AWS service and choose a use case (e.g., EC2).
- Click Next: Permissions.

**Attach the ABAC Policy:**
- Search for and select the `ABACFinancePolicy` created earlier.
- Click Next: Tags to add tags if needed, then Next: Review.
- Enter a role name (e.g., `FinanceRole`) and click Create role.

## Part 2: Constructing Role-Based Access Control (RBAC) Policies

RBAC assigns permissions to roles based on job functions.

### Step 1: Create RBAC Policies
**Navigate to IAM Policies:**
- In the IAM console, click on Policies from the left-hand navigation pane.
- Click Create policy.

**Define Developer Policy Using JSON:** Switch to the JSON tab and enter the following policy:

```json
{
  "Version": "2012-10-17",
  "Statement": [
    {
      "Effect": "Allow",
      "Action": [
        "ec2:DescribeInstances",
        "s3:ListBucket",
        "s3:GetObject"
      ],
      "Resource": "*"
    }
  ]
}
```

**Review and Create Policy:**
- Click Next: Tags, add any tags if necessary, then click Next: Review.
- Enter a name for the policy (e.g., `DeveloperPolicy`) and click Create policy.

### Step 2: Create RBAC Roles
**Create a Role for Developers:**
- In the IAM console, click on Roles from the left-hand navigation pane.
- Click Create role.
- Select AWS service and choose a use case (e.g., EC2).
- Click Next: Permissions.

**Attach Developer Policy:**
- Search for and select the `DeveloperPolicy` created earlier.
- Click Next: Tags to add tags if needed, then Next: Review.
- Enter a role name (e.g., `DeveloperRole`) and click Create role.

### Step 3: Assign Users to Roles
**Assign Role to User:**
- Navigate to the Users section in the IAM console.
- Select the user (e.g., JohnDoe) who will be assigned the `DeveloperRole`.
- Click on the Add permissions button.
- Choose Attach policies directly and select the `DeveloperPolicy`.

- Alternatively, choose Add permissions boundary and select the `DeveloperRole`.

This hands-on lab guides you through creating and applying ABAC and RBAC policies in AWS. ABAC uses tags to dynamically manage access based on user attributes, while RBAC uses predefined roles to manage access based on job functions. Regularly review and update these policies to ensure they meet your organization's security and access requirements.

## 4.8.3 Troubleshooting Authorization Issues

In this lab, you will learn how to troubleshoot common authorization issues in AWS using CloudTrail, IAM Access Advisor, and IAM Policy Simulator. These tools help identify and resolve permissions-related problems, ensuring secure and efficient access to AWS resources.

**Prerequisites**
- Access to AWS Management Console
- Basic understanding of IAM policies and AWS services

### Step 1: Using AWS CloudTrail to Identify Authorization Issues

**Step 1.1: Enable CloudTrail Logging**
**Navigate to CloudTrail Console**: Open the AWS Management Console and go to the CloudTrail service.

**Create a Trail**:
- Click on **Trails** in the left-hand navigation pane.
- Click **Create trail**.
- Enter a trail name (e.g., `MyTrail`).
- For **Storage location**, choose an S3 bucket where the logs will be stored.
- Enable logging for both management and data events if needed.
- Click **Create trail**.

**Step 1.2: Review CloudTrail Logs**
**Access Event History:**
- In the CloudTrail console, click on Event history.

**Filter Events:**
- Use filters to narrow down the events. For example, filter by Event name (e.g., `AccessDenied`), Event source (e.g., `s3.amazonaws.com`), or `User name`.

**Analyze Event Details:**
- Click on a specific event to view details such as the `eventName`, `eventSource`, `userIdentity`, and `errorCode`.
- Look for `AccessDenied` errors and review the `requestParameters` and `responseElements` to understand why the request was denied.

### Step 2: Using IAM Access Advisor to Understand Permissions

**Step 2.1: Review Access Advisor Data**
**Navigate to IAM Console:** Open the IAM service in the AWS Management Console.

**Select an IAM User or Role:**
- Click on Users or Roles from the left-hand navigation pane.
- Select a user (e.g., `JohnDoe`) or a role to review.

112

**Access Access Advisor:**
- In the user or role details page, click on the Access Advisor tab.
- Review the list of AWS services accessed by the user or role and the last accessed timestamp.

**Identify Unused Permissions:**
- Look for permissions that are not being used or are rarely accessed. This can help identify unnecessary permissions that might be causing authorization issues or security risks.

## Step 3: Using IAM Policy Simulator to Test and Troubleshoot Policies

**Step 3.1: Access the IAM Policy Simulator:** Navigate to IAM Policy Simulator. In the IAM console, click on Policy Simulator from the left-hand navigation pane.

**Step 3.2: Simulate a Policy**
**Select an IAM Entity:**
- Choose the type of IAM entity to test: User, Group, or Role.
- For example, select a user (e.g., `JohnDoe`).

**Choose Policies to Simulate**: Select the policies attached to the user, group, or role you are testing.

**Define Simulation Settings:**
- Specify the AWS services and actions to test. For example, test `s3:ListBucket`, `s3:GetObject`, and `s3:PutObject` actions.
- Enter the ARNs of the resources to test against, such as `arn:aws:s3:::example-bucket` and `arn:aws:s3:::example-bucket/*`.

**Run the Simulation:**
- Click Simulate to run the test.
- Review the results to see whether the actions are allowed or denied based on the current policies.

**Step 3.3: Analyze and Adjust Policies**
**Review Simulation Results:** Check which actions are allowed or denied and identify the policies affecting these decisions.

**Adjust Policies as Needed:**
- If an action is incorrectly denied, update the relevant policies to include the necessary permissions.
- If an action is incorrectly allowed, tighten the policy by adding conditions or removing unnecessary permissions.

## Example Scenario

Suppose `JohnDoe` reports that he cannot upload objects to a specific S3 bucket (`example-bucket`). Here's how to troubleshoot this issue:

**Review CloudTrail Logs:**
- Filter CloudTrail logs for `s3:PutObject` actions by `JohnDoe` on `example-bucket`.
- Look for `AccessDenied` errors and analyze the event details.

**Check IAM Access Advisor:**
- Review the services `JohnDoe` has accessed recently to ensure that S3 is included.

- Identify any unused permissions that might be irrelevant.

**Simulate Policies Using IAM Policy Simulator:**
- Test s3:PutObject action for `JohnDoe` on `example-bucket`.
- Analyze the simulation results to identify which policy statements are denying the action.
- Adjust the policies to grant the necessary permissions, ensuring they adhere to the principle of least privilege.

By following these steps, you can effectively troubleshoot common authorization issues in AWS using CloudTrail, IAM Access Advisor, and IAM Policy Simulator. These tools provide comprehensive insights into access patterns, permissions usage, and policy configurations, enabling you to identify and resolve authorization problems efficiently. Regularly using these tools helps maintain a secure and well-managed AWS environment.

# 4.9 Key Exam Tips

**IAM Policies and Types:** Understand the different types of IAM policies: Managed Policies (AWS-managed and customer-managed), Inline Policies (directly embedded in a user, group, or role), Identity-Based Policies (attached to a user, group, or role), and Resource-Based Policies (attached to AWS resources like S3 buckets). Be clear on how each works and when to use them.

**Policy Structure:** Master the components of IAM policies: Effect, Action, Resource, and Condition. Be prepared to analyze and interpret the impact of a policy on access control. You may encounter questions that require you to read and understand complex policy structures.

**Resource-Based vs. Identity-Based Policies:** Know the key difference between Resource-Based Policies (attached to resources and define who can access that resource) and Identity-Based Policies (attached to IAM users, groups, or roles). Understand when to use each and how they work together.

**Session Policies with AWS STS:** Familiarize yourself with Session Policies, which are temporary and used with AWS STS (Security Token Service). These policies can limit the permissions of a temporary session and are critical for implementing fine-grained security controls.

**Understand different access control models:**
- Attribute-Based Access Control (ABAC): Based on user attributes (tags). Understand how ABAC policies are constructed and their advantages for large, dynamic environments.
- Role-Based Access Control (RBAC): Based on roles that grant specific permissions. Know how to design RBAC policies to grant access based on the user's role.

**Implementing Least Privilege:** The Principle of Least Privilege is crucial for limiting access to only what is needed. Understand how to enforce Separation of Duties (ensuring no single user has excessive access) and implement policies that follow least privilege best practices.

**Troubleshooting Authorization Issues:**
- Be proficient in using AWS CloudTrail to troubleshoot authorization issues by reviewing API calls and changes to IAM policies.
- Learn how to use IAM Access Advisor to review permissions and IAM Policy Simulator to test policies and their effects.

**Analyzing Access Errors:** Be able to identify and troubleshoot access errors based on denied permissions. Understanding IAM policy evaluation logic and how policies are evaluated will help you quickly resolve access issues.

**Regular Policy Audits:** Ensure that policies are regularly audited to verify they are up to date and enforce least privilege. Pay attention to the need for continuous monitoring and logging to detect unauthorized access attempts or policy misconfigurations.

**Best Practices for Authorization:** Conduct regular reviews of IAM policies, keep logging enabled for critical resources, and monitor AWS CloudTrail for changes. Use policy versioning to maintain control over changes and ensure policies align with organizational compliance.

## 4.10 Chapter Review Questions

**Question 1:**
Which of the following best describes a managed policy in AWS IAM?
A. A policy that is directly attached to an individual user or role
B. A policy that is created and managed by AWS
C. A policy that is used to control access to S3 buckets
D. A policy that is created and managed by the customer only

**Question 2:**
What is a key difference between identity-based policies and resource-based policies?
A. Identity-based policies are attached to resources, and resource-based policies are attached to users
B. Identity-based policies are attached to users or roles, while resource-based policies are attached to resources
C. Resource-based policies are always more restrictive than identity-based policies
D. Identity-based policies cannot be used with IAM roles

**Question 3:**
What is the primary purpose of session control policies in AWS?
A. To allow users temporary access to AWS resources
B. To enforce the least privilege principle
C. To specify permissions that can limit or modify the default policies during a session
D. To troubleshoot access control issues

**Question 4:**
Which IAM policy component is responsible for defining whether access is allowed or denied?
A. Action
B. Resource
C. Effect
D. Condition

**Question 5:**
Which of the following is an example of Attribute-Based Access Control (ABAC)?
A. Granting access to a resource based on a user's job title or department
B. Creating a custom policy that specifies individual permissions
C. Granting access based on predefined roles
D. Creating policies that apply to specific resources only

**Question 6:**
Which AWS service would you use to troubleshoot and analyze issues related to IAM policies and permissions?
A. IAM Policy Simulator
B. AWS Trusted Advisor
C. AWS Shield
D. AWS Macie

**Question 7:**
What is the purpose of enforcing separation of duties in IAM policies?
A. To allow multiple users to share the same set of credentials
B. To reduce the risk of unauthorized access by dividing tasks among multiple users
C. To consolidate all IAM policies into a single master policy
D. To allow users to access resources across multiple regions

**Question 8:**
Which IAM feature helps you identify unused permissions and roles for a user or group?
A. AWS CloudTrail
B. IAM Access Advisor
C. Amazon Inspector
D. AWS Config

**Question 9:**
What is the principle of least privilege?
A. Allowing users to access only the resources necessary for their tasks
B. Granting users full access to AWS resources by default
C. Providing users temporary credentials for accessing AWS services
D. Allowing administrators to bypass all security policies

**Question 10:**
Which tool can be used to simulate the effect of a policy and test its impact on user permissions?
A. AWS CloudTrail
B. IAM Access Advisor
C. AWS IAM Policy Simulator
D. AWS Artifact

**Question 11:**
Your organization has multiple AWS accounts under a consolidated billing structure. You want to give an external auditor temporary access to view specific S3 buckets across multiple accounts for a security audit. Which policy structure and service would you use to grant access?
A. Managed Policies with AWS STS
B. Inline Policies with AWS IAM Roles
C. Resource-Based Policies with AWS STS
D. Identity-Based Policies with AWS CloudTrail

**Question 12:**
You've created a custom IAM policy for a developer team that grants access to an S3 bucket. However, the team is unable to upload files despite having the required permissions. Upon review, you discover that an S3 bucket policy denies uploads from any source except a specific IP range. Which tool can you use to simulate and troubleshoot the effect of both the IAM and resource-based policies?
A. IAM Access Advisor
B. AWS Trusted Advisor
C. AWS IAM Policy Simulator
D. AWS Artifact

**Question 13:**
Your security team needs to enforce separation of duties to prevent any single individual from having too much control over critical resources. You want to ensure that different administrators manage IAM roles and EC2 instances. Which IAM feature can you use to implement this requirement?
A. Role-Based Access Control (RBAC)

B. Attribute-Based Access Control (ABAC)
C. Session Control Policies
D. AWS CloudTrail Auditing

**Question 14:**
A developer is assigned an IAM role that grants full access to DynamoDB and EC2 services. However, after reviewing their activities, you discover that they have only been using DynamoDB, leaving the EC2 permissions unused. How can you identify and remove the unused permissions?
A. Use IAM Access Advisor to review service usage
B. Use AWS CloudTrail to track API calls
C. Use the IAM Policy Simulator to modify the policies
D. Use AWS Shield to block access to EC2

**Question 15:**
You need to grant temporary access to an external consultant who requires permission to access several AWS resources during a 2-week period. What is the best approach to provide secure access while ensuring that permissions are automatically revoked after this period?
A. Create an IAM user with long-term credentials
B. Use AWS STS to issue temporary security credentials and define a session policy
C. Use a managed policy with unrestricted access
D. Enable resource-based policies with time-limited access

## 4.11 Answers to Chapter Review Questions

1. B. A policy that is created and managed by AWS
Explanation: Managed policies are created and managed by AWS, allowing customers to apply predefined policies to users, groups, or roles without needing to create them from scratch.

2. B. Identity-based policies are attached to users or roles, while resource-based policies are attached to resources
Explanation: Identity-based policies are attached to users, groups, or roles to specify their permissions, while resource-based policies are attached directly to resources (such as S3 buckets) to control access.

3. C. To specify permissions that can limit or modify the default policies during a session
Explanation: Session control policies define additional permissions that can be applied or limited during an active session, allowing more granular control over user actions while a session is in progress.

4. C. Effect
Explanation: The Effect element in an IAM policy determines whether the specified action is allowed ("Allow") or denied ("Deny"). It controls the overall impact of the policy on the resource.

5. A. Granting access to a resource based on a user's job title or department
Explanation: Attribute-Based Access Control (ABAC) allows access to be granted based on attributes such as a user's department, job title, or other characteristics.

6. A. IAM Policy Simulator
Explanation: The IAM Policy Simulator allows users to simulate and test IAM policies to ensure that permissions are correctly configured and that access control policies behave as intended.

7. B. To reduce the risk of unauthorized access by dividing tasks among multiple users
Explanation: Separation of duties ensures that critical tasks are divided among multiple users, reducing the risk of one individual gaining complete control over sensitive operations or resources.

8. B. IAM Access Advisor
Explanation: IAM Access Advisor shows service permissions granted to a user and highlights any unused permissions, helping administrators refine and tighten access controls.

9. A. Allowing users to access only the resources necessary for their tasks
Explanation: The principle of least privilege ensures that users are granted only the minimum permissions necessary to perform their assigned tasks, minimizing the risk of unauthorized actions.

10. C. AWS IAM Policy Simulator
Explanation: The IAM Policy Simulator allows you to simulate policies and test their effects on user access, helping ensure that policies are correctly configured before implementation.

11. C. Resource-Based Policies with AWS STS
Explanation: Resource-Based Policies allow you to grant access to specific AWS resources like S3 buckets. AWS STS can be used to generate temporary security credentials, enabling the auditor to access the resources for a limited time.

12. C. AWS IAM Policy Simulator
Explanation: The IAM Policy Simulator allows you to simulate the effects of both identity-based and resource-based policies to troubleshoot and test how policies interact, helping you identify why certain permissions are being denied.

13. A. Role-Based Access Control (RBAC)
Explanation: RBAC allows you to assign roles based on the specific tasks or responsibilities, ensuring that critical tasks are divided among different administrators, implementing separation of duties.

14. A. Use IAM Access Advisor to review service usage
Explanation: IAM Access Advisor helps you review which AWS services are being accessed by a particular role, allowing you to identify unused permissions and refine policies to implement the principle of least privilege.

15. B. Use AWS STS to issue temporary security credentials and define a session policy
Explanation: AWS STS (Security Token Service) allows you to issue temporary credentials that can expire after a specified period, ensuring that the consultant's access will be automatically revoked after the 2-week period.

# Chapter 5. Detective Controls

**This chapter addresses the following exam objectives:**
Domain 1: Threat Detection and Incident Response
Skills in: Deploying security services (for example, AWS Config, AWS CloudTrail, Amazon CloudWatch, Amazon Inspector, Amazon GuardDuty, AWS Security Hub)

◆◆◆◆◆◆

Detective controls are essential security measures designed to detect potential security threats or incidents that may have already occurred within a system or network. These controls monitor, analyze, and report on security events or anomalies, making them a critical component of any cybersecurity strategy. Tools and techniques used in detective controls include intrusion detection systems (IDS), security information and event management (SIEM) systems, log analysis, and network traffic monitoring. These tools identify potential security incidents and provide real-time alerts to security teams.

The primary goal of detective controls is to help organizations detect security incidents as early as possible, enabling quick and effective responses to minimize damage and prevent further attacks. They also aid in understanding the scope and impact of security incidents, helping organizations develop strategies to prevent similar incidents in the future.

AWS Security Detective Controls are a suite of features provided by Amazon Web Services (AWS) that allow users to monitor and detect potential security threats within their AWS infrastructure. These controls ensure prompt and effective detection and response to security incidents.

As a security expert, it is crucial to understand what is happening in your environment. This can be compared to noticing a tree falling in a forest, even if it makes no sound. Security professionals need to detect such events as they could indicate underlying issues or potential future risks. This is why monitoring devices, such as sensors, are strategically placed to gather information and infer system activities through generated events, a practice known as observability.

In AWS, resources are considered observable objects, and protecting these resources and the data they manage is a security expert's primary goal. Detective controls involve gathering information about the status of resources and the events they generate, including interactions with external elements and internal changes. The detection process goes beyond merely presenting observable records; AWS capabilities include leveraging big data analytics to extract meaningful findings from raw data and deliver processed events as observable records. Furthermore, automation can transform the detection process from a passive viewer role to an active security enforcer.

# 5.1 AWS Security Detective Controls

Some of the key AWS Security Detective Controls include:

**AWS CloudTrail**: This service allows users to log, continuously monitor, and retain account activity related to actions taken within their AWS account. It provides visibility into who has accessed resources and when and how they were accessed. This helps users to detect potential security incidents, investigate them, and respond appropriately.

**AWS Config**: This service allows users to assess, audit, and evaluate the configuration of their AWS resources. It provides a detailed inventory of resources and their configuration settings and helps to identify non-compliant or misconfigured resources.

**Amazon GuardDuty**: This threat detection service continuously monitors and analyzes AWS account activity for potential security threats. It uses machine learning and anomaly detection to identify and prioritize threats and provides detailed findings to help users investigate and respond to potential incidents.

**AWS Security Hub:** This service provides a central place to manage security and compliance across an AWS environment. It aggregates and prioritizes security alerts and findings from multiple AWS services and provides a consolidated view of security posture.

**Amazon Macie:** This security service uses machine learning to automatically discover, classify, and protect sensitive data within an AWS environment. It provides alerts and notifications when sensitive data is detected and helps users to protect data from unauthorized access.

Overall, AWS Security Detective Controls provide users with comprehensive tools to detect and respond to potential security incidents within their AWS environment. By leveraging these controls, users can gain better visibility into their environment, quickly identify potential threats, and respond more effectively to security incidents.

# 5.2 Detective Controls Process Flow Framework

To explain the various detective controls, we will follow the framework presented in the form of a flow, as shown in the diagram below.

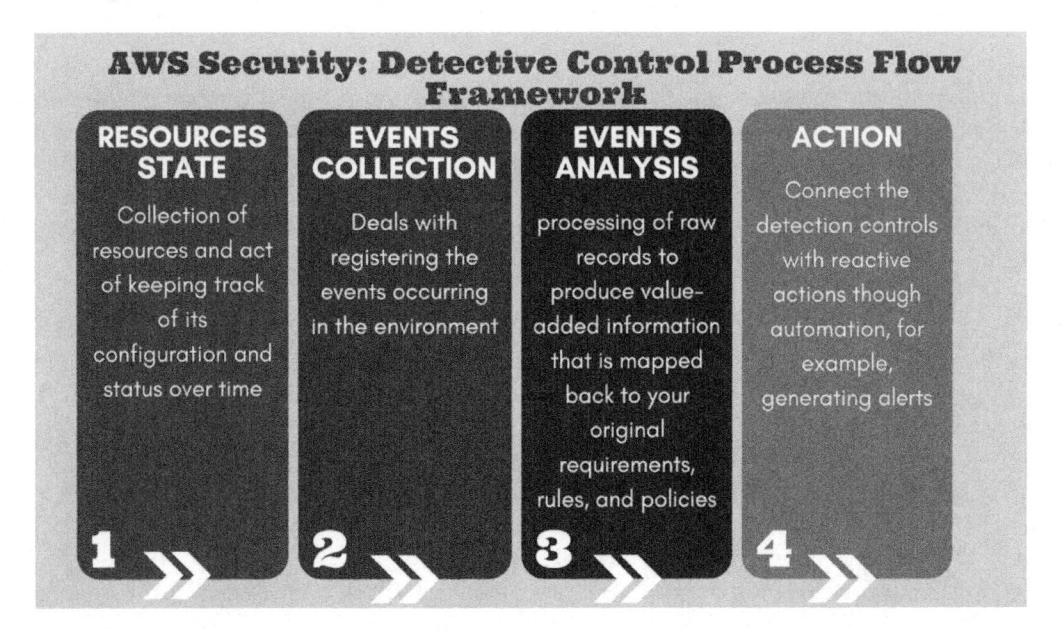

**AWS Security: Detective Control Process Flow Framework**

| 1. RESOURCES STATE | 2. EVENTS COLLECTION | 3. EVENTS ANALYSIS | 4. ACTION |
|---|---|---|---|
| Collection of resources and act of keeping track of its configuration and status over time | Deals with registering the events occurring in the environment | processing of raw records to produce value-added information that is mapped back to your original requirements, rules, and policies | Connect the detection controls with reactive actions though automation, for example, generating alerts |

As you notice in the diagram, the framework is divided into four main process stages: resource state, events collection, events analysis, and action.

### Resources State, Events, and Observable Records

The first stage in the framework is the *resources state,* which deals with keeping track of resource configuration and status over time. These resources are the "objects" that are under observation for detective controls. These resources can be running EC2 instances, published REST API-based microservices on API Gateway, or custom applications. The important point to understand in this stage is that resources don't focus on detecting their changes but establish a series of static pictures. The concept is similar to a movie if we have enough snapshots over a period of time, we should be able to observe progression by watching the sequence of these pictures.

These resources are not of static nature – they change over time due to the intrinsic automation nature of the cloud computing environment or to scale the system to handle additional request processing. All of it represents movement [movie analogy], or in more simple words, modifications in the environment.

As changes or actions occur in the environment, these changes can be represented in the form of events. An *event* is a representation of such a change or action in the environment. Any change or action, an event, can happen at any time in a cloud environment which is live 24x7. We need the right software tools to record these events as observable records.

### Events Collection

Events collection is the second stage of the detective controls process flow framework. This stage deals with the changes or actions occurring in the environment, in other words, dealing with event records, such as storing them. These event records can be passive or active. An example of passive records is when external sources are responsible for sending event notifications to the detective control. However, in the case of active records, the detective control itself is responsible for looking into event records and dealing with them. AWS provides services to deal with both types of records -- passive and active event records.

### Events Analysis

The raw event records typically contain many types of valuable information. However, depending on the type of analysis, not all information may be needed to analyze events. That's where the events analysis stage is valuable to the framework. The raw records can be filtered and processed in this stage to produce value-added information.

The events analysis is one of key stages of the detective control framework. The event analysis can be done in different ways. One of the ways is to compare the event with the best practices if there are differences. Or in another example, the event can be compared against the rules and policies and if it violates the rules or policies.

The event analysis can also use statistics to determine if the event is deviating from normal-looking events. Or the event analysis can also leverage machine learning to find out if the event is of a suspicious type. After event analysis, event records are stored as input for the next stage, which is *action* stage.

### Action

In the *action* stage, the framework reacts to events based on events analysis, such as sending alerts in the form of emails, SMS, etc. In this stage, automation can also be leveraged. For example, Amazon EventBridge can connect the source of events with consumers who can respond to those events.

In this chapter, we will look into many AWS Cloud services that support detective control activities:

AWS Config, AWS Systems Manager [Resources State Stage]
AWS CloudTrail, Amazon CloudWatch Logs, Amazon CloudWatch, AWS Health [Events Collection Stage]

AWS Config Rules, Amazon Inspector, Amazon GaurdDuty, AWS Security Hub, AWS Trusted Advisor [Events Analysis Stage]
AWS Systems Manager, Amazon EventBridge [Action Stage]

## 5.3 Stage 1: Resources State

The Resources State, as we discussed earlier, is the first stage in the detective control framework. It deals with keeping track or focusing on the configuration and status of the monitored resource over time. We will look into how AWS Config and AWS Systems Manager services can be leveraged at this stage.

### 5.3.1 AWS Config

AWS resources inside your account have their configurations at each point in time. And as we talked about that, changes can occur in AWS resources, such as changes in their configurations, over time. AWS Config enables you to track changes in AWS resources in your account over time. It provides a detailed inventory of AWS resources and records configuration changes that occur over time, allowing you to view a timeline of resource configuration changes.

For example, you could create an AWS Config rule to check that all Amazon Elastic Compute Cloud (EC2) instances are launched with the required security group attached. If an instance is launched without the required security group, AWS Config can detect this and trigger an alert, allowing you to take action before a security breach occurs.

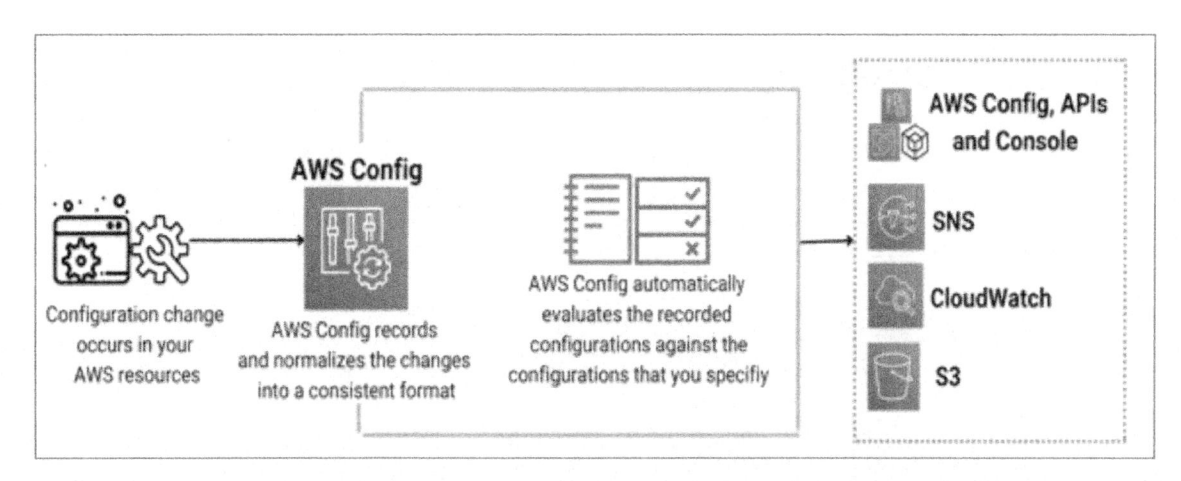

AWS Config continually assesses, audits, and evaluates the configurations and relationships of your resources. That way, it helps with auditing and recording compliance of your AWS resources and recording configurations and changes over time. It simplifies operational troubleshooting by correlating configuration changes to particular events in your accounts.

For example, questions that AWS Config can answer:
- Is there unrestricted SSH access to my security groups?
- Do my buckets have any public access?
- How has my ALB configuration changed over time?

When changes occur, you can access change history and compliance results using console or APIs, CloudWatch Events, or SNS alerts. You can deliver change history and snapshot files to your S3 bucket, which you can analyze by Athena.

AWS Config is a per-region service. It can be aggregated across regions and accounts.

*As of this writing, you pay $0.003 per configuration item recorded in your AWS account per AWS Region. A configuration item is recorded whenever a resource undergoes a configuration change or a relationship change.*

## 5.3.2 Configuration Recorder

In AWS Config, you start with Configuration Recorder. Configuration Recorder records configuration changes made to AWS resources. It continuously monitors and records the configuration changes and details of resources that are part of your AWS account, and then stores that information as Configuration Items (CIs) in an Amazon S3 bucket. The service provides one configuration recorder per account per region.

You can configure the Configuration Recorder to capture configuration changes for specific AWS resources or for all resources in your account. Additionally, you can specify the frequency at which configuration changes are recorded and the retention period for configuration history.

## 5.4 Stage 2: Events Collection

In a dynamic environment, events -- activities that affect resources -- are continuously happening. A detective system should capture those changes and convert them into observable records, which we discussed in the previous section. Based on the Detective Control framework we discussed earlier, in the second stage, all events – irrespective of what it is, good or bad – are collected as observable records and stored.

Now let's talk about AWS services, that we can leverage at this stage.

## 5.4.1 AWS CloudTrail

AWS CloudTrail enables your AWS account's governance, compliance, operational, and risk auditing. It records and logs all the API (Application Programming Interface) activity performed in your AWS account, creating a history of events that occurred within your cloud environment. These logs are crucial for security and monitoring purposes, as they provide a detailed record of actions taken by users, roles, services, or any other entities interacting with your AWS resources. Here is an example of a CloudTrail event

```
{
  "eventVersion": "1.08",
  "userIdentity": {
    "type": "IAMUser",
    "principalId": "EXAMPLEID:JohnDoe",
    "arn": "arn:aws:iam::123456789012:user/JohnDoe",
    "accountId": "123456789012",
    "accessKeyId": "AKIEXAMPLEKEY",
    "userName": "JohnDoe"
  },
  "eventTime": "2023-07-22T12:34:56Z",
  "eventSource": "s3.amazonaws.com",
  "eventName": "PutObject",
  "awsRegion": "us-west-2",
  "sourceIPAddress": "203.0.113.12",
  "userAgent": "aws-cli/1.20.40 Python/3.8.8 Linux/4.14.243-185.433.amzn2.x86_64 botocore/1.21.40",
  "requestParameters": {
    "bucketName": "example-bucket",
    "key": "example-file.txt"
  },
  "responseElements": {
    "x-amz-request-id": "EXAMPLEREQUESTID",
    "x-amz-id-2": "EXAMPLEAMZID"
  },
  "requestID": "EXAMPLEREQUESTID",
  "eventID": "EXAMPLEEVENTID",
  "readOnly": false,
  "resources": [
    {
      "type": "AWS::S3::Object",
      "ARN": "arn:aws:s3:::example-bucket/example-file.txt"
    }
  ],
  "eventType": "AwsApiCall",
  "recipientAccountId": "123456789012"
}
```

Explanation of Key Components:

- eventVersion: The version of the CloudTrail event record format.
- userIdentity: Contains information about the identity of the user or entity that performed the API call.
- type: The type of identity, in this case, an IAM user.
- principalId: A unique identifier for the IAM user.
- arn: The Amazon Resource Name (ARN) of the IAM user.
- accountId: The AWS account ID of the user.
- accessKeyId: The access key ID used for the API call.
- userName: The name of the IAM user.
- eventTime: The timestamp when the API call was made.
- eventSource: The AWS service or entity that the API call was made to, in this case, Amazon S3.
- eventName: The name of the API call that was performed, in this case, "PutObject" (indicating an object was uploaded to an S3 bucket).
- awsRegion: The AWS region in which the API call was made, here it's "us-west-2".
- sourceIPAddress: The IP address from which the API call originated.
- userAgent: Information about the tool or application that made the API call, in this case, the AWS CLI version, Python version, and OS details.
- requestParameters: Parameters associated with the API call, such as the bucket name ("example-bucket") and the key of the object ("example-file.txt") uploaded.
- responseElements: Elements in the response received after the API call.
- requestID and eventID: Unique identifiers for the API request and the CloudTrail event.
- readOnly: Indicates if the API call was a read-only operation (e.g., Describe, List) or not (read-only is false in this example).
- resources: Information about the AWS resources affected by the API call. In this case, it's an object in an S3 bucket with the specified ARN.
- eventType: Indicates the type of event; here, it's "AwsApiCall" indicating an API call event.
- recipientAccountId: The AWS account ID of the recipient, which is the same as the user's account ID in this example.

## CloudTrail Event Record

This CloudTrail event record provides detailed information about an API call to upload an object to an S3 bucket, including the user identity, timestamp, event details, and the resource affected. This data is valuable for auditing, monitoring, and troubleshooting AWS activities within your environment. AWS CloudTrail captures and logs API calls made by various AWS services and tools, such as the AWS Management Console, AWS Command Line Interface (CLI), AWS SDKs, and AWS CloudFormation. This includes actions like creating, modifying, and deleting resources, granting permissions, and more. By recording this data, CloudTrail provides an audit trail for security and compliance analysis.

The logs contain valuable information about user and resource activity, including the source IP address, the time of the API call, the identity of the caller, and the parameters used in the request. Security teams can use this information to identify unusual or unauthorized behavior, potentially indicating security threats or suspicious activities. In the event of a security incident, AWS CloudTrail logs can be invaluable for conducting investigations and forensic analysis. The detailed records of API calls help in understanding what actions were taken and by whom, aiding in identifying the incident's root cause.

Many compliance standards and regulations require organizations to maintain an audit trail of activities related to sensitive data and critical infrastructure. AWS CloudTrail assists in meeting these requirements by providing a complete history of actions performed on AWS resources. CloudTrail logs API activities and changes made to AWS resources, allowing administrators to track resource modifications and ensure the integrity of their infrastructure. Additionally, CloudTrail can be integrated with other AWS services like AWS CloudWatch and AWS Config, enabling real-time monitoring and alerting for specific events to help respond quickly to security incidents or policy violations. To ensure data integrity, CloudTrail logs are digitally signed and stored in an S3 bucket, providing an additional layer of security and ensuring that log files have not been tampered with.

## 5.4.1.1 CloudTrail Event Types

Actions taken by an IAM principal (IAM user, role, or an AWS service) are recorded as events in AWS CloudTrail, with an event being the basic recording unit. Various types of events are logged as records, each corresponding to a specific AWS API call or action performed on AWS resources or services. Understanding different event types is crucial for analyzing CloudTrail logs and gaining insights into activities within an AWS account. CloudTrail logs are generated in JSON format, and each log entry contains information about the event type along with other relevant details.

Common event types in AWS CloudTrail include management events, which capture API calls related to managing AWS resources, such as creating, modifying, or deleting resources like EC2 instances, S3 buckets, IAM users, and security groups. These events provide insights into infrastructure changes and help track resource configurations. Data events are specific to certain AWS services and capture data-level operations, such as S3 object-level actions (e.g., GetObject, PutObject), Lambda function invocations, and DynamoDB table operations, providing visibility into who accessed or modified specific data within AWS resources.

AWS service events capture calls made to AWS services in your account, including activities related to service health checks, AWS Support actions, and AWS Marketplace operations. Global service events apply to AWS services used globally, such as AWS Identity and Access Management (IAM), and capture actions affecting resources in multiple AWS regions. Insights events are generated when anomaly detection or insights are enabled for CloudTrail, providing information about suspicious API activities or notable patterns identified by CloudTrail Insights.

Control Tower events capture activity related to AWS Control Tower operations, such as creating, updating, or deleting Control Tower resources. CloudFront events capture actions related to the Amazon CloudFront content delivery network, including cache invalidations and origin requests. EventBridge events capture actions related to the AWS EventBridge service, used for event routing and event-driven application architectures.

Each event type contains specific information, including the time of the event, the identity of the caller (user or service), the source IP address, the event name, the AWS region, and additional parameters relevant to the specific event. By understanding these different event types, AWS users can effectively analyze and monitor their AWS environment, detect security issues, troubleshoot operational problems, and ensure compliance with organizational policies and industry regulations.

## 5.4.1.2 CloudTrail Integration

AWS CloudTrail integrates with various AWS services to help analyze event records and gain deeper insights into your AWS environment. These integrations allow you to use the event data captured by CloudTrail with other AWS services for real-time monitoring, auditing, and incident analysis. Key AWS services that integrate with AWS CloudTrail include:

AWS CloudWatch, which enables real-time monitoring and alerting based on specific API activity by creating CloudWatch Alarms to trigger notifications or automated actions when certain API calls or patterns are detected in CloudTrail logs. AWS Config integrates with CloudTrail to track changes to AWS resources over time, providing a comprehensive audit trail of changes made to your AWS environment by recording resource configuration details and API activity.

AWS EventBridge (formerly Amazon CloudWatch Events) allows building event-driven architectures and automating workflows based on events in your AWS environment. CloudTrail can be used as a source of events in EventBridge, triggering actions or notifications based on specific API activity. AWS Lambda captures events related to Lambda function invocations and can trigger Lambda functions based on specific API calls, enabling programmatic responses to events.

AWS Athena allows running ad-hoc queries on CloudTrail logs stored in Amazon S3, enabling custom analysis and insights from event data. AWS Glue can create ETL (Extract, Transform, Load) jobs to transform and analyze CloudTrail logs for further processing or data analysis. Amazon S3 and Amazon CloudFront can store CloudTrail logs, and securely deliver these logs to desired locations, centralizing log storage for efficient access.

AWS Partner Solutions provide advanced monitoring, reporting, and compliance capabilities by integrating with CloudTrail. Leveraging these integrations, you can harness the power of AWS CloudTrail data in combination with other AWS services to build a robust security and monitoring framework for your AWS resources. This enables effective management of your AWS environment, detection and response to security incidents, and compliance with industry regulations and organizational policies.

## 5.4.1.3 How AWS CloudTrail Protects Records

AWS CloudTrail employs several mechanisms to protect the integrity, confidentiality, and availability of the event records it captures. To ensure secure transmission of event records over the network, CloudTrail uses HTTPS (TLS) for encryption in transit between the AWS service generating the event and the CloudTrail service. For encryption at rest, CloudTrail supports server-side encryption (SSE) using AWS Key Management Service (KMS) or an Amazon S3-managed key (SSE-S3), ensuring that event records are encrypted and protected while stored in S3.

CloudTrail also allows fine-grained access controls through AWS Identity and Access Management (IAM), enabling the restriction of access to CloudTrail trails and log files to specific users, roles, or AWS services. This ensures that only authorized personnel can view and manage the event records. Additionally, to prevent tampering or accidental deletion of log files, S3 bucket policies can be used to enforce write-once-read-many (WORM) protection, making log files immutable.

CloudTrail log files contain digital signatures to verify their authenticity and integrity, ensuring that the log files have not been altered or tampered with. For disaster recovery and redundancy, CloudTrail can be configured to replicate event logs to a different AWS region, ensuring availability even if the primary region faces issues. Periodic integrity checks are performed on log files stored in S3 to identify any modifications or unauthorized changes, with alerts triggered if discrepancies are detected.

Retention management allows you to define the retention period for your CloudTrail logs, enabling efficient log storage management by automatically deleting logs after a specific duration. CloudTrail Insights enhances the detection of suspicious activities by using machine learning algorithms to identify unusual patterns or potential security threats in event data. Additionally, CloudTrail records and logs API calls made to the CloudTrail service, ensuring a complete audit trail of actions performed on the CloudTrail configuration, settings, and access.

By incorporating these protective measures, AWS CloudTrail ensures that event records remain secure and reliable. Organizations can confidently use CloudTrail to audit and monitor their AWS environments while adhering to best data protection and compliance practices.

## 5.4.1.4 Regional Scoped Service

AWS CloudTrail is a regional-scoped service. That being the case, events reported at the event history level are related to your account and region. You can also consolidate events from different regions in a single trail by creating a multi-region trail. A multi-region trail is configured to capture event records from all the AWS Regions, which is recommended configuration. However, if a trail is not chosen to apply to all regions, it will exist only in the current region. The trail will receive event logs only from the region where it was created.

If a trail applies for all AWS Regions, when a new AWS Region is added and enabled in the account, AWS CloudTrail will automatically start creating event logs for that region.

### 5.4.1.5 AWS Organizations Scope

A trial can also have an organization scope. You can create a trail in an organization's master account that will log events from all the accounts under the master account. An organization scope is independent of the Regional scope. All of the organization's member accounts will be able to see the trail, but they will need privileges to modify it. By default, they won't have privileges to access the trail's S3 bucket either.

Another way you can centralize logs is by letting different accounts store log files in centralized Amazon S3 buckets. In this case will have to configure the right access privileges for the different accounts to put objects in that centralized S3 bucket.

## 5.4.2 Amazon CloudWatch

Amazon CloudWatch is a monitoring and observability service that offers a comprehensive set of functionalities to help monitor, collect, analyze, and act on various metrics, logs, and events from AWS resources and applications. It provides real-time insights into the performance, health, and operational behavior of an AWS environment. As an event collection service for detection control, Amazon CloudWatch functions as a metric repository, recording numbers (metrics) in a time sequence for each period. It receives data from AWS services or custom data sources and uses the CloudWatch Agent to collect metrics, logs, and additional system-level information from both Amazon EC2 instances and on-premises servers. This allows for efficient and streamlined operational data collection, which can then be analyzed, visualized, and acted upon.

Key functionalities of Amazon CloudWatch include Metrics and Alarms, which allow for the collection and monitoring of metrics from various AWS services, such as EC2 instances, RDS databases, and S3 buckets, along with the creation of custom metrics. Users can set alarms based on these metrics to notify them when certain threshold conditions are met, enabling proactive monitoring and automated actions. Logs Insights enables interactive searching and analysis of log data from various sources using a simple query language to quickly identify patterns, troubleshoot issues, and gain insights into application and infrastructure behavior. CloudWatch Dashboards allow for the creation of customizable visualizations of metrics and logs data, displaying real-time graphs and charts for a unified view of AWS resources.

EventBridge (formerly CloudWatch Events) allows users to respond to changes in their AWS environment by setting up event rules to capture events from various sources and trigger actions such as invoking AWS Lambda functions or sending notifications via SNS. CloudWatch Synthetics enables the creation of canaries, configurable scripts that run on a schedule to monitor endpoints and APIs, helping proactively detect and troubleshoot issues related to application availability and functionality. Anomaly Detection uses machine learning algorithms to detect anomalous behavior in metric data automatically, alerting users to unusual patterns or potential issues.

Application Insights provides automated application monitoring for AWS and Microsoft workloads, helping detect and troubleshoot issues in applications hosted on AWS resources or Microsoft Windows and SQL Server environments. Container Insights offers in-depth monitoring and analysis of containerized applications running on Amazon ECS (Elastic Container Service) and Amazon EKS (Elastic Kubernetes Service), providing detailed performance metrics and logs. Tracing Insights helps analyze and troubleshoot performance issues in distributed applications by analyzing traces from AWS X-Ray. These functionalities collectively enable comprehensive monitoring, proactive issue detection, and effective troubleshooting for AWS resources and applications.

## Standard and High Resolution

Amazon CloudWatch offers two different resolutions for monitoring metrics: Standard Resolution and High Resolution. Standard Resolution provides data points at 1-minute intervals and is available for up to 15 months, making it suitable for most general monitoring needs by balancing granularity and storage costs effectively. High Resolution, in contrast, provides data points at intervals of either 1 second or 5 seconds, available for up to 3 hours. This resolution is designed for scenarios requiring more granular monitoring of rapidly changing metrics, allowing you to capture transient spikes or anomalies not visible within 1-minute intervals.

The choice between Standard Resolution and High Resolution depends on specific monitoring requirements. Standard Resolution is generally sufficient for most use cases, offering a good overview of resource performance and operational behavior. High Resolution is beneficial for workloads with rapidly changing metrics, as it captures more fine-grained details and provides a more accurate representation of resource performance during short-term bursts or high-frequency changes. However, High-Resolution metrics are more resource-intensive and can generate higher costs due to the increased data points and storage requirements. Therefore, it is crucial to consider specific monitoring needs, performance expectations, and budget constraints when deciding which resolution to use for CloudWatch metrics.

## 5.4.3 Amazon CloudWatch Logs

Amazon CloudWatch Logs enables you to collect, store, and analyze log data from various sources throughout their lifecycle, helping you centralize and manage logs generated by systems, applications, and AWS services. This provides valuable insights into the health, performance, and operational behavior of your resources.

Log data can be collected from AWS services, applications running on Amazon EC2 instances, AWS Lambda functions, containers, and custom applications. Data is sent to CloudWatch Logs using SDKs, AWS CLI, or CloudWatch Logs agents installed on instances. The logs are organized into "log groups," which act as containers for log streams. Each log group typically represents a specific application or resource, while individual "log streams" within the group represent sources of log data.

CloudWatch Logs supports real-time log streaming, making log data available for analysis as soon as it is received. This enables real-time monitoring and alerts for critical events and issues. You can configure the retention period for log data in each log group, with CloudWatch Logs automatically archiving data for long-term retention to ensure access to historical logs for compliance and auditing.

The "CloudWatch Logs Insights" feature allows interactive searching and analysis of log data using a simple query language. This helps you quickly identify patterns, errors, and anomalies in your logs. Metric filters can be created to extract specific data from log events and convert them into CloudWatch metrics, which can be used to create alarms that notify you when certain log events or thresholds are met, enabling proactive monitoring and automated responses.

CloudWatch Logs integrates seamlessly with other AWS services, such as triggering AWS Lambda functions for log data processing, integrating with Amazon Elasticsearch for log data indexing and search, or archiving log data to Amazon S3 for long-term storage and analysis. It provides fine-grained access control using AWS Identity and Access Management (IAM) to define permissions for accessing and managing log data, ensuring data security and compliance.

You can also create custom dashboards using CloudWatch Metrics and Logs Insights queries to visualize log data with line charts, bar graphs, and pie charts, enhancing the visibility and understanding of your log data.

## 5.4.4 Amazon Log Group, Log Steams, and Log Event

In Amazon CloudWatch Logs, an Amazon Log Group is a container for log data that organizes and stores log data for specific applications, resources, or system components. Log groups act as the top-level hierarchy for organizing logs in CloudWatch Logs. Within each log group, there are multiple Amazon Log Streams, which represent the log data from individual resources or instances. Log streams are sequences of log events that share the same source and are contained within log groups.

An Amazon Log Event represents a single log entry or event within a log stream, containing specific information about an activity, operation, or event that occurred within the system. Each log event includes a timestamp, a message, and other optional fields containing valuable log data.

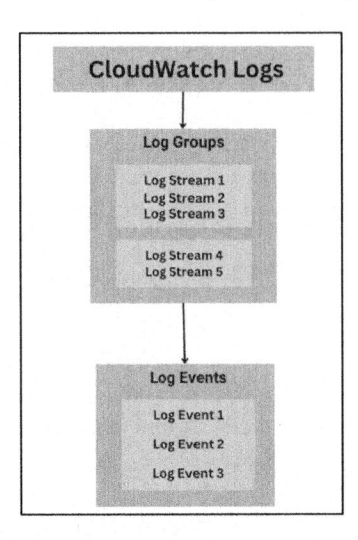

The top-level hierarchy in the diagram is the Amazon CloudWatch Logs service. Under CloudWatch Logs, there are multiple Amazon Log Groups, each representing a specific application, resource, or system component. Within each log group, there are multiple Amazon Log Streams, typically representing the log data from individual resources or instances. Within each log stream, there are multiple Amazon Log Events, each representing a single log entry or event containing specific log data.

Key characteristics of an Amazon Log Event include a timestamp indicating when the event occurred, a message containing the actual content of the log entry, and an event ID that uniquely identifies each log event. In contrast, an Amazon Log Group is a logical grouping of related log streams representing a specific application, resource, or system component. Log groups organize and categorize log data, allowing efficient management and analysis of logs.

Key characteristics of an Amazon Log Group include a unique group name, configurable retention settings determining how long log data is retained, and log streams representing a series of log events from the same log source within the log group. Permissions and access control are managed through AWS Identity and Access Management (IAM), allowing you to define who has permission to create, read, and manage log groups and log streams.

Amazon Log Groups and Log Events work together to create a structured and organized approach to log management in CloudWatch Logs. Log events are collected and stored within log streams, which belong to specific log groups. This hierarchy allows efficient management, searching, and analysis of log data for various applications and resources in your AWS environment.

# 5.4.5 AWS Health

AWS Health provides personalized information and guidance regarding the status of your AWS resources and services. AWS Health is designed to keep you informed about the health of your AWS environment and to help you quickly assess and respond to any potential issues that may affect your applications and workloads.

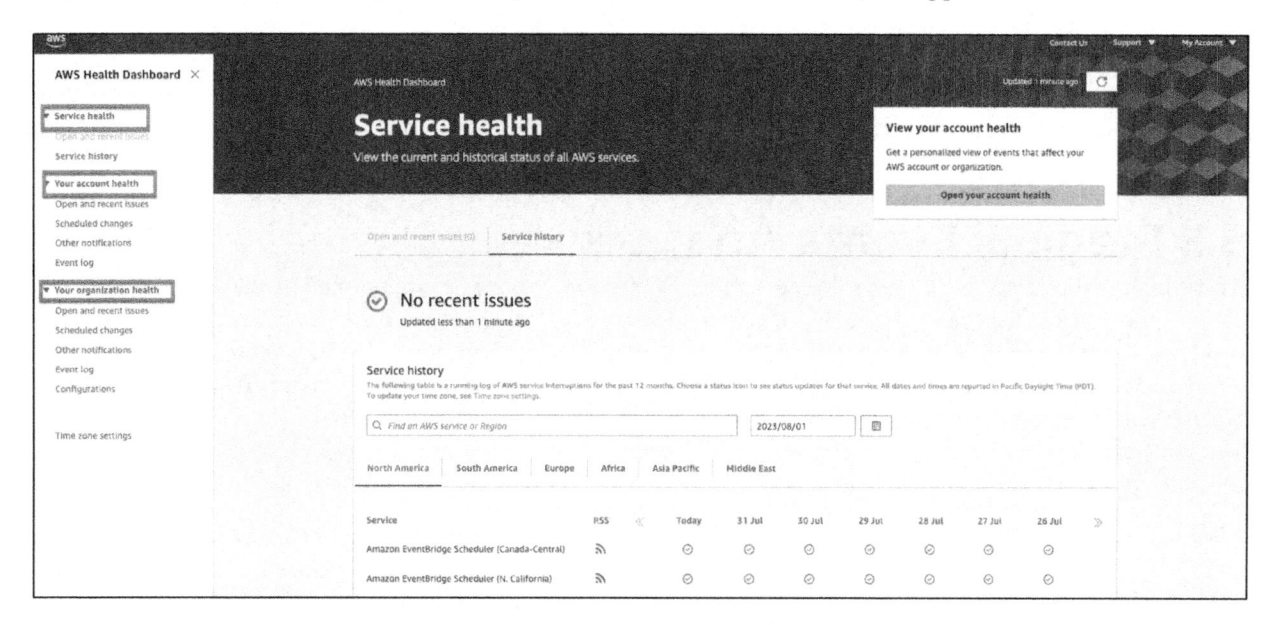

AWS Health Dashboard has three options as you can notice in the screenshot at the left: *Service health, Your account health, Your organization health*.

***Service health*** shows the overall health of AWS services. In other words, the Service Health Dashboard is the single place to find out about the availability and health of AWS services. In addition, you can view the overall status of AWS services. Amazon Web Services publishes up-to-the-minute information on service availability using its Health Dashboard page. You can check the page to get current status information about AWS services or subscribe to an RSS feed to be notified about any interruption of AWS services.

***Your account health*** offers alerts and remediation guidance when AWS is having issues that might impact your workloads or any other access issues. While the ***Service health*** provides the general availability status of AWS services, ***Your account health*** gives you a personalized view of the performance and availability of the AWS services underlying your AWS resources.

With ***Your account health***, alerts are triggered by changes in the health of AWS resources. The alerts provide you with event visibility and guidance to help quickly diagnose and resolve issues. For example, in the event of an AWS hardware failure, which impacts one of your EBS volumes, you will get an alert that includes a list of your affected resources and a recommendation to restore your volume.

***Your organization health***, in the AWS Health Dashboard provides an aggregated view of the AWS service health status for all AWS accounts associated with an organization in AWS Organizations. This feature allowed administrators and organization managers to get a comprehensive overview of the health of AWS services across all accounts within their organization.

AWS Health sends event-based notifications to keep you informed about the health of your AWS environment, including alerts about service issues, scheduled maintenance, and updates related to your AWS resources. It provides advanced notifications for planned maintenance events, helping you plan and prepare for maintenance windows.

AWS Health integrates with AWS Trusted Advisor, offering best-practice recommendations to optimize your AWS infrastructure's reliability, security, and performance. It also supports integration with third-party applications and services through Amazon CloudWatch Events, enabling automated responses based on AWS Health events.

Covering all AWS regions globally by default, AWS Health provides a comprehensive view of the health status of your resources across different regions within your AWS account. You can create filters to check specific events of interest and use the organizational view API for consolidated information about events across all accounts in your AWS organization, provided you have a business or enterprise support plan.

## 5.5 Stage 3: Events Analysis

According to the Detective Control Process Flow Framework, which we mentioned at the beginning of this chapter, once we collect the events, the next step is to analyze collected events. In other words, process the collected events -- execute an analytical process to produce a list of findings. In this section, with respect to event analysis, you will learn about AWS Config Rules, Amazon Inspector, Amazon GaurdDuty, AWS Security Hub, AWS Systems Manager, and AWS Trusted Advisor.

## 5.5.1 AWS Config Rules

AWS Config enables continuous assessment, auditing, and evaluation of AWS resource configurations. It tracks configuration changes over time, providing a detailed inventory and configuration timeline for each resource. This is valuable for infrastructure insights, policy compliance, and troubleshooting. AWS Config rules specify which resources to evaluate, the timing, and remediation actions. Rules can be triggered by configuration changes or at regular intervals.

There are three types of Config Rules: AWS Config Managed Rules, Custom Rules, and Service-linked Rules. Managed Rules are predefined by AWS and customizable, with over 84 available. Custom Rules allow users to create their own using AWS Guard or Lambda functions, for instance, to evaluate EBS disk types or EC2 instance types. Service-linked Rules are created and deployed by AWS services and cannot be modified by users, representing best practices defined by AWS development teams.

### 5.5.1.1 Config Rules Notifications

AWS Config is notified when a change happens. This notification allows the service to establish if the change impacts the monitored resource with respect to its "compliant" or "noncompliant" state by comparing it with a template that defines the desired configuration.

AWS Config rule can be configured to be notified (triggered) in three ways - not mutually exclusive. The AWS Config rule can be triggered on a *periodic* basis, for example, you can have it trigger after every 1, 6, 12, or 24 hours when a *configuration change is detected*—that way, it sets up a continuous audit of your monitored resources. You can also set up to trigger it *on-demand* -- either by an API call or via the Management Console.

Let's look into two typical notification use cases:

You can EventBridge to trigger notifications when AWS resources have become non-compliant due to configuration changes.

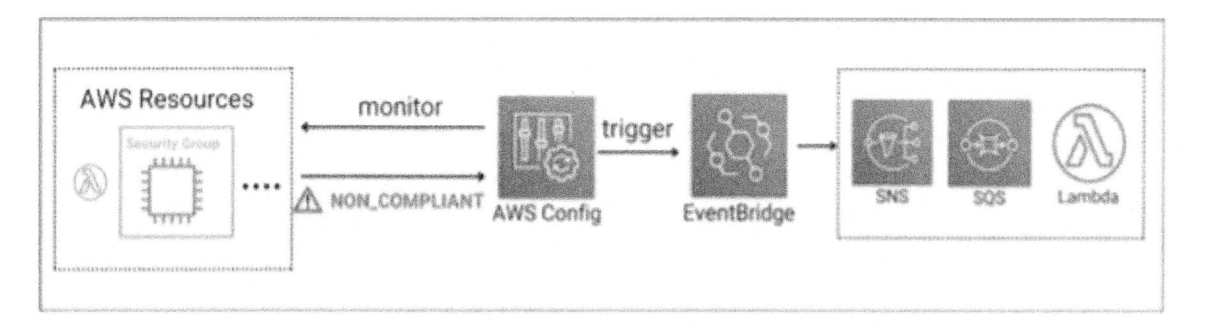

You can send configuration changes and compliance state notifications to SNS for all events. You can also use SNS Filtering or filter on the client side.

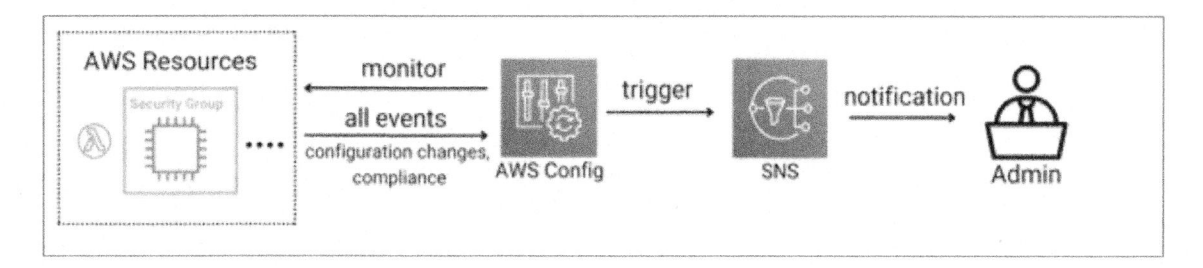

## 5.5.2 Amazon Inspector

Amazon Inspector identifies potential security vulnerabilities on Amazon EC2 instances using automated reasoning technology to assess issues like vulnerabilities, exposed ports, and insecure configurations. It provides actionable findings and recommendations to enhance security.

To use Amazon Inspector, install its agent on your EC2 instances (Assessment Targets). The agent collects data on the instance's configuration, software packages, network, and other relevant information. You can initiate an assessment run from the Amazon Inspector console, AWS CLI, or SDK, triggering the security assessment.

Amazon Inspector uses pre-built rules packages to perform the security assessment, evaluating configurations and behaviors against security best practices and industry standards. The assessment identifies potential vulnerabilities, deviations from standards, and compliance violations.

After the assessment, Amazon Inspector generates detailed findings for each EC2 instance, including detected security issues, their severity, and suggested remediation actions. You can address these issues manually or automate the remediation process by integrating Amazon Inspector with other AWS services.

Amazon Inspector provides valuable insights into the security status of EC2 instances, allowing proactive management of vulnerabilities and compliance violations. It enhances overall security and ensures the protection of resources and data. Additionally, it integrates with AWS services like AWS Systems Manager, AWS CloudFormation, and AWS Security Hub to facilitate the automation of security remediation and streamline security management processes.

### 5.5.2.1 Amazon Inspector Assessment Template

Amazon Inspector Assessment Templates are reusable configurations that define the scope and behavior of security assessments performed by Amazon Inspector. These templates standardize and streamline the process of running security assessments on your Amazon EC2 instances and other AWS resources. By creating an assessment template with predefined settings and rules packages, you can conduct consistent security evaluations across your environment without configuring assessment runs from scratch each time.

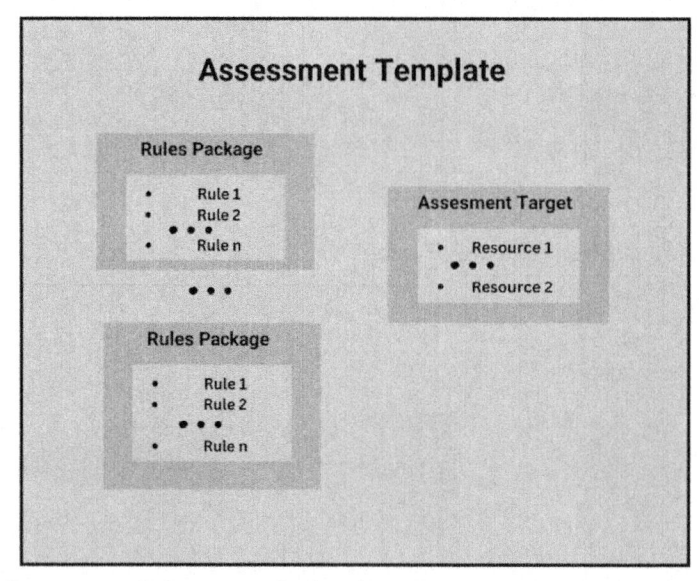

Assessment templates allow you to define a standardized configuration for your security assessments, including specifying the rules packages, assessment targets (resources to be assessed), duration, and other settings. You can select specific Amazon Inspector rule packages to use in the assessments, which determine the security checks performed during the assessment.

These templates specify the target resources, such as Amazon EC2 instances, that should be assessed, allowing you to define inclusion or exclusion criteria for the resources. You can use Amazon Inspector's automated scheduling feature to trigger assessment runs based on the defined template automatically, eliminating the need for manual intervention each time you want to perform an assessment.

After running an assessment using the template, you can generate a documented report (in PDF or HTML format) with the findings information. Amazon Inspector collects telemetry data from instances in JSON format and stores them in an Inspector-owned S3 bucket, where they are retained for 30 days before being automatically deleted. Assessment results can be viewed in the Amazon Inspector console or retrieved programmatically using AWS APIs, including details on findings, severity levels, and remediation recommendations.

For real-time notifications, you can define an Amazon SNS topic to receive alerts when a finding is reported in the assessment template, as well as notifications when an assessment run starts, completes, or changes its state.

## 5.5.3 Amazon GuardDuty

Amazon GuardDuty is a threat detection service that continuously monitors your AWS environment for malicious activity and unauthorized behavior. It analyzes events from various AWS data sources, including AWS CloudTrail logs, VPC Flow Logs, and DNS logs, to detect potential security threats and suspicious activities. By using machine learning and anomaly detection algorithms, GuardDuty identifies patterns and behaviors indicative of malicious activities, such as unauthorized access, compromised instances, and communication with known malicious IP addresses. This enables real-time threat detection and analysis, allowing for quick responses to potential security incidents and proactive measures to protect resources.

GuardDuty leverages threat intelligence from AWS, third-party providers, and the global AWS customer base to enhance its detection capabilities. It helps meet compliance requirements by detecting potential security issues and providing detailed findings for auditing and reporting. Users can create lists of trusted and malicious IPs (threat lists), where activity from trusted IPs will not generate findings, while activity involving IP addresses on threat lists will generate findings.

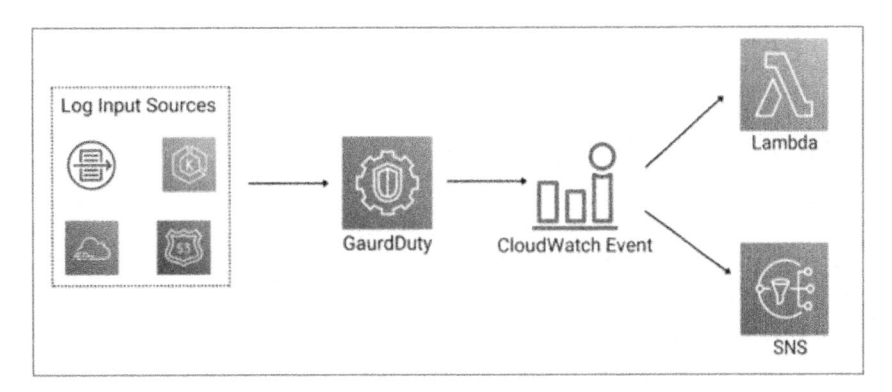

The core entity in GuardDuty is a detector, which collects information and generates security findings in a unified console, providing a comprehensive view of potential threats within a specific AWS account and region. Findings include attributes such as ID, time, severity, type, affected resources, and action details. GuardDuty is fully managed, requiring no infrastructure setup or configuration, and can be enabled with a few clicks in the AWS Management Console or through AWS APIs. It integrates with other AWS services, such as AWS CloudWatch and AWS Security Hub, to enhance security monitoring, incident response, and overall security posture.

Once a detector is enabled, GuardDuty starts reporting findings, accessible through the management console or via the GetFindings API. The GetFindingsStatistics API provides findings statistics. GuardDuty's pricing model is based on the number of AWS events analyzed, making it a cost-effective solution for continuous threat detection. It offers multiple benefits, including improved visibility into potential security threats, quicker incident response times, and enhanced protection for AWS workloads, complementing other AWS security services like AWS WAF and AWS IAM.

## Amazon GuardDuty Findings

Amazon GuardDuty provides a workflow to manage findings. The workflow enables you to document the manual actions taken as a response to a finding. You can archive findings. You can also automatically send findings to an archive by creating suppression rules, which is essentially a filter. When a finding matches the filter, the finding is automatically marked archived. You can visualize current, archived or all findings.

You can also export findings in JSON format. You can configure the automate the export process of sending findings to an S3 bucket. Amazon GuardDuty will export active findings (not the one matching with suppressed rules) within five minutes of its first occurrence. If the same finding occurs again, you can configure how frequently those events you want to get reported (for example, every 15 mins/hourly/or every other x hour).

Exported findings are encrypted with an AWS KMS key that you select.

## Amazon GuardDuty with Organizations

Amazon GuardDuty uses the concept of master account. What it means, the master account receives findings from all the member accounts. The master account has the ability to manage (for example, enable, disable, or suspend) the detectors and manage the findings workflow (archiving, suppression rules), and also can configure threat lists for the member accounts.

## 5.5.4 AWS Security Hub

AWS Security Hub is a comprehensive security service that gives you a centralized view of your security posture across your AWS accounts and workloads. It collects, organizes, and prioritizes security findings from various AWS services (such as Amazon GaurdDuty, Amazon Inspector, AWS Config, Amazon Macie, AWs Firewall Manager, and IAM Access Analyzer), integrated partner solutions, and AWS-native security tools.

Security Hub acts as a central hub where security findings from multiple sources are aggregated and correlated. It provides a single pane of glass to view and manage security alerts and compliance status across your AWS accounts. You can also use *GetFindings* API. These findings contain information about potential security issues, compliance violations, and best practice deviations detected in your AWS resources. Security Hub helps you assess your AWS environment's compliance against industry standards and best practices. It provides insights and recommendations to address any compliance issues.

Security Hub automatically prioritizes findings based on their severity and potential impact. This helps you focus on addressing the most critical security issues first. It integrates with AWS Systems Manager Automation, enabling you to automate responses to security findings and implement corrective actions.

You can create custom insights and dashboards in Security Hub to gain deeper visibility into specific security aspects of your environment. This enables you to tailor the view of security data based on your organization's needs. For each finding, Security Hub provides detailed information about the issue and actionable recommendations for remediation. This empowers you to take prompt action to resolve security concerns.

### AWS Security Hub Workflow

The AWS Security Hub also provides a workflow to manage findings. It involves several steps, starting from collecting security findings from various sources and ending with actionable insights and responses to address potential security issues. Each finding contains an attribute called WorkflowStatus, which has the following values: New, Notified, Suppressed or Resolved. You have the flexibility to modify the workflow status of a finding, giving you the flexibility to implement your own process to handle the findings.

There is also an important point to mention about Findings. Findings also contain an attribute "RecordState" which can have value Active or Archived. By default, Archived ones are not shown on the Management Console. You can modify the visualization filter, though.

### AWS Security Hub and Organizations

AWS Security Hub has a Region scope. It uses the concept of a master-member like Amazon GuardDuty and Amazon Macie. The master account can invite other accounts. The master account can view findings from the member accounts and can also execute actions on those findings.

### AWS Security Hub Integrations

AWS Security Hub supports both ingress and egress way of integrations. Ingress integrations allow AWS services, third party applications, or custom applications to send events to Security Hub and generate findings. On the other have, egress integrations allow Security Hub to send events to AWS services, third party applications, or custom applications so that you can track them in the external systems.

## 5.5.5 AWS Systems Manager

AWS Systems Manager is a comprehensive service that provides visibility and control over AWS infrastructure and automates infrastructure management tasks. It simplifies the management of Windows and Linux instances, whether they are running on EC2 or on-premises. With AWS Systems Manager, you can perform tasks such as collecting system inventory, applying OS patches, creating Amazon Machine Images (AMIs), and configuring operating systems and applications at scale.

It is particularly useful for managing a large fleet of instances, providing a unified interface and tools for configuring and managing resources across multiple AWS accounts and regions. Previously known as AWS EC2 Simple Systems Manager or AWS SSM, this service enhances operations, improves security, and reduces costs by offering powerful tools for managing infrastructure and applications at scale.

> **NOTE** For AWS Systems Manager, SSM Agent needs to be running. AWS Systems Manager comes with no additional charge. However, you will pay based on the pay-as-you-model – the resources you use.

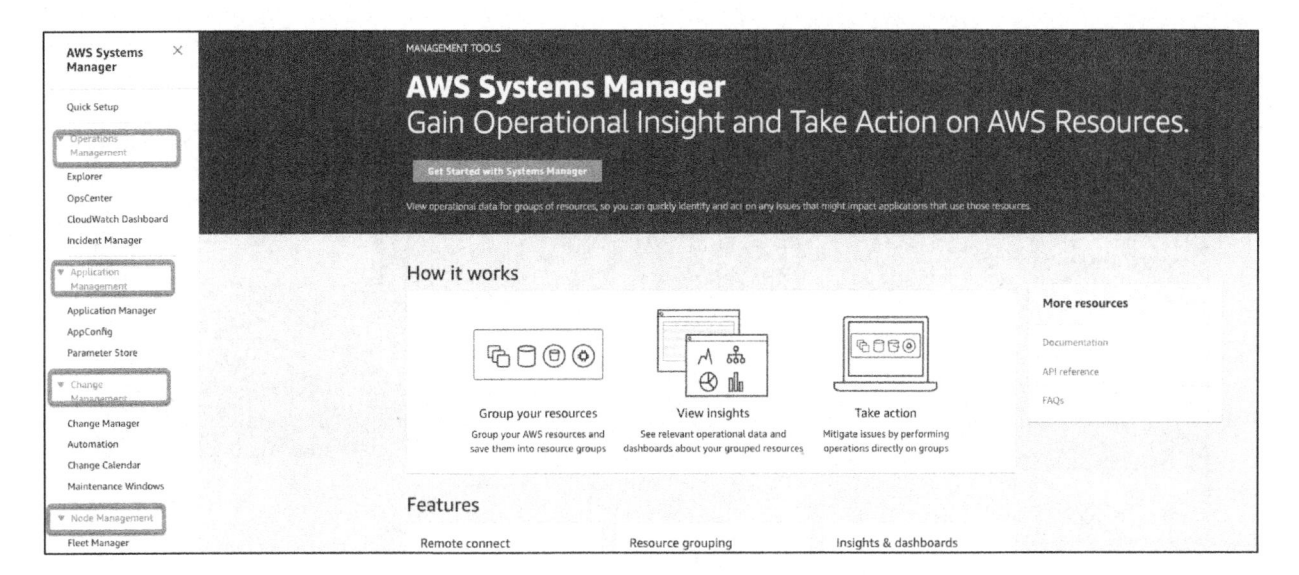

As mentioned earlier, AWS Systems Manager's capabilities are grouped into operations management, applications management, change management, and node management. Let's look into each of these categories in a brief:

## Operations Management
It groups together AWS Systems Manager's features that help understand your environment's current state and its components' performance. Explorer, OpsCenter, and CloudWatch Dashboard services are grouped under Operations Management.

## Applications Management
It groups together AWS Systems Manager's features that help in the administration of applications that are distributed along several components and AWS accounts. Applications Manager, AppConfig, and Parameter Store services are grouped under Applications Management.

## Change Management
It groups together AWS Systems Manager's features that allow you to specify a sequence of actions to be executed on your managed instances and how to control execution. Change Manager, Automation, Change Calendar, and Maintenance Windows are grouped under Change Management.

## Node Management
It groups AWS Systems Manager's features together *to manage instances and nodes at scale.*
Fleet Manager, Compliance, Inventory, Hybrid Activations, Session Manager, Run Command, State Manager, Patch Manager, and Distributor *are grouped under Node Management.*

With regard to detective control, AWS Systems Manager provides capabilities that allow you to interact with monitored resources at deeper levels—for example, gathering information about the EC2 instances or applications, executing commands on the operating system, or establishing a terminal administration channel (ssh) into the instance. You need to install *SSM Agent* on the EC2 instances to enable this feature. The *SSM Agent* acts as the representative of the service inside the instance.

Let's look into some of the important services/modules/features of AWS Systems Managers.

**Inventory**
AWS Systems Manager Inventory enables you to collect metadata from your Amazon Elastic Compute Cloud (Amazon EC2) instances and on-premises servers and track changes over time. This metadata includes information about applications, AWS components, network configurations, instance detailed information, operating system patches, and other system details.

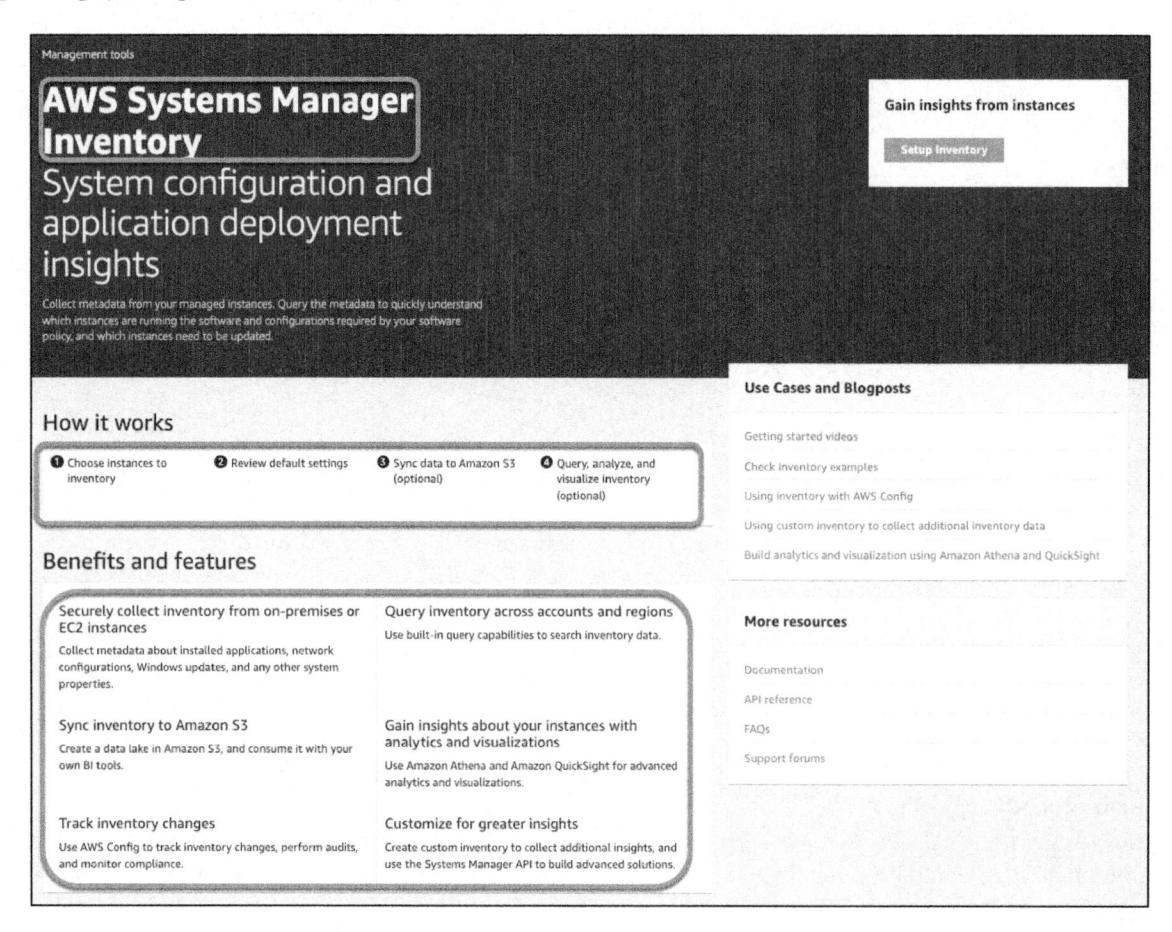

With Inventory, you can simplify the process of collecting and tracking system information using a single, centralized solution. You can also use the service to automate patch management, compliance monitoring, and software inventory tracking tasks. You can specify targets by selecting all managed instances in your account, specifying a tag, or manually specifying instances.

```
Targets
Specify targets by
○ Selecting all managed instances in this account
○ Specifying a tag
● Manually selecting instances

[i-00b10c94887d206dd  X]
```

| ☑ | Name | Instance ID | Instance state | Availability zone | Ping status | Last ping time (UTC) | Agent version |
|---|------|-------------|----------------|-------------------|-------------|----------------------|---------------|
| ☑ | My Test Server | i-00b10c94887d206dd | running | us-east-1a | ⊘ Online | Tue, 09 May 2023 03:05:46 GMT | 3.1.1927.0 |

```
Schedule
(Requires SSMAgent version 2.0.790.0 and above)

Collect inventory data every  [30]   [Minute(s) ▼]
```

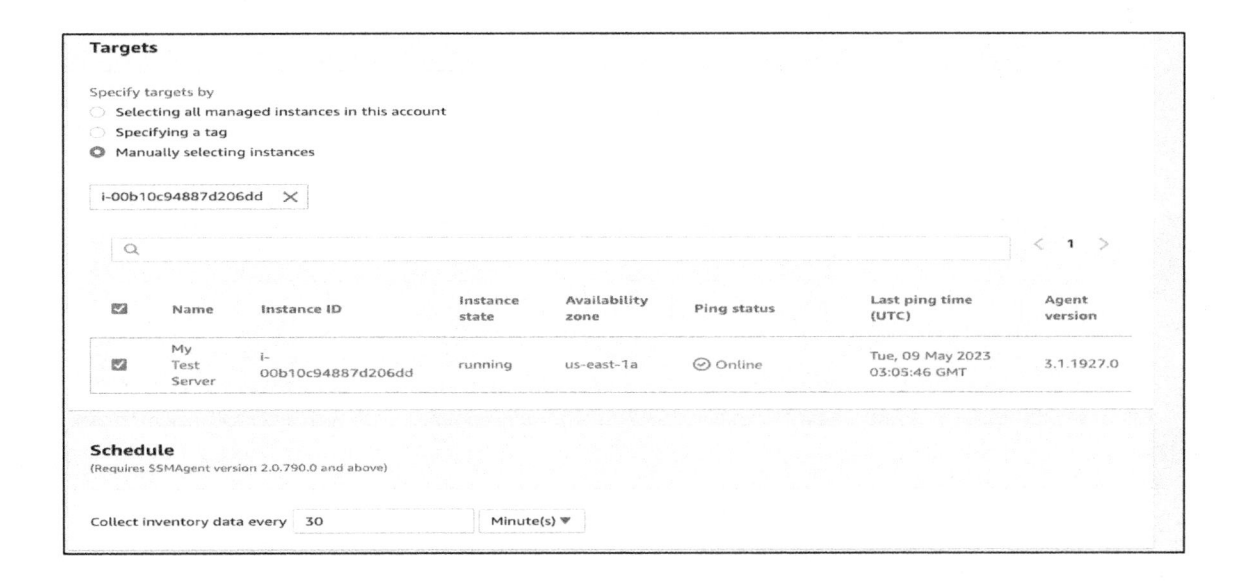

To add an EC2 instance to appear on the SSM, make sure that the SSM Agent is running on the instance. Some AMI type comes installed with SSM Agent such as Amazon Linux.
In addition, you also need to make sure to attach an IAM role with SSM as a Trust relationship.

For example. In the screenshot above, the EC2 instance has been assigned a role with the Trust relationship, as shown below.

| Permissions | Trust relationships | Tags | Access Advisor | Revoke sessions |

**Trusted entities**
Entities that can assume this role under specified conditions.

```json
{
    "Version": "2012-10-17",
    "Statement": [
        {
            "Effect": "Allow",
            "Principal": {
                "Service": [
                    "ec2.amazonaws.com",
                    "ssm.amazonaws.com"
                ]
            },
            "Action": "sts:AssumeRole"
        }
    ]
}
```

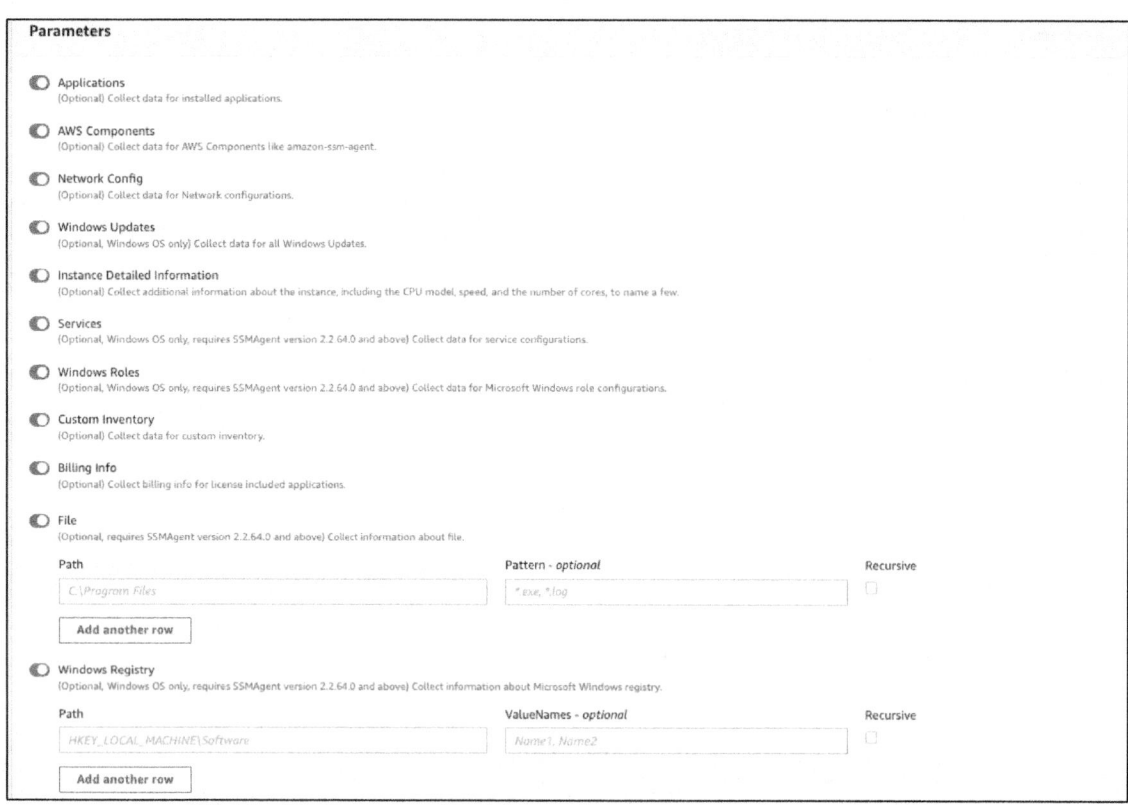

SSM Set Up Inventory Partial Snapshot– what metadata can it collect

Once the information is collected, SSM can export it to an S3 bucket you own by configuring sync inventory execution logs to an S3 bucket. In SSM Inventory, you can define how frequently you want the inventory data to be collected. For example, you configure it to collect inventory data every 30 mins.

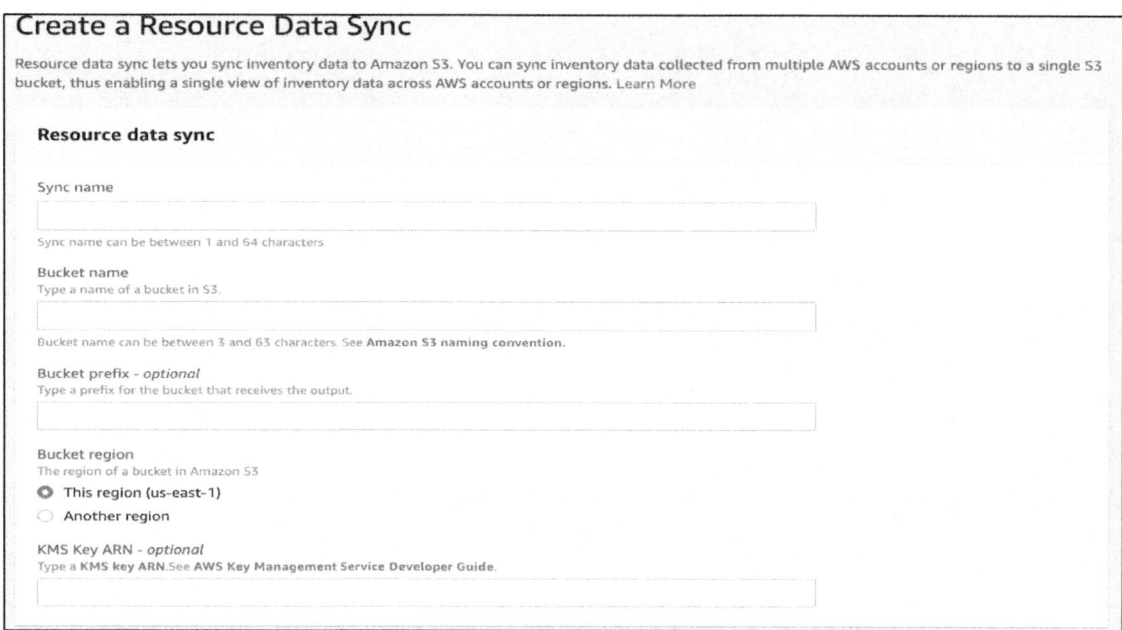

Inventory is integrated with other AWS services, such as AWS Systems Manager Patch Manager, AWS Config, and AWS Resource Groups, and it supports both Linux and Windows instances. The service can also be extended to collect custom data using AWS Config rules and AWS Lambda functions.

AWS Certified Security – Specialty Exam Guide

Bucket Policy when setting up Resource Data Sync to write to the S3 bucket.

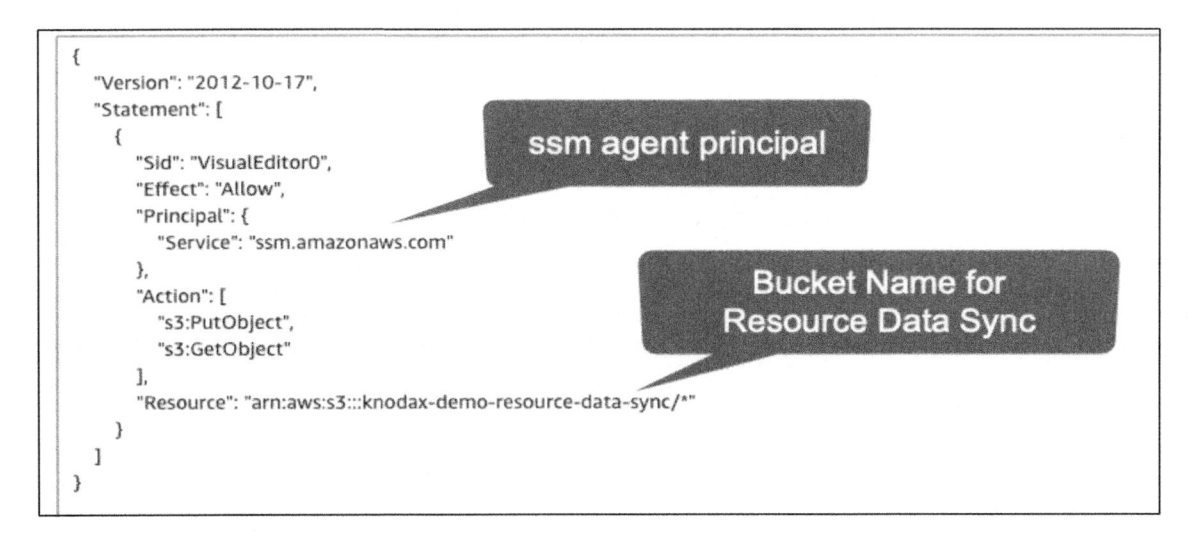

```json
{
    "Version": "2012-10-17",
    "Statement": [
        {
            "Sid": "VisualEditor0",
            "Effect": "Allow",
            "Principal": {
                "Service": "ssm.amazonaws.com"
            },
            "Action": [
                "s3:PutObject",
                "s3:GetObject"
            ],
            "Resource": "arn:aws:s3:::knodax-demo-resource-data-sync/*"
        }
    ]
}
```

*ssm agent principal*

*Bucket Name for Resource Data Sync*

The screenshot below shows the SSM inventory dashboard after a running EC2 is set up as a resource to monitor.

## Patch Manager

AWS Systems Manager Patch Manager automates patching for managed instances (EC2 instances with SSM Agent) to handle security and other updates. It can apply patches for both operating systems and applications, although on Windows Server, application support is limited to Microsoft applications. Patch operations are performed in the background, requiring a snapshot with approved updates in the patch baseline for deployment. The list of approved updates is sent to the Windows or Linux APIs to determine what needs to be applied.

We create a patch baseline with Patch Manager or use default ones provided by SSM. Based on requirements, we select and approve patches using auto-approval rules, specifying patches to be uploaded after a certain number of days or up to a specific date. Patches not required for the system can be rejected.

### Run Command
AWS Systems Manager Run Command is a crucial service that allows you to remotely and securely manage configurations of managed instances (EC2 instances with SSM Agent). Managed instances include any EC2 instance or on-premises machine in a hybrid environment configured for Systems Manager.

Run Command automates common administrative tasks and performs ad hoc configuration changes at scale. For example, it enables you to run Ansible playbook Docker containers, shell scripts, or PowerShell scripts on EC2 instances via the AWS Systems Manager dashboard. To use it, create an IAM Role with Systems Manager access and apply it to the EC2 instances.

You can use Run Command from the AWS Management Console, AWS CLI, AWS Tools for Windows PowerShell, or AWS SDKs, which are offered for free.

### Session Manager
AWS Systems Manager Session Manager enables secure, browser-based or CLI access to AWS Cloud and on-premises instances without needing SSH or RDP connections. It allows management through the AWS Management Console or AWS CLI and uses IAM policies for access control.

Session Manager enhances security, auditability, and simplifies management by eliminating the need for inbound ports or bastion hosts, reducing the attack surface, and logging all session activity for compliance. It supports both Linux and Windows instances and integrates with AWS CloudTrail, AWS CloudWatch Logs, and AWS Identity and Access Management (IAM).

### Parameter Store
AWS Systems Manager Parameter Store securely stores and manages configuration data and secrets, like database connection strings, API keys, and passwords, accessible by AWS services and on-premises applications. Parameters can be stored as plaintext or encrypted data, with defined access policies for control. Features include versioning and tagging for tracking changes and managing large parameters.

Parameter Store is useful for storing parameters for EC2 instances, Lambda functions, and other AWS services. It integrates with AWS CloudFormation, AWS CodePipeline, and AWS CodeBuild to automate application and infrastructure deployment.

## 5.6 Stage 4: Action
Remediation in security refers to the process of addressing and resolving security issues, vulnerabilities, or weaknesses in a system or environment to mitigate potential risks and protect against threats. When security vulnerabilities are identified, whether through manual assessments or automated security tools, remediation involves taking corrective actions to reduce or eliminate the impact of those vulnerabilities on the system's security posture. The goal of remediation is to ensure that security risks are properly managed and minimized and that the system is returned to a secure and compliant state. In this section, we will learn about services and features related to the remediation aspect of detective controls.

## 5.6.1 AWS Systems Manager: SSM Automation

AWS Systems Manager SSM documents define steps and actions to achieve automation goals, written in YAML or JSON format with predefined steps and parameters. They are crucial for automating responses to security findings or operational issues in AWS environments.

SSM Automation integrates with AWS services like AWS Security Hub, AWS Config, and AWS CloudFormation to trigger remediation actions when issues are detected. AWS provides pre-built "public documents" for common use cases, and custom documents can be created to meet specific needs.

SSM Automation documents define sequences for remediation tasks such as restarting EC2 instances, applying patches, modifying security group rules, and adjusting IAM policies. They support parameterization for dynamic values and can be executed manually or automatically based on events. The execution is tracked and logged in AWS Systems Manager, with error handling and rollback mechanisms included to ensure reliability and consistency.

Using SSM Automation documents accelerates remediation, reduces human error, and ensures prompt and efficient handling of security and operational issues across AWS environments.

## 5.6.2 AWS Config Rules: Remediation

Once an AWS Config Rule executes a check, and if the result of an evaluation is a non-compliant status, the rule can apply a remediation action.

You can automate the remediation of non-compliant resources using SSM Automation Documents. You can use AWS-Managed Automation Documents or create custom Automation Documents. You can create custom Automation Documents that invoke a Lambda function. You can set Remediation Retries if the resource is still non-compliant after auto-remediation

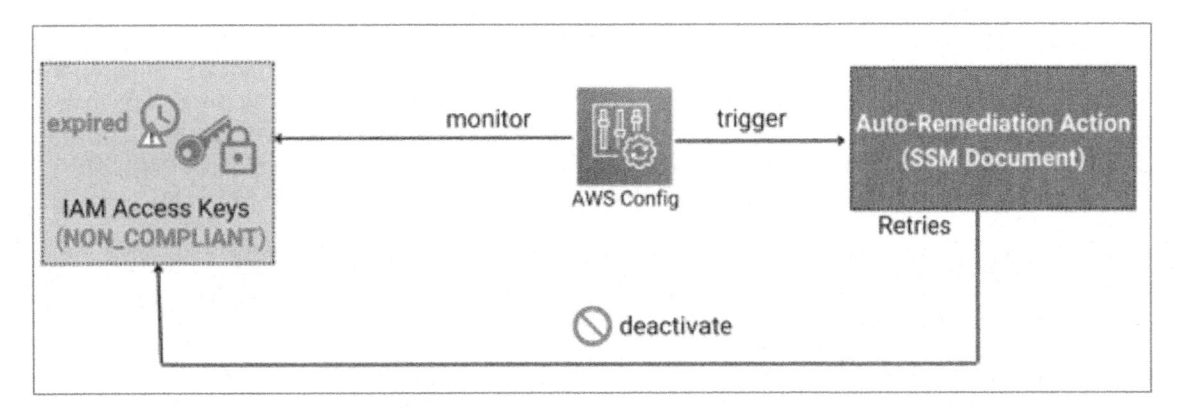

## 5.6.3 Amazon EventBridge

Amazon EventBridge is a fully managed event bus service that enables event-driven architectures by allowing applications to respond to events from various AWS services, SaaS applications, custom applications, and other sources. It facilitates real-time reactions to events, decoupling application components through event communication.

EventBridge operates on an event bus model, routing events from sources to targets like AWS Lambda, SQS, and Step Functions based on defined rules. It supports numerous event sources, including AWS services like CloudTrail and S3, and integrates with SaaS and custom applications. EventBridge allows event replay for testing and debugging, provides a schema registry for defining event structures and enforcing validation, and supports IAM for access control and CloudTrail for auditing.

EventBridge extends Amazon CloudWatch with additional features, such as managed event buses that can receive events from external sources, whereas CloudWatch Events only provides a default bus. EventBridge is preferred for managing events from AWS resources due to its enhanced capabilities.

## 5.6.3.1 EventBridge Generic Workflow

Let's try to understand how Amazon EventBridge handles actions with respect to detection controls with the Amazon EventBridge generic workflow diagram given below.

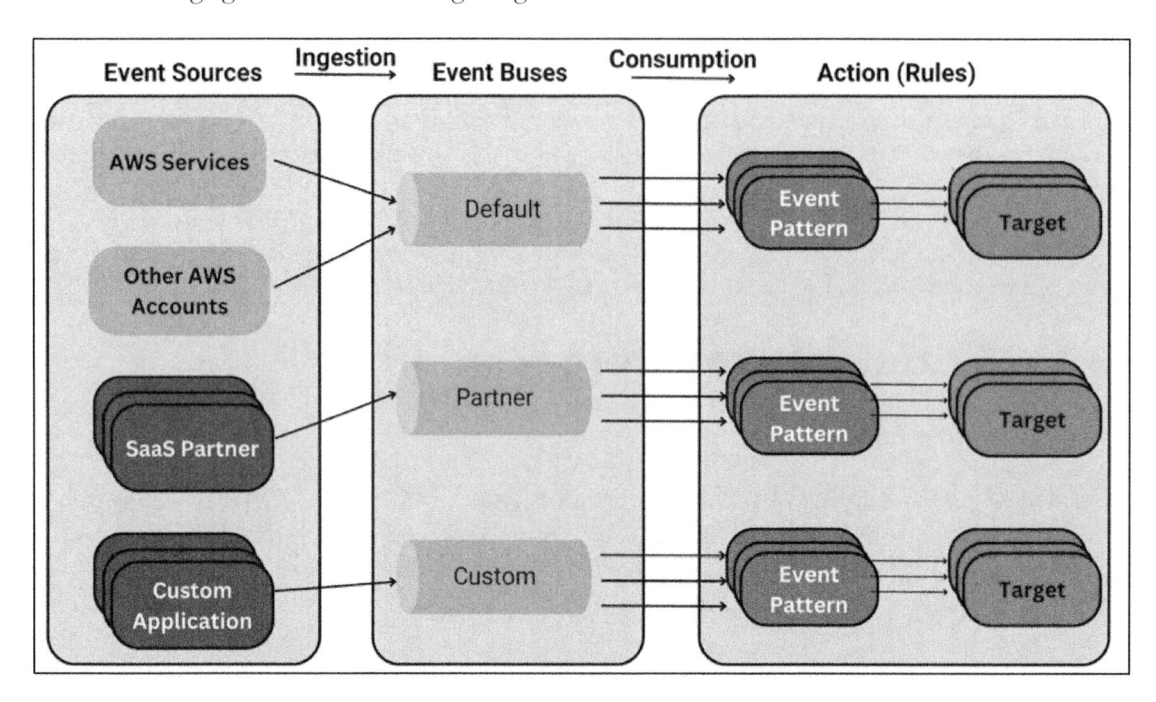

In the workflow, the first is the ingestion of events, which represents changes in resources generated by different sources, such as AWS services, SaaS, or custom applications. Events are ingested into an event bus. In Amazon EventBridge there are three types of buses: Default, Partner, and Custom. And finally, the events trigger actions on targets based on the matching rules.

You can think of Amazon EventBridge as a service that connects event sources to action executors (targets) view event buses. Additionally, Amazon EventBridge can also trigger actions at a scheduled time periodically.

### EventBridge Event Buses

Amazon EventBridge offers three types of event buses: Default, Partner, and Custom. The default event bus receives events from AWS resources and is region-specific per account. It cannot be deleted.

The Partner event bus ingests events from third-party applications. To set up, you provide an AWS account to the partner application that sends events to EventBridge. Each Partner event bus receives events from only one partner event source.

Custom event buses are created for ingesting custom events through the PutEvents API. These buses allow building event-driven architectures that trigger actions and workflows based on user-defined event types, providing flexibility and scalability.

## Example of Amazon EventBridge Custom Event

```
{
  "version": "0",
  "id": "1a234567-1234-5678-1234-567812345678",
  "detail-type": "MyCustomEvent",
  "source": "com.example.myapp",
  "account": "123456789012",
  "time": "2023-07-22T12:34:56Z",
  "region": "us-west-2",
  "resources": [
    "arn:aws:s3:::my-bucket"
  ],
  "detail": {
    "eventName": "PutObject",
    "bucketName": "my-bucket",
    "objectKey": "example.txt",
    "userIdentity": {
      "principalId": "A1B2C3D4E5F6G7H8I9J0"
    }
  }
}
```

- **version:** The version of the event. Use "0" for custom events.
- **id:** A unique identifier for the event.
- **detail-type:** A string that identifies the type of event detail.
- **source:** The identifier of the event source. It can be your application or service name.
- **account:** The AWS account ID where the event originated.
- **time:** The timestamp when the event occurred in ISO 8601 format.
- **region:** The AWS region where the event occurred.
- **resources:** An array of resource ARNs related to the event.
- **detail:** The detailed information about the event. In this example, we have a custom event with the detail type `MyCustomEvent` and the event source `com.example.myapp`. The event occurred in the "us-west-2" region of AWS, and the resources array contains the ARN of the S3 bucket "my-bucket". The detail section provides additional information specific to this event, such as the event name `PutObject`, the bucket name "my-bucket", the object key "example.txt", and the user identity "A1B2C3D4E5F6G7H8I9J0".

You can customize the content of the custom event according to your specific use case and application needs. When publishing custom events to Amazon EventBridge, you can use the PutEvents API or SDKs provided by AWS in various programming languages.

### 5.6.3.2 Integration of Amazon GuardDuty and AWS Security Hub

Amazon GuardDuty and AWS Security Hub use Amazon EventBridge to deliver their findings. GuardDuty delivers new events to EventBridge within five minutes and updates recurrent events based on a configured export frequency to S3.

For AWS Security Hub integration with EventBridge, there are two options: using the default bus or configuring custom actions. Custom actions involve setting a unique ID related to the custom action name in Security Hub. When findings are sent to EventBridge, attributes distinguish these events as custom actions with the unique ID, allowing EventBridge to apply different actions based on defined patterns. This allows applying custom actions for up to 20 findings and 100 resource identifiers simultaneously.

## Summary

Detection services are fundamental for enhancing cloud security and implementing AWS Cloud Security principles effectively. These services align with security principles and help organizations adopt robust security practices.

AWS Trusted Advisor recommends security best practices, including IAM policies and permissions. AWS CloudTrail tracks API calls to AWS Key Management Service (KMS), monitoring key usage and unauthorized access attempts. AWS Config detects unencrypted resources and configuration changes affecting encryption. Amazon GuardDuty identifies data breaches and suspicious activities, while AWS Security Hub provides a comprehensive view of security findings, including data protection issues.

Amazon CloudWatch monitors resources and applications, allowing alarms and notifications for potential security issues. AWS Config records configuration changes and tracks resource history. Amazon GuardDuty offers real-time threat detection and automated remediation actions, while AWS Systems Manager Automation creates automated responses to security findings.

These detection services monitor resources and maintain an up-to-date status, covering both AWS's and the user's responsibilities. They capture events as observable records, process them using cloud analytics, and produce security insights. Additionally, they can automatically respond to different situations to remediate findings, leveraging cloud integration capabilities.

## 5.7 Lab Exercises
### 5.7.1 How to Enable Configuration Recorder

To enable AWS Configuration Recorder, on the AWS Config page, on the left side, click on Settings. By default, the Recorder is off. You may find that you go AWS Config, it can ask you to set up or set up with 1-click.

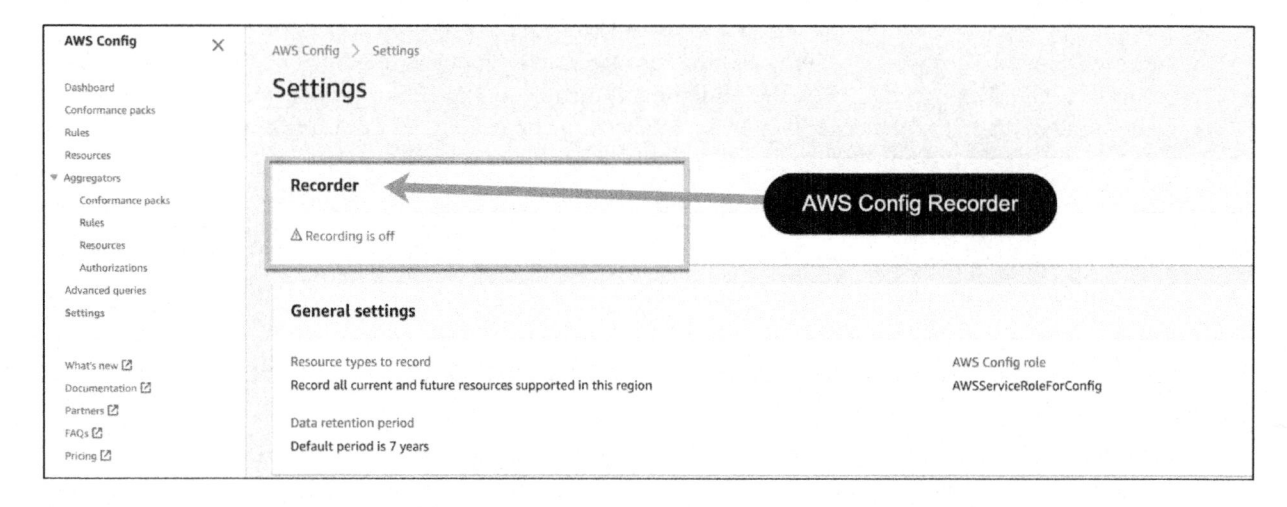

To turn on the Recorder, click on the Edit button (on the top right side) on the Settings page and make sure "Enable recording" is checked. You will have to configure if you need to record all current and future resources or specific resource types. You need to configure the retention period (default is 7 years), or you can also set a custom retention period.

You will have to configure the config rule. Here, you can use the existing AWS Config service-lined rule or choose from your account. Additionally, you need to define the delivery method: Amazon S3 and SNS topic *(if you need to stream configuration changes and notifications to an Amazon SNS topic)*. You can also define the Amazon CloudWatch Events rule. And then click on the Save button. This will turn your AWS Configuration Recorder.

After the configuration recorder is successfully enabled, it starts tracking changes of the monitored resources by recording when a change is detected either in the monitored resource or in the configuration of any of its related resources (both of them charged – change in relationship or change in the configuration of monitored resources).

To check the Configuration Recorder status – whether it is enabled it or not in your account -- you can use AWS CLI command: *aws configservice describe-configuration-recorder-status*

```
sksingh:~$ aws configservice describe-configuration-recorder-status
{
    "ConfigurationRecordersStatus": [
        {
            "name": "default",
            "lastStartTime": 1683225422.523,
            "recording": true,
            "lastStatus": "SUCCESS",
            "lastStatusChangeTime": 1683229034.781
        }
    ]
}
```

For example, as you see in the screenshot about that, the Config Recorder is enabled in my account. Once the Configuration Recorder is turned on, it starts storing each monitored resource's configuration and updates any detected changes.

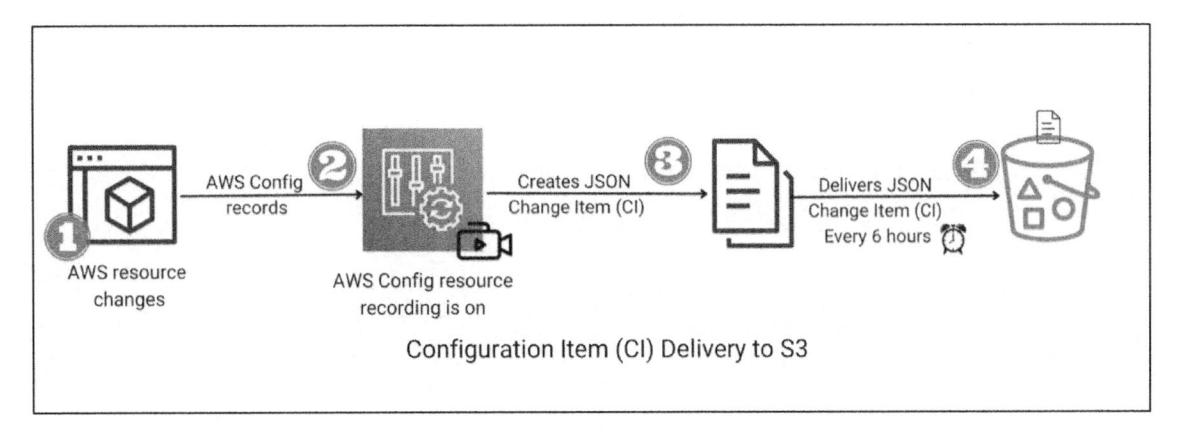

Configuration Item (CI) Delivery to S3

After every 6 hours, the AWS Config service uploads the history of change items to the S3 bucket as well, which you configure when turning on the recording.

146

```
{
    "version": "1.3",
    "accountId": "383246081810",
    "configurationItemCaptureTime": "2023-05-04T18:37:13.721Z",
    "configurationItemStatus": "ResourceDiscovered",
    "configurationStateId": "1683225433721",
    "configurationItemMD5Hash": "",
    "arn": "arn:aws:ec2:us-east-1:383246081810:instance/i-0a8cbf6c58ac68aec",
    "resourceType": "AWS::EC2::Instance",
    "resourceId": "i-0a8cbf6c58ac68aec",
    "awsRegion": "us-east-1",
    "availabilityZone": "us-east-1a",
    "resourceCreationTime": "2023-05-04T18:32:36.000Z",
    "tags": {
        "Name": "MyTestServer"
    },
    "relatedEvents": [],
    "relationships": [
        {
            "resourceType": "AWS::EC2::VPC",
            "resourceId": "vpc-ee413f93",
            "relationshipName": "Is contained in Vpc"
        },
```

The Configuration Recorder stores the changes in the monitored resources in the *configuration item* in JSON form, as shown above in a screenshot of the configuration item of a monitored resource (EC2 instance). The JSON file about the configuration item contains information metadata, attributes (such as resourceId, ARN, awsRegion, availabilityZone, resourceCreationTime, tags), relationships, and current configuration.

```
"relationships": [
    {
        "resourceType": "AWS::EC2::VPC",
        "resourceId": "vpc-ee413f93",
        "relationshipName": "Is contained in Vpc"
    },
    {
        "resourceType": "AWS::EC2::SecurityGroup",
        "resourceId": "sg-05a7016cc9febe9b6",
        "relationshipName": "Is associated with SecurityGroup"
    },
    {
        "resourceType": "AWS::EC2::Subnet",
        "resourceId": "subnet-9a1931bb",
        "relationshipName": "Is contained in Subnet"
    },
    {
        "resourceType": "AWS::EC2::Volume",
        "resourceId": "vol-09b9f74774610aafc",
        "relationshipName": "Is attached to Volume"
    },
    {
        "resourceType": "AWS::EC2::NetworkInterface",
        "resourceId": "eni-0b9757c04282cba3d",
        "relationshipName": "Contains NetworkInterface"
    }
],
```

Let's talk about the relationships section of the configuration item in the JSON, as shown in the partial screenshot of a monitored EC2 resource.

Relationships element contains different relationships (connections) that the monitored resource has. For example, in the screenshot, the EC2 instance has a relationship with the VPC (the VPC in which it is launched), and the instance has a relationship with the security group as this security group is attached to the instance. And there are other relationships also shown in the screenshot for this monitored resource, such as Volume, NetworkInterface etc. The key point to note down is that you can find the current configuration of each monitored resource in AWS Config under the Resources menu (AWS Config >Resources > resourceID). You can also use BatchGetResourceConfig API.

**Advanced Queries**
You can also use SQL-Like syntax to query the current configuration of the monitored resource.

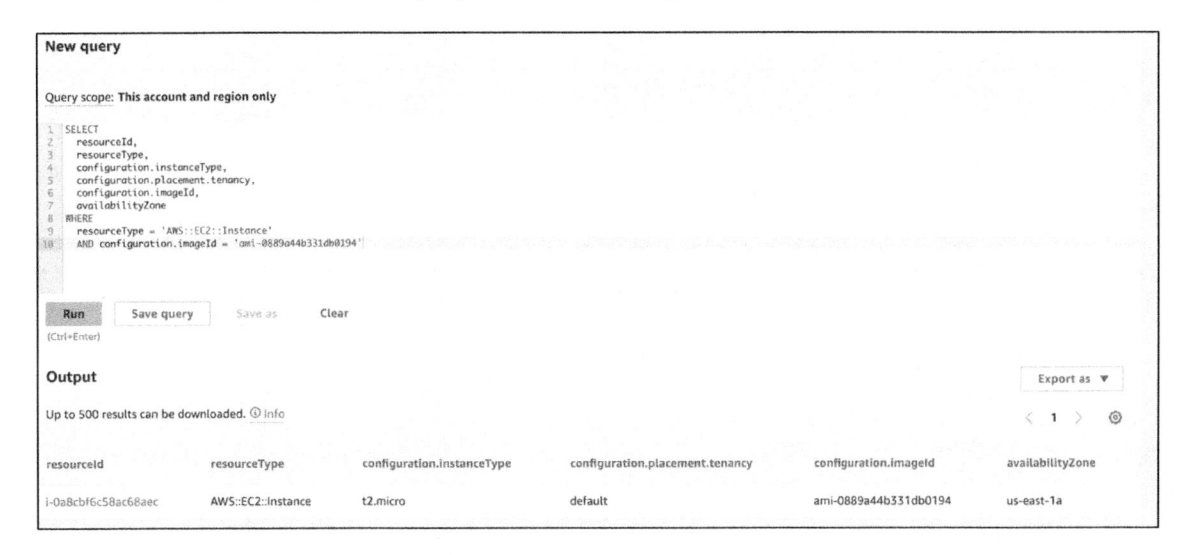

In the screenshot given about, SQL query is executed directly with the AWS Management Console. However, you can also use SelectResourceConfig API.

**Configuration Snapshot of Monitored Resource in Amazon S3**
AWS Config can provide a configuration snapshot of all monitored resources in the Amazon S3 bucket. This bucket you define at the time of enabling the config recording.

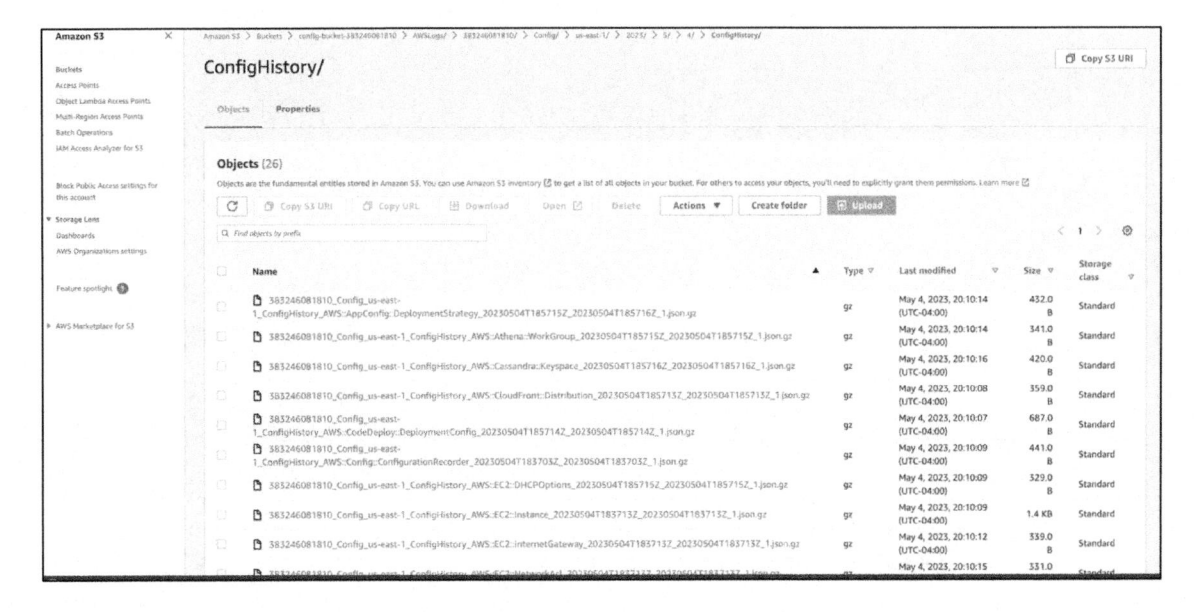

You can also manually create such a configuration snapshot by calling the DeliverConfigSnapshot API.

### View Configuration Item and Resource Timeline
View Configuration item and Resource Timeline are two important items on the AWS Config I would like to discuss regarding the recourse state of detective control.

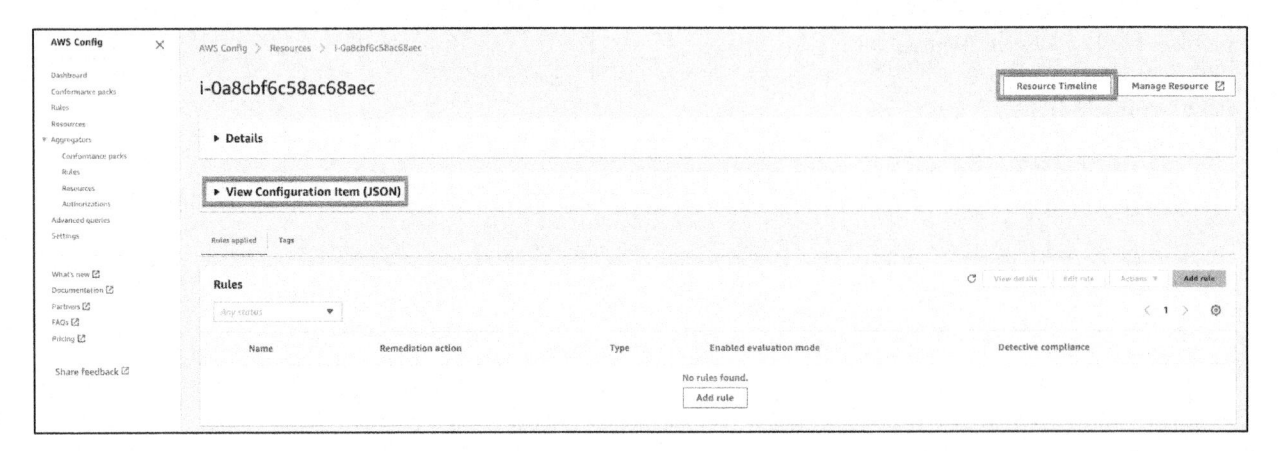

Using the View Configuration item, you can find the very detailed current configuration of the resource, as we talked about earlier when talking about Configuration Recorder.

The other important item is Resource Time, which is extremely important as we can find here the history of all the changes in a resource, and along with AuditTrail [who did it, source, the timing of the change, etc.] of the resource.

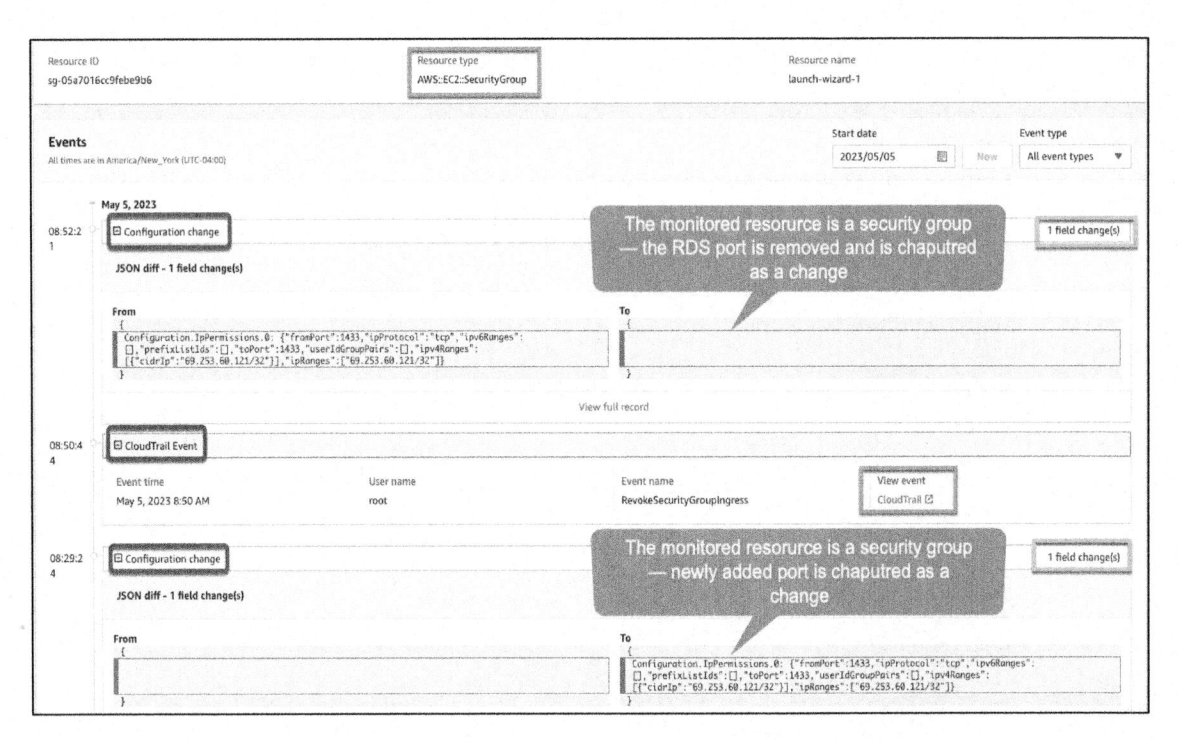

As you can see in the screenshot above for the Resource Timeline of a Security Group, it shows that the RDS port is added, and then that port is removed. The point is that Resource Time shows the capture change on the resource. You can also click on the CloudTrail link to find the audit aspect of the change: who did that, what time etc.

AWS Certified Security – Specialty Exam Guide

## 5.7.2 How to Set Up a Trail in CloudTrail

You can practice how to create Tail in your AWS account. Setting up a trail in AWS CloudTrail involves a few straightforward steps. Trails are configurations that enable CloudTrail to record and store event logs for your AWS account. Here's steps about how to set up a trail in CloudTrail:

**Sign in to the AWS Management Console:** Go to the AWS Management Console (https://aws.amazon.com/console/) and sign in to your AWS account using your credentials.

**Open the CloudTrail Service:** Once logged in, navigate to the CloudTrail service by searching for "CloudTrail" in the AWS Management Console's search bar, or you can find it under the "Management & Governance" section.

**Create a New Trail:** In the CloudTrail dashboard, click on the "Trails" link in the left navigation pane. Then click the "Create trail" button.

**Configure Trail Settings:** Provide a name for your trail to identify it uniquely. You can also choose an S3 bucket where you want the CloudTrail logs to be stored. If you haven't created an S3 bucket for this purpose, you can do it through the CloudTrail setup or pre-create the bucket in the S3 service. Optionally, you can also specify a prefix for the S3 log file names.

**Choose Trail Management Events:** You can select whether you want to record "Management events," which include all AWS API calls related to management operations on resources (e.g., creating, deleting, modifying), "Data events," which include specific data-level events like S3 object-level operations, or both. Make your selection based on your monitoring and auditing needs.

**Enable S3 Data Events (Optional):** If you chose to record data events in the previous step, you can now specify which S3 buckets or Lambda functions you want to monitor for data-level activity. Choose the specific resources you want to track, or you can leave this section blank to record data events for all S3 buckets and Lambda functions in your account.

**Configure Advanced Event Settings (Optional):** In this section, you can choose to enable "CloudTrail Insights" for anomaly detection and intelligent monitoring of your event data. You can also enable "Log file validation" to ensure the integrity of log files through digital signatures.

**Select CloudWatch Logs Integration (Optional):** If you want to send CloudTrail events to CloudWatch Logs for real-time monitoring and alerting, you can enable this integration and choose an existing CloudWatch Logs group or create a new one.

**Choose an Encryption Key (Optional):** You can choose to encrypt your CloudTrail logs using AWS Key Management Service (KMS). If you select this option, you can specify an existing KMS key or create a new one for encrypting your log files at rest.

**Review Settings and Create Trail:** Review all the settings you've configured for the trail. If everything looks correct, click the "Create" button to create the trail.

Once the trail is created, CloudTrail will start recording and storing event logs according to the specified settings. You can monitor the trail's activity and access the log data in the chosen S3 bucket or view it in CloudWatch Logs if you enabled that integration. You can also manage your trails, update settings, or delete trails through the CloudTrail dashboard in the AWS Management Console.

## 5.7.3 Create Amazon CloudWatch Alarm

Let's do a hands-on exercise of setting up an Amazon CloudWatch alarm.

CloudWatch Alarms allow you to monitor metrics and trigger actions or notifications when certain threshold conditions are met. The following are the steps:

**Sign into the AWS Management Console:** Go to the AWS Management Console (and sign in to your AWS account using your credentials.

**Open the CloudWatch Service:** Once logged in, navigate to the CloudWatch service by searching for "CloudWatch" in the AWS Management Console's search bar, or you can find it under the "Management & Governance" section.

**Select "Alarms" from the CloudWatch Dashboard:** In the CloudWatch dashboard, click "Alarms" in the left navigation pane. This will take you to the Alarms page, where you can manage your alarms.

**Create Alarm:** Click on the "Create alarm" button to start creating a new CloudWatch Alarm.

**Select a Metric:** Choose the metric you want to monitor and set up an alarm for. You can select from pre-existing metrics or create custom metrics.

**Define the Conditions:** Set the conditions for the alarm based on the chosen metric. You can specify the threshold value, comparison operator (greater than, less than, etc.), and the duration for which the condition must be met.

**Choose Actions:** Select the actions to be taken when the alarm state is triggered. You can send a notification to an Amazon SNS topic, stop or terminate an Amazon EC2 instance, or invoke an AWS Lambda function, among other options.

**Configure the Alarm Name and Description:** Provide a descriptive name and optional description for the alarm to help identify its purpose and context.

**Set Up Alarm State Actions:** You can choose to configure actions for the alarm's various states, such as "OK," "ALARM," or "INSUFFICIENT_DATA." For example, you can set up an action to automatically recover the resource when it enters the "ALARM" state. This is an optional step.

**Review and Create the Alarm:** Review all the settings you've configured for the alarm. If everything looks correct, click the "Create alarm" button to create the CloudWatch Alarm.

Once the CloudWatch Alarm is created, it will start monitoring the specified metric. If the conditions that are set for the alarm are met, the state will be transitioned to the "ALARM" state, and the configured actions will be triggered. If the conditions are no longer met, the alarm will transition back to the "OK" state.

You can manage your CloudWatch Alarms from the CloudWatch console and modify or delete them as needed. CloudWatch Alarms helps you proactively monitor your AWS resources and automate responses to potential issues or events.

## 5.7.4 AWS CloudTrail and CloudWatch Logs integration

AWS CloudTrail and Amazon CloudWatch Logs can be integrated to deliver events to a log group. This integration allows you to centralize and analyze the AWS CloudTrail event logs using the powerful capabilities of Amazon CloudWatch Logs. You can set up AWS CloudTrail to deliver events to a log group in Amazon CloudWatch Logs:

**Create a CloudWatch Logs Log Group**: First, if you haven't already done so, start by creating a log group in Amazon CloudWatch Logs to store the CloudTrail events. You can create a log group using the AWS Management Console or the AWS Command Line Interface (CLI).

**Create an S3 Bucket for CloudTrail Logs:** Ensure that you have an S3 bucket configured to receive CloudTrail logs. If you don't have an S3 bucket, you can create one using the AWS Management Console or the AWS CLI.

**Enable CloudTrail and Configure Logging:** In the AWS Management Console, navigate to the AWS CloudTrail service. Create or select a trail that captures the AWS API events you want to monitor and log. Ensure that you choose the "Yes" option for "Create a new S3 bucket" or "Specify an existing S3 bucket for log file delivery." Select the S3 bucket you created in the previous step.

**Configure CloudWatch Logs Integration**: In the CloudTrail trail configuration, under "CloudWatch Logs," select "Yes" to enable CloudWatch Logs integration. Choose the CloudWatch Logs log group where you want to send the CloudTrail events.

**Create the CloudTrail Trail:** Review your CloudTrail trail settings and create the trail. After creating the trail, it will start delivering CloudTrail events to the specified log group in Amazon CloudWatch Logs.

**Accessing and Analyzing CloudTrail Events**: Once CloudTrail events are delivered to the log group in CloudWatch Logs, you can use CloudWatch Logs Insights to query and analyze the log data. CloudWatch Logs Insights provides a powerful and interactive query language that allows you to search, filter, and analyze log events based on specific patterns or fields.

By integrating AWS CloudTrail with Amazon CloudWatch Logs, you can efficiently monitor, search, and analyze your AWS API activity and log data in a centralized and structured manner. This integration is beneficial for security, compliance, and operational purposes, providing real-time visibility into AWS account activity and helping you detect and respond to potential security threats or operational issues.

## 5.7.5 Enable Amazon GuardDuty in Your AWS Account

Enabling Amazon GuardDuty in your AWS account is a simple process that you can through the AWS Management Console. The steps are provided below:

**Sign in to the AWS Management Console:** Go to the AWS Management Console (and sign in to your AWS account using your credentials.

**Open the GuardDuty Service:** Once logged in, navigate to the Amazon GuardDuty service by searching for "GuardDuty" in the AWS Management Console's search bar.

**Choose Your AWS Region:** Ensure you are in the desired AWS region where you want to enable GuardDuty. GuardDuty operates independently in each region, so you need to enable it separately for each region if needed.

**Enable GuardDuty:** In the GuardDuty console, you will see an introduction screen that provides information about the service. You will notice a message "You can evaluate GuardDuty and its threat detection capabilities with a 30-day free trial." Click on Get Started button. Click on the "Get Started" button to proceed with enabling GuardDuty.

**Review and Enable GuardDuty:** Here you can view Service role permissions and pricing. You can click on the "Enable GuardDuty" button to enable the service for the account and the selected Region.

**Wait for Activation:** After enabling GuardDuty, it may take a few minutes for the service to become active and start analyzing events to detect potential threats and security issues.

Once GuardDuty is enabled, it will automatically start analyzing AWS CloudTrail logs, VPC Flow Logs, and DNS logs to identify suspicious activities and potential threats in your AWS environment. You can access the findings in the GuardDuty console and take appropriate actions to address any security concerns. Additionally, you can integrate GuardDuty with other AWS services, such as AWS CloudWatch and AWS Security Hub, for enhanced security monitoring and response capabilities.

## 5.7.6 How to Enable AWS Security Hub in your AWS Account

You can enable AWS Security Hub in your AWS account through the AWS Management Console. Here are the steps about how to enable AWS Security Hub:

**Sign in to the AWS Management Console:** Go to the AWS Management Console (https://aws.amazon.com/console/) and sign in to your AWS account using your credentials.

**Open the Security Hub Service:** Once logged in, navigate to the AWS Security Hub service by searching for "Security Hub" in the AWS Management Console's search bar.

**Set Up AWS Security Hub**: In the Security Hub console, you will see an introduction screen that provides information about the service. Click on the "Go to Security Hub" button to start the setup process.

**Choose Your AWS Region:** Select the AWS region in which you want to enable Security Hub. Note that Security Hub operates independently in each region, so you may need to enable it separately for multiple regions if required.

**Enable Security Hub:** You can enable AWS Security Hub for the current AWS account on the next screen. You will also need to enable AWS Config if you have not enabled it. You will need to select Security Standards (default AWS Foundational Security Best Practices v1.0.0 and CIS AWS Foundations Benchmark v1.2.0 are checked.) Click on the "Enable Security Hub" button to enable the service for your account(s).

Wait for Activation: After enabling AWS Security Hub, it may take a few moments for the service to become active and start collecting and analyzing security findings from integrated services and partners.

**Configure Settings (Optional):** Once Security Hub is enabled, you can further configure settings such as automated response actions, custom insights, and custom actions based on your organization's security requirements.

## 5.7.7 AWS Config Rules Remediation

In this exercise, you will learn how to configure an AWS Config Rule to take action when a resource is reported to be in non-compliant status.

To configure an AWS Config rule to take action when a resource is reported to be in a non-compliant status, you can use AWS Config's Remediation actions feature. Remediation actions automatically correct the non-compliant resources based on the rules you define. Here are the steps about how to set up a remediation action for a non-compliant resource using AWS Config:

**Enable AWS Config:** First, ensure that AWS Config is enabled for your AWS account and the desired AWS resources. You can enable AWS Config through the AWS Management Console or AWS CLI commands.

**Create an AWS Config Rule:** Create an AWS Config rule that checks for compliance with the specific resource or resource type you want to monitor. You can create a custom rule or use one of the built-in AWS-managed rules. For example, you could use a managed rule like "required-tags" to check for compliance with specific resource tags.

**Enable Remediation for the Rule:** In the AWS Config console, select the rule you want to configure for remediation. In the rule details page, look for the "Remediation action" section, and click the "Add remediation action" button.

**Configure Remediation Action:** In the "Add remediation action" window, select the type of remediation action you want to perform when a non-compliant resource is detected. AWS Config supports several remediation action types, including "AWS Systems Manager Automation" (to use SSM Automation documents for remediation) and "AWS Lambda Function" (to use Lambda functions for remediation).

**Configure the Parameters:** Depending on the selected remediation action type, you will need to configure the necessary parameters for the action. For example, if you choose "AWS Systems Manager Automation," you'll need to specify the SSM Automation document and any required input parameters. If you choose "AWS Lambda Function," you'll need to select the Lambda function and specify any input parameters required for the function.

**Save the Remediation Action:** After configuring the remediation action, click the "Save" button to save the settings.

**Monitor and Review:** Once the remediation action is configured, AWS Config will automatically detect non-compliant resources based on the rule evaluation. When a non-compliant resource is detected, the remediation action will be triggered, and the specified action will be taken to correct the resource automatically.

Please note that the specific steps and options may vary depending on the AWS Config rule and your remediation action type. Additionally, consider testing the remediation action in a non-production environment before implementing it in a production environment to ensure that it works as expected and does not cause unintended consequences.

## 5.7.8 AWS CloudTrail Integration with Amazon EventBridge

Integrating AWS CloudTrail with Amazon EventBridge allows you to receive and process CloudTrail events in real-time, enabling you to build event-driven workflows and take automated actions based on CloudTrail events. To set up this integration, follow these steps:

**Enable AWS CloudTrail:** If you haven't already enabled AWS CloudTrail, start by creating a new CloudTrail trail or modifying an existing one to capture the specific events you want to process. Ensure that the trail is configured to send events to CloudWatch.

**Create an Amazon EventBridge Rule:** In the AWS Management Console, navigate to the Amazon EventBridge service. Click on "Create rule" to define a new rule that will match the CloudTrail events you want to process.

**Configure Rule Details:** In the "Create rule", configure the rule details: For "Event Source," choose "Event Pattern." For "Service Name," select "CloudTrail." For "Event Type," select the specific CloudTrail event type or pattern you want to capture (e.g., "CreateTrail" or "DeleteTrail").

**Define Event Pattern (Optional):** If you want to filter events based on specific criteria, you can define an event pattern. You can filter based on attributes like the resource, region, or event name. If you want to capture all events of a certain type, you can leave this step empty.

**Add Target:** After defining the event pattern (if needed), click on "Add target" to specify what action should be taken when the CloudTrail event matches the rule. You have several target options, such as AWS Lambda function, Step Functions, SNS topic, etc. For example, you can choose a Lambda function to process the CloudTrail event.

**Configure Target Parameters:** If you selected a Lambda function as the target, specify the input parameters that should be passed to the function when the event is processed. These parameters can include event details and context.

**Enable the Rule:** Once you've configured the rule and target, click on "Create rule" to enable the integration between AWS CloudTrail and Amazon EventBridge.

Now, whenever a CloudTrail event that matches the rule is generated, it will be forwarded to Amazon EventBridge and processed according to the target you defined. For example, if you selected a Lambda function as the target, the Lambda function will be triggered and receive the CloudTrail event as input, allowing you to take automated actions based on the event.

## 5.8 Key Exam Tips

**Understanding Detective Controls:** Detective controls help detect security violations and events in real time. Be familiar with how AWS security detective controls work, such as AWS Config, CloudTrail, Amazon CloudWatch, and AWS Security Hub, and know how they integrate for a comprehensive security monitoring solution.

**AWS Config and Configuration Recorder:** Know how AWS Config continuously records configurations of AWS resources and provides an audit trail for compliance purposes. Understand the importance of the Configuration Recorder, which records changes in resource configurations and helps detect misconfigurations or non-compliance in real time.

**AWS CloudTrail:** CloudTrail is crucial for tracking API calls and actions across your AWS account. Ensure you understand CloudTrail event types and the integration with other AWS services like CloudWatch Logs for real-time monitoring. Be familiar with how CloudTrail stores logs securely and integrates with AWS Organizations for multi-account logging.

**Amazon CloudWatch Logs:** CloudWatch Logs play a key role in collecting and storing log data from AWS resources and applications. Understand how to create Log Groups, Log Streams, and Log Events, and how to use them to monitor resource activity and detect anomalies. Be aware of how CloudWatch Alarms are set up to notify when thresholds are breached.

**AWS Health and EventBridge:** AWS Health provides personalized information on AWS resource availability and performance. Understand how AWS Health integrates with Amazon EventBridge to automate responses to health events, helping to streamline remediation efforts.

**AWS Config Rules:** Config Rules help assess AWS resource compliance. Be prepared to answer questions on how Config Rules enforce compliance by triggering actions when resources deviate from best practices. Understand the integration of Config Rules with remediation actions, such as invoking Lambda functions to correct configuration drifts.

**Amazon GuardDuty:** GuardDuty is AWS's threat detection service. Understand how it monitors malicious or unauthorized behavior using threat intelligence and machine learning. Be prepared to explain how GuardDuty findings are categorized (e.g., low, medium, high severity), and how it integrates with AWS Security Hub for a unified security dashboard.

**Amazon Inspector:** Amazon Inspector provides automated security assessments of EC2 instances for vulnerabilities and deviations from best practices. Familiarize yourself with how Inspector assessment templates work and how findings are reported and remediated.

**AWS Systems Manager:** AWS Systems Manager provides operational data and automation capabilities for AWS resources. Learn how SSM Automation is used for automated remediation workflows based on security events. For example, how Systems Manager can apply patches or update configurations automatically in response to a security incident.

## 5.9 Chapter Review Questions

**Question 1:**
Which of the following is the primary purpose of AWS Config?
A. To automatically fix security vulnerabilities
B. To assess, audit, and evaluate the configurations of AWS resources
C. To store and manage user credentials securely
D. To automate patch management across AWS resources

**Question 2:**
What is the role of AWS CloudTrail in detective controls?
A. To monitor real-time performance metrics of applications
B. To log and record API calls made within an AWS environment
C. To enforce encryption on all AWS resources
D. To optimize costs and resource utilization

**Question 3:**
Which service provides continuous security assessments to help identify vulnerabilities in your AWS infrastructure?
A. Amazon GuardDuty
B. AWS Systems Manager
C. Amazon Inspector
D. AWS Security Hub

**Question 4:**
What are CloudTrail event types used for?
A. To encrypt CloudTrail logs automatically
B. To categorize and organize different types of AWS API activity logs
C. To monitor user login activities only
D. To ensure CloudTrail records are deleted after 30 days

**Question 5:**
Which service can you use to create customizable Config Rules to evaluate compliance of your AWS resources?

A. AWS Systems Manager
B. Amazon CloudWatch
C. AWS Config
D. Amazon GuardDuty

**Question 6:**
What is the purpose of Amazon GuardDuty?
A. To provide detailed access control policies for resources
B. To provide continuous threat detection and monitoring for malicious activities
C. To create audit reports for compliance
D. To automatically encrypt all data stored in AWS services

**Question 7:**
How does Amazon EventBridge help in the Action stage of detective controls?
A. By sending email alerts for security violations
B. By responding to events and triggering automated workflows based on security events
C. By creating IAM roles for security administrators
D. By storing detailed logs in CloudWatch Logs

**Question 8:**
Which service is designed to aggregate findings from multiple AWS security services like GuardDuty, Inspector, and AWS Config for a unified security view?
A. AWS CloudTrail
B. AWS Security Hub
C. AWS Systems Manager
D. AWS Config Rules

**Question 9:**
What is the primary function of AWS CloudWatch Logs?
A. To monitor and collect log data from AWS resources and applications
B. To store IAM roles for security auditing
C. To evaluate the effectiveness of security policies
D. To provide encryption of stored log data

**Question 10:**
Which tool would you use to automate the remediation of non-compliant AWS resources detected by AWS Config rules?
A. AWS Security Hub
B. Amazon GuardDuty
C. AWS Systems Manager Automation
D. AWS CloudTrail

**Question 11:**
Your organization has deployed multiple resources in AWS, and you need to ensure that all EC2 instances comply with security configuration requirements. You want to be notified whenever a configuration deviates from the defined security policy. Which service should you use to continuously monitor and enforce these configuration standards?
A. Amazon CloudWatch
B. AWS CloudTrail
C. AWS Config
D. Amazon GuardDuty

**Question 12:**
You are conducting a security audit for your AWS environment and need to review all the API activity in your account over the last three months. This includes changes to IAM policies and S3 bucket configurations. Which AWS service would you use to gather this historical data?
A. Amazon CloudWatch Logs
B. AWS Config
C. AWS CloudTrail
D. AWS Systems Manager

**Question 13:**
You have been alerted by Amazon GuardDuty of a potential unauthorized login attempt from an unusual IP address. You want to investigate which other resources or services this IP has interacted with in the past. Which service will provide detailed logging of API calls across your AWS resources?
A. AWS CloudTrail
B. Amazon CloudWatch
C. AWS Security Hub
D. AWS Health

**Question 14:**
You have set up AWS Config to monitor the compliance of your AWS resources. Recently, an EC2 instance was found to be non-compliant with the security group's inbound rules. You want to automatically remediate this issue by updating the security group. Which AWS service should you use to automate this remediation process?
A. Amazon EventBridge
B. AWS Systems Manager Automation
C. AWS CloudTrail
D. Amazon Inspector

**Question 15:**
Your team is using Amazon GuardDuty and AWS Security Hub to monitor and analyze security threats in your AWS environment. A specific threat was detected, and you need to trigger a response workflow to mitigate the risk. Which AWS service should you use to create and manage an automated response to this security event?
A. AWS Config
B. AWS Systems Manager Automation
C. Amazon EventBridge
D. Amazon CloudWatch

## 5.10 Answers to Chapter Review Questions

1. B. To assess, audit, and evaluate the configurations of AWS resources
Explanation: AWS Config enables you to continuously monitor and record AWS resource configurations and helps you evaluate whether these configurations comply with your security policies.

2. B. To log and record API calls made within an AWS environment
Explanation: AWS CloudTrail records and logs API activity and account events within an AWS environment, providing visibility into user actions for auditing and troubleshooting.

3. C. Amazon Inspector
Explanation: Amazon Inspector provides automated security assessments of applications running on AWS, helping to identify vulnerabilities and assess compliance with best practices.

4. B. To categorize and organize different types of AWS API activity logs

Explanation: CloudTrail event types categorize different API activities, such as management events and data events, helping you track and audit AWS API calls.

5. C. AWS Config
Explanation: AWS Config allows you to define Config Rules to evaluate the compliance of your AWS resources based on internal and external security policies.

6. B. To provide continuous threat detection and monitoring for malicious activities
Explanation: Amazon GuardDuty is a managed threat detection service that continuously monitors for malicious activities and unauthorized behavior across AWS accounts.

7. B. By responding to events and triggering automated workflows based on security events
Explanation: Amazon EventBridge helps automate responses to specific security events by triggering workflows, such as executing Lambda functions, when particular conditions are met.

8. B. AWS Security Hub
Explanation: AWS Security Hub aggregates and centralizes security findings from multiple AWS services (like GuardDuty, Inspector, and Config) to provide a unified view of security posture.

9. A. To monitor and collect log data from AWS resources and applications
Explanation: AWS CloudWatch Logs is used to monitor, store, and access log data generated by applications, services, and AWS resources.

10. C. AWS Systems Manager Automation
Explanation: AWS Systems Manager Automation can be used to automatically remediate non-compliant resources identified by AWS Config Rules, ensuring that security best practices are enforced across your environment.

11. C. AWS Config
Explanation: AWS Config provides continuous monitoring of AWS resources, ensuring that they comply with security policies. It allows you to set up Config Rules that trigger notifications or actions when resources deviate from the defined standards.

12. C. AWS CloudTrail
Explanation: AWS CloudTrail logs all API calls made in your AWS environment, including changes to IAM policies, S3 configurations, and other activities. You can review historical data of the past three months to audit API actions.

13. A. AWS CloudTrail
Explanation: AWS CloudTrail provides a detailed log of all API activity in your AWS environment. It will allow you to trace the activities associated with the unusual IP address across multiple resources.

14. B. AWS Systems Manager Automation
Explanation: AWS Systems Manager Automation allows you to automate the remediation of non-compliant resources. In this case, you can configure automation to update the security group rules when a compliance issue is detected by AWS Config.

15. C. Amazon EventBridge
Explanation: Amazon EventBridge allows you to create event-driven workflows. It can be used to automatically trigger responses, such as running a Lambda function or initiating a remediation process, in response to security threats detected by GuardDuty or Security Hub.

# Chapter 6. Threat Detection and Incident Response

**This chapter addresses the following exam objectives:**
Domain 1: Threat Detection and Incident Response
Task Statement 1.1: Design and implement an incident response plan.
Knowledge of:
- AWS best practices for incident response
- Cloud incidents
- Roles and responsibilities in the incident response plan
- AWS Security Finding Format (ASFF)

Skills in:
Implementing credential invalidation and rotation strategies in response to compromises (for example, by using AWS Identity and Access Management [IAM] and AWS Secrets Manager)
- Isolating AWS resources
- Designing and implementing playbooks and runbooks for responses to security incidents
- Deploying security services (for example, AWS Security Hub, Amazon Macie,
- Amazon GuardDuty, Amazon Inspector, AWS Config, Amazon Detective,
- AWS Identity and Access Management Access Analyzer)
- Configuring integrations with native AWS services and third-party services
- (for example, by using Amazon EventBridge and the ASFF)

◆◆◆◆◆◆

In the ever-evolving landscape of cloud security, the ability to detect threats and respond effectively to incidents is paramount. This chapter delves into the essential strategies and tools for managing security incidents within AWS environments. This chapter provides a comprehensive guide to designing, implementing, and continually improving your incident response capabilities to safeguard your AWS resources.

We begin with an introduction to threat detection and incident response, highlighting the critical need for proactive and reactive measures in maintaining cloud security. The chapter then guides you through designing an incident response plan, following AWS best practices. Understanding cloud-specific incidents and clearly defining roles and responsibilities in incident response are crucial components of this planning process. We also explore the AWS Security Finding Format (ASFF), which standardizes security findings for better integration and response.

Implementing incident response strategies involves several key actions, including credential invalidation and rotation, and isolating compromised AWS resources. These strategies are essential for mitigating the impact of security breaches and preventing further damage.

The chapter also covers the creation and use of playbooks and runbooks, which provide structured procedures for responding to various types of security incidents. Designing effective playbooks and runbooks ensures that your response teams can act quickly and efficiently during an incident.

Deploying AWS security services is a critical part of threat detection and incident response. We provide an in-depth look at services such as AWS Security Hub, Amazon GuardDuty, Amazon Macie, Amazon Inspector, AWS Config, Amazon Detective, and AWS IAM Access Analyzer. Each service offers unique capabilities for detecting and responding to security threats.

Configuring integrations with native and third-party services enhances the effectiveness of your incident response strategies. Using Amazon EventBridge and integrating AWS services with third-party tools can streamline your security operations and improve response times.

Best practices for threat detection and incident response are emphasized throughout the chapter, including continuous monitoring and alerting, conducting regular incident response drills, and performing post-incident analysis and improvement. These practices ensure that your incident response plan remains effective and evolves with emerging threats.

To reinforce the theoretical concepts, the chapter concludes with lab exercises that provide hands-on experience in creating an incident response plan, deploying AWS security services, configuring event-driven security automation, and simulating and responding to security incidents. These exercises are designed to enhance your practical skills and prepare you for real-world security challenges.

By the end of this chapter, readers will have a thorough understanding of how to design, implement, and improve threat detection and incident response strategies within AWS, ensuring robust protection for their cloud environments.

## 6.1 Introduction to Threat Detection and Incident Response

In AWS environments, threat detection and incident response are critical components of maintaining a secure and resilient infrastructure. Threat detection involves continuously monitoring the environment to identify potential security threats and anomalies. This is particularly crucial in a cloud context where resources are dynamic, constantly changing, and can be accessed from various locations. Therefore, it is imperative to have real-time visibility into the security posture, ensuring that any unusual activity is quickly identified and addressed.

On the other hand, incident response is the process of managing and addressing security breaches or attacks. A robust incident response strategy is essential to mitigate the impact of security incidents, prevent data loss, and ensure business continuity. This strategy should include predefined plans and procedures for identifying, containing, and eradicating threats, steps for recovering from incidents, and post-incident analysis to prevent future occurrences.

The importance of these processes in AWS environments cannot be overstated, as they help organizations protect sensitive data, comply with regulatory requirements, and maintain customer trust. Key concepts in threat detection and incident response include the use of AWS services like Amazon GuardDuty for threat detection, AWS CloudTrail for logging and monitoring, and AWS Security Hub for centralized security management. These tools, combined with a well-defined incident response plan, enable organizations to effectively detect, respond to, and recover from security incidents, enhancing their AWS environments' overall security posture.

## 6.2 Designing an Incident Response Plan

In today's digital landscape, the ability to swiftly and effectively respond to security incidents is crucial for maintaining the integrity and availability of organizational assets. Designing a robust incident response plan involves detecting, analyzing, and mitigating security threats. This plan ensures that organizations are prepared to handle incidents efficiently, minimizing potential damage and facilitating a rapid return to normal operations.

## 6.2.1 AWS Best Practices for Incident Response

AWS best practices for incident response are fundamental to ensuring a resilient and secure cloud environment. These practices revolve around a structured and proactive approach to managing security incidents.

The first crucial step is **preparation**, which involves establishing a comprehensive incident response plan and ensuring that all team members are trained and aware of their roles. This plan should include detailed response procedures, communication strategies, and escalation paths.

**Detection** is the next critical phase, where the AWS environment is continuously monitored to identify potential threats and anomalies promptly. AWS provides several tools for this purpose, such as Amazon GuardDuty, AWS CloudTrail, and AWS Config, which help detect suspicious activities and ensure that configurations comply with best security practices.

Once a potential incident is detected, the **analysis** phase begins. This involves a thorough investigation to understand the incident's scope, origin, and impact. Accurate analysis is crucial for making informed decisions on how to respond effectively. AWS CloudWatch and AWS Security Hub are instrumental in aggregating and analyzing security data to facilitate this process.

Following analysis, the **containment** phase focuses on preventing the incident from causing further damage. This could involve isolating affected resources, applying temporary security controls, or redirecting traffic. Swift containment is vital to minimize the impact of the incident.

**Eradication** involves eliminating the root cause of the incident. This might include removing malware, correcting misconfigurations, or patching vulnerabilities. Ensuring that the underlying issues are fully resolved is essential to prevent recurrence.

The final phase, **recovery**, focuses on restoring affected systems and services to normal operation. This includes validating that the environment is secure and that systems function correctly. Conducting a **post-incident review** is critical to identifying lessons learned and improving the incident response plan. Regular drills and updates to the incident response plan are also part of best practices, ensuring preparedness for future incidents.

By adhering to these AWS best practices for incident response—preparation, detection, analysis, containment, eradication, and recovery—organizations can effectively manage security incidents, minimize their impact, and enhance their overall security posture.

## 6.2.2 Understanding Cloud Incidents

Cloud incidents differ significantly from traditional on-premises incidents due to the inherent nature of cloud environments. In traditional on-premises setups, organizations have complete control over their infrastructure, including physical access to servers, networking equipment, and storage. This level of control allows for direct and immediate responses to incidents, such as isolating compromised systems or adjusting physical security measures. However, this control also comes with the responsibility of maintaining and securing the entire infrastructure, which can be resource-intensive.

Cloud environments operate on a shared responsibility model, a key concept that underlines the need for a clear understanding of roles and responsibilities. Cloud service providers (CSPs) handle the security of the cloud infrastructure, while the customers are responsible for securing their data, applications, and configurations within the cloud. This division introduces unique challenges that require a different approach to incident response.

An example of a cloud-specific incident is an Amazon S3 bucket misconfiguration that leads to data exposure. In an on-premises environment, misconfigurations might be limited to internal network permissions, but in the cloud, such errors can result in publicly accessible data if not properly secured. This highlights a significant challenge in cloud security: the ease of deploying and scaling resources can lead to oversight or misconfigurations that have wide-reaching impacts. Moreover, cloud environments are highly dynamic, with resources frequently created and destroyed, making maintaining continuous visibility and control difficult.

Another challenge in cloud environments is the potential for complex, multi-tenant scenarios where resources are shared among different customers. This necessitates robust isolation mechanisms, a critical component that prevents one customer's incident from affecting others. Additionally, cloud incidents can involve sophisticated attack vectors like account hijacking, where attackers gain access to cloud accounts through compromised credentials, exploiting the extensive privileges often associated with these accounts.

The ephemeral nature of cloud resources also complicates incident response. For example, an attacker might use auto-scaling features to propagate malicious instances rapidly, making it challenging to track and contain the threat. Moreover, the integration of various cloud services and APIs can introduce additional vulnerabilities, requiring vigilant monitoring and security practices.

In summary, while cloud environments offer flexibility, scalability, and reduced infrastructure management burdens, they also introduce specific challenges such as visibility, control, and the need for stringent configuration management. Addressing these challenges requires a deep understanding of the cloud provider's security model, continuous monitoring, and robust incident response strategies tailored to the cloud's unique characteristics.

## 6.2.3 Roles and Responsibilities in Incident Response

Defining roles and responsibilities within an incident response team is essential for clear accountability and effective coordination during incidents. An incident response team comprises members with distinct roles that contribute to a comprehensive response strategy. The Incident Response Manager oversees the entire process, coordinating team efforts and communicating with senior management to ensure the response plan is executed effectively and actions are documented. Security Analysts are on the frontline, monitoring systems for suspicious activity, analyzing threats, determining the scope and impact of incidents, gathering and preserving evidence, performing forensic analysis, and providing detailed reports.

Forensic Investigators specialize in in-depth analysis, performing digital forensics to understand the nature of attacks, how they were executed, and what data or systems were compromised. IT Support staff offer technical assistance, implementing containment measures, applying patches, and restoring systems to operational status while ensuring backups are functional for quick recovery. Legal and Compliance Officers ensure adherence to relevant laws and regulations, handling legal implications, such as data breach notifications, and guiding the team on compliance issues to avoid legal repercussions.

Communication Officers manage internal and external communications, ensuring accurate information dissemination to stakeholders, including employees, customers, and the media, and handling public relations to maintain the organization's reputation. The Crisis Management Team, which includes senior executives and business continuity planners, makes critical decisions about the organization's response to an incident, ensuring business operations can continue or resume quickly to minimize impact. The Incident Response Coordinator ensures all team members are informed and efforts are synchronized, facilitating communication, managing the incident response plan, and ensuring resource availability as needed.

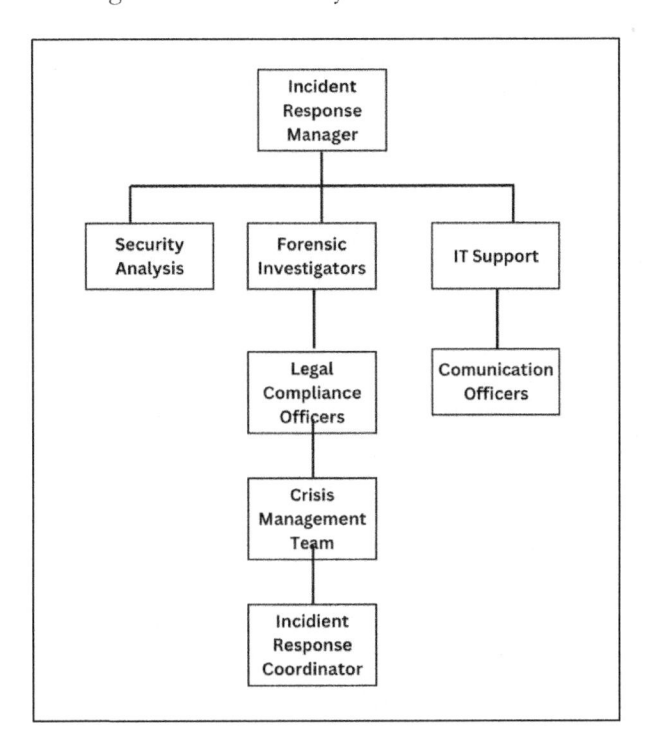

In this diagram, the Incident Response Manager is at the top, overseeing the entire operation. The Security Analysts, Forensic Investigators, and IT Support staff form the core technical team, each reporting to the Incident Response Manager. The Legal and Compliance Officers and Communication Officers provide essential support and ensure compliance and effective communication. The Crisis Management Team handles high-level decisions and business continuity, while the Incident Response Coordinator ensures that all team members are aligned and that the response is well-coordinated.

This structured approach ensures that all aspects of an incident are managed effectively, with clear responsibilities and coordinated efforts to minimize the impact and facilitate recovery.

## 6.2.4 AWS Security Finding Format (ASFF)

The Amazon Security Finding Format (ASFF) is a standardized schema used to present security findings across various AWS services and third-party tools, enabling seamless integration and interoperability. ASFF facilitates a unified view of security data, allowing security teams to efficiently manage, analyze, and respond to threats.

This format provides a structured way to capture essential details about security findings, such as the nature of the issue, its severity, affected resources, and recommended remediation steps.

ASFF is particularly valuable in environments that leverage multiple security tools and services, as it ensures that all findings are presented consistently, regardless of their source. This consistency simplifies the process of aggregating and correlating security data from diverse sources, enhancing the overall effectiveness of threat detection and incident response strategies. The key components of an ASFF finding include:

**Title:** A brief description of the security issue.

**Description:** Detailed information about the finding, including the context and potential impact.
**Severity:** The level of threat posed by the issue, typically categorized as low, medium, high, or critical.
**Resources:** Information about the affected AWS resources, such as instance IDs, S3 bucket names, or other relevant identifiers.
**Remediation:** Suggested actions to resolve the issue and mitigate risk.
**Compliance:** Information about how the finding relates to specific compliance frameworks or standards.
**Timestamp:** The time when the finding was detected.

By standardizing these elements, ASFF enables tools like Amazon GuardDuty, AWS Security Hub, and various third-party security solutions to share and process security data in a coherent manner. This integration capability helps organizations create comprehensive security dashboards, automate incident response workflows, and ensure compliance with regulatory requirements.

Here's a simple diagram illustrating how ASFF facilitates integration between AWS services and third-party tools:

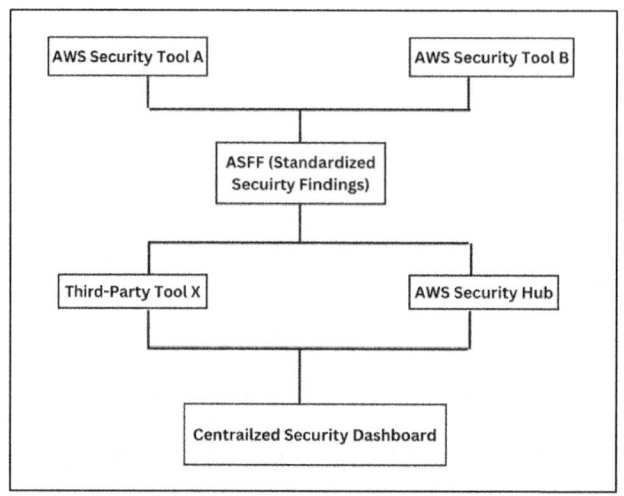

In this diagram, various AWS security tools (Tool A and Tool B) generate findings in ASFF format. These findings are then integrated into both third-party security tools and AWS Security Hub, creating a centralized security dashboard that provides a comprehensive view of the organization's security posture.

ASFF's standardized format ensures that all security findings, regardless of their source, can be interpreted and acted upon consistently, enabling more efficient threat management and incident response. This interoperability is crucial for maintaining a robust and cohesive security strategy in complex, multi-vendor environments.

# 6.3 Implementing Incident Response Strategies
## 6.3.1 Credential Invalidation and Rotation

Invalidating and rotating credentials promptly in response to compromises is a critical security practice in AWS environments. Using AWS IAM and AWS Secrets Manager, organizations can effectively manage and secure their credentials, ensuring that any compromised credentials are swiftly rendered useless and replaced with new ones.

### AWS IAM Techniques
**Disabling User Accounts:** When a user's credentials are suspected to be compromised, the first step is to disable the user account to prevent further access. This can be done through the AWS Management Console or programmatically via AWS CLI or SDKs.

**Rotating IAM Access Keys:** AWS IAM allows you to create, rotate, and disable access keys for users. When rotating access keys, follow these steps:
- Create a new access key: Generate a new access key for the IAM user.
- Update applications: Update all applications and scripts to use the new access key.
- Disable the old access key: Temporarily disable the old access key to ensure the new key works as expected.
- Delete the old access key: Once confirmed, delete the old access key to complete the rotation process.

### AWS Secrets Manager Techniques

AWS Secrets Manager can automatically rotate secrets, such as database credentials, API keys, and other sensitive information. This process involves setting up a rotation schedule and specifying a Lambda function that handles the rotation. The Lambda function updates the secret in AWS Secrets Manager and the associated resource, such as a database, with the new credentials.

For secrets requiring manual intervention, follow these steps: First, retrieve the current secret value from AWS Secrets Manager. Next, generate a new secret value, such as a new password. Then, update the associated resource with the new secret. Finally, store the new secret value in AWS Secrets Manager, replacing the old one.

When dealing with AWS IAM, you should first disable the compromised IAM user or access key to prevent unauthorized access. Then, create a new access key for the affected IAM user. Update all applications and scripts to use the new access key, verify that the new access key works as expected, and delete the old access key to finalize the rotation.

For AWS Secrets Manager, retrieve the compromised secret from the service. Generate a new secret, such as a new password or API key. Update the associated resource with the new secret and store it in AWS Secrets Manager. Verify that the resource is accessible with the new secret and delete the old secret to complete the rotation process.

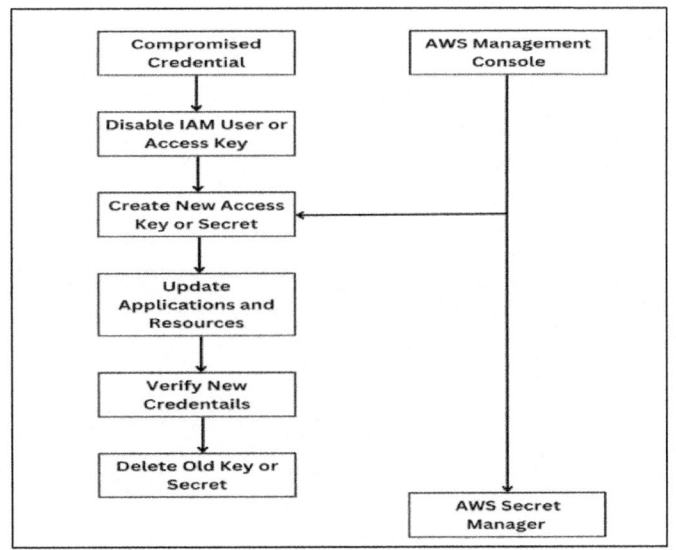

The diagram above illustrates the workflow for invalidating and rotating credentials using AWS IAM and AWS Secrets Manager.

## 6.3.2 Isolating AWS Resources

Isolating compromised resources quickly is crucial to contain the impact of a security incident in AWS environments. Effective containment methods include using security groups, network access control lists

(ACLs), and other network segmentation techniques. These tools help limit the spread of the compromise, protect unaffected resources, and provide a controlled environment for investigation and remediation.

## Security Groups

Security groups act as virtual firewalls for your EC2 instances, controlling inbound and outbound traffic. To isolate a compromised resource using security groups, follow these steps:
- **Identify the compromised instance:** Determine the specific instance or resource that has been compromised.
- **Create a new security group:** Set up a security group with restrictive rules, allowing only essential traffic or no traffic at all.
- **Attach the security group:** Apply this new security group to the compromised instance to restrict its network communication.

For example, if an EC2 instance is compromised, you can create a security group that only allows SSH access from a specific IP address (e.g., the IP address of your incident response team) and then attach this group to the compromised instance. This ensures that only authorized personnel can access the instance while investigation and remediation are underway.

## Network ACLs

Network ACLs provide an additional layer of security at the subnet level. Unlike security groups, which are stateful, network ACLs are stateless, meaning that you need to explicitly allow both inbound and outbound traffic. To isolate a compromised subnet using network ACLs:

- **Identify the compromised subnet:** Locate the subnet where the compromised resources are deployed.
- **Modify the network ACL:** Adjust the network ACL rules to block all inbound and outbound traffic to and from the compromised subnet.
- **Apply the updated ACL:** Ensure that the modified ACL is associated with the compromised subnet.

For example, if an entire subnet within your VPC is compromised, you can modify the network ACL to deny all traffic (using rules that explicitly deny all inbound and outbound IP ranges). This effectively isolates the entire subnet, preventing any communication until further investigation is conducted.

## Example Scenario

Imagine a scenario where a web server in your AWS environment has been compromised due to a vulnerability in the web application. Here's how you can isolate the compromised server:

**Create a Restrictive Security Group:**
- Allow only SSH traffic from the incident response team's IP address.
- Deny all other inbound traffic.

**Apply the Security Group:**
- Detach the existing security group from the compromised web server.
- Attach the new restrictive security group to the server.

**Modify Network ACL:**
Configure the network ACL associated with the subnet to deny all inbound and outbound traffic, effectively isolating the entire subnet if needed.

By using security groups and network ACLs, you can quickly and effectively isolate compromised resources, limiting the potential damage and providing a secure environment for remediation efforts. This layered approach enhances your ability to respond to incidents and maintain the security and integrity of your AWS environment.

## 6.4 Playbooks and Runbooks

### 6.4.1 Playbook

A playbook is a high-level document that provides a general strategy and set of guidelines for responding to specific types of incidents or scenarios. It outlines the overall approach, objectives, and roles and responsibilities of team members during an incident. Playbooks are typically used by incident response teams to ensure a consistent and coordinated response to various security threats and operational issues.

Key features of a playbook include incident identification, which describes the types of incidents the playbook covers, such as phishing attacks, malware outbreaks, and data breaches. The objectives section specifies the goals for handling the incident, like containing the threat, mitigating damage, and restoring normal operations. Roles and responsibilities are defined to clarify who is responsible for what during an incident response, such as the Incident Response Manager, Security Analysts, and IT Support. Additionally, the playbook provides high-level steps, offering a broad overview of the actions to be taken during the incident, including detection, assessment, containment, eradication, recovery, and post-incident review.

Playbooks are used in various contexts, such as Security Operations Centers (SOCs) to guide teams in responding to security incidents, IT operations to handle operational issues like system outages or performance degradation, and business continuity planning to manage responses to major disruptions like natural disasters or significant technology failures.

### 6.4.2 Runbook

A runbook is a detailed document that provides step-by-step instructions for performing specific tasks or processes. Runbooks are more granular than playbooks and are used to execute particular procedures within the broader framework provided by a playbook. They ensure that tasks are carried out consistently and accurately, often used by technical staff for routine operations, troubleshooting, and incident response.

Key features of a runbook include step-by-step instructions, which offer detailed procedures for specific tasks such as resetting a password or reconfiguring a firewall. It specifies the exact tools, scripts, and commands to be used, including antivirus software and network monitoring tools. The runbook also includes instructions for documenting actions taken, evidence collected, and outcomes achieved. Additionally, it provides guidance on troubleshooting common issues or errors that might arise during task execution.

Runbooks are used in various scenarios, such as day-to-day operations for routine tasks like system maintenance, software updates, and backups. They are also essential for incident response, handling specific incidents as part of the response outlined in a playbook, such as steps to isolate a compromised server or remediate a malware infection. Furthermore, runbooks are often used in conjunction with automation tools to script and automate repeatable tasks.

### 6.4.3 Example Scenario: Phishing Attack

**Playbook for Phishing Attack**

**Objective:** Mitigate the impact of phishing emails, protect sensitive information, and educate users.

Roles and Responsibilities:
- Incident Response Manager: Oversees the process.
- Security Analysts: Analyze the emails and identify affected accounts.
- IT Support: Assist with user account management and system clean-up.
- Communication Officer: Manages communications with stakeholders.

**High-Level Steps:**
- Detection: Identify phishing emails through user reports or automated systems.
- Assessment: Determine the scope and impact.
- Containment: Block sender and isolate affected accounts.
- Eradication: Remove phishing emails and clean systems.
- Recovery: Restore normal operations and secure accounts.
- Post-Incident Review: Analyze the incident and update training materials.

**Runbook for Phishing Attack Containment**

Detection:
- Use email security tools to scan for phishing emails.
- Instruct users to report suspicious emails.

Assessment:
- Review email headers and content to confirm phishing.
- Identify affected users and systems.

Containment:
- Block the sender's email domain in the email security system.
- Reset passwords for compromised accounts.
- Disconnect affected systems from the network.

Eradication:
- Use antivirus tools to scan and clean affected systems.
- Remove phishing emails from user inboxes.

Recovery:
- Reconnect cleaned systems to the network.
- Restore user access with new credentials.
- Monitor systems for residual compromise.

Documentation:
- Record actions taken, evidence collected, and outcomes achieved.

## 6.4.4 Designing Playbooks and Runbooks

Designing and implementing playbooks and runbooks for responding to specific types of security incidents is an essential part of an organization's incident response strategy. Playbooks provide high-level guidance on handling different categories of incidents, while runbooks offer detailed, step-by-step instructions for specific scenarios. Together, they ensure that security teams can respond quickly and effectively to various threats.

**Designing Playbooks**
- **Identify Incident Types:** Start by categorizing potential security incidents. Common categories include malware infections, data breaches, phishing attacks, DDoS attacks, and insider threats.
- **Define Objectives:** For each incident type, outline the primary objectives. For example, the objective for a data breach might be to contain the breach, protect sensitive data, and notify affected parties.
- **High-Level Response Steps:** Describe the overall approach for handling each type of incident. This includes initial detection, assessment, containment, eradication, recovery, and post-incident review.
- **Roles and Responsibilities:** Clearly define the roles and responsibilities of the incident response team members for each type of incident. Ensure that there are designated leads for different tasks such as communication, technical response, and legal compliance.

**Implementing Runbooks**
- **Detailed Procedures:** For each type of incident identified in the playbooks, create runbooks that provide detailed, step-by-step procedures. These should cover every aspect of the incident response process.

- **Tools and Commands:** Include specific tools, scripts, and commands that responders will use. For example, if dealing with malware, specify the antivirus tools and the exact commands to run scans and remove malware.
- **Communication Protocols:** Outline communication protocols, including who should be notified at each stage of the incident response and how the communication should be conducted.
- **Documentation:** Ensure that each step includes instructions for documenting actions taken, evidence collected, and decisions made. This is crucial for post-incident analysis and compliance.

## Example: Responding to a Phishing Attack
### Playbook
**Objective:** Identify and mitigate the impact of phishing emails, prevent data loss, and educate users to avoid future attacks.

**High-Level Response Steps:**
- Detection: Identify phishing emails through user reports or automated email filtering systems.
- Assessment: Determine the scope and potential impact of the phishing attack.
- Containment: Block the sender's email address and isolate affected user accounts.
- Eradication: Remove phishing emails from user inboxes and clean any compromised systems.
- Recovery: Restore normal operations and ensure that affected accounts are secure.
- Post-Incident Review: Analyze the attack to improve future defenses and update user training.

**Roles and Responsibilities:**
- Incident Response Manager: Oversees the entire response.
- Security Analysts: Perform technical analysis and remediation.
- IT Support: Assist with user account management and system clean-up.
- Communication Officer: Manages internal and external communications.
- Legal and Compliance Officer: Ensures compliance with regulatory requirements.

### Runbook
**Detection:**
- Use email security tools to scan for phishing emails.
- Instruct users to forward suspicious emails to the security team.

**Assessment:**
- Review email headers and content to confirm phishing.
- Identify affected users and systems.

**Containment:**
- Block the sender's email domain in the email security system.
- Reset passwords for compromised accounts.
- Disconnect affected systems from the network.

**Eradication:**
- Use antivirus and anti-malware tools to scan and clean affected systems.
- Remove phishing emails from all user inboxes using email administration tools.

**Recovery:**
- Reconnect cleaned systems to the network.
- Restore user access with new, secure credentials.
- Monitor affected systems for any signs of residual compromise.

**Post-Incident Review:**

- Document the incident and response actions.
- Conduct a meeting to discuss lessons learned and update training materials.
- Adjust email filters and security policies based on findings.

### Diagram: Phishing Incident Response Workflow

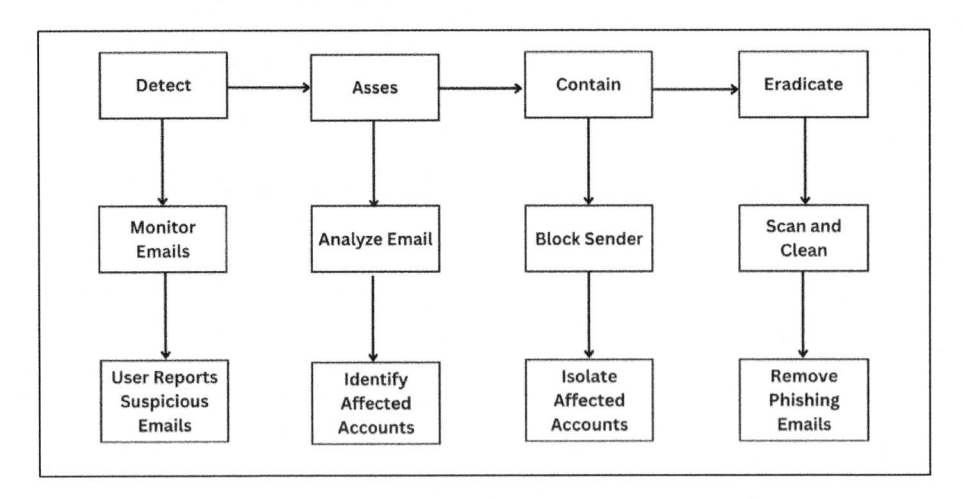

```
Detect  →  Asses  →  Contain  →  Eradicate
  ↓         ↓          ↓            ↓
Monitor   Analyze    Block       Scan and
Emails    Email     Sender        Clean
  ↓         ↓          ↓            ↓
User      Identify   Isolate      Remove
Reports   Affected   Affected     Phishing
Suspicious Accounts  Accounts     Emails
Emails
```

In this diagram, each step of the incident response process for a phishing attack is visualized, showing the flow from detection to post-incident review. This structured approach ensures that all necessary actions are taken to mitigate the impact of the attack and prevent future occurrences.

By implementing comprehensive playbooks and runbooks, organizations can ensure a consistent and effective response to security incidents, reducing the impact of attacks and improving overall security posture.

# 6.5 Deploying AWS Security Services

Deploying AWS Security Services involves implementing a suite of tools and services designed to enhance the security of your AWS environment. These services, such as AWS Identity and Access Management (IAM), Amazon GuardDuty, AWS Security Hub, and AWS Key Management Service (KMS), provide comprehensive solutions for identity management, threat detection, compliance monitoring, and data protection. By leveraging these services, organizations can effectively secure their cloud infrastructure, protect sensitive data, and ensure compliance with industry standards and regulations.

# 6.5.1 AWS Security Hub

AWS Security Hub is a comprehensive security service designed to provide a centralized view of your security state within AWS, enabling efficient management and improvement of your security posture. It integrates with various AWS services and third-party tools to aggregate, prioritize, and remediate security findings, giving you a holistic understanding of your security landscape.

One of its key features is centralized security management, which consolidates security findings from multiple AWS services such as Amazon GuardDuty, Amazon Inspector, AWS Config, and supported third-party security products. This centralization simplifies security management by providing a single pane of glass for all security-related information.

Security Hub also offers automated compliance checks, continuously monitoring your AWS environment against industry best practices and compliance standards like CIS AWS Foundations Benchmark, PCI DSS, and AWS Foundational Security Best Practices. It provides detailed reports and insights to help maintain compliance and identify areas for improvement.

The service integrates seamlessly with various AWS security services, including GuardDuty for threat detection, Inspector for vulnerability assessments, and AWS Config for resource configuration management. It also supports numerous third-party security products, enhancing its capability to provide comprehensive security insights.

Security Hub aggregates and normalizes findings from various integrated sources, presenting them in a standardized format. This helps in quickly identifying and understanding potential security issues across your AWS accounts and regions. The service uses predefined severity levels and filters to prioritize findings, allowing you to focus on the most critical security issues first. Its dashboard provides visualizations such as bar charts and heat maps to help you quickly grasp your security posture and trends.

Furthermore, Security Hub enables automated response and remediation of security findings through integration with AWS Lambda and AWS Systems Manager. This capability helps in quickly addressing security issues, reducing the time to resolution, and minimizing potential damage.

### How AWS Security Hub Aggregates and Prioritizes Findings

AWS Security Hub collects security findings from various AWS services and third-party products using the Amazon Security Finding Format (ASFF), a standardized format that ensures consistency for easy aggregation and analysis. Once collected, Security Hub normalizes these findings by removing duplicates and categorizing them based on predefined rules.

Findings are prioritized based on their severity and potential impact, with each assigned a severity score (low, medium, high, critical) and additional metadata such as resource details, remediation steps, and compliance status. This prioritization helps security teams quickly identify and address the most critical security issues. The service provides a dashboard that visualizes the aggregated findings, offering insights into the overall security posture of the AWS environment. Users can filter findings by severity, resource type, account, and other criteria, enabling focused investigations and efficient incident response.

### Diagram: AWS Security Hub Workflow

```
┌─────────────────────────────────────────────────────────────┐
│   ┌──────────────────────┐      ┌──────────────────────┐    │
│   │    AWS Services      │      │   Third-Party Tools  │    │
│   │ (GaurdDuty, Inspector│      │  (Security Products) │    │
│   │    AWS Config, etc.) │      │                      │    │
│   └──────────┬───────────┘      └──────────┬───────────┘    │
│              ▼                             ▼                │
│   ┌──────────────────────┐      ┌──────────────────────┐    │
│   │   Findings in ASFF   │      │   Findings in ASFF   │    │
│   └──────────┬───────────┘      └──────────┬───────────┘    │
│              └──────────────┬──────────────┘                │
│                             ▼                               │
│              ┌──────────────────────────┐                   │
│              │    AWS Security Hub      │                   │
│              └──────────────┬───────────┘                   │
│                             ▼                               │
│              ┌──────────────────────────┐                   │
│              │ Aggregations & Normalization │               │
│              └──────────────┬───────────┘                   │
│                             ▼                               │
│              ┌──────────────────────────┐                   │
│              │  Prioritization & Filtering │                │
│              └──────────────┬───────────┘                   │
│                             ▼                               │
│              ┌──────────────────────────┐                   │
│              │  Dashboard & Visualization │                 │
│              └──────────────┬───────────┘                   │
│                             ▼                               │
│              ┌──────────────────────────────┐               │
│              │ Automated Response & Remediation │           │
│              └──────────────────────────────┘               │
└─────────────────────────────────────────────────────────────┘
```

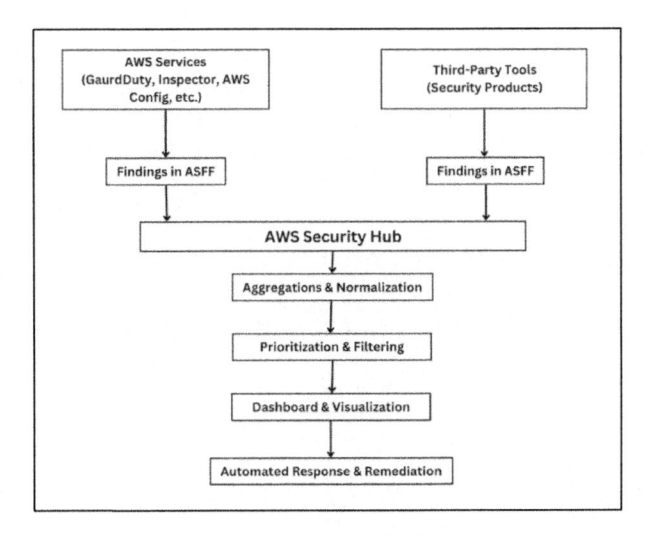

In this diagram, AWS Security Hub aggregates findings from both AWS services and third-party tools, normalizes the data, and prioritizes findings based on severity. The dashboard visualizes these findings, providing insights into the security posture. Automated response and remediation capabilities help in addressing security issues efficiently.

## 6.5.2 Amazon GuardDuty

Amazon GuardDuty is a managed threat detection service that continuously monitors your AWS environment for malicious activity and unauthorized behavior, providing an essential layer of security to help protect your AWS resources. Leveraging machine learning, anomaly detection, and integrated threat intelligence, GuardDuty identifies potential security threats and enables proactive incident response. It analyzes various data sources, including AWS CloudTrail event logs, Amazon VPC Flow Logs, and DNS logs, to detect a wide range of potential threats. By utilizing machine learning algorithms, GuardDuty can identify anomalous patterns and behaviors that might indicate a compromised account or instance. It also incorporates threat intelligence feeds from AWS Security, CrowdStrike, and Proofpoint to enhance its detection capabilities, providing context and insights into known malicious IP addresses, domains, and other indicators of compromise.

GuardDuty operates continuously, providing real-time threat detection without the need for manual intervention. It automatically analyzes and correlates log data from across your AWS environment, ensuring that any unusual activity is quickly identified and flagged. This continuous monitoring helps organizations maintain a robust security posture by ensuring that threats are detected promptly, even as the environment scales and evolves. Key features of GuardDuty include anomaly detection, which identifies deviations from historical baseline data that may signify a security threat, such as unusual API calls, unauthorized access attempts, or data exfiltration activities.

GuardDuty also integrates threat intelligence from multiple sources, enhancing its ability to detect known bad actors and malicious activities. When a threat is detected, GuardDuty generates detailed findings that include information about the affected resources, the nature of the threat, and recommended remediation steps. These findings are presented in a standardized format that integrates seamlessly with other AWS security services and third-party tools. As a managed service, GuardDuty is easy to set up and does not require complex configuration or ongoing maintenance. It automatically scales with your AWS environment, providing continuous threat detection without additional infrastructure or operational overhead. Additionally, GuardDuty findings can be aggregated and prioritized in AWS Security Hub, allowing for a centralized view of your security posture and streamlined incident response.

### Example Use Case

Consider a scenario where an unauthorized user gains access to your AWS account and starts launching EC2 instances in an unusual region. GuardDuty would detect this anomalous behavior by comparing it to your account's typical activity patterns. It would generate a finding detailing the suspicious activity, including the IP addresses involved, the regions affected, and the specific actions taken. This finding would then be available in the GuardDuty console and could be forwarded to AWS Security Hub or a third-party SIEM for further analysis and response.

### Diagram: Amazon GuardDuty Monitoring Workflow

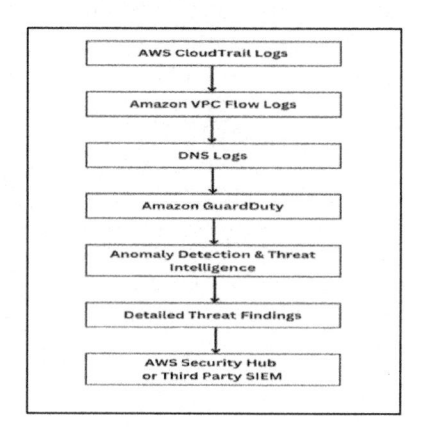

In the diagram, GuardDuty continuously monitors and analyzes data from AWS CloudTrail, VPC Flow Logs, and DNS logs. It applies machine learning and threat intelligence to detect anomalies and malicious activities, generating detailed findings that can be further investigated and remediated using AWS Security Hub or other security tools.

Amazon GuardDuty's proactive threat detection capabilities and continuous monitoring make it a vital component of a comprehensive security strategy, helping organizations detect and respond to security threats quickly and effectively.

## 6.5.3 Amazon Macie

Amazon Macie is a fully managed data security and data privacy service designed to help organizations discover and protect sensitive data stored in AWS. Macie uses machine learning and pattern matching to automatically identify and classify sensitive data, such as personally identifiable information (PII), financial data, and intellectual property. By continuously monitoring and analyzing data stored in Amazon S3, Macie helps organizations ensure their data security and compliance with regulatory requirements.

Key features of Macie include automated data discovery, where it scans and analyzes the contents of Amazon S3 buckets to identify sensitive data using machine learning algorithms and pattern matching techniques. Once sensitive data is discovered, Macie classifies and labels it according to predefined categories, helping organizations understand the nature and location of their sensitive data for better management and protection strategies. Macie provides continuous monitoring of S3 buckets, automatically updating its findings as new data is added or existing data is modified, ensuring up-to-date visibility into the data landscape.

When Macie detects sensitive data, it generates detailed findings, including information about the data, the type of sensitivity detected, and the S3 bucket where the data resides. These findings can be integrated with AWS Security Hub or third-party security information and event management (SIEM) systems for centralized management and response. Macie also helps organizations implement data protection measures by identifying unencrypted sensitive data or data with overly permissive access controls, enabling corrective actions such as encrypting data or tightening access permissions. Additionally, Macie aids organizations in meeting regulatory compliance requirements, such as GDPR, HIPAA, and CCPA, by providing detailed insights into the location and type of sensitive data, supporting data governance efforts across the AWS environment.

**Example Use Case**

Consider a scenario where a company stores large amounts of customer data in Amazon S3. Using Amazon Macie, the company can automatically discover and classify sensitive customer information, such as social security numbers and credit card details. Macie generates findings that indicate where sensitive data is stored and whether it is properly protected. For example, if Macie detects sensitive data stored in an unencrypted S3 bucket or a bucket with public access, it generates an alert, allowing the company to quickly remediate the issue by encrypting the data and adjusting access controls.

**Diagram: Amazon Macie Workflow**

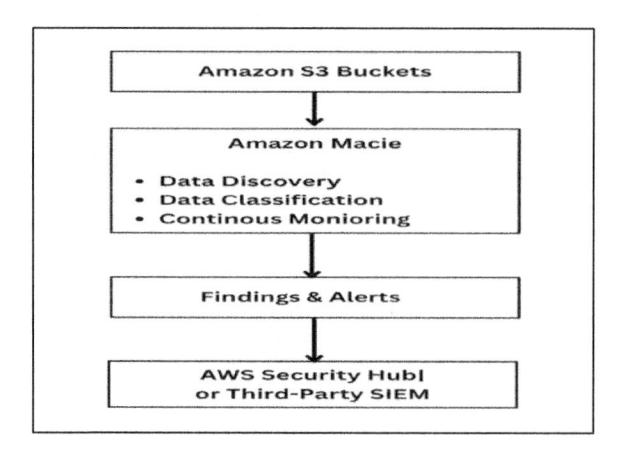

```
┌─────────────────────────────────┐
│        Amazon S3 Buckets        │
└─────────────────────────────────┘
              │
              ▼
┌─────────────────────────────────┐
│         Amazon Macie            │
│   • Data Discovery              │
│   • Data Classification         │
│   • Continous Monioring         │
└─────────────────────────────────┘
              │
              ▼
┌─────────────────────────────────┐
│        Findings & Alerts        │
└─────────────────────────────────┘
              │
              ▼
┌─────────────────────────────────┐
│        AWS Security Hub│        │
│      or Third-Party SIEM        │
└─────────────────────────────────┘
```

In this diagram, Amazon Macie continuously monitors Amazon S3 buckets to discover and classify sensitive data. It generates findings and alerts that can be integrated with AWS Security Hub or third-party SIEM systems for centralized management and response.

By leveraging Amazon Macie, organizations can gain deep visibility into their sensitive data stored in AWS, enhance data protection, and ensure compliance with data privacy regulations. Macie's automated and continuous monitoring capabilities significantly reduce the risk of data breaches and unauthorized access, helping organizations maintain a robust security posture.

## 6.5.4 Amazon Inspector

Amazon Inspector is a comprehensive automated security assessment service designed to enhance the security and compliance of applications deployed on Amazon Web Services (AWS). It identifies vulnerabilities and deviations from best practices in applications by performing automated security assessments and generating detailed reports. This allows organizations to proactively address security issues and improve their overall security posture. Amazon Inspector analyzes the behavior and configuration of applications running on Amazon EC2 instances using various techniques, including static and dynamic analysis, to evaluate the security of the operating system, network configurations, and application code.

Key capabilities of Amazon Inspector include vulnerability assessment, where it scans for known vulnerabilities in the operating system and installed applications, comparing findings against a continuously updated database of known vulnerabilities (CVE database). It also performs best practice assessments by evaluating applications against AWS security best practices and industry standards, checking for common security misconfigurations and providing recommendations on rectifying them. Additionally, Inspector monitors the runtime behavior of applications to detect suspicious activities that could indicate a security breach, analyzing network traffic, system calls, and other behavioral patterns to identify anomalies and potential threats. Inspector can also be configured to perform compliance checks based on specific regulatory requirements, such as PCI DSS or CIS benchmarks, helping organizations ensure their applications meet relevant compliance standards.

Amazon Inspector simplifies the process of identifying and mitigating vulnerabilities in applications through its automated and continuous assessment capabilities. Users define assessment targets by specifying the Amazon EC2 instances they want to analyze, grouping them based on criteria such as instance tags, resource groups, or specific configurations. Assessment templates are created to define the rules and checks to be performed during the assessment, which can be customized to include specific rules for vulnerability detection, best practice adherence, and compliance checks. Inspector runs the assessments according to the defined templates and schedules, automatically scanning the selected EC2 instances, analyzing the collected data, and identifying potential security issues. Detailed findings are generated for each identified issue, including a description of the vulnerability, its severity, affected resources, and recommended remediation steps, presented in a comprehensive report accessible through the AWS Management Console or via API. For each finding, Inspector provides clear remediation guidance, including links to relevant documentation and best practice guidelines. Inspector findings can be integrated with other AWS security services, such as AWS Security Hub and AWS Lambda, to enable automated incident response and centralized security management.

**Diagram: Amazon Inspector Workflow**

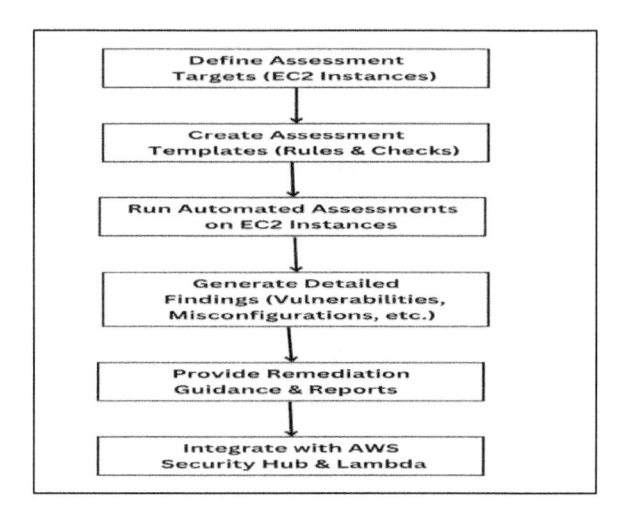

```
┌─────────────────────────────┐
│   Define Assessment         │
│   Targets (EC2 Instances)   │
└─────────────┬───────────────┘
              ↓
┌─────────────────────────────┐
│   Create Assessment         │
│   Templates (Rules & Checks)│
└─────────────┬───────────────┘
              ↓
┌─────────────────────────────┐
│   Run Automated Assessments │
│   on EC2 Instances          │
└─────────────┬───────────────┘
              ↓
┌─────────────────────────────┐
│   Generate Detailed         │
│   Findings (Vulnerabilities,│
│   Misconfigurations, etc.)  │
└─────────────┬───────────────┘
              ↓
┌─────────────────────────────┐
│   Provide Remediation       │
│   Guidance & Reports        │
└─────────────┬───────────────┘
              ↓
┌─────────────────────────────┐
│   Integrate with AWS        │
│   Security Hub & Lambda     │
└─────────────────────────────┘
```

In the diagram, Amazon Inspector's workflow is outlined, starting with the definition of assessment targets and creation of assessment templates. Automated assessments are then run on the specified EC2 instances, generating detailed findings and providing remediation guidance. Integration with other AWS services enables automated response and centralized security management.

By leveraging Amazon Inspector, organizations can proactively identify and address security vulnerabilities in their applications, ensuring a higher level of security and compliance in their AWS environment. Its automated and continuous assessment capabilities significantly reduce the time and effort required to maintain a secure application landscape.

# 6.5.5 AWS Config

AWS Config is a powerful service that provides comprehensive visibility into the configuration of AWS resources, enabling organizations to manage and maintain their AWS environment effectively. It offers detailed inventory and configuration history, making it a crucial tool for assessing compliance, detecting configuration changes, and troubleshooting issues. AWS Config continuously monitors and records the configuration settings of AWS resources, creating a complete inventory of these resources and their relationships. It captures and stores configuration details such as security group rules, instance types, and bucket policies. This detailed inventory is updated whenever a configuration change is detected, ensuring the information remains current.

Additionally, AWS Config maintains a historical record of configuration changes, allowing users to track and audit the evolution of their AWS resources over time. This historical data can be queried to understand past states and configurations, which is invaluable for forensic analysis and compliance audits. By providing a clear and precise history of configuration changes, AWS Config helps organizations ensure that their resources are configured according to their policies and best practices.

AWS Config plays a critical role in assessing compliance by allowing organizations to define and evaluate rules that represent their desired configurations. These rules can be based on AWS best practices, industry standards, or specific organizational policies. Config continuously evaluates the current state of AWS resources against these rules and generates compliance reports, highlighting resources that do not comply with the defined standards. For example, a company can create rules to ensure that all S3 buckets have server-side encryption enabled or that EC2 instances are not using deprecated instance types. AWS Config evaluates these rules and provides real-time compliance status, enabling organizations to quickly identify and remediate non-compliant resources. This continuous compliance assessment helps organizations maintain security, avoid misconfigurations, and meet regulatory requirements.

One of AWS Config's key features is its ability to detect configuration changes in real time. Whenever a change occurs to an AWS resource, such as a security group modification or an IAM policy update, AWS Config records the change and triggers a notification. These notifications can be used to alert administrators about unexpected changes, allowing them to take immediate action if necessary. AWS Config integrates with Amazon SNS (Simple Notification Service) to send alerts and notifications, ensuring that the right personnel are informed about configuration changes. It also integrates with AWS Lambda, enabling automated responses to specific changes. For example, if an unauthorized change to a security group is detected, a Lambda function can be triggered to revert the change automatically.

**Diagram: AWS Config Workflow**

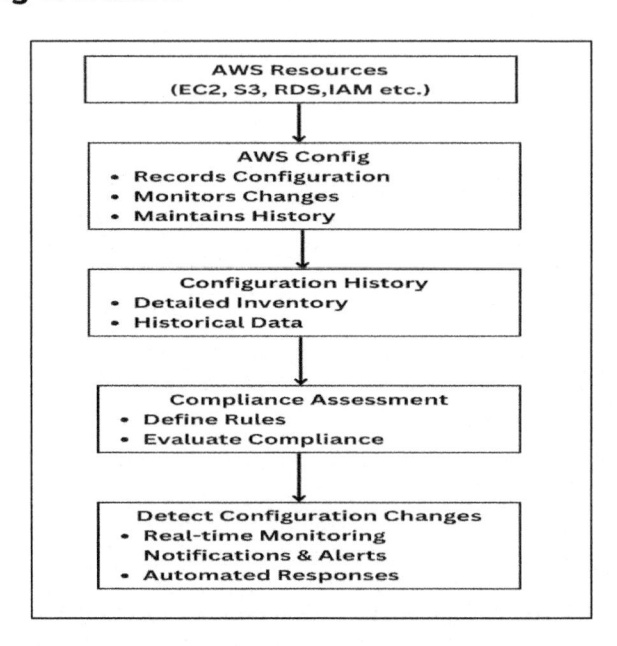

```
┌─────────────────────────────────┐
│         AWS Resources           │
│    (EC2, S3, RDS, IAM etc.)     │
└─────────────────────────────────┘
                │
                ▼
┌─────────────────────────────────┐
│           AWS Config            │
│     • Records Configuration     │
│     • Monitors Changes          │
│     • Maintains History         │
└─────────────────────────────────┘
                │
                ▼
┌─────────────────────────────────┐
│      Configuration History      │
│     • Detailed Inventory        │
│     • Historical Data           │
└─────────────────────────────────┘
                │
                ▼
┌─────────────────────────────────┐
│     Compliance Assessment       │
│     • Define Rules              │
│     • Evaluate Compliance       │
└─────────────────────────────────┘
                │
                ▼
┌─────────────────────────────────┐
│  Detect Configuration Changes   │
│     • Real-time Monitoring      │
│       Notifications & Alerts    │
│     • Automated Responses       │
└─────────────────────────────────┘
```

In this diagram, AWS Config continuously records and monitors the configuration of AWS resources, maintaining a detailed inventory and historical record. It assesses compliance by evaluating resources against defined rules and detects configuration changes in real-time, triggering notifications and automated responses as necessary.

AWS Config's ability to provide detailed inventory and configuration history, assess compliance, and detect configuration changes makes it an indispensable tool for managing AWS environments. It enhances visibility, ensures compliance, and helps organizations maintain a secure and well-configured cloud infrastructure.

## 6.5.6 Amazon Detective

Amazon Detective is an advanced security service designed to simplify and accelerate security investigations by leveraging machine learning and graph analysis. It automatically collects and processes data from various AWS sources to provide a comprehensive view of potential security issues, enabling security teams to conduct faster and more efficient investigations. Key features and capabilities include automated data collection, where

Detective continuously gathers log data from AWS CloudTrail, Amazon VPC Flow Logs, and Amazon GuardDuty. This data is then processed and organized into a graph model depicting relationships between various entities in the AWS environment, such as users, IP addresses, and resources.

Detective uses machine learning algorithms to analyze the collected data, identifying patterns and anomalies that might indicate security threats. Its graph-based approach allows for the visualization of complex relationships and interactions over time, making it easier to understand the context of an incident and track the chain of events leading up to it. The service provides interactive visualizations that help security analysts explore and investigate findings, enabling them to drill down into specific details, uncover hidden connections, and gain a deeper understanding of incidents.

Amazon Detective integrates seamlessly with other AWS security services, such as AWS Security Hub and Amazon GuardDuty, allowing for the easy ingestion of findings from these services into Detective, providing a unified platform for investigating and correlating security data. It significantly reduces the time and effort required to investigate security incidents by automating data collection and providing powerful analytical tools. This enables security teams to quickly triage alerts, identify root causes, and take corrective actions without manually sifting through large volumes of log data.

In modern security operations, Amazon Detective enhances the efficiency and effectiveness of security investigations. When a potential security incident is detected, such as unauthorized access or data exfiltration, Detective helps security analysts quickly understand the incident by providing a consolidated view of relevant data and highlighting key relationships. Analysts can identify root causes by tracing the incident to its origin and correlating related events to reveal a coherent picture of the attacker's activities and methods. With access to detailed insights and contextual information, security teams can make informed decisions about containment, mitigation, and remediation efforts, reducing the impact of the incident

## Diagram: Amazon Detective Workflow

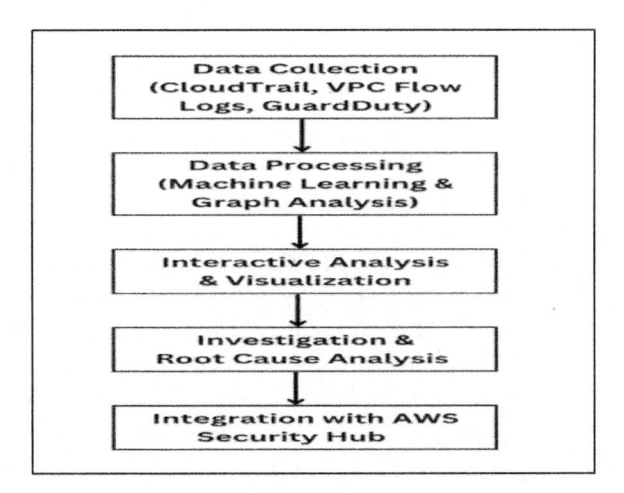

```
┌─────────────────────────────┐
│   Data Collection           │
│   (CloudTrail, VPC Flow     │
│   Logs, GuardDuty)          │
└─────────────┬───────────────┘
              ↓
┌─────────────────────────────┐
│   Data Processing           │
│   (Machine Learning &       │
│   Graph Analysis)           │
└─────────────┬───────────────┘
              ↓
┌─────────────────────────────┐
│   Interactive Analysis      │
│   & Visualization           │
└─────────────┬───────────────┘
              ↓
┌─────────────────────────────┐
│   Investigation &           │
│   Root Cause Analysis       │
└─────────────┬───────────────┘
              ↓
┌─────────────────────────────┐
│   Integration with AWS      │
│   Security Hub              │
└─────────────────────────────┘
```

In this diagram, Amazon Detective collects and processes log data from various AWS sources, applies machine learning and graph analysis to organize the data, and provides interactive visualizations for detailed investigation and root cause analysis. It integrates with AWS Security Hub to streamline the investigation process.

By leveraging the advanced capabilities of Amazon Detective, organizations can enhance their security posture, respond to threats more effectively, and minimize the time and resources required for security investigations.

## 6.5.7 AWS IAM Access Analyzer

AWS IAM Access Analyzer is a powerful tool designed to enhance the security and governance of AWS resources by identifying and evaluating resources that are shared with external entities. It helps organizations ensure that their resource policies do not unintentionally grant access to unauthorized users, thereby mitigating potential security risks.

### Key Features and Capabilities

- **Automated Resource Analysis:** Access Analyzer automatically scans resource policies to identify resources that are accessible from outside the AWS account. This includes resources such as Amazon S3 buckets, AWS KMS keys, IAM roles, AWS Lambda functions, and more. Access Analyzer helps maintain a secure and compliant AWS environment by performing this analysis continuously.
- **Detailed Findings:** Access Analyzer provides detailed findings for each resource that is identified as being shared with external entities. These findings include information about the resource, the specific policies that allow external access, and the external entities that have access. This level of detail helps security teams understand the context and potential impact of the shared access.
- **Risk Assessment:** Access Analyzer helps assess the risk associated with shared resources by categorizing findings based on the level of access granted and the sensitivity of the resource. For example, it can highlight high-risk findings where sensitive data is accessible to external parties or where broad permissions are granted.
- **Integration with AWS Organizations:** Access Analyzer integrates with AWS Organizations, enabling centralized analysis across multiple accounts within an organization. This helps security teams maintain a holistic view of resource sharing and access policies across their entire AWS environment.
- **Actionable Insights:** Access Analyzer's findings are actionable, providing clear recommendations on how to remediate potential security issues. This includes suggestions for modifying resource policies to restrict access or using more granular permissions to minimize risk.

### Role in Security and Compliance

AWS IAM Access Analyzer plays a critical role in ensuring the security and compliance of AWS environments by providing visibility into resource sharing practices. Organizations can use Access Analyzer to:

- **Identify Unintended Access:** Detect resources that are unintentionally shared with external entities, helping to prevent data leaks and unauthorized access.
- **Enhance Compliance:** Ensure that resource sharing practices comply with internal policies and regulatory requirements by continuously monitoring and analyzing resource policies.
- **Improve Security Posture:** Reduce the attack surface by identifying and remediating overly permissive policies, thereby enhancing the overall security posture of the AWS environment.
- **Streamline Audits:** Simplify the audit process by providing a comprehensive view of resource access and sharing, along with detailed findings and remediation recommendations.

### Example Scenario

Consider a scenario where an organization has multiple S3 buckets, some of which are used to store sensitive data. Using Access Analyzer, the organization can automatically identify any S3 buckets that are shared with external accounts or made publicly accessible. Access Analyzer provides detailed findings for each identified bucket, such as the specific bucket policies that allow external access and the entities that have access. The security team can then assess the risk associated with each finding and take appropriate actions, such as modifying bucket policies to restrict access or using bucket policies to enforce more granular permissions.

**Diagram: AWS IAM Access Analyzer Workflow**

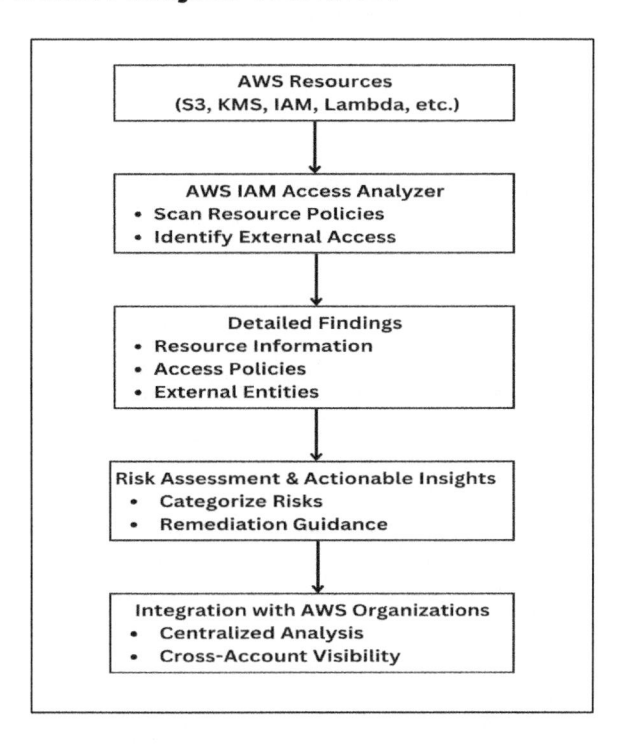

```
┌─────────────────────────────────────┐
│          AWS Resources              │
│     (S3, KMS, IAM, Lambda, etc.)    │
└─────────────────────────────────────┘
                  ↓
┌─────────────────────────────────────┐
│       AWS IAM Access Analyzer       │
│   • Scan Resource Policies          │
│   • Identify External Access        │
└─────────────────────────────────────┘
                  ↓
┌─────────────────────────────────────┐
│         Detailed Findings           │
│   • Resource Information            │
│   • Access Policies                 │
│   • External Entities               │
└─────────────────────────────────────┘
                  ↓
┌─────────────────────────────────────┐
│  Risk Assessment & Actionable Insights │
│   • Categorize Risks                │
│   • Remediation Guidance            │
└─────────────────────────────────────┘
                  ↓
┌─────────────────────────────────────┐
│   Integration with AWS Organizations │
│   • Centralized Analysis            │
│   • Cross-Account Visibility        │
└─────────────────────────────────────┘
```

In this diagram, AWS IAM Access Analyzer continuously scans resource policies to identify external access. It generates detailed findings and categorizes risks, providing actionable insights and remediation guidance. Integration with AWS Organizations allows for centralized analysis across multiple accounts.

AWS IAM Access Analyzer helps organizations maintain a secure and compliant AWS environment by providing visibility into resource sharing practices, assessing risks, and offering actionable recommendations for improving security.

# 6.6 Configuring Integrations with Native and Third-Party Services

Configuring integrations with native and third-party services in AWS allows organizations to extend the functionality of their AWS environment, enabling seamless communication and data exchange between various tools and platforms. By leveraging these integrations, businesses can enhance their workflows, automate processes, and improve overall efficiency and security. Integrations can include native AWS services like Amazon SNS, AWS Lambda, and AWS Security Hub, as well as third-party applications such as Splunk, Datadog, and ServiceNow.

## 6.6.1 Using Amazon EventBridge

Amazon EventBridge is a serverless event bus service that simplifies building event-driven architectures by enabling seamless integration between AWS services and third-party applications. It allows you to route and manage events from various sources to different destinations, facilitating automation and improving the responsiveness of your applications.

Configuring Amazon EventBridge involves several steps. First, you create an event bus, a logical entity that receives, stores, and routes events. Each AWS account has a default event bus, but you can create custom event buses for different applications or use cases. Next, you define event sources. EventBridge supports a wide range of event sources, including AWS services, custom applications, and third-party SaaS partners. To use an AWS service as an event source, you need to enable it in EventBridge. For custom applications, you can use the AWS SDKs or the EventBridge API to put events into the event bus. Setting up integration for third-party applications involves providing necessary permissions and configurations.

Then, you create event rules to match incoming events and route them to target destinations. Each rule consists of an event pattern that specifies the conditions under which the rule is triggered. You can create rules to filter events based on specific criteria, such as event source, detail type, or custom attributes. Once an event rule is triggered, the matched events are sent to one or more targets. EventBridge supports various target types, including AWS Lambda functions, Amazon SNS topics, Amazon SQS queues, AWS Step Functions, and more. You can also configure event targets to be HTTP endpoints or other SaaS applications.

Finally, after configuring the event bus, event sources, rules, and targets, you deploy your configuration. It is crucial to thoroughly test the event flow to ensure that events are correctly matched and routed to their intended destinations.

### Example Use Case

Consider a scenario where you want to automate the process of resizing images uploaded to an S3 bucket. Here's how you can configure EventBridge to achieve this:

- **Create an Event Bus:** Use the default event bus or create a new custom event bus for your application.
- **Define Event Source:** Enable Amazon S3 as an event source to send events to EventBridge whenever a new object is created in the S3 bucket.
- **Create Event Rule:** Define an event rule with a pattern that matches S3 object creation events. For example:

```
{
  "source": ["aws.s3"],
  "detail-type": ["Object Created"],
  "detail": {
    "bucket": {
      "name": ["my-image-bucket"]
    }
  }
}
```

- **Specify Target:** Configure the target to be an AWS Lambda function that resizes images. When the event rule matches an S3 object creation event, it triggers the Lambda function to perform the image resizing.
- **Deploy and Test:** Deploy and test the configuration by uploading an image to the S3 bucket. Verify that EventBridge and the Lambda function capture the event and are triggered to resize the image.

**Diagram: Amazon EventBridge Workflow**

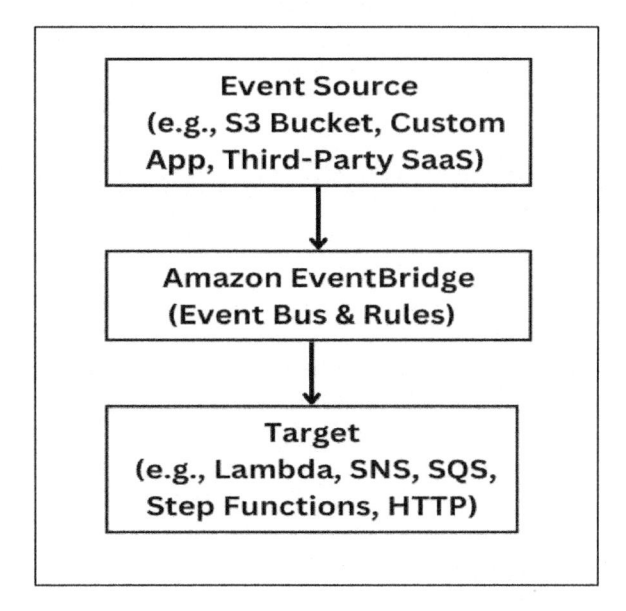

```
┌─────────────────────────────────┐
│   ┌─────────────────────────┐   │
│   │      Event Source       │   │
│   │ (e.g., S3 Bucket, Custom│   │
│   │  App, Third-Party SaaS) │   │
│   └─────────────────────────┘   │
│                │                │
│                ▼                │
│   ┌─────────────────────────┐   │
│   │   Amazon EventBridge    │   │
│   │   (Event Bus & Rules)   │   │
│   └─────────────────────────┘   │
│                │                │
│                ▼                │
│   ┌─────────────────────────┐   │
│   │         Target          │   │
│   │ (e.g., Lambda, SNS, SQS,│   │
│   │  Step Functions, HTTP)  │   │
│   └─────────────────────────┘   │
└─────────────────────────────────┘
```

This diagram sends events from various sources, such as an S3 bucket, custom applications, or third-party SaaS providers, to Amazon EventBridge. EventBridge uses event rules to match and route events to appropriate targets, such as AWS Lambda functions or other AWS services.

Configuring Amazon EventBridge allows you to create sophisticated event-driven architectures that integrate AWS services and third-party applications. This allows for highly automated, scalable, and responsive applications that react to real-time events.

## 6.6.2 Integrating AWS Services with Third-Party Tools

Integrating AWS security services with third-party security tools is essential for enhancing incident response capabilities, providing a comprehensive security posture, and enabling seamless detection, investigation, and remediation of security incidents. By leveraging the strengths of both AWS-native services and third-party solutions, organizations can build robust, scalable, and efficient security operations.

**Key Techniques for Integration**
- **Centralized Monitoring and Management:** AWS Security Hub is a central service that aggregates, organizes, and prioritizes security findings from multiple AWS services such as Amazon GuardDuty, AWS Config, and Amazon Inspector, as well as third-party security tools. By integrating third-party tools like Splunk, Palo Alto Networks, and CrowdStrike with Security Hub, organizations can achieve a unified view of their security posture, streamline monitoring, and enhance incident response workflows.
- **Automated Incident Response:** AWS services like AWS Lambda and AWS Step Functions can be integrated with third-party security tools to automate incident response actions. For example, when GuardDuty detects a potential threat, it can trigger a Lambda function that interacts with third-party tools like ServiceNow or PagerDuty to create incident tickets, notify security teams, and execute predefined remediation scripts, thereby reducing response times and minimizing the impact of incidents.
- **Real-time Alerting and Notification:** Amazon SNS (Simple Notification Service) can be used to send real-time alerts and notifications from AWS security services to third-party tools. For instance, GuardDuty findings can be sent to an SNS topic, which then routes the alerts to third-party platforms

like Slack, Microsoft Teams, or email systems, ensuring that security teams are promptly informed of potential threats.
- **Data Enrichment and Correlation**: Integrating AWS security services with third-party SIEM (Security Information and Event Management) systems such as Splunk, IBM QRadar, or ArcSight allows for data enrichment and correlation. By combining AWS security data with logs and alerts from on-premises and other cloud environments, organizations can gain deeper insights into security events, identify complex attack patterns, and improve threat hunting capabilities.
- **Threat Intelligence Sharing:** AWS security services like GuardDuty and AWS WAF (Web Application Firewall) can be integrated with third-party threat intelligence platforms to enhance detection capabilities. By incorporating threat intelligence feeds from providers like CrowdStrike, ThreatConnect, or Recorded Future, these services can identify and respond to emerging threats more effectively.
- **Compliance and Reporting:** AWS Config and third-party compliance tools can be integrated to ensure continuous compliance and generate comprehensive reports. Tools like Evident.io or Dome9 can work alongside AWS Config to assess configuration compliance, detect deviations, and provide detailed audit trails, helping organizations meet regulatory requirements and maintain security best practices.

## Example Integration Workflow

Consider a scenario where an organization wants to enhance its incident response capabilities by integrating AWS GuardDuty with Splunk for real-time threat detection and response:
- **Detect Threats:** GuardDuty continuously monitors for suspicious activities and generates security findings.
- **Send Findings to Splunk:** Use AWS Lambda to automatically send GuardDuty findings to Splunk for further analysis and correlation with other security data.
- **Trigger Automated Responses:** Configure Splunk to trigger automated response actions via AWS Lambda or third-party tools like ServiceNow when specific threats are detected.
- **Notify Security Teams:** Use Amazon SNS to send real-time notifications to security teams via Slack or email.
- **Analyze and Remediate:** Security analysts use Splunk to investigate the incident, enrich it with data from GuardDuty and other sources, and take appropriate remediation actions.

## Diagram: AWS and Third-Party Integration Workflow

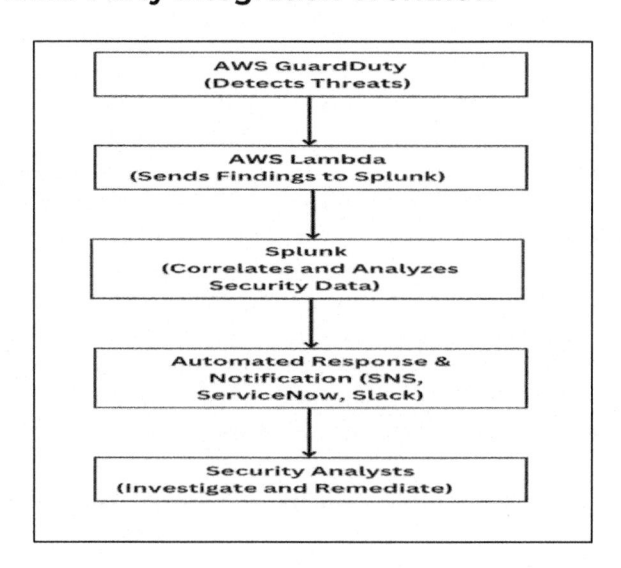

```
┌─────────────────────────┐
│    AWS GuardDuty        │
│   (Detects Threats)     │
└───────────┬─────────────┘
            ↓
┌─────────────────────────┐
│      AWS Lambda         │
│ (Sends Findings to Splunk)│
└───────────┬─────────────┘
            ↓
┌─────────────────────────┐
│        Splunk           │
│  (Correlates and Analyzes│
│     Security Data)      │
└───────────┬─────────────┘
            ↓
┌─────────────────────────┐
│  Automated Response &   │
│   Notification (SNS,    │
│  ServiceNow, Slack)     │
└───────────┬─────────────┘
            ↓
┌─────────────────────────┐
│   Security Analysts     │
│(Investigate and Remediate)│
└─────────────────────────┘
```

AWS GuardDuty detects threats in this diagram and sends findings to Splunk via AWS Lambda. Splunk analyzes the data, triggering automated responses and notifications through SNS, ServiceNow, or Slack. Security analysts then investigate and remediate the incident.

By integrating AWS security services with third-party security tools, organizations can create a robust, cohesive security ecosystem that enhances their ability to detect, investigate, and respond to incidents efficiently and effectively. This integration helps ensure a comprehensive security posture and improves the overall resilience of the IT infrastructure.

## 6.7 Best Practices for Threat Detection and Incident Response

Implementing best practices for threat detection and incident response is essential to maintaining a secure and resilient IT environment. These practices include continuous monitoring for anomalies, leveraging automation to streamline response processes, and conducting regular training and drills to ensure preparedness. By adopting a proactive and systematic approach, organizations can effectively identify and mitigate threats, minimizing potential damage and ensuring rapid recovery.

### 6.7.1 Continuous Monitoring and Alerting

Continuous monitoring and real-time alerting are essential for maintaining a secure and resilient IT environment. They enable organizations to detect and respond to threats swiftly. Continuous monitoring involves collecting and analyzing security data from various sources within an organization's IT infrastructure. This proactive approach ensures that any anomalies or suspicious activities are identified promptly, providing a comprehensive view of the security posture at all times.

Real-time alerting, a key component of continuous monitoring, reduces the time between threat detection and response initiation. It ensures that security teams are immediately notified when a potential threat is detected, thereby reducing the time for initiating a response. This instant notification system is vital for swift threat mitigation. By receiving alerts in real time, security professionals can quickly investigate and mitigate threats, preventing them from escalating into more serious incidents.

Continuous monitoring and real-time alerting are crucial practices that enhance the speed and effectiveness of incident response. Rapid detection and alerting allow for quick containment of threats, thereby minimizing the potential impact on the organization. This is particularly crucial in today's dynamic threat landscape, where cyber-attacks can unfold in a matter of minutes. Moreover, these practices help ensure compliance with regulatory requirements, as many standards mandate timely detection and response to security incidents.

**Best Practices for Continuous Monitoring and Real-Time Alerting**
- **Comprehensive Data Collection:** Ensure that all critical assets and endpoints are monitored. This includes network traffic, system logs, application logs, and user activities. The more comprehensive the data collection, the better the visibility into potential threats.
- **Centralized Logging and Analysis:** Utilize centralized logging solutions like SIEM (Security Information and Event Management) systems to aggregate and analyze logs from various sources. This centralization enables efficient correlation and analysis of security events.
- **Automated Threat Detection:** Implement automated threat detection mechanisms that use machine learning and behavioral analytics to identify anomalies and potential threats. Automated systems can process vast amounts of data more quickly and accurately than manual analysis.
- **Defined Alerting Thresholds:** Set clear thresholds for alerts to avoid alert fatigue. Ensure that alerts are meaningful and actionable, prioritizing critical threats that require immediate attention.

- **Regular Tuning and Updates:** Continuously tune monitoring and alerting systems to adapt to the evolving threat landscape. Regular updates and fine-tuning help maintain the effectiveness of detection and alerting mechanisms.
- **Integration with Incident Response Plans:** Ensure that real-time alerts are integrated into the organization's incident response plans. This integration ensures that alerts trigger predefined response actions, enabling swift and coordinated incident management.
- **Training and Awareness:** Regularly train security teams on the use of monitoring and alerting tools. Awareness and proficiency in handling alerts and initiating response actions are crucial for effective incident management.
- **Testing and Drills:** Conduct regular testing and drills to evaluate the effectiveness of continuous monitoring and real-time alerting systems. Simulated attacks and incident response exercises help identify gaps and improve readiness.

In summary, continuous monitoring and real-time alerting are essential for quickly detecting and responding to threats. Adopting best practices for these processes enhances an organization's ability to maintain a robust security posture, ensuring the integrity and availability of critical systems and data while minimizing the impact of security incidents.

## 6.7.2 Regular Incident Response Drills

Conducting regular incident response drills is crucial to ensuring the effectiveness of an organization's incident response plan and the readiness of the response team. These drills simulate real-world cyber-attacks and security incidents, allowing teams to practice their response procedures, identify gaps in their processes, and improve their overall preparedness.

### Importance of Incident Response Drills
- **Validate Response Plans:** Drills help validate the current incident response plans by testing them against realistic scenarios. This ensures that the documented procedures are practical and effective in mitigating actual threats.
- **Identify Weaknesses:** By conducting drills, organizations can identify weaknesses and gaps in their incident response strategies. This includes detecting issues such as unclear roles, ineffective communication channels, and insufficient technical controls.
- **Enhance Team Coordination:** Regular drills foster better coordination and communication within the incident response team. They provide an opportunity for team members to practice working together, improving their ability to respond swiftly and effectively during a real incident.
- **Improve Response Time:** Practicing incident response helps teams to become more familiar with their roles and responsibilities, leading to faster and more efficient responses when a real incident occurs. This can significantly reduce the impact of an incident.
- **Boost Confidence:** Regular drills build confidence within the incident response team. Knowing that they have successfully handled simulated incidents can prepare them psychologically and technically for real-world events.

### Best Practices for Incident Response Drills
- **Realistic Scenarios:** Design drills based on realistic scenarios reflecting the current threat landscape and the organization's risk profile. This ensures that the drills are relevant and valuable.
- **Clear Objectives:** Define clear objectives for each drill. Whether it's testing a specific aspect of the response plan or evaluating the team's communication skills, having specific goals helps measure the drill's success.
- **Involve All Stakeholders:** Include all relevant stakeholders in the drills, including IT, security, legal, and executive teams. This ensures comprehensive testing and highlights the importance of cross-functional collaboration.

- **Simulate Entire Response Process:** Conduct drills that simulate the entire incident response process, from detection and analysis to containment, eradication, recovery, and post-incident review. This comprehensive approach tests all aspects of the response plan.
- **Document and Review:** Thoroughly document the drill process and outcomes. Conduct a review session after each drill to discuss what went well, what didn't, and how the response plan can be improved. Use these insights to update the plan and procedures.
- **Regular Frequency:** Schedule drills at regular intervals to keep the team prepared and the response plan up-to-date. Frequency can vary based on the organization's risk environment, but quarterly or bi-annual drills are common.
- **Evaluate Against Metrics:** Establish metrics to evaluate the effectiveness of the drills, such as response times, communication efficiency, and the accuracy of incident detection. Use these metrics to track improvements over time.

### Example Scenario
Imagine a scenario where a drill simulates a ransomware attack. The objectives are to test the incident detection capabilities, the effectiveness of the communication plan, and the technical response procedures. During the drill, the incident response team detects the ransomware, isolates affected systems, communicates with stakeholders, and begins recovery processes. Post-drill, the team reviews their performance, identifies areas for improvement, and updates the incident response plan accordingly.

By conducting regular incident response drills and adhering to best practices, organizations can ensure their response teams are well-prepared to handle actual security incidents. This level of preparedness not only minimizes potential damage and maintains business continuity but also provides a sense of security and peace of mind, instilling confidence in the team and the organization as a whole.

## 6.7.3 Post-Incident Analysis and Improvement
Conducting post-incident analysis is essential for identifying lessons learned and improving incident response processes. This analysis helps organizations understand the root causes of incidents, assess the effectiveness of their response, and implement measures to prevent future occurrences. Here are some techniques and best practices for conducting effective post-incident analysis.

### Techniques for Post-Incident Analysis
- **Incident Review Meeting:** Schedule a meeting with all relevant stakeholders, including incident responders, IT staff, and management, to discuss the incident. This collaborative approach ensures that different perspectives are considered and all aspects of the incident are examined.
- **Root Cause Analysis (RCA):** Perform a detailed RCA to identify the underlying causes of the incident. Techniques such as the "5 Whys" or Fishbone (Ishikawa) diagrams can be used to systematically explore and document the contributing factors.
- **Timeline Reconstruction:** Reconstruct the timeline of events leading up to, during, and after the incident. This helps in understanding the sequence of actions and decisions made, and identifies any delays or missteps in the response process.
- **Data Collection and Analysis:** Gather and analyze all relevant data, including logs, alerts, communication records, and incident documentation. This data-driven approach provides objective insights into what happened and why.
- **Performance Metrics Evaluation:** Evaluate the performance metrics associated with the incident response, such as detection times, response times, and resolution times. Comparing these metrics against predefined benchmarks can highlight areas for improvement.
- **Stakeholder Feedback:** Collect feedback from all stakeholders involved in the incident response. This includes technical staff, management, and affected users. Feedback can provide valuable insights into the practical challenges faced and suggest areas for enhancement.

### Best Practices for Post-Incident Analysis

- Structured Approach: Use a structured framework or methodology for conducting post-incident analysis. This ensures consistency, thoroughness, and comprehensiveness in the review process.
- Documentation: Thoroughly document the findings of the post-incident analysis, including the root causes, timeline, performance metrics, and stakeholder feedback. Detailed documentation serves as a reference for future incidents and helps in tracking improvements over time.
- Actionable Recommendations: Develop actionable recommendations based on the analysis. These should address the identified weaknesses and include specific, measurable, and time-bound actions for improvement.
- Follow-Up: Implement a follow-up process to ensure that the recommendations are acted upon. Regularly review the progress of the implemented actions and assess their effectiveness in preventing similar incidents.
- Continuous Improvement: Treat post-incident analysis as an ongoing process. Regularly update the incident response plan based on the lessons learned from each incident, and continuously refine procedures and controls to enhance readiness.
- Training and Awareness: Use the findings from post-incident analysis to inform training and awareness programs. Educate the incident response team and broader organization on the lessons learned and best practices identified.

### Example Scenario

Consider a scenario where an organization experienced a data breach due to a phishing attack. During the post-incident analysis, the following steps are taken:

- Incident Review Meeting: The incident response team, IT staff, and management gather to discuss the breach.
- Root Cause Analysis: The team uses the "5 Whys" technique to determine that the breach occurred because an employee clicked on a malicious link, leading to the compromise of their credentials.
- Timeline Reconstruction: The team reconstructs the timeline, noting when the phishing email was received, when the link was clicked, and when the breach was detected.
- Data Collection and Analysis: Logs from email servers, security systems, and endpoint devices are analyzed to understand the extent of the breach and the attacker's actions.
- Performance Metrics Evaluation: Response times are compared against benchmarks, revealing delays in detection and response.
- Stakeholder Feedback: Feedback from the affected employee and IT staff highlights the need for better phishing awareness training.

**Diagram: Post-Incident Analysis Workflow**

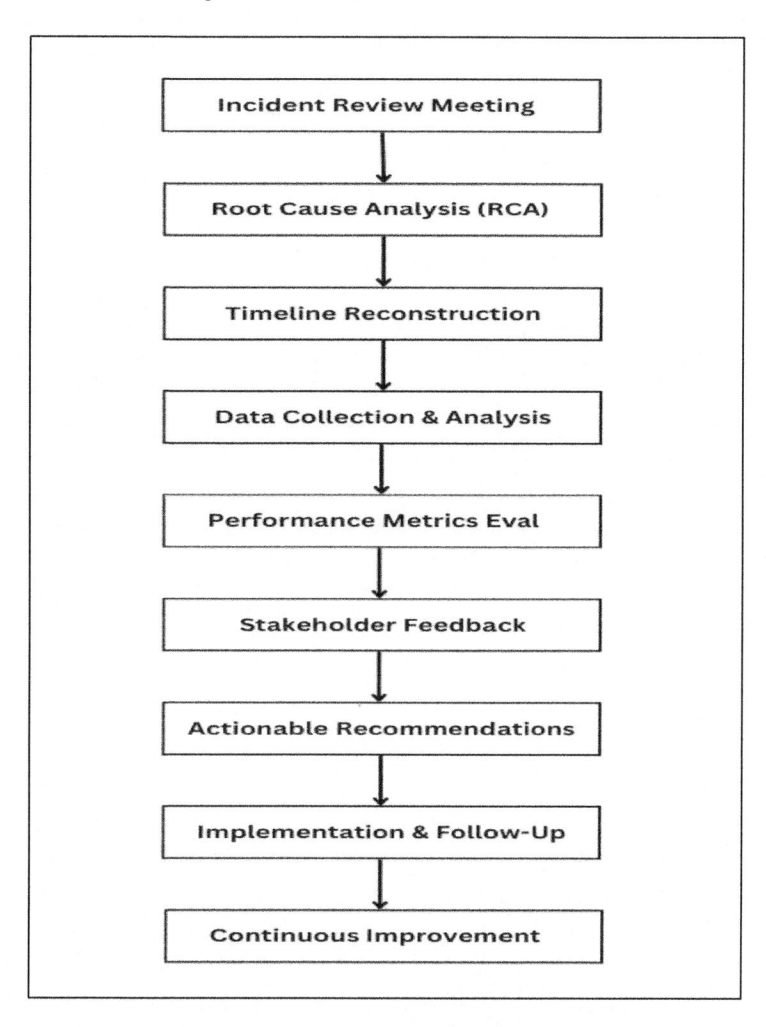

```
Incident Review Meeting
          ↓
Root Cause Analysis (RCA)
          ↓
Timeline Reconstruction
          ↓
Data Collection & Analysis
          ↓
Performance Metrics Eval
          ↓
Stakeholder Feedback
          ↓
Actionable Recommendations
          ↓
Implementation & Follow-Up
          ↓
Continuous Improvement
```

In this workflow, each step of the post-incident analysis process is connected, leading to actionable recommendations and continuous improvement. This structured approach ensures that lessons learned are effectively applied to enhance incident response processes.

By conducting thorough post-incident analysis and adhering to best practices, organizations can significantly improve their incident response capabilities, reduce the likelihood of future incidents, and enhance their overall security posture.

# 6.8 Lab Exercises
## 6.8.1 Creating an Incident Response Plan

Creating a comprehensive incident response plan tailored to an AWS environment involves several key steps, from understanding the specific requirements of your organization to implementing and testing the plan. Here is a step-by-step guide to create such a plan.

### Step 1: Define the Scope and Objectives
- Identify Assets: List all critical AWS resources (EC2 instances, S3 buckets, RDS databases, etc.) and their roles in your organization.

- Determine Objectives: Clearly define what the incident response plan aims to achieve, such as minimizing downtime, protecting sensitive data, and ensuring regulatory compliance.

### Step 2: Establish an Incident Response Team
- Assign Roles: Identify team members and assign roles, including Incident Response Manager, Security Analysts, IT Support, and Communication Officers.
- Define Responsibilities: Outline the specific responsibilities of each team member during an incident.

### Step 3: Develop Incident Response Procedures
**Preparation:**
- Ensure all team members are trained and have access to necessary tools.
- Set up AWS CloudTrail for logging and monitoring account activity.
- Implement AWS Config to monitor changes to resources and configurations.

**Detection and Analysis:**
- Enable Amazon GuardDuty for continuous threat detection.
- Set up Amazon SNS to receive real-time alerts from GuardDuty and other security services.
- Define procedures for analyzing alerts and determining the severity of incidents.

**Containment, Eradication, and Recovery:**
- Develop containment strategies for different types of incidents (e.g., isolate compromised instances).
- Create eradication procedures to remove threats (e.g., using AWS Systems Manager to run scripts).
- Outline recovery steps to restore systems to normal operation (e.g., restore from backups in AWS Backup).

**Post-Incident Analysis:**
- Define steps for conducting a post-incident review, including root cause analysis and documentation of lessons learned.
- Update incident response plans based on findings.

### Step 4: Implement Security Tools and Services
**Configure AWS CloudTrail:**
- Enable CloudTrail in all regions to log API calls and account activity.
- Store CloudTrail logs in an S3 bucket and ensure the bucket is properly secured.

**Set Up Amazon GuardDuty:**
- Enable GuardDuty in the AWS Management Console.
- Configure GuardDuty to monitor all supported data sources (VPC Flow Logs, DNS logs, CloudTrail events).

**Set Up AWS Config Rules:**
- Enable AWS Config to track changes to resources.
- Define and implement AWS Config rules to enforce compliance with your organization's security policies.

### Step 5: Develop Communication Plan
**Internal Communication:**
- Create a communication matrix that includes contact information for all team members.
- Define protocols for internal communication during an incident (e.g., secure chat channels, email).

**External Communication:**
- Develop templates for external communication, including notifications to customers and regulatory bodies.
- Define criteria for when and how to communicate with external parties.

### Step 6: Conduct Training and Simulated Drills
**Training:**
- Provide regular training sessions for the incident response team on tools and procedures.
- Conduct tabletop exercises to discuss hypothetical scenarios and responses.

**Simulated Drills:**
- Plan and execute simulated incident response drills to test the effectiveness of the plan.
- Use AWS tools like AWS IAM Access Analyzer and AWS Security Hub to simulate incidents and monitor the team's response.

### Step 7: Review and Update the Plan
**Post-Drill Review:**
- After each drill, conduct a debriefing session to discuss what worked well and what needs improvement.
- Document any issues identified and update the incident response plan accordingly.

**Continuous Improvement:**
- Regularly review and update the incident response plan to adapt to new threats and changes in the AWS environment.
- Stay informed about new AWS security services and features that can enhance your incident response capabilities.

By following these steps, you can create a robust incident response plan to detect, respond to, and recover from security incidents in an AWS environment.

## 6.8.2 Deploying AWS Security Services

This exercise will guide you through deploying and configuring key AWS security services: Security Hub, GuardDuty, Macie, Inspector, Config, Detective, and IAM Access Analyzer. Each section will include step-by-step instructions to help you set up and utilize these services effectively.

### AWS Security Hub
**Enable AWS Security Hub:**
- Open the AWS Management Console.
- Navigate to Security Hub.
- Click Enable Security Hub.

**Configure Security Standards:**
- In the Security Hub console, go to the Standards section.
- Enable desired security standards like CIS AWS Foundations, PCI DSS, or AWS Foundational Security Best Practices.

**Integrate with AWS Services:**
Security Hub automatically integrates with services like GuardDuty, Inspector, Macie, and IAM Access Analyzer. Ensure these integrations are active in the Integrations section.

### Amazon GuardDuty
**Enable GuardDuty:**
- Open the AWS Management Console.
- Navigate to GuardDuty.
- Click Get Started and then Enable GuardDuty.

**Configure Data Sources**: Ensure GuardDuty is monitoring CloudTrail logs, VPC Flow Logs, and DNS logs.

**Set Up Notifications:**
- Configure Amazon SNS to send notifications for GuardDuty findings.
- Create an SNS topic and subscribe your email or other notification endpoints.

## Amazon Macie
**Enable Macie:**
- Open the AWS Management Console.
- Navigate to Macie.
- Click Get started and then Enable Macie.

**Set Up Data Discovery:**
- Configure Macie to scan S3 buckets.
- Select the S3 buckets you want Macie to monitor for sensitive data.

**Create Findings and Alerts:**
- Configure alerting in Macie for sensitive data discoveries.
- Integrate Macie findings with Security Hub for centralized management.

## Amazon Inspector
**Enable Inspector:**
- Open the AWS Management Console.
- Navigate to Inspector.
- Click Get Started and then Create assessment target.

**Create Assessment Templates:**
- Define assessment targets by selecting EC2 instances to be scanned.
- Create assessment templates specifying rules packages (CVE database, CIS benchmarks, etc.).

**Run Assessments:**
- Start an assessment run using the created template.
- Review findings and recommendations in the Inspector console.

## AWS Config
**Enable AWS Config:**
- Open the AWS Management Console.
- Navigate to Config.
- Click Get Started and follow the setup wizard.

**Configure Rules:**
- Define Config rules to monitor compliance (e.g., ensuring S3 buckets are encrypted).
- Enable automatic remediation actions for specific rule violations.

**Review Compliance Reports:**
- Access compliance reports in the Config dashboard.
- Integrate Config findings with Security Hub for centralized visibility.

## AWS Detective
**Enable Detective:**
- Open the AWS Management Console.
- Navigate to Detective.
- Click Get Started and then Enable Detective.

**Analyze Findings:**
- Review findings imported from GuardDuty and other sources.
- Use the Detective console to investigate incidents and understand their scope.

## IAM Access Analyzer
**Enable IAM Access Analyzer:**
- Open the AWS Management Console.
- Navigate to IAM.
- In the Access Analyzer section, click Get Started and follow the prompts to create an analyzer.

**Review Findings:**
- Access findings in the IAM Access Analyzer console.
- Identify resources with public or cross-account access and review their policies.

**Remediate Issues:**
- Follow recommendations to secure resources identified by Access Analyzer.
- Integrate findings with Security Hub for a unified view of security issues.

To summarize, By following these steps, you will have deployed and configured AWS Security Hub, GuardDuty, Macie, Inspector, Config, Detective, and IAM Access Analyzer. These services provide comprehensive security monitoring, threat detection, compliance assessment, and incident investigation capabilities, helping you maintain a robust security posture in your AWS environment.

## 6.8.3 Configuring Event-Driven Security Automation

Objective of this exercise is to demonstrate the use of event-driven architecture for automated incident response by configuring Amazon EventBridge to trigger security responses based on specific events.

### Prerequisites
- AWS account with administrative access.
- Basic knowledge of AWS services: EventBridge, Lambda, SNS, and IAM.
- AWS CLI installed and configured on your local machine.

### Step 1: Create an IAM Role for Lambda

1. **Navigate to IAM** in the AWS Management Console.
2. **Create a new role**:
    - Choose **AWS service** and then **Lambda**.
    - Attach the following policies: `AWSLambdaBasicExecutionRole` and `AmazonSNSFullAccess`.
    - Name the role (e.g., `LambdaEventBridgeRole`) and create it.

### Step 2: Create an Amazon SNS Topic

1. **Navigate to SNS** in the AWS Management Console.
2. **Create a new topic**:
    - Choose **Standard** type.
    - Name the topic (e.g., SecurityAlerts).
3. **Create a subscription**:
    - Choose the protocol (e.g., **Email**).
    - Enter the endpoint (your email address).
    - Confirm the subscription from your email.

### Step 3: Create an AWS Lambda Function

1. **Navigate to Lambda** in the AWS Management Console.
2. **Create a new function**:
    - Choose **Author from scratch**.
    - Name the function (e.g., SecurityAlertFunction).
    - Select the runtime (e.g., **Python 3.9**).
    - Choose the execution role created earlier (LambdaEventBridgeRole).
3. **Add the following code** to your Lambda function:

```
1. import json
2. import boto3
3.
4. def lambda_handler(event, context):
5.     sns_client = boto3.client('sns')
6.     topic_arn = 'arn:aws:sns:your-region:your-account-id:SecurityAlerts'
7.     message = json.dumps(event)
8.     sns_client.publish(TopicArn=topic_arn, Message=message)
9.     return {
10.        'statusCode': 200,
11.        'body': json.dumps('Alert sent successfully')
12.    }
```

4. Deploy the Lambda function.

### Step 4: Create an EventBridge Rule

1. **Navigate to EventBridge** in the AWS Management Console.
2. **Create a new rule**:
    - Name the rule (e.g., SecurityAlertRule).
    - Choose the **Event Source** that will trigger the rule. For example, select **GuardDuty** as the event source to trigger on security findings.
    - Define the **Event Pattern**. For example, to trigger on all GuardDuty findings:

```
1. {
2.   "source": ["aws.guardduty"],
3.   "detail-type": ["GuardDuty Finding"]
4. }
```

3. **Add Targets**:
    - Select **Lambda function**.
    - Choose the Lambda function you created (SecurityAlertFunction).

4. **Create the rule**.

### Step 5: Test the Configuration

1. **Generate a GuardDuty finding**:
   o Simulate a finding by enabling GuardDuty and waiting for it to detect an event, or manually triggering a test event in EventBridge.
2. **Check for Alerts**:
   o Verify that the Lambda function is triggered, and an alert is sent to the SNS topic.
   o Check your email for the alert notification from SNS.

To summarize, by following these steps, you have configured Amazon EventBridge to automate security responses based on specific events. This setup demonstrates how event-driven architecture can enhance incident response by automatically triggering actions when certain conditions are met.

### Diagram: EventBridge Workflow

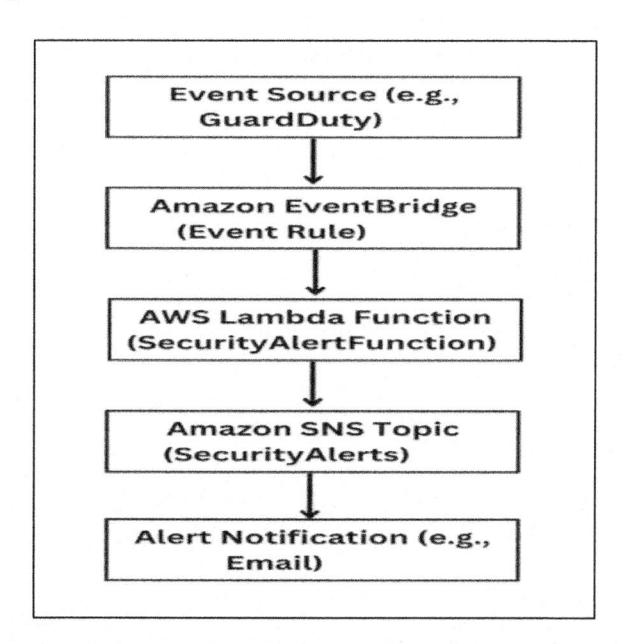

```
┌─────────────────────────┐
│ Event Source (e.g.,     │
│ GuardDuty)              │
└───────────┬─────────────┘
            ↓
┌─────────────────────────┐
│ Amazon EventBridge      │
│ (Event Rule)            │
└───────────┬─────────────┘
            ↓
┌─────────────────────────┐
│ AWS Lambda Function     │
│ (SecurityAlertFunction) │
└───────────┬─────────────┘
            ↓
┌─────────────────────────┐
│ Amazon SNS Topic        │
│ (SecurityAlerts)        │
└───────────┬─────────────┘
            ↓
┌─────────────────────────┐
│ Alert Notification (e.g.,│
│ Email)                  │
└─────────────────────────┘
```

This workflow illustrates how events from GuardDuty trigger an EventBridge rule, which invokes a Lambda function to send an alert via SNS, ultimately notifying the appropriate personnel.

## 6.8.4 Simulating and Responding to Security Incidents

The objective of this exercise to develop hands-on incident response skills in a controlled environment by practicing isolation, credential rotation, and deploying playbooks and runbooks.

### Prerequisites
- AWS account with administrative access
- Basic knowledge of AWS services: EC2, IAM, Lambda, EventBridge, and SNS
- AWS CLI installed and configured on your local machine

You will simulate a security incident where an EC2 instance is compromised. The exercise involves isolating the instance, rotating IAM credentials, and deploying predefined playbooks and runbooks to mitigate the incident.

### Step 1: Set Up the Environment
To launch an EC2 instance, open the AWS Management Console and navigate to the EC2 service. From there, launch a new instance with the required configurations, ensuring that you tag the instance with "Name=CompromisedInstance."

Next, create an IAM user and role by navigating to the IAM service. Set up a new IAM user with programmatic access, attaching policies that grant limited access to necessary services. Additionally, create an IAM role with the appropriate permissions for your Lambda function to execute.

### Step 2: Simulate the Compromise
To simulate unauthorized activity, SSH into the EC2 instance. Once inside, run a script that performs suspicious actions, such as installing unauthorized software, to mimic unauthorized activity on the instance.

### Step 3: Isolate the Compromised Instance
To create a security group for isolation, navigate to EC2 and create a new security group named IsolationGroup with no inbound rules. Once the security group is created, detach the current security group from the compromised instance and attach the IsolationGroup to the instance to isolate it from any incoming traffic.

### Step 4: Rotate IAM Credentials
**Create a Lambda Function for Credential Rotation:**
- Navigate to Lambda and create a new function named RotateCredentials.
- Use the following code to rotate the IAM credentials:

```
1. import boto3
2. import json
3.
4. def lambda_handler(event, context):
5.    iam_client = boto3.client('iam')
6.    user_name = 'CompromisedUser'
7.
8.    # Create new access key
9.    response = iam_client.create_access_key(UserName=user_name)
10.   new_access_key = response['AccessKey']
11.
12.   # Deactivate old access keys
13.   old_keys = iam_client.list_access_keys(UserName=user_name)['AccessKeyMetadata']
14.   for key in old_keys:
15.      if key['AccessKeyId'] != new_access_key['AccessKeyId']:
16.           iam_client.update_access_key(UserName=user_name, AccessKeyId=key['AccessKeyId'], Status='Inactive')
17.
18.   return {
19.      'statusCode': 200,
20.      'body': json.dumps('Credentials rotated successfully')
21.   }
22.
```

**Create an EventBridge Rule**: Navigate to EventBridge and create a rule that triggers the Lambda function when specific events occur (e.g., unauthorized API calls detected by GuardDuty).

## Step 5: Deploy Playbooks and Runbooks

To define playbooks and runbooks, it is essential to create a document that outlines the steps involved in detecting, containing, and eradicating potential threats. This document should clearly define tasks assigned to different team members. Moreover, the playbook must have sections dedicated to preparation, detection, analysis, containment, eradication, and recovery to ensure a comprehensive approach to incident response.

Once the playbooks and runbooks are created, it is important to deploy them effectively. Share these documents with your incident response team to ensure everyone is on the same page. Tools such as AWS Systems Manager can be utilized to distribute and execute the runbooks, facilitating a smoother incident response process.

## Step 6: Test the Response

To trigger an event, simulate an occurrence that matches the criteria set in the EventBridge rule, such as an unauthorized API call. After the event is triggered, verify the isolation of the compromised instance by checking its security group settings. Additionally, confirm that IAM credentials have been rotated by reviewing the IAM user's access keys.

Next, proceed to execute the playbooks and runbooks, ensuring that all documented steps are followed accurately. After completing the response, conduct a post-incident review to assess the effectiveness of the procedures and identify areas for improvement.

To summarize, by following these steps, you will have practiced isolating a compromised instance, rotating IAM credentials, and deploying playbooks and runbooks in response to a simulated security incident. This exercise helps develop practical skills in incident response, ensuring readiness for real-world scenarios.

# 6.9 Key Exam Tips

**Understand the Incident Response Lifecycle:** Be familiar with the phases of the Incident Response Lifecycle, which include preparation, detection and analysis, containment, eradication, recovery, and post-incident activity. AWS best practices stress building a robust incident response plan and ensuring ongoing testing.

**AWS Security Finding Format (ASFF):** Learn the structure and importance of the AWS Security Finding Format (ASFF). This standardized format helps normalize findings from multiple security services such as AWS Security Hub, GuardDuty, and Macie. Ensure you know how to interpret ASFF for effective threat detection and response.

**Credential Invalidation and Rotation:** Understand the significance of rotating credentials and invalidating compromised credentials during incident response. Familiarize yourself with AWS services like AWS IAM for managing credentials and how to implement temporary credentials with AWS STS for security.

**Isolating AWS Resources:** When responding to a security breach, isolating affected resources is critical to contain the threat. Understand how to use VPC Security Groups, Network ACLs, and Instance Isolation techniques in AWS to achieve quick containment of compromised resources.

**Playbooks and Runbooks:** Playbooks and Runbooks are essential tools in automating and streamlining incident responses. Playbooks define the overall strategy, while runbooks detail step-by-step procedures. Learn how to design and implement these to handle various scenarios like phishing attacks or compromised credentials.

**AWS Security Hub:** Security Hub is a centralized platform for managing security across AWS services. Ensure you know how to use Security Hub to aggregate findings from services like GuardDuty, Inspector, and Macie, and how to automate responses using Security Hub Insights and custom actions.

**Amazon GuardDuty:** GuardDuty is AWS's intelligent threat detection service. Understand how GuardDuty monitors for malicious or unauthorized activity in AWS environments, leveraging machine learning and threat intelligence. Ensure you know how to configure and interpret GuardDuty findings.

**Amazon Macie and Amazon Inspector:** Macie is used for identifying and protecting sensitive data (like personally identifiable information), while Inspector performs security assessments of EC2 instances. Be familiar with how both tools contribute to your overall incident detection strategy and integrate with AWS Security Hub.

**Integrating AWS Services with Third-Party Tools:** AWS services such as Amazon EventBridge can be used to integrate with third-party security tools for enhanced threat detection and response automation. Know how to set up and configure these integrations for a holistic security posture.

**Regular Incident Response Drills:** AWS recommends regular incident response drills to ensure your team and systems are prepared for real incidents. These simulations help identify weaknesses and improve response times. Understand the importance of post-incident reviews to improve security strategies.

## 6.10 Chapter Review Questions

**Question 1:**
What is the primary purpose of an Incident Response Plan in AWS?
A. To ensure that AWS resources are automatically optimized for cost
B. To outline the steps to detect, respond to, and recover from security incidents
C. To prevent security breaches by encrypting data automatically
D. To monitor the performance of AWS applications

**Question 2:**
Which of the following AWS services is primarily used for continuous threat detection and security monitoring across AWS accounts?
A. AWS Security Hub
B. Amazon Inspector
C. Amazon GuardDuty
D. AWS IAM Access Analyzer

**Question 3:**
What does AWS Security Finding Format (ASFF) help with in incident response?
A. It standardizes how security findings are represented across AWS services
B. It ensures that security findings are encrypted
C. It automatically remediates all security vulnerabilities
D. It integrates with third-party auditing tools to manage billing

**Question 4:**
Which AWS service can you use to automatically detect and classify sensitive data stored in S3 buckets?
A. Amazon GuardDuty
B. Amazon Macie
C. AWS Config
D. Amazon Detective

**Question 5:**
In the context of threat detection and response, what is a runbook?
A. A set of pre-configured alerts for AWS services
B. A document that outlines step-by-step instructions for responding to specific incidents
C. An AWS feature that automatically triggers incident responses
D. A manual process for evaluating cloud security posture

**Question 6:**
What is the purpose of credential invalidation and rotation in incident response?
A. To log out inactive users automatically
B. To prevent unauthorized access by invalidating compromised credentials and rotating them
C. To optimize cost usage for AWS accounts
D. To track the creation of new IAM roles

**Question 7:**
Which of the following is a best practice for threat detection and incident response?
A. Disabling continuous monitoring to reduce costs
B. Regular incident response drills to prepare for real-world scenarios
C. Using only manual tools for incident detection
D. Ignoring post-incident analysis to save time

**Question 8:**
Which service can aggregate security findings from multiple sources to provide a comprehensive view of your AWS security posture?
A. Amazon Macie
B. Amazon Detective
C. AWS Security Hub
D. AWS Config

**Question 9:**
How does Amazon Detective assist in incident response?
A. It provides automated responses to threats
B. It helps investigate and visualize security issues by analyzing and correlating log data
C. It generates encryption keys for securing sensitive data
D. It sends real-time alerts for failed login attempts

**Question 10:**
What is the role of playbooks in incident response?
A. To provide a high-level strategy for responding to common security incidents
B. To configure security policies for AWS accounts
C. To automatically encrypt sensitive data at rest
D. To notify users of application downtime

**Question 11:**
A malicious actor has compromised one of your IAM user accounts. The compromised account is making unauthorized API calls. What is the first step you should take to respond to this incident?
A. Monitor the API calls through AWS CloudWatch
B. Rotate the compromised user's credentials immediately
C. Review the user's activities using AWS CloudTrail
D. Disable logging temporarily to prevent further exposure

**Question 12:**

Your team receives a security alert from Amazon GuardDuty about an unauthorized instance communication with a known malicious IP address. What should be your first action to isolate this threat?
A. Delete the affected EC2 instance
B. Disconnect the instance from the network by modifying its security group
C. Enable AWS Shield to protect the instance
D. Review all IAM roles associated with the instance

**Question 13:**
A company is using AWS Security Hub to centralize and manage security findings across multiple accounts. After a potential phishing attack, how would you automate the process of notifying your security team and remediating affected resources?
A. Create a CloudWatch Alarm and manually notify the security team
B. Use AWS Config Rules to automatically remediate the resources
C. Set up an Amazon EventBridge rule to trigger a Lambda function that handles notifications and remediation
D. Enable GuardDuty to block all external traffic to affected instances

**Question 14:**
Your organization's Amazon Macie service has detected sensitive data stored in an S3 bucket that violates your company's data policy. You need to take immediate action to prevent further access to this bucket. What would be the best course of action?
A. Delete the bucket immediately
B. Encrypt the bucket using AWS KMS
C. Remove public access to the bucket and review its permissions
D. Transfer the sensitive data to an encrypted database

**Question 15:**
During a security incident involving unauthorized access to your EC2 instances, you need to gather and analyze log data to investigate the incident thoroughly. Which service would provide you with detailed logging information and help visualize the attack?
A. Amazon Macie
B. Amazon Detective
C. AWS IAM Access Analyzer
D. AWS Config

# 6.11 Answers to Chapter Review Questions

1. B. To outline the steps to detect, respond to, and recover from security incidents
Explanation: An Incident Response Plan ensures a structured and well-documented approach to detecting, responding to, and recovering from security incidents to minimize damage and restore normal operations.

2. C. Amazon GuardDuty
Explanation: Amazon GuardDuty is a continuous threat detection service that monitors AWS environments for malicious or unauthorized activities, helping to protect your AWS workloads.

3. A. It standardizes how security findings are represented across AWS services
Explanation: AWS Security Finding Format (ASFF) is a standardized format for security findings, making it easier to analyze and respond to issues across different AWS security services.

4. B. Amazon Macie
Explanation: Amazon Macie automatically detects, classifies, and protects sensitive data, such as personally identifiable information (PII), in Amazon S3 buckets.

5. B. A document that outlines step-by-step instructions for responding to specific incidents
Explanation: A runbook provides detailed, step-by-step instructions for handling specific security incidents, helping teams respond quickly and effectively.

6. B. To prevent unauthorized access by invalidating compromised credentials and rotating them
Explanation: In incident response, credential invalidation and rotation ensure that compromised credentials are no longer valid and new ones are issued, preventing further unauthorized access.

7. B. Regular incident response drills to prepare for real-world scenarios
Explanation: Conducting regular incident response drills ensures that teams are well-prepared to respond quickly and effectively to real-world security incidents.

8. C. AWS Security Hub
Explanation: AWS Security Hub aggregates security findings from services like GuardDuty, Inspector, and third-party tools to provide a comprehensive view of your security posture.

9. B. It helps investigate and visualize security issues by analyzing and correlating log data
Explanation: Amazon Detective assists in the investigation of security issues by analyzing and correlating data from logs to visualize suspicious activities and security threats.

10. A. To provide a high-level strategy for responding to common security incidents
Explanation: Playbooks are high-level strategies that guide teams in responding to common security incidents by outlining key steps and considerations.

11. B. Rotate the compromised user's credentials immediately
Explanation: In the event of a compromised IAM user account, the first action should be to rotate the credentials to prevent further unauthorized access. Afterward, you can review the activities using AWS CloudTrail and take additional steps to mitigate the impact.

12. B. Disconnect the instance from the network by modifying its security group
Explanation: The best immediate action is to modify the security group to isolate the instance by disconnecting it from the network. This helps contain the threat without deleting the instance, allowing you to investigate further.

13. C. Set up an Amazon EventBridge rule to trigger a Lambda function that handles notifications and remediation
Explanation: Amazon EventBridge can be used to create rules that automatically trigger responses to security findings. In this case, it can notify the security team and invoke a Lambda function to remediate affected resources.

14. C. Remove public access to the bucket and review its permissions
Explanation: Amazon Macie detects sensitive data, and the immediate action should be to remove public access and review permissions to ensure that the bucket is secured and no further unauthorized access occurs.

15. B. Amazon Detective
Explanation: Amazon Detective helps investigate and visualize security incidents by analyzing and correlating data from logs and other AWS sources. It assists in identifying the root cause and pattern of unauthorized activities.

# Chapter 7. Detecting Security Threats and Anomalies

**This chapter addresses the following exam objectives:**
Domain 1: Threat Detection and Incident Response
Task Statement 1.2: Detect security threats and anomalies by using AWS services.
Knowledge of:
- AWS managed security services that detect threats Anomaly and correlation techniques to join data across services
- Visualizations to identify anomalies
- Strategies to centralize security findings

Skills in:
- Evaluating findings from security services (for example, GuardDuty, Security Hub, Macie, AWS Config, IAM Access Analyzer)
- Searching and correlating security threats across AWS services (for example, by using Detective)
- Performing queries to validate security events (for example, by using Amazon Athena)
- Creating metric filters and dashboards to detect anomalous activity (for example, by using Amazon CloudWatch)

◆◆◆◆◆◆

In today's dynamic threat landscape, the ability to detect security threats and anomalies in real-time is crucial for maintaining the integrity and security of your AWS environment. This chapter provides a comprehensive guide to understanding and implementing effective threat detection strategies using AWS tools and services.

We begin with an introduction to security threat detection, highlighting its importance in a proactive security posture. The chapter then explores AWS managed security services, including Amazon GuardDuty, AWS Security Hub, Amazon Macie, AWS Config, and IAM Access Analyzer. Each of these services offers unique capabilities for identifying and mitigating security threats.

Anomaly and correlation techniques are essential for detecting unusual patterns and behaviors that may indicate security breaches. We delve into anomaly detection techniques and the use of Amazon Detective to investigate and correlate security findings effectively.

Visualizing security threats is another critical aspect of threat detection. The chapter covers creating visualizations, dashboards, and metric filters to monitor security events and trends. These tools help in quickly identifying and responding to potential threats.

Centralizing security findings improves the efficiency and effectiveness of threat detection. We discuss strategies for centralization and how to integrate various AWS security services with AWS Security Hub to consolidate and manage security findings from multiple sources.

Validating security events is crucial for distinguishing between false positives and genuine threats. We explore performing queries with Amazon Athena and other analysis and investigation techniques to validate and respond to security events accurately.

Best practices for threat detection, such as continuous monitoring, real-time alerts, regular audits, and reviews, are emphasized throughout the chapter. These practices ensure that your threat detection mechanisms remain robust and up-to-date with evolving threats.

To reinforce the theoretical knowledge, the chapter concludes with lab exercises that provide hands-on experience in setting up Amazon GuardDuty, creating visualizations with CloudWatch, using Amazon Athena for log analysis, and integrating various AWS security services. These exercises are designed to enhance your practical skills and prepare you for real-world security challenges.

By the end of this chapter, readers will have a thorough understanding of how to detect security threats and anomalies using AWS services and best practices, ensuring a strong and proactive security posture for their AWS environments.

## 7.1 Introduction to Security Threat Detection

Detecting security threats and anomalies in AWS environments is critical for maintaining the integrity, confidentiality, and availability of cloud resources. The dynamic nature of AWS, with its scalable and flexible infrastructure, makes it a prime target for various cyber threats. Therefore, proactive monitoring and quick identification of potential security issues are essential to safeguard against data breaches, unauthorized access, and other malicious activities.

Proactive monitoring involves continuously observing AWS environments for unusual patterns or behaviors that might indicate a security threat. This can include unexpected changes in configurations, unusual API calls, or anomalous network traffic. Organizations can implement robust threat detection mechanisms that provide real-time alerts and detailed insights into security events by leveraging AWS-native tools like Amazon GuardDuty, AWS CloudTrail, Amazon Macie, and AWS Security Hub.

Quick identification of potential security issues allows organizations to respond promptly, mitigating the impact of any detected threats. This includes isolating compromised resources, rotating credentials, and deploying predefined incident response playbooks. Effective threat detection not only helps in preventing data loss and service disruptions but also ensures compliance with industry regulations and standards.

Understanding AWS's foundational concepts of threat detection mechanisms is essential for security professionals. It includes knowledge of how AWS services integrate to provide a comprehensive security posture, the types of threats and anomalies that can occur in cloud environments, and best practices for implementing and managing these security services. This knowledge empowers organizations to build resilient security architectures that can adapt to evolving threats and ensure the continuous protection of their AWS infrastructure.

## 7.2 AWS Managed Security Services

AWS Managed Security Services offer a suite of security solutions designed to protect cloud environments through continuous monitoring, threat detection, and automated responses. These services, including AWS

Security Hub, Amazon GuardDuty, AWS Shield, and AWS WAF, provide organizations with robust, scalable security measures that help safeguard their data and applications against evolving cyber threats. By leveraging AWS Managed Security Services, organizations can enhance their security posture while reducing the operational burden of managing security infrastructure.

## 7.2.1 Amazon GuardDuty

Amazon GuardDuty is a managed threat detection service that continuously monitors your AWS environment for malicious activity and unauthorized behavior, providing an essential layer of security to help protect your cloud infrastructure. Leveraging machine learning, anomaly detection, and integrated threat intelligence, GuardDuty analyzes various data sources, including AWS CloudTrail event logs, Amazon VPC Flow Logs, and DNS logs, to detect a wide range of potential threats such as compromised instances, unusual API activity, and unauthorized data exfiltration attempts.

GuardDuty's threat detection capabilities are built on several key features. Firstly, it uses machine learning to establish a baseline of normal activity within your AWS environment, allowing it to identify deviations that may indicate suspicious behavior. Secondly, it integrates threat intelligence from both AWS and external sources to identify known malicious IP addresses, domains, and malware signatures. This combination of anomaly detection and threat intelligence enables GuardDuty to provide high-fidelity alerts with minimal false positives.

Once a threat is detected, GuardDuty generates detailed findings that include information about the affected resources, the nature of the threat, and recommended remediation steps. These findings can be viewed in the GuardDuty console, sent to AWS Security Hub for centralized management, or forwarded to other AWS services like Amazon SNS for automated notifications and incident response workflows.

As part of AWS's suite of managed security services, GuardDuty complements other tools designed to enhance security posture. AWS Security Hub aggregates and prioritizes security findings from GuardDuty and other services, providing a comprehensive view of your security state. Amazon Macie helps identify and protect sensitive data by scanning S3 buckets for personally identifiable information (PII) and other critical data. AWS Shield and AWS WAF protect against DDoS attacks and web application threats.

In summary, Amazon GuardDuty is a powerful tool for detecting threats and monitoring malicious activity in your AWS environment. Its continuous monitoring, advanced threat detection capabilities, and integration with other AWS security services make it a crucial component of a robust cloud security strategy. Understanding and utilizing these managed security services can significantly enhance your ability to detect, respond to, and mitigate security threats in the cloud.

## 7.2.2 AWS Security Hub

AWS Security Hub is a comprehensive security service designed to provide a unified view of security across your AWS environment. It integrates with various AWS security services and third-party products to aggregate, prioritize, and manage security findings from multiple accounts, offering a holistic approach to threat detection and response.

**Key Features of AWS Security Hub**
**Centralized Security Management:** AWS Security Hub consolidates security findings from multiple sources, including Amazon GuardDuty, Amazon Inspector, AWS Config, and third-party security products. This centralized management allows for a single pane of glass to view and manage security alerts.

**Automated Compliance Checks:** Security Hub continuously assesses your AWS environment against industry standards and best practices such as CIS AWS Foundations Benchmark and PCI DSS. It provides detailed compliance reports and highlights areas that require attention, helping organizations maintain compliance and improve their security posture.

**Security Findings Aggregation:** Security Hub collects and normalizes findings from integrated sources, presenting them in a standardized format. This aggregation enables quick identification and understanding of security issues across different AWS accounts and regions.

**Prioritization and Visualization:** Security Hub uses predefined severity levels to prioritize findings. It provides visualizations such as dashboards and charts to help security teams quickly grasp the security state of their AWS environment, focusing on the most critical issues first.

**Automated Response and Remediation:** By integrating with AWS Lambda and AWS Systems Manager, Security Hub allows for automated responses to security findings. This capability helps in reducing the time to remediate issues, enhancing the overall security posture.

### How AWS Security Hub Aggregates and Prioritizes Findings

AWS Security Hub collects security findings from various AWS services and third-party tools through a standardized format known as the Amazon Security Finding Format (ASFF). This format ensures consistency and facilitates the aggregation of data from different sources. Security Hub normalizes these findings, categorizing them based on predefined rules to eliminate duplicates and provide a clear overview of the security state.

The findings are prioritized based on their severity, potential impact, and relevance to compliance standards. Each finding is assigned a severity score (low, medium, high, critical) and includes detailed metadata such as resource information, remediation steps, and compliance status. This prioritization allows security teams to focus on the most critical issues, enabling efficient and effective incident response.

### Integration with AWS Managed Security Services

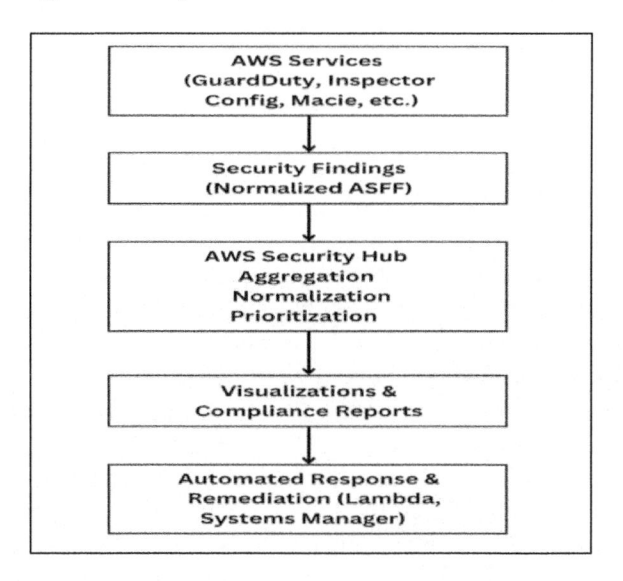

```
┌─────────────────────────┐
│   AWS Services          │
│ (GuardDuty, Inspector   │
│  Config, Macie, etc.)   │
└───────────┬─────────────┘
            ↓
┌─────────────────────────┐
│   Security Findings     │
│   (Normalized ASFF)     │
└───────────┬─────────────┘
            ↓
┌─────────────────────────┐
│   AWS Security Hub      │
│   Aggregation           │
│   Normalization         │
│   Prioritization        │
└───────────┬─────────────┘
            ↓
┌─────────────────────────┐
│   Visualizations &      │
│   Compliance Reports    │
└───────────┬─────────────┘
            ↓
┌─────────────────────────┐
│ Automated Response &    │
│ Remediation (Lambda,    │
│ Systems Manager)        │
└─────────────────────────┘
```

- AWS Security Hub integrates seamlessly with other AWS managed security services to enhance its threat detection and response capabilities:
- Amazon GuardDuty: Provides continuous threat detection by monitoring AWS resources for unusual and unauthorized behavior. Findings from GuardDuty are aggregated into Security Hub for centralized management.
- Amazon Inspector: Conducts automated security assessments to identify vulnerabilities and deviations from best practices. Inspector findings are integrated into Security Hub for a comprehensive view.

- **AWS Config:** Monitors and records AWS resource configurations and evaluates them against compliance rules. Config findings are aggregated into Security Hub to ensure compliance and security best practices are maintained.
- **Amazon Macie:** Identifies and protects sensitive data stored in S3 buckets. Macie findings are included in Security Hub to manage data protection issues.

To summarize, AWS Security Hub provides a centralized and comprehensive solution for managing security across AWS environments. By aggregating and prioritizing security findings from multiple sources, it enables organizations to quickly identify, understand, and respond to potential threats. Integrating with other AWS managed security services, Security Hub enhances threat detection and response capabilities, helping maintain a robust and compliant security posture.

## 7.2.3 Amazon Macie

Amazon Macie is a fully managed data security and privacy service that uses ML and pattern matching to discover, classify, and protect sensitive data stored in Amazon S3. By continuously monitoring S3 buckets, Macie helps organizations gain visibility into the location and security of their sensitive information, ensuring compliance with data privacy regulations and minimizing the risk of data breaches.

### Key Features
- **Data Discovery:** Macie automatically scans S3 buckets to identify sensitive data, such as personally identifiable information (PII), financial data, and intellectual property. By leveraging machine learning, Macie can accurately recognize and classify various types of sensitive information.
- **Data Classification:** Once sensitive data is discovered, Macie classifies it based on predefined categories. This classification enables organizations to understand the type and amount of sensitive data they hold, facilitating better data management and protection strategies.
- **Continuous Monitoring:** Macie continuously monitors S3 buckets for sensitive data and any changes to the data, ensuring that organizations maintain an up-to-date understanding of their data landscape. It also detects changes to bucket policies and configurations that might affect the security of the data.
- **Security Alerts:** Macie generates detailed findings when sensitive data is discovered or when there are policy violations, such as overly permissive access settings. These findings include information about the type of data, its location, and the associated risk level, allowing organizations to take immediate action to secure the data.
- **Compliance Reporting:** Macie helps organizations comply with data privacy regulations, such as GDPR, HIPAA, and CCPA, by providing insights into where sensitive data is stored and how it is being accessed. The service also supports compliance reporting by generating detailed audit reports.

### Integration with AWS Managed Security Services
Amazon Macie integrates seamlessly with other AWS managed security services to provide a comprehensive security posture:
- **AWS Security Hub:** Macie findings are integrated with AWS Security Hub, allowing for centralized management and prioritization of security alerts across multiple AWS accounts and regions. Security Hub aggregates findings from Macie and other services, providing a unified view of the security state.
- **Amazon GuardDuty:** While Macie focuses on data security, GuardDuty provides continuous threat detection across AWS accounts by monitoring for malicious activity and unauthorized behavior. Findings from both services can be viewed and managed in Security Hub, enhancing threat detection and response capabilities.
- **AWS CloudTrail:** Macie leverages AWS CloudTrail logs to monitor API calls and detect changes to S3 bucket configurations. This integration helps identify unauthorized access and policy changes that could compromise sensitive data.

- **AWS Config:** Macie works with AWS Config to track changes to S3 bucket configurations and ensure they comply with organizational policies and best practices. AWS Config rules can trigger Macie scans when specific changes are detected, ensuring continuous compliance.

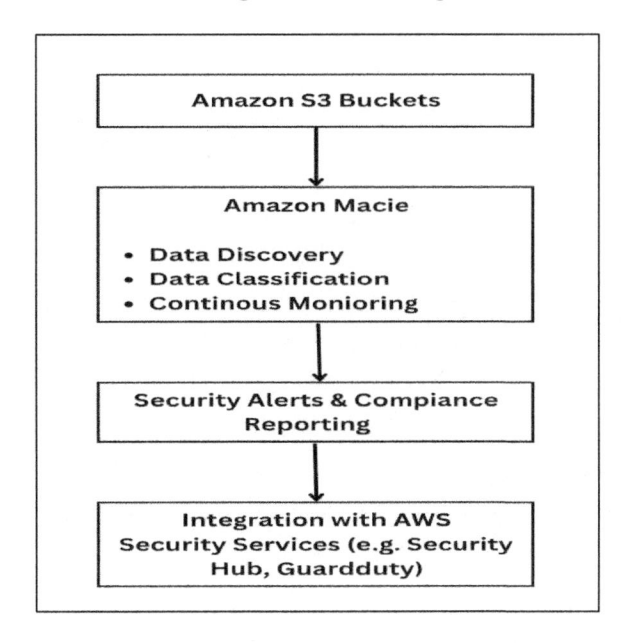

```
┌─────────────────────────────────┐
│        Amazon S3 Buckets        │
└─────────────────────────────────┘
              │
              ▼
┌─────────────────────────────────┐
│         Amazon Macie            │
│  • Data Discovery               │
│  • Data Classification          │
│  • Continous Monioring          │
└─────────────────────────────────┘
              │
              ▼
┌─────────────────────────────────┐
│  Security Alerts & Compliance   │
│            Reporting            │
└─────────────────────────────────┘
              │
              ▼
┌─────────────────────────────────┐
│      Integration with AWS       │
│  Security Services (e.g. Security│
│       Hub, Guardduty)           │
└─────────────────────────────────┘
```

Amazon Macie provides essential capabilities for discovering and protecting sensitive data stored in AWS. Its use of machine learning for data discovery and classification, combined with continuous monitoring and security alerts, helps organizations maintain robust data security and compliance with data privacy regulations. Macie enhances the overall security posture by integrating with other AWS managed security services like AWS Security Hub, Amazon GuardDuty, and AWS Config, ensuring comprehensive protection of sensitive information in the cloud.

## 7.2.4 AWS Config

AWS Config is a powerful service that provides detailed inventory and configuration history of AWS resources, playing a critical role in assessing compliance and detecting configuration changes. By continuously monitoring and recording the configurations of your AWS resources, AWS Config helps you maintain a comprehensive view of your infrastructure's state over time.

**Detailed Inventory and Configuration History**

AWS Config captures configuration snapshots and changes in your AWS resources, such as EC2 instances, S3 buckets, and IAM roles. This data is stored in a centralized repository, allowing you to view historical configurations and understand how your resources have evolved. The configuration history includes details such as security group rules, instance types, and bucket policies, enabling you to track changes and identify misconfigurations.

**Role in Assessing Compliance**

AWS Config is instrumental in ensuring compliance with internal policies and external regulatory requirements. It provides a set of pre-built rules, known as Config Rules, that can be customized to evaluate your resources against best practices and compliance standards. For example, you can create rules to ensure that all S3 buckets are encrypted or that IAM users do not have overly permissive policies. AWS Config continuously evaluates your resources against these rules and generates compliance reports, highlighting non-compliant resources and providing remediation guidance.

**Detecting Configuration Changes**

One of AWS Config's key features is its ability to detect configuration changes in real-time. When a change is detected, AWS Config records the new configuration and triggers notifications, enabling you to respond promptly to unauthorized or unexpected changes. This is crucial for maintaining security and operational stability, as it allows you to quickly identify and address potential issues before they escalate.

**Integration with Other AWS Managed Security Services**
AWS Config integrates seamlessly with other AWS managed security services to enhance threat detection and response capabilities:
- **AWS Security Hub:** Aggregates and prioritizes security findings from AWS Config and other services, providing a comprehensive view of your security posture. Security Hub helps you manage compliance findings and take action on non-compliant resources.
- **Amazon GuardDuty:** Provides continuous threat detection by monitoring for anomalous and unauthorized activities. Findings from GuardDuty can be correlated with configuration changes detected by AWS Config to identify potential security incidents.
- **AWS CloudTrail:** Logs API calls and provides visibility into user activities and resource changes. AWS Config uses CloudTrail logs to track configuration changes and correlate them with specific API calls and users.
- **AWS Lambda:** Automates remediation actions for non-compliant resources detected by AWS Config. For example, you can create Lambda functions that automatically revert unauthorized changes or enforce compliance policies.

In summary, AWS Config provides invaluable capabilities for maintaining a detailed inventory and configuration history of AWS resources, assessing compliance, and detecting configuration changes. By integrating with other AWS managed security services, AWS Config enhances your ability to detect and respond to threats, ensuring a secure and compliant cloud environment. This comprehensive visibility and real-time monitoring are essential for maintaining the integrity and security of your AWS infrastructure.

## 7.2.5 IAM Access Analyzer

AWS IAM Access Analyzer is a security tool designed to help organizations identify resources that are shared with external entities and assess the associated risks. By analyzing resource policies, Access Analyzer provides insights into unintended and potentially risky resource sharing, enabling organizations to enhance their security posture and prevent data leaks.

**Key Features of IAM Access Analyzer**
**Policy Analysis:** IAM Access Analyzer examines resource policies to identify any resources that are shared outside of your AWS account. This includes S3 buckets, IAM roles, KMS keys, Lambda functions, and more. The analysis helps detect unintended access that could lead to security vulnerabilities.
**Detailed Findings:** The service generates findings for resources that are shared with external entities. Each finding includes detailed information about the resource, the type of access granted, and the external entities involved. This allows security teams to quickly understand and remediate potential risks.
**Continuous Monitoring:** IAM Access Analyzer continuously monitors resource policies and updates findings in real-time. This ensures that any changes to resource sharing configurations are immediately detected, providing ongoing protection against unauthorized access.
**Actionable Insights:** Findings from IAM Access Analyzer include recommendations for remediation. These insights help organizations adjust resource policies to limit external access, ensuring that only authorized entities have access to sensitive resources.
**Integration with AWS Security Services:** IAM Access Analyzer integrates with other AWS security services, such as AWS Security Hub, to provide a centralized view of security findings. This integration helps streamline security management and enhances the ability to detect and respond to threats.

**Role in Threat Detection**

IAM Access Analyzer plays a critical role in threat detection by identifying potential security risks associated with resource sharing. In cloud environments, inadvertent sharing of resources can lead to data breaches and unauthorized access. By continuously monitoring resource policies and identifying risky configurations, IAM Access Analyzer helps organizations mitigate these risks and maintain a secure AWS environment.

**Integration with AWS Managed Security Services**
IAM Access Analyzer works in conjunction with other AWS managed security services to provide comprehensive threat detection and response capabilities:
- **AWS Security Hub:** Aggregates findings from IAM Access Analyzer and other security services, providing a centralized dashboard for managing security alerts and compliance status. Security Hub helps prioritize findings and coordinate response efforts.
- **Amazon GuardDuty:** Detects anomalous and unauthorized behavior across AWS accounts. Findings from GuardDuty can complement IAM Access Analyzer by identifying suspicious activities that may result from unauthorized access detected by Access Analyzer.
- **AWS Config:** Monitors configuration changes and evaluates compliance with defined rules. IAM Access Analyzer findings can be correlated with AWS Config rules to ensure that resource policies adhere to security best practices and compliance requirements.

In summary, IAM Access Analyzer is a vital tool for identifying and mitigating risks associated with resource sharing in AWS environments. By providing detailed findings and continuous monitoring, it helps organizations ensure that their resource policies are secure and compliant. Integration with other AWS managed security services further enhances the ability to detect, respond to, and remediate security threats, maintaining a robust and secure cloud infrastructure.

# 7.3 Anomaly and Correlation Techniques

Anomaly and correlation techniques are critical components of modern cybersecurity strategies, enabling organizations to detect unusual patterns and relationships within their data that may indicate potential security threats. Anomaly detection focuses on identifying deviations from normal behavior, while correlation techniques analyze the relationships between different events to uncover complex attack patterns. Together, these techniques enhance the ability to proactively identify and respond to security incidents, improving overall threat detection and response capabilities.

## 7.3.1 Anomaly Detection Techniques

Detecting anomalies in AWS environments involves leveraging various techniques to analyze patterns and identify deviations from normal behavior. Organizations can join data across different services by focusing on anomaly and correlation techniques to gain comprehensive insights into their cloud infrastructure's security state.

**Techniques for Anomaly Detection**
- **Machine Learning-Based Anomaly Detection:** AWS services like Amazon GuardDuty and AWS CloudTrail use machine learning algorithms to identify unusual patterns in data. These algorithms learn from historical data to establish a baseline of normal behavior. Any deviation from this baseline, such as unexpected API calls or irregular network traffic, is flagged as an anomaly. For example, GuardDuty can detect instances of unusual login attempts, changes in user behavior, or communication with known malicious IP addresses.
- **Statistical Analysis:** Statistical methods involve using metrics such as mean, standard deviation, and percentiles to detect anomalies. AWS CloudWatch enables the creation of custom metrics and alarms that trigger when monitored values deviate significantly from expected ranges. This approach is useful for monitoring resource utilization, such as CPU usage or network throughput, where significant deviations could indicate potential security incidents.

- **Rule-Based Detection:** Predefined rules and thresholds can be used to identify anomalies. AWS Config allows users to define rules that assess whether AWS resources comply with specified configurations. Deviations from these configurations are flagged as non-compliant, potentially indicating security risks. For example, a rule might check if all S3 buckets are encrypted, and any deviation would trigger an alert.

## Correlation Techniques

- **Event Correlation:** Correlation involves linking related events to uncover complex attack patterns. AWS Security Hub aggregates findings from multiple AWS services and third-party tools, enabling correlation across different data sources. By correlating events such as IAM policy changes, network traffic anomalies, and GuardDuty findings, Security Hub provides a comprehensive view of potential security incidents.
- **Cross-Service Data Integration:** Integrating data from various AWS services enhances anomaly detection and correlation. For instance, combining VPC Flow Logs, CloudTrail logs, and GuardDuty findings can provide a more complete picture of network and user activities. AWS Lake Formation allows for centralized data lakes, facilitating the integration and analysis of data across services.
- **Temporal Correlation:** This technique involves analyzing the timing of events to identify patterns that might indicate an ongoing attack. AWS CloudTrail logs, which record API activity, can be correlated with GuardDuty findings to detect sequences of events that may suggest an attacker's presence, such as simultaneous login attempts from different locations.

## Example Scenario

Consider a scenario where multiple unsuccessful login attempts are detected, followed by a successful login and an unexpected change in IAM policies. Using machine learning-based anomaly detection, GuardDuty flags unusual log in attempts. Correlation techniques then link these events with the subsequent IAM policy changes logged by CloudTrail, indicating a potential account compromise. AWS Security Hub aggregates these findings, prioritizing the incident for immediate investigation.

**Anomaly Detection and Correlation Workflow**

```
Data Resources
(CloudTrail, VPC Flow Logs,
GuardDuty, etc.)
         ↓
Anomaly Detection
- Machine Learning
- Statistical Analysis
- Rule-Based Detection
         ↓
Event Corelation
- Event Correlation
- Cross-Service Data
- Temporal Correlation
         ↓
Security Findings
(AWS Security Hub)
         ↓
Incident Response
(Investigate and Remediate)
```

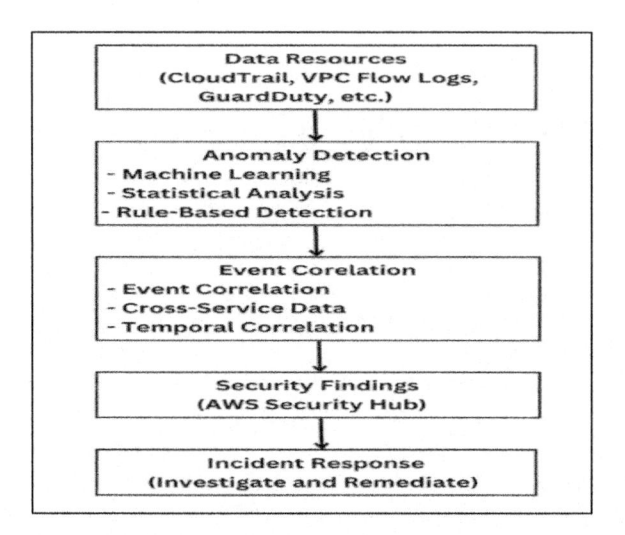

To summarize, detecting anomalies in AWS environments requires a combination of techniques to analyze patterns and identify deviations from normal behavior. Machine learning, statistical analysis, and rule-based detection are key methods used to detect anomalies. Correlation techniques, such as event correlation and cross-service data integration, enhance the ability to link related events and uncover complex security incidents. By leveraging these techniques, organizations can improve their threat detection and response capabilities, ensuring a robust security posture in their AWS environments.

## 7.3.2 Using Amazon Detective

Amazon Detective simplifies security investigations by analyzing and visualizing data from multiple sources, enabling security teams to uncover the root cause of potential security issues more efficiently. By leveraging machine learning, statistical analysis, and graph theory, Amazon Detective automatically collects and organizes data from AWS services, providing a detailed and interactive view of activities and relationships within your AWS environment.

### Analyzing and Visualizing Data

- Amazon Detective ingests data from key AWS services, including Amazon GuardDuty, AWS CloudTrail, and Amazon VPC Flow Logs. It then processes this data to create a unified and context-rich view of your AWS resources and their interactions. The service uses machine learning models to detect patterns, anomalies, and correlations within the data, which helps in identifying suspicious activities and potential security threats.
- The visualization capabilities of Amazon Detective are particularly powerful. It provides an intuitive graphical interface that displays the relationships and interactions between various AWS resources. This visual representation helps security analysts quickly understand the scope and context of an incident, making it easier to trace the sequence of events leading up to and following a security issue.

### Searching and Correlating Security Threats

- One of the core strengths of Amazon Detective is its ability to correlate data from multiple sources to provide comprehensive insights into security threats. For instance, when a GuardDuty finding indicates a potential security issue, Amazon Detective automatically correlates this finding with relevant CloudTrail logs and VPC Flow Logs. This correlation helps identify the specific actions and network traffic associated with the threat, providing a complete picture of the incident.
- Amazon Detective's search functionality allows security teams to query historical data and investigate specific activities or resources. Analysts can search for particular events, such as API calls, network connections, or changes in resource configurations. The results are presented in a detailed timeline, showing how different events are related and helping to pinpoint the root cause of the issue.

**Example Scenario**

Consider a scenario where GuardDuty detects suspicious API calls indicating potential credential compromise. Amazon Detective automatically correlates this finding with CloudTrail logs to show the sequence of API calls made by the compromised credentials. It also correlates VPC Flow Logs to highlight any unusual network activity originating from the affected resources. By visualizing these relationships, Detective helps the security team understand how the credentials were compromised, what actions were taken by the attacker, and what other resources may be affected.

**Diagram: Amazon Detective Workflow**

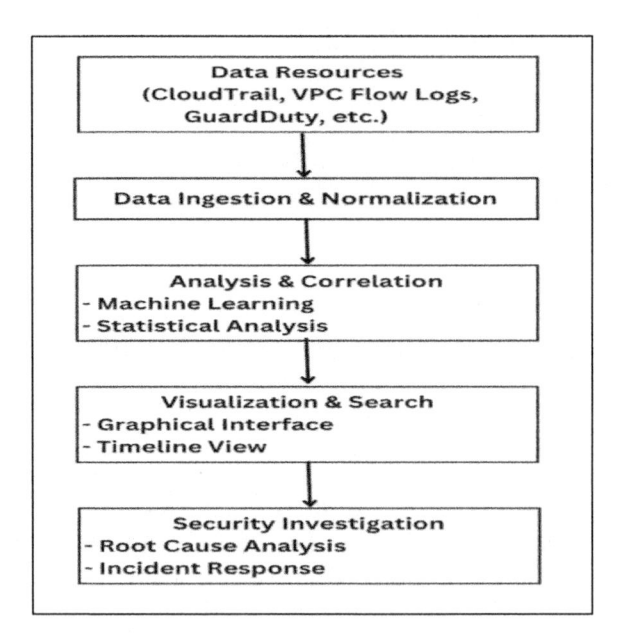

```
Data Resources
(CloudTrail, VPC Flow Logs,
GuardDuty, etc.)
          ↓
Data Ingestion & Normalization
          ↓
Analysis & Correlation
- Machine Learning
- Statistical Analysis
          ↓
Visualization & Search
- Graphical Interface
- Timeline View
          ↓
Security Investigation
- Root Cause Analysis
- Incident Response
```

In summary, Amazon Detective enhances the efficiency and effectiveness of security investigations by automating the analysis and correlation of data from multiple AWS sources. Its ability to visualize complex relationships and provide a detailed context around security incidents simplifies the process of uncovering the root cause of potential security issues. By integrating with other AWS security services, Amazon Detective enables comprehensive threat detection and response, helping organizations maintain a secure and resilient cloud environment.

# 7.4 Visualizing Security Threats

Visualizing security threats involves using graphical representations to understand and analyze the nature, scope, and impact of potential security incidents. By transforming complex data into intuitive visual formats, such as charts, graphs, and network maps, security teams can quickly identify patterns, anomalies, and relationships, enhancing their ability to detect, investigate, and respond to threats effectively. This approach aids in comprehending the overall security posture and making informed decisions to protect the organization's assets.

## 7.4.1 Creating Visualizations

Creating visualizations to identify security anomalies and trends is a crucial aspect of maintaining a robust security posture in AWS environments. Tools like Amazon QuickSight and AWS CloudWatch provide powerful capabilities for transforming raw security data into actionable insights through intuitive visual formats.

### Techniques for Creating Visualizations
**Amazon QuickSight**
- Data Integration: QuickSight allows you to integrate data from multiple AWS services, such as CloudTrail logs, VPC Flow Logs, and GuardDuty findings. By consolidating this data into a single dashboard, you can gain a comprehensive view of your security landscape.
- Custom Dashboards: Create custom dashboards that highlight key security metrics and indicators. For example, you can visualize the frequency of specific API calls, the distribution of security findings by severity, or the trend of network traffic over time.

- Interactive Visualizations: Utilize QuickSight's interactive capabilities to drill down into specific data points. For instance, clicking on a spike in login attempts can reveal the source IP addresses, the times of attempts, and any associated GuardDuty findings, helping to identify potential brute force attacks.
- Alerts and Notifications: Set up visual thresholds and alerts within QuickSight to notify you of unusual activities. For example, you can configure alerts for when the number of denied API calls exceeds a certain threshold, indicating possible reconnaissance activities.

**AWS CloudWatch**
- CloudWatch Metrics and Alarms: Use CloudWatch to create and monitor custom metrics that are relevant to your security posture. Metrics such as CPU utilization, network in/out, and disk read/write operations can indicate anomalous behavior when they deviate from established baselines.
- Log Insights: CloudWatch Log Insights enables you to run queries on your log data and create visualizations based on the results. For example, you can query CloudTrail logs to visualize the frequency of specific API calls or to identify patterns in failed login attempts.
- Dashboards: Build CloudWatch dashboards to display real-time data and historical trends. These dashboards can include widgets for metrics, alarms, and log insights, providing a centralized view of your security metrics.
- Anomaly Detection: Leverage CloudWatch Anomaly Detection to automatically apply machine learning models to your metrics. This feature helps you identify deviations from normal behavior, such as sudden spikes in traffic or unexpected changes in resource utilization.

**Example Scenario**
Imagine you want to monitor for unusual login activities and data access patterns. By using Amazon QuickSight and AWS CloudWatch, you can create visualizations that provide insights into these activities:
- QuickSight Dashboard: Integrate data from GuardDuty and CloudTrail into QuickSight to visualize login attempts and data access. Create bar charts showing the number of login attempts by source IP and time of day. Use heat maps to highlight regions with the most frequent access attempts.
- CloudWatch Metrics: Monitor metrics such as the number of login failures and the volume of data transferred. Set up CloudWatch alarms to alert you when login failures exceed a predefined threshold, indicating possible brute force attacks.
- Log Insights Queries: Use CloudWatch Log Insights to query CloudTrail logs for patterns in API calls. Create visualizations that show the distribution of API calls by user, highlighting any unusual activities by specific users or roles.

## Diagram: Visualization Workflow

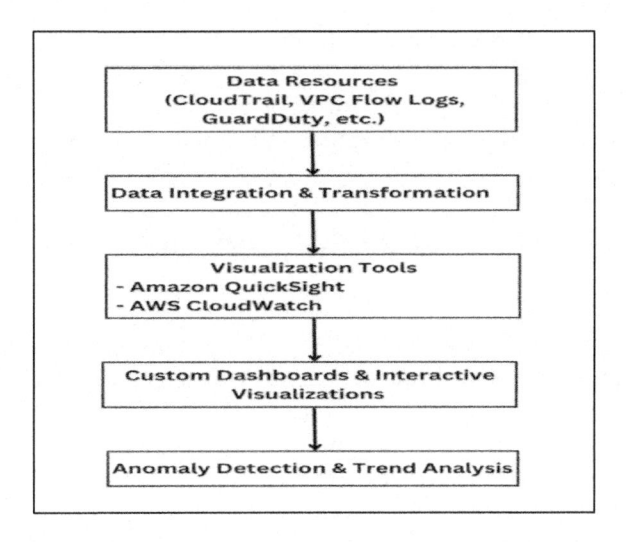

In summary, using tools like Amazon QuickSight and AWS CloudWatch to create visualizations helps identify security anomalies and trends by transforming raw data into meaningful insights. Custom dashboards, interactive visualizations, and real-time alerts enable security teams to monitor their AWS environments effectively, quickly identify potential threats, and respond to incidents with greater accuracy. By leveraging these visualization techniques, organizations can enhance their ability to detect and mitigate security anomalies, ensuring a robust security posture.

## 7.4.2 Dashboards and Metric Filters

Creating dashboards and metric filters in Amazon CloudWatch is a powerful way to detect and respond to anomalous activity in your AWS environment. These tools enable you to monitor real-time data, set up alerts, and visualize trends and patterns, helping you quickly identify and address potential security issues.

### Creating Metric Filters in Amazon CloudWatch

**Define Log Group:** First, ensure that you have a log group that collects the relevant logs, such as CloudTrail logs for API activity or VPC Flow Logs for network traffic.

**Create a Metric Filter:**
To set up a metric filter in CloudWatch, start by navigating to the CloudWatch console and selecting Logs. Choose the log group where your logs are stored. Click on "Create Metric Filter" and provide a filter pattern, which determines which log events trigger the metric. For instance, to monitor unauthorized API calls, you might use a pattern that matches "AccessDenied" in CloudTrail logs. Next, define a name for the metric filter and specify a namespace and metric name. Set the Metric Value to 1 to count each matching log event.

**Assign a Metric Filter to a Log Group:** Choose the log group to which you want to assign the metric filter. Click Create Filter and review the configuration.

### Creating Dashboards in Amazon CloudWatch

**Create a Dashboard:** Navigate to the CloudWatch console and select Dashboards. Click Create Dashboard, enter a name for your dashboard, and choose a layout (e.g., single value, line, or bar graph).

**Add Widgets to the Dashboard:** After creating the dashboard, add widgets to visualize your metrics. Click Add Widget and select the type of widget you want to use, such as a time series graph or a single number widget. Configure the widget by selecting the namespace and the metric name you defined with your metric filter. For example, choose the namespace and metric for unauthorized API calls.

**Customize the Widgets:** Customize the widgets to display relevant information. You can adjust the time range, set thresholds, and add annotations to highlight specific events or periods of interest. Repeat the process to add more widgets for different metrics, such as failed login attempts or unusual data transfer volumes.

### Example Scenario: Detecting Unauthorized API Calls

Imagine you want to monitor for unauthorized API calls to detect potential security breaches:

**Set Up a Metric Filter:** Create a metric filter for your CloudTrail log group with the filter pattern { $.errorCode = "AccessDenied" }. This filter captures all log entries where an API call was denied due to insufficient permissions. Define the metric filter with a namespace (e.g., SecurityMetrics) and a metric name (e.g., UnauthorizedAPICalls).

**Create a CloudWatch Dashboard:** Create a new dashboard named SecurityMonitoring. Add a widget to the dashboard to display the UnauthorizedAPICalls metric as a time series graph. This graph shows the number of unauthorized API calls over time. Set alarms on this metric to notify you when the number of unauthorized calls exceeds a certain threshold, indicating a potential security issue.

### Responding to Anomalous Activity

**Set Up Alarms:** Create CloudWatch alarms for critical metrics to receive notifications when anomalous activity is detected. For example, set an alarm on the UnauthorizedAPICalls metric to trigger if the count exceeds a predefined limit within a specific time frame. Configure the alarm actions to notify your incident response team via Amazon SNS, triggering an automated response or sending an email notification.

**Investigate and Respond:** Use the dashboard to investigate the anomalies. Drill down into specific time periods to view detailed log data and identify the root cause of the anomalies. Take appropriate action to mitigate the issue, such as revoking compromised credentials, blocking malicious IP addresses, or tightening IAM policies.

### Diagram: CloudWatch Monitoring Workflow

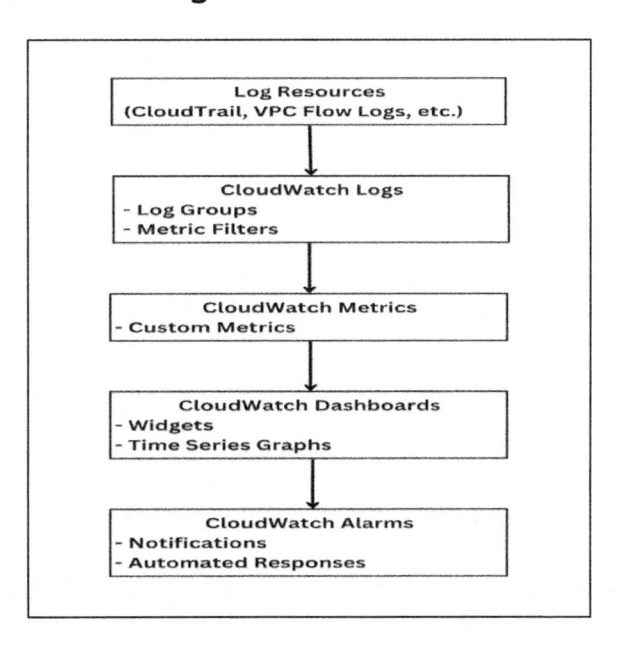

```
┌─────────────────────────────────┐
│         Log Resources           │
│ (CloudTrail, VPC Flow Logs, etc.)│
└─────────────────────────────────┘
              │
              ▼
┌─────────────────────────────────┐
│        CloudWatch Logs          │
│ - Log Groups                    │
│ - Metric Filters                │
└─────────────────────────────────┘
              │
              ▼
┌─────────────────────────────────┐
│       CloudWatch Metrics        │
│ - Custom Metrics                │
└─────────────────────────────────┘
              │
              ▼
┌─────────────────────────────────┐
│      CloudWatch Dashboards      │
│ - Widgets                       │
│ - Time Series Graphs            │
└─────────────────────────────────┘
              │
              ▼
┌─────────────────────────────────┐
│        CloudWatch Alarms        │
│ - Notifications                 │
│ - Automated Responses           │
└─────────────────────────────────┘
```

To summarize, creating metric filters and dashboards in Amazon CloudWatch enables you to detect and respond to anomalous activities effectively. By defining metric filters to capture specific log events and visualizing these metrics on dashboards, you can monitor your AWS environment in real-time and quickly identify potential security threats. Coupled with CloudWatch alarms, this approach ensures that you are promptly notified of any anomalies, allowing you to investigate and mitigate security incidents swiftly.

## 7.5 Centralizing Security Findings

Centralizing security findings involves consolidating security alerts and insights from various sources into a single, unified view. This approach enhances the ability to monitor, analyze, and respond to potential threats efficiently. By centralizing security findings, organizations can streamline incident response, reduce the complexity of managing multiple security tools, and improve their overall security posture.

## 7.5.1 Strategies for Centralization

Centralizing security findings from various AWS services is a critical strategy for streamlining threat detection and response. By aggregating security alerts and insights into a single, cohesive view, organizations can enhance their ability to monitor, analyze, and act on potential threats more effectively. Here are key strategies for achieving centralized security findings:

### Utilize AWS Security Hub

AWS Security Hub is designed to aggregate and prioritize security findings from multiple AWS services and third-party tools. By enabling Security Hub, you can collect data from services like Amazon GuardDuty, AWS Config, and Amazon Macie, consolidating them into a single dashboard. Ensure that all relevant AWS services and third-party security tools are integrated with Security Hub for seamless data collection and aggregation. Security Hub also provides automated insights by running compliance checks and security standards, such as CIS AWS Foundations Benchmark and PCI DSS, giving a comprehensive view of your security posture. Use the Security Hub console to centrally manage and prioritize findings, ensuring that critical issues are addressed promptly.

### Implement AWS CloudWatch for Centralized Logging

AWS CloudWatch can be used to collect and aggregate logs from various AWS services, providing a centralized view of security-related events. You can create log groups and streams to organize logs from different services, such as CloudTrail, VPC Flow Logs, and application logs. Additionally, metric filters can be set up to monitor specific patterns in the logs, and alarms can be created to notify you of potential security incidents. CloudWatch dashboards allow for real-time visualization of log data and metrics, enabling continuous monitoring and in-depth analysis.

### Leverage Amazon EventBridge for Event Correlation

Amazon EventBridge (formerly CloudWatch Events) allows you to create rules that trigger actions based on specific events from AWS services. You can define event rules to capture events from services like GuardDuty, CloudTrail, and AWS Config, which can trigger automated responses such as invoking AWS Lambda functions or sending notifications via Amazon SNS. Additionally, using a centralized event bus helps collect and route events from multiple sources, providing a single point of integration for managing security events effectively.

### Integrate with Third-Party Security Information and Event Management (SIEM) Tools

Integrating AWS services with third-party SIEM tools can enhance centralized security monitoring and analysis. You can export data using AWS service integrations or custom data export solutions to send logs and security findings to your SIEM tool. The SIEM's advanced correlation and analysis capabilities can detect complex attack patterns and anomalies. Additionally, the SIEM's unified dashboard provides a comprehensive view of security across your AWS environment and other on-premises or cloud resources.

### Enable Amazon Detective for In-Depth Investigation

Amazon Detective simplifies security investigations by automatically collecting and organizing data from AWS services. Detective analyzes data from GuardDuty, CloudTrail, and VPC Flow Logs to create visualizations that help trace the root cause of security issues. Using the interactive interface, you can explore relationships and patterns in your data, facilitating a deeper understanding of security incidents.

### Centralized Security Findings Workflow

```
         AWS Services
   (GuardDuty, CloudTrail, Config,
          Macie, etc.)
              │
              ▼
       Data Aggregation
  (Security Hub, CloudWatch Logs,
          EventBridge)
              │
              ▼
       Centralized Analysis
   (SIEM Integration, Amazon
           Detective)
              │
              ▼
    Unified Security Dashboard
       (Security Hub, SIEM)
              │
              ▼
        Incident Response
 (Automated Actions, Notifications)
```

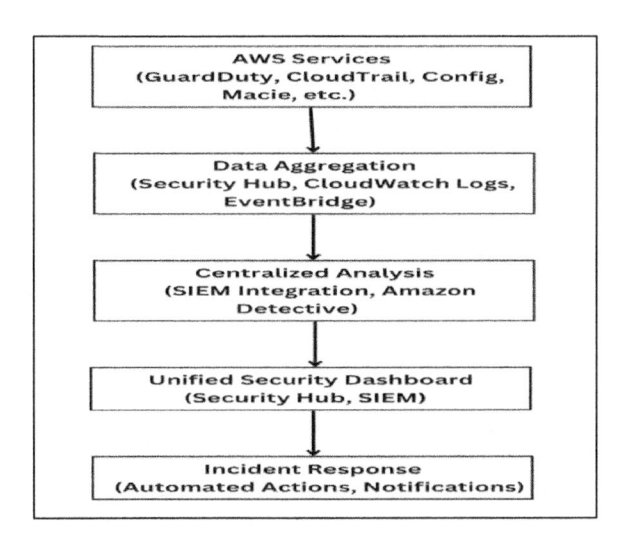

In summary, centralizing security findings from various AWS services enhances threat detection and response by providing a unified view of security events. Strategies such as utilizing AWS Security Hub, implementing CloudWatch for centralized logging, leveraging EventBridge for event correlation, integrating with third-party SIEM tools, and enabling Amazon Detective for in-depth investigation are crucial. These approaches streamline monitoring, analysis, and incident response, helping organizations maintain a robust and proactive security posture.

## 7.5.2 Integrating with AWS Security Hub

Integrating various AWS security services with AWS Security Hub enables organizations to aggregate findings and gain a comprehensive security overview. This integration facilitates centralized management of security alerts and compliance checks, allowing for more efficient threat detection, analysis, and response. Here's how to integrate key AWS security services with Security Hub and evaluate the findings from these services.

### Integrating AWS Security Services with Security Hub

**Amazon GuardDuty:** GuardDuty is a threat detection service that continuously monitors for malicious activity and unauthorized behavior. To integrate GuardDuty with Security Hub, enable both services and navigate to the Security Hub console. In the Integrations section, ensure GuardDuty is listed and enabled. GuardDuty findings will automatically be forwarded to Security Hub.

**AWS Config:** AWS Config provides detailed inventory and configuration history and evaluates resource configurations against predefined rules. Enable AWS Config and Security Hub. In the Security Hub console, enable the Config integration in the Integrations section. Config compliance findings, such as non-compliant resource configurations, will be sent to Security Hub for centralized management.

**Amazon Macie:** Macie is a data security service that uses machine learning to discover, classify, and protect sensitive data stored in S3. Enable Macie and Security Hub, then configure the integration through the Security Hub console. Macie findings, such as sensitive data discoveries and policy violations, will be aggregated in Security Hub.

**AWS Inspector:** Amazon Inspector performs automated security assessments to identify vulnerabilities and deviations from best practices. Enable Inspector and Security Hub, then set up the integration in the Security Hub console. Inspector findings, including identified vulnerabilities and security issues, will be displayed in Security Hub.

**AWS IAM Access Analyzer:** IAM Access Analyzer helps identify resources shared with external entities and assesses their risk. Enable Access Analyzer and integrate it with Security Hub through the console. Findings from Access Analyzer, such as potential security risks due to external sharing, will be available in Security Hub.

## Evaluating Findings from Integrated Security Services

**Centralized Dashboard:** Use the Security Hub dashboard to get a centralized view of all security findings. The dashboard aggregates alerts and insights from all integrated services, providing a unified overview. Visualize trends, prioritize high-severity findings, and track compliance status across your AWS environment.

**Finding Details and Context:** Each finding in Security Hub includes detailed information, such as the affected resource, the nature of the issue, and recommended remediation steps. By clicking on a finding, you can view its full details, including links to the original finding in the integrated service (e.g., GuardDuty or Macie).

**Automated Remediation:** Use AWS Lambda and AWS Systems Manager to automate responses to security findings. For example, you can create Lambda functions to automatically isolate compromised instances or revoke compromised IAM credentials based on specific findings. Security Hub can trigger these automated actions based on predefined criteria, streamlining incident response.

**Compliance Checks:** Security Hub evaluates your AWS environment against industry standards and best practices, such as CIS AWS Foundations Benchmark and PCI DSS. Findings related to compliance can help you identify gaps in your security posture and take corrective actions to ensure adherence to regulatory requirements.

**Custom Insights and Filters:** Create custom insights in Security Hub to focus on specific types of findings or areas of concern. For example, you can filter findings to only show high-severity threats or non-compliant resources. Use these insights to prioritize and manage security incidents more effectively.

## Integration and Evaluation Workflow

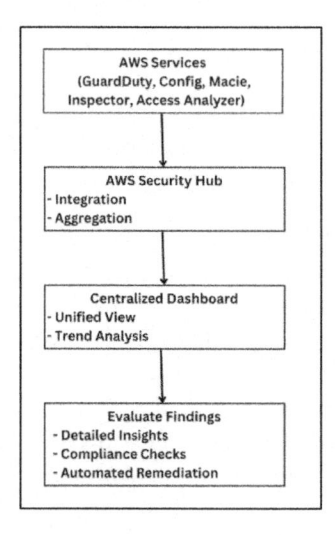

```
┌─────────────────────────────┐
│     AWS Services            │
│ (GuardDuty, Config, Macie,  │
│  Inspector, Access Analyzer)│
└─────────────┬───────────────┘
              ↓
┌─────────────────────────────┐
│     AWS Security Hub        │
│ - Integration               │
│ - Aggregation               │
└─────────────┬───────────────┘
              ↓
┌─────────────────────────────┐
│    Centralized Dashboard    │
│ - Unified View              │
│ - Trend Analysis            │
└─────────────┬───────────────┘
              ↓
┌─────────────────────────────┐
│     Evaluate Findings       │
│ - Detailed Insights         │
│ - Compliance Checks         │
│ - Automated Remediation     │
└─────────────────────────────┘
```

In summary, integrating AWS security services with AWS Security Hub is essential for achieving a comprehensive security overview. By aggregating findings from services like GuardDuty, AWS Config, Amazon Macie, AWS Inspector, and IAM Access Analyzer, Security Hub provides a centralized dashboard for monitoring and managing security alerts. This integration enables detailed evaluation of findings, automated remediation, and compliance checks, enhancing the overall security posture and streamlining threat detection and response processes.

# 7.6 Validating Security Events

Validating security events is a crucial process that involves verifying the legitimacy and severity of detected security alerts to ensure accurate incident response. By validating events, security teams can distinguish between true positives, false positives, and benign activities, allowing them to prioritize and respond effectively to genuine threats. This step enhances the efficiency and accuracy of the overall security operations.

## 7.6.1 Performing Queries with Amazon Athena

Using Amazon Athena to perform queries on log data stored in Amazon S3 is an effective method for validating and investigating security events. Athena, a serverless interactive query service, allows you to analyze vast amounts of data using standard SQL without the need to set up or manage any infrastructure. This makes it particularly useful for querying log data to validate and scrutinize security incidents.

### Steps to Perform Queries Using Amazon Athena

**Store Log Data in S3:** Ensure that all relevant log data, such as AWS CloudTrail logs, VPC Flow Logs, and application logs, are stored in Amazon S3. Organize these logs in a structured manner, often by service, date, and other relevant criteria.

**Create a Database and Table in Athena:** Open the Amazon Athena console and create a database if one does not already exist. Define tables that map to the log data stored in S3. This involves specifying the schema, including the columns and data types that match the structure of your log files. For example, to create a table for CloudTrail logs, you might use a `CREATE TABLE` statement that includes columns such as `eventTime`, `eventName`, `userIdentity`, `sourceIPAddress`, and `errorCode`.

**Run SQL Queries to Validate Security Events:** Once the tables are defined, you can use SQL queries to analyze the log data. For instance, to validate suspicious login attempts, you can query the CloudTrail logs for failed login events:

```sql
SELECT eventTime, userIdentity.userName, sourceIPAddress, errorCode
FROM cloudtrail_logs
WHERE eventName = 'ConsoleLogin'
AND errorCode IS NOT NULL
ORDER BY eventTime DESC;
```

This query retrieves recent failed login attempts, providing details about the time, user, source IP address, and error code. Such information is crucial for validating whether the login failures indicate a brute force attack or a potential compromise.

**Investigate Security Events:** To investigate an identified security event, you can perform more detailed queries. For example, if a particular user shows suspicious activity, you can query all actions taken by that user:

```sql
SELECT eventTime, eventName, sourceIPAddress, requestParameters
FROM cloudtrail_logs
WHERE userIdentity.userName = 'suspiciousUser'
ORDER BY eventTime DESC;
```

This query helps trace the actions of the suspicious user, revealing what operations they attempted and from which IP addresses. Such detailed insights enable thorough investigation and help determine the scope and impact of the security event.

**Automate and Schedule Queries:** You can automate and schedule these queries to run at regular intervals using AWS services like AWS Lambda and Amazon CloudWatch. This setup ensures continuous monitoring and validation of security events, providing timely alerts and insights.

### Example Scenario

Consider a scenario where an unusual spike in failed login attempts is detected. By using Athena, you can quickly validate this security event:

**Query Failed Logins:** Run a query to list all failed login attempts over the past 24 hours. This helps confirm whether the spike is due to repeated failed logins from the same IP addresses or different ones, indicating potential brute force attacks.

**Identify Patterns:** Use Athena to correlate these logins with other events, such as changes in IAM policies or unusual data transfer activities, to identify patterns that may suggest coordinated attacks or unauthorized access attempts.

**Detailed Investigation:** For a specific failed login attempt, drill down into the details by querying the associated events around the same time frame. This can reveal if there were successful logins or suspicious API calls following the failed attempts.

### Workflow for Validating Security Events with Athena

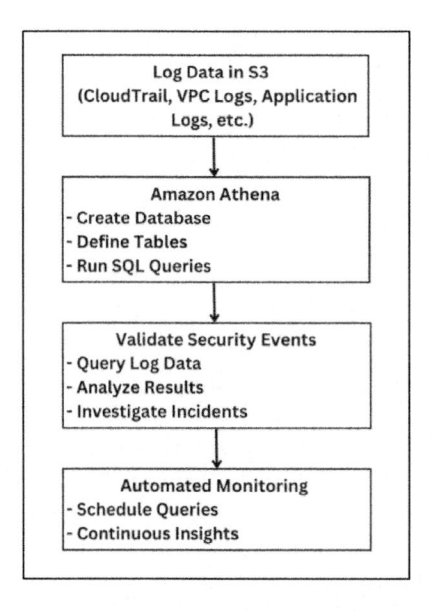

```
┌─────────────────────────────────┐
│       Log Data in S3            │
│ (CloudTrail, VPC Logs, Application │
│         Logs, etc.)             │
└─────────────────────────────────┘
              │
              ▼
┌─────────────────────────────────┐
│        Amazon Athena            │
│ - Create Database               │
│ - Define Tables                 │
│ - Run SQL Queries               │
└─────────────────────────────────┘
              │
              ▼
┌─────────────────────────────────┐
│     Validate Security Events    │
│ - Query Log Data                │
│ - Analyze Results               │
│ - Investigate Incidents         │
└─────────────────────────────────┘
              │
              ▼
┌─────────────────────────────────┐
│      Automated Monitoring       │
│ - Schedule Queries              │
│ - Continuous Insights           │
└─────────────────────────────────┘
```

To summarize, using Amazon Athena to perform queries on log data stored in Amazon S3 provides a powerful method for validating and investigating security events. By leveraging Athena's SQL query capabilities, you can efficiently analyze vast amounts of log data, validate the legitimacy of security alerts, and gain detailed insights into potential incidents. This approach enhances your ability to respond promptly to security threats and maintain a secure AWS environment.

## 7.6.2 Analysis and Investigation Techniques

Analyzing and investigating security events to determine their validity and potential impact is a critical aspect of maintaining a secure AWS environment. Evaluating findings from various security services involves a combination of techniques that help differentiate between true and false positives, understand the context of the events, and assess their potential impact on the organization.

## Techniques for Analyzing Security Events

Cross-service correlation involves integrating data from multiple AWS security services, such as Amazon GuardDuty, AWS Config, Amazon Macie, and AWS CloudTrail, to provide a comprehensive view of a security event. Cross-referencing findings from these services can help identify patterns and correlations that may suggest a genuine threat. For instance, a GuardDuty finding of unusual API activity can be verified against CloudTrail logs to determine the source and legitimacy of the activity, while AWS Config can be used to check for recent changes in resource configurations.

Contextual analysis is essential for accurately validating security events. This involves examining the event's context, such as the time it occurred, the resources involved, and usual behavior patterns. Services like Amazon Detective can provide deeper insights by visualizing relationships and interactions between AWS resources, helping to determine whether the event is part of normal operations or an anomaly.

Behavioral analysis focuses on detecting deviations from established baselines by analyzing user and system behavior. Services like Amazon GuardDuty and AWS CloudWatch Anomaly Detection use machine learning models to identify unusual behaviors that might indicate a security incident. For example, an unexpected spike in data transfers from an S3 bucket flagged by Macie can be cross-checked against normal usage patterns to assess if it's malicious or a legitimate spike.

Detailed log analysis can be performed using Amazon Athena or CloudWatch Logs Insights, enabling an in-depth examination of specific events like failed login attempts, changes to IAM policies, or suspicious network traffic. By analyzing logs, you can trace the sequence of actions leading up to the security event and identify any anomalies or unauthorized activities.

Finally, an impact assessment should be conducted once the validity of the security event is confirmed. This assessment evaluates the affected resources, the sensitivity of the data involved, and the potential consequences of the security breach. AWS Security Hub can help prioritize findings based on severity and compliance standards, ensuring that high-severity incidents affecting critical resources are addressed immediately.

## Example Scenario

Consider a scenario where GuardDuty detects an unusual pattern of API calls from an IP address not previously seen. To analyze and investigate this event, start with correlation by checking CloudTrail logs to verify the details of the API calls. This helps determine which resources were accessed and by whom. AWS Config can be used to review any recent changes to the resource configurations involved. Next, consider the context by using Amazon Detective to visualize the sequence of API calls and the interactions between the affected resources, providing deeper insights into the event's legitimacy.

Behavioral analysis comes next, where the detected pattern is compared with established behavior baselines using GuardDuty's machine learning models to identify deviations. For detailed insights, perform log analysis by querying CloudTrail logs with Athena to get a timeline of actions performed by the suspicious IP address, including any failed attempts and subsequent successful accesses.

Finally, assess the impact of the event by evaluating the sensitivity of the accessed data and the criticality of the involved resources. Use Security Hub to prioritize the event based on its severity, ensuring the highest-risk findings are addressed promptly.

## Security Event Analysis Workflow

```
        Security Findings
    (GuardDuty, Macie, Config,
         CloudTrail, etc.)
                │
                ▼
    Cross-Service Correlation
                │
                ▼
        Contextual Analysis
                │
                ▼
        Behavioral Analysis
                │
                ▼
       Detailed Log Analysis
                │
                ▼
         Impact Assessment
                │
                ▼
    Incident Response & Remed
```

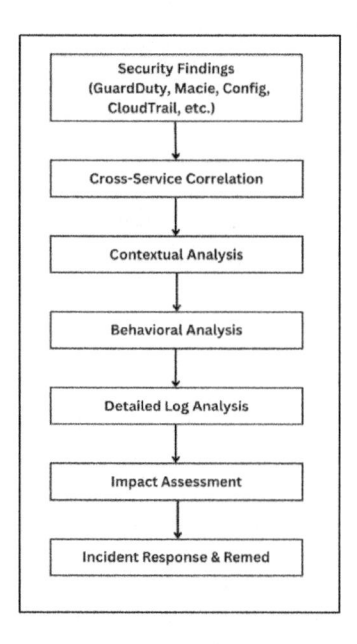

To summarize, analyzing and investigating security events involves multiple techniques to validate their authenticity and assess their impact. Cross-service correlation, contextual analysis, behavioral analysis, detailed log analysis, and impact assessment are essential steps in this process. By leveraging AWS security services like GuardDuty, Config, Macie, CloudTrail, Athena, and Detective, organizations can efficiently identify genuine threats, understand their context, and take appropriate actions to mitigate potential risks, ensuring a robust security posture.

## 7.7 Best Practices for Threat Detection

Best practices for threat detection involve implementing robust and proactive measures to identify and respond to potential security threats effectively. This includes continuous monitoring, leveraging advanced threat detection tools, integrating data from multiple sources, and maintaining a well-trained security team. By following these practices, organizations can enhance their ability to detect and mitigate threats, ensuring a strong security posture.

### 7.7.1 Continuous Monitoring and Real-Time Alerts

Best practices for setting up continuous monitoring and real-time alerts are essential for quickly identifying and responding to security threats. Implementing these practices involves leveraging a combination of advanced tools, automation, and a proactive approach to security management.

To start, leverage advanced monitoring tools. Use comprehensive monitoring services like AWS CloudWatch for real-time monitoring of your AWS environment. Set up custom metrics and dashboards to track critical performance indicators and security metrics. Implement AWS Config to monitor configuration changes and ensure compliance with security policies. AWS Config continuously evaluates your resources and generates alerts for non-compliance or unauthorized changes. Also, integrate AWS security services by enabling Amazon GuardDuty to detect threats and malicious activity within your AWS accounts. GuardDuty uses machine learning, anomaly detection, and integrated threat intelligence to identify potential security issues. Additionally, AWS CloudTrail should be used to log all API calls and user activities in your AWS environment. These CloudTrail logs are invaluable for forensic analysis and understanding the context of security events.

Automating alerts and responses is another critical practice. Set up real-time alerts by configuring CloudWatch Alarms to trigger notifications based on predefined thresholds for specific metrics. For instance, alarms can be set up for high CPU usage, unusual network activity, or a spike in failed login attempts. Utilize Amazon SNS

(Simple Notification Service) to send alerts via email, SMS, or push notifications to your incident response team, ensuring they are immediately notified of potential issues. Automate remediation by implementing AWS Lambda functions to respond to specific security events, such as isolating compromised instances, revoking compromised IAM credentials, or enforcing security group rules. Use AWS Systems Manager Automation to create and manage runbooks that define automated workflows for common incident response tasks.

Proactive monitoring and analysis also play a crucial role. Engage in continuous log analysis by using Amazon Athena to perform ad-hoc queries on log data stored in S3. Regularly query and analyze logs to identify patterns and anomalies that might indicate security threats. AWS CloudWatch Logs Insights can be implemented for real-time log analysis and creating custom queries for specific security events. Additionally, establish behavioral baselines using historical data. Services like Amazon GuardDuty and AWS CloudWatch Anomaly Detection can help identify deviations from these baselines. Regularly review and update these baselines to reflect changes in your environment and improve the accuracy of anomaly detection.

Lastly, centralized management is essential. Use AWS Security Hub to aggregate findings from various AWS security services. Security Hub provides a centralized view of your security posture, enabling you to manage and prioritize security findings effectively. It also offers automated compliance checks to ensure adherence to industry standards and best practices. For cross-account monitoring, set up AWS Organizations to enable centralized monitoring across multiple AWS accounts. Use AWS CloudWatch cross-account dashboards to visualize and monitor metrics from all accounts in one place.

### Example Scenario
Consider a scenario where you need to monitor for unauthorized access attempts. First, set up CloudWatch Alarms for metrics such as the number of failed login attempts or denied API calls. You can configure these alarms to trigger alerts when the metrics exceed normal limits, ensuring that any unusual activity is promptly flagged. Next, configure real-time alerts using Amazon SNS to send immediate notifications to your security team when an alarm is triggered. These alerts should include detailed information about the event to facilitate a quick investigation. Finally, automate responses by implementing Lambda functions that can automatically disable IAM credentials or isolate affected resources when unauthorized access attempts are detected. This helps to swiftly mitigate potential security threats.

To summarize, setting up continuous monitoring and real-time alerts involves leveraging advanced tools, automating responses, and adopting a proactive approach to security management. By using services like AWS CloudWatch, AWS Config, Amazon GuardDuty, and AWS Security Hub, organizations can achieve comprehensive visibility into their AWS environments, quickly detect security threats, and respond effectively. These best practices ensure a robust security posture, minimizing the risk of security breaches and enhancing overall resilience.

## 7.7.2 Regular Audits and Reviews
Conducting regular audits and reviews of security configurations and findings is essential for maintaining ongoing security and compliance in any AWS environment. These audits help identify potential vulnerabilities, ensure that security policies are being adhered to, and verify that configurations remain aligned with best practices and regulatory requirements. Here are the best practices for conducting regular audits and reviews:

### Best Practices for Regular Audits and Reviews
To ensure a robust security posture, start by scheduling regular audits. These audits can be conducted monthly, quarterly, or as required by your compliance framework. Regular audits allow you to proactively identify and mitigate potential security risks.

Leverage automated tools such as AWS Config and AWS Security Hub to continuously monitor your AWS environment. AWS Config allows for the definition of rules and continuously evaluates the configuration of

AWS resources. Security Hub aggregates findings from multiple AWS services, offering a comprehensive view of your security posture. These tools can be used to generate reports and alerts for any deviations from established security policies.

Regularly review IAM roles, policies, and permissions to ensure that they adhere to the principle of least privilege. Identify and remove any unnecessary permissions that could be exploited. Utilize IAM Access Analyzer to identify resources shared with external entities and assess the associated risks.

Evaluate security groups and network ACL configurations to ensure that they are restricting traffic properly. Check for overly permissive rules that could allow unauthorized access. AWS Firewall Manager can be used to enforce security group policies across multiple accounts within your organization.

Assess logging and monitoring configurations to ensure that logging is enabled for all critical AWS services, including CloudTrail, VPC Flow Logs, and AWS Config. Regularly review these logs to detect anomalies or suspicious activities. Ensure that CloudWatch Alarms and SNS notifications are set up to alert your security team of any critical events.

Conduct compliance checks using AWS Security Hub to automate checks against industry standards and best practices such as CIS AWS Foundations Benchmark and PCI DSS. Review the compliance status regularly and address any non-compliant resources promptly. Ensure that your AWS environment meets regulatory requirements and organizational policies through regular compliance assessments.

Ensure incident response preparedness by reviewing and updating your incident response plan regularly. Conduct mock drills and simulations to make sure the team is prepared to respond effectively to security incidents. AWS Systems Manager Automation can be used to create runbooks for common incident response tasks, ensuring they are documented and easily executable.

Maintain detailed records of all audits, findings, and actions taken. Proper documentation helps track progress, ensures accountability, and provides evidence of compliance during external audits. Use AWS Config to maintain a historical record of configuration changes, and AWS Security Hub to document security findings and remediation steps.

### Example Scenario

Consider an organization that conducts quarterly security audits. The security team schedules these audits for the first week of each quarter to review IAM policies, security groups, logging configurations, and compliance status. Automated tools like AWS Config are used to continuously evaluate resource configurations, while AWS Security Hub aggregates findings from services such as GuardDuty, Macie, and Inspector.

During the audit, the team reviews IAM policies using IAM Access Analyzer to identify and mitigate any overly permissive policies or external sharing risks. For security group assessments, the team ensures the rules are not overly permissive and uses AWS Firewall Manager to enforce consistent policies across all accounts.

In terms of logging and monitoring, the team verifies that CloudTrail and VPC Flow Logs are enabled and that CloudWatch Alarms are configured to alert on critical events. They also conduct compliance checks using Security Hub and promptly address any non-compliant findings to ensure adherence to regulatory requirements.

Finally, the incident response plan is reviewed and updated based on the latest findings. The team conducts mock drills to test their readiness and ensure that they are prepared to respond effectively to any security incidents.

In summary, regular audits and reviews of security configurations and findings are vital for ensuring ongoing security and compliance in AWS environments. By following best practices such as scheduled audits, leveraging automated tools, reviewing IAM policies, assessing security groups, ensuring comprehensive logging and monitoring, conducting compliance checks, and maintaining incident response preparedness, organizations can proactively manage security risks and maintain a robust security posture. Detailed documentation of findings and actions taken further enhances accountability and compliance, providing a solid foundation for continuous security improvement.

## 7.8 Lab Exercises
### 7.8.1 Setting Up Amazon GuardDuty

This hands-on lab will guide you through the process of setting up Amazon GuardDuty and configuring it to detect security threats in your AWS environment.

**Prerequisites:** An AWS account with necessary permissions to create and manage AWS resources. Basic understanding of AWS services and security concepts.

**Step-by-Step Instructions**
**Step 1: Enable Amazon GuardDuty**
Log in to the AWS Management Console by navigating to the console and entering your credentials. Once logged in, access GuardDuty by typing "GuardDuty" into the search bar and selecting Amazon GuardDuty from the dropdown menu. To enable GuardDuty, go to the GuardDuty dashboard and click the "Get started" button. Review the features presented and then click "Enable GuardDuty" to complete the process.

**Step 2: Configure GuardDuty**
To set up data sources for GuardDuty, it automatically integrates with AWS CloudTrail, VPC Flow Logs, and DNS logs. Ensure these services are enabled: For CloudTrail, verify that logging is enabled for your AWS account; for VPC Flow Logs, create flow logs for the relevant VPCs; and for DNS logs, make sure that Route 53 Resolver query logging is enabled. Once GuardDuty is enabled, it will begin analyzing the data and generating findings. You can review these findings by navigating to the GuardDuty dashboard and accessing the "Findings" section to check for any detected security threats.

**Step 3: Configure Notifications and Alerts**
To create an SNS topic, navigate to the SNS (Simple Notification Service) dashboard in the AWS Management Console. Click "Create topic" and select "Standard." Enter a name for the topic, such as "GuardDutyAlerts," and click "Create topic." Next, subscribe to the SNS topic by clicking on the newly created topic and selecting "Create subscription." Choose the protocol as "Email," and provide your email address. Once you've clicked "Create subscription," confirm the subscription through the email you receive.

To set up CloudWatch alarms, navigate to CloudWatch in the AWS Management Console. Go to "Alarms" and click "Create Alarm." Select the relevant GuardDuty metrics, such as "Threats detected." Configure the alarm to trigger when the metric exceeds a set threshold. Choose to "Send notification to an SNS topic" and select the SNS topic created earlier. Finally, click "Create Alarm" to complete the process.

**Step 4: Simulate and Test GuardDuty**
To generate test findings in GuardDuty, navigate to the GuardDuty dashboard and click on "Settings." In the "Sample findings" section, click on "Generate sample findings." After generating these sample findings, go to the "Findings" section to review them. Ensure that the alerts and notifications are functioning correctly by checking the email associated with the SNS topic to confirm that you received the notifications.

**Step 5: Respond to GuardDuty Findings**
To investigate findings, click on a specific finding in the GuardDuty dashboard to view detailed information, such as the affected resources, threat type, and recommended actions. Based on these findings, take appropriate

remedial actions to mitigate the security threats, which could involve isolating affected resources, revoking compromised credentials, or modifying security group rules. Additionally, you can automate responses by using AWS Lambda. Create Lambda functions to perform actions like isolating instances or notifying security personnel. To make this process more efficient, configure CloudWatch Events to trigger Lambda functions based on GuardDuty findings.

To summarize, setting up Amazon GuardDuty and configuring it to detect security threats involves enabling the service, configuring data sources, setting up notifications and alerts, simulating findings, and responding to detected threats. By following these steps, you can enhance the security posture of your AWS environment and ensure proactive threat detection and response.

## 7.8.2 Creating Visualizations with CloudWatch

This exercise will guide you through creating metric filters and dashboards in Amazon CloudWatch to monitor for anomalies. By completing this exercise, you will develop skills in visualizing and detecting anomalous activity.

**Prerequisites:** An AWS account with necessary permissions to create and manage CloudWatch resources. Basic understanding of AWS services and monitoring concepts.

### Step 1: Enable Logging for AWS Services

To enable CloudTrail, navigate to the AWS Management Console, type "CloudTrail" in the search bar, and select CloudTrail. Make sure CloudTrail is enabled and logging is set up to an S3 bucket. Next, to enable VPC Flow Logs, go to the VPC service in the AWS Management Console. Select the VPC you wish to monitor, and under the Actions menu, choose "Create Flow Log." Configure the flow log to either log to an S3 bucket or CloudWatch Logs for further analysis.

### Step 2: Create a Log Group in CloudWatch

**Access CloudWatch Logs:** In the AWS Management Console, type "CloudWatch" in the search bar and select CloudWatch. Navigate to Logs and click Log groups.

**Create Log Group:** Click Create log group. Enter a name for your log group, e.g., "MyAppLogGroup", and click Create.

### Step 3: Create Metric Filters in CloudWatch

**Create a Metric Filter for Login Failures:** In the CloudWatch console, navigate to Logs and select your log group (e.g., "MyAppLogGroup"). Click Create metric filter. Enter a filter pattern to match failed login attempts. For example, to match login failures in CloudTrail logs:

```
{ $.eventName = "ConsoleLogin" && $.errorMessage = "Failed authentication" }
```

Click Next.

**Define Metric Filter Details:** Enter a name for your filter, e.g., "FailedLogins". Define a namespace, e.g., "MyAppMetrics". Define a metric name, e.g., "FailedLogins". Set the Metric Value to 1.

**Create Metric Filter:** Review the settings and click Create filter.

### Step 4: Create CloudWatch Alarms

**Set Up Alarm for Metric Filter:** In the CloudWatch console, navigate to Alarms and click Create Alarm. Select the metric filter you created (FailedLogins) from the MyAppMetrics namespace. Click Select metric.

**Configure Alarm Settings:** Define the threshold for triggering the alarm. For example, set the threshold to 5 to trigger the alarm if there are 5 or more failed login attempts within a specified period. Configure the alarm state and notification settings. For example, choose Send notification to an SNS topic and select or create an SNS topic to receive alerts.

**Create Alarm:** Review the settings and click Create alarm.

## Step 5: Create CloudWatch Dashboard
**Access Dashboards:** In the CloudWatch console, navigate to Dashboards and click Create dashboard. Enter a name for your dashboard, e.g., "SecurityMonitoringDashboard", and click Create dashboard.

**Add Widgets to Dashboard:** Click Add widget and select the type of widget you want to add, such as a Line graph or Number. Select the MyAppMetrics namespace and the FailedLogins metric. Configure the widget settings, such as time range and visualization options.

**Save Dashboard:** Add additional widgets as needed to monitor other metrics or log groups. Click Save dashboard to finalize the configuration.

## Step 6: Test the Configuration
**Generate Test Log Events:** Simulate failed login attempts or other events to generate log entries that match your metric filter pattern. Verify that the metric filter detects the log events and updates the metric value.

**Verify Alarms and Notifications:** Check the CloudWatch Alarms dashboard to ensure that the alarm is triggered when the threshold is met. Confirm that notifications are sent to the specified SNS topic.

**Review Dashboard:** Access the CloudWatch Dashboard to view the visualizations and ensure that the metrics are displayed correctly.

To summarize, creating metric filters and dashboards in Amazon CloudWatch is a powerful way to monitor for anomalies and visualize security-related metrics. By following these steps, you can set up comprehensive monitoring, create alarms for critical events, and visualize data using CloudWatch Dashboards. This practical exercise enhances your ability to detect and respond to anomalous activities in your AWS environment, ensuring robust security monitoring and incident response capabilities.

# 7.8.3 Using Amazon Athena for Log Analysis
This lab exercise will guide you through using Amazon Athena to query and analyze log data stored in Amazon S3. By the end of this exercise, you will be able to validate security events and gain insights into potential security issues within your AWS environment.

**Prerequisites:** An AWS account with necessary permissions to access Amazon S3 and Amazon Athena. Basic understanding of AWS services and SQL queries.

## Step 1: Prepare Your Log Data
**Ensure Logging is Enabled:** Verify that AWS CloudTrail, VPC Flow Logs, and other relevant logs are enabled and configured to store data in an S3 bucket.

**Organize Your Log Data in S3:** Structure your S3 bucket to store log files in a logical manner, such as by service, date, and region. For example:

```
1. s3://your-bucket-name/cloudtrail/AWSLogs/123456789012/CloudTrail/us-east-1/2021/07/29/
```

```
2. s3://your-bucket-name/vpcflowlogs/AWSLogs/123456789012/VPCFlowLogs/us-east-1/2021/07/29/
```

## Step 2: Create a Database and Table in Athena

**Access Amazon Athena:** In the AWS Management Console, type "Athena" in the search bar and select Amazon Athena.

**Create a Database:** In the Athena console, click on Query Editor. Enter the following SQL query to create a new database:

```
CREATE DATABASE security_logs;
```

Click Run Query.

**Create a Table for CloudTrail Logs:** Enter the following SQL query to create a table for CloudTrail logs. Adjust the LOCATION to match your S3 bucket structure:

```
CREATE EXTERNAL TABLE cloudtrail_logs (
  eventVersion STRING,
  userIdentity STRUCT<type:STRING,principalId:STRING,arn:STRING,accountId:STRING,invokedBy:STRING,accessKeyId:STRING,userName:STRING,sessionContext:STRUCT<attributes:STRUCT<mfaAuthenticated:STRING,creationDate:STRING>,sessionIssuer:STRUCT<type:STRING,principalId:STRING,arn:STRING,accountId:STRING,userName:STRING>>>,
  eventTime STRING,
  eventSource STRING,
  eventName STRING,
  awsRegion STRING,
  sourceIPAddress STRING,
  userAgent STRING,
  errorCode STRING,
  errorMessage STRING,
  requestParameters STRING,
  responseElements STRING,
  additionalEventData STRING,
  requestId STRING,
  eventId STRING,
  resources ARRAY<STRUCT<arn:STRING,accountId:STRING,type:STRING>>,
  eventType STRING,
  recipientAccountId STRING,
  sharedEventID STRING,
  vpcEndpointId STRING
)
ROW FORMAT SERDE 'com.amazon.emr.hive.serde.CloudTrailSerde'
STORED AS INPUTFORMAT
'com.amazon.emr.cloudtrail.CloudTrailInputFormat'
OUTPUTFORMAT
'org.apache.hadoop.hive.ql.io.HiveIgnoreKeyTextOutputFormat'
LOCATION 's3://your-bucket-name/cloudtrail/';
```

Click Run Query.

**Create a Table for VPC Flow Logs:** Enter the following SQL query to create a table for VPC Flow Logs. Adjust the LOCATION to match your S3 bucket structure:

```sql
CREATE EXTERNAL TABLE vpc_flow_logs (
  version INT,
  account_id STRING,
  interface_id STRING,
  srcaddr STRING,
  dstaddr STRING,
  srcport INT,
  dstport INT,
  protocol INT,
  packets BIGINT,
  bytes BIGINT,
  start BIGINT,
  end BIGINT,
  action STRING,
  log_status STRING
)
ROW FORMAT DELIMITED
FIELDS TERMINATED BY ' '
STORED AS TEXTFILE
LOCATION 's3://your-bucket-name/vpcflowlogs/';
```

Click Run Query.

## Step 3: Query Log Data Using Athena

**Query for Failed Login Attempts in CloudTrail Logs:** Enter the following SQL query to find failed login attempts:

```sql
SELECT eventTime, userIdentity.userName, sourceIPAddress, errorCode, errorMessage
FROM cloudtrail_logs
WHERE eventName = 'ConsoleLogin' AND errorCode IS NOT NULL
ORDER BY eventTime DESC;
```

Click Run Query and review the results to identify any suspicious login failures.

**Query for Unusual Traffic in VPC Flow Logs:** Enter the following SQL query to detect high traffic from a specific source IP:

```sql
SELECT srcaddr, SUM(bytes) as total_bytes
FROM vpc_flow_logs
WHERE action = 'ACCEPT' AND end > UNIX_TIMESTAMP() - 3600
GROUP BY srcaddr
HAVING total_bytes > 1000000000
ORDER BY total_bytes DESC;
```

Click Run Query and review the results to detect any unusual traffic patterns.

## Step 4: Create Saved Queries and Automate Analysis

**Save Queries for Future Use:** In the Athena console, click the Save button above the query editor to save your frequently used queries. Provide a name and description for each query.

**Automate Query Execution with AWS Lambda and CloudWatch:** Create a Lambda function that runs your Athena queries on a schedule using CloudWatch Events. Configure the Lambda function to send the query results to an SNS topic or an S3 bucket for further analysis and alerting.

### Step 5: Visualize Query Results

**Integrate with Amazon QuickSight:** In the AWS Management Console, type "QuickSight" in the search bar and select Amazon QuickSight. Create a new dataset using Athena as the data source. Select the database and tables you created. Use QuickSight to create visualizations and dashboards based on your Athena query results.

**Create Dashboards for Monitoring:** In QuickSight, create dashboards to visualize key metrics such as failed login attempts, high traffic sources, and other security events. Share the dashboards with your security team for continuous monitoring and analysis.

Using Amazon Athena to query and analyze log data stored in Amazon S3 provides powerful capabilities for validating security events. By following these steps, you can set up databases and tables in Athena, run SQL queries to identify and investigate potential security issues, automate query execution, and visualize results using Amazon QuickSight.

## 7.8.4 Integrating AWS Security Services

This exercise will guide you through the steps to integrate various AWS security services with AWS Security Hub to centralize and manage security findings effectively. By completing this exercise, you will reinforce your understanding of centralizing security findings to improve visibility and response capabilities.

**Prerequisites:** An AWS account with necessary permissions to access and manage AWS Security Hub and other AWS security services. Basic understanding of AWS security services and their functions.

### Step 1: Enable AWS Security Hub

**Access AWS Security Hub:** In the AWS Management Console, type "Security Hub" in the search bar and select AWS Security Hub.

**Enable Security Hub:** On the Security Hub dashboard, click the Get started button. Review the features and click Enable Security Hub.

### Step 2: Integrate Amazon GuardDuty with Security Hub

**Enable GuardDuty:** In the AWS Management Console, type "GuardDuty" in the search bar and select Amazon GuardDuty. On the GuardDuty dashboard, click Get started and then Enable GuardDuty.

**Integrate with Security Hub:** Navigate back to the Security Hub dashboard. In the Integrations section, ensure GuardDuty is listed and enabled. Findings from GuardDuty will now be automatically forwarded to Security Hub.

### Step 3: Integrate AWS Config with Security Hub

**Enable AWS Config:** In the AWS Management Console, type "Config" in the search bar and select AWS Config. Follow the prompts to set up AWS Config, ensuring that configuration recording is enabled.

**Integrate with Security Hub:** Navigate back to the Security Hub dashboard. In the Integrations section, ensure AWS Config is listed and enabled. Findings from AWS Config compliance checks will now be automatically forwarded to Security Hub.

### Step 4: Integrate Amazon Macie with Security Hub
**Enable Amazon Macie:** In the AWS Management Console, type "Macie" in the search bar and select Amazon Macie. On the Macie dashboard, click Get started and then Enable Macie.

**Integrate with Security Hub:** Navigate back to the Security Hub dashboard. In the Integrations section, ensure Macie is listed and enabled. Findings from Macie, such as sensitive data discoveries, will now be automatically forwarded to Security Hub.

### Step 5: Integrate AWS IAM Access Analyzer with Security Hub
**Enable IAM Access Analyzer:** In the AWS Management Console, type "IAM" in the search bar and select IAM. Navigate to Access Analyzer and click Create analyzer. Follow the prompts to set up the analyzer.

**Integrate with Security Hub:** Navigate back to the Security Hub dashboard. In the Integrations section, ensure IAM Access Analyzer is listed and enabled. Findings from IAM Access Analyzer, such as potential security risks due to external sharing, will now be automatically forwarded to Security Hub.

### Step 6: Integrate Amazon Inspector with Security Hub
**Enable Amazon Inspector:** In the AWS Management Console, type "Inspector" in the search bar and select Amazon Inspector. On the Inspector dashboard, click Get started and follow the prompts to set up Amazon Inspector.

**Integrate with Security Hub:** Navigate back to the Security Hub dashboard. In the Integrations section, ensure Amazon Inspector is listed and enabled. Findings from Inspector, such as identified vulnerabilities, will now be automatically forwarded to Security Hub.

### Step 7: Review Centralized Findings in Security Hub
**Navigate to Findings:** In the Security Hub dashboard, navigate to the Findings section. Review the aggregated findings from GuardDuty, AWS Config, Macie, IAM Access Analyzer, and Amazon Inspector.

**Analyze and Respond to Findings:** Click on individual findings to view detailed information, including the affected resources, threat type, and recommended actions.Use the Insights section in Security Hub to prioritize high-severity findings and compliance issues.

### Step 8: Automate Responses to Findings
**Set Up CloudWatch Events:** In the AWS Management Console, type "CloudWatch" in the search bar and select CloudWatch. Navigate to Events and click Create rule. Choose Event Source as Security Hub Findings.

**Configure Rule Details:** Define the event pattern to match specific findings, such as high-severity threats or compliance failures. Set the target as an AWS Lambda function to automate responses, such as isolating compromised instances or notifying the security team.

**Create Lambda Function:** In the AWS Management Console, type "Lambda" in the search bar and select AWS Lambda. Create a new Lambda function and configure it to perform automated actions based on the findings from Security Hub.

**Link Lambda Function to CloudWatch Events:** Return to CloudWatch Events and select the Lambda function as the target for your rule. Save the rule to enable automated responses to specific findings in Security Hub.

# 7.9 Key Exam Tips

## Familiarize Yourself with AWS Managed Security Services

**Amazon GuardDuty:** Understand how GuardDuty detects security threats using machine learning and threat intelligence. Be familiar with the types of findings it generates and how to integrate them with other AWS services.

**AWS Security Hub:** Focus on how Security Hub aggregates security findings from multiple AWS services like GuardDuty, Macie, and Inspector, and provides a comprehensive view of your AWS environment's security posture.

**Amazon Macie:** Know how Macie automatically discovers and classifies sensitive data such as PII in your AWS environment, especially in S3.

**AWS Config:** Understand how Config continuously monitors AWS resource configurations and detects configuration changes that could pose security risks.

**IAM Access Analyzer:** Remember that IAM Access Analyzer helps identify resources shared with external entities and flags potential risks to ensure secure access controls.

## Master Anomaly and Correlation Techniques

**Anomaly Detection:** Learn how to detect abnormal behavior and unexpected changes in your AWS environment using services like GuardDuty and CloudWatch Anomaly Detection. Machine learning plays a key role here in flagging unusual activities.

**Amazon Detective:** Grasp how Detective helps in deep investigations by automatically collecting and analyzing data from GuardDuty, CloudTrail, and VPC Flow Logs, enabling easier threat analysis and correlation of security events.

## Visualization and Dashboards

**Creating Visualizations:** Be aware of how to use CloudWatch to create dashboards and metric filters that allow you to visualize and monitor security threats in real time. Understanding dashboards will help you track threats more efficiently.

**Dashboards and Metric Filters:** Practice creating filters that focus on specific log patterns to quickly identify issues such as unauthorized API calls or network anomalies.

## Centralizing Security Findings

**Security Hub Integration:** Focus on integrating Security Hub with AWS services to centralize security findings and improve incident management. This step helps to consolidate alerts and findings from different services into a single pane of glass.

**Strategies for Centralization:** Learn how centralizing security findings helps with quicker detection, validation, and response to security events. Understand the importance of setting up a central security operations dashboard.

## Validating Security Events

**Queries with Amazon Athena:** Know how to use Amazon Athena to run queries on CloudTrail, VPC Flow Logs, or other data sources to investigate suspicious activities. This can help validate whether a security event is genuine or a false positive.

**Analysis and Investigation Techniques:** Be familiar with the techniques for investigating security incidents, such as analyzing log data and correlating findings from multiple AWS services to understand the context and severity of the threat.

## Best Practices for Threat Detection

**Continuous Monitoring and Real-Time Alerts:** Implement continuous monitoring across your AWS environment and set up real-time alerts for high-severity events. This includes configuring GuardDuty, CloudWatch Alarms, and SNS notifications for immediate action on security threats.

**Regular Audits and Reviews:** Understand the importance of conducting regular audits of your security configurations, access policies, and monitoring setups. Regular audits ensure that your environment remains secure as it evolves.

## 7.10 Chapter Review Questions

**Question 1:**
Which AWS service is primarily used to continuously monitor your AWS environment for malicious activities and unauthorized behavior?
A. AWS Config
B. Amazon GuardDuty
C. AWS IAM Access Analyzer
D. Amazon Macie

**Question 2:**
What is the role of AWS Security Hub in threat detection?
A. To store and encrypt sensitive data
B. To automatically remediate security issues
C. To aggregate, organize, and prioritize security findings across AWS accounts
D. To create custom IAM roles for security administrators

**Question 3:**
Which AWS service helps you detect and protect sensitive data, such as personally identifiable information (PII), in your Amazon S3 buckets?
A. Amazon GuardDuty
B. AWS Config
C. Amazon Macie
D. Amazon Detective

**Question 4:**
What does IAM Access Analyzer help you detect in your AWS environment?
A. Misconfigured EC2 instances
B. Potential unauthorized access to AWS resources
C. Non-compliant security groups
D. Exposed credentials in S3 buckets

**Question 5:**
Which service helps you investigate security threats by analyzing log data and visualizing suspicious activities?
A. Amazon GuardDuty
B. AWS Security Hub
C. Amazon Macie
D. Amazon Detective

**Question 6:**
Which technique is used to identify unexpected patterns or unusual behavior in your AWS environment that could indicate a security threat?
A. Session management
B. Anomaly detection
C. Encryption key rotation
D. Disaster recovery planning

**Question 7:**
What is the purpose of dashboards and metric filters in AWS security monitoring?
A. To store sensitive data
B. To visualize and track security metrics and incidents
C. To encrypt data at rest
D. To configure IAM roles and policies

**Question 8:**
How can Amazon Athena be used to help with security event validation?
A. By querying and analyzing AWS CloudTrail logs and other data sources
B. By encrypting log data from Amazon S3
C. By visualizing security trends and incidents in real time
D. By storing access keys securely

**Question 9:**
Which service helps centralize security findings and integrates with AWS Security Hub to provide a comprehensive view of security alerts across multiple AWS accounts?
A. Amazon Macie
B. Amazon GuardDuty
C. Amazon Detective
D. AWS Config

**Question 10:**
Which of the following is considered a best practice for threat detection in AWS environments?
A. Disabling real-time alerts to reduce noise
B. Continuous monitoring with real-time alerts
C. Limiting the use of automation tools
D. Relying solely on manual monitoring

**Question 11:**
Your security team receives an alert from Amazon GuardDuty indicating a possible data exfiltration from an EC2 instance. Upon further inspection, you find the instance is communicating with an IP address linked to malicious activity. What should be your next step to ensure the security of the instance and stop the data leak?
A. Terminate the instance immediately
B. Disconnect the instance from the network using its security group
C. Use Amazon Detective to gather more data and visualize the instance's activity
D. Block all external traffic using AWS Shield

**Question 12:**
Your company uses Amazon Macie to scan S3 buckets for sensitive data. A recent scan detected sensitive customer information stored in an unencrypted S3 bucket. What would be the best course of action to remediate this issue quickly and secure the data?
A. Enable default encryption for the S3 bucket
B. Remove public access from the S3 bucket
C. Enable logging on the S3 bucket
D. Delete the data from the bucket immediately

**Question 13:**
You have set up AWS Security Hub to centralize and track security findings across multiple AWS accounts. After reviewing the findings, you discover several accounts with non-compliant security groups allowing inbound traffic from any IP. How can you quickly address this issue across multiple accounts?
A. Use AWS Config to automatically remediate non-compliant security groups

B. Manually delete the security groups from each account
C. Set up Amazon Macie to block access to the resources
D. Use Amazon Detective to investigate the affected resources

**Question 14:**
During a security audit, your team noticed multiple instances of IAM roles allowing external access to AWS resources. You need to detect and investigate if any of these roles have been used to grant unauthorized access. Which AWS service can help you identify and investigate the potential security risk?
A. Amazon GuardDuty
B. IAM Access Analyzer
C. Amazon Inspector
D. AWS Config

**Question 15:**
Your team uses Amazon Detective to investigate a security incident involving unusual API calls. After identifying the root cause, you want to ensure similar incidents are caught in the future by setting up real-time alerts. Which AWS service should you integrate to continuously monitor for suspicious API activity and trigger alerts?
A. Amazon Macie
B. Amazon GuardDuty
C. AWS Security Hub
D. IAM Access Analyzer

# 7.11 Answers to Chapter Review Questions

1. B. Amazon GuardDuty
Explanation: Amazon GuardDuty continuously monitors for malicious activities and unauthorized behavior by analyzing AWS CloudTrail logs, VPC flow logs, and DNS logs to identify potential security threats.

2. C. To aggregate, organize, and prioritize security findings across AWS accounts
Explanation: AWS Security Hub provides a central location to aggregate, organize, and prioritize security findings from AWS services like GuardDuty, Inspector, and third-party tools.

3. C. Amazon Macie
Explanation: Amazon Macie is a managed security service that helps you detect and protect sensitive data, such as personally identifiable information (PII), in your Amazon S3 buckets.

4. B. Potential unauthorized access to AWS resources
Explanation: IAM Access Analyzer helps detect potential unauthorized access to your AWS resources by analyzing policies and configurations to identify public or cross-account access.

5. D. Amazon Detective
Explanation: Amazon Detective helps you analyze and investigate potential security threats by using machine learning and data analysis to visualize suspicious activities and patterns.

6. B. Anomaly detection
Explanation: Anomaly detection techniques help identify unexpected patterns or unusual behavior in your AWS environment, which may indicate a potential security threat.

7. B. To visualize and track security metrics and incidents
Explanation: Dashboards and metric filters in AWS services like CloudWatch allow you to create visualizations and track important security metrics and incidents, improving visibility into your security posture.

8. A. By querying and analyzing AWS CloudTrail logs and other data sources
Explanation: Amazon Athena allows you to query AWS CloudTrail logs and other data sources to validate security events by performing detailed analysis and investigations.

9. B. Amazon GuardDuty
Explanation: Amazon GuardDuty integrates with AWS Security Hub, allowing security findings from GuardDuty to be centralized and correlated with findings from other AWS security services.

10. B. Continuous monitoring with real-time alerts
Explanation: A best practice for threat detection in AWS environments is to implement continuous monitoring with real-time alerts to ensure that security threats are identified and addressed promptly.

11. B. Disconnect the instance from the network using its security group
Explanation: Disconnecting the instance by modifying its security group is the best immediate action to contain the threat without terminating the instance. This allows time to investigate the issue using tools like Amazon Detective while stopping the data exfiltration.

12. A. Enable default encryption for the S3 bucket
Explanation: Amazon Macie detected sensitive data, and the most effective way to protect it is to enable default encryption for the S3 bucket to ensure that all future objects are encrypted at rest.

13. A. Use AWS Config to automatically remediate non-compliant security groups
Explanation: AWS Config can be used to define and enforce compliance rules for security groups, and automatic remediation can be triggered to fix non-compliant resources across multiple accounts.

14. B. IAM Access Analyzer
Explanation: IAM Access Analyzer helps detect and investigate external access to AWS resources by analyzing permissions and access policies, allowing you to identify and address potential security risks.

15. B. Amazon GuardDuty
Explanation: Amazon GuardDuty is a threat detection service that continuously monitors API calls, network activity, and other logs for suspicious behavior, and it can trigger real-time alerts based on defined detection rules.

# Chapter 8. Responding to Compromised Resources

**This chapter addresses the following exam objectives:**
Domain 1: Threat Detection and Incident Response
Task Statement 1.3: Respond to compromised resources and workloads.
Knowledge of:
- AWS Security Incident Response Guide
- Resource isolation mechanisms
- Techniques for root cause analysis
- Data capture mechanisms
- Log analysis for event validation

Skills in:
- Automating remediation by using AWS services (for example, AWS Lambda,
- AWS Step Functions, EventBridge, AWS Systems Manager runbooks, Security Hub, AWS Config)
- Responding to compromised resources (for example, by isolating Amazon EC2 instances)
- Investigating and analyzing to conduct root cause analysis (for example, by using Detective)
- Capturing relevant forensics data from a compromised resource (for example, Amazon Elastic Block Store [Amazon EBS] volume snapshots, memory dump)
- Querying logs in Amazon S3 for contextual information related to security events (for example, by using Athena)
- Protecting and preserving forensic artifacts (for example, by using S3
- Object Lock, isolated forensic accounts, S3 Lifecycle, and S3 replication)
- Preparing services for incidents and recovering services after incidents

❖❖❖❖❖❖

In the face of a security breach, effective incident response is critical to minimizing damage and restoring normal operations. This chapter provides a detailed roadmap for managing security incidents within AWS environments, emphasizing the importance of a structured and timely response to compromised resources.

We begin with an introduction to incident response, outlining the key concepts and objectives involved in addressing security incidents. The AWS Security Incident Response Guide is introduced, providing an overview of its contents and detailing the incident response lifecycle, which includes preparation, detection, analysis, containment, eradication, recovery, and post-incident activities.

Resource isolation mechanisms are crucial for containing the impact of a security breach. This section covers various techniques for isolating compromised resources, as well as methods for automating resource isolation to ensure swift and effective containment.

Root cause analysis is essential for understanding the underlying issues that led to the incident. We discuss how to conduct a root cause analysis and leverage tools like Amazon Detective for thorough investigations, enabling a deeper understanding of the incident.

Data capture mechanisms are vital for preserving evidence and conducting forensic analysis. We explore techniques for capturing forensic data and preserving forensic artifacts, which are crucial for post-incident investigations and legal compliance.

Log analysis plays a significant role in validating security events and understanding the scope of an incident. This section covers techniques for log analysis and the use of Amazon Athena for performing detailed log queries, aiding in the validation and investigation of security events.

Automating remediation can significantly enhance the speed and effectiveness of your response. We discuss the use of AWS Lambda for automated remediation, implementing AWS Step Functions, and event-driven remediation with EventBridge, providing practical examples of how to automate incident response tasks.

Preparing and recovering services after an incident is essential for maintaining business continuity. This section offers guidance on preparing services for potential incidents and the steps needed to recover services after an incident has occurred.

Best practices for incident response are emphasized throughout the chapter, including continuous monitoring, regular incident response drills, and ongoing improvement of response strategies. These practices help ensure that your incident response capabilities remain effective and up-to-date.

The chapter concludes with lab exercises that provide hands-on experience in simulating a security incident, automating incident response with AWS Lambda and EventBridge, using Amazon Detective for investigations, and capturing and analyzing forensic data. These exercises are designed to solidify your understanding and enhance your practical skills in incident response.

By the end of this chapter, readers will be well-equipped with the knowledge and tools necessary to respond effectively to compromised resources, ensuring a swift and organized recovery from security incidents within their AWS environments.

## 8.1 Introduction to Incident Response

Incident response within AWS involves a structured approach to identifying, managing, and mitigating security incidents to protect cloud resources and workloads. The dynamic nature of cloud environments, combined with the shared responsibility model, makes it crucial to implement effective incident response strategies tailored to AWS. This ensures quick detection, isolation, and resolution of security threats, minimizing potential damage and maintaining business continuity.

In AWS, incident response revolves around several foundational components and services designed to enhance visibility and control over your cloud environment. Key services include AWS CloudTrail, which provides detailed logging of API calls and user activities; Amazon GuardDuty, which uses machine learning and threat intelligence to detect anomalies and potential threats; AWS Config, which monitors and records AWS resource configurations and compliance status; and AWS Security Hub, which aggregates security findings from various AWS services and provides a unified view of your security posture.

## Importance of Effective Incident Response Strategies
**Early Detection and Alerting:**
Early detection of security incidents is vital to minimize impact. AWS provides robust monitoring and alerting capabilities through services like Amazon CloudWatch and AWS CloudTrail, enabling real-time detection of suspicious activities and policy violations.

**Rapid Containment and Mitigation:**
Once an incident is detected, it's crucial to quickly contain the threat to prevent further damage. AWS services like IAM for access control and AWS Firewall Manager for managing firewall rules help isolate compromised resources and block malicious traffic.

**Automated Response:**
Automation plays a significant role in incident response. AWS Lambda and AWS Systems Manager Automation can be used to automate repetitive tasks, such as revoking compromised credentials, isolating instances, or applying security patches, ensuring swift and consistent responses.

**Comprehensive Analysis and Forensics:**
Post-incident analysis is essential for understanding the root cause and impact of the incident. AWS services like Amazon Athena allow you to query and analyze log data stored in Amazon S3, facilitating detailed forensic investigations.

**Continuous Improvement:**
Incident response is an iterative process. Regularly reviewing and updating incident response plans based on lessons learned from past incidents ensures continuous improvement and preparedness for future threats.

## Foundational Knowledge for AWS Incident Response
**Understanding the Shared Responsibility Model:**
AWS operates under a shared responsibility model, where AWS manages the security of the cloud, and customers are responsible for security in the cloud. This means customers must implement and manage their own security controls, while AWS ensures the underlying infrastructure is secure.

**Familiarity with AWS Security Best Practices:**
Adhering to AWS security best practices, such as the AWS Well-Architected Framework's Security Pillar, helps build a secure cloud environment. This includes identity and access management, infrastructure protection, data protection, and incident response.

**Leveraging AWS Native Security Services:**
Utilizing AWS native security services like GuardDuty, Macie, and Inspector enhances your ability to detect and respond to security incidents. These services integrate seamlessly with AWS Security Hub, providing a centralized view of security findings.

**Developing a Comprehensive Incident Response Plan:**
A well-defined incident response plan tailored to AWS environments should include roles and responsibilities, communication protocols, and detailed response procedures for different types of incidents. Regularly testing the plan through simulations and drills ensures team readiness.

**Utilizing AWS Security Automation and Orchestration:**
Automating incident response processes using AWS Lambda, Step Functions, and Systems Manager Automation improves response times and reduces human error. Implementing security orchestration workflows enables coordinated and efficient handling of complex incidents.

In conclusion, effective incident response within AWS involves leveraging AWS's comprehensive suite of security services, understanding the shared responsibility model, and continuously improving response strategies through automation and regular testing. By implementing these foundational concepts, organizations can enhance their ability to protect cloud resources and workloads, ensuring a robust and resilient security posture.

## 8.2 AWS Security Incident Response Guide

The AWS Security Incident Response Guide provides comprehensive guidelines for managing and responding to security incidents in AWS environments. It emphasizes best practices for preparing, detecting, responding to, and recovering from security threats, ensuring robust protection and resilience of cloud resources. The guide is essential for building an effective incident response strategy that leverages AWS-native tools and services to maintain a secure cloud infrastructure.

### 8.2.1 Overview of the AWS Security Incident Response Guide

The AWS Security Incident Response Guide offers a comprehensive framework for effectively managing security incidents within AWS environments. This guide outlines best practices and procedures to ensure a robust incident response capability tailored to the cloud's dynamic and scalable nature. It is designed to help organizations prepare for, detect, respond to, and recover from security incidents while leveraging AWS-native tools and services.

**Key Principles of the AWS Security Incident Response Guide**

**Preparation:**
- Readiness: Ensures organizations are prepared to handle security incidents by establishing incident response plans, defining roles and responsibilities, and training the incident response team.
- Tooling: Recommends deploying AWS-native security services like AWS CloudTrail for logging and monitoring API calls, Amazon GuardDuty for threat detection, AWS Config for configuration monitoring, and AWS Security Hub for centralized security management.

**Detection and Analysis:**
- Monitoring: Emphasizes continuous monitoring of the AWS environment using services like Amazon CloudWatch, AWS CloudTrail, and Amazon GuardDuty to detect anomalous activities and potential security threats.
- Analysis: Guides on analyzing detected incidents to determine the scope and impact. It includes steps to comprehensively correlate findings across various AWS services to view the incident.

**Containment, Eradication, and Recovery:**
- Containment: Focuses on isolating affected systems to prevent the spread of the incident. It suggests using AWS Identity and Access Management (IAM) to revoke compromised credentials and AWS Firewall Manager to block malicious traffic.
- Eradication: Details the process of removing the incident's root cause, such as cleaning up malware or closing vulnerabilities. It highlights the importance of using AWS Systems Manager for automated remediation tasks.
- Recovery: Outlines the steps to restore systems to normal operations. It includes validating that systems are secure before returning to production and continuously monitoring for any signs of recurrence.

**Post-Incident Activity:**
- Review: Encourages conducting a thorough review of the incident to understand what happened, why it happened, and how it was handled. This involves documenting lessons learned and identifying areas for improvement.

- Improvement: Recommends updating incident response plans based on insights gained from the review. This continuous improvement cycle ensures that organizations are better prepared for future incidents.

### Utilizing AWS-Native Tools

The use of AWS-native tools and services to can enhance incident response capabilities. Services like AWS CloudFormation can automate the deployment of security infrastructure, while AWS Lambda can be used to create automated responses to specific security events. Integrating these tools allows for a more cohesive and efficient incident response strategy.

### Conclusion

The AWS Security Incident Response Guide is essential for organizations looking to strengthen their cloud security posture. Organizations can effectively manage and mitigate security incidents by following its principles and utilizing AWS-native services, ensuring minimal impact and swift recovery. The guide provides a structured approach to incident response, emphasizing preparation, detection, analysis, containment, eradication, recovery, and continuous improvement, all tailored for the unique characteristics of AWS environments.

## 8.2.2 Incident Response Lifecycle

The incident response lifecycle is a structured approach to handling security incidents systematically and effectively. It consists of six stages: preparation, detection, analysis, containment, eradication, and recovery. Each stage plays a critical role in ensuring a swift and coordinated response to security threats, minimizing potential damage, and restoring normal operations.

### Preparation

Preparation is the foundation of an effective incident response strategy. It involves establishing and training an incident response team, defining roles and responsibilities, and developing detailed incident response plans and playbooks. Preparation also includes setting up necessary tools and infrastructure, such as logging and monitoring systems, to ensure the organization is ready to detect and respond to incidents. Regular training, simulations, and drills are conducted to ensure team readiness and to continuously improve the incident response capabilities.

### Detection

Detection focuses on identifying potential security incidents as early as possible. This involves continuous monitoring of systems, networks, and applications for signs of malicious activity, anomalies, or policy violations. Tools such as intrusion detection systems (IDS), intrusion prevention systems (IPS), security information and event management (SIEM) systems, and AWS services like Amazon GuardDuty and AWS CloudTrail play a crucial role in this stage. Effective detection requires well-defined baselines of normal behavior to accurately identify deviations that could indicate a security incident.

### Analysis

Once an incident is detected, the analysis stage involves determining the nature, scope, and impact of the incident. This stage requires a thorough investigation to understand how the incident occurred, what systems or data were affected, and the severity of the threat. Incident responders analyze logs, network traffic, and other relevant data to gather evidence and establish a timeline of events. The goal is to gain a comprehensive understanding of the incident to inform subsequent response actions.

### Containment

Containment aims to isolate the affected systems or networks to prevent the incident from spreading and causing further damage. This stage may involve implementing firewall rules, disabling compromised accounts, or isolating infected machines from the network. Containment can be performed in two phases: short-term containment, which provides immediate isolation, and long-term containment, which involves more thorough measures to ensure the threat is fully controlled. Effective containment strategies help limit the impact of the incident while allowing for continued investigation and remediation.

**Eradication**
Eradication involves removing the root cause of the incident from the affected systems. This could include deleting malware, closing vulnerabilities, or applying patches to prevent the incident from reoccurring. Eradication requires careful validation to ensure that all traces of the threat have been eliminated. This stage also involves restoring affected systems to their pre-incident state, ensuring they are secure and operational. Comprehensive testing and verification are critical to confirm the success of eradication efforts.

**Recovery**
Recovery focuses on restoring normal operations and ensuring that affected systems are fully functional and secure. This stage includes reintroducing the cleaned and secured systems back into the production environment, closely monitoring them for any signs of residual issues. Recovery also involves conducting a post-incident review to document lessons learned and update incident response plans and procedures accordingly. Effective recovery ensures that the organization can resume its business operations with minimal disruption and enhanced security measures in place.

Summary
The incident response lifecycle provides a structured and systematic approach to managing and mitigating security incidents. Each stage—preparation, detection, analysis, containment, eradication, and recovery—plays a critical role in ensuring a coordinated and effective response to security threats. By following these stages, organizations can minimize the impact of security incidents, protect their assets, and continuously improve their incident response capabilities.

## 8.3 Resource Isolation Mechanisms

Resource isolation mechanisms are critical techniques used to limit the impact of security incidents by segregating compromised or high-risk components from the rest of the system. These mechanisms include the use of security groups, network access control lists (ACLs), and virtual private clouds (VPCs) in AWS to control and restrict network traffic, ensuring that potential threats are contained and do not spread to unaffected resources. Implementing robust isolation strategies helps maintain the integrity and availability of essential services while addressing security issues.

### 8.3.1 Techniques for Isolating Compromised Resources

Isolating compromised resources is a critical step in mitigating security incidents and preventing the spread of threats within an AWS environment. AWS provides several tools and mechanisms for effective resource isolation, including security groups, network access control lists (ACLs), and other AWS-native services.

**Security Groups**
Security groups in AWS act as virtual firewalls that control inbound and outbound traffic to AWS resources, such as EC2 instances. They are stateful, meaning that if an inbound request is allowed, the response is automatically allowed. For example, if an EC2 instance is suspected to be compromised, you can immediately update the security group rules to block all inbound and outbound traffic. This action isolates the instance from the network, preventing it from communicating with other instances or services and thus containing the threat.

**Network Access Control Lists (ACLs)**
Network ACLs provide an additional layer of security by controlling traffic at the subnet level. Unlike security groups, network ACLs are stateless, meaning both inbound and outbound rules must be explicitly defined. If a subnet within your VPC is compromised, you can update the network ACL to deny all inbound and outbound traffic, effectively isolating all resources within that subnet. This broad isolation method is particularly useful for quickly containing threats that might affect multiple resources.

**VPC Isolation**
Virtual Private Clouds (VPCs) allow for the creation of isolated network environments within AWS. During a security incident, compromised resources can be segregated into a separate VPC, often referred to as a quarantine VPC. This can be done by modifying route tables, security groups, and network ACLs to restrict network access, or by physically moving instances to the quarantine VPC. This method ensures that compromised resources are fully isolated from the rest of the infrastructure, minimizing the risk to other resources.

**AWS Lambda and Automation**
AWS Lambda can automate the isolation process, ensuring a swift response to security incidents. For instance, a Lambda function can be triggered by a CloudWatch Event or a GuardDuty finding, which then automatically updates security group rules or network ACLs to isolate the compromised resource. Automation ensures consistent and rapid isolation, reducing the potential for human error and minimizing response times.

**AWS Systems Manager**
AWS Systems Manager offers comprehensive management and automation capabilities. Using Systems Manager, you can create automation runbooks that isolate compromised instances. For example, a runbook might change the security group of a compromised EC2 instance to one that blocks all traffic, or move the instance to a quarantine VPC. This ensures that isolation procedures are performed consistently and reliably, enhancing overall incident response effectiveness.

## Example Scenario
Consider a scenario where an EC2 instance shows signs of compromise, such as unusual outbound traffic detected by Amazon GuardDuty. An immediate response would involve updating the security group of the EC2 instance to block all inbound and outbound traffic, effectively isolating the instance. Next, AWS Systems Manager can be used to run an automation script that moves the instance to a quarantine VPC. This script could be triggered by an AWS Lambda function in response to the GuardDuty alert. This combination of tools ensures that the compromised instance is quickly isolated, preventing further spread of the threat while allowing for detailed investigation and remediation.

By leveraging these AWS tools and mechanisms, organizations can effectively isolate compromised resources, contain security threats, and protect their cloud environments from further damage. Implementing these strategies as part of a comprehensive incident response plan ensures a robust and resilient approach to cloud security.

# 8.3.2 Automating Resource Isolation
Automating the isolation of compromised resources is essential for minimizing the impact of security incidents and ensuring a swift response. AWS provides several services, such as AWS Lambda and AWS Systems Manager, which can be leveraged to automate remediation tasks, ensuring that compromised resources are isolated quickly and effectively without manual intervention.

### AWS Lambda
AWS Lambda allows you to run code in response to events, such as changes in data or system states, without provisioning or managing servers. Lambda functions can be triggered by AWS services such as Amazon CloudWatch Events, AWS Config, or Amazon GuardDuty findings. For example, when Amazon GuardDuty detects suspicious activity on an EC2 instance, it can generate a finding that triggers a Lambda function. This function can then automate the isolation process by modifying the instance's security group to block all inbound and outbound traffic, effectively isolating the compromised instance from the network.

**AWS Systems Manager**
AWS Systems Manager provides a unified user interface to manage and automate operational tasks across AWS resources. Systems Manager includes Automation, which enables the creation and execution of runbooks to automate common tasks. When integrated with AWS Lambda, you can create a comprehensive automation solution for isolating compromised resources.

### Example Scenario
Consider a scenario where Amazon GuardDuty detects unusual outbound traffic from an EC2 instance, indicating a potential compromise. Here's how AWS Lambda and AWS Systems Manager can be used to automate the isolation process:

- **GuardDuty Detection**: Amazon GuardDuty detects suspicious activity and generates a finding.
- **Triggering Lambda Function**: The GuardDuty finding triggers an AWS Lambda function through Amazon CloudWatch Events.
- **Lambda Function Execution**: The Lambda function executes the following steps:
    - Updates the security group of the compromised EC2 instance to block all inbound and outbound traffic, immediately isolating the instance from the network.
    - Invokes an AWS Systems Manager Automation runbook to perform additional isolation tasks.
- **Systems Manager Automation**: The Systems Manager runbook can perform various tasks, such as:
    - Moving the EC2 instance to a quarantine VPC with strict network controls.
    - Capturing a snapshot of the instance's EBS volume for forensic analysis.
    - Running predefined commands on the instance to terminate malicious processes or collect further data for investigation.

This automated workflow ensures that the compromised instance is isolated swiftly, minimizing the potential for further damage or lateral movement within the network. The combination of AWS Lambda and AWS Systems Manager enables a robust, repeatable, and scalable approach to incident response, reducing the reliance on manual processes and improving overall security posture.

By utilizing AWS Lambda and AWS Systems Manager, organizations can automate the isolation of compromised resources, ensuring quick and effective responses to security incidents. This automation not only helps contain threats but also frees up valuable time for security teams to focus on more complex tasks and investigations.

## 8.4 Root Cause Analysis
## 8.4.1 Conducting Root Cause Analysis
Investigating and analyzing incidents to determine the root cause is a critical aspect of effective incident response. Root cause analysis (RCA) involves identifying the underlying issues that led to a security incident, allowing organizations to implement measures to prevent recurrence. Several techniques can be employed to conduct a thorough root cause analysis, leveraging AWS tools and best practices.

### Techniques for Root Cause Analysis
**Data Collection:** The first step in root cause analysis is gathering relevant data from various sources. This includes logs, system metrics, and alerts from monitoring tools. AWS services like AWS CloudTrail, AWS Config, and Amazon CloudWatch provide detailed logging and monitoring capabilities. CloudTrail logs all API calls made in your AWS environment, while Config tracks changes to AWS resources and their configurations. CloudWatch collects and tracks metrics, sets alarms, and provides insights through dashboards.

**Timeline Reconstruction:** Creating a timeline of events helps visualize the sequence of actions leading up to the incident. By correlating data from different sources, such as CloudTrail logs and CloudWatch metrics, you can reconstruct what happened before, during, and after the incident. This step is crucial for understanding the incident's progression and identifying potential entry points or vulnerabilities.

**Event Correlation:** Correlating events across multiple data sources helps identify patterns and anomalies. Tools like Amazon Detective can assist in this process by analyzing and visualizing data from AWS CloudTrail, Amazon VPC Flow Logs, and GuardDuty findings. Detective uses machine learning and graph analysis to uncover relationships and identify the root cause of potential security issues.

**Anomaly Detection:** Analyzing logs and metrics for anomalies can provide insights into unusual activities that may have contributed to the incident. AWS services like Amazon GuardDuty and Amazon Macie can detect threats and anomalies in your environment. GuardDuty identifies potential security threats by analyzing VPC Flow Logs, DNS logs, and CloudTrail events, while Macie uses machine learning to detect sensitive data exposure and anomalies in S3 buckets.

**Forensic Analysis:** Conducting a forensic analysis involves examining compromised systems and artifacts to gather evidence and identify malicious activities. AWS provides tools like AWS Systems Manager to automate the collection of logs and other forensic data from compromised instances. You can also use Amazon S3 to store and analyze forensic data.

**Root Cause Identification:** Once the data is collected and analyzed, the next step is to identify the root cause. This involves determining the initial point of compromise, the attack vector used, and any underlying vulnerabilities. Techniques like the "5 Whys" or Fishbone Diagram (Ishikawa) can be applied to systematically identify the root cause by asking a series of "why" questions or mapping out potential causes.

### Example Scenario
Consider a scenario where an EC2 instance is found to be communicating with a known malicious IP address. The following steps outline how root cause analysis could be conducted:

- **Data Collection:** Use AWS CloudTrail to review API call logs for the EC2 instance, CloudWatch for instance metrics, and VPC Flow Logs for network traffic details.
- **Timeline Reconstruction:** Correlate the data to create a timeline of events leading up to the suspicious communication, identifying any abnormal activities or changes in the instance's behavior.
- **Event Correlation**: Use Amazon Detective to analyze the relationships between different events, such as unauthorized access attempts or configuration changes, to identify patterns.
- **Anomaly Detection:** Leverage Amazon GuardDuty to detect any anomalies or threats that may have contributed to the compromise.
- **Forensic Analysis:** Use AWS Systems Manager to collect forensic data from the compromised instance, such as logs, memory dumps, and running processes.
- **Root Cause Identification:** Apply the "5 Whys" technique to determine why the instance communicated with the malicious IP address, identifying the initial vulnerability (e.g., unpatched software, weak credentials) and taking corrective actions to prevent future incidents.

By employing these techniques and leveraging AWS tools, organizations can conduct comprehensive root cause analyses, identify underlying issues, and implement measures to enhance their security posture and prevent future incidents.

## 8.4.2 Using Amazon Detective for Investigations
Amazon Detective simplifies and accelerates security investigations by automatically collecting and analyzing log data from AWS resources, helping to identify the root cause of security incidents more efficiently. It uses machine learning, statistical analysis, and graph theory to build a linked set of data that enables security teams

to investigate and understand potential security issues quickly. Here's how Amazon Detective can be used to conduct root cause analysis effectively.

### Key Features of Amazon Detective

**Data Aggregation:** Amazon Detective aggregates data from AWS CloudTrail logs, Amazon VPC Flow Logs, and Amazon GuardDuty findings. This comprehensive dataset provides a detailed view of activities and interactions within your AWS environment.

**Visualizations:** Detective presents data in an intuitive, interactive visual interface. This helps investigators quickly identify relationships and anomalies.

**Behavioral Baselines:** It establishes baselines of normal behavior for entities (users, roles, IP addresses, etc.), making it easier to spot deviations that might indicate a security incident.

**Entity Profiles:** Detective creates detailed profiles for entities, aggregating historical activity and security findings related to each entity.

### Example Scenario

Consider a scenario where Amazon GuardDuty detects suspicious activity, such as an EC2 instance making unusual API calls. Here's how Amazon Detective can be used to investigate and perform root cause analysis:

- **GuardDuty** Finding: GuardDuty detects suspicious API calls from an EC2 instance and generates a security finding.
- **Detective Investigation:** The security team uses Amazon Detective to investigate the finding. Detective automatically links the GuardDuty finding to related AWS CloudTrail logs and VPC Flow Logs.
- **Data Visualization:** Detective's visual interface shows the sequence of API calls made by the EC2 instance, highlighting any anomalies or patterns. Investigators can see related entities, such as the IAM role associated with the instance and any external IP addresses it communicated with.
- **Behavioral Analysis:** Detective's behavioral baselines indicate whether the detected activity is typical for the instance or significantly deviates from its normal behavior.
- **Root Cause Analysis:** By examining the linked data, investigators determine that the EC2 instance's IAM role was compromised, allowing unauthorized API calls. The investigation reveals that the credentials were exposed due to a misconfigured application that inadvertently leaked sensitive information.

### Steps to Use Amazon Detective for Root Cause Analysis

1. **Enable Amazon Detective:** Ensure that Detective is enabled in your AWS environment and integrated with AWS CloudTrail, Amazon GuardDuty, and Amazon VPC Flow Logs.
2. **Investigate Findings:** When a security finding is detected (e.g., by GuardDuty), use Amazon Detective to start an investigation. The service automatically correlates and visualizes relevant data.
3. **Analyze Entity Profiles:** Review the profiles of entities involved in the incident. These profiles provide a comprehensive view of each entity's activities and historical security findings.
4. **Identify Anomalies:** Use Detective's visualizations and behavioral baselines to identify anomalous activities and potential entry points for the compromise.
5. **Determine Root Cause:** Correlate the data to trace the incident back to its root cause, such as a compromised IAM role or exposed credentials.

By leveraging Amazon Detective, security teams can streamline their investigations, quickly identify the root cause of security incidents, and take appropriate measures to mitigate risks. Detective's automated data aggregation, powerful visualizations, and machine learning capabilities make it an invaluable tool for efficient and effective root cause analysis in AWS environments.

# 8.5 Data Capture Mechanisms

Data capture mechanisms are essential tools and processes used to collect and log data across an organization's IT environment. In AWS, these mechanisms include services like AWS CloudTrail, Amazon CloudWatch, and VPC Flow Logs, which provide detailed records of API calls, system metrics, and network traffic. Implementing robust data capture mechanisms ensures comprehensive monitoring and auditing capabilities, enabling organizations to detect, analyze, and respond to security incidents effectively.

## 8.5.1 Capturing Forensic Data

Capturing relevant forensic data from compromised resources is a crucial step in investigating and understanding security incidents. AWS provides several tools and methods to gather this data, including EBS snapshots and memory dumps. These techniques ensure that critical information is preserved for analysis, helping to identify the root cause of the incident and mitigate future risks.

### EBS Snapshots

EBS (Elastic Block Store) snapshots are point-in-time backups of EBS volumes. They are particularly useful for capturing the state of a compromised instance's storage, allowing for detailed forensic analysis. By creating an EBS snapshot, you can preserve the current state of the volume without impacting the running instance. This snapshot can then be attached to a different instance for analysis, ensuring that the forensic investigation does not interfere with the compromised system.

**Example:** If an EC2 instance shows signs of compromise, such as unexpected outbound traffic, you can take an EBS snapshot of the instance's root volume and any attached data volumes. This snapshot can be analyzed to identify malicious files, unauthorized changes, or other indicators of compromise. Using AWS Systems Manager, you can automate the creation of these snapshots as part of your incident response process.

### Memory Dumps

Memory dumps capture the contents of an instance's RAM, providing a snapshot of its current state. This data can be invaluable for forensic investigations, as it may contain information about running processes, network connections, and potentially malicious code. AWS provides tools like Amazon EC2Rescue, which can be used to create memory dumps from EC2 instances.

**Example:** When an instance is suspected of being compromised, you can use EC2Rescue to capture a memory dump. This dump can then be analyzed using forensic tools to examine the processes that were running at the time of the incident, identify any malware, and understand the actions taken by an attacker. Memory dumps are particularly useful for identifying in-memory threats that may not be present on disk.

### AWS Systems Manager

AWS Systems Manager provides automation capabilities to streamline the process of capturing forensic data. Using Systems Manager Automation, you can create runbooks that automatically perform tasks such as taking EBS snapshots, capturing memory dumps, and collecting logs from compromised instances. This ensures a consistent and reliable approach to data capture during an incident.

**Example:** A Systems Manager runbook can be created to automate the response to a GuardDuty finding. When a finding is generated, the runbook can be triggered to take an EBS snapshot of the compromised instance, capture a memory dump, and gather CloudWatch logs. This comprehensive data capture ensures that all relevant information is collected for analysis without manual intervention.

By utilizing these methods and tools, organizations can effectively capture forensic data from compromised resources, ensuring that comprehensive information is available for incident analysis. Implementing automated data capture mechanisms using AWS Systems Manager further enhances the efficiency and reliability of the incident response process, enabling quick and accurate root cause analysis.

## 8.5.2 Preserving Forensic Artifacts

Protecting and preserving forensic artifacts is crucial for ensuring the integrity and availability of evidence during and after a security investigation. AWS provides several services and features, such as S3 Object Lock and S3 Lifecycle policies, to help secure and manage forensic data effectively. These tools ensure that forensic artifacts are tamper-proof and can be retained for the necessary duration to support ongoing investigations and potential legal proceedings.

### S3 Object Lock

S3 Object Lock allows you to store objects in Amazon S3 using a write-once-read-many (WORM) model. This means that once an object is written, it cannot be overwritten or deleted for a specified period or indefinitely. This feature is particularly useful for preserving forensic artifacts, as it ensures that the data remains unchanged and available for the duration of the investigation.

**Example:** After capturing an EBS snapshot or memory dump as part of a forensic investigation, you can store these artifacts in an S3 bucket with Object Lock enabled. By applying a retention period, you ensure that the data cannot be modified or deleted until the retention period expires, protecting the integrity of the forensic evidence.

### S3 Lifecycle Policies

S3 Lifecycle policies enable you to automate the management of objects in your S3 buckets. You can define rules to transition objects to different storage classes or expire objects after a specified period. This helps manage the storage costs associated with long-term retention of forensic data while ensuring that artifacts are preserved according to organizational policies or regulatory requirements.

**Example:** You can create an S3 Lifecycle policy that transitions forensic artifacts to a more cost-effective storage class, such as S3 Glacier, after a certain period. This ensures that the data is preserved at a lower cost while remaining accessible for long-term analysis. Additionally, you can set policies to automatically delete artifacts after a specified retention period, ensuring compliance with data retention policies.

### Combining S3 Object Lock and Lifecycle Policies

Combining S3 Object Lock with Lifecycle policies provides a robust solution for protecting and preserving forensic artifacts. Object Lock ensures data integrity by preventing modification or deletion, while Lifecycle policies help manage storage costs and automate data retention.

**Example Scenario:** Following a security incident, EBS snapshots and memory dumps are captured and stored in an S3 bucket. S3 Object Lock is applied with a retention period of one year to protect the artifacts from tampering. Simultaneously, an S3 Lifecycle policy transitions these artifacts to S3 Glacier after 30 days, reducing storage costs while maintaining data availability for long-term analysis. After the one-year retention period, the artifacts are automatically deleted in accordance with the organization's data retention policy.

By leveraging AWS services like S3 Object Lock and S3 Lifecycle policies, organizations can effectively protect and preserve forensic artifacts. These techniques ensure that critical evidence remains intact and available throughout the investigation process, supporting thorough analysis and compliance with legal and regulatory requirements.

# 8.6 Log Analysis for Event Validation

Log analysis for event validation involves scrutinizing system logs to verify the authenticity and impact of security events. By examining logs from various sources, such as application logs, server logs, and network logs, organizations can identify patterns, detect anomalies, and confirm whether an event is a legitimate security threat or a false positive. Effective log analysis is critical for validating events and ensuring accurate incident response.

## 8.6.1 Techniques for Log Analysis

Analyzing logs to validate security events is a fundamental aspect of incident response. By leveraging various log sources and applying systematic analysis methods, organizations can confirm the legitimacy of security events and take appropriate actions. Common log sources include application logs, server logs, and network logs, each providing critical insights into different aspects of the IT environment. Effective log analysis techniques ensure comprehensive event validation and help mitigate potential threats.

### Common Log Sources

**Application Logs:** These logs capture events generated by applications running on servers. They often include information about user activities, application errors, and other significant events. Analyzing application logs helps identify unusual user behaviors or application errors that might indicate a security incident.

**Server Logs:** Server logs, such as those from web servers (e.g., Apache, Nginx) or database servers (e.g., MySQL, PostgreSQL), provide detailed records of server activities. These logs can reveal unauthorized access attempts, SQL injection attacks, or other suspicious activities.

**Network Logs:** Network logs, including firewall logs, VPC Flow Logs, and IDS/IPS logs, record traffic data and network events. They are crucial for detecting and analyzing network-based attacks, such as port scanning, DDoS attacks, or unauthorized data exfiltration.

### Analysis Methods

**Pattern Matching:** Pattern matching involves searching logs for known indicators of compromise (IOCs), such as specific error codes, IP addresses, or command sequences. Tools like AWS CloudWatch Logs Insights can be used to query and filter logs for these patterns.

**Anomaly Detection:** Anomaly detection methods identify deviations from normal behavior. Machine learning algorithms can be employed to establish baselines of typical activity and flag anomalies. For instance, Amazon GuardDuty uses machine learning to detect unusual activities that might indicate a compromise.

**Correlation Analysis:** Correlating events across multiple log sources helps build a comprehensive picture of the incident. For example, correlating application login failures with firewall logs showing multiple connection attempts from a single IP can confirm a brute-force attack.

**Timeline Reconstruction:** Creating a timeline of events helps visualize the sequence of activities leading up to and following the incident. This technique is essential for understanding the progression of an attack and identifying the initial point of compromise.

### Example Scenario

Consider an example where unusual outbound traffic is detected from an EC2 instance. The following steps outline how log analysis can validate this security event:

**Collect Logs:** Gather relevant logs from various sources, including VPC Flow Logs for network traffic, AWS CloudTrail logs for API calls, and application logs from the compromised instance.

**Pattern Matching:** Use AWS CloudWatch Logs Insights to search for known IOCs in the logs, such as connections to known malicious IP addresses or specific error messages indicating compromise.

**Anomaly Detection:** Employ Amazon GuardDuty to detect any deviations from normal network traffic patterns. GuardDuty might flag the outbound traffic as suspicious based on historical baselines.

**Correlation Analysis:** Correlate the findings from CloudTrail logs showing unusual API calls with VPC Flow Logs indicating outbound traffic. This correlation confirms that the instance was compromised and used to exfiltrate data.

**Timeline Reconstruction:** Reconstruct the timeline of events, starting from the initial compromise (e.g., a successful login from an unusual location) to the detected outbound traffic. This helps understand the attack vector and the sequence of actions taken by the attacker.

By employing these techniques, organizations can effectively analyze logs to validate security events, ensuring that they respond to actual threats while minimizing false positives. Systematic log analysis provides deep insights into security incidents, enabling a swift and accurate response to protect critical assets.

## 8.6.2 Using Amazon Athena for Log Queries

Amazon Athena is a powerful tool for querying logs stored in Amazon S3, providing valuable contextual information related to security events. Athena allows you to use standard SQL queries to analyze large datasets quickly, making it an essential tool for security investigations and incident response.

### Using Amazon Athena for Log Analysis

**Set Up Athena:** To start using Athena, you need to set up an S3 bucket to store your logs and configure Athena to use this bucket. This involves creating a database and tables that map to the log data stored in S3.

**Create a Table:** Define a table in Athena that matches the structure of your log data. For example, if you have Apache web server logs, you would create a table with columns corresponding to the fields in the log files, such as IP address, request time, request method, and status code.

**Query the Logs:** Use SQL queries to analyze the log data. Athena's SQL syntax supports a wide range of queries, from simple SELECT statements to complex joins and aggregations. You can filter logs by specific criteria, aggregate data to find patterns, and join different datasets to gain comprehensive insights.

### Example Scenario

Suppose you need to investigate a potential security breach where an unusual number of failed login attempts were detected. Here's how you could use Amazon Athena to query logs stored in S3 for contextual information:

**Store Logs in S3:** Ensure that all relevant logs, such as application logs, web server logs, and authentication logs, are stored in an S3 bucket.

**Create Athena Table:** Define an Athena table for your authentication logs. For instance, if your logs are in JSON format, your table definition might look like this:

```
CREATE EXTERNAL TABLE IF NOT EXISTS auth_logs (
  timestamp STRING,
  user STRING,
  ip_address STRING,
  action STRING,
```

```
    status STRING
)
ROW FORMAT SERDE 'org.openx.data.jsonserde.JsonSerDe'
LOCATION 's3://your-log-bucket/auth-logs/';
```

**Run Queries:** Use SQL queries to analyze the log data. To find all failed login attempts within a specific timeframe, you could run a query like:

```
SELECT timestamp, user, ip_address, action, status
FROM auth_logs
WHERE status = 'FAILURE'
  AND timestamp BETWEEN '2024-07-01T00:00:00' AND '2024-07-01T23:59:59';
```

**Contextual Information:** To gain more context, you might want to correlate these failed login attempts with other logs. For example, you could join the authentication logs with web server logs to see if the same IP addresses accessed other parts of the system:

```
SELECT a.timestamp, a.user, a.ip_address, w.request_uri, w.status_code
FROM auth_logs a
JOIN web_logs w
ON a.ip_address = w.ip_address
WHERE a.status = 'FAILURE'
  AND a.timestamp BETWEEN '2024-07-01T00:00:00' AND '2024-07-01T23:59:59';
```

**Analyze Results:** Review the query results to identify patterns or anomalies. For instance, you might find that multiple failed login attempts originated from the same IP address, indicating a potential brute-force attack.

By using Amazon Athena to query logs stored in Amazon S3, organizations can efficiently analyze large volumes of log data to extract contextual information related to security events. This enables more informed decision-making during incident response and helps ensure that potential threats are identified and mitigated promptly.

# 8.7 Automating Remediation
## 8.7.1 Using AWS Lambda for Remediation

AWS Lambda is a powerful serverless compute service that allows you to run code in response to events without provisioning or managing servers. By integrating AWS Lambda with other AWS services, you can automate remediation actions in response to security incidents, enhancing your incident response capabilities and reducing the time to mitigate threats.

### Automating Remediation with AWS Lambda

AWS Lambda can be triggered by various events, such as changes in data, system state, or user activity, making it ideal for automated responses to security incidents. Common triggers include AWS CloudWatch Alarms, AWS Config rules, and AWS Security Hub findings. Once triggered, Lambda functions can execute predefined actions to remediate security issues.

### Example Scenario: Automating Response to Unauthorized Access

Consider a scenario where an unauthorized access attempt is detected on an EC2 instance. Here's how AWS Lambda can automate the remediation process:

**Detect the Incident:** Use Amazon GuardDuty to detect suspicious activity, such as unauthorized access attempts. GuardDuty continuously monitors your AWS environment and generates findings when it detects potential security threats.

**Trigger Lambda Function:** Configure an Amazon CloudWatch Event rule to trigger an AWS Lambda function when GuardDuty generates a finding for unauthorized access. The event rule specifies the condition under which the Lambda function should be invoked.

**Remediation Action:** Write a Lambda function that performs the necessary remediation actions. In this example, the function could isolate the compromised instance by modifying its security group to restrict inbound and outbound traffic.

```
1. import boto3
2.
3. def lambda_handler(event, context):
4.     ec2 = boto3.client('ec2')
5.
6.     # Extract instance ID from the GuardDuty finding
7.     instance_id = event['detail']['resource']['instanceDetails']['instanceId']
8.
9.     # Define the security group to isolate the instance
10.    security_group_id = 'sg-xxxxxxxx'
11.
12.    # Revoke all inbound and outbound rules for the security group
13.    ec2.revoke_security_group_ingress(GroupId=security_group_id, IpPermissions=[])
14.    ec2.revoke_security_group_egress(GroupId=security_group_id, IpPermissions=[])
15.
16.    # Attach the security group to the instance
17.    ec2.modify_instance_attribute(InstanceId=instance_id, Groups=[security_group_id])
18.
19.    return {
20.        'statusCode': 200,
21.        'body': f'Instance {instance_id} isolated successfully'
22.    }
23.
```

**Deploy and Test:** Deploy the Lambda function and configure the necessary permissions for it to modify security groups and instance attributes. Test the setup by simulating a GuardDuty finding and verifying that the instance is isolated as expected.

### Enhancing Remediation with AWS Systems Manager

AWS Systems Manager can be used alongside Lambda to provide more comprehensive remediation capabilities. For example, you can use Systems Manager Automation to orchestrate complex remediation workflows that involve multiple steps and services.

**Example Enhancement:** Extend the previous Lambda function to execute a Systems Manager Automation document that performs additional actions, such as capturing a memory dump and taking an EBS snapshot of the compromised instance.

```
1. import boto3
2.
3. def lambda_handler(event, context):
4.     ssm = boto3.client('ssm')
5.
6.     # Extract instance ID from the GuardDuty finding
7.     instance_id = event['detail']['resource']['instanceDetails']['instanceId']
8.
```

```
9.      # Execute an SSM Automation document for additional remediation steps
10.     ssm.start_automation_execution(
11.         DocumentName='AWS-StartEC2Rescue',
12.         Parameters={'InstanceId': [instance_id]}
13.     )
14.
15.     return {
16.         'statusCode': 200,
17.         'body': f'Remediation actions initiated for instance {instance_id}'
18.     }
```

## 8.7.2 Implementing AWS Step Functions

AWS Step Functions is a serverless orchestration service that enables you to coordinate multiple AWS services into flexible workflows. These workflows are composed of a series of steps, with each step representing a discrete task or function. Step Functions can be used to build robust, scalable, and fault-tolerant workflows, making them ideal for automating complex remediation processes in response to security incidents.

### Overview of AWS Step Functions

AWS Step Functions uses a visual workflow to connect various AWS services and automate tasks based on a predefined sequence of steps. This orchestration service ensures that each step is executed in order, handling retries, error handling, and state management automatically. By using Step Functions, you can create workflows that integrate with other AWS services such as Lambda, ECS, SNS, SQS, and more, allowing for comprehensive and automated incident response strategies.

### Role in Orchestrating Complex Remediation Workflows

When a security incident occurs, multiple remediation actions may be required, such as isolating compromised resources, capturing forensic data, and notifying relevant stakeholders. AWS Step Functions can orchestrate these actions seamlessly, ensuring that each step is completed successfully before proceeding to the next. This reduces manual intervention, minimizes errors, and speeds up the incident response process.

### Example Scenario: Automating Remediation for a Compromised EC2 Instance

Consider a scenario where a security incident is detected on an EC2 instance, and you need to perform several remediation actions:

**Detect the Incident:** Use Amazon GuardDuty to detect suspicious activity, such as unauthorized access or unusual network traffic.
**Trigger the Workflow:** Configure an Amazon CloudWatch Event rule to trigger a Step Functions workflow when GuardDuty generates a finding.
**Isolate the Instance:** Use AWS Lambda to modify the security group of the compromised instance, restricting its network access.
**Capture Forensic Data:** Use AWS Systems Manager to execute commands on the instance, such as taking an EBS snapshot and capturing a memory dump.
**Notify Stakeholders:** Use Amazon SNS to send notifications to the security team and other relevant stakeholders.

### Example Workflow Definition

Below is an example of a Step Functions workflow definition (in Amazon States Language) for the above scenario:

```
1.  {
2.      "Comment": "Workflow to remediate a compromised EC2 instance",
3.      "StartAt": "IsolateInstance",
4.      "States": {
```

```
5.      "IsolateInstance": {
6.        "Type": "Task",
7.        "Resource": "arn:aws:lambda:region:account-id:function:isolate-instance",
8.        "Next": "CaptureForensicData"
9.      },
10.     "CaptureForensicData": {
11.       "Type": "Task",
12.       "Resource": "arn:aws:ssm:region:account-id:automation-definition/capture-forensic-data",
13.       "Next": "NotifyStakeholders"
14.     },
15.     "NotifyStakeholders": {
16.       "Type": "Task",
17.       "Resource": "arn:aws:sns:region:account-id:topic/notify-stakeholders",
18.       "End": true
19.     }
20.   }
21. }
22.
```

In this example:
- **IsolateInstance** is a Lambda function that isolates the EC2 instance by modifying its security group.
- **CaptureForensicData** is an SSM Automation document that captures forensic data from the instance.
- **NotifyStakeholders** is an SNS topic that sends notifications to relevant parties.

AWS Step Functions provides a powerful framework for orchestrating complex remediation workflows, ensuring that security incidents are handled efficiently and effectively. By automating the coordination of various AWS services, Step Functions enables organizations to respond to threats swiftly and systematically, improving their overall security posture.

## 8.7.3 Event-Driven Remediation with EventBridge

Amazon EventBridge is a serverless event bus that makes it easy to connect applications using data from your own applications, integrated Software-as-a-Service (SaaS) applications, and AWS services. By configuring EventBridge, you can trigger automated remediation actions based on specific events, streamlining your incident response processes and improving overall security posture.

### Configuring Amazon EventBridge for Automated Remediation

EventBridge can be configured to respond to various types of events, such as security findings, state changes, or system errors. When a specified event occurs, EventBridge can trigger AWS Lambda functions, Step Functions workflows, or other AWS services to automatically remediate the issue.

### Example Scenario: Automated Remediation for Unauthorized Access

Consider a scenario where you need to automate the remediation of unauthorized access attempts detected by Amazon GuardDuty:

**Detect the Incident:** GuardDuty continuously monitors your AWS environment and generates findings for potential security threats, such as unauthorized access attempts.
**Set Up EventBridge Rule:** Create an EventBridge rule to capture specific GuardDuty findings. The rule will match events based on criteria such as severity, finding type, or resource type.
**Trigger Lambda Function:** Configure the EventBridge rule to trigger an AWS Lambda function that performs the necessary remediation actions, such as isolating the compromised instance or revoking temporary access.

### Example Configuration
1. **Create an EventBridge Rule:**

- Open the Amazon EventBridge console.
- Choose "Create rule."
- Enter a name and description for the rule.
- Under "Define pattern," select "Event pattern."
- Choose "AWS services" as the event source.
- Select "GuardDuty" as the service name.
- Define the event pattern to match specific GuardDuty findings. For example, to match unauthorized access findings:

```
{
  "source": ["aws.guardduty"],
  "detail-type": ["GuardDuty Finding"],
  "detail": {
    "severity": [{
      "numeric": [4.0, 8.0]
    }],
    "type": ["UnauthorizedAccess:EC2/SSHBruteForce"]
  }
}
```

2. **Add Target:**
   - Choose "Add target."
   - Select "Lambda function" as the target type.
   - Choose the Lambda function that will handle the remediation.

3. **Create Lambda Function:**
   - Write a Lambda function that isolates the compromised instance by modifying its security group. For example:

```python
import boto3

def lambda_handler(event, context):
    ec2 = boto3.client('ec2')

    # Extract instance ID from the GuardDuty finding
    instance_id = event['detail']['resource']['instanceDetails']['instanceId']

    # Define the security group to isolate the instance
    security_group_id = 'sg-xxxxxxxx'

    # Revoke all inbound and outbound rules for the security group
    ec2.revoke_security_group_ingress(GroupId=security_group_id, IpPermissions=[])
    ec2.revoke_security_group_egress(GroupId=security_group_id, IpPermissions=[])

    # Attach the security group to the instance
    ec2.modify_instance_attribute(InstanceId=instance_id, Groups=[security_group_id])

    return {
        'statusCode': 200,
        'body': f'Instance {instance_id} isolated successfully'
    }
```

4. **Deploy and Test:**
   - Deploy the Lambda function and ensure it has the necessary permissions to modify security groups and instance attributes.
   - Test the setup by simulating a GuardDuty finding and verifying that the instance is isolated as expected.

# 8.8 Preparing and Recovering Services

Preparing and recovering services is a critical aspect of maintaining business continuity and resilience in the face of disruptions. This involves proactive planning, implementing disaster recovery strategies, and ensuring rapid restoration of services following an incident. By preparing effectively, organizations can minimize downtime, protect data integrity, and maintain operational stability.

## 8.8.1 Preparing Services for Incidents

Preparing AWS services to handle security incidents involves implementing robust backup and failover mechanisms to ensure data integrity and service availability. By proactively configuring these mechanisms, organizations can mitigate the impact of security incidents and enhance their ability to recover quickly.

### Techniques for Preparing AWS Services
#### Configuring Backups
- **Amazon S3 Versioning and Object Lock:** Enable versioning on Amazon S3 buckets to preserve, retrieve, and restore every version of every object stored. Use S3 Object Lock to prevent objects from being deleted or overwritten, ensuring data immutability.
- **AWS Backup:** Use AWS Backup to automate and manage backups across various AWS services, including Amazon EC2, RDS, EFS, DynamoDB, and others. AWS Backup centralizes and automates backup scheduling, retention management, and backup monitoring.
- **EBS Snapshots:** Regularly take snapshots of Amazon Elastic Block Store (EBS) volumes to create point-in-time backups of your data. EBS snapshots are incremental, reducing storage costs and enabling efficient backups.

#### Configuring Failover Mechanisms
- **Auto Scaling Groups:** Configure Auto Scaling groups for your EC2 instances to automatically adjust the number of instances based on demand. This ensures that your application can handle increased load and recover from instance failures.
- **Amazon RDS Multi-AZ Deployments:** Enable Multi-AZ deployments for Amazon RDS to provide high availability and failover support. In case of a database instance failure, Amazon RDS automatically switches to a standby replica in another Availability Zone.
- **Amazon Route 53 Health Checks and DNS Failover:** Use Amazon Route 53 to configure health checks and DNS failover. Route 53 can monitor the health of your endpoints and automatically route traffic to healthy endpoints in case of a failure.

### Example Scenario: Preparing an EC2-Based Application
Consider a web application hosted on EC2 instances with a backend database in Amazon RDS:

#### Configuring Backups
- **EBS Snapshots:** Schedule regular EBS snapshots for the EC2 instances to ensure that data can be restored to a previous state in case of an incident.
- **RDS Automated Backups:** Enable automated backups for the RDS database to take daily snapshots and transaction logs, ensuring point-in-time recovery.

#### Configuring Failover Mechanisms
- **Auto Scaling Group:** Create an Auto Scaling group with a minimum and maximum number of instances to ensure that the application can scale in response to traffic spikes and recover from instance failures.
- **RDS Multi-AZ Deployment:** Configure the RDS instance for Multi-AZ deployment to provide high availability and automatic failover support.

- **Route 53 DNS Failover:** Set up Route 53 health checks to monitor the application endpoints. Configure DNS failover to route traffic to a secondary endpoint if the primary endpoint becomes unavailable.

## 8.8.2 Recovering Services After Incidents

Recovering AWS services following a security incident requires a structured approach to ensure minimal downtime and data loss. The process involves several steps, including assessing the impact, isolating compromised resources, restoring from backups, and verifying the integrity of restored services.

### Steps for Recovering AWS Services

**Assessing the Impact**
- Incident Detection: Use AWS CloudTrail, Amazon GuardDuty, and AWS Security Hub to detect and assess the extent of the security incident.
- Incident Triage: Prioritize the incident based on its severity, the affected resources, and the potential impact on the business. This involves identifying critical services and data that need immediate attention.

**Isolating Compromised Resources**
- Security Groups and Network ACLs: Immediately update security groups and network ACLs to isolate compromised instances. This prevents further spread of the incident and limits unauthorized access.
- AWS Systems Manager: Use AWS Systems Manager to execute automation documents for isolating compromised resources. For example, use the "AWSSupport-TroubleshootSSH" automation document to investigate and isolate instances with suspicious SSH activity.

**Restoring from Backups**
- EBS Snapshots: Restore compromised EC2 instances from the latest known good EBS snapshots. This ensures that you are rolling back to a clean state before the incident occurred.
- RDS Point-in-Time Recovery: Use Amazon RDS point-in-time recovery to restore the database to a specific time before the incident. This minimizes data loss by restoring to the closest point before the compromise.
- S3 Versioning: Utilize S3 versioning to restore previous versions of objects that might have been tampered with or deleted during the incident.

**Verifying the Integrity of Restored Services**
- Service Validation: Validate the integrity and functionality of restored services. This includes running automated tests and manual checks to ensure services are operational and data integrity is maintained.
- Security Review: Conduct a thorough security review to ensure that all compromised resources have been isolated and that restored services are secure. Update IAM policies, rotate access keys, and ensure that security best practices are implemented.

### Example Scenario: Recovering a Compromised Web Application

**Assessing the Impact:** The web application hosted on EC2 instances shows signs of unauthorized access. AWS CloudTrail logs and Amazon GuardDuty alerts indicate suspicious activity on specific instances.

**Isolating Compromised Resources:** Update security groups to block all inbound traffic to the compromised instances. Use AWS Systems Manager to disconnect the instances from the network.

**Restoring from Backups:** Identify the latest clean EBS snapshots for the compromised instances and launch new instances from these snapshots. Restore the database to the last known good state using RDS point-in-time recovery.

**Verifying the Integrity of Restored Services:** Run automated tests to verify that the application is functioning correctly. Conduct a manual review to ensure no suspicious activity remains. Rotate access keys and update IAM policies to prevent future incidents.

## 8.9 Best Practices for Incident Response

Incident response best practices in AWS involve preparing in advance with a well-defined incident response plan, continuous monitoring using services like Amazon CloudWatch and AWS Security Hub, and regularly conducting incident response drills. Effective incident response also requires automating remediation tasks with AWS Lambda and Step Functions to minimize manual intervention and ensure a swift and coordinated response to security incidents.

## 8.9.1 Continuous Monitoring and Improvement

Continuous monitoring and regular review of incident response plans are critical for ensuring the effectiveness and readiness of an organization to handle security incidents. Continuous monitoring involves using tools such as Amazon CloudWatch, AWS Security Hub, and GuardDuty to keep an ongoing check on system activities and detect any anomalies or potential threats in real-time. This proactive approach helps in identifying and mitigating issues before they escalate into significant incidents.

Regular review of incident response plans involves periodically revisiting and updating the plan to reflect the current security landscape, technological advancements, and changes within the organization. This ensures that the response strategies are up-to-date and capable of addressing new types of threats. For instance, an organization might discover through monitoring that a new type of malware is targeting their industry. By reviewing and updating their incident response plan, they can incorporate specific detection and response strategies for this threat.

An example of the importance of these practices can be seen in a scenario where a company uses AWS to host its e-commerce platform. Through continuous monitoring with AWS CloudWatch and GuardDuty, the security team detects unusual login attempts from multiple IP addresses, indicating a potential brute-force attack. Because the incident response plan is regularly reviewed and includes up-to-date procedures for such scenarios, the team quickly isolates the affected instances using security groups and network ACLs, rotates the credentials, and mitigates the attack with minimal disruption to the business.

**Best practices for incident response include:**
- **Automation:** Automate as many detection and response tasks as possible using AWS Lambda and Step Functions. This reduces the time taken to respond and minimizes human error.
- **Regular Drills:** Conduct regular incident response drills to test the effectiveness of the plan and the readiness of the team. This helps in identifying any gaps or weaknesses in the plan.
- **Collaboration and Communication:** Ensure clear communication channels and collaboration tools are in place. This is essential for coordinated efforts during an incident.
- **Documentation and Learning:** Document every incident and the response actions taken. Analyze these incidents to learn and improve the response plan continuously.

## 8.9.2 Incident Response Drills

Regular incident response drills are essential for testing the readiness and effectiveness of an incident response team and their plan. These drills simulate real-world security incidents, providing a controlled environment to practice and evaluate the procedures and coordination required to respond effectively. The primary objective of these drills is to ensure that the team can quickly identify, contain, and mitigate security threats, minimizing the impact on the organization.

One of the best practices for conducting incident response drills is creating realistic scenarios that mimic the organization's potential security threats. For example, a drill could simulate a ransomware attack in which the team must detect the intrusion, isolate affected systems, and recover from backups. This not only tests the team's technical capabilities but also their ability to communicate and coordinate under pressure.

Another critical aspect of effective drills is to include all relevant stakeholders, not just the IT and security teams. This ensures that everyone understands their role in the event of an incident and can contribute to a swift and effective response. For example, involving the legal team can help address compliance and regulatory concerns, while the public relations team can manage communication with customers and the media.

Documentation and debriefing are also crucial components of incident response drills. After each drill, conducting a thorough debrief is important to discuss what went well, what didn't, and what improvements can be made. This feedback loop helps to continuously refine the incident response plan and enhance the team's readiness. For instance, if a drill reveals a delay in detecting an intrusion due to insufficient monitoring, the organization can invest in better tools or improve existing ones.

**An example of a successful incident response** drill can be seen in how a financial services company might prepare for a data breach. By conducting regular drills that simulate different breach scenarios, the company can ensure that its incident response team is well-prepared to handle various threats, from phishing attacks to insider threats. These drills help the team practice critical tasks such as forensic analysis, evidence preservation, and communication with regulatory bodies.

# 8.10 Lab Exercises
## 8.10.1 Simulating a Security Incident

The objective of this exercise is to provide practical experience with incident response techniques by simulating a security incident, practicing resource isolation, remediation, and performing root cause analysis.

**Prerequisites:**
- AWS account with administrative access
- Basic knowledge of AWS services (EC2, IAM, CloudWatch, AWS Lambda)
- AWS CLI installed and configured

### Step 1: Setting Up the Environment
1. **Create a New EC2 Instance**
   - Navigate to the EC2 Dashboard.
   - Launch a new EC2 instance with Amazon Linux 2 AMI.
   - Configure instance details, add storage, and configure security group to allow SSH access.
   - Launch the instance and connect using SSH.

2. **Install a Vulnerable Web Application**
   - Connect to the EC2 instance via SSH.
   - Install Apache and PHP:

```
1. sudo yum update -y
2. sudo yum install -y httpd php
3. sudo systemctl start httpd
4. sudo systemctl enable httpd
```

   - Download a vulnerable web application (e.g., DVWA):

```
1. cd /var/www/html
2. sudo wget https://github.com/digininja/DVWA/archive/master.zip
3. sudo unzip master.zip
```

```
4. sudo mv DVWA-master/* .
5. sudo chown -R apache:apache /var/www/html
6. sudo systemctl restart httpd
```

## Step 2: Simulating a Security Incident
1. **Simulate Unauthorized Access**
    - Assume an attacker exploits a vulnerability in the web application.
    - To simulate, run a script on the instance that mimics malicious activity (e.g., downloading sensitive files).

```
1. sudo touch /var/log/sensitive_data.txt
2. sudo chmod 777 /var/log/sensitive_data.txt
3. echo "Confidential data" | sudo tee /var/log/sensitive_data.txt
```

## Step 3: Detecting the Incident
1. **Enable CloudWatch Logs for the EC2 Instance:** Install and configure the CloudWatch agent on the EC2 instance:

```
1. sudo yum install -y amazon-cloudwatch-agent
2. sudo /opt/aws/amazon-cloudwatch-agent/bin/amazon-cloudwatch-agent-config-wizard
3. sudo systemctl start amazon-cloudwatch-agent
```

Configure CloudWatch to monitor /var/log/httpd/access_log and /var/log/httpd/error_log.

2. **Create a CloudWatch Alarm**
    - In the CloudWatch console, create an alarm that triggers when there is unusual activity in the access logs.
    - Set up an SNS topic to receive notifications.

## Step 4: Isolating the Compromised Resource
1. **Modify the Security Group**
    - Navigate to the EC2 instance's security group.
    - Remove all inbound rules except for essential access (e.g., SSH from a specific IP).

2. **Stop the Instance**: As a more drastic measure, stop the EC2 instance from the console to prevent further damage.

## Step 5: Remediating the Incident
1. **Analyze Logs**
    - Use CloudWatch to review logs and identify the scope of the incident.
    - Determine if other instances or services are affected.

2. **Patch Vulnerabilities:** Update the web application and underlying software to the latest, most secure versions.

```
sudo yum update -y httpd php
```

## Step 6: Root Cause Analysis
1. **Capture Forensic Data**
    - Create an EBS snapshot of the compromised instance for further analysis.
    - Capture memory dumps using tools like Volatility.

2. **Analyze the Snapshot:** Attach the snapshot to a new instance and investigate files and logs for traces of the attack.

3. **Review IAM Policies**: Review IAM policies and roles to ensure that the principle of least privilege is followed.

### Step 7: Documentation and Reporting
- **Create an Incident Report**: Document the incident details, including detection, isolation, remediation steps, and findings from the root cause analysis.
- **Update Incident Response Plan**: Based on the lessons learned, update the incident response plan to improve readiness for future incidents.

## 8.10.2 Automating Incident Response with AWS Lambda and EventBridge

The objective of this exercise is to provide hands-on experience with automating incident response actions using AWS Lambda and Amazon EventBridge. This exercise focuses on creating automated remediation for security incidents.

**Prerequisites:**
- AWS account with administrative access
- Basic knowledge of AWS services (Lambda, EventBridge, CloudWatch)
- AWS CLI installed and configured

### Step 1: Setting Up the Environment
**Create an IAM Role for Lambda**
- Navigate to the IAM console.
- Create a new role with the following policies:
    - AWSLambdaBasicExecutionRole
    - Additional policies as needed for the Lambda function (e.g., permissions to isolate EC2 instances).

### Step 2: Creating a Lambda Function
**1. Navigate to the Lambda Console**
- Click on "Create function."
- Choose "Author from scratch."
- Name the function AutoRemediationFunction.
- Choose the runtime (e.g., Python 3.8).
- Assign the IAM role created earlier.

**2. Write the Lambda Function Code:** Implement the code to isolate an EC2 instance. Here is an example:

```python
import boto3
import json

ec2 = boto3.client('ec2')

def lambda_handler(event, context):
    instance_id = event['detail']['instance-id']
    response = ec2.modify_instance_attribute(InstanceId=instance_id, DisableApiTermination={'Value': True})
    print(f'Instance {instance_id} is now isolated.')
    return {
        'statusCode': 200,
        'body': json.dumps('Isolation successful')
    }

```

3. **Deploy the Lambda Function:** Save and deploy the function.

### Step 3: Creating an EventBridge Rule
1. **Navigate to the EventBridge Console**
    - Click on "Create rule."
    - Name the rule SecurityIncidentResponseRule.
    - Define the event pattern. For example, to trigger on specific CloudWatch alarms:

```
{
  "source": ["aws.cloudwatch"],
  "detail-type": ["CloudWatch Alarm State Change"],
  "detail": {
    "state": {
      "value": ["ALARM"]
    }
  }
}
```

2. **Add Targets:** Add the Lambda function created earlier as the target.

### Step 4: Testing the Automation
1. **Simulate an Incident**
    - Create a CloudWatch alarm that triggers based on specific conditions (e.g., high CPU usage on an EC2 instance).
    - Trigger the alarm manually or adjust thresholds to simulate an incident.

2. **Verify the Lambda Function Execution**
    - Check the Lambda console for execution logs.
    - Verify that the EC2 instance specified in the alarm was isolated successfully.

### Step 5: Clean Up
1. **Remove the EventBridge Rule:** Navigate to the EventBridge console and delete the rule.
2. **Delete the Lambda Function:** Navigate to the Lambda console and delete the function.
3. **Delete the IAM Role:** Navigate to the IAM console and delete the role if no longer needed.

This exercise provides a comprehensive approach to automating incident response actions, leveraging AWS Lambda and EventBridge to handle security incidents effectively.

## 8.10.3 Using Amazon Detective for Investigations

The objective of this exercise is to provide hands-on experience in using Amazon Detective for investigating and analyzing security incidents, focusing on understanding root cause analysis and investigation techniques.

**Prerequisites:**
- AWS account with administrative access
- Basic knowledge of AWS services (Amazon Detective, CloudTrail, GuardDuty)

### Step 1: Setting Up Amazon Detective
**Enable Amazon Detective**
- Navigate to the Amazon Detective console.
- Click on "Enable Amazon Detective."
- Ensure that Detective has permissions to access data from AWS services like GuardDuty, CloudTrail, and VPC Flow Logs.

## Step 2: Generating Data for Investigation
1. **Enable GuardDuty**
    - Navigate to the GuardDuty console.
    - Click on "Enable GuardDuty."
    - Ensure that GuardDuty is set up to monitor your AWS environment.

2. **Simulate a Security Incident**
    - Trigger a GuardDuty finding by simulating a security incident. This can be done using AWS tools or manual triggers.
    - Example: Create an EC2 instance with a known vulnerability or configure security groups to allow unauthorized access temporarily.

## Step 3: Investigating the Incident with Amazon Detective
1. **Accessing the Findings**
    - Navigate to the Amazon Detective console.
    - Go to the "Overview" tab to see the summary of recent activities and findings.
2. **Drill Down into Findings**
    - Select a specific finding from GuardDuty that you want to investigate.
    - Click on the finding to view detailed information.
3. **Using the Graph Interface**
    - Amazon Detective provides a visual graph interface to explore the relationships between different entities (e.g., IP addresses, EC2 instances, AWS accounts).
    - Follow the graph to investigate the root cause of the incident. Identify which resources were compromised and how the attack was carried out.

## Step 4: Analyzing the Data
1. **Reviewing CloudTrail Logs**
    - Use Amazon Detective to analyze CloudTrail logs for unusual API calls and user activities.
    - Identify any unauthorized access or suspicious activities that align with the GuardDuty findings.
2. **Examining VPC Flow Logs**
    - Review VPC Flow Logs to trace the network traffic associated with the incident.
    - Look for unusual patterns or unexpected connections to compromised resources.

## Step 5: Documenting the Findings
1. **Create a Report**
    - Document the findings of your investigation, including the timeline of events, involved entities, and root cause analysis.
    - Highlight any vulnerabilities or misconfigurations that led to the incident.
2. **Suggest Remediation Steps**
    - Provide recommendations for mitigating the identified vulnerabilities and preventing future incidents.
    - Example: Implement stricter IAM policies, update security group configurations, or patch vulnerable systems.

## Step 6: Clean Up
1. **Disable GuardDuty (if not needed):** Navigate to the GuardDuty console and disable it if it was enabled only for the exercise.

2. **Disable Amazon Detective (if not needed):** Navigate to the Amazon Detective console and disable it if it was enabled only for the exercise.

This lab exercise helps reinforce the understanding of root cause analysis and investigation techniques using Amazon Detective, providing practical experience in handling security incidents effectively.

## 8.10.4 Capturing and Analyzing Forensic Data

The objective of this exercise is to provide hands-on experience in capturing forensic data from compromised resources and analyzing it using AWS tools, focusing on data capture and log analysis for incident response.

**Prerequisites:**
- AWS account with administrative access
- Basic knowledge of AWS services (EC2, S3, CloudWatch, Athena)

### Step 1: Simulating a Security Incident
**1. Create an EC2 Instance**
- Launch an EC2 instance with a basic Amazon Linux 2 AMI.
- Ensure that the instance is in a security group that allows inbound SSH access (port 22).

**2. Compromise the EC2 Instance**
- Simulate a compromise by running a script that mimics malicious activity.
- Example script:

```
1. #!/bin/bash
2. sudo yum install -y httpd
3. sudo systemctl start httpd
4. sudo systemctl enable httpd
5. echo "Compromised!" > /var/www/html/index.html
6.
```

### Step 2: Capturing Forensic Data
**1. Create an EBS Snapshot**
- Navigate to the EC2 console.
- Select the compromised instance and go to the "Description" tab.
- Under "Block devices," select the root volume (e.g., /dev/xvda).
- Click on "Create Snapshot" to capture the current state of the instance's storage.

**2. Capture Memory Dump**
- SSH into the compromised EC2 instance.
- Use LiME (Linux Memory Extractor) to capture the memory:

```
1. sudo yum install -y git kernel-devel-$(uname -r)
2. git clone https://github.com/504ensicsLabs/LiME.git
3. cd LiME/src
4. make
5. sudo insmod lime-$(uname -r).ko "path=/tmp/memory.lime format=lime"
6. sudo cp /tmp/memory.lime /var/log/
7.
```

### Step 3: Analyzing Forensic Data
**1. Store Data in S3**
- Create an S3 bucket to store forensic data.
- Upload the EBS snapshot and memory dump to the S3 bucket.

**2. Analyze EBS Snapshot**
- Use AWS EC2 to create a new volume from the EBS snapshot.
- Attach the volume to a forensic analysis EC2 instance.

- Mount the volume and analyze the filesystem for signs of compromise.

**3. Analyze Memory Dump:** Use Volatility or similar tools to analyze the memory dump:

```
1. sudo yum install -y python3
2. sudo pip3 install volatility3
3. vol -f /var/log/memory.lime --profile=Linux analyze
```

## Step 4: Log Analysis for Event Validation

**1. Enable CloudWatch Logs:** Ensure CloudWatch Logs is enabled for the EC2 instance to capture system logs.

**2. Query Logs Using Amazon Athena**
- Navigate to the Athena console.
- Create a new database and table to catalog CloudWatch Logs stored in S3:

```
1. CREATE DATABASE forensic_logs;
2. CREATE EXTERNAL TABLE IF NOT EXISTS forensic_logs.cloudwatch_logs (
3.   timestamp string,
4.   message string
5. )
6. ROW FORMAT SERDE 'org.openx.data.jsonserde.JsonSerDe'
7. LOCATION 's3://<your-s3-bucket>/CloudWatchLogs/';
8.
```

Query the logs for suspicious activities:

```sql
SELECT * FROM forensic_logs.cloudwatch_logs WHERE message LIKE '%UnauthorizedAccess%';
```

## Step 5: Documenting Findings

**1. Create an Incident Report**
- Document the steps taken, data captured, and analysis performed.
- Include details such as the timeline of events, compromised resources, and root cause analysis.

**2. Recommend Remediation Actions**
- Provide recommendations to prevent future incidents.
- Examples: Update IAM policies, patch vulnerabilities, enhance monitoring.

## Step 6: Clean Up

**1. Delete Forensic Data:** Remove the EBS snapshots and memory dumps from S3 to avoid storage costs.
**2. Terminate EC2 Instances:** Terminate any EC2 instances used during the exercise.

This exercise provides practical experience in capturing and analyzing forensic data, reinforcing the importance of thorough incident response procedures.

# 8.11 Key Exam Tips

## Understand the AWS Security Incident Response Guide

**Incident Response Lifecycle:** Focus on the stages of incident response: preparation, detection, analysis, containment, eradication, and recovery. Understanding this lifecycle will help you respond effectively to security events in the AWS environment.

**Roles and Responsibilities:** Ensure you're familiar with the roles involved in incident response, including security teams, developers, and operations. Knowing who should handle what tasks in a security incident is essential for effective response.

## Master Resource Isolation Mechanisms

**Techniques for Isolating Compromised Resources:** Practice isolating resources by modifying security group rules, detaching network interfaces, or using AWS Systems Manager to take actions like stopping EC2 instances.

**Automating Resource Isolation:** Learn how to use AWS Lambda to automate the process of isolating resources. For example, you can write Lambda functions triggered by GuardDuty or Security Hub findings that isolate compromised instances or revoke compromised credentials.

## Perform Root Cause Analysis Effectively

**Conducting Root Cause Analysis:** Focus on the process of investigating a security event by analyzing logs, resource changes, and user activity. This includes determining how the breach occurred, what systems were affected, and the extent of the compromise.

**Using Amazon Detective:** Familiarize yourself with Amazon Detective, which simplifies security investigations by providing a visual representation of security incidents. Know how to use Detective to correlate security findings from GuardDuty, CloudTrail, and VPC Flow Logs.

## Forensic Data Collection and Preservation

**Capturing Forensic Data:** Understand the importance of capturing and preserving forensic data during a security incident, such as application logs, network traffic, and system snapshots. AWS services like CloudTrail and VPC Flow Logs can help capture critical information.

**Preserving Forensic Artifacts:** Practice using AWS tools like S3 and CloudTrail to preserve evidence that may be needed for post-incident investigation or legal purposes.

## Log Analysis for Event Validation

**Techniques for Log Analysis:** Learn how to analyze logs using CloudWatch Logs, VPC Flow Logs, and CloudTrail to investigate security events. You should know how to identify unauthorized actions, changes to resources, or abnormal network traffic.

**Using Amazon Athena for Log Queries:** Practice writing queries in Amazon Athena to search through logs efficiently. This can be useful for validating whether a security event was a legitimate threat or a false positive.

## Automating Remediation

**AWS Lambda for Remediation:** Get comfortable with writing Lambda functions to automate remediation actions. For example, Lambda can automatically shut down compromised EC2 instances or rotate IAM credentials.

**AWS Step Functions:** Understand how Step Functions can orchestrate multiple remediation actions in response to an event. This can help automate complex workflows such as multi-step incident response tasks.

**Event-Driven Remediation with EventBridge:** Learn how to use Amazon EventBridge to trigger remediation actions based on events detected by AWS services like GuardDuty, Security Hub, or Macie.

### Prepare for and Recover from Incidents
**Preparing Services for Incidents:** Ensure you're familiar with preparing AWS services for security incidents by implementing measures like logging, backups, and role-based access controls.
**Recovering Services After Incidents:** Know the steps required to recover services after an incident, including restoring from backups, rotating compromised credentials, and revalidating security controls.

### Best Practices for Incident Response
**Continuous Monitoring and Improvement:** Implement continuous monitoring to detect security issues in real-time using tools like CloudWatch, GuardDuty, and Security Hub. Regularly review and improve your incident response processes.
**Incident Response Drills:** Regularly conduct incident response drills or simulations to ensure that your team is prepared to respond effectively to actual incidents. AWS Systems Manager Automation can be used to run these simulations.

## 8.12 Chapter Review Questions

**Question 1:**
What is the primary objective of the AWS Security Incident Response Guide?
A. To monitor application performance
B. To automate AWS resource provisioning
C. To provide a structured approach to detecting and responding to security incidents
D. To handle cloud cost optimization

**Question 2:**
Which AWS service can help in investigating and analyzing the root cause of a security incident by visualizing relationships between resources?
A. Amazon Macie
B. Amazon Detective
C. AWS CloudTrail
D. AWS Systems Manager

**Question 3:**
What is the key benefit of automating resource isolation during a security incident?
A. It reduces human error in manually isolating compromised resources
B. It prevents future cost overruns in AWS accounts
C. It automatically encrypts data in compromised resources
D. It creates IAM roles for the security team

**Question 4:**
Which of the following tools can be used to capture and preserve forensic data during a security incident in AWS?
A. Amazon CloudFront
B. AWS Config
C. AWS CloudTrail
D. AWS Lambda

**Question 5:**
When using Amazon Athena, what is its primary role in the incident response process?
A. Querying and analyzing logs for event validation
B. Encrypting logs at rest
C. Automating log storage
D. Creating IAM policies for resource access

**Question 6:**
Which service would you use for event-driven remediation during a security incident in AWS?
A. AWS Lambda
B. Amazon EventBridge
C. Amazon CloudWatch
D. Amazon Detective

**Question 7:**
What is the purpose of root cause analysis in incident response?
A. To automatically remediate incidents
B. To determine the underlying factors that caused the security incident
C. To prevent future costs associated with compromised resources
D. To manage IAM roles for security personnel

**Question 8:**
What is one of the best practices for continuous improvement in incident response?
A. Running periodic incident response drills
B. Disabling AWS CloudTrail logging
C. Manually rotating access keys every week
D. Isolating every resource manually during an incident

**Question 9:**
Which AWS service can be used to automate remediation actions such as rotating compromised credentials or blocking unauthorized access during an incident?
A. Amazon CloudWatch Logs
B. AWS Lambda
C. Amazon S3
D. AWS Security Hub

**Question 10:**
In the context of incident response, what is the role of AWS Step Functions?
A. To automatically update IAM policies
B. To orchestrate and automate complex remediation workflows
C. To track user activity logs
D. To store forensic data during incidents

**Question 11:**
Your team has detected unusual network activity coming from an EC2 instance, which appears to have been compromised. What is the first step you should take to isolate the compromised instance without shutting it down?
A. Terminate the instance
B. Create an IAM role with no permissions and apply it to the instance
C. Modify the security group to block all inbound and outbound traffic
D. Enable CloudTrail logging for the instance

**Question 12:**
During a root cause analysis of a recent security incident, you need to analyze historical API calls to determine what actions were performed by the compromised IAM user. Which service would you use to retrieve and analyze this information?
A. Amazon Macie
B. AWS Config

C. AWS CloudTrail
D. AWS Lambda

**Question 13:**
After identifying a compromised resource in your AWS environment, you want to automate the remediation process by disabling the compromised credentials and rotating new ones. Which AWS service would be the best option for automating this task?
A. Amazon EventBridge
B. AWS Lambda
C. Amazon GuardDuty
D. AWS Systems Manager

**Question 14:**
Your security team needs to collect forensic data from a compromised EC2 instance to analyze the potential breach without affecting the data on the instance. Which of the following actions should you take to preserve forensic artifacts while continuing the investigation?
A. Create an AMI image of the instance
B. Terminate the instance
C. Restart the instance
D. Modify the instance type

**Question 15:**
During a security incident, you need to validate that the suspicious API activity was performed by an external actor. You want to correlate logs from multiple AWS services to confirm the incident. Which AWS service is best suited to perform this correlation and analysis of security logs?
A. Amazon Macie
B. Amazon Detective
C. Amazon S3
D. AWS Config

## 8.13 Answers to Chapter Review Questions

1. C. To provide a structured approach to detecting and responding to security incidents
Explanation: The AWS Security Incident Response Guide outlines the best practices and processes to follow when dealing with security incidents to ensure swift detection, response, and recovery.

2. B. Amazon Detective
Explanation: Amazon Detective helps investigate and visualize the relationships between resources, making it easier to analyze and understand the root cause of security incidents.

3. A. It reduces human error in manually isolating compromised resources
Explanation: Automating resource isolation ensures that compromised resources are quickly and accurately isolated, minimizing human error and reducing response time.

4. C. AWS CloudTrail
Explanation: AWS CloudTrail captures detailed log data about AWS API calls and can be used to gather forensic evidence during and after a security incident.

5. A. Querying and analyzing logs for event validation
Explanation: Amazon Athena is used to run SQL queries on log data stored in Amazon S3, enabling detailed analysis of logs during incident investigations.

6. B. Amazon EventBridge
Explanation: Amazon EventBridge enables event-driven architectures, allowing you to automatically trigger remediation actions in response to security events.

7. B. To determine the underlying factors that caused the security incident
Explanation: Root cause analysis is performed to identify the primary factors that led to the security incident, helping organizations take steps to prevent similar issues in the future.

8. A. Running periodic incident response drills
Explanation: Regular incident response drills help prepare your team for real-world security incidents, improving their ability to respond quickly and effectively.

9. B. AWS Lambda
Explanation: AWS Lambda can be used to automatically execute remediation actions such as rotating credentials or blocking unauthorized access during a security incident.

10. B. To orchestrate and automate complex remediation workflows
Explanation: AWS Step Functions help orchestrate complex workflows by automating remediation tasks and managing dependencies between different steps during incident response.

11. C. Modify the security group to block all inbound and outbound traffic
Explanation: Modifying the security group to block all traffic isolates the compromised EC2 instance, preventing it from communicating with other systems while allowing for investigation and analysis without shutting it down.

12. C. AWS CloudTrail
Explanation: AWS CloudTrail records all API activity within your AWS environment. You can retrieve and analyze the logs to determine what actions were performed by the compromised IAM user during a security incident.

13. B. AWS Lambda
Explanation: AWS Lambda can automate the remediation process, such as disabling compromised credentials and rotating new ones, as part of an automated incident response workflow.

14. A. Create an AMI image of the instance
Explanation: Creating an AMI image of the compromised EC2 instance preserves the current state of the instance and its data, allowing the forensic team to analyze it without affecting the original instance.

15. B. Amazon Detective
Explanation: Amazon Detective helps investigate security incidents by analyzing and correlating data from AWS services, such as CloudTrail, VPC Flow Logs, and GuardDuty, making it the best option for validating suspicious API activity.

# Chapter 9. Security Logging and Monitoring

**This chapter addresses the following exam objectives:**
Domain 2: Security Logging and Monitoring
Task Statement 2.1: Design and implement monitoring and alerting to address security events.
Knowledge of:
- AWS services that monitor events and provide alarms (for example, CloudWatch, EventBridge)
- AWS services that automate alerting (for example, Lambda, Amazon Simple Notification Service [Amazon SNS], Security Hub)
- Tools that monitor metrics and baselines (for example, GuardDuty, Systems
- Manager)
- Analyzing architectures to identify monitoring requirements and sources of data for security monitoring
- Analyzing environments and workloads to determine monitoring requirements
- Designing environment monitoring and workload monitoring based on business and security requirements
- Setting up automated tools and scripts to perform regular audits (for example, by creating custom insights in Security Hub)
- Defining the metrics and thresholds that generate alerts

Task Statement 2.2: Troubleshoot security monitoring and alerting.
Knowledge of:
- Configuration of monitoring services (for example, Security Hub)
- Relevant data that indicates security events

Skills in:
- Analyzing the service functionality, permissions, and configuration of resources after an event that did not provide visibility or alerting
- Analyzing and remediating the configuration of a custom application that is not reporting its statistics
- Evaluating logging and monitoring services for alignment with security requirements

Task Statement 2.3: Design and implement a logging solution.
Knowledge of:
- AWS services and features that provide logging capabilities (for example, VPC Flow Logs, DNS logs, AWS CloudTrail, Amazon CloudWatch Logs)
- Attributes of logging capabilities (for example, log levels, type, verbosity)
- Log destinations and lifecycle management (for example, retention period)

Skills in:

- Configuring logging for services and applications
- Identifying logging requirements and sources for log ingestion
- Implementing log storage and lifecycle management according to AWS best practices and organizational requirements

Task Statement 2.4: Troubleshoot logging solutions.
Knowledge of:
- Capabilities and use cases of AWS services that provide data sources (for example, log level, type, verbosity, cadence, timeliness, immutability)
- AWS services and features that provide logging capabilities (for example, VPC Flow Logs, DNS logs, CloudTrail, CloudWatch Logs)
- Access permissions that are necessary for logging

Skills in:
- Identifying misconfiguration and determining remediation steps for absent access permissions that are necessary for logging (for example, by managing read/write permissions, S3 bucket permissions, public access, and integrity)
- Determining the cause of missing logs and performing remediation steps

Task Statement 2.5: Design a log analysis solution.
Knowledge of:
- Services and tools to analyze captured logs (for example, Athena, CloudWatch Logs filter)
- Log analysis features of AWS services (for example, CloudWatch Logs Insights, CloudTrail Insights, Security Hub insights)
- Log format and components (for example, CloudTrail logs)

Skills in:
- Identifying patterns in logs to indicate anomalies and known threats
- Normalizing, parsing, and correlating logs

❖❖❖❖❖❖

Effective security logging and monitoring are crucial components of a robust security posture in any cloud environment. This chapter delves into the principles and practices that enable continuous visibility, threat detection, and proactive management of security incidents within AWS environments. This chapter provides a comprehensive guide to designing, implementing, and troubleshooting logging and monitoring solutions to safeguard your cloud infrastructure.

We start with an introduction to security logging and monitoring, emphasizing their importance in maintaining a secure and compliant AWS environment. The chapter then explores the design of monitoring and alerting solutions, covering AWS services for monitoring and alarms, automated alerting services, monitoring metrics and baselines, and the identification of monitoring requirements. Designing effective monitoring solutions and setting up automated audits, along with defining metrics and thresholds, are key topics that ensure timely detection and response to security events.

Troubleshooting monitoring and alerting is critical for maintaining the efficacy of your security solutions. We discuss the configuration of monitoring services, analyzing security events, evaluating service functionality and permissions, troubleshooting custom applications, and aligning monitoring configurations with security requirements.

Designing and implementing logging solutions is another vital aspect covered in this chapter. We examine the logging capabilities of various AWS services, attributes of logging, log destinations, lifecycle management, and configuring logging for services and applications. Identifying logging requirements and implementing log storage and management strategies are essential for comprehensive log collection and retention.

Troubleshooting logging solutions involves understanding the capabilities and use cases of logging services, ensuring proper access permissions, identifying and remediating misconfigurations, and determining the causes of missing logs. These troubleshooting skills are necessary for maintaining reliable and complete logging infrastructure.

Designing log analysis solutions includes leveraging services and tools for log analysis, understanding log analysis features of AWS services, working with log formats and components, and identifying patterns in logs. Techniques for normalizing, parsing, and correlating logs are crucial for deriving actionable insights from log data.

To reinforce these concepts, the chapter concludes with lab exercises that provide hands-on experience in setting up CloudWatch Alarms, configuring AWS Security Hub, implementing VPC Flow Logs and analyzing data, troubleshooting logging and monitoring issues, and creating log analysis dashboards. These practical exercises are designed to enhance your skills and confidence in managing security logging and monitoring within AWS.

By the end of this chapter, readers will be equipped with the knowledge and tools to design, implement, and troubleshoot effective security logging and monitoring solutions, ensuring continuous visibility and proactive management of security within their AWS environments.

## 9.1 Introduction to Security Logging and Monitoring

Security logging and monitoring are essential practices in managing and safeguarding cloud environments. They involve capturing detailed records of events and continuously observing the infrastructure to detect anomalies, performance issues, and security threats. In the context of AWS, these practices leverage various AWS services designed to ensure your cloud resources' visibility, integrity, and security. AWS offers tools like CloudTrail, CloudWatch, and VPC Flow Logs to provide comprehensive logging and monitoring capabilities.

Logging and monitoring play a crucial role in maintaining the security and compliance of AWS environments. Effective logging ensures that every action within the AWS infrastructure is recorded, providing a detailed trail of user activities and API calls. This is vital for auditing, forensics, and accountability. AWS CloudTrail, for instance, logs all API calls made in the environment, allowing administrators to track user changes and actions, which is essential for both security and compliance.

On the other hand, monitoring involves continuously observing the environment to detect and respond to security incidents in real time. AWS CloudWatch collects and tracks metrics, collects and monitors log files, and sets alarms to automatically react to changes in the AWS resources. This real-time observability helps in promptly identifying unusual activity patterns, potential security breaches, and operational issues, thereby mitigating risks before they escalate.

The combined power of logging and monitoring enhances the ability to detect security incidents and ensures system integrity. For example, by setting up CloudWatch alarms to monitor CloudTrail logs for unauthorized access attempts, administrators can receive immediate alerts and take swift action to contain threats. Additionally, VPC Flow Logs provide visibility into the network traffic, helping identify and investigate suspicious network activities.

Another significant aspect of effective logging and monitoring is maintaining compliance. Many regulatory standards, such as GDPR, HIPAA, and SOC 2, require rigorous logging and monitoring practices to ensure data protection and privacy. By leveraging AWS's logging and monitoring services, organizations can meet these regulatory requirements and demonstrate their commitment to security and compliance.

In conclusion, security logging and monitoring are foundational to any robust security strategy in AWS environments. They provide the necessary visibility and control to detect and respond to security incidents effectively, ensure the integrity of the systems, and maintain compliance with regulatory standards. Understanding and implementing these mechanisms are crucial for securing AWS resources and protecting sensitive data.

## 9.2 Designing Monitoring and Alerting Solutions

Designing monitoring and alerting solutions is essential for maintaining the security, performance, and reliability of AWS environments. These solutions involve setting up systems to continuously track the health and activity of resources and configuring alerts to promptly notify administrators of any anomalies or issues. Effective monitoring and alerting enable quick detection and response to potential threats and operational problems, ensuring that the infrastructure remains robust and compliant with security policies.

### 9.2.1 AWS Services for Monitoring and Alarms

AWS provides several services that help monitor events and generate alarms to ensure your applications and infrastructure's security, performance, and reliability. Two key services in this domain are Amazon CloudWatch and Amazon EventBridge.

**Amazon CloudWatch** is a comprehensive monitoring and observability service. It allows you to collect various operational data and track metrics, monitor log files, and set alarms. CloudWatch collects operational data in the form of logs, metrics, and events. These data are then used to provide a unified view of AWS resources, applications, and services that run on AWS and on-premises servers. For example, CloudWatch can monitor CPU utilization, memory usage, and application logs, and it can trigger alarms when specified thresholds are breached, notifying administrators through Amazon SNS (Simple Notification Service) or triggering automated actions through AWS Lambda.

**Amazon EventBridge**, formerly known as Amazon CloudWatch Events, is a serverless event bus service that makes it easy to connect applications using data from your applications, integrated software-as-a-service (SaaS) applications, and AWS services. EventBridge allows you to build event-driven architectures that react to changes in your data. For instance, you can configure EventBridge to trigger an AWS Lambda function when an Amazon EC2 instance enters a stopped state, enabling automated remediation or notification processes.

#### Example Scenario

Consider a scenario where you want to monitor an application hosted on an EC2 instance and receive alerts when its CPU utilization exceeds 80%. Here's how you can set it up:

**Create a CloudWatch Alarm:**
- Navigate to the CloudWatch console and create an alarm.
- Choose the EC2 instance as the metric source.
- Set the threshold to 80% CPU utilization.
- Configure the alarm actions to send notifications via Amazon SNS or trigger a Lambda function.

**Set Up EventBridge Rule:**
- Navigate to the EventBridge console.
- Create a rule that matches the desired event pattern, such as EC2 state change notifications.

- Configure the target to be an SNS topic or a Lambda function to perform specific actions, like sending notifications or executing remediation scripts.

By using CloudWatch for real-time monitoring and EventBridge for event-driven automation, you can maintain a robust monitoring and alerting system that ensures timely responses to critical events.

## 9.2.2 Automated Alerting Services

AWS offers several services that automate alerting, ensuring that any security events or operational issues are promptly addressed. Key services in this domain include AWS Lambda, Amazon SNS, and AWS Security Hub.

**AWS Lambda** is a serverless compute service that runs code in response to events. Additionally, AWS Lambda automatically manages the underlying compute resources. AWS Lambda functions can be triggered by various AWS services, including CloudWatch alarms, S3 bucket events, and DynamoDB streams. For example, a Lambda function can be set up to respond to a CloudWatch alarm indicating high CPU usage on an EC2 instance. The Lambda function could take actions such as scaling up resources, notifying administrators, or even stopping the instance if necessary.

**Amazon Simple Notification Service (SNS)** is a fully managed pub/sub messaging service that is architecture-built to make it easy to decouple and scale microservices, distributed systems, and serverless applications. SNS can be used to send notifications to users or systems via email, SMS, or HTTP endpoints. For instance, a CloudWatch alarm can use SNS to trigger an email to the operations team whenever a threshold is breached. SNS ensures that alerts are delivered reliably and promptly to the right recipients.

**AWS Security Hub** provides a comprehensive view of high-priority security alerts and compliance status across AWS accounts. It aggregates, organizes, and prioritizes security findings from multiple AWS services like Amazon GuardDuty, Amazon Inspector, and AWS IAM Access Analyzer, as well as from supported third-party security products. Security Hub can automate alerting by integrating with EventBridge, which can trigger Lambda functions or SNS notifications based on specific findings. For example, if Security Hub detects a critical vulnerability through Amazon Inspector, it can automatically send an alert via SNS or invoke a Lambda function to remediate the issue.

### Example Scenario

Consider an example where you want to automate alerting for suspicious activity detected by Amazon GuardDuty:

**GuardDuty Finding:** GuardDuty detects a potential security threat, such as unauthorized access attempts.

**EventBridge Rule:** Configure an EventBridge rule to listen for GuardDuty findings with a specific severity level (e.g., high or critical). The rule triggers an action when a matching event is detected.

**AWS Lambda:** The EventBridge rule triggers a Lambda function designed to handle the finding. The Lambda function could perform actions like isolating the compromised resource by modifying security group rules, logging details for forensic analysis, and notifying the security team.

**Amazon SNS:** The Lambda function publishes a notification to an SNS topic. The SNS topic sends an email or SMS to the security team with details of the incident and steps being taken.

**AWS Security Hub:** The finding is also sent to AWS Security Hub, which aggregates it with other findings for a comprehensive view of your security posture. Security Hub can further trigger additional automation or alerting mechanisms through EventBridge and Lambda.

This setup ensures a comprehensive, automated response to security threats, leveraging the integration capabilities of AWS services to maintain security and operational efficiency.

## 9.2.3 Monitoring Metrics and Baselines

AWS offers a variety of tools for monitoring metrics and baselines to ensure robust security monitoring. Two key services in this domain are Amazon GuardDuty and AWS Systems Manager. These tools play critical roles in detecting and managing security threats, ensuring compliance, and maintaining the integrity of AWS environments.

**Amazon GuardDuty** is a threat detection service that continuously monitors for malicious activity and unauthorized behavior. It uses machine learning, anomaly detection, and integrated threat intelligence to identify potential threats. For example, GuardDuty can detect unusual API calls, potentially unauthorized deployments, or compromised EC2 instances based on established baselines of normal activity. When such anomalies are detected, GuardDuty generates detailed security findings that are sent to the AWS Security Hub or other monitoring systems for further analysis and remediation .

**AWS Systems Manager** provides a unified interface to view operational data from multiple AWS services and automate operational tasks across AWS resources. It includes features like Systems Manager Automation and Run Command, which help in maintaining security baselines by automating the application of patches, updates, and configuration changes. For instance, using Systems Manager, an administrator can create automation documents to enforce security baselines across all EC2 instances, ensuring they meet compliance requirements. Additionally, Systems Manager can be configured to alert administrators about deviations from these baselines, enabling prompt corrective actions .

These tools exemplify AWS's approach to integrating comprehensive security monitoring with automated alerting and response capabilities, thereby helping organizations maintain a strong security posture.

## 9.2.4 Identifying Monitoring Requirements

Analyzing architectures to identify monitoring requirements and sources of data is a fundamental step in establishing effective security monitoring within AWS environments. This process involves understanding the various components of an architecture, the data they generate, and how this data can be leveraged to ensure security and compliance.

### Map Out the Architecture and Pinpoint the Critical Resources

Firstly, it's essential to map out the architecture and pinpoint the critical resources, such as EC2 instances, RDS databases, S3 buckets, and Lambda functions. Each of these resources generates specific types of data that are valuable for monitoring. For example, EC2 instances produce CloudWatch logs and VPC Flow Logs, which can be used to monitor system performance and network traffic patterns. Similarly, S3 buckets can generate access logs that provide insight into who accessed the data and from where, which is crucial for detecting unauthorized access or data exfiltration attempts.

### Establishing the Monitoring Requirements

Once the key components and data sources are identified, the next step is establishing the monitoring requirements. This involves determining what needs to be monitored, such as unauthorized access attempts, data breaches, performance anomalies, or compliance violations. For instance, in a web application architecture, monitoring requirements include tracking changes to security group configurations, detecting anomalous API calls using AWS CloudTrail, and identifying unusual traffic patterns with Amazon GuardDuty.

### Example Scenario
Consider an example of an e-commerce application hosted on AWS. The architecture includes EC2 instances for the web and application servers, RDS for the database, and S3 for storing product images and logs. To ensure comprehensive security monitoring, one would:
- Enable CloudTrail to log all API calls made within the AWS account, providing a history of changes to the environment.
- Configure VPC Flow Logs to capture detailed information about IP traffic going to and from network interfaces in the VPC. This helps detect suspicious activities like port scanning or data exfiltration.
- Set up Amazon GuardDuty to continuously monitor for malicious activities and unauthorized behavior, such as compromised instances or reconnaissance attempts.
- Use AWS Config to track and evaluate the configurations of AWS resources, ensuring they comply with security best practices and regulatory requirements.

By analyzing the architecture and identifying the relevant data sources, organizations can set up a robust monitoring framework that detects security incidents in real-time, helps maintain compliance, and improves overall security posture.

## 9.2.5 Designing Monitoring Solutions
Designing environment and workload monitoring solutions based on business and security requirements is critical to maintaining a secure and compliant AWS infrastructure. This process involves understanding the business's specific needs, threats, and compliance requirements. By aligning monitoring solutions with these requirements, organizations can ensure they have the visibility and insights needed to protect their workloads and respond effectively to incidents.

### Identify the Business Requirements and Security Objectives
To begin, it is essential to identify the business requirements and security objectives. This involves understanding the critical assets that need protection, the types of data being handled, and the potential risks and threats. For example, a financial services company might need to monitor for data breaches, unauthorized access to sensitive customer information, and compliance with regulations such as PCI-DSS.

### Design Monitoring Solution
Once the requirements are clear, the next step is to design a monitoring solution that covers the entire environment and specific workloads. This includes selecting and configuring the appropriate AWS services to meet the identified needs. For instance, consider an e-commerce platform hosted on AWS, which includes web servers on EC2 instances, a database on RDS, and a data lake on S3.

### Environment Monitoring
- **AWS CloudTrail:** Enable CloudTrail to capture all API calls across the AWS environment. This provides a detailed log of actions taken by users, roles, or AWS services, helping to detect unauthorized changes or access attempts.
- **Amazon CloudWatch:** Set up CloudWatch to monitor key metrics such as CPU utilization, memory usage, and disk I/O for EC2 instances. Create CloudWatch Alarms to notify the operations team when these metrics exceed defined thresholds, indicating potential performance issues or attacks.
- **AWS Config:** Use AWS Config to assess and record the continuous configuration of AWS resources. Comparing resource configurations against predefined rules helps identify and address compliance issues.

### Workload Monitoring
- **Amazon GuardDuty:** Enable GuardDuty to monitor the AWS environment for malicious activity and unauthorized behavior. GuardDuty analyzes VPC Flow Logs, CloudTrail logs, and DNS logs to detect threats such as compromised instances or anomalous API calls.
- **AWS WAF:** Implement AWS WAF to protect web applications from common web exploits—Configure WAF rules to block malicious traffic and monitor WAF logs for attack patterns.
- **Amazon RDS Enhanced Monitoring:** Enable Enhanced Monitoring for RDS to gain deeper insights into database performance. This provides real-time metrics on CPU, memory, and storage, helping to detect and troubleshoot performance issues.

### Business-Specific Monitoring
- **Custom CloudWatch Metrics**: Develop custom metrics that align with business-specific requirements. For an e-commerce platform, this might include monitoring the number of successful and failed user logins, transaction volumes, and shopping cart abandonment rates.
- **AWS Lambda and EventBridge:** Use Lambda functions and EventBridge to automate responses to specific events. For example, they automatically trigger an incident response workflow when suspicious activity is detected, such as multiple failed login attempts from a single IP address.

By designing monitoring solutions tailored to business and security requirements, organizations can ensure they have comprehensive visibility into their AWS environment. This enables them to detect and respond to threats promptly, maintain compliance, and optimize the performance and security of their workloads.

## 9.2.6 Setting Up Automated Audits

Implementing automated tools and scripts to perform regular security audits is essential for maintaining AWS environments' security and compliance. Automating these processes helps organizations quickly identify and mitigate security vulnerabilities, ensuring that security postures remain robust over time. AWS provides several services and features that facilitate the automation of security audits, including AWS Security Hub, AWS Lambda, and AWS Config.

AWS Security Hub serves as a central location for managing and viewing the security posture of AWS environments. It aggregates, organizes, and prioritizes security findings from various AWS services such as Amazon GuardDuty, Amazon Inspector, and AWS Config. Custom insights in AWS Security Hub can be created to automate security audits, enabling organizations to focus on specific security requirements and compliance standards.

For example, consider an organization that needs to ensure all its S3 buckets are encrypted and that public access is restricted. They can create custom insights in AWS Security Hub to regularly check the compliance of their S3 buckets against these criteria.

### Creating Custom Insights in AWS Security Hub
**Identify Key Security Requirements:** Determine the specific security configurations and compliance standards that need to be audited regularly. In this example, the focus is on S3 bucket encryption and public access settings.

**Create a Custom Insight:** Use AWS Security Hub to create a custom insight. Navigate to the Insights tab, click on "Create insight," and define the filters based on security requirements. For S3 bucket encryption, the filter can be set to check for buckets where the encryption is not enabled. Similarly, for public access, the filter can identify buckets with ACLs or policies allowing public read or write access.

```
1. {
2.     "Findings": [
3.         {
```

```
4.          "Title": "S3 Buckets Without Encryption",
5.          "Description": "List of S3 buckets that do not have encryption enabled.",
6.          "Filters": {
7.              "ResourceType": [{ "Value": "AWS::S3::Bucket", "Comparison": "EQUALS" }],
8.              "Configuration": [{ "Value": "false", "Comparison": "EQUALS", "Field":
"S3BucketServerSideEncryptionConfigurationEnabled" }]
9.          }
10.     },
11.     {
12.         "Title": "S3 Buckets with Public Access",
13.         "Description": "List of S3 buckets with public read or write access.",
14.         "Filters": {
15.             "ResourceType": [{ "Value": "AWS::S3::Bucket", "Comparison": "EQUALS" }],
16.             "Configuration": [{ "Value": "true", "Comparison": "EQUALS", "Field":
"S3BucketPublicAccess" }]
17.         }
18.     }
19.  ]
20. }
```

### Automating Audits with AWS Lambda and EventBridge

**Scheduled Audits:** Use Amazon EventBridge to create rules that trigger AWS Lambda functions at regular intervals (e.g., daily or weekly) to perform security audits. These Lambda functions can query AWS Security Hub for findings and generate reports or notifications if any issues are detected.

```
1. import boto3
2.
3. def lambda_handler(event, context):
4.     securityhub = boto3.client('securityhub')
5.     response = securityhub.get_findings(
6.         Filters={
7.             'RecordState': [{'Value': 'ACTIVE', 'Comparison': 'EQUALS'}],
8.             'ProductArn': [{'Value': 'arn:aws:securityhub:::product/aws/securityhub',
'Comparison': 'EQUALS'}],
9.             'AwsAccountId': [{'Value': '123456789012', 'Comparison': 'EQUALS'}]
10.        }
11.    )
12.
13.    findings = response['Findings']
14.    for finding in findings:
15.        print(finding['Title'], finding['Description'])
16.
17.    # Notify or remediate based on findings
```

### AWS Config Rules

**Automated Compliance Checks:** AWS Config can be used to create rules that automatically check resource configurations against the desired settings. For instance, an AWS Config rule can be set to ensure all S3 buckets have server-side encryption enabled and that no buckets are publicly accessible. Non-compliant resources can be flagged, and remediation actions can be automated using AWS Systems Manager or Lambda.

By implementing these automated tools and scripts, organizations can ensure continuous monitoring and auditing of their AWS environments. This proactive approach not only enhances security but also ensures compliance with regulatory standards, reducing the risk of security breaches and data loss.

## 9.2.7 Defining Metrics and Thresholds

Defining the appropriate metrics and thresholds to generate alerts is crucial for ensuring timely detection of security events in AWS environments. Effective monitoring requires identifying the key performance indicators

(KPIs) and security metrics that reflect the health and security posture of the environment. Setting thresholds involves determining the values at which these metrics indicate a potential security issue, thus triggering alerts that enable prompt investigation and response.

Metrics are quantifiable measures that can reflect various aspects of system performance and security. For example, in an AWS environment, common security metrics might include the number of failed login attempts, unusual API activity, changes to security group rules, and data transfer volumes. Thresholds are specific values or conditions for these metrics that, when crossed, trigger alerts. Setting these thresholds requires a balance between being sensitive enough to catch actual issues and avoiding too many false positives that could lead to alert fatigue.

For instance, consider monitoring failed login attempts to detect potential brute-force attacks. Using Amazon CloudWatch, an administrator can set up a metric to track the number of failed login attempts to the AWS Management Console. A threshold might be defined where more than five failed login attempts within a minute triggers an alert. This can be implemented using a CloudWatch alarm that monitors the "Failed login attempts" metric and uses Amazon SNS to send notifications when the threshold is crossed.

```
import boto3

cloudwatch = boto3.client('cloudwatch')
sns = boto3.client('sns')

response = cloudwatch.put_metric_alarm(
    AlarmName='FailedLoginAttemptsAlarm',
    ComparisonOperator='GreaterThanOrEqualToThreshold',
    EvaluationPeriods=1,
    MetricName='FailedLoginAttempts',
    Namespace='AWS/CloudTrail',
    Period=60,
    Statistic='Sum',
    Threshold=5,
    ActionsEnabled=True,
    AlarmActions=[
        'arn:aws:sns:us-west-2:123456789012:MySNSTopic'
    ],
    AlarmDescription='Alarm when there are more than 5 failed login attempts within a minute',
    Dimensions=[
        {
            'Name': 'EventName',
            'Value': 'ConsoleLogin'
        },
        {
            'Name': 'EventSource',
            'Value': 'signin.amazonaws.com'
        }
    ]
)
```

Another example is monitoring changes to security group rules. Unauthorized changes to security groups can indicate potential security breaches. AWS Config can be used to track these changes, and a CloudWatch metric can be created to monitor the count of "UnauthorizedSecurityGroupChanges." A threshold could be set to alert if any unauthorized change is detected.

```
response = cloudwatch.put_metric_alarm(
    AlarmName='UnauthorizedSecurityGroupChangeAlarm',
    ComparisonOperator='GreaterThanOrEqualToThreshold',
    EvaluationPeriods=1,
    MetricName='UnauthorizedSecurityGroupChanges',
```

```
6.      Namespace='AWS/Config',
7.      Period=300,
8.      Statistic='Sum',
9.      Threshold=1,
10.     ActionsEnabled=True,
11.     AlarmActions=[
12.         'arn:aws:sns:us-west-2:123456789012:SecurityAlerts'
13.     ],
14.     AlarmDescription='Alarm when there is any unauthorized change to security group rules',
15.     Dimensions=[
16.         {
17.             'Name': 'ComplianceType',
18.             'Value': 'NON_COMPLIANT'
19.         }
20.     ]
21. )
```

In summary, defining metrics and thresholds that generate alerts is a vital aspect of security monitoring in AWS environments. It involves selecting relevant metrics that reflect potential security threats and setting appropriate thresholds that balance sensitivity and specificity. Examples include monitoring failed login attempts and unauthorized security group changes using CloudWatch alarms and AWS Config rules. Properly configured metrics and thresholds enable timely detection and response to security events, helping to maintain the security and integrity of the AWS environment.

## 9.3 Troubleshooting Monitoring and Alerting

Troubleshooting, monitoring, and alerting in AWS environments is crucial to maintaining security and operational oversight effectiveness. It involves diagnosing issues with the monitoring setup, ensuring that alerts are correctly configured and functioning as expected, and fine-tuning the system to minimize false positives and negatives. Proper troubleshooting helps ensure timely detection and response to security incidents, enhancing system reliability and security.

### 9.3.1 Configuration of Monitoring Services

Configuring monitoring services such as AWS Security Hub to provide accurate and timely alerts is essential for maintaining a secure AWS environment. AWS Security Hub aggregates and prioritizes security findings from various AWS services, such as Amazon GuardDuty, Amazon Inspector, and AWS Config, as well as from third-party security solutions. To ensure these alerts are accurate and timely, it is crucial to properly configure the integrated services and customize the Security Hub settings to meet the specific needs of your environment.

For example, to configure AWS Security Hub to monitor for potential security threats, you first need to enable it in your AWS account and region. After activation, integrate it with services like GuardDuty and Inspector. GuardDuty provides intelligent threat detection by continuously monitoring for malicious or unauthorized behavior, while Inspector assesses the security and compliance of applications running on AWS.

Next, configure custom insights in AWS Security Hub to focus on specific security issues relevant to your environment. For instance, you can create an insight to identify EC2 instances with findings related to unauthorized port scans. Setting appropriate severity levels and defining custom actions ensures that critical alerts are prioritized and promptly addressed.

To further refine alert accuracy, regularly review and adjust the thresholds and parameters of the integrated services. For instance, in GuardDuty, you can fine-tune the sensitivity of the anomaly detection models to balance between detecting genuine threats and minimizing false positives.

### Configuration Example
**Consider the following configuration example:** Enable AWS Security Hub in your AWS Management Console. Integrate Amazon GuardDuty, Amazon Inspector, and AWS Config with Security Hub. Create a custom insight in Security Hub to monitor for specific threats, such as unauthorized port scans on EC2 instances. Set the severity levels for different types of findings to prioritize critical alerts. Define custom actions, such as invoking AWS Lambda functions to automate incident response.

Regularly reviewing and adjusting these configurations ensures that AWS Security Hub provides accurate and timely alerts, enabling your security team to respond effectively to potential threats.

## 9.3.2 Analyzing Security Events
Identifying relevant data that indicates security events and understanding its significance is crucial for effective security monitoring and incident response in AWS environments. This process involves collecting and analyzing various types of data, such as logs, metrics, and configuration changes, to detect potential security incidents and understand their impact.

For example, Amazon GuardDuty uses data from AWS CloudTrail logs, VPC Flow Logs, and DNS logs to detect anomalies and potential threats. CloudTrail logs provide a history of AWS API calls made on your account, which can reveal unauthorized access attempts or unusual API activity. VPC Flow Logs capture information about the IP traffic going to and from network interfaces in your VPC, which can help identify unusual traffic patterns or communication with known malicious IP addresses. DNS logs record DNS queries from your resources, indicating attempts to communicate with malicious domains.

Understanding the significance of these data sources allows you to configure GuardDuty effectively to detect relevant security events. For instance, if GuardDuty detects an API call from an unusual geographic location, this might indicate a compromised credential. Similarly, a spike in outbound traffic to an unfamiliar IP address could suggest data exfiltration attempts.

Consider a scenario where GuardDuty generates an alert for a suspected port scan. By analyzing VPC Flow Logs, you can determine the source and target of the scan, the frequency of the attempts, and whether the traffic matches known attack patterns. This information helps you understand the scope and potential impact of the threat, allowing you to take appropriate mitigation steps, such as blocking the IP address or tightening security group rules.

Regularly reviewing and correlating data from these logs enhances your ability to promptly identify and respond to security events. AWS Security Hub can further aggregate and prioritize findings from multiple services, providing a centralized view of your security posture.

## 9.3.3 Evaluating Service Functionality and Permissions
Analyzing the functionality, permissions, and configuration of resources after an event that did not provide visibility or alerting is essential for understanding why the event was not detected and for enhancing the monitoring setup. This process involves a thorough examination of resource settings and their interaction with monitoring tools to identify gaps in visibility and alerting mechanisms.

For example, consider a scenario where an unauthorized user accessed sensitive data in an S3 bucket, but no alerts were triggered. To analyze this, start by reviewing the bucket's permissions and access control lists (ACLs). Check if the bucket was publicly accessible or if specific IAM roles and policies granted unintended access. This step helps understand how the unauthorized user gained access and whether permissions were overly permissive.

Next, evaluate the configuration of AWS CloudTrail, which should log all API calls made to the S3 bucket. Ensure CloudTrail is enabled and configured to log the bucket's management events and data events. If CloudTrail was not logging these events, you would not have visibility into who accessed the data and when. Verify the CloudTrail trail's configuration and confirm that it is delivering logs to an S3 bucket or CloudWatch Logs for further analysis.

Additionally, examine the functionality and configuration of AWS Config to ensure it is monitoring changes to the bucket's settings and ACLs. AWS Config provides a detailed history of resource configurations and can trigger rules to detect non-compliant changes. Check if AWS Config rules were in place to monitor for changes in S3 bucket policies and if those rules were correctly configured to alert to policy violations.

For instance, AWS Config was not set up to monitor S3 bucket policies. In that case, you need to create a new Config rule that checks for public access settings and triggers an alert if a bucket becomes publicly accessible. Similarly, ensure that Amazon GuardDuty is enabled and configured to detect anomalous access patterns, such as access from unusual IP addresses or locations.

By analyzing these resources' functionality, permissions, and configuration, you can identify why the event did not trigger an alert and take corrective actions. Implementing more stringent IAM policies, enabling detailed logging, configuring AWS Config rules, and using GuardDuty can enhance visibility and ensure timely detection of similar incidents in the future.

## 9.3.4 Troubleshooting Custom Applications

Analyzing and remediating the configuration of custom applications that are not reporting their statistics correctly is crucial for maintaining an effective monitoring and alerting system. This process involves identifying the root cause of the reporting issues, adjusting configurations, and implementing best practices to ensure accurate data collection and reporting.

For example, consider a custom application running on AWS EC2 instances that is supposed to send performance metrics to Amazon CloudWatch but is failing to report these metrics correctly. The first step in analyzing this issue is to review the application's configuration settings related to metric reporting. Check the CloudWatch agent configuration files to ensure they are correctly set up to capture the necessary metrics. This includes verifying the log files and system metrics paths specified in the configuration files.

Next, examine the IAM roles and policies assigned to the EC2 instances. The CloudWatch agent requires specific permissions to send metrics to CloudWatch. Ensure that the IAM role attached to the EC2 instances includes the necessary permissions, such as `cloudwatch:PutMetricData`, `logs:CreateLogStream`, and `logs:PutLogEvents`. If the IAM policies are insufficient, update them to grant the required permissions.

Review the application's logs to identify any errors or warnings related to metric reporting. Application logs can provide valuable insights into why metrics are not being sent to CloudWatch. Common issues may include network connectivity problems, misconfigured endpoints, or missing dependencies. Addressing these errors can often resolve the reporting issues.

For instance, if the logs indicate that the CloudWatch agent cannot reach the CloudWatch endpoint, ensure that the EC2 instances have the necessary network access to the CloudWatch service. This may involve configuring security groups, network ACLs, or VPC endpoints to allow outbound traffic to CloudWatch.

After identifying and addressing the root cause:
- Validate the changes by testing the application.
- Monitor CloudWatch to confirm that the custom application metrics are now being reported correctly.

- Use CloudWatch dashboards to visualize the metrics and set up alarms to notify you of any future issues with metric reporting.

By thoroughly analyzing and remediating the configuration of custom applications, you can ensure that they report their statistics accurately. This process improves the effectiveness of your monitoring and alerting system and helps maintain the overall security and performance of your AWS environment.

## 9.3.5 Aligning with Security Requirements

Evaluating logging and monitoring services to ensure they align with organizational security requirements is essential for maintaining a robust security posture. This process involves assessing the capabilities of existing services, ensuring compliance with security policies, and implementing necessary enhancements to address any gaps.

For example, consider an organization that relies on AWS CloudWatch and AWS Security Hub to log and monitor its AWS infrastructure. The first step in the evaluation process is to review the organization's security requirements and policies. These may include requirements for log retention, data encryption, access controls, and incident response capabilities.

Next, the current configuration of CloudWatch and Security Hub will be assessed. Verify that CloudWatch is configured to collect logs from all relevant sources, such as EC2 instances, Lambda functions, and VPC flow logs. Ensure that log data is being retained for the required period and that it is encrypted both in transit and at rest. Review the permissions and access controls to ensure that only authorized personnel can access and manage the logs.

For AWS Security Hub, evaluate its integration with other AWS security services like GuardDuty, Macie, and Inspector. Ensure that Security Hub aggregates findings from these services and provides a comprehensive view of the security posture. Check that the Security Hub's findings are mapped to the organization's security policies and that they trigger appropriate alerts and actions.

An example of improving the alignment with organizational security requirements is enabling AWS CloudTrail to log all API calls and integrating it with CloudWatch for real-time monitoring. By doing so, the organization can ensure that every action taken within the AWS environment is recorded and monitored, providing a complete audit trail. Configuring CloudTrail logs to be stored in an encrypted S3 bucket with strict access controls ensures compliance with data protection policies.

Furthermore, setting up automated alerts using Amazon SNS (Simple Notification Service) can enhance the incident response capabilities. For instance, CloudWatch alarms can be configured to monitor specific metrics or log patterns that indicate potential security incidents. When an alarm is triggered, SNS can send notifications to the security team, ensuring timely response to security events.

In summary, evaluating and aligning logging and monitoring services with organizational security requirements involves a comprehensive review of current configurations, ensuring compliance with security policies, and implementing enhancements to address any gaps. This process ensures that the organization's security posture is robust and capable of effectively detecting and responding to security incidents.

## 9.4 Designing and Implementing Logging Solutions

Designing and implementing logging solutions is crucial for maintaining robust security and operational visibility in an AWS environment. Effective logging solutions capture detailed records of activities across the infrastructure, enabling organizations to monitor, detect, and respond to potential security incidents promptly.

By ensuring comprehensive log collection and storage, organizations can meet compliance requirements and enhance their overall security posture.

## 9.4.1 Logging Capabilities of AWS Services

AWS provides a comprehensive suite of services and features for logging capabilities, enhancing security and operational visibility across various AWS resources. For instance, VPC Flow Logs capture information about the IP traffic passing to and from network interfaces in a VPC, aiding in network monitoring and troubleshooting. DNS logs from Amazon Route 53 provide visibility into DNS queries, useful for detecting and investigating DNS-related issues. AWS CloudTrail is essential for governance, compliance, and operational auditing of your AWS account, as it records AWS API calls made on your account. Lastly, Amazon CloudWatch Logs enable you to monitor, store, and access log files from Amazon EC2 instances, CloudTrail, and other sources. Together, these services provide a robust framework for logging and monitoring, ensuring that critical data is captured and available for analysis to maintain security and compliance .

**Example:** Suppose an organization wants to monitor and investigate API activity within its AWS environment. By enabling AWS CloudTrail, the organization can capture detailed logs of every API call made, including who made the call, when it was made, and which resources were affected. These logs can be sent to Amazon CloudWatch Logs for storage and analysis, allowing the security team to set up alerts for unusual activities, such as unauthorized access attempts, and respond promptly to potential security incidents.

## 9.4.2 Attributes of Logging

Understanding log levels, types, verbosity, and other attributes of logging capabilities is crucial for effectively managing and utilizing logs for security and operational insights. Log levels, such as DEBUG, INFO, WARN, ERROR, and FATAL, categorize the severity and importance of log messages. DEBUG logs, for instance, contain detailed information used for diagnosing problems, while ERROR logs capture issues that need immediate attention. Different log types include application logs, which record events within an application; system logs, which track system-level events; and security logs, which log security-related incidents.

The verbosity of logs refers to the amount of detail captured. High-verbosity logs provide in-depth details, useful for troubleshooting but can result in large volumes of data, while low-verbosity logs capture only essential information, reducing data volume but potentially missing crucial details.

Example: Consider an e-commerce application running on AWS. The application can generate different types of logs:
- **Application logs:** Record user interactions, such as product searches, order placements, and payment processing.
- **System logs:** Capture events related to the underlying infrastructure, like server restarts, CPU usage, and memory allocation.
- **Security logs:** Monitor access control events, such as successful and failed login attempts and changes to user permissions.

The application can ensure that only relevant information is captured at each level by configuring log levels appropriately. For instance, during routine operations, the system might log INFO and WARN messages, while DEBUG logs are enabled only during troubleshooting sessions to avoid excessive data generation.

## 9.4.3 Log Destinations and Lifecycle Management

Managing log destinations and lifecycle management is essential to ensure logs are stored securely, retained appropriately, and comply with regulatory requirements. Log destinations can include services like Amazon S3, Amazon CloudWatch Logs, and Amazon Elasticsearch Service. Effective lifecycle management involves defining retention periods and archival strategies and ensuring logs are accessible for auditing and compliance purposes.

**Example:** An organization using AWS CloudTrail for logging API activity might configure CloudTrail to deliver logs to an Amazon S3 bucket. To manage the log lifecycle, they could use S3 Object Lifecycle policies to automatically transition older logs to cheaper storage classes (e.g., S3 Glacier) and eventually delete them after a specified period. This approach ensures that logs are retained for the necessary duration to meet compliance requirements, such as GDPR or HIPAA, while also optimizing storage costs.

For instance, the organization could set a policy where logs are retained in S3 Standard for 30 days, transitioned to S3 Glacier for archival storage after 30 days, and then deleted after 365 days. This ensures logs are readily available for recent analysis and compliance audits while minimizing storage costs for long-term retention.

Compliance considerations also play a crucial role in log management. Different regulations may require logs to be retained for specific periods, kept immutable, or encrypted at rest. AWS services like S3 Object Lock can enforce write-once-read-many (WORM) policies, ensuring that logs cannot be altered or deleted during their retention period, which is critical for compliance with regulations like SEC Rule 17a-4.

## 9.4.4 Configuring Logging for Services and Applications

Configuring logging for AWS services and custom applications involves several steps to ensure that all relevant events are captured and stored for analysis and compliance. Here's a detailed process using AWS CloudTrail, Amazon CloudWatch Logs, and a custom application as examples:

### Enable AWS CloudTrail
- AWS CloudTrail provides comprehensive logging for API calls and activities across your AWS account.
- Go to the AWS Management Console, navigate to CloudTrail, and create a new trail.
- Specify the trail name, enable logging for all regions, and choose an S3 bucket to store the logs.
- Optionally, configure the trail to send logs to CloudWatch Logs for real-time monitoring and alerting.

### Set Up Amazon CloudWatch Logs for AWS Services
- Many AWS services can send logs to CloudWatch Logs, such as Amazon EC2, AWS Lambda, and Amazon RDS.
- For EC2 instances, install the CloudWatch Logs agent on the instance, configure the agent to monitor specific log files, and define the log group and log stream to send the logs.
- For Lambda functions, go to the Lambda console, select your function, and under Monitoring and Operations Tools, ensure that CloudWatch Logs is enabled.

### Configure VPC Flow Logs
- VPC Flow Logs capture information about the IP traffic going to and from network interfaces in your VPC.
- Navigate to the VPC console, select your VPC, and choose Create Flow Log.
- Select the log destination (either an S3 bucket or a CloudWatch Logs group) and define the log format and aggregation interval.

### Configure Logging for Custom Applications
- Custom applications can send logs to CloudWatch Logs using the AWS SDKs.
- Integrate the CloudWatch Logs SDK into your application code. For example, in a Node.js application, use the AWS SDK to create a CloudWatch Logs client and send log events to a specified log group.

- Example code snippet in Node.js

```
1.  const AWS = require('aws-sdk');
2.  const cloudwatchlogs = new AWS.CloudWatchLogs({region: 'us-west-2'});
3.
4.  function logToCloudWatch(logGroupName, logStreamName, message) {
5.    const params = {
6.      logGroupName: logGroupName,
7.      logStreamName: logStreamName,
8.      logEvents: [{message: message, timestamp: Date.now()}]
9.    };
10.
11.   cloudwatchlogs.putLogEvents(params, function(err, data) {
12.     if (err) console.log(err, err.stack);
13.     else console.log(data);
14.   });
15. }
16.
17. logToCloudWatch('my-log-group', 'my-log-stream', 'This is a log message.');
```

### Implement Lifecycle Management
- Configure S3 Object Lifecycle policies to manage log retention and transition to cost-effective storage.
- For CloudWatch Logs, set retention policies on log groups to automatically delete logs after a specified period.

### Compliance and Security
- Ensure logs are encrypted at rest and in transit.
- Use S3 Object Lock for compliance requirements, enforcing WORM policies to prevent log tampering.

### Example Scenario
A company uses CloudTrail to log all API activities, VPC Flow Logs to monitor network traffic, and custom application logs sent to CloudWatch Logs. They configure lifecycle policies to retain logs for 90 days in S3 Standard, transition to S3 Glacier after 90 days, and delete logs after 365 days. This setup ensures comprehensive logging, cost-effective storage management, and compliance with data retention policies.

## 9.4.5 Identifying Logging Requirements

Identifying the logging requirements and sources necessary for effective log ingestion and analysis is crucial for maintaining robust security and operational visibility in AWS environments. Logging requirements typically include understanding what needs to be logged, determining the appropriate log sources, and setting up efficient log collection and storage mechanisms.

First, it is essential to determine what activities and events need to be logged. Common logging requirements include recording API calls, user activities, network traffic, and system events. For example, AWS CloudTrail logs provide detailed records of all API calls made within an AWS account, capturing who made the call, when it was made, and what actions were performed. These logs are vital for auditing and forensic investigations.

Next, identifying the appropriate log sources is crucial. AWS provides several services that generate valuable logs. For instance, Amazon VPC Flow Logs capture IP traffic information going to and from network interfaces in a VPC. These logs can be used to monitor network traffic and detect suspicious activities. AWS CloudWatch Logs can collect log data from various AWS services like AWS Lambda, Amazon RDS, and custom applications. By setting up CloudWatch Logs, you can centralize log data from multiple sources, making analyzing and correlating events easier.

An **example scenario** involves setting up comprehensive logging for a web application hosted on AWS. The application uses Amazon EC2 instances, an Amazon RDS database, and is fronted by an Application Load Balancer (ALB). The logging setup would include:

- Enabling CloudTrail to log all API calls across the AWS account.
- Setting up VPC Flow Logs to capture network traffic for the VPC containing the EC2 instances and RDS database.
- Configuring ALB access logs to capture detailed information about requests sent to the load balancer.
- Using the CloudWatch Logs agent on EC2 instances to collect application and system logs.
- Enabling RDS Enhanced Monitoring to gather detailed metrics and logs from the database.

By aggregating these logs in CloudWatch Logs, you can perform centralized analysis and set up alerts for specific events, such as unauthorized access attempts or unusual traffic patterns.

## 9.4.6 Implementing Log Storage and Management

Implementing log storage and lifecycle management according to AWS best practices and organizational requirements is crucial for ensuring data availability, security, and compliance. Following these best practices helps maintain the integrity and accessibility of log data while optimizing storage costs and adhering to regulatory requirements.

One of the primary best practices is to centralize log storage. AWS recommends using Amazon S3 as a centralized repository for log data due to its durability, scalability, and cost-effectiveness. By storing logs in S3, you can take advantage of features like versioning, which helps protect against accidental deletions or modifications, and S3 Object Lock, which can enforce write-once-read-many (WORM) policies for regulatory compliance.

Another critical practice is to define and implement appropriate log retention policies. Retention policies determine how long logs should be kept before they are deleted or archived. For example, AWS CloudTrail logs can be set to expire after a certain period using S3 lifecycle policies. These policies can automatically transition older logs to lower-cost storage classes like S3 Glacier or delete them when they are no longer needed. This helps manage storage costs while ensuring compliance with data retention regulations.

Encryption is also a key best practice for securing log data. AWS recommends encrypting logs both in transit and at rest. Logs stored in S3 can be encrypted using server-side encryption with AWS Key Management Service (KMS) keys. Additionally, enabling encryption for logs collected by services like AWS CloudWatch Logs and VPC Flow Logs helps protect sensitive information from unauthorized access.

Access control is another essential aspect of log management. Implementing strict access policies using AWS Identity and Access Management (IAM) ensures that only authorized users and services can access log data. Using IAM roles and policies, you can grant granular permissions to different teams or applications, minimizing the risk of unauthorized access.

An example scenario involves setting up log storage and lifecycle management for a web application hosted on AWS. The application generates various logs, including CloudTrail logs, VPC Flow Logs, and application logs collected via CloudWatch Logs.

To implement best practices:
- **Centralize Log Storage:** Configure CloudTrail, VPC Flow Logs, and CloudWatch Logs to send log data to a centralized S3 bucket.
- **Implement Retention Policies:** Use S3 lifecycle policies to transition logs older than 30 days to S3 Glacier and delete logs older than one year.

- **Encrypt Logs:** Use AWS KMS to enable server-side encryption for the S3 bucket and Configure CloudWatch Logs and VPC Flow Logs to use encryption.
- **Control Access:** Create IAM policies that restrict access to the S3 bucket and logs to specific roles and users. Use AWS Organizations to enforce policies across multiple accounts if necessary.

By following these best practices, organizations can ensure that their log data is secure, accessible, and compliant with regulatory requirements.

## 9.5 Troubleshooting Logging Solutions

Troubleshooting logging solutions is essential for maintaining effective security monitoring and ensuring system integrity. It involves identifying and resolving issues related to log collection, storage, and analysis. By addressing these problems promptly, organizations can ensure that their logging infrastructure provides accurate and timely insights into security events and system performance.

### 9.5.1 Capabilities and Use Cases of Logging Services

AWS offers a comprehensive suite of logging services catering to various use cases, from security monitoring to performance optimization. AWS CloudTrail, for example, provides detailed logs of API calls made in an AWS account, helping track changes and ensuring compliance by maintaining a history of AWS account activity. This service is particularly useful for auditing purposes, as it allows administrators to see who did what and when across the AWS infrastructure.

**Amazon CloudWatch Logs** is another powerful tool that collects and stores log data from AWS resources, applications, and services. It enables real-time monitoring and alerting based on log data, making it indispensable for performance monitoring and troubleshooting. For instance, developers can use CloudWatch Logs to track application errors, monitor system performance, and set alarms to notify them of specific events, such as when the error rate exceeds a predefined threshold.

**VPC Flow Logs** provide network-level logging, capturing information about the IP traffic going to and from network interfaces in a VPC. This service is essential for network troubleshooting and security analysis, as it helps identify anomalous traffic patterns that could indicate a security breach or misconfiguration. For example, VPC Flow Logs can help detect unauthorized access attempts or data exfiltration by logging detailed information about network traffic flows.

AWS also offers specialized logging services like **AWS Config**, which provides a detailed inventory of AWS resources and their configurations. This service helps maintain configuration compliance by recording configuration changes and allowing for continuous monitoring and assessment of resource configurations against desired configurations. AWS Config is particularly useful in environments that require stringent compliance with regulatory standards, as it enables automatic evaluation of resource configurations against best practices and compliance rules.

In summary, AWS logging services such as AWS CloudTrail, Amazon CloudWatch Logs, VPC Flow Logs, and AWS Config offer robust capabilities for security monitoring, performance optimization, and compliance auditing. By leveraging these tools, organizations can gain deep visibility into their AWS environments, ensuring efficient operation and adherence to security and compliance requirements.

### 9.5.2 Access Permissions for Logging

Understanding and managing access permissions for logging in AWS is crucial to ensure both security and proper functionality. Access permissions determine who can view, modify, and manage log data, which is vital for maintaining the integrity and confidentiality of logs. AWS Identity and Access Management (IAM) plays a central role in controlling access to logging services such as AWS CloudTrail, Amazon CloudWatch Logs, and VPC Flow Logs.

In AWS, permissions are granted through IAM policies, which define the actions that are allowed or denied for specific AWS services and resources. For example, to allow a user to create, view, and delete log streams in CloudWatch Logs, an IAM policy might include permissions for `logs:CreateLogStream`, `logs:PutLogEvents`, and `logs:DeleteLogStream`. Ensuring that only authorized users have these permissions helps prevent unauthorized access and potential tampering with log data.

One best practice is to follow the principle of least privilege, which means granting users only the permissions they need to perform their job functions. For instance, a developer who needs to monitor application performance might be granted permissions to view CloudWatch Logs but not to delete them. This approach minimizes the risk of accidental or malicious modifications to log data.

Another important aspect is managing access permissions for AWS CloudTrail, which records API calls made within an AWS account. To view CloudTrail logs, users need permissions for `cloudtrail:LookupEvents`. However, configuring CloudTrail itself, such as setting up new trails or modifying existing ones, requires more extensive permissions, including `Cloudtrail:CreateTrail` and `Cloudtrail:UpdateTrail`. Using IAM roles and policies, administrators can ensure that only trusted personnel have the ability to configure CloudTrail, thereby protecting the integrity of audit logs.

AWS Organizations can be leveraged to manage permissions across multiple AWS accounts centrally. By using service control policies (SCPs), administrators can define permissions boundaries for all accounts within an organization. This is particularly useful for large enterprises that need to enforce consistent security policies across various teams and departments.

In summary, effectively managing access permissions for AWS logging services involves:
- IAM policies are used to grant the necessary permissions.
- Adhering to the principle of least privilege.
- Utilizing AWS Organizations for centralized management.

These practices help secure log data, ensuring that only authorized users can access and manage it, thereby maintaining the security and integrity of AWS environments.

## 9.5.3 Identifying and Remediating Misconfigurations

Identifying and correcting misconfigurations in logging setups is crucial for ensuring effective security monitoring and compliance in AWS environments. Misconfigurations can lead to insufficient logging coverage, incomplete log data, or unauthorized access to log files. The process involves a thorough review of the logging configurations and permissions to detect and rectify any issues.

One common issue is the absence or incorrect configuration of AWS CloudTrail, which logs API activity across an AWS account. If CloudTrail is not enabled or is misconfigured, it can result in critical gaps in audit logs. To identify such misconfigurations, administrators can use AWS Config to check whether CloudTrail is enabled and correctly configured. AWS Config provides rules that can automatically detect when CloudTrail logging is disabled or not set up according to best practices.

For example, an AWS Config rule like cloud-trail-enabled can ensure that CloudTrail is active in all regions. If this rule is violated, the remediation step involves enabling CloudTrail and configuring it to capture all API calls across all regions. This can be done via the AWS Management Console, AWS CLI, or AWS CloudFormation templates.

Another issue can arise from incorrect permissions in Amazon CloudWatch Logs. Suppose an application is expected to send logs to CloudWatch, but logs are missing. This could be due to inadequate permissions for the application to create log streams or put log events. To diagnose this, an IAM policy review is necessary. The IAM user or role used by the application should have permissions like `logs:CreateLogStream`, `logs:PutLogEvents`, and `logs:DescribeLogStreams`.

For example, if a Lambda function is not logging to CloudWatch as expected, you might find that the associated IAM role needs the necessary permissions. The remediation involves updating the IAM policy to include the required CloudWatch Logs actions.

Here's an example of such a policy:

```
1.  {
2.    "Version": "2012-10-17",
3.    "Statement": [
4.      {
5.        "Effect": "Allow",
6.        "Action": [
7.          "logs:CreateLogGroup",
8.          "logs:CreateLogStream",
9.          "logs:PutLogEvents"
10.       ],
11.       "Resource": "*"
12.     }
13.   ]
14. }
```

Misconfigurations can also occur in log retention settings. Logs might be set to an insufficient retention period, causing valuable data to be deleted prematurely. AWS CloudWatch Logs allows for setting log retention policies, which can be audited through AWS Config rules or manual checks. If a log group has a retention policy of just a few days but needs to retain logs for compliance purposes (e.g., 90 days), the retention settings need to be updated.

Lastly, ensuring that log data is encrypted at rest is essential for compliance and security. For instance, CloudTrail logs should be encrypted using AWS Key Management Service (KMS). A misconfiguration in encryption settings can be identified by reviewing the CloudTrail configuration in the AWS Management Console or using AWS Config rules that check for encryption compliance. If encryption is not enabled, the remediation step involves configuring CloudTrail to use KMS for log encryption.

In summary, identifying and remediating misconfigurations in logging setups involves a comprehensive review of CloudTrail, CloudWatch Logs, and IAM policies. Automated tools like AWS Config can significantly aid in detecting issues, while remediation steps typically involve updating configurations and permissions to align with best practices and compliance requirements.

## 9.5.4 Determining Causes of Missing Logs

Determining the causes of missing logs and performing the necessary remediation steps is critical for ensuring comprehensive security monitoring and compliance in AWS environments. Missing logs can result from several issues, including misconfigurations in logging services, insufficient permissions, or resource constraints. Identifying the root causes and implementing appropriate remediation measures can help maintain the integrity and completeness of log data.

One common cause of missing logs is the misconfiguration of AWS CloudTrail, which captures API activity across an AWS account. For example, some logs might need to be included if CloudTrail is not enabled in all regions or if the logging bucket is misconfigured. To diagnose this issue, administrators can use AWS Config rules to check CloudTrail configurations. The cloud-trail-enabled rule ensures CloudTrail is enabled across all regions. If this rule indicates a violation, the remediation step involves enabling CloudTrail in the missing regions and verifying the logging bucket configuration to ensure it is correctly set up and has the necessary permissions.

For instance, if CloudTrail logs are missing for specific regions, you can enable logging by navigating to the CloudTrail console, selecting "Trails," and configuring the trail to cover all regions. Additionally, ensure the S3 bucket used for storing CloudTrail logs has the correct bucket policy to allow CloudTrail to write logs.

```
1.  {
2.    "Version": "2012-10-17",
3.    "Statement": [
4.      {
5.        "Sid": "AWSCloudTrailAclCheck",
6.        "Effect": "Allow",
7.        "Principal": { "Service": "cloudtrail.amazonaws.com" },
8.        "Action": "s3:GetBucketAcl",
9.        "Resource": "arn:aws:s3:::your-cloudtrail-bucket-name"
10.     },
11.     {
12.       "Sid": "AWSCloudTrailWrite",
13.       "Effect": "Allow",
14.       "Principal": { "Service": "cloudtrail.amazonaws.com" },
15.       "Action": "s3:PutObject",
16.       "Resource": "arn:aws:s3:::your-cloudtrail-bucket-name/AWSLogs/your-account-id/*",
17.       "Condition": { "StringEquals": { "s3:x-amz-acl": "bucket-owner-full-control" } }
18.     }
19.   ]
20. }
```

Another area for improvement could be more permissions for services like Amazon CloudWatch Logs. For example, if an EC2 instance is supposed to send logs to CloudWatch but logs still need to be included, it might be due to inadequate IAM role permissions. To diagnose this, check the IAM role associated with the EC2 instance to ensure it has the necessary permissions to create log streams and put log events.

```
1.  {
2.    "Version": "2012-10-17",
3.    "Statement": [
4.      {
5.        "Effect": "Allow",
6.        "Action": [
7.          "logs:CreateLogStream",
8.          "logs:PutLogEvents"
9.        ],
10.       "Resource": "arn:aws:logs:region:account-id:log-group:log-group-name:*"
11.     }
12.   ]
13. }
```

If the IAM role lacks these permissions, update the role's policy to include them. This ensures the EC2 instance can create log streams and send log events to CloudWatch Logs.

Resource constraints can also cause missing logs. For instance, if the CloudWatch Logs agent on an EC2 instance is configured with insufficient memory or disk space, it might fail to send logs. To diagnose this, check the CloudWatch Logs agent's configuration and logs on the EC2 instance. If you notice errors related to resource constraints, adjust the configuration to allocate more resources.

```
1.  {
2.    "logs": {
```

```
3.      "log_stream_name": "my-log-stream",
4.      "log_group_name": "my-log-group",
5.      "region": "us-west-2",
6.      "file": "/var/log/my-application.log",
7.      "buffer_duration": "5000",
8.      "initial_position": "start_of_file",
9.      "timestamp_format": "%b %d %H:%M:%S",
10.     "multi_line_start_pattern": "{datetime_format}",
11.     "batch_size": "1024",
12.     "use_gzip_http_content_encoding": true
13.   }
14. }
15.
```

Adjusting parameters like `buffer_duration` or `batch_size` can help manage the resource usage of the CloudWatch Logs agent.

In summary, diagnosing and remediating missing logs involves checking the configuration and permissions of logging services like AWS CloudTrail and Amazon CloudWatch Logs, as well as ensuring sufficient resources for log agents. By systematically reviewing and correcting these aspects, you can maintain comprehensive and reliable logging in your AWS environment.

## 9.6 Designing Log Analysis Solution

Designing a log analysis solution involves creating a systematic approach to collecting, storing, and analyzing log data to gain actionable insights. This process ensures effective monitoring of system health, security incidents, and operational performance. Key aspects include identifying relevant log sources, choosing appropriate storage solutions, and implementing tools for real-time analysis and visualization to support proactive incident response and compliance requirements.

### 9.6.1 Services and Tools for Log Analysis

Analyzing captured logs is crucial for maintaining security, compliance, and operational efficiency in AWS environments. AWS offers several tools and services to facilitate this process, including Amazon Athena and CloudWatch Logs filter.

**Amazon Athena** is a powerful service that allows you to run SQL queries on data stored in Amazon S3. It is particularly useful for log analysis because it can process structured, semi-structured, and unstructured data without the need for complex ETL processes. For example, you can store your application logs in S3 and use

Athena to run queries that identify patterns, anomalies, or specific events of interest. By setting up partitions and using proper schemas, you can optimize the performance of your queries, making Athena a flexible and efficient tool for deep log analysis.

**CloudWatch Logs filter**, on the other hand, provides real-time monitoring capabilities by allowing you to define metric filters based on specific patterns in your log data. These filters can be used to create CloudWatch Alarms, which trigger notifications or automated responses when certain conditions are met. For instance, you can set up a filter to detect failed login attempts or unusual API activity, and an alarm can be configured to notify your security team or initiate an automated remediation action using AWS Lambda.

Combining these tools allows you to leverage real-time monitoring and historical data analysis strengths. For example, you might use the CloudWatch Logs filter to catch immediate threats and Athena to conduct a thorough investigation afterward. This multi-layered approach ensures that you have comprehensive visibility into your AWS environment, enabling you to respond promptly and effectively to security incidents.

In summary, Amazon Athena and CloudWatch Logs filter provide robust solutions for log analysis in AWS, each catering to different aspects of monitoring and investigation. Their integration helps organizations maintain a secure and compliant infrastructure by facilitating both proactive and reactive security measures.

## 9.6.2 Log Analysis Features of AWS Services

AWS offers a suite of services that provide detailed log analysis features to help organizations monitor, analyze, and secure their environments. Key services include CloudWatch Logs Insights, CloudTrail Insights, and Security Hub Insights, each offering unique capabilities for different log analysis and security monitoring aspects.

**CloudWatch Logs** Insights is an interactive query service enabling users to analyze real-time log data. It allows you to run queries on log data stored in CloudWatch Logs to identify patterns, detect anomalies, and troubleshoot issues. For example, you can use CloudWatch Logs Insights to query application logs for error rates over a specified period, helping you quickly pinpoint issues that require immediate attention. The service provides a simple query language that is easy to learn and use, making it accessible for developers and operations teams alike.

**CloudTrail Insights** builds on the standard AWS CloudTrail service, which logs API calls made in your AWS account. CloudTrail Insights automatically detects unusual API activities, such as spikes in resource provisioning or unexpected changes in permissions. For example, if there is a sudden increase in the number of EC2 instances launched in your account, CloudTrail Insights will detect this anomaly and generate an event. This feature helps organizations identify potential security threats and operational issues by highlighting deviations from normal activity .

**AWS Security Hub** aggregates organizes and prioritizes security findings from multiple AWS services, including CloudWatch, GuardDuty, and others. Security Hub Insights uses these findings to view your security posture comprehensively. For instance, it can consolidate findings related to misconfigured security groups, exposed S3 buckets, and compromised EC2 instances into a single dashboard. This centralized approach simplifies the process of monitoring and responding to security threats, enabling security teams to focus on the most critical issues first .

These log analysis features provide a robust framework for maintaining security and compliance in AWS environments. CloudWatch Logs Insights offers real-time log querying and analysis capabilities. At the same time, CloudTrail Insights detects anomalies in API activity, and Security Hub Insights provides a holistic view of security findings across multiple services. By leveraging these tools, organizations can improve their ability to detect, investigate, and respond to security incidents effectively.

## 9.6.3 Log Formats and Components

Understanding log formats and components is crucial for effective log analysis and security monitoring. Each log entry typically includes various pieces of information that detail events occurring within a system. For example, AWS CloudTrail logs provide a comprehensive record of API calls made within an AWS account, which can be instrumental in auditing and monitoring activities.

A CloudTrail log entry is structured in JSON format and contains several key components, each serving a specific purpose. These components include:

- **Event Time:** Indicates the exact timestamp when the event occurred. This is essential for chronological analysis and correlating events over time.
- **Event Name:** Specifies the API action that was invoked, such as RunInstances for launching an EC2 instance or PutObject for uploading an object to S3.

- **Event Source:** Identifies the AWS service that the event pertains to, such as ec2.amazonaws.com or s3.amazonaws.com.
- **User Identity:** Provides details about the user or entity that performed the action. This can include the IAM user, role, or AWS service.
- **Source IP Address:** Records the IP address from which the request originated, useful for identifying unusual access patterns or potential unauthorized access.
- **User Agent:** Describes the application or service that made the request, helping to differentiate between requests made from different sources.
- **Request Parameters:** Contains the parameters that were passed with the API request, providing context about the specific action taken.
- **Response Elements:** Details the response returned by AWS for the API call, including any error messages or status codes.

Here is an example of a CloudTrail log entry:

```
1.  {
2.    "eventVersion": "1.05",
3.    "userIdentity": {
4.      "type": "IAMUser",
5.      "principalId": "EXAMPLEPRINCIPALID",
6.      "arn": "arn:aws:iam::123456789012:user/Alice",
7.      "accountId": "123456789012",
8.      "accessKeyId": "EXAMPLEKEYID",
9.      "userName": "Alice"
10.   },
11.   "eventTime": "2021-09-15T12:34:56Z",
12.   "eventSource": "ec2.amazonaws.com",
13.   "eventName": "RunInstances",
14.   "awsRegion": "us-west-2",
15.   "sourceIPAddress": "203.0.113.0",
16.   "userAgent": "aws-cli/1.18.69 Python/3.7.4 Linux/5.4.0-1045-aws botocore/1.16.19",
17.   "requestParameters": {
18.     "minCount": 1,
19.     "maxCount": 1,
20.     "instanceType": "t2.micro",
21.     "imageId": "ami-0abcdef1234567890"
22.   },
23.   "responseElements": {
24.     "instancesSet": {
25.       "items": [
26.         {
27.           "instanceId": "i-0123456789abcdef0"
28.         }
29.       ]
30.     }
31.   },
32.   "requestID": "e6b678dd-26d1-4ba2-bd36-7c1e11cde1ef",
33.   "eventID": "7b4a3128-1e4c-4a29-8c50-03c7e78ed9e4"
34. }
```

In this example, the log entry records the `RunInstances` API call made by the IAM user `Alice` from IP address `203.0.113.0`. It includes the request parameters such as `instanceType` and `imageId`, and the response indicating the instance ID of the newly launched EC2 instance.

Understanding these log components enables administrators and security analysts to perform detailed forensic analysis, identify potential security incidents, and maintain compliance with organizational policies. By analyzing log entries like the example above, organizations can detect unusual activities, troubleshoot issues, and ensure that their AWS environments are secure and well-monitored.

## 9.6.4 Identifying Patterns in Logs

Identifying patterns in logs that indicate anomalies and known threats is a critical aspect of maintaining security in AWS environments. Techniques for detecting these patterns involve both automated tools and manual analysis. The goal is to recognize deviations from normal behavior that could signify security incidents such as unauthorized access, data exfiltration, or other malicious activities.

One effective technique is the use of anomaly detection algorithms, which are often part of security monitoring services like Amazon GuardDuty. GuardDuty continuously analyzes AWS CloudTrail logs, VPC Flow Logs, and DNS logs to identify unusual patterns. For example, if GuardDuty detects a spike in API calls from an IP address that has never interacted with your AWS account, it flags this as a potential threat. The service uses machine learning models to establish a baseline of normal activity, making it easier to spot deviations.

Another technique involves the use of pattern matching and correlation rules. AWS CloudWatch Logs Insights allows you to run queries on your log data to find specific patterns. For example, you can create queries to detect failed login attempts that exceed a certain threshold within a specific timeframe, which might indicate a brute-force attack. Here is an example of a CloudWatch Logs Insights query to detect multiple failed login attempts:

```
1. fields @timestamp, @message
2. | filter @message like /Failed login/
3. | stats count() by bin(5m)
4. | filter count > 10
5. | sort @timestamp desc
```

This query filters log messages for failed login attempts, counts the occurrences within 5-minute intervals, and lists those intervals where the count exceeds 10, sorted by timestamp. Such queries help quickly identify potential brute-force attacks or other login-related anomalies.

Correlation engines are also used to link events across multiple sources. AWS Security Hub aggregates findings from various AWS services and third-party tools, providing a centralized view of security threats. Security Hub can automatically generate insights by correlating data, such as identifying if an IAM policy change is followed by unusual API activity from the same user account.

Additionally, manual analysis can complement automated tools. Analysts can create custom dashboards in Amazon CloudWatch that visualize metrics and logs. For instance, monitoring an application's average response time and correlating it with API call patterns can reveal performance degradation due to potential DDoS attacks.

Here is an example scenario: An organization notices a sudden increase in the volume of data being transferred out of its S3 buckets. By analyzing CloudTrail logs, it discovers that an IAM user, which typically does not perform large data transfers, initiated these actions. Further investigation reveals that the user's credentials were compromised, and a malicious actor was exfiltrating data. This pattern of unusual data transfer activity helps the organization quickly identify and respond to security threats.

In summary, identifying patterns in logs that indicate anomalies and known threats involves a combination of machine learning algorithms, pattern matching, correlation rules, and manual analysis. Services like Amazon GuardDuty, CloudWatch Logs Insights, and Security Hub provide robust tools for detecting and responding to these patterns, enhancing the security and integrity of AWS environments.

# 9.6.5 Normalizing, Parsing, and Correlating Logs

**Normalizing logs** involves standardizing log data from various sources into a consistent format. This process is crucial because logs can come from different systems, applications, and devices, each with its own format. Normalization ensures that the log data can be easily compared and analyzed, regardless of its origin. For example, normalizing timestamps into a common format (e.g., ISO 8601) allows for accurate chronological analysis of events across different logs.

**Parsing logs** refers to extracting specific data fields from log entries. This involves breaking down raw log data into structured components, such as IP addresses, user names, timestamps, and error codes. Parsing enables detailed analysis by allowing security tools to focus on relevant log attributes. For instance, parsing HTTP logs to extract status codes and URLs helps identify patterns like frequent 404 errors that might indicate a web scraping attempt.

**Correlating logs** is the process of linking related log events across different sources to identify patterns and detect potential security threats. Correlation helps in understanding the context of events, making it easier to spot anomalies that single log entries might not reveal. For example, correlating firewall logs with authentication logs can help detect a pattern where failed login attempts are followed by attempts to access restricted resources.

Best Practices for Normalizing, Parsing, and Correlating Logs
- **Consistent Log Formats:** Implement consistent logging formats across all systems and applications. Use structured logging formats like JSON or XML, which facilitate easier normalization and parsing. Consistency ensures that all logs adhere to a common schema, simplifying downstream analysis.
- **Use Centralized Log Management:** Utilize centralized log management solutions like AWS CloudWatch Logs, ELK Stack (Elasticsearch, Logstash, Kibana), or Splunk. These tools help aggregate, normalize, parse, and correlate logs from diverse sources. For example, AWS CloudWatch Logs can centralize logs from EC2 instances, Lambda functions, and VPC Flow Logs, providing a unified view of log data.
- **Automate Parsing:** Automate the parsing process using log management tools. Tools like AWS CloudWatch Logs Insights, Logstash, and Fluentd can parse logs based on predefined patterns. For instance, Logstash can be configured with GROK patterns to extract fields from log entries, making it easier to analyze specific log attributes.
- **Correlation Rules:** Define correlation rules that link related events across different log sources. Security Information and Event Management (SIEM) systems like Splunk, AWS Security Hub, and Azure Sentinel offer capabilities to create and manage correlation rules. For example, a rule might correlate VPN login failures with subsequent successful logins from unusual locations, indicating a possible credential compromise.
- **Time Synchronization:** Ensure all systems are synchronized to a common time source, such as an NTP server. Consistent timestamps across logs are essential for accurate event correlation. Discrepancies in timestamps can lead to incorrect conclusions about the sequence of events.
- **Log Enrichment:** Enhance logs with additional context before ingestion. This can include metadata such as geographic location of an IP address or the application name generating the log. Enriched logs provide more context for analysis, making it easier to detect and understand anomalies.
- **Regular Audits and Updates:** Regularly audit and update parsing and correlation rules to adapt to new threat patterns and changes in the environment. As new types of logs are introduced, ensure that parsing and correlation configurations are updated accordingly.

## Example Scenario

Consider a scenario where a company uses multiple AWS services, including EC2 instances, S3 buckets, and AWS CloudTrail for logging API calls. To monitor for potential data exfiltration, the company can normalize, parse, and correlate logs as follows:
- **Normalization:** Convert all log timestamps to ISO 8601 format.

- **Parsing:** Use AWS CloudWatch Logs Insights to parse CloudTrail logs, extracting fields like `eventName`, `sourceIPAddress`, and `userIdentity`.
- **Correlation:** Create a correlation rule in AWS Security Hub that links S3 `GetObject` events with CloudTrail login events from the same IP address within a short timeframe. If multiple S3 downloads occur shortly after a login from a suspicious IP address, an alert is generated.

By following these practices, the company can effectively analyze logs to detect and respond to security threats, ensuring a robust security posture.

## 9.7 Lab Exercises
### 9.7.1 Setting Up CloudWatch Alarms

Setting up Amazon CloudWatch alarms to alert on specific metrics and thresholds is an essential skill for monitoring and maintaining the health and security of your AWS environment. This hands-on lab will guide you through the process step-by-step. We will use an example where we set up an alarm to monitor the CPU utilization of an EC2 instance and send an alert if it exceeds 80%.

#### Step 1: Sign in to AWS Management Console
Open the AWS Management Console and sign in to your account. Navigate to the Amazon CloudWatch service.

#### Step 2: Create a Metric Alarm
In the CloudWatch dashboard, click on "Alarms" in the left-hand menu. Click on the "Create Alarm" button.

#### Step 3: Select the Metric
Click on "Select metric". In the "Browse" tab, navigate to "EC2" and then "Per-Instance Metrics". Select the EC2 instance you want to monitor. Choose the "CPUUtilization" metric. Click "Select metric".

#### Step 4: Configure the Alarm
Set the "Period" to a time interval suitable for your monitoring needs (e.g., 5 minutes). Under "Conditions", set the threshold type to "Static". Enter "80" in the "Threshold value" field to set the alarm to trigger when CPU utilization exceeds 80%. Configure "Additional configuration" if needed, such as evaluation periods and datapoints to alarm.

#### Step 5: Configure Actions
Under "Configure actions", click on "Add notification". Choose "In alarm" as the condition. Select "Send a notification to an SNS topic". Click on "Create new topic" if you don't have an existing one. Enter a topic name (e.g., "HighCPUAlert") and an email address to receive the notifications. Click "Create topic". You will need to confirm the subscription by checking your email and clicking on the confirmation link sent by AWS SNS.

#### Step 6: Add Alarm Name and Description
Provide a name for the alarm (e.g., "High CPU Utilization Alarm"). Optionally, add a description to help identify the purpose of the alarm.

#### Step 7: Review and Create Alarm
Review the alarm configuration. Click on "Create alarm".

#### Example: Setting Up a CloudWatch Alarm for EC2 CPU Utilization
In this example, we set up an alarm for an EC2 instance to alert when its CPU utilization exceeds 80% for more than two 5-minute periods.

**Select Metric:** Navigate to EC2 > Per-Instance Metrics, and select the "CPUUtilization" metric for your specific instance.

**Set Conditions:**
- Period: 5 minutes
- Threshold type: Static
- Threshold value: Greater than 80%
- Datapoints to alarm: 2 out of 2

**Configure Actions:** Notification: Send a notification to an SNS topic "HighCPUAlert". Subscription: Add your email address to receive alerts.

**Add Alarm Name and Description:** Alarm Name: "High CPU Utilization Alarm" Description: "Alarm when CPU utilization exceeds 80% for more than 10 minutes"

Setting up CloudWatch alarms is a straightforward process that significantly enhances your ability to monitor and maintain AWS resources. By following these steps, you can create alarms that alert you to potential issues, allowing you to respond quickly and maintain system stability and security.

## 9.7.2 Configuring AWS Security Hub

Configuring AWS Security Hub and integrating it with other AWS security services provides a centralized view of security alerts and compliance status across your AWS environment. This practical exercise will guide you through the steps of setting up AWS Security Hub and integrating it with AWS services like GuardDuty, Inspector, and Macie for centralized monitoring.

### Step 1: Enable AWS Security Hub
- **Sign in to the AWS Management Console**.
- **Navigate to the Security Hub service:** In the AWS Management Console, type "Security Hub" in the search bar and select it from the dropdown menu.
- **Enable Security Hub:** On the Security Hub dashboard, click on the "Enable Security Hub" button. Follow the prompts to enable Security Hub in your AWS account and select the region where you want to enable it.

### Step 2: Enable Integrations with AWS Security Services
- **Navigate to the Integrations page:** In the Security Hub dashboard, click on "Settings" in the left-hand menu and then select "Integrations".
- **Enable AWS GuardDuty:** Find "Amazon GuardDuty" in the list of available integrations and click on "Enable". Follow the prompts to enable GuardDuty and integrate it with Security Hub.
- **Enable AWS Inspector:** Find "Amazon Inspector" in the list of available integrations and click on "Enable". Follow the prompts to enable Inspector and integrate it with Security Hub.
- **Enable AWS Macie:** Find "Amazon Macie" in the list of available integrations and click on "Enable". Follow the prompts to enable Macie and integrate it with Security Hub.

### Step 3: Configure AWS Security Hub Settings
**Set up AWS Config:** AWS Security Hub relies on AWS Config to provide a detailed inventory of your AWS resources and their configurations. Navigate to the AWS Config service and ensure it is enabled in your account. Follow the prompts to set up AWS Config if it is not already enabled.

**Configure Findings and Insights:** In the Security Hub dashboard, click on "Settings" and then "Standards". Enable the security standards you wish to use, such as the CIS AWS Foundations Benchmark or AWS Foundational Security Best Practices. Review and configure the specific controls and findings for each standard.

### Step 4: View and Analyze Security Findings
**Navigate to the Findings page:** In the Security Hub dashboard, click on "Findings" in the left-hand menu.
**Review Security Findings:** Security Hub aggregates findings from GuardDuty, Inspector, Macie, and other integrated services. Use the filters and search functionality to review and analyze security findings.

**Investigate Findings:** Click on individual findings to view detailed information, including the affected resources, severity, and remediation steps.

### Example: Integrating AWS GuardDuty with Security Hub
In this example, we will integrate AWS GuardDuty with Security Hub to centralize the monitoring of security findings.

**Enable GuardDuty:** Navigate to the GuardDuty service in the AWS Management Console. Click on "Get started" and enable GuardDuty for your account and region.

**Enable Integration in Security Hub:** In the Security Hub dashboard, go to "Settings" > "Integrations". Find "Amazon GuardDuty" and click "Enable".

**Review GuardDuty Findings in Security Hub:** After enabling the integration, navigate to the "Findings" page in Security Hub. Use the filter options to view findings sourced from GuardDuty.

Integrating AWS Security Hub with other AWS security services like GuardDuty, Inspector, and Macie enables centralized monitoring and provides a comprehensive view of your AWS environment's security posture. By following these steps, you can ensure that all critical security findings are aggregated in one place, making it easier to manage and respond to potential security threats.

## 9.7.3 Implementing VPC Flow Logs and Analyzing Data
Implementing VPC Flow Logs allows you to capture information about the IP traffic going to and from network interfaces in your VPC. You can analyze this data using CloudWatch Logs Insights to gain insights into your network traffic. This exercise will guide you through setting up VPC Flow Logs, capturing network traffic data, and analyzing it using CloudWatch Logs Insights.

### Step 1: Enable VPC Flow Logs
**Sign in to the AWS Management Console.**
**Navigate to the VPC service:** In the AWS Management Console, type "VPC" in the search bar and select it from the dropdown menu.
**Select Your VPC:** In the VPC Dashboard, click on "Your VPCs" in the left-hand menu. Select the VPC for which you want to enable Flow Logs.
**Create a Flow Log:** Click on the "Actions" button, then select "Create flow log".
**Configure Flow Log Settings:**
- Filter: Choose "All" to capture all traffic or "Reject" to capture only rejected traffic.
- Destination: Select "Send to CloudWatch Logs".
- Log Group: Create a new log group or choose an existing one (e.g., /aws/vpc/flow-logs).
- IAM Role: Create a new IAM role if one does not exist, with permissions to publish flow logs to CloudWatch Logs.
- Click "Create flow log".

## Step 2: Verify Flow Logs in CloudWatch
**Navigate to the CloudWatch service:** In the AWS Management Console, type "CloudWatch" in the search bar and select it from the dropdown menu.
**Check Log Groups:** In the CloudWatch dashboard, click on "Logs" in the left-hand menu. Verify that the log group you specified earlier (e.g., /aws/vpc/flow-logs) exists and is receiving data.

## Step 3: Analyze VPC Flow Logs using CloudWatch Logs Insights
**Navigate to CloudWatch Logs Insights:** In the CloudWatch dashboard, click on "Logs Insights" in the left-hand menu.
**Select Log Group:** Select the log group containing your VPC Flow Logs (e.g., /aws/vpc/flow-logs).
**Run a Query:** Use CloudWatch Logs Insights to run queries on your VPC Flow Logs. Example Query: To analyze the top talkers (source IP addresses) in your network:

```
1. fields @timestamp, srcAddr, dstAddr, srcPort, dstPort, action, bytes
2. | stats sum(bytes) as totalBytes by srcAddr
3. | sort totalBytes desc
4. | limit 20
```

## Step 4: Advanced Analysis with CloudWatch Logs Insights
**Identify Unusual Traffic Patterns:** Example Query: To identify traffic to a specific port:

```
1. fields @timestamp, srcAddr, dstAddr, srcPort, dstPort, action, bytes
2. | filter dstPort = 22
3. | sort @timestamp desc
4. | limit 20
```

**Investigate Dropped Traffic:** Example Query: To filter for rejected traffic:

```
1. fields @timestamp, srcAddr, dstAddr, srcPort, dstPort, action, bytes
2. | filter action = 'REJECT'
3. | sort @timestamp desc
4. | limit 20
```

## Example: Capturing and Analyzing SSH Traffic
In this example, we will capture and analyze SSH traffic (port 22) using VPC Flow Logs and CloudWatch Logs Insights.

**Create a Flow Log:** Follow the steps in Step 1 to create a flow log for your VPC.
**Verify Flow Logs:** Follow the steps in Step 2 to verify that flow logs are being captured in CloudWatch Logs.
**Run a Query to Analyze SSH Traffic:**
- Navigate to CloudWatch Logs Insights.
- Select the log group containing your VPC Flow Logs.
- Run the following query to analyze SSH traffic:

```
1. fields @timestamp, srcAddr, dstAddr, srcPort, dstPort, action, bytes
2. | filter dstPort = 22
3. | stats count(*) as connectionCount, sum(bytes) as totalBytes by srcAddr, dstAddr
4. | sort connectionCount desc
5. | limit 10
```

This query will display the top 10 source and destination IP pairs with the highest number of SSH connections.

By enabling VPC Flow Logs and analyzing them using CloudWatch Logs Insights, you can gain valuable insights into your network traffic. This exercise demonstrated how to set up VPC Flow Logs, verify data capture, and perform basic to advanced traffic analysis using CloudWatch Logs Insights. This approach helps in monitoring network activity, identifying potential security issues, and ensuring compliance with organizational policies.

## 9.7.4 Troubleshooting Logging and Monitoring Issues

This exercise will guide you through troubleshooting common issues with logging and monitoring configurations in AWS. By the end of this exercise, you will be able to identify, analyze, and resolve common issues to ensure your logging and monitoring systems are functioning correctly.

### Step 1: Identify Missing Logs in CloudWatch

**Check Log Group Configuration** Sign in to the AWS Management Console. Navigate to CloudWatch and click on "Logs" in the left-hand menu. Verify that the log group for your application or service exists.

**Verify Log Stream Configuration:** Within the log group, ensure that the relevant log streams are present. If log streams are missing, check the configuration of your application or service to ensure it is sending logs to the correct log group.

### Step 2: Troubleshoot IAM Permissions Issues

**Check IAM Role Permissions:** Navigate to the IAM service in the AWS Management Console. Identify the IAM role associated with your application or service. Verify that the IAM role has the necessary permissions to write logs to CloudWatch.

Example Policy:

```
1.  {
2.    "Version": "2012-10-17",
3.    "Statement": [
4.      {
5.        "Effect": "Allow",
6.        "Action": [
7.          "logs:CreateLogGroup",
8.          "logs:CreateLogStream",
9.          "logs:PutLogEvents"
10.       ],
11.       "Resource": "*"
12.     }
13.   ]
14. }
```

**Update IAM Role Permissions:** If the IAM role lacks the necessary permissions, update the policy to include the required actions. Save the changes and redeploy your application or service if necessary.

### Step 3: Analyze Log Data Issues

**Check Log Format and Structure:** Navigate to CloudWatch Logs and select the log group. Open a few log streams and examine the log events. Verify that the logs are in the expected format and contain the necessary information.

**Verify Application Logging Configuration:** Check the logging configuration of your application or service. Ensure that log levels (e.g., INFO, ERROR) and log formats are correctly set.

**Example Configuration for an EC2 Instance Running a Web Server (Apache):** SSH into the EC2 instance. Open the Apache configuration file (e.g., /etc/httpd/conf/httpd.conf). Ensure the ErrorLog and CustomLog directives are correctly configured:

```
1. ErrorLog /var/log/httpd/error_log
2. CustomLog /var/log/httpd/access_log combined
```

Restart Apache to apply the changes:

```
1. sudo service httpd restart
```

### Step 4: Validate Log Ingestion and Analysis
**Verify CloudWatch Log Insights Queries:** Navigate to CloudWatch Logs Insights. Select the log group and run a basic query to validate log ingestion:

```
1. fields @timestamp, @message
2. | sort @timestamp desc
3. | limit 20
4.
```

Ensure that recent log events are displayed.

**Check Log Stream Activity:** In CloudWatch Logs, select a log stream and check for recent activity. If log events are missing or delayed, investigate the application or service to ensure it is actively generating logs.

### Step 5: Troubleshoot Specific Log Issues
**Handling Missing Log Events:** If specific log events are missing, verify that the application or service is configured to log those events. For example, if database query logs are missing, ensure the database logging is enabled and configured correctly.

**Resolve Log Formatting Issues:** If logs are not formatted correctly, update the application or service logging configuration.

Example: For a Python application using the logging module, ensure the log format is specified correctly:

```
1. import logging
2. logging.basicConfig(
3.     level=logging.INFO,
4.     format='%(asctime)s %(levelname)s %(message)s',
5.     handlers=[
6.         logging.FileHandler("app.log"),
7.         logging.StreamHandler()
8.     ]
9. )
```

By following these step-by-step instructions, you can troubleshoot and resolve common issues with logging and monitoring configurations in AWS. Ensuring that logs are correctly captured, formatted, and analyzed is critical for maintaining the security and compliance of your AWS environments.

## 9.7.5 Creating Log Analysis Dashboards
This hands-on lab will guide you through creating dashboards in Amazon CloudWatch and using Amazon Athena to query and analyze log data. By the end of this lab, you will have a comprehensive understanding of how to visualize and analyze your AWS logs.

## Part 1: Creating Dashboards in CloudWatch

### Step 1: Create a CloudWatch Dashboard
**Sign in to the AWS Management Console.**
**Navigate to the CloudWatch service:** In the AWS Management Console, type "CloudWatch" in the search bar and select it from the dropdown menu.

**Create a New Dashboard:** In the CloudWatch dashboard, click on "Dashboards" in the left-hand menu. Click on the "Create dashboard" button. Enter a name for your dashboard (e.g., "MyDashboard") and click "Create dashboard".

### Step 2: Add Widgets to the Dashboard
**Add a Line Graph Widget:** In the "Add widget" dialog, select "Line" and click "Configure". Choose the metric you want to visualize (e.g., EC2 CPU Utilization). Configure the metric settings, such as period and statistic (e.g., Average). Click "Create widget".

**Add a Text Widget:** Click "Add widget" again. Select "Text" and click "Configure". Enter the desired text, such as a summary or description of the dashboard. Click "Create widget".

**Add Other Widgets:** Repeat the process to add other widgets, such as "Number", "Stacked area", or "Query results", depending on your needs.

### Step 3: Save and View the Dashboard
**Save the Dashboard:** After adding all desired widgets, click "Save dashboard".
**View the Dashboard:** The dashboard will now display real-time metrics based on the widgets you added. You can edit or add more widgets at any time by clicking the "Actions" button on the dashboard.

## Part 2: Using Athena to Query and Analyze Log Data

### Step 1: Set Up Athena
**Navigate to the Athena service:** In the AWS Management Console, type "Athena" in the search bar and select it from the dropdown menu.
**Set Up a Query Result Location:** If this is your first time using Athena, you need to set up a query result location. Click on "Get Started". In the "Settings" dialog, specify an S3 bucket where query results will be stored (e.g., s3://my-athena-query-results/). Click "Save".

### Step 2: Create a Database and Table for Log Data
**Create a Database:** In the Athena query editor, enter the following SQL statement to create a database:

```
1. CREATE DATABASE my_log_data;
```

Click "Run query".

**Create a Table for Log Data:** Assume you have CloudTrail logs stored in an S3 bucket (e.g., s3://my-cloudtrail-logs/). Create a table to query these logs:

```
1.  CREATE EXTERNAL TABLE my_log_data.cloudtrail_logs (
2.    eventVersion STRING,
3.    userIdentity STRUCT<
4.      type: STRING,
5.      principalId: STRING,
6.      arn: STRING,
7.      accountId: STRING,
8.      invokedBy: STRING,
9.      accessKeyId: STRING,
10.     userName: STRING,
11.     sessionContext: STRUCT<
12.       attributes: STRUCT<
13.         mfaAuthenticated: STRING,
14.         creationDate: STRING
15.     >,
```

```
16.          sessionIssuer: STRUCT<
17.            type: STRING,
18.            principalId: STRING,
19.            arn: STRING,
20.            accountId: STRING,
21.            userName: STRING
22.          >
23.        >
24.    >,
25.    eventTime STRING,
26.    eventSource STRING,
27.    eventName STRING,
28.    awsRegion STRING,
29.    sourceIPAddress STRING,
30.    userAgent STRING,
31.    errorCode STRING,
32.    errorMessage STRING,
33.    requestParameters STRING,
34.    responseElements STRING,
35.    additionalEventData STRING,
36.    requestId STRING,
37.    eventId STRING,
38.    readOnly STRING,
39.    resources ARRAY<STRUCT<
40.      arn: STRING,
41.      accountId: STRING,
42.      type: STRING
43.    >>,
44.    eventType STRING,
45.    apiVersion STRING,
46.    managementEvent STRING,
47.    recipientAccountId STRING,
48.    sharedEventID STRING,
49.    vpcEndpointId STRING
50. )
51. ROW FORMAT SERDE 'com.amazon.emr.hive.serde.CloudTrailSerde'
52. STORED AS INPUTFORMAT 'com.amazon.emr.cloudtrail.CloudTrailInputFormat'
53. OUTPUTFORMAT 'org.apache.hadoop.hive.ql.io.HiveIgnoreKeyTextOutputFormat'
54. LOCATION 's3://my-cloudtrail-logs/';
55.
```

Adjust the LOCATION parameter to point to your CloudTrail logs in S3. Click "Run query".

## Step 3: Query the Log Data

**Run a Basic Query:** Enter the following SQL query to retrieve the first 10 records from the CloudTrail logs:

```
1. SELECT * FROM my_log_data.cloudtrail_logs
2. LIMIT 10;
```

Click "Run query". Review the results in the query output pane.

**Analyze Specific Events:** Run a query to identify specific events, such as failed login attempts:

```
1. SELECT eventTime, eventName, userIdentity.userName, sourceIPAddress
2. FROM my_log_data.cloudtrail_logs
3. WHERE eventName = 'ConsoleLogin' AND errorMessage = 'Failed authentication';
```

Click "Run query" and analyze the results.

By following these step-by-step instructions, you can create dashboards in CloudWatch to visualize important metrics and use Athena to query and analyze log data for detailed insights. This hands-on lab equips you with the skills to monitor and analyze your AWS environment effectively, helping you maintain security and operational efficiency.

## 9.8 Key Exam Tips

### Master AWS Services for Monitoring and Alarms

**CloudWatch:** Know how to use CloudWatch for setting up alarms, dashboards, and monitoring metrics related to security events. You should be able to create custom metrics, set up thresholds for specific alarms, and configure notification systems like Amazon SNS for alerts.

**AWS Config:** Understand how AWS Config tracks configuration changes and provides compliance reports. Focus on its ability to detect changes in your environment that may indicate security issues.

**CloudTrail:** CloudTrail is crucial for logging API calls and user activities across AWS. Know how to analyze CloudTrail logs for suspicious activities such as unauthorized access or configuration changes.

### Set Up Automated Alerts

**Automated Alerts with CloudWatch:** Be prepared to configure CloudWatch Alarms to send alerts when security thresholds are breached (e.g., unauthorized API calls, changes in security group configurations).

**AWS Security Hub:** Familiarize yourself with how Security Hub aggregates and prioritizes security findings from services like GuardDuty, AWS Config, and Macie. Learn to integrate it into your monitoring workflow to streamline alerts.

**SNS for Notifications:** Use Amazon SNS to send alerts and notifications based on CloudWatch Alarms or Security Hub findings. Ensure you understand how to set up cross-account alerts for a centralized view of your organization's security.

### Understand Monitoring Metrics and Baselines

**Metric Baselines:** Know how to establish baselines for normal system behavior to detect anomalies. For example, setting a baseline for CPU usage, network traffic, or the number of failed login attempts can help detect unusual patterns.

**Anomaly Detection:** Explore the use of Amazon GuardDuty and AWS CloudWatch Anomaly Detection to automatically detect outliers in metrics and trigger alerts.

### Design Monitoring Solutions

**Centralized Monitoring:** Learn how to design a centralized monitoring solution using CloudWatch to gather logs and metrics from various services, and CloudWatch Logs Insights to query log data for detailed analysis.

**Cross-Account Monitoring:** Know how to implement cross-account monitoring using AWS Organizations, CloudWatch cross-account dashboards, and AWS Security Hub to track security incidents across multiple AWS accounts.

### Implement Automated Audits

**AWS Config Rules:** Familiarize yourself with AWS Config Rules to automatically evaluate whether your AWS resources comply with best practices or organizational policies.

**Security Audits:** Use Security Hub to run automated security checks and compliance reports. Be sure to understand how to audit your environment for regulatory compliance (e.g., PCI DSS, CIS AWS Foundations Benchmark).

### Log Management and Configuration

**CloudWatch Logs:** Ensure you know how to set up CloudWatch Logs to capture logs from services like CloudTrail, VPC Flow Logs, and custom application logs. Know how to configure retention periods and apply lifecycle management policies.

**S3 for Log Storage:** Be familiar with best practices for storing logs in Amazon S3, including the use of S3 lifecycle policies for archiving and deleting old logs.
**Log Group and Stream Organization:** Organize logs into appropriate log groups and log streams for easier management and querying.

### Troubleshooting Monitoring and Logging Issues
**Analyzing Security Events:** Know how to troubleshoot security events by reviewing logs using CloudWatch Logs Insights or Athena for deep log analysis. This could involve investigating unauthorized access, network traffic anomalies, or service misconfigurations.
**Log Misconfigurations:** Learn how to troubleshoot missing logs, improper log storage, or logs that are not being generated by services like CloudTrail or VPC Flow Logs. Ensure that logging is enabled and configured correctly.
**Access Permissions for Logging:** Understand the importance of setting appropriate IAM permissions for accessing and managing logs to avoid unauthorized access.

### Design Log Analysis Solutions
**Tools for Log Analysis:** Be proficient in using tools like Amazon Athena, CloudWatch Logs Insights, and AWS Lambda for automating log analysis and responding to security events.
**Log Formats:** Understand the common log formats generated by AWS services (e.g., JSON for CloudTrail logs) and know how to parse these logs for useful information.
**Correlation of Logs:** Be prepared to correlate data across multiple logs (e.g., VPC Flow Logs, CloudTrail, and GuardDuty) to get a full picture of a security incident.

### Best Practices for Logging and Monitoring
**Logging Best Practices:** Enable logging for all critical services, such as CloudTrail, VPC Flow Logs, and S3 Access Logs. Regularly review these logs to detect any anomalies or unauthorized access.
**Monitoring Solutions:** Ensure continuous monitoring by using automated tools like AWS Config, CloudWatch, and GuardDuty. Use dashboards to visualize real-time metrics and security events.
**Secure Log Storage:** Securely store logs by using S3 encryption (KMS keys) and restricting access via IAM roles. Ensure logs are immutable by using S3 Object Lock or Glacier Vault Lock.

### Incident Response Preparedness
**Real-Time Alerts:** Configure real-time alerts for critical security events, ensuring your security team is notified immediately when incidents occur.
**Runbooks for Logging:** Develop incident response runbooks that detail how to respond to security events based on logs and alerts. Automate these processes using AWS Lambda and EventBridge.

### Summary
Mastering the logging and monitoring features of AWS services like CloudWatch, AWS Config, Security Hub, and Athena is critical for success in the exam. You need to be able to design solutions that provide visibility into your AWS environment, automate monitoring and auditing processes, and ensure logs are properly managed and analyzed. Understanding how to troubleshoot issues with logging and monitoring is equally important to ensure continuous security operations in your AWS environment.

## 9.9 Chapter Review Questions
**Question 1:**
Which AWS service is primarily used for collecting, monitoring, and analyzing log files from various AWS resources and applications?
A. AWS Config
B. AWS CloudTrail

C. Amazon CloudWatch Logs
D. AWS Lambda

**Question 2:**
What is the role of AWS CloudTrail in security logging and monitoring?
A. Encrypts data at rest
B. Logs API calls made to AWS services
C. Automatically remediates security issues
D. Manages access to AWS resources

**Question 3:**
Which service can be used to set alarms based on metric thresholds to automatically alert administrators of security anomalies?
A. Amazon Macie
B. AWS Config
C. Amazon CloudWatch
D. AWS Security Hub

**Question 4:**
What is one of the key elements to consider when designing a monitoring solution for AWS resources?
A. Choosing appropriate encryption algorithms
B. Identifying metrics and baselines for normal behavior
C. Creating IAM roles for all users
D. Automating backups of all EC2 instances

**Question 5:**
Which service can be used to automate security audits by continuously checking the compliance of AWS resources?
A. AWS Config
B. Amazon GuardDuty
C. AWS CloudTrail
D. AWS Lambda

**Question 6:**
Which of the following is a best practice for log lifecycle management in AWS?
A. Retaining all logs indefinitely
B. Automatically archiving logs to Amazon S3
C. Storing logs on EC2 instances
D. Enabling logging only for critical services

**Question 7:**
In the context of logging and monitoring, what is the primary function of Amazon CloudWatch Logs Insights?
A. Encrypting log data
B. Automating log retention policies
C. Providing interactive queries and real-time log analysis
D. Managing permissions for logging services

**Question 8:**
Which AWS service allows you to monitor and track changes to your AWS resources and trigger alerts for non-compliance?
A. AWS Lambda
B. AWS Config

C. Amazon Macie
D. Amazon S3

**Question 9:**
When setting up a monitoring solution, why is it important to define appropriate thresholds for metrics?
A. To determine when resources should be archived
B. To identify deviations from normal behavior and trigger alerts
C. To minimize costs associated with data retention
D. To reduce the number of IAM policies created

**Question 10:**
Which AWS service can be used to troubleshoot missing log data by analyzing access permissions and identifying misconfigurations?
A. AWS Security Hub
B. AWS Config
C. AWS CloudTrail
D. Amazon CloudWatch

**Question 11:**
You have deployed an application in AWS, and your team has noticed performance degradation during peak traffic. To ensure that you can quickly detect similar performance issues in the future, you want to set up an automated monitoring and alerting system. Which AWS service should you use, and how can it help detect such issues?
A. Amazon Macie for sensitive data monitoring
B. AWS Config to audit resource configurations
C. Amazon CloudWatch to monitor performance metrics and trigger alerts
D. AWS Lambda to automatically scale resources

**Question 12:**
During a security audit, you discovered that logs from some critical EC2 instances are missing. After investigating, you find that logging was not enabled on these instances. What steps should you take to troubleshoot and resolve this issue to ensure logs are consistently collected in the future?
A. Reboot the EC2 instances to generate new logs
B. Enable CloudWatch Logs for the EC2 instances and verify log group permissions
C. Terminate the instances and deploy new ones
D. Configure CloudTrail logging and rerun the audit

**Question 13:**
Your security team has set up CloudWatch alarms to monitor unusual activity in your VPC. You have received multiple alerts indicating potential unauthorized access attempts from different IP addresses. How can you automate the response to these alerts to block the suspicious IPs?
A. Use AWS Config to automatically apply new security group rules
B. Manually update the network ACLs to block the IP addresses
C. Use Amazon CloudWatch with AWS Lambda to trigger automated security group updates based on alarms
D. Deploy AWS Shield Advanced to block the IP addresses

**Question 14:**
You are responsible for designing a centralized logging solution for multiple AWS accounts. Your goal is to consolidate and analyze all logs in one location to detect security threats across your organization. Which AWS service should you use to achieve this, and what key feature will assist you in analyzing the logs?
A. AWS Systems Manager for centralized configuration
B. Amazon S3 for long-term log storage

C. AWS Security Hub for centralized security findings
D. Amazon CloudWatch Logs Insights for querying and analyzing logs from multiple accounts

**Question 15:**
Your team has implemented a logging solution for an application, but during an incident investigation, you realize that certain logs are missing critical security details. How can you troubleshoot this issue and ensure future logs contain the required information for security analysis?
A. Review IAM permissions for log access
B. Analyze log format requirements and update logging configurations
C. Enable multi-factor authentication (MFA) on the instances
D. Increase the instance type for the application

## 9.10 Answers to Chapter Review Questions

1. C. Amazon CloudWatch Logs
Explanation: Amazon CloudWatch Logs is the primary AWS service used for collecting, monitoring, and analyzing log files from AWS resources and applications, providing real-time monitoring and alerting based on log data.

2. B. Logs API calls made to AWS services
Explanation: AWS CloudTrail logs API calls made to AWS services, providing detailed records of who accessed what resources, which is essential for auditing and security monitoring.

3. C. Amazon CloudWatch
Explanation: Amazon CloudWatch allows you to set alarms based on specific metric thresholds, helping administrators monitor resource performance and detect anomalies in real-time.

4. B. Identifying metrics and baselines for normal behavior
Explanation: Identifying metrics and establishing baselines for normal behavior helps in detecting anomalies or deviations, which can indicate potential security incidents or performance issues.

5. A. AWS Config
Explanation: AWS Config helps automate security audits by continuously checking the compliance of AWS resources against defined configuration rules and alerting administrators of non-compliance.

6. B. Automatically archiving logs to Amazon S3
Explanation: A best practice for log lifecycle management is to automatically archive logs to Amazon S3 to ensure cost-effective long-term storage and easy access for auditing purposes.

7. C. Providing interactive queries and real-time log analysis
Explanation: Amazon CloudWatch Logs Insights provides an interactive query engine for real-time analysis of logs, enabling administrators to filter, search, and visualize log data.

8. B. AWS Config
Explanation: AWS Config monitors and tracks changes to AWS resources and can trigger alerts for non-compliance based on predefined rules, ensuring that your environment meets security and compliance requirements.

9. B. To identify deviations from normal behavior and trigger alerts
Explanation: Defining appropriate thresholds for metrics allows you to detect deviations from expected behavior, helping to identify potential security issues or performance anomalies.

10. B. AWS Config
Explanation: AWS Config can be used to troubleshoot missing log data by analyzing access permissions and identifying misconfigurations that may have prevented logging from working correctly.

11. C. Amazon CloudWatch to monitor performance metrics and trigger alerts
Explanation: Amazon CloudWatch can monitor key performance metrics (CPU, memory, etc.) and set alarms to notify administrators when thresholds are breached, enabling timely detection and response to performance issues.

12. B. Enable CloudWatch Logs for the EC2 instances and verify log group permissions
Explanation: Enabling CloudWatch Logs for your EC2 instances and ensuring that the correct permissions are set for log groups will allow you to collect and store logs consistently, preventing future log loss.

13. C. Use Amazon CloudWatch with AWS Lambda to trigger automated security group updates based on alarms
Explanation: You can set up Amazon CloudWatch to monitor specific security events and use AWS Lambda to automate the response, such as updating security groups to block suspicious IP addresses in real time.

14. D. Amazon CloudWatch Logs Insights for querying and analyzing logs from multiple accounts
Explanation: Amazon CloudWatch Logs Insights allows you to query and analyze logs across multiple AWS accounts, providing visibility into security events and enabling centralized log analysis for threat detection.

15. B. Analyze log format requirements and update logging configurations
Explanation: If logs are missing critical information, reviewing and updating the log format and configurations ensures that future logs include the necessary details for effective security monitoring and analysis.

# Chapter 10. AWS Networking Essentials

**This chapter addresses the following exam objectives:**
Domain 3: Infrastructure Security
Task Statement 3.2: Design and implement network security controls.

◆◆◆◆◆◆

Networking forms the backbone of any cloud infrastructure, and understanding its fundamentals is crucial for designing and managing robust AWS environments. This chapter provides a comprehensive guide to key networking concepts and services within AWS, enabling you to build secure, efficient, and scalable network architectures.

We begin with an exploration of Classless Inter-Domain Routing (CIDR) for IPv4, breaking down its components and the importance of subnet masks in IP address allocation. Understanding the difference between public and private IP addresses sets the stage for more complex networking concepts.

The chapter delves into AWS Virtual Private Cloud (VPC), a fundamental service that allows you to launch AWS resources in a logically isolated virtual network. We discuss VPC subnets and the role of the Internet Gateway (IGW) in enabling communication between VPC resources and the internet.

Routing within VPCs is covered in detail, including considerations for VPC resources communicating with the internet and the significance of private subnets. Bastion hosts and NAT gateways are introduced as essential components for securing and managing access to your VPC.

AWS network security is a critical topic, encompassing security groups, network access control lists (NACLs), ephemeral ports, and the flow of requests and responses through these security mechanisms. We provide guidance on troubleshooting issues related to security groups and NACLs, highlighting the differences between them.

VPC Flow Logs and their creation, analysis, and usage are discussed, providing insights into monitoring and troubleshooting network traffic By the end of this chapter, readers will have a thorough understanding of AWS networking essentials.

## 10.1 Understanding CIDR – IPv4

CIDR (Classless Inter-Domain Routing) is a method for allocating IP addresses that improves the efficiency of address distribution in a network. The CIDR is used in Security Groups rules and AWS networking in general.

| IP version | Type | Protocol | Port range | Source | Description |
|---|---|---|---|---|---|
| IPv4 | HTTPS | TCP | 443 | 0.0.0.0/0 | - |
| IPv4 | HTTP | TCP | 80 | 0.0.0.0/0 | - |
| IPv4 | SSH | TCP | 22 | 73.81.154.236/32 | - |

They help to define an IP address range.
- For example, in XX.YY.ZZ.WW/32. The CIDR XX.YY.ZZ.WW/32 has an IP address range for one IP. In 0.0.0.0/0. the CIDR 0.0.0.0/0 has an IP address range for all IPs.
- We can also define, for example, 192.168.0.0/27. The CIDR 192.168.0.0/27 has an IP address range from 192.168.0.0 – 192.168.0.31 (32 IP addresses). It means if you use this CIDR, you will be able to allocate 32 different IP addresses for different machines in your network.

## 10.1.1 CIDR Components

A CIDR has two components: base IP address and subnet mask.

**Base IP:** Base IP represents an IP address part in the range -- similar to what would be seen in a normal IP address, such as 192.168.0.0, 10.0.0.0, etc.

**Subnet Mask:** CIDR notation is just shorthand for the subnet mask and represents the number of bits available to the IP address. For instance, the /24 in 192.168.0.101/24 is equivalent to the IP address 192.168.0.101 and the subnet mask 255.255.255.0 Or we can also understand it in another way, as a subnet mask defines how many bits can be changed in the CIDR. For example:
- /8 ⇔ 255.0.0.0 [ last three octets can change]
- /16 ⇔ 255.255.0.0 [ last two octets can change]
- /24 ⇔ 255.255.255.0 [ last octets can change]
- /32 ⇔ 255.255.255.255 [no octet can change]

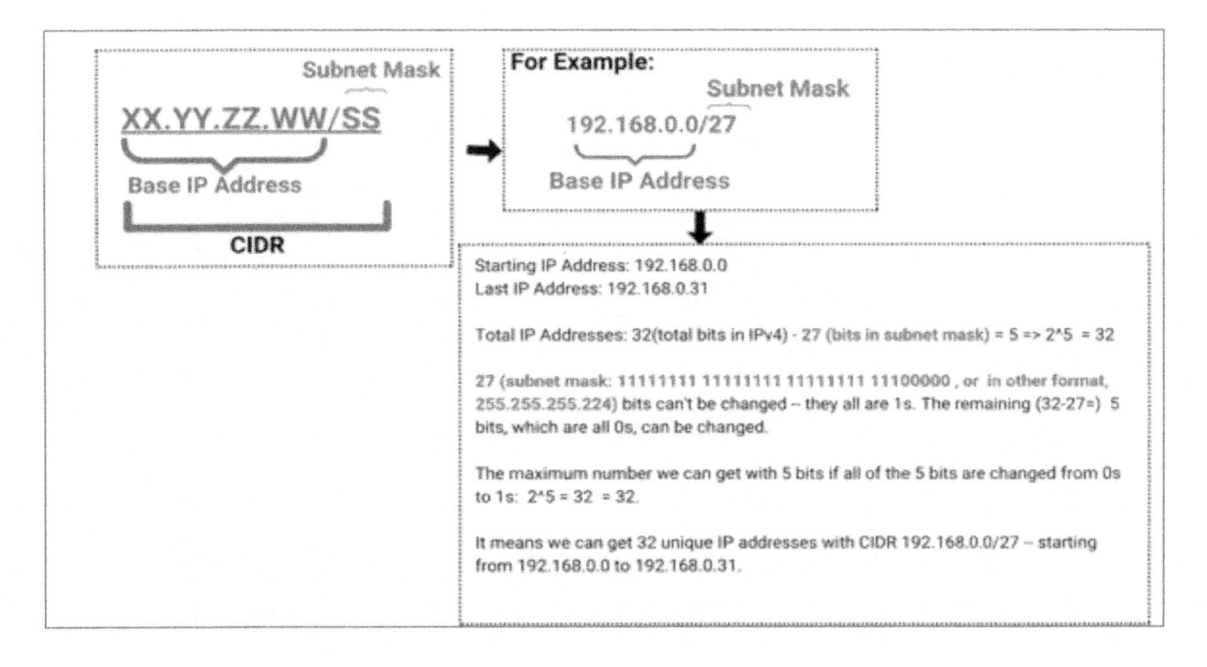

XX.YY.ZZ.WW/SS
- Base IP Address
- Subnet Mask
- CIDR

For Example: 192.168.0.0/27
- Base IP Address
- Subnet Mask

Starting IP Address: 192.168.0.0
Last IP Address: 192.168.0.31

Total IP Addresses: 32(total bits in IPv4) - 27 (bits in subnet mask) = 5 => 2^5 = 32

27 (subnet mask: 11111111 11111111 11111111 11100000, or in other format, 255.255.255.224) bits can't be changed -- they all are 1s. The remaining (32-27=) 5 bits, which are all 0s, can be changed.

The maximum number we can get with 5 bits if all of the 5 bits are changed from 0s to 1s: 2^5 = 32 = 32.

It means we can get 32 unique IP addresses with CIDR 192.168.0.0/27 – starting from 192.168.0.0 to 192.168.0.31.

## 10.1.2 Subnet Mask
The Subnet mask allows to the allocation of a range of IP addresses starting from the base IP. The concept depends on changing bits that can be changed. For example, if the subnet mask is /27, we can change 32-27 = 5 bits from 0 to 1 to get different IP addresses. The one permutation is when all 5 bits are 1s. and that will be the last IP address for the CIDR having subnet mask /27. Let's see in detail to get a better understanding.

```
198.198.0.0 /32 => allows for (32-32 = 0 ) => 2^0 = 1 IP address => 192.168.0.0
198.198.0.0 /31 => allows for (32-31 = 1 ) => 2^1 = 2 IP addresses => 192.168.0.0 -> 192.168.0.1
198.198.0.0 /30 => allows for (32-32 = 2 ) => 2^2 = 4 IP addresses => 192.168.0.0 -> 192.168.0.3
198.198.0.0 /29 => allows for (32-29 = 3 ) => 2^3 = 8 IP addresses => 192.168.0.0 -> 192.168.0.7
198.198.0.0 /28 => allows for (32-28 = 4 ) => 2^4 = 16 IP addresses => 192.168.0.0 -> 192.168.0.15
198.198.0.0 /27 => allows for (32-27 = 5 ) => 2^5 = 32 IP addresses => 192.168.0.0 -> 192.168.0.31
198.198.0.0 /26 => allows for (32-26 = 6 ) => 2^6 = 64 IP addresses => 192.168.0.0 -> 192.168.0.63
198.198.0.0 /25 => allows for (32-25 = 7 ) => 2^7 = 128 IP addresses => 192.168.0.0 -> 192.168.0.127
198.198.0.0 /24 => allows for (32-24 = 8 ) => 2^8 = 256 IP addresses => 192.168.0.0 -> 192.168.0.255
...
198.198.0.0 /16 => allows for (32-16 = 16 ) => 2^16 = 65536 IP addresses => 192.168.0.0 -> 192.168.255.255
...
198.198.0.0 / 1 => allows for (32-1= 31 ) => 2^31 = 214,748,364,8 IP addresses => 192.168.0.0 ->255.255.255.255
```

## 10.1.3 CIDR – Review Exercise
192.168.0.0/24 =? => 192.168.0.0 – 192.168.0.255 (256 IPs)
192.168.0.0/16 = ? => 192.168.0.0 – 192.168.255.255 (65,536 IPs)
134.56.78.123/32 =? => just 134.56.78.123
0.0.0.0/0 => All IPs!

When you need a quick look-up, you can use: https://www.ipaddressguide.com/cidr

## 10.2 Public vs. Private IP Address
### Public IP Address
A public IP address is a unique identifier assigned to your internet connection (or router) by your ISP (Internet Service Provider). Your router uses its public IP address to communicate with the rest of the internet. This address is unique, meaning other devices do not use it. Public IP addresses are used to communicate with sites and servers on the internet. They are traceable by ISPs, advertisers, governments, and hackers. You can find your public IP address by searching for "What is my IP address" on Google.

### Private IP Address
On the other hand, the private IP address identifies different devices connected to the same local network. Once your router has received information from the global network to send to one of the devices on your network, it needs to know which device to send it to. The private IP address helps the router identify different devices on your network to forward the response. Private IP addresses are not unique; different routers can reuse them. These addresses are used to communicate between devices on a local network and are traceable by other devices on the same network. You can find a private IP address by using system settings and preferences.

### IP Addresses for Public and Private IP
The Internet Assigned Numbers Authority (IANA) established certain blocks of IPv4 addresses for the use of private (LAN) and public (Internet) addresses.
- Private IP can only allow specific values:
- 10.0.0.0 – 10.255.255.255 (10.0.0.0/8) [ Used commonly in big networks which need lots of IP addresses]
- 172.16.0.0 – 172.31.255.255 (172.16.0.0/12) [AWS default VPC range]
- 192.168.0.0 – 192.168.255.255 (192.168.0.0/16) [Used commonly in home networks]
- All the rest of the IP addresses on the internet are Public IP addresses.

## 10.3 AWS VPC
Virtual Private Cloud (VPC) is conceptually like a traditional network in a data center, with the additional benefits of leveraging the massively scalable infrastructure of AWS. Virtual Private Cloud (VPC) enables you to launch AWS resources into the network you have set up.

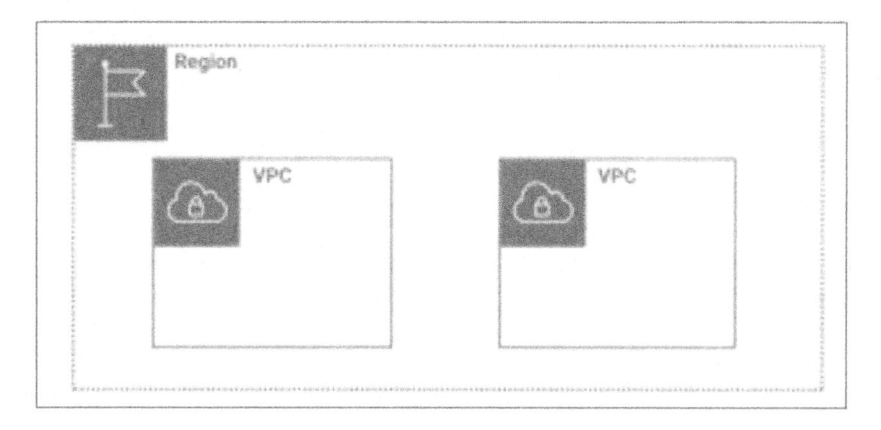

A Virtual Private Cloud (VPC) allows selecting your IP address range, creating subnets, and configure route tables and network gateways. A Virtual Private Cloud (VPC) controls how the AWS resources inside your network are exposed to the Internet.

### IP Address CIDR Block
Let's start with IP addresses. At the time of AWS account creation, you get a default VPC. So, for example, in my AWS account, with N. Virginia is the default AWS Region, and the CIDR range for the VPC is 172.31.0.0/16.

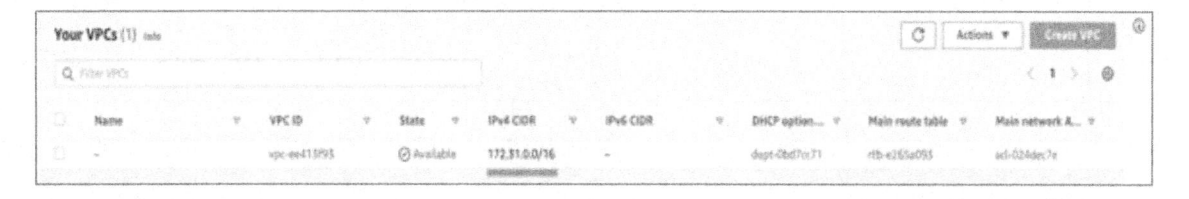

In the CIDR block (172.31.0.0/16.), the first half portion of the first two octets ("172.31") describes the network portion of the IP address, and the next two octets ("0.0") represent the host portion of the IP address. The "172.31.*" is a private IP range. If you use this IP range in your private VPC, you will not have overlapping or conflict with any other IP address on the Internet. We should not have overlapping IP addresses because overlapping IP addresses can't talk to each other.

Let's talk about the host portion of the CIDR block (172.31.0.0/16). In the host portion of the CIDR block, we have "0.0/16," -- which means we can get around 65536 IP addresses. There are many IP addresses to launch resources in a private network. When defining your IP CIDR block, think about how many resources you will be launching and choose the IP address CIDR block accordingly.

## 10.4 VPC Subnets

What is a subnet? -- A subnet is a range of IP addresses in your VPC. You can launch AWS resources into a specific subnet, such as EC2 instances. When you create a subnet, you specify a subset of the VPC CIDR block for the subnet. Each subnet must reside entirely within one Availability Zone (AZ) and cannot span zones. Launching instances in separate Availability Zones can protect your applications from the failure of a single zone.

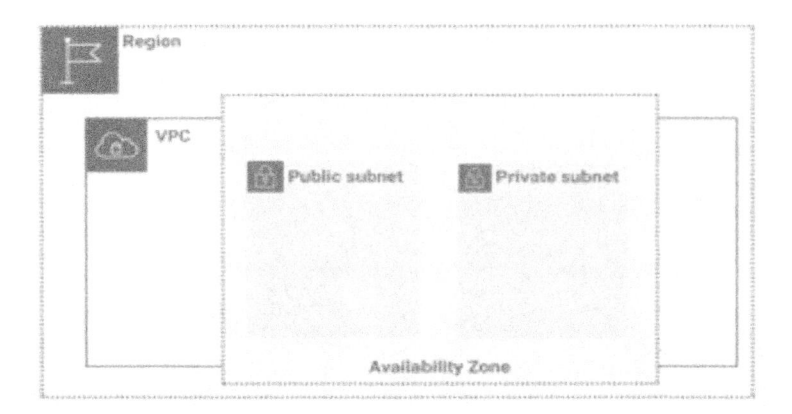

When a default VPC is created, AWS creates subnets based on the number of Availability Zones (AZs) and assigns a CIDR range to each subnet. It establishes one subnet for each AZ. When creating yourself, assign IP address CIDR to each subnet of the VPC and make sure there are no overlapping IP addresses.

As you can see in the screenshot, in the default VPC with six subnets – there are six AZs in the us-east-1 (N. Virginia) Region. Each of them has been assigned a CIDR range. Each AZ has one or more data centers with a separate power grid, away from the city to avoid floods or other natural calamities.

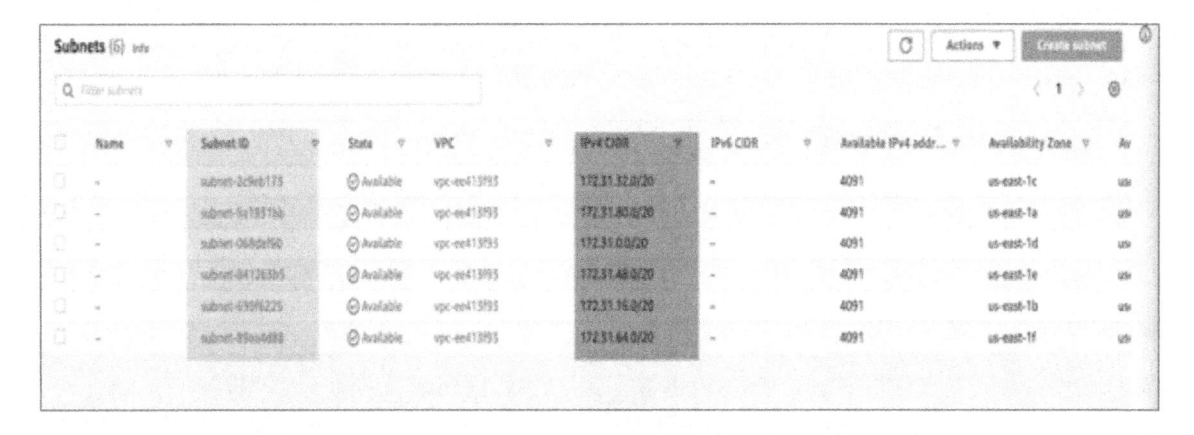

Each AZ is associated with a subnet in a Region. This subnet association with an AZ helps resources in a subnet talk to resources in the other subnet using their private address yet having logical separation.

When defining your subnet, we need to put subnet in AZs so that they can talk to a subnet of other AZs in the same Region. To do that, we need to divide the CIDR range of VPC into different subnets. For example, from the screenshot of the subnets given above, in the case of subnet-2c9eb173, the IPv4 CIDR is 172.31.32.0/20. That means the network address for this subnet is 172.31.32.0 and starting IP address for the first host is 172.31.33.0, and the ending IP address is 172.31.46.255, with the max possible hosts in this subnet being 4094.

You can use the CIDR calculator https://codebeautify.org/cidr-calculator to get the ideal network address and max hosts about other subnets based on the CIDR block address. As you can see in the default setting with VPC IP CIDR (172.31.0.0/16), the first two octets are used for the network portion of subnets.

### Private Subnet
You need a private subnet when you want your AWS resources not reachable from the Internet. In the case of a private subnet, the Route table associated with the subnet doesn't have an association with the Internet Gateway. In other words, there will be no entry for the Internet Gateway in the Route table.

**KEY POINTS**
- You can have multiple VPCs in an AWS region -- the maximum of 5 VPCs per region, which is a soft limit.
- For each CIDR, the minimum size is /28 (16 IP addresses), and the maximum size is /16 (65536 IP addresses).
- Because VPC is private, only Private IPv4 ranges are allowed:
    - 10.0.0.0 – 10.255.255.255 (10.0.0.0/8)
    - 172.16.0.0 – 172.31.255.255 (172.16.0.0/12)
    - 192.168.0.0 – 192.168.255.255 (192.168.0.0/16
- VPC CIDRs should NOT overlap.
- AWS reserves 5 IP addresses in each subnet – the first four and the last one from the CIDR range. These 5 IP addresses are unavailable for use and can't be assigned to an EC2 instance.
- Example: if a subnet has CIDR block 10.0.0.0/24, then reserved IP addresses are:
    - 10.0.0.0 – network address
    - 10.0.0.1 – reserved by AWS for the VPC router
    - 10.0.0.2 – reserved by AWS for mapping to Amazon-provided DNS
    - 10.0.0.3 – reserved by AWS for future use
    - 10.0.0.255 – Network broadcast addresses AWS does not support broadcast in a VPC; therefore, the address is reserved.
    
    (Reference: https://docs.aws.amazon.com/vpc/latest/userguide/configure-subnets.html)

- For example: if you need 30 IP addresses for EC2 instances:
    - You can't choose a subnet of size /27, which is 32 IP addresses (32 – 5 = 27 < 30)
    - You need to choose a subnet of size /26, which is 64 IP addresses (64 – 5 = 59 > 30)

# 10.5 Internet Gateway (IGW)
Internet Gateway allows resources (such as EC2 Instances) in a VPC to connect to the Internet. It scales horizontally and is highly available.

A default VPC comes with a public subnet in each AZ, an internet gateway, and the main route table. In other words, there is an Internet Gateway in your default VPC. But for other VPCs, an internet gateway needs to be created separately because one internet gateway can be attached to only one VPC.

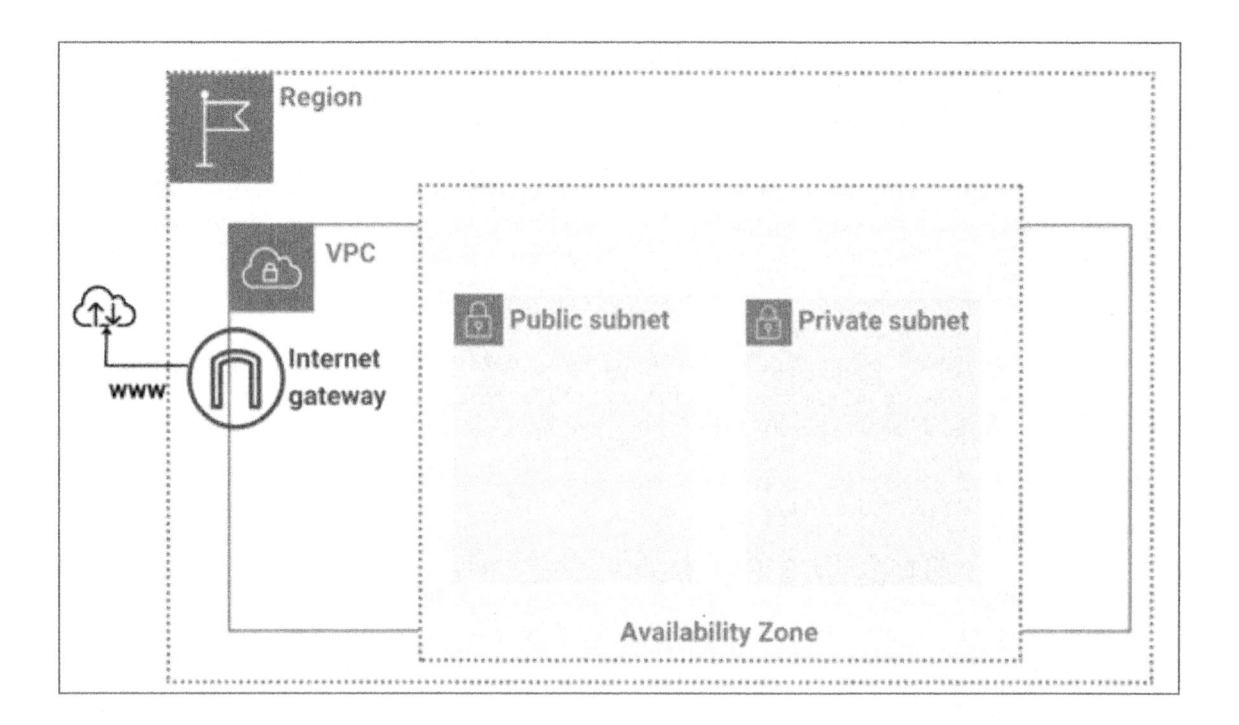

Just creating an internet gateway will not default allow access to resources from VPC to the Internet. You will need to add/edit an entry in the Route table.

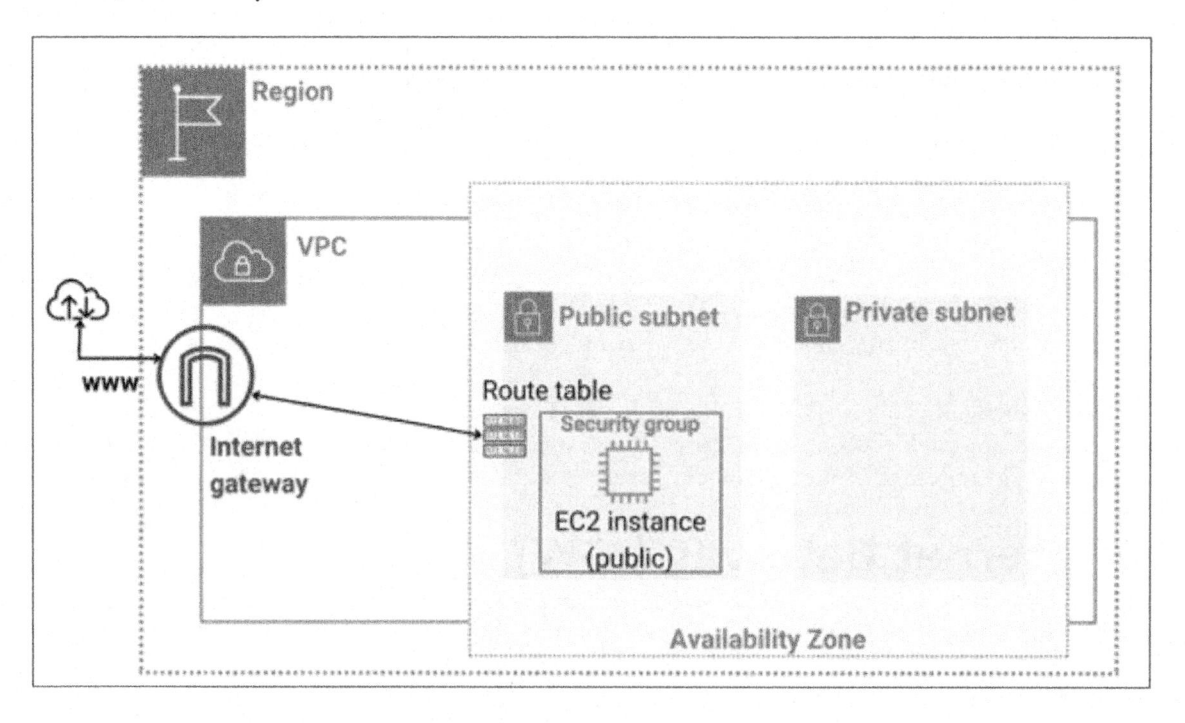

## 10.6 Routing in VPC

Routing is critical to talk to two addresses on a VPC. How two IP addresses talk to each other – the rules – are contained in a Route table. In other words, a Route table includes rules about how two IP addresses talk to each other on a VPC or where to send the next packet.

A routing table specifies how packets are forwarded between the subnets within your VPC, the internet, and your VPN connection. Every VPC has a default Route table, in which a rule says a target for every request in CIDR range is inside the VPC.

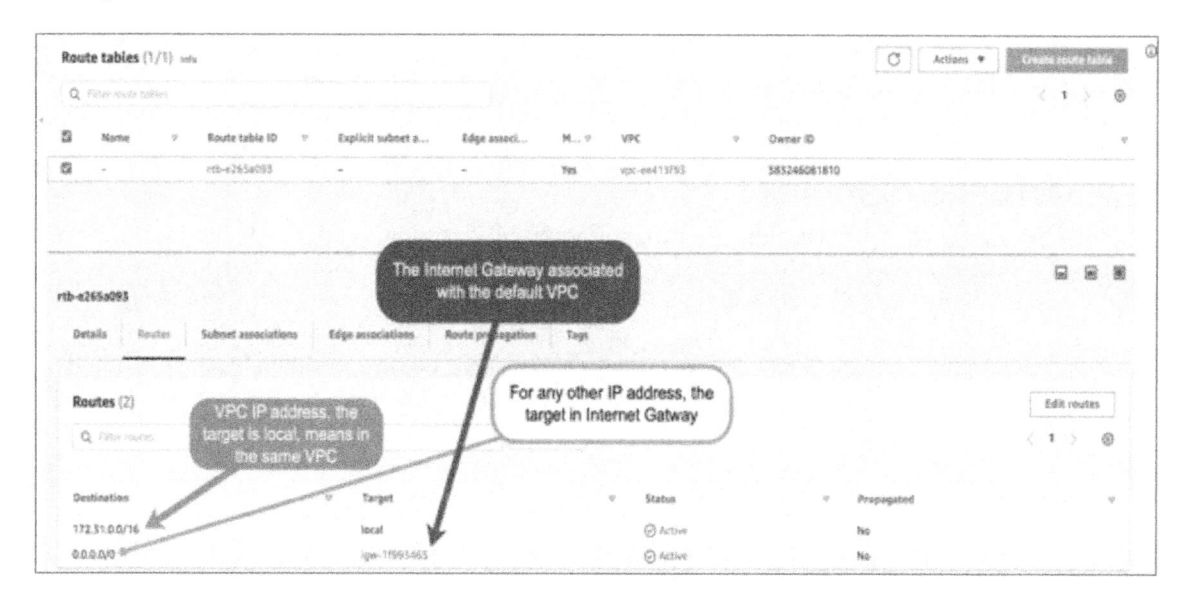

As you can see, this is the screenshot of the default Route table for the default VPC. When a destination is the IP address of the VPC, the target is local – means in the VPC. If the destination IP address is not from the VPC IP address CIDR, the target is Internet Gateway, associated with the default VPC.

You can also create a Route table and assign it to any subnet in your VPC. Then that Route table will replace the default route table of the VPC.

## 10.6.1 What About VPC Resources Communicating to the Internet

For resources in VPC to connect to the Internet: Your VPC needs to have a connection to the Internet. You will get the default Internet Gateway when you get your AWS account. You need a route to the Internet Gateway from the Route table associated with the subnet. Next, you need to have a public IP address for the resource in the subnet trying to connect to the Internet.

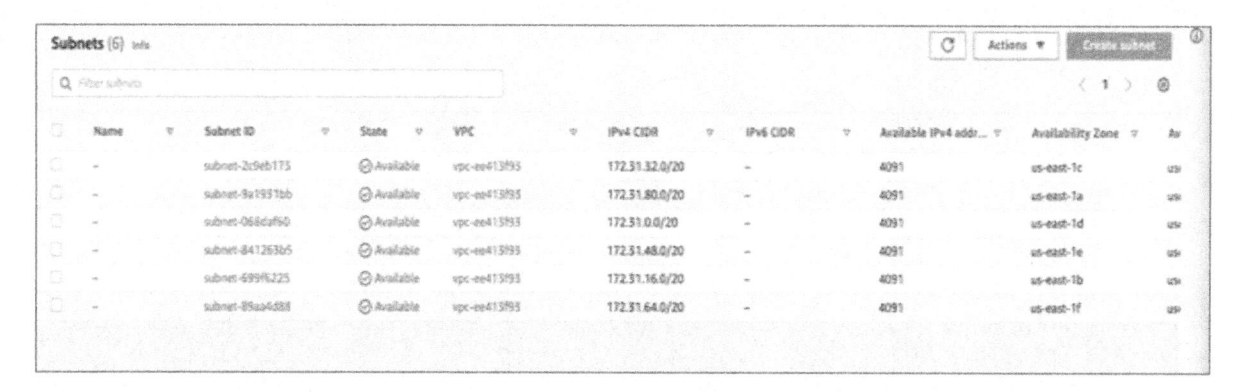

The above screenshot shows all the subnets in the N. Virginia Region in my AWS account. Since there are six AZs in the N. Virginia, that's why if you notice in the screenshot, there are six subnets.

318

In the case of default subnets that AWS creates for the default VPC, each of them, by default, is associated with the default route table. As you saw earlier, that default Route table has an entry to the Internet Gateway. In other words, if we launch an EC2 instance in a subnet created by AWS for the default VPC, the EC2 instance will get a public IP address.

Please keep in mind that any subnet in which the Route table has an entry for the Internet Gateway means the subnet is public. Therefore, all subnets associated with default VPC is, by default, a public subnet unless we add a different Route table that doesn't have an entry for Internet Gateway.

### 10.6.2 Private Subnet

In many use cases, you need a private subnet where you want AWS resources not reachable from the Internet. In the case of a private subnet, the Route table associated with the subnet doesn't have association with the Internet Gateway. In other words, there will be no entry for the Internet Gateway in the Route table.

A typical use case for EC2 instances running in a private subnet is a scenario in which instances should not be accessible from the Internet. Still, they are, however, allowed to connect to the Internet to download any software or get an update about their installed software. The question is how to allow a host inside a private subnet to access the Internet. The answer is NAT Gateway. Unfortunately, there is no default NAT Gateway created with the default VPC.

## 10.7 Bastion Hosts

If you have worked in complex big enterprise projects, particularly with many Unix servers, you have come across or used bastion hosts to SSH to Unix servers such as database / Hadoop servers. Because of their functions, these servers do not typically allow inbound connections from any machines on the network and are typically behind a company firewall. In other words, you cannot SSH to them directly -- you will have to use a Bastion host to SSH to them. On AWS, you can set up bastion hosts inside a public subnet to connect to (SSH) EC2 instances running in a private subnet.

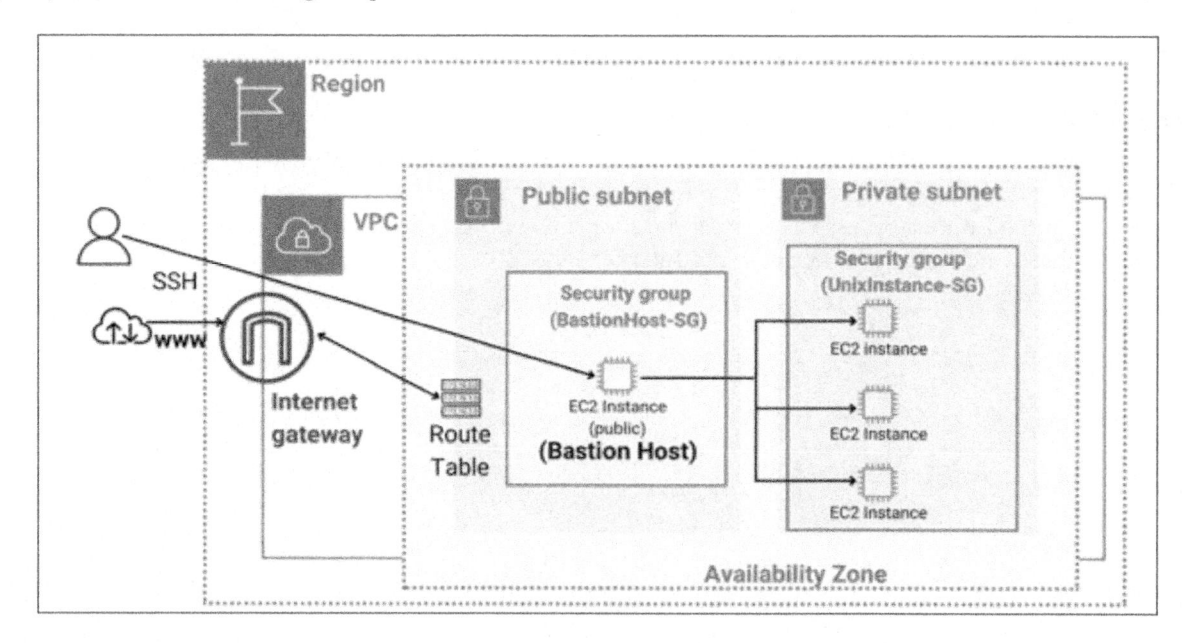

The bastion host is in the public subnet, which then can be used to connect to all other EC2 instances running in a private subnet. Bastion Host security group must allow inbound connection from the internet on port 22 from restricted CIDR, for example, the public CIDR of your corporation. Security Group of the EC2 Instances must allow the Security Group of the Bastion Host or the private IP of the Bastion host.

## 10.8 NAT Gateway

What is NAT Gateway? A NAT gateway is a Network Address Translation (NAT) service. You can use a NAT gateway so that instances in a private subnet can connect to services outside of your VPC. However, the external services cannot initiate a connection with instances inside the private subnet. Typically used for connecting EC2 instances in a private subnet to the Internet. For example, if the instances in the private subnet want to download software from the Internet. They can use NAT Gateway connectivity to connect to the Internet.

When you create a NAT gateway, you specify one of the following connectivity types:

**Public** – (Default) Instances in private subnets can connect to the internet through a public NAT gateway but cannot receive unsolicited inbound connections from the internet. You create a public NAT gateway in a public subnet and must associate an elastic IP address with the NAT gateway at creation. Then, you route traffic from the NAT gateway to the internet gateway for the VPC. Alternatively, you can use a public NAT gateway to connect to other VPCs or your on-premises network. In this case, you route traffic from the NAT gateway through a transit gateway or a virtual private gateway.

**Private** – Instances in private subnets can connect to other VPCs or your on-premises network through a private NAT gateway. You can route traffic from the NAT gateway through a transit gateway or a virtual private gateway. You cannot associate an elastic IP address with a private NAT gateway. You can attach an internet gateway to a VPC with a private NAT gateway, but if you route traffic from the private NAT gateway to the internet gateway, the internet gateway drops the traffic. Suppose you would like hosts in the private subnet to connect to the Internet. You will need to create NAT Gateway and associate the NAT Gateway to the subnet.

*Please note that the NAT Gateway is one way street to connect. What it means inbound traffic from the Internet to the NAT Gateway is not allowed.*

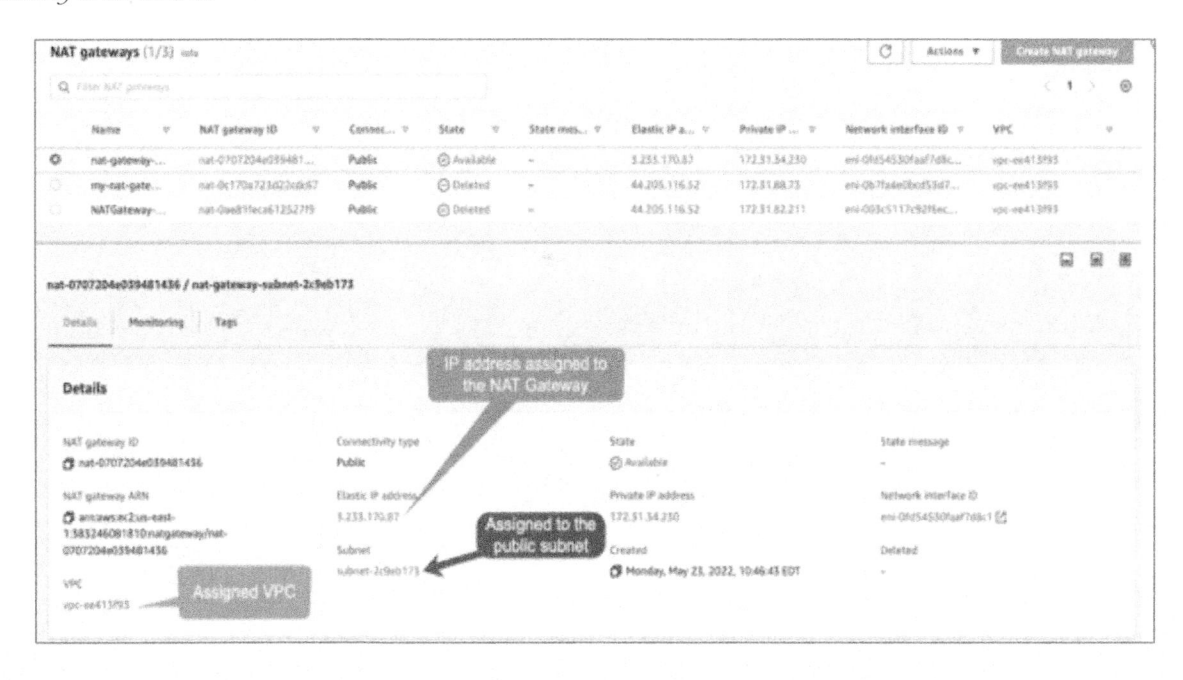

The above screenshot is related to a NAT Gateway. The NAT Gateway is assigned an Elastic IP address, which is a must. For devices to connect to the Internet and find and talk to other devices or machines on the Internet, a public IP address is necessary.

The next point to notice is that it is assigned to a VPC, and VPC is connected to the Internet Gateway.

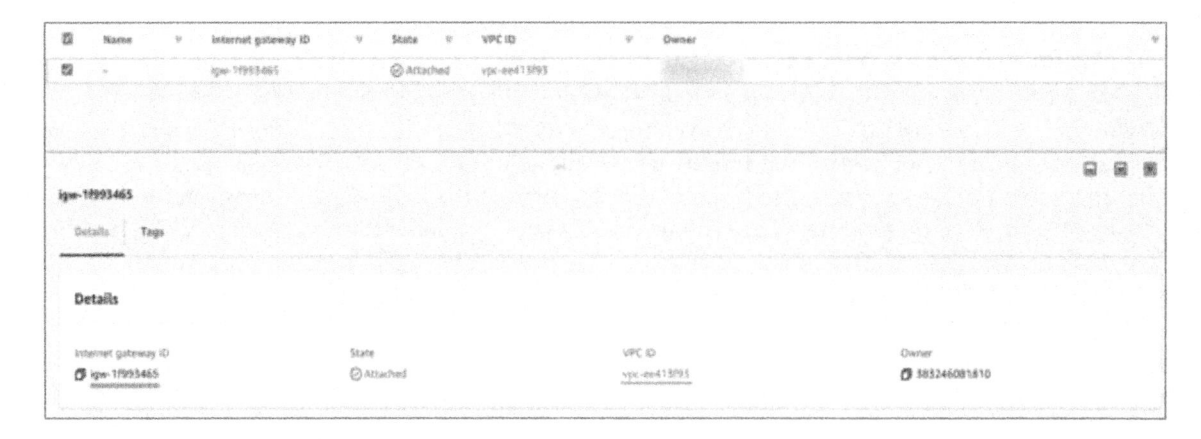

As you can notice in the above screenshot of an Internet Gateway, it is connected to a VPC. Going back to the screenshot of the NAT Gateway, another vital point to notice is that it is assigned a public subnet. It is an important point – a NAT Gateway must be associated with a public subnet.

You have created a NAT Gateway in the public subnet. The NAT Gateway is associated with a VPC assigned Internet Gateway, which will take care of Internet traffic. Please keep in mind that NAT Gateway is a device for one-way traffic. In other words, a NAT Gateway allows making outbound calls to the Internet from resources in the private subnet -- not the inbound calls from the Internet to the subnet. The typical use case is to get patches or install software on the machines in a private subnet.

The next question is: how will a host in a private subnet connect to the NAT Gateway to go to the Internet, for example, download a patch or a software.

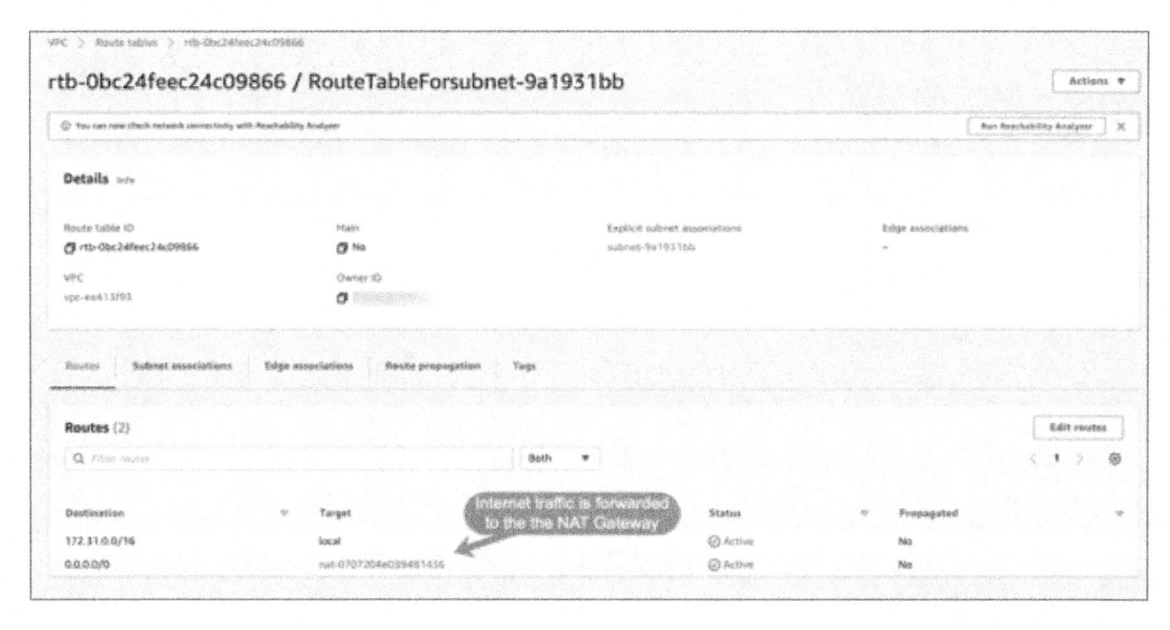

The answer in the Route Table of the private subnet is straightforward: add an entry for the Internet traffic to forward to the NAT Gateway, as you can see in the screenshot above.

For hosts in a private subnet to make outbound requests to the Internet, in the Route table associated with the private subnet, an entry will be added to direct Internet 0.0.0.0/0 traffic to the NAT Gateway, as you can notice in the screenshot above.

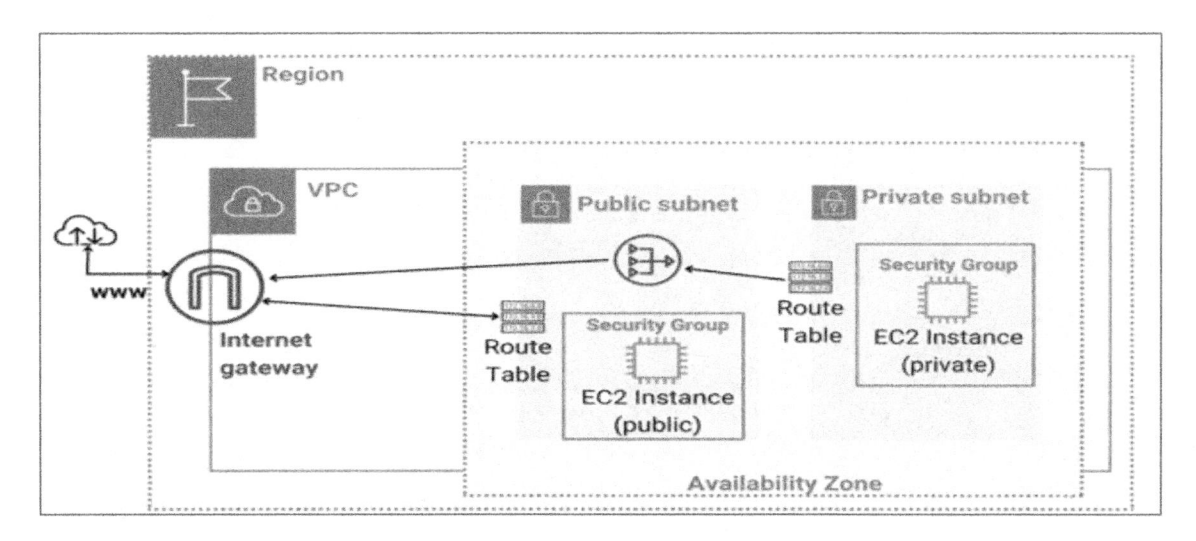

The above diagram shows setting up NAT Gateway in the public subnet to access the Internet from the hosts in the private subnet. If you notice, traffic from the private subnet goes to the NAT Gateway. And from there, then, it is sent to the Internet Gateway connected to the Internet.

# 10.9 AWS Network Security
When we talk about AWS network security, it is essential to understand security group, Network Access Control List (NACLs), and VPC Flow Logs.

## 10.9.1 Security Group
What is a security group? Security groups are AWS distributed firewalls. The important point to know about the AWS Security Group, or in general, about any firewall, is that they are stateful. So, for example, if a request is allowed, a response is automatically allowed.

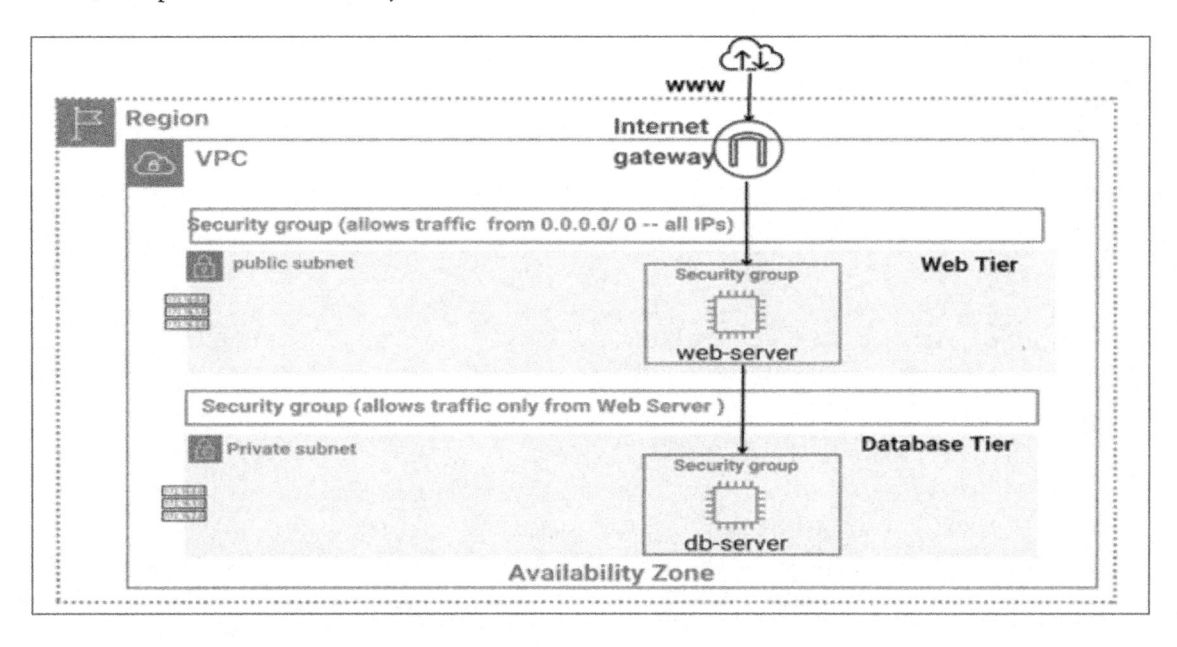

Let's try to understand Security Group with the diagram shown above. One EC2 instance runs a web server, and one EC2 instance is for the database. It's always a good practice to protect your databases. So EC2 instances running database servers are in a private subnet. And they only accept traffic from the web server. On the other

322

hand, the EC2 instance running the web server is in a public subnet. The reason is that the web server needs to be accessed from the Internet.

Now that was the concept of the security group. How will you create it? You can create it by clicking on the Security Group link on VPC or EC2 instance. Also, when you launch an EC2 instance, you can assign a default security group, create a new one, or choose from the existing ones.

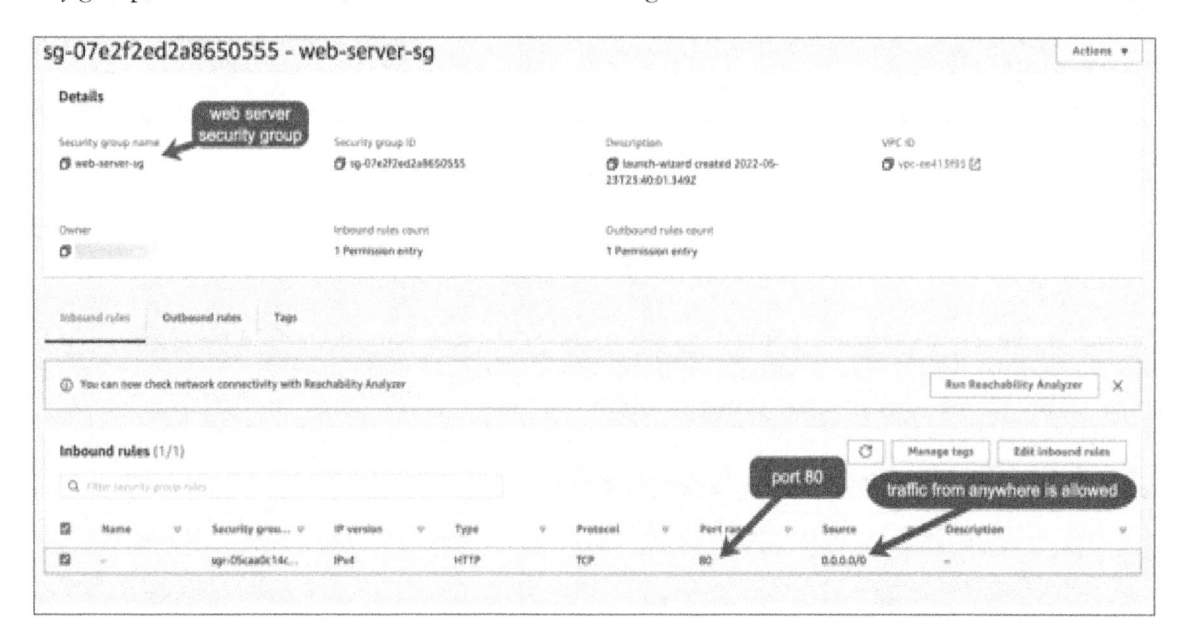

This is the screenshot of the security group of the web tier. If you notice, inbound traffic from anywhere is allowed at port 80.

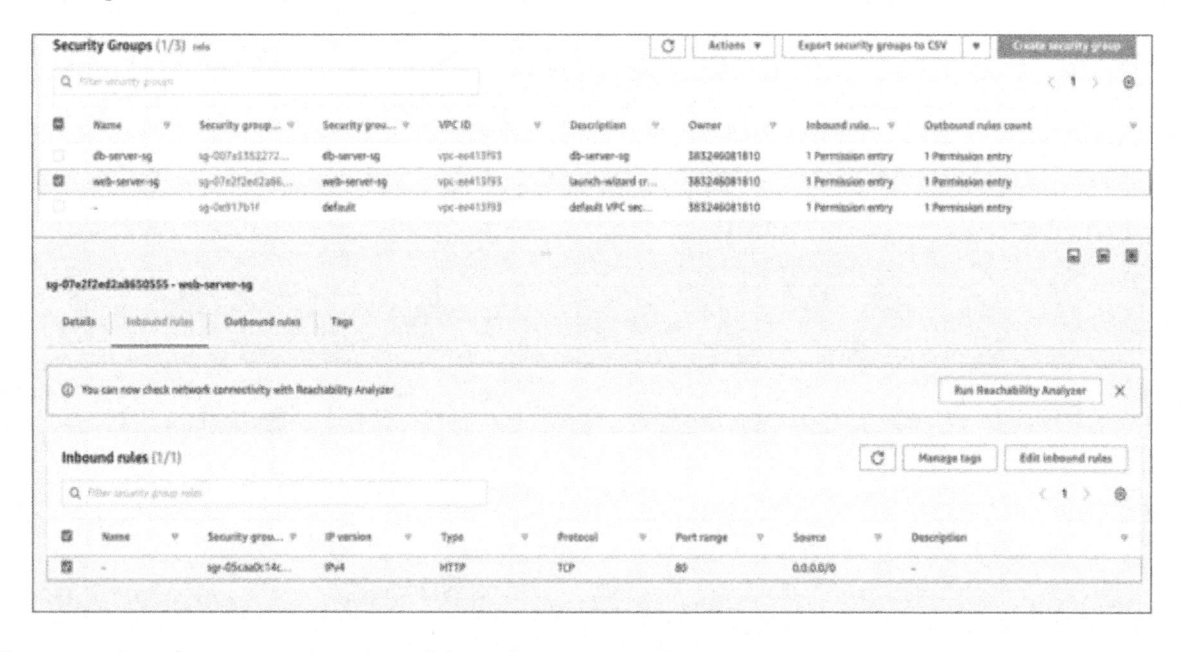

The screenshot above is another view of the web server security group

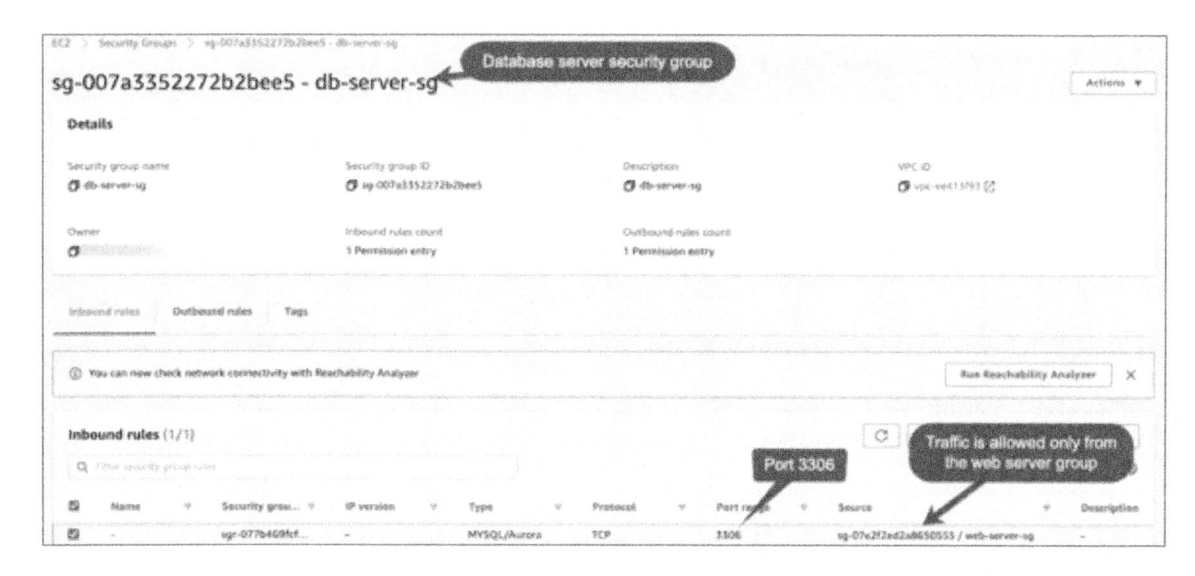

[Screenshot of AWS EC2 Security Group details page for sg-007a3352272b2bee5 - db-server-sg, with annotations: "Database server security group", "Port 3306", and "Traffic is allowed only from the web server group"]

The above screenshot is for the security group of the database server. This security group allows traffic only from the web server security group- an excellent concept. First, providing a security group as a source protects the input traffic by ensuring that the input is allowed from the machines that have that security group (for example, web-server-sg in this case) traffic. And secondly, if more web servers are added to the webserver group, you will not have to change the database security group – imagine a scenario where you have to provide the IP address of each web server machine.

(Note: the example is for explaining security groups. Standard implementations have an application load balancer that forwards web traffic to web server instances in an auto-scaling group.)

Adding a security group as a source is a scalable solution. The screenshot below is another view of the database server security group.

[Screenshot of AWS Security Groups list showing db-server-sg, web-server-sg, and default security groups, with inbound rules for db-server-sg displayed]

Another critical point is that though more than one security group can be assigned to one EC2 instance, at least, one security group must be assigned to an EC2 instance. *A security group can be modified, changed, and deleted.*

324

## 10.9.2 Default Inbound Rule

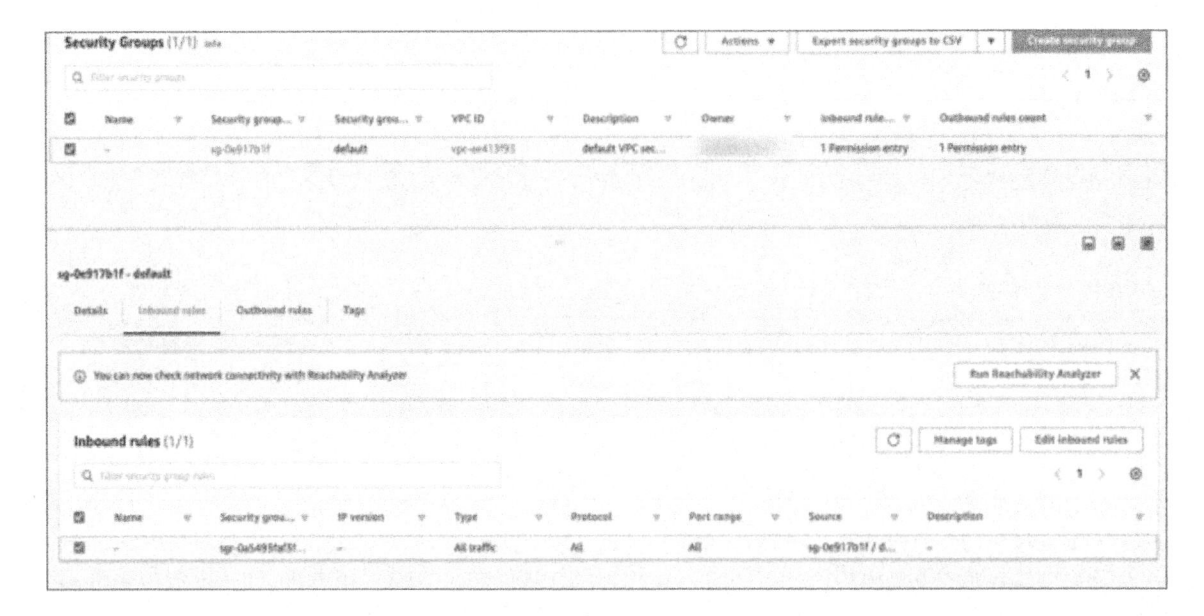

When you create a security group, it has no inbound rules. Therefore, no inbound traffic originating from another host to your instance is allowed until you add inbound rules to the security group.

## 10.9.3 Default Outbound Rule

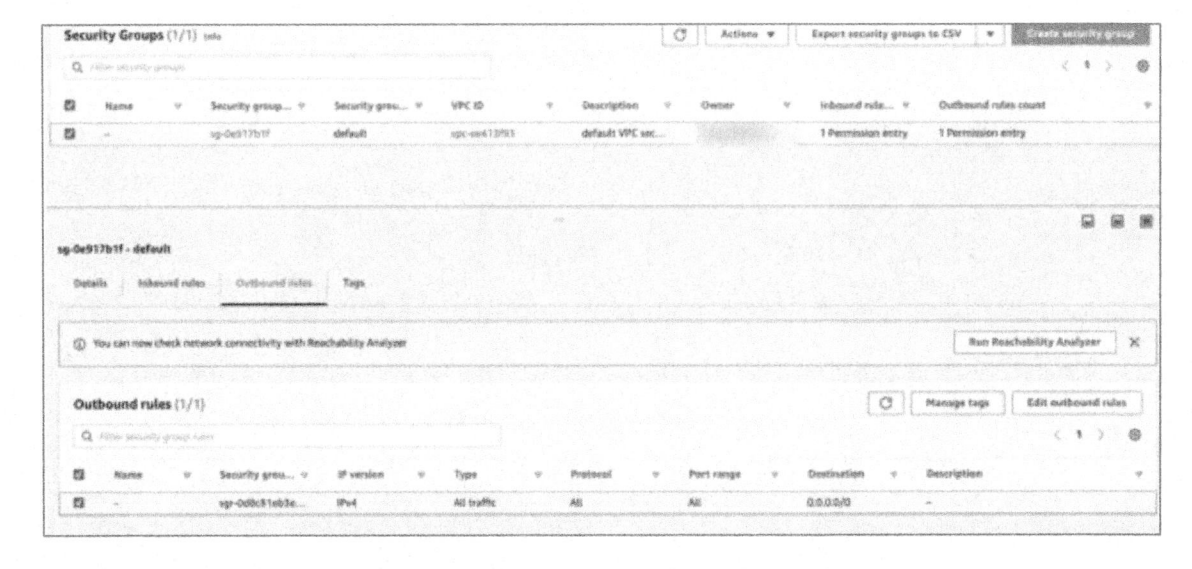

A security group includes an outbound rule that allows all outbound traffic by default. It is best to remove this default rule and add outbound rules that would enable specific outbound traffic only.

### KEY POINTS

- Security Group acts as a virtual firewall controlling inbound and outbound traffic on an EC2 instance. When you create VPC, it comes with a default security group. You can modify the default security group or create an additional security group. The default security group has no inbound rules until you add inbound rules. You only add Allow rules – not Deny rules. For each security group, you add rules that control the traffic based on protocols and port numbers. There are a separate set of rules for inbound and outbound traffic.

- There are quotas about how many security groups can be created in a VPC, how many rules can be added to a security group, and how many security groups can be associated with a network interface. A security group can only be assigned to the resources in the security group's VPC.

- Security groups are stateful. What it means for each allowed inbound request, the response is also allowed.

- You can assign multiple security groups. Based on the aggregation of rules, it is decided whether particular traffic is allowed or not on a resource.

## 10.9.4 Network Access Control List (NACLs)

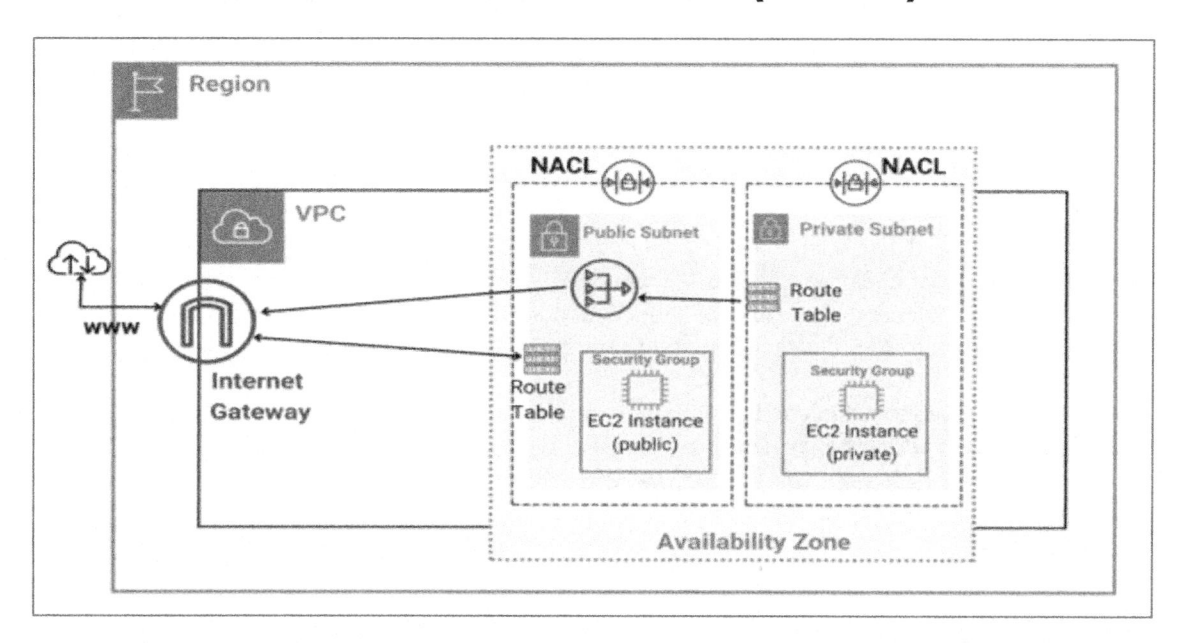

![Diagram showing a Region containing a VPC with Internet Gateway connected to www. Inside an Availability Zone are a Public Subnet and Private Subnet, each protected by a NACL. The Public Subnet contains a Route Table and an EC2 Instance (public) with a Security Group. The Private Subnet contains a Route Table and an EC2 Instance (private) with a Security Group.]

To understand the Network Access Control List, it would be better if we go through the differences between security group and Network ACL.

| Security Group | Network ACL |
| --- | --- |
| Security groups operate at *instance level* | Network ACLs operate at *subnet level* |
| Security groups support *allow rules* only | Network ACLs support *allow and deny rules* |
| Security groups are *stateful* – the return traffic is automatically allowed regardless of any rules | Network ACLs are *stateless* – the return traffic must be allowed by rules. |
| *All rules are evaluated* before deciding if the traffic is allowed | Rules are *evaluated in order (low to high)* in deciding whether to allow traffic |
| Applies only to *instances explicitly associated* with the security group | Automatically applies *all instances* launched into associated subnet |

Network Access Control List are coarse-grained controls, and they should be allowed to work at the edges of the network. However, suppose you have too many complex sets of rules configured in NACLs. It could be highly likely that you are using NACLs as a security group. If this is the case, it is better to review them to ensure that you are not configuring security groups in the NACLs. To understand the Network Access Control List (NACLs), it would be better if we go through the differences between a security group and NACLs.

*NACLs should be coarse grained.*

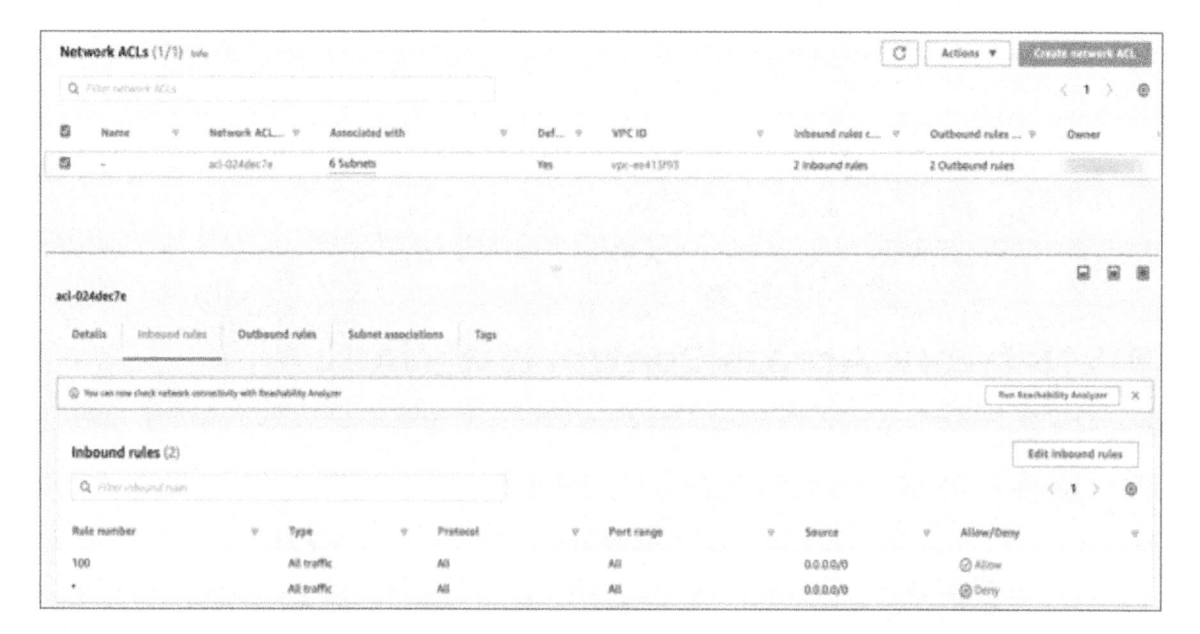

The above is the screenshot showing default Network ACLs inbound rules. You can notice that the NACLs are associated with six subnets. There are six subnets because my default Region is N. Virginia which has 6 AZs. Another important to notice is that inbound traffic is allowed from anywhere.

Below is the screenshot showing NACLs outbound rules -- this is the default setup. In the screenshot, the outbound traffic is allowed from anywhere.

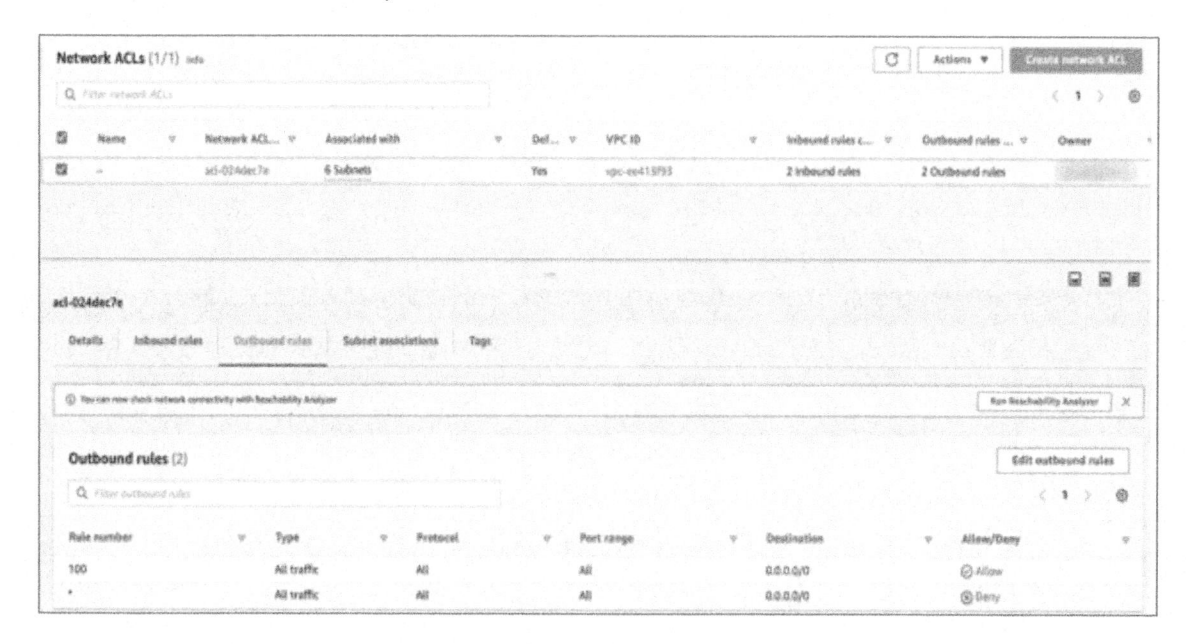

## 10.9.5 Security Groups & NACLs Request Response Flow

**Incoming Request**

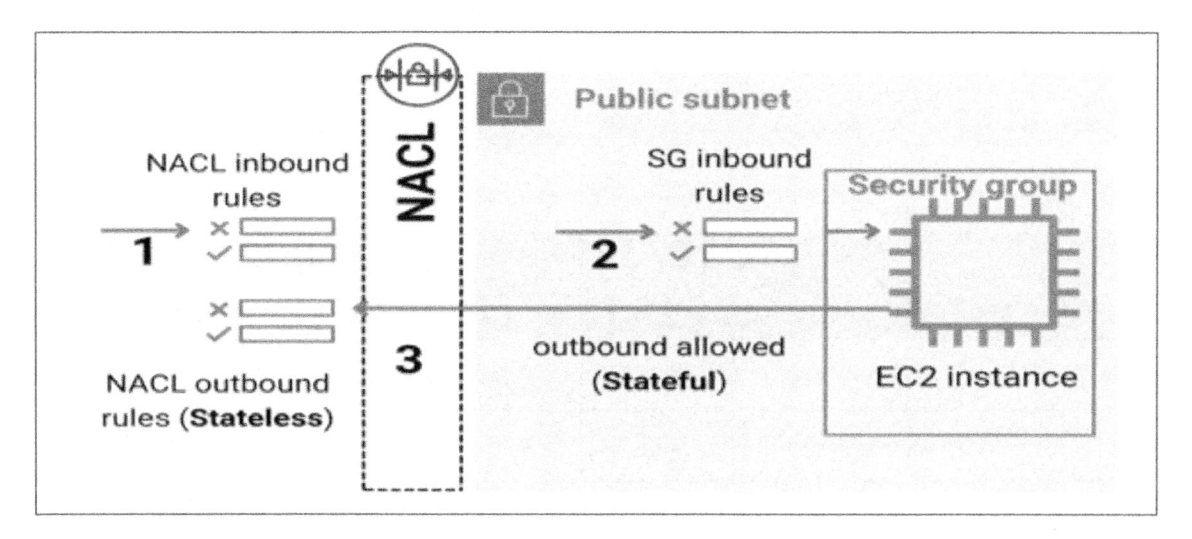

Let's understand how an incoming request is handled with NACL and Security Group. In the diagram, the request (1) is first checked by NACL rules whether the request is allowed.

Then the request (2) is checked at the instance level security group rules whether the request is allowed.

Then the outgoing response (3) is not checked by the security group as the security groups are stateful (if a request is allowed, its outgoing response is allowed). However, the outgoing response is evaluated at the NACL whether the outgoing response is allowed as the NACLs are stateless (which means both a request and its response are checked against the NACL rules).

**Outgoing Request**

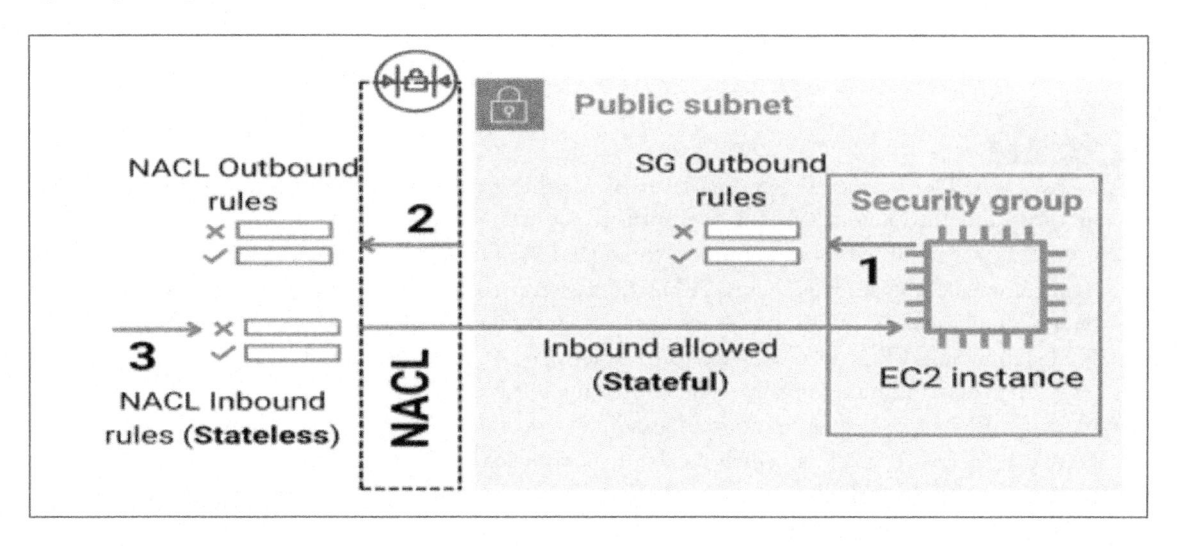

Handling of the outgoing request by Security Group and NACLs are conceptually the same – it's just the reverse of how an incoming request is handled.

From the diagram above, request (1) is first handled by the security group rules. Then the request is checked at the NACL (2). Regarding response, since NACLs are stateless, response (3) is checked against NACL rules. However, when the response goes through the security group, it is allowed as Security Groups are stateful.

**Default NACL**

By default, your VPC has default Network ACLs that allow all inbound and outbound traffic.

Inbound Rules

| Rule# | Type | Protocol | Port Range | Source | Allow / Deny |
|---|---|---|---|---|---|
| 100 | All IPv4 Traffic | ALL | ALL | 0.0.0.0/0 | ALLOW |
| * | All IPv4 Traffic | ALL | ALL | 0.0.0.0/0 | Deny |

Outboud Rules

| Rule# | Type | Protocol | Port Range | Source | Allow / Deny |
|---|---|---|---|---|---|
| 100 | All IPv4 Traffic | ALL | ALL | 0.0.0.0/0 | ALLOW |
| * | All IPv4 Traffic | ALL | ALL | 0.0.0.0/0 | Deny |

Though the default Network ACL can be modified, Do NOT modify the Default NACL. Instead, create custom NACLs.

**KEY POINTS**

- Network ACLs provide an optional layer of security for your VPC. It acts as a firewall controlling inbound and outbound traffic for one or more subnets.
- One NACL per subnet. New subnets are assigned the Default NACL.
- You can create a custom Network ACL and assign it to a subnet. By default, each custom Network denies all inbound and outbound rules until you add rules.
- Each subnet in a VPC must be assigned to a Network ACL. If the subnet is not assigned to a Network ACL, the subnet is automatically assigned to a default Network ACL.
- Network ACLs have separate inbound and outbound rules -- each rule can deny or allow traffic.
- Network ACLs are stateless, which means the response to inbound traffic is only allowed if outbound traffic is permitted and vice-versa.
- NACL rules:
  o Network ACL contains numbered rules (1 – 32766) highest number can be 32766. The order is evaluated for the lowest numbers; as soon as the lowest number rule matches, it is applied, and higher number rules are ignored.
  o Example: if you define #100 ALLOW 10.0.0.10/32 and #200 DENY 10.0.0.10/32, the IP address will be allowed because 100 has higher precedence over 200.

- o The last rule is an asterisk (*) and denies a request in case of no rule match.
- o AWS recommends adding rules by increments of 100.
- Network ACLs are different from security groups – security groups are applied at the instance level, while Network ACLs are used at the subnet level.
- NACLs are an excellent way of blocking a specific IP address at the subnet level.

## 10.9.6 Ephemeral Ports

In networking, two devices must establish a connection to communicate on an endpoint and use ports. Client devices connect to a defined fixed destination port and expect a response on an ephemeral port.

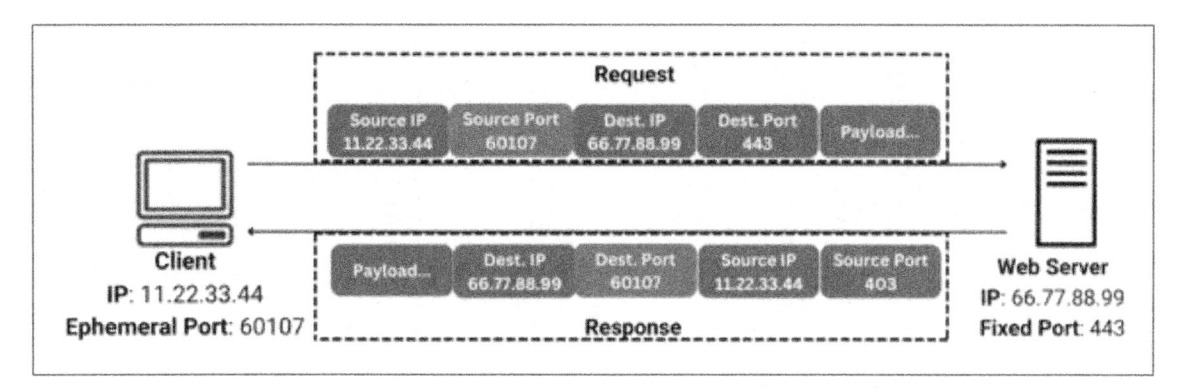

As you can see in the diagram, the client machine uses its port 60107 (ephemeral port) to connect to the web server at 443 and expects a response on its port 60107.

Different operating systems use different port ranges as ephemeral ports. For example, MS Windows uses ports between 49152 and 65535, and many Linux kernels use between 32768 and 60999.

## 10.9.7 Ephemeral Ports with NACL Example Diagram

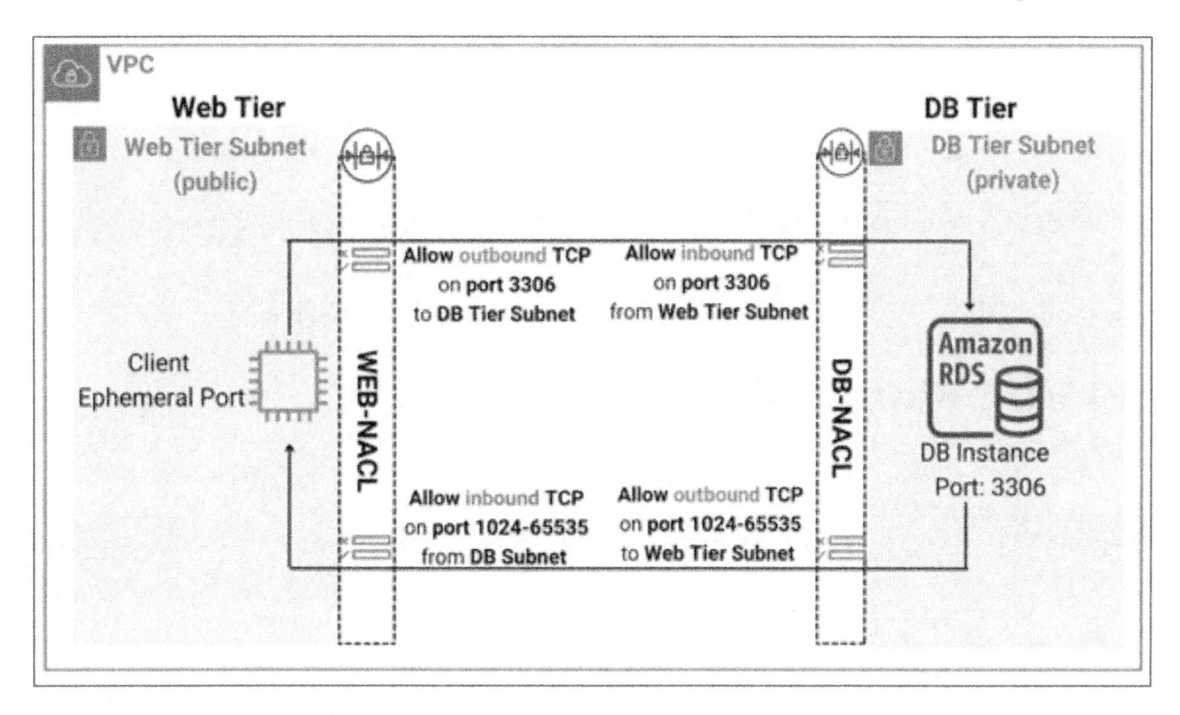

## 10.9.8 Troubleshoot SG & NACL Related Issues

Analyze the "Action" field in flow logs.

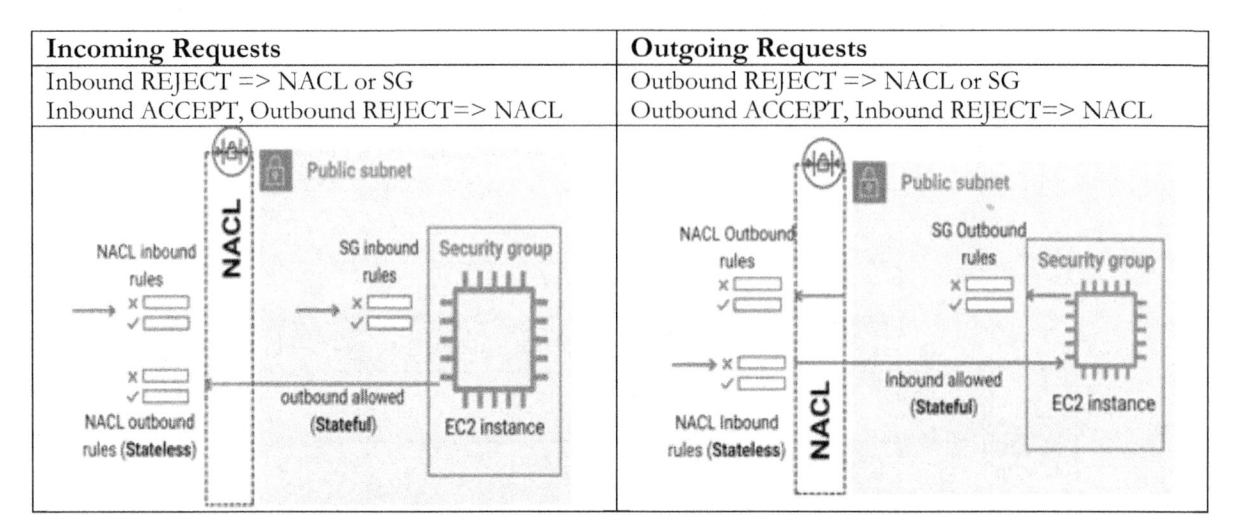

| Incoming Requests | Outgoing Requests |
| --- | --- |
| Inbound REJECT => NACL or SG | Outbound REJECT => NACL or SG |
| Inbound ACCEPT, Outbound REJECT=> NACL | Outbound ACCEPT, Inbound REJECT=> NACL |

## 10.9.9 Security Groups vs. NACLs

| Security Group | NACL |
| --- | --- |
| Operates at the instance level | Operates at the subnet level |
| Supports "allow" rules only | Supports both "allow" and "deny" rules |
| All rules are evaluated before deciding whether to allow traffic | Rules are evaluated in order from lowest to highest when deciding whether to allow traffic, the first match is used. |
| **Stateful**: response traffic is automatically allowed regardless of any rules. | **Stateless**: response traffic must be explicitly allowed by rules – think of ephemeral ports |
| Applies to an EC2 instance when specified | Automatically applies to all EC2 instances in the subnet |

Reference: https://docs.aws.amazon.com/vpc/latest/userguide/vpc-network-acls.html

# 10.10 VPC Flow Logs

In the previous sections, we discussed ensuring that correct traffic is allowed to the subnet (via NACLs) and instances (via Security Groups). But the question is how to look into traffic: the question is Flow Logs. We can create Flow Logs at the VPC and the Subnet levels. When we create Flow Logs at a VPC, it applies to all subnets in the VPC. However, when we create Flow Logs at the subnet, it applies only to the associated subnet.

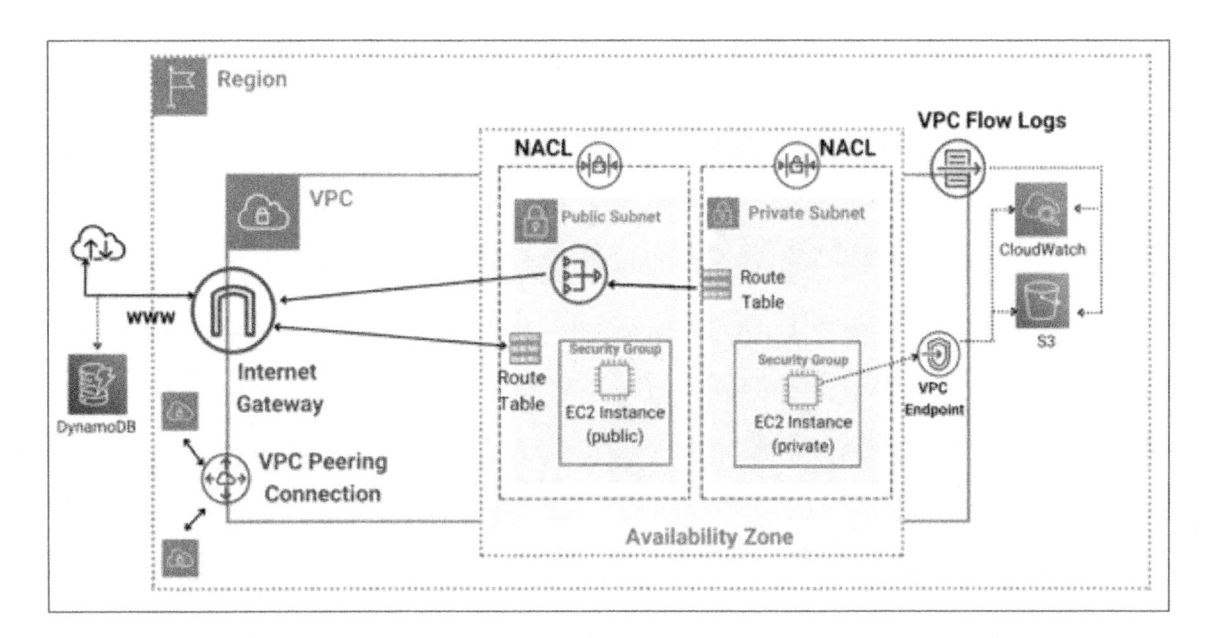

The VPC Flow Logs can be written either to a CloudWatch group or an S3 bucket. It provides visibility about what's going on in your VPC, such as troubleshooting if wrong rules are set up or analyzing traffic flows. One important point is that Flow Logs do not contain the payload of a request and response. Instead, the Flow Logs only include a packet description, such as a source and destination address, port, payload size, and whether the request is denied or accepted.

## 10.10.1 How to Create VPC Flow Logs

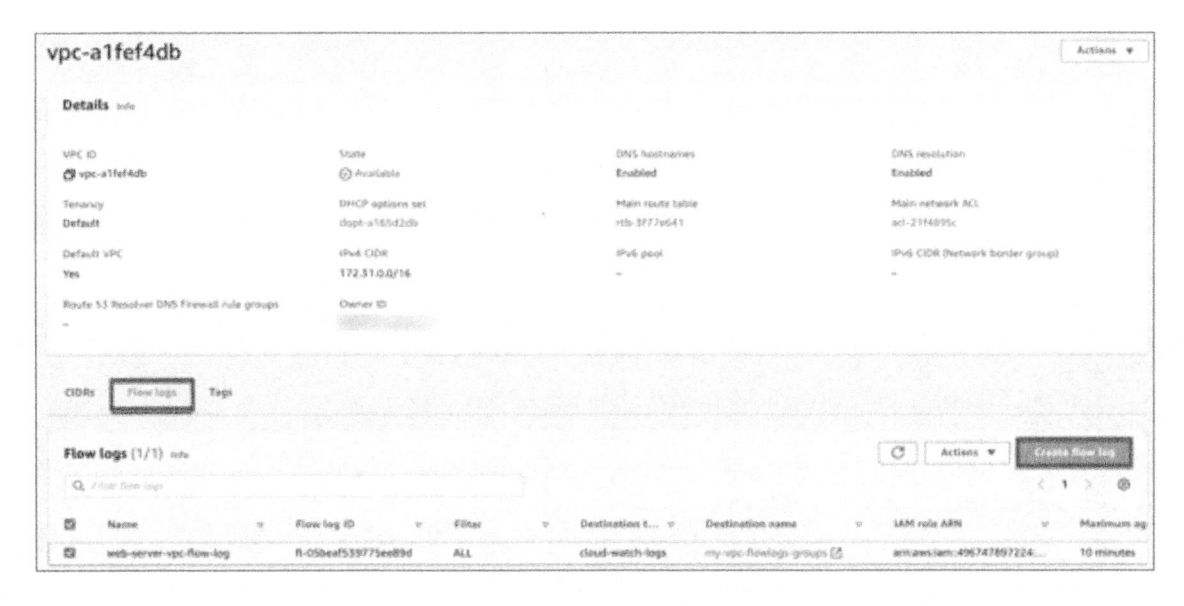

Go to VPC, click on the Flow Logs tab and then click on Create flow Log button. You can notice in the screenshot above that the Flow Log is associated with the VPC, and the destination is CloudWatch logs.

## 10.10.2 How to Create Subnet Flow Logs

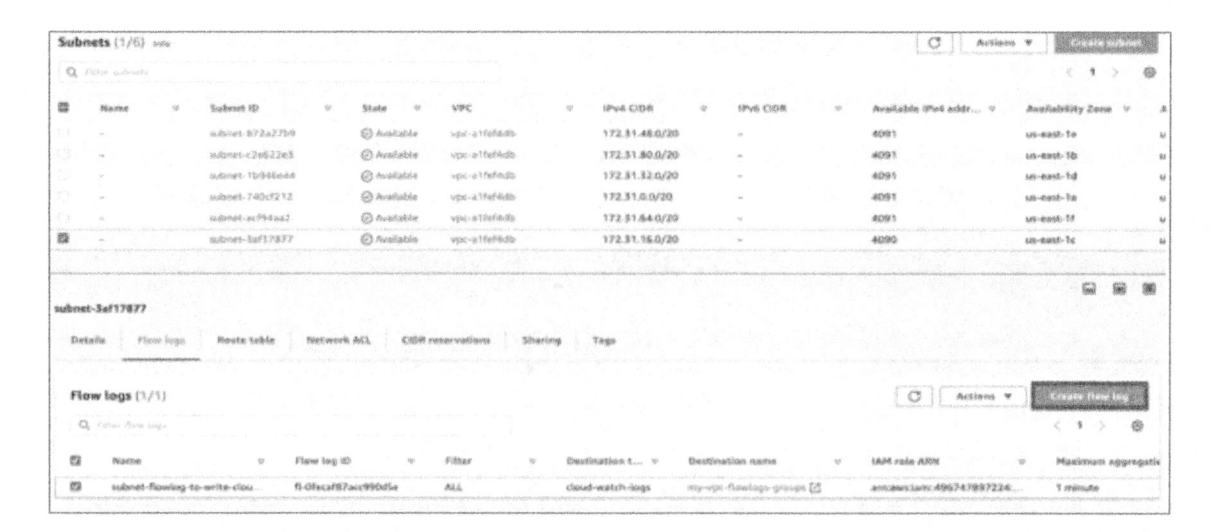

You can also create flow logs for the subnet as well. Go to VPC and select subnets. Select the subnet to which you would like to add a flow log. Then click on the Flow Logs tab and the Create flow log button. You can notice in the screenshot above shows a flow log associated with the subnet subnet-3af17877, and the destination is CloudWatch logs.

## 10.10.3 Analyzing Flow Log Record

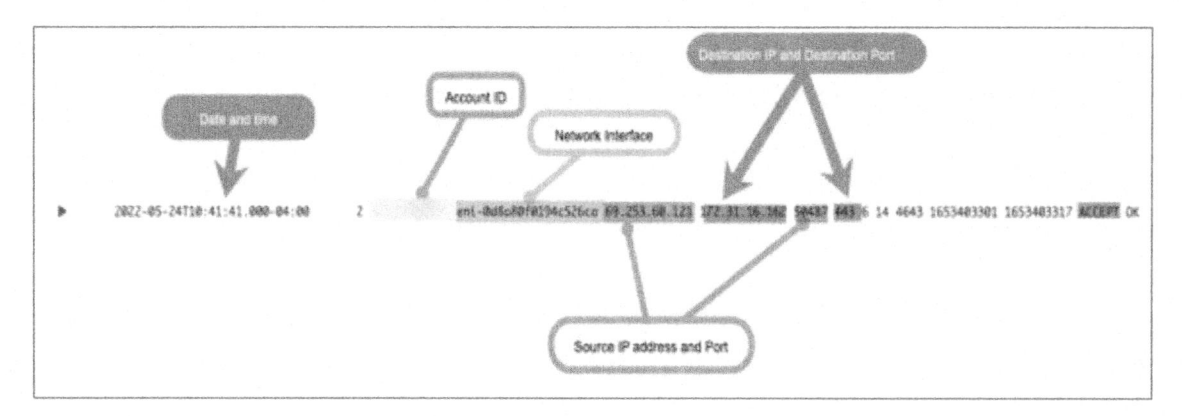

The above screenshot is for one sample Flow Log record. You can notice different parts of a request in the Flow Log.
- Source IP address and Port – help identify the problematic source.
- Destination IP and Destination Port - help identify the problematic destination.
- Action – success or failure of the request due to Security Group / NACL. It can be used for analytics on usage patterns or malicious behavior.
- You can query VPC flow logs using Athena on S3 or CloudWatch Logs Insights.

# Chapter 11. Infrastructure Security

**This chapter addresses the following exam objectives:**
Domain 3: Infrastructure Security
Task Statement 3.1: Design and implement security controls for edge services.
Knowledge of:
- Security features on edge services (for example, AWS WAF, load balancers, Amazon Route 53, Amazon CloudFront, AWS Shield)
- Common attacks, threats, and exploits (for example, Open Web Application Security Project [OWASP] Top 10, DDoS)
- Layered web application architecture
- Defining edge security strategies for common use cases (for example, public website, serverless app, mobile app backend)
- Selecting appropriate edge services based on anticipated threats and attacks (for example, OWASP Top 10, DDoS)
- Selecting appropriate protections based on anticipated vulnerabilities and risks (for example, vulnerable software, applications, libraries)
- Defining layers of defense by combining edge security services (for example, CloudFront with AWS WAF and load balancers)
- Applying restrictions at the edge based on various criteria (for example, geography, geolocation, rate limit)
- Activating logs, metrics, and monitoring around edge services to indicate attacks

Task Statement 3.2: Design and implement network security controls.
Knowledge of:
- VPC security mechanisms (for example, security groups, network ACLs, AWS Network Firewall)
- Inter-VPC connectivity (for example, AWS Transit Gateway, VPC endpoints)
- Security telemetry sources (for example, Traffic Mirroring, VPC Flow Logs)
- VPN technology, terminology, and usage
- On-premises connectivity options (for example, AWS VPN, AWS Direct Connect)

Skills in:
- Implementing network segmentation based on security requirements (for example, public subnets, private subnets, sensitive VPCs, on-premises connectivity)
- Designing network controls to permit or prevent network traffic as required
- (for example, by using security groups, network ACLs, and Network Firewall)
- Designing network flows to keep data off the public internet (for example, by using Transit Gateway, VPC endpoints, and Lambda in VPCs)

- Determining which telemetry sources to monitor based on network design, threats, and attacks (for example, load balancer logs, VPC Flow Logs, Traffic
- Mirroring)
- Determining redundancy and security workload requirements for communication between on-premises environments and the AWS Cloud
- (for example, by using AWS VPN, AWS VPN over Direct Connect, and MACsec)
- Identifying and removing unnecessary network access
- Managing network configurations as requirements change (for example, by using AWS Firewall Manager)

Task Statement 3.3: Design and implement security controls for compute workloads.
Knowledge of:
- Provisioning and maintenance of EC2 instances (for example, patching, inspecting, creation of snapshots and AMIs, use of EC2 Image Builder)
- IAM instance roles and IAM service roles
- Services that scan for vulnerabilities in compute workloads (for example, Amazon Inspector, Amazon Elastic Container Registry [Amazon ECR])
- Host-based security (for example, firewalls, hardening)

Skills in:
- Creating hardened EC2 AMIs
- Applying instance roles and service roles as appropriate to authorize compute workloads
- Scanning EC2 instances and container images for known vulnerabilities
- Applying patches across a fleet of EC2 instances or container images
- Activating host-based security mechanisms (for example, host-based firewalls)
- Analyzing Amazon Inspector findings and determining appropriate mitigation techniques
- Passing secrets and credentials securely to compute workloads

Task Statement 3.4: Troubleshoot network security.
Knowledge of:
- How to analyze reachability (for example, by using VPC Reachability Analyzer and Amazon Inspector)
- Fundamental TCP/IP networking concepts (for example, UDP compared with TCP, ports, Open Systems Interconnection [OSI] model, network operating system utilities)
- How to read relevant log sources (for example, Route 53 logs, AWS WAF logs, VPC Flow Logs)

Skills in:
- Identifying, interpreting, and prioritizing problems in network connectivity
- (for example, by using Amazon Inspector Network Reachability)
- Determining solutions to produce desired network behavior
- Analyzing log sources to identify problems
- Capturing traffic samples for problem analysis (for example, by using Traffic Mirroring)

◆◆◆◆◆◆

In the cloud environment, securing infrastructure is a paramount concern to protect against an ever-growing array of threats. This chapter provides an in-depth exploration of the strategies, tools, and best practices necessary to safeguard AWS infrastructure. This chapter covers a broad spectrum of security controls for edge services, network security, and compute workloads, offering a comprehensive guide to fortifying your AWS environments.

We begin with an introduction to infrastructure security, establishing the foundation for understanding the critical elements involved in securing cloud infrastructure. The chapter then delves into security controls for edge services, offering an overview of edge security services, common attacks and threats, and the importance of a layered web application architecture. Strategies for defining edge security, selecting appropriate edge services, applying restrictions, and monitoring are discussed to ensure robust protection at the perimeter.

Network security controls are examined in detail, including VPC security mechanisms, inter-VPC connectivity, VPN technology, on-premises connectivity options, network segmentation, and the design of network controls and flows. Emphasis is placed on monitoring network telemetry, ensuring redundancy and security for on-premises communication, and managing network configurations to remove unnecessary access and enhance security.

Security controls for compute workloads focus on the provisioning and maintenance of EC2 instances, IAM instance and service roles, vulnerability scanning, host-based security mechanisms, and the creation of hardened EC2 AMIs. We discuss applying patches across EC2 instances, analyzing Amazon Inspector findings, and securely passing secrets and credentials to ensure the security of compute resources.

Troubleshooting network security is a critical aspect covered in this chapter. We explore analyzing reachability with tools like VPC Reachability Analyzer, understanding TCP/IP networking concepts, reading relevant log sources, and identifying and interpreting network connectivity problems. Solutions for achieving desired network behavior, analyzing log sources, and capturing traffic samples are provided to aid in diagnosing and resolving security issues.

To reinforce the concepts discussed, the chapter concludes with lab exercises that offer hands-on experience in implementing edge security controls, designing network security configurations, hardening EC2 instances, and troubleshooting network issues. These exercises are structured to enhance practical skills and confidence in managing and securing AWS infrastructure.

By the end of this chapter, readers will have a thorough understanding of infrastructure security principles, best practices, and tools, enabling them to design, implement, and manage robust security measures for their AWS environments.

## 11.1 Introduction to Infrastructure Security

Infrastructure security is critical to maintaining robust and secure AWS environments. It involves implementing comprehensive security controls across various infrastructure layers, including network, compute, storage, and application layers. Ensuring infrastructure security is essential to protecting sensitive data, maintaining compliance with regulatory requirements, and safeguarding against cyber threats.

In AWS environments, infrastructure security starts with a shared responsibility model, where AWS manages the security of the cloud infrastructure, including hardware, software, networking, and facilities that run AWS services. At the same time, customers are responsible for securing the data and applications they deploy on AWS. This model necessitates a layered security approach, often referred to as defense in depth, which involves multiple security controls at different layers to protect against a wide range of threats.

**Network Security:** One of the foundational layers of infrastructure security is network security. AWS provides various tools and services to secure network traffic, such as Virtual Private Cloud (VPC) to create isolated networks, Security Groups and Network Access Control Lists (NACLs) to control inbound and outbound traffic, and AWS Shield and AWS WAF (Web Application Firewall) to protect against DDoS attacks and other web-based threats. For example, configuring Security Groups to allow only necessary traffic to and from EC2 instances and using NACLs to add an additional layer of stateless traffic filtering can significantly enhance network security.

**Compute Security:** Securing compute resources involves protecting instances, containers, and serverless functions. AWS provides several features and best practices to secure compute resources, such as using IAM roles to control access, enabling logging and monitoring with AWS CloudTrail and Amazon CloudWatch, and employing encryption to protect data at rest and in transit. For instance, deploying EC2 instances with IAM roles ensures that instances only have the permissions they need to function, reducing the risk of unauthorized access.

**Storage Security:** Protecting data stored in AWS is crucial. AWS offers various services to secure storage, such as Amazon S3, EBS, and RDS. Security features include encryption, access controls, and logging. For example, enabling server-side encryption for S3 buckets ensures that data is encrypted at rest, and configuring bucket policies and IAM policies controls who can access the data. Additionally, enabling S3 access logging provides detailed records of requests made to the bucket, which is essential for auditing and compliance.

**Application Security:** Securing applications running on AWS involves implementing best practices for software development and deployment, such as using secure coding practices, performing regular security assessments, and employing tools like AWS CodePipeline and AWS CodeBuild for continuous integration and delivery with security checks integrated into the pipeline. For example, integrating static code analysis tools into the CI/CD pipeline can help identify and remediate security vulnerabilities before they reach production.

An example of comprehensive infrastructure security in AWS is a multi-tier application where each layer (web, application, and database) is deployed in separate subnets within a VPC, with Security Groups and NACLs configured to restrict traffic between layers. AWS WAF protects the web layer, the application layer uses IAM roles to access AWS services securely, and the database layer employs encryption and automated backups with RDS.

In conclusion, infrastructure security in AWS environments requires a holistic approach that incorporates multiple security controls across different layers of the infrastructure. Organizations can build resilient, secure, and compliant cloud environments by leveraging AWS's built-in security features and following best practices. This foundational knowledge is essential for understanding and implementing effective infrastructure security mechanisms in AWS.

## 11.2 Security Controls for Edge Services

Edge services refer to computing infrastructure that resides closer to the end-users or data sources, typically at the edge of the network, rather than in a centralized data center. This approach helps reduce latency, improve response times, and enhance the user experience by processing data locally or closer to where it is generated. In the context of AWS, edge services often include content delivery networks (CDNs) like Amazon CloudFront, AWS IoT services, and AWS Wavelength for mobile edge computing.

Implementing security controls for edge services is crucial to protecting data, ensuring privacy, and maintaining compliance, as these services often handle sensitive and critical information closer to the source. Security measures must be robust and comprehensive to mitigate risks such as data breaches, unauthorized access, and cyberattacks, which can occur at these decentralized points in the network.

### 11.2.1 Overview of Edge Security Services

Edge services in AWS, such as AWS WAF, load balancers, Amazon Route 53, Amazon CloudFront, and AWS Shield, come equipped with several key security features designed to protect applications and data. AWS WAF (Web Application Firewall) helps protect web applications from common exploits and vulnerabilities by allowing users to create custom security rules. It integrates seamlessly with services like Amazon CloudFront and Application Load Balancer, providing a powerful defense against SQL injection, cross-site scripting (XSS), and other threats.

Load balancers, including the Application Load Balancer (ALB) and Network Load Balancer (NLB), distribute incoming application traffic across multiple targets, such as EC2 instances. They help enhance application availability and fault tolerance while also providing SSL/TLS termination for secure communications. Amazon Route 53 is a scalable DNS web service that offers high availability and automatic failover. It ensures users are directed to healthy endpoints, which enhances applications' overall resilience and security.

Amazon CloudFront is a content delivery network (CDN) that securely delivers various types of content (data, video, applications) and APIs to customers globally with low latency and high transfer speeds. It integrates with AWS Shield, a managed Distributed Denial of Service (DDoS) protection service, to safeguard applications against DDoS attacks. AWS Shield provides two levels of protection: Standard, which is automatically included at no extra cost, and Advanced, which offers additional detection and mitigation against larger and more sophisticated attacks.

For example, a company hosting a global e-commerce platform can use AWS WAF to block malicious requests, CloudFront to deliver content quickly and securely, and AWS Shield Advanced to protect against DDoS attacks. By leveraging these edge services, the company can ensure a secure, high-performance experience for its users while maintaining robust security and compliance controls.

## 11.2.2 Understanding Common Attacks and Threats

Understanding common attacks, threats, and exploits is crucial for maintaining the security of web applications and services. The OWASP (Open Web Application Security Project) Top 10 is a widely recognized list that highlights the most critical security risks to web applications. These include:

**Injection Attacks:** These include SQL, NoSQL, and command injection, where untrusted data is sent to an interpreter as part of a command or query. This can lead to data theft, loss, or corruption. For example, a poorly implemented login form can be exploited by SQL injection to bypass authentication mechanisms and access unauthorized data.

Injection attacks occur when untrusted data is sent to an interpreter as part of a command or query. The most common form is SQL injection, where an attacker can manipulate a query to execute unintended commands. For example, if a web application uses user input directly in an SQL query without proper sanitization, an attacker might input '; DROP TABLE users; -- to delete the entire users table.

**Broken Authentication:** This threat involves vulnerabilities that allow attackers to compromise passwords, keys, or session tokens. An example is when a website's login system does not limit the number of failed login attempts, allowing attackers to perform brute-force attacks until they guess the correct password.

**Sensitive Data Exposure:** There is insufficient protection of sensitive data, such as credit card information and personal identifiers. An example is the lack of encryption for data in transit or at rest, making it susceptible to interception and theft.

Sensitive data exposure happens when applications do not adequately protect sensitive information such as credit card numbers or personal data. For example, storing passwords in plain text rather than hashing them can lead to data breaches if the database is compromised.

**XML External Entities (XXE):** Exploiting vulnerabilities in XML parsers to execute harmful requests. This can lead to the exposure of internal files and other sensitive data. XXE attacks exploit vulnerabilities in XML parsers that process user-provided XML input. An attacker can include external entities in the XML input that the parser retrieves, potentially exposing sensitive internal files. For instance, an XXE attack could exploit an XML parser to read sensitive data from the server's file system.

**Broken Access Control:** Failures that allow unauthorized users to access restricted resources, such as URL-based access control checks that can be bypassed by manipulating the URL This type of attack occurs when restrictions on what authenticated users are allowed to do are not properly enforced. An example is when users can access other users' accounts by simply changing a user ID in the URL.

**Security Misconfiguration:** Security misconfiguration refers to improper configurations of security settings, which can be exploited by attackers. Poorly configured security settings, such as default passwords or incomplete configurations. For example, leaving default configurations and passwords unchanged can allow attackers easy access to systems.

**Cross-Site Scripting (XSS):** XSS attacks occur when an attacker injects malicious scripts into content that other users can view. For instance, an attacker could inject JavaScript into a comment section, which then runs in the browser of anyone who views the comment, potentially stealing session cookies or other sensitive information.

**Insecure Deserialization:** This vulnerability arises when applications deserialize data from untrusted sources without proper validation. An attacker can exploit this to execute arbitrary code. For example, if a web application unserializes data directly from user input, an attacker might craft a serialized object to execute malicious code on the server.

**Using Components with Known Vulnerabilities:** Many applications use third-party libraries and frameworks. If these components have known vulnerabilities and are not updated, attackers can exploit them. For instance, an application using an outdated version of a library with a critical vulnerability can be compromised by attackers exploiting that vulnerability. Incorporating libraries, frameworks, or other software components that contain known vulnerabilities can expose the application to attacks.

**Insufficient Logging and Monitoring:** Failing to log and monitor activities can prevent the detection of security breaches. For example, not logging failed login attempts can allow a brute-force attack to go unnoticed until the attacker gains access.

Another prevalent threat is **Distributed Denial of Service (DDoS)** attacks. These attacks aim to disrupt the normal traffic of a targeted server, service, or network by overwhelming it with a flood of internet traffic. DDoS attacks are executed using multiple compromised computer systems as sources of attack traffic. For example, a botnet can be used to send millions of requests to a website, causing it to slow down or crash, rendering it unavailable to legitimate users.

Organizations can employ various security measures to mitigate these threats, including web application firewalls (WAF) like AWS WAF, which can filter out malicious traffic, and DDoS protection services like AWS Shield, which can detect and mitigate large-scale DDoS attacks. Regular security assessments, patch management, and adherence to security best practices are essential for protecting web applications from these common threats.

## 11.2.3 Layered Web Application Architecture

Layered web application architecture is a design pattern that segments an application into distinct layers, each with its specific responsibilities and roles. The primary layers typically include:
- The presentation layer (user interface).
- The application layer (business logic).
- The data layer (data access).
- Sometimes an additional service layer (for web services and external integrations).

This architectural approach is crucial for securing edge services, as it provides multiple lines of defense against potential attacks.

In a layered architecture, each layer is designed to handle specific types of threats and can enforce its own security controls. For example, the presentation layer can implement input validation to prevent injection attacks, while the application layer can enforce business rules and access control to ensure that only authorized users can perform certain actions. The data layer can be secured with encryption and access controls to protect sensitive information from unauthorized access.

Edge services, such as AWS WAF (Web Application Firewall), AWS Shield, and Amazon CloudFront, play a critical role in this architecture by providing additional security at the boundary of the application. AWS WAF helps protect web applications from common web exploits by filtering and monitoring HTTP requests. It allows the implementation of rules to block malicious traffic before it reaches the application. AWS Shield offers DDoS protection, ensuring that the application remains available even during large-scale attacks. Amazon CloudFront, a content delivery network (CDN), can be configured to serve static and dynamic content securely, reducing the attack surface and improving performance.

For example, consider an e-commerce application built using a layered architecture. The application leverages Amazon CloudFront to deliver static content, such as images and scripts, from edge locations closer to users, reducing latency and exposure to attacks. AWS WAF is configured to inspect incoming traffic, blocking SQL injection and cross-site scripting (XSS) attempts. AWS Shield provides additional DDoS protection, ensuring that the application remains available during traffic surges.

By separating concerns into different layers, organizations can apply specific security measures at each level, making it harder for attackers to penetrate the system. This layered defense strategy ensures that additional layers provide continued protection if one layer is compromised.

In summary, layered web application architecture is essential for securing edge services, as it enables a robust and flexible security model. Each layer can enforce specific security controls, and edge services like AWS WAF, Shield, and CloudFront provide critical protection at the boundary of the application. This approach enhances the overall security posture, making it more challenging for attackers to exploit vulnerabilities.

## 11.2.4 Defining Edge Security Strategies

Defining edge security strategies for common use cases such as public websites, serverless applications, and mobile app backends is crucial to protecting data, ensuring user privacy, and maintaining system integrity. Edge security involves implementing protective measures at the boundary between an internal network and external networks, like the Internet. This includes the use of services and tools such as AWS WAF, Amazon CloudFront, AWS Shield, and Amazon Route 53.

For **public websites**, implementing a Content Delivery Network (CDN) like Amazon CloudFront is essential to enhance performance and security. CloudFront can be configured to use AWS WAF, which allows you to create rules to block common attack patterns, such as SQL injection or cross-site scripting (XSS). Additionally, integrating AWS Shield provides protection against Distributed Denial of Service (DDoS) attacks, which can overwhelm your website with traffic and cause downtime. For example, setting up rate-based rules in AWS WAF can help mitigate DDoS attacks by limiting the number of requests from a single IP address within a specified time period .

For **serverless applications** using AWS Lambda to run code without provisioning or managing servers, security must focus on both the API gateway and the Lambda functions themselves. Amazon API Gateway can be secured using AWS WAF to protect against malicious requests. Implementing fine-grained permissions with AWS Identity and Access Management (IAM) ensures that Lambda functions have the minimum required permissions, following the principle of least privilege. For example, IAM roles and policies should be defined to restrict access to specific resources and actions needed by the Lambda functions. Monitoring and logging using AWS CloudTrail and Amazon CloudWatch can help detect and respond to unauthorized access attempts and other suspicious activities.

For **mobile app backends**, security strategies should include protecting APIs and data stored in the backend. Using Amazon Cognito for authentication and authorization provides a secure way to manage user sign-ups, sign-ins, and access controls. Amazon API Gateway and AWS WAF can protect backend APIs from common web exploits. Encrypting data at rest using AWS Key Management Service (KMS) and in transit using TLS ensures data security. For instance, you can configure Amazon S3 buckets to enforce server-side encryption and use bucket policies to restrict access to authenticated users only.

Defining edge security strategies for different use cases involves leveraging AWS services to implement robust security measures. Organizations can protect their applications from various threats, ensure data integrity, and maintain high availability by using services like AWS WAF, Amazon CloudFront, AWS Shield, and Amazon Cognito.

## 11.2.5 Selecting Appropriate Edge Services

Selecting appropriate edge services based on anticipated threats and attacks is a critical step in securing an AWS environment. The selection process involves understanding the specific security requirements of your applications and infrastructure, identifying the potential threats and attacks they might face, and then choosing the right combination of AWS services to mitigate these risks.

One essential technique is to conduct a **threat modeling exercise**. This involves identifying the types of attacks that are most likely to target your application, such as SQL injection, cross-site scripting (XSS), distributed denial of service (DDoS) attacks, and unauthorized access. For example, a public-facing e-commerce website might be more susceptible to DDoS attacks and web application exploits like SQL injection.

**AWS WAF (Web Application Firewall)** is highly effective for protecting web applications against common web exploits that could affect application availability, compromise security, or consume excessive resources. It allows you to create custom rules to filter out specific patterns of traffic. For instance, you can create rules to block requests that contain malicious SQL code to prevent SQL injection attacks.

For applications that need protection against large-scale DDoS attacks, **AWS Shield** is a crucial service. AWS Shield Standard is automatically included at no extra cost and provides protection against most common network and transport layer DDoS attacks. For more advanced protection, AWS Shield Advanced offers additional detection and mitigation against larger, more sophisticated attacks, near real-time visibility into attacks, and integration with AWS WAF to automate incident response .

**Amazon CloudFront**, a content delivery network (CDN), improves performance by caching content closer to users and provides an additional layer of security. It integrates with AWS WAF and AWS Shield to protect against application-layer attacks and DDoS attacks. CloudFront's integration with AWS Certificate Manager (ACM) allows for easy management of SSL/TLS certificates, ensuring that data in transit is encrypted.

For **API protection**, especially in serverless architectures, Amazon API Gateway combined with AWS WAF can help secure API endpoints. This is crucial for preventing unauthorized access and attacks like cross-site scripting (XSS) and man-in-the-middle (MITM) attacks. Amazon API Gateway can be configured to require API keys, authenticate requests using AWS Identity and Access Management (IAM), and validate incoming requests to prevent injection attacks.

In the context of **mobile backends**, using **Amazon Cognito** to manage user authentication and authorization can significantly enhance security. Cognito supports multi-factor authentication (MFA) and can integrate with AWS Lambda to customize authentication flows and enforce fine-grained access control policies .

By carefully selecting and configuring these AWS edge services based on the specific threats and attacks anticipated, organizations can build a robust security posture that protects their applications and data from a wide range of vulnerabilities.

## 11.2.6 Defining Layers of Defense

The concept of "layers of defense" in cybersecurity refers to implementing multiple security measures at different points in the network to protect against potential threats. This multi-layered approach ensures that additional layers are in place if one layer is compromised to mitigate the risk. Key layers of defense include network security, application security, data protection, and endpoint security. Each layer addresses specific threats and employs different technologies and strategies to protect the system as a whole.

### Combining Edge Security Services for Multiple Layers of Defense

AWS offers several edge security services, such as Amazon CloudFront, AWS WAF (Web Application Firewall), and Elastic Load Balancing (ELB), which can be combined to create robust, multi-layered defense mechanisms.

### Amazon CloudFront

Amazon CloudFront is a content delivery network (CDN) that distributes content globally with low latency. It acts as the first layer of defense by serving cached content closer to the end users, reducing the load on the origin servers and protecting them from direct attacks. CloudFront integrates with AWS Shield for DDoS protection and AWS WAF to filter malicious requests before they reach their origin.

Example: A public website utilizing CloudFront can benefit from its edge locations to cache content and mitigate DDoS attacks. When combined with AWS WAF, it can also block malicious requests at the edge.

### AWS WAF (Web Application Firewall)

AWS WAF provides application layer protection by filtering incoming traffic based on customizable rules that can block common attack patterns, such as SQL injection or cross-site scripting (XSS). Placing AWS WAF in front of your web applications ensures that only legitimate traffic is allowed through to the application layer.

Example: An e-commerce application can use AWS WAF to create rules that block requests containing SQL injection attempts, protecting the application from data breaches.

### Elastic Load Balancing (ELB)

Elastic Load Balancing distributes incoming application traffic across multiple targets in one or more Availability Zones, such as EC2 instances, containers, and IP addresses. ELB adds an additional layer of security by managing traffic flow and providing an extra buffer against attacks. It can also be configured to use SSL/TLS certificates to encrypt traffic between the load balancer and the clients.

Example: A web application using ELB can handle increased traffic and provide failover capabilities, ensuring high availability and reducing the risk of a single point of failure.

## Combining Edge Security Services for a Multi-Layered Defense

### Edge Layer - Amazon CloudFront
Deploy CloudFront to cache content at edge locations globally. This reduces latency and protects the origin servers from direct attacks. Enable AWS Shield Standard for DDoS protection.

Example: A news website uses CloudFront to serve static content, reducing the load on its origin servers and protecting them from DDoS attacks.

### Application Layer - AWS WAF
Integrate AWS WAF with CloudFront to filter malicious requests before they reach the origin. Create custom rules to block specific attack patterns.

Example: The same news website configures AWS WAF to block requests with common SQL injection patterns, ensuring that malicious traffic is filtered out at the edge.

### Load Balancing Layer - Elastic Load Balancing (ELB)
Use ELB to distribute incoming traffic across multiple instances, ensuring high availability and fault tolerance. Configure SSL/TLS certificates to encrypt traffic.

Example: The news website uses ELB to manage traffic across several EC2 instances, ensuring that the site remains available even during traffic spikes or if one instance fails.

By combining Amazon CloudFront, AWS WAF, and Elastic Load Balancing, organizations can create a multi-layered defense strategy that enhances their applications' security, availability, and performance. This layered approach ensures that even if one security measure is bypassed, additional layers are in place to protect against threats, providing comprehensive security coverage.

## 11.2.7 Applying Restrictions at the Edge
Implementing security restrictions at the edge based on criteria such as geography, geolocation, and rate limits is crucial for enhancing the protection and performance of web applications. These restrictions help mitigate specific threats, manage traffic more effectively, and ensure compliance with regional regulations.

### Geographic Restrictions
Geographic restrictions involve limiting or allowing access to content based on the user's geographical location. This technique is particularly useful for complying with legal requirements, restricting content availability, or mitigating risks from regions known for high levels of cyberattacks.

Example:
An e-commerce website targeting customers in the United States can use geographic restrictions to block access from other countries. This reduces the attack surface and ensures compliance with licensing or regulatory requirements that restrict content distribution to specific regions.

Amazon CloudFront provides a feature called geo-restriction, which allows you to whitelist or blacklist specific countries, controlling who can access your content based on their location.

Steps to configure geographic restrictions in CloudFront:
- Open the CloudFront console.
- Select the distribution you want to update.
- Go to the 'Restrictions' tab.
- Under 'Geo-Restriction,' choose 'Whitelist' or 'Blacklist' and select the countries accordingly.

## Geolocation Restrictions
Geolocation restrictions apply security policies based on users' geographical locations. These policies can include blocking requests, redirecting users, or displaying location-specific content. Geolocation data helps customize user experiences and enhance security by blocking regions known for malicious activities.

Example:
A streaming service can use geolocation restrictions to provide different content libraries to users in different countries, ensuring compliance with content licensing agreements.

## Rate Limiting
Rate limiting involves controlling the number of requests a user or IP address can make to a server within a specific time frame. This technique helps prevent abuse, such as Denial of Service (DoS) attacks, brute force attacks, and API abuse.

Example:
A banking application can implement rate limiting to ensure that a user can only attempt to log in a certain number of times within a minute. If the user exceeds this limit, their IP address is temporarily blocked, mitigating brute force attacks.

**Implementing Rate Limiting with AWS WAF:**
AWS WAF provides rate-based rules to limit the number of requests an IP address can make within a predefined time period.

**Steps to configure rate limiting in AWS WAF:**
- Open the AWS WAF console.
- Create a new web ACL or select an existing one.
- Add a new rate-based rule.
- Set the rate limit threshold and specify the conditions that trigger the rule.
- Associate the web ACL with CloudFront, an Application Load Balancer, or an API Gateway.

## Combining Restrictions for Enhanced Security
By combining geographic, geolocation, and rate limiting restrictions, organizations can significantly enhance the security and performance of their web applications.

Example:
An online gaming platform can use geographic restrictions to allow access only from regions where it operates, geolocation restrictions to customize the gaming experience based on user location, and rate limiting to prevent abuse and ensure fair usage.

**Steps to combine these restrictions:**
- **Geographic Restrictions:** Configure geographic restrictions in CloudFront to block access from certain countries.
- **Geolocation Restrictions:** Use AWS Lambda@Edge to implement custom geolocation-based logic that tailors content delivery based on user location.
- **Rate Limiting:** Implement rate-limiting rules in AWS WAF to control the number of requests from individual IP addresses.

Applying restrictions at the edge based on geography, geolocation, and rate limits provides a robust security framework that enhances protection, optimizes performance, and ensures compliance with regional regulations.

Leveraging AWS services such as CloudFront, AWS WAF, and Lambda@Edge enables organizations to implement these restrictions effectively, safeguarding their applications from various threats.

## 11.2.8 Monitoring Edge Services

Activating logs, metrics, and monitoring around edge services is crucial for detecting and indicating potential attacks. AWS provides various services and tools to facilitate this. For instance, you can use AWS CloudTrail, Amazon CloudWatch, and AWS WAF logs to monitor and log activities around edge services like Amazon CloudFront, AWS WAF, and Amazon Route 53.

**AWS CloudTrail** enables logging of API calls made on your account, providing a comprehensive history of user activity and API usage across your AWS infrastructure. For example, enabling CloudTrail logging for Amazon CloudFront will log every request made to the CloudFront distribution, including details about the requester, the type of request, and the response. This helps in identifying unusual patterns or unauthorized access attempts.

**Amazon CloudWatch** provides monitoring and observability services, enabling you to collect and track metrics, collect and monitor log files, and set alarms. For instance, you can set up CloudWatch metrics to monitor the number of requests, latency, and error rates for your CloudFront distributions. Alarms can be configured to notify you when certain thresholds are breached, such as a sudden spike in request rates or increased error rates, which may indicate a DDoS attack.

**AWS WAF** logs are invaluable for monitoring and analyzing web traffic to detect and block malicious requests. By enabling AWS WAF logging, you can capture detailed information about traffic that is analyzed by your web ACLs. This includes details about the rule that triggered, the action taken, and the HTTP request that matched the rule. For example, you can create a CloudWatch dashboard to visualize WAF metrics and logs, helping to identify patterns such as repeated attempts to exploit a specific vulnerability.

### Example Scenario

To illustrate, consider a scenario where you are running a public website using Amazon CloudFront, protected by AWS WAF, and you want to monitor for potential attacks:

- **Enable CloudTrail** for logging API calls and CloudFront access logs. This will provide a detailed record of all the requests and responses, helping you trace back any suspicious activities.
- **Set up CloudWatch metrics and alarms** for your CloudFront distribution to monitor request rates, error rates, and latency. For instance, you can set an alarm to notify you if the request rate exceeds a certain threshold, indicating a potential DDoS attack.
- **Activate AWS WAF** logging to capture detailed logs of web requests that are analyzed by your WAF rules. These logs can be sent to Amazon S3, where you can analyze them using Amazon Athena to detect patterns of malicious activity.

By combining these logging and monitoring services, you can gain comprehensive visibility into your edge services, enabling prompt detection and response to potential attacks, thus enhancing the security posture of your AWS environment.

## 11.3 Network Security Controls

Network security controls are essential for protecting data integrity, confidentiality, and availability within an AWS environment. These controls encompass a range of measures designed to safeguard network infrastructure from threats and vulnerabilities. By implementing robust network security strategies, organizations can ensure that their systems are resilient against attacks and unauthorized access, providing a secure foundation for their operations.

## 11.3.1 VPC Security Mechanisms

Virtual Private Cloud (VPC) security mechanisms in AWS are fundamental components that ensure secure and efficient management of network traffic within your cloud environment. These mechanisms include security groups, network access control lists (ACLs), and AWS Network Firewall. Together, they provide a multi-layered security model that helps protect AWS resources from unauthorized access and various types of network-based attacks.

Security Groups act as virtual firewalls for your EC2 instances, controlling both inbound and outbound traffic at the instance level. They work by defining a set of rules that permit or deny traffic based on IP addresses, ports, and protocols. For instance, you might configure a security group to allow HTTP and HTTPS traffic from the internet to a web server instance, while restricting all other types of traffic. This allows for fine-grained control over the network traffic that reaches your instances, enhancing their security posture.

Network ACLs, on the other hand, operate at the subnet level, providing an additional layer of defense. Unlike security groups, network ACLs can be used to allow or deny traffic to and from entire subnets. They are stateless, meaning each request and response is evaluated against the rules separately, which can be particularly useful for blocking specific IP addresses or ranges. For example, you could use a network ACL to deny all traffic from a known malicious IP range, thereby protecting all resources within a subnet from potential attacks originating from those addresses.

AWS Network Firewall is a managed service that offers enhanced protection by providing stateful, managed, network firewall and intrusion detection and prevention capabilities. It can be used to establish network security policies for entire VPCs, allowing for the inspection and filtering of both inbound and outbound traffic at the VPC perimeter. This is especially beneficial for complex environments where comprehensive traffic analysis and more advanced security measures are required. For example, AWS Network Firewall can help detect and block sophisticated threats like malware and data exfiltration attempts, ensuring that your network traffic adheres to your security policies.

By combining these VPC security mechanisms, organizations can create robust and flexible security architectures tailored to their specific needs. Security groups and network ACLs provide fundamental traffic control at the instance and subnet levels, respectively, while AWS Network Firewall offers advanced protection for the entire VPC. Together, they help ensure that AWS environments are secure and resilient against a wide range of network-based threats.

## 11.3.2 Inter-VPC Connectivity

Establishing secure inter-VPC connectivity is crucial for maintaining secure and efficient communication between multiple Virtual Private Clouds (VPCs) in an AWS environment. AWS offers several techniques to achieve this, with AWS Transit Gateway and VPC endpoints being two of the most effective solutions.

### AWS Transit Gateway

AWS Transit Gateway is a highly scalable service that enables you to connect multiple VPCs and on-premises networks through a central hub. This service simplifies network architecture by reducing the number of connections required and providing a single point for managing and monitoring traffic. To establish secure inter-VPC connectivity using AWS Transit Gateway, you would typically follow these steps:

- **Create a Transit Gateway:** First, create a transit gateway in your AWS account. This acts as the central hub for all your VPC and on-premises connections.

- **Attach VPCs to the Transit Gateway:** Next, attach each VPC to the transit gateway. This process involves creating a transit gateway attachment for each VPC. By doing so, you enable traffic routing between the VPCs through the transit gateway.
- **Configure Route Tables:** Once the attachments are in place, configure the route tables for the transit gateway and the attached VPCs. These route tables determine how traffic is directed between the VPCs and any connected on-premises networks.
- **Implement Security Controls:** To secure the connectivity, implement security groups and network ACLs to control traffic flow and ensure only authorized traffic is allowed. Additionally, you can use AWS Transit Gateway's built-in security features, such as route propagation and route table association, to further secure and manage your network traffic.

**Example:** Suppose you have three VPCs in different regions that need to communicate securely with each other and with an on-premises network. By using AWS Transit Gateway, you can create a central hub that connects all three VPCs and the on-premises network, simplifying the architecture and enhancing security.

### VPC Endpoints

VPC Endpoints provide another technique for secure inter-VPC connectivity, particularly for accessing AWS services and private applications within your VPCs without exposing traffic to the public internet. VPC endpoints come in two types: Interface endpoints and Gateway endpoints.

- **Interface Endpoints:** These are ENIs (Elastic Network Interfaces) with private IP addresses that serve as entry points to AWS services powered by AWS PrivateLink. Interface endpoints can be used to connect to services like Amazon S3, DynamoDB, or any AWS Marketplace services.
- **Gateway Endpoints:** These are used to route traffic to AWS services like Amazon S3 and DynamoDB using route tables. They are more cost-effective for high-throughput services as they leverage the AWS network.

**Example:** If you have a private application running in one VPC that needs to securely access Amazon S3 buckets in another VPC, you can set up a VPC endpoint for S3. This allows the application to connect to S3 directly over the AWS network without traversing the public internet, thus enhancing security and reducing latency.

By combining AWS Transit Gateway and VPC endpoints, you can establish robust, secure, and efficient inter-VPC connectivity tailored to your specific network architecture and security requirements.

## 11.3.3 Security Telemetry Sources

Security telemetry sources such as Traffic Mirroring and VPC Flow Logs are key tools for monitoring and securing network traffic within AWS environments. These tools provide valuable insights into network traffic behavior, helping to detect anomalies, troubleshoot issues, and ensure compliance with security policies.

**Traffic Mirroring** enables you to capture and inspect network traffic in your VPC. By mirroring traffic from Elastic Network Interfaces (ENIs) of Amazon EC2 instances, you can analyze the traffic for security threats, performance issues, and other network-related events. This feature is particularly useful for deep packet inspection, network forensics, and real-time threat detection.

Example: Suppose you have a critical application running on an EC2 instance and need to monitor its network traffic for potential threats. You can configure Traffic Mirroring to capture traffic from the ENI associated with the EC2 instance and send it to a monitoring appliance or security tool for analysis. This setup allows you to gain deep visibility into the network traffic, helping you to identify and mitigate threats promptly.

**VPC Flow Logs** provide detailed information about the IP traffic flowing into and out from network interfaces in your VPC. By capturing metadata about the traffic, including source and destination IP addresses, ports, protocols, and packet counts, VPC Flow Logs enable you to monitor and troubleshoot network connectivity issues and audit network traffic for security purposes.

Example: Consider an organization that needs to audit network traffic for compliance and security monitoring. By enabling VPC Flow Logs, the organization can capture detailed logs of all traffic flowing in and out of their VPC. These logs can be stored in Amazon S3, analyzed using Amazon Athena, or visualized with Amazon CloudWatch Logs Insights to gain insights into network traffic patterns and detect any suspicious activity.

In summary, Traffic Mirroring and VPC Flow Logs are powerful telemetry sources that provide comprehensive visibility into network traffic within AWS environments. By leveraging these tools, organizations can enhance their security posture, perform detailed traffic analysis, and ensure compliance with security policies.

## 11.3.4 VPN Technology and Usage

A Virtual Private Network (VPN) creates a secure and encrypted connection over a less secure network, such as the Internet. The main purpose of a VPN is to provide privacy, security, and anonymity by encrypting data transmitted between the user's device and the VPN server. Key terminology associated with VPN technology includes:

- **Tunneling Protocols:** These protocols establish the secure tunnel through which data is transmitted. Common tunneling protocols include IPsec (Internet Protocol Security), SSL/TLS (Secure Sockets Layer/Transport Layer Security), and L2TP (Layer 2 Tunneling Protocol).
- **Encryption:** Encryption is the process of converting data into a code to prevent unauthorized access. VPNs use various encryption methods, such as AES (Advanced Encryption Standard), to ensure data confidentiality.
- **VPN Gateway:** This network device or software application terminates the VPN connection and decrypts incoming data. It is typically deployed on the edge of the network.

In a corporate setting, VPNs are commonly used to provide secure on-premises connectivity for remote employees, ensuring that sensitive data is protected while being transmitted over the internet. For example, a company might use a VPN to allow employees to securely access the company's internal network and resources, such as file servers, applications, and databases, from remote locations.

Amazon Web Services (AWS) offers VPN solutions, such as AWS Site-to-Site VPN, to facilitate secure connections between on-premises networks and AWS environments. AWS Site-to-Site VPN creates an encrypted tunnel between an on-premises VPN gateway and the AWS Virtual Private Gateway (VGW). This setup ensures that data transmitted between the on-premises network and AWS is protected from interception and tampering.

For instance, an organization can establish a Site-to-Site VPN connection to extend its on-premises data center to the AWS cloud securely. This allows the organization to leverage AWS services while maintaining a secure and seamless network experience for its users. Additionally, AWS provides:
- Features like VPN CloudHub.
- Enabling multiple on-premises sites to connect securely to AWS.
- Facilitating a hub-and-spoke model for secure, scalable connectivity

## 11.3.5 On-Premises Connectivity Options

On-premises connectivity options like AWS VPN and AWS Direct Connect are essential for securely linking on-premises infrastructure with AWS cloud resources. Depending on an organization's specific requirements, these connectivity options provide different benefits and use cases.

**AWS VPN:** AWS VPN provides a secure and encrypted connection between an on-premises network and an AWS Virtual Private Cloud (VPC). It uses IPsec to establish a secure tunnel over the internet, ensuring data privacy and integrity during transmission. AWS offers two types of VPN connections: AWS Site-to-Site VPN and AWS Client VPN.

- **AWS Site-to-Site VPN:** This option is ideal for connecting entire on-premises networks to AWS. It allows organizations to securely extend their data centers to the cloud. For example, a company with an on-premises data center can use a Site-to-Site VPN to connect its network to an AWS VPC, enabling secure access to AWS resources such as Amazon EC2 instances, S3 storage, and RDS databases.
- **AWS Client VPN:** This service is designed for individual users to have remote access. It allows employees to securely connect to AWS resources from any location using their devices. For instance, remote workers can use AWS Client VPN to securely access the corporate network hosted on AWS, enabling them to work from anywhere with the same security as if they were in the office.

**AWS Direct Connect:** AWS Direct Connect provides a dedicated network connection between an on-premises environment and AWS. It bypasses the internet, offering more consistent network performance, reduced latency, and higher bandwidth.

- **Dedicated and Hosted Connections:** Direct Connect offers two types of connections: Dedicated (a physical Ethernet connection) and Hosted (a connection provided by an AWS Direct Connect partner). For example, a financial services company requiring low-latency and high-bandwidth connectivity for data-intensive applications can use AWS Direct Connect to establish a private, dedicated link to AWS. This setup ensures secure, reliable, and fast access to AWS services without relying on the public internet.
- **Use Case:** A media company streaming high-definition content to users worldwide might use AWS Direct Connect to handle large volumes of data transfer between its on-premises video storage systems and AWS. The dedicated connection ensures minimal latency and high transfer speeds, improving the user experience for content delivery.

AWS VPN and Direct Connect provide secure connectivity options tailored to different scenarios. AWS VPN is well-suited for quick, cost-effective setups with secure internet-based connections. At the same time, AWS Direct Connect is ideal for enterprises requiring high-performance, dedicated links for critical workloads.

## 11.3.6 Implementing Network Segmentation

Network segmentation is a crucial technique for enhancing security within a cloud environment. It divides the network into smaller, isolated segments, each with its own security controls. This approach limits the spread of attacks and provides greater control over data traffic. In AWS, network segmentation can be implemented using several methods, including Virtual Private Clouds (VPCs), subnets, security groups, and network ACLs.

A common network segmentation technique is creating multiple VPCs for different applications or departments within an organization. Each VPC can be designed with its own set of subnets, further segmenting the network based on security needs. For instance, public-facing applications might be placed in a public subnet, while sensitive data and backend applications reside in private subnets.

**Security groups** act as virtual firewalls for instances to control inbound and outbound traffic at the instance level. For example, a security group can be configured to allow SSH access only from a specific IP range, thus limiting access to authorized personnel. Network ACLs, on the other hand, operate at the subnet level and can be used to set rules that allow or deny traffic to and from subnets, providing an additional layer of security.

**AWS Transit Gateway** facilitates secure inter-VPC connectivity by acting as a central hub that simplifies the management of multiple VPCs and on-premises networks. Traffic between VPCs can be routed securely, ensuring that only legitimate and necessary communication occurs between segments.

For enhanced security, AWS Network Firewall can be used to define firewall rules and apply them across multiple VPCs. It provides network protection at the perimeter of a VPC and helps manage and control outbound traffic to prevent data exfiltration.

### Example
Consider an organization with a multi-tier web application. The frontend web servers are placed in a public subnet, and the application and database servers are in private subnets. Security groups are configured to allow HTTP/HTTPS traffic to the web servers, while the application servers accept traffic only from them. The database servers allow connections only from the application servers, ensuring that each tier is isolated and protected.

AWS Network Firewall can be deployed to monitor and filter traffic at the VPC boundaries, and AWS Transit Gateway can manage secure communication between different VPCs within the organization. By implementing network segmentation, the organization ensures that the attack is contained even if one segment is compromised and does not spread to other parts of the network.

## 11.3.7 Designing Network Controls

Designing network controls to permit or prevent network traffic as required is essential for maintaining a secure and efficient cloud environment. In AWS, this is achieved through the use of security groups, network access control lists (ACLs), and AWS Network Firewall. These tools provide granular control over the flow of traffic within and between Virtual Private Clouds (VPCs).

### Security Groups
Security groups are stateful, meaning they automatically allow return traffic. They act as virtual firewalls for EC2 instances to control inbound and outbound traffic at the instance level. Each security group can be configured with rules that specify the allowed protocols, ports, and IP address ranges.

**Example:** Suppose you have a web server running on an EC2 instance. You can create a security group and sets up rule that allows inbound HTTP (port 80) and HTTPS (port 443) traffic from anywhere (0.0.0.0/0), but restricts SSH access (port 22) to a specific IP address or range. This security group rule ensures that only authorized personnel can manage the server remotely, while the web application remains accessible to all users.

```
1. Inbound Rules:
2. - Type: HTTP, Port: 80, Source: 0.0.0.0/0
3. - Type: HTTPS, Port: 443, Source: 0.0.0.0/0
4. - Type: SSH, Port: 22, Source: <Your IP Address>
```

### Network ACLs
Network ACLs are stateless, meaning return traffic must be explicitly allowed by rules. They operate at the subnet level and can be used to set rules that either allow or deny traffic based on protocols, ports, and IP address ranges.

**Example:** To secure a subnet containing a database server, you can create a network ACL that allows inbound traffic on the database port (e.g., MySQL on port 3306) only from the application server subnet, while denying all other traffic. Similarly, you can restrict outbound traffic from the database subnet to the application server subnet.

```
1. Inbound Rules:
2. - Rule #100: Allow, Protocol: TCP, Port Range: 3306, Source: <Application Subnet CIDR>
3. - Rule #* : Deny, All Traffic
4.
5. Outbound Rules:
6. - Rule #100: Allow, Protocol: TCP, Port Range: 3306, Destination: <Application Subnet CIDR>
7. - Rule #* : Deny, All Traffic
```

### AWS Network Firewall

AWS Network Firewall provides advanced protection by allowing you to define and enforce rules to control both ingress and egress traffic at the VPC level. It supports stateful inspection, intrusion prevention, and web filtering.

**Example:** To protect against SQL injection attacks, you can configure AWS Network Firewall with rules that block known malicious patterns in web requests. You can also set up firewall rules to allow only specific IP ranges to access sensitive resources within your VPC.

By combining these network control mechanisms, you can create a layered defense strategy that enhances the security posture of your AWS environment. Each tool serves a specific purpose, allowing you to design flexible and robust controls tailored to your security requirements.

## 11.3.8 Designing Network Flows

Designing network flows to keep data off the public internet is crucial for maintaining data security and privacy within AWS environments. This can be achieved using AWS Transit Gateway, VPC endpoints, and AWS Lambda within VPCs. These components help ensure that data traffic remains within the AWS network, reducing the risk of exposure to public internet threats.

### AWS Transit Gateway

AWS Transit Gateway is a hub connecting multiple VPCs and on-premises networks through a central point, facilitating efficient and secure data transfer without the need to route traffic over the public internet. It simplifies network architecture by enabling seamless connectivity across various VPCs.

**Example:** Suppose you have multiple VPCs in different AWS regions that need to communicate with each other. By using AWS Transit Gateway, you can establish peering connections between these VPCs. This setup allows data to flow securely within the AWS network without traversing the public internet. Additionally, Transit Gateway supports high bandwidth and low latency, making it ideal for inter-region data transfer.

### VPC Endpoints

VPC endpoints enable private connections between VPCs and AWS services without exposing data to the public internet. There are two types of VPC endpoints: interface endpoints and gateway endpoints.
Interface Endpoints: These provide private connectivity to AWS services using AWS PrivateLink. They create an elastic network interface in your VPC that serves as an entry point to the service.
Gateway Endpoints: These are used to connect to AWS services like Amazon S3 and DynamoDB, routing traffic through a gateway within the VPC.

**Example:** To securely access Amazon S3 from within your VPC, you can create a gateway endpoint for S3. This allows your instances to connect to S3 directly over the AWS network, avoiding the public internet. Similarly, you can use interface endpoints to access services like AWS Lambda, Amazon Kinesis, and AWS Systems Manager.

```
1. - Create a VPC endpoint for Amazon S3.
2. - Update route tables to direct S3 traffic to the endpoint.
```

```
3. - Ensure that security groups and network ACLs allow traffic to the endpoint.
```

### AWS Lambda in VPCs

Running AWS Lambda functions within VPCs ensures secure access to resources without needing to traverse the public Internet. Lambda functions can access VPC resources such as RDS databases, EC2 instances, and other VPC endpoints.

**Example:** Suppose you have a Lambda function that processes data stored in an RDS database within a VPC. By configuring the Lambda function to run within the VPC, you can ensure that all data transfers between the function and the database occur within the secure VPC network.

```
1. - Create a Lambda function and configure it to run within the VPC.
2. - Assign the function to the appropriate subnets and security groups.
3. - Ensure the security groups allow traffic between the Lambda function and the database.
```

You can design secure network flows that keep data off the public internet by leveraging AWS Transit Gateway, VPC endpoints, and Lambda within VPCs. This approach enhances data security and privacy, ensuring that sensitive information remains within the controlled AWS network environment.

## 11.3.9 Monitoring Network Telemetry

Determining which telemetry sources to monitor is crucial in designing an effective network security strategy. The selection of telemetry sources should be based on the specific network design, potential threats, and types of attacks the organization will likely face. Monitoring the right telemetry sources ensures that security teams have the necessary visibility to detect, analyze, and respond to security incidents effectively.

### Network Design Considerations

The network's architecture and components play a significant role in identifying the appropriate telemetry sources. Different parts of the network, such as the perimeter, internal segments, and cloud environments, will require distinct monitoring strategies. **Example:** In a hybrid cloud environment, telemetry sources may include VPC Flow Logs for monitoring traffic within AWS VPCs, firewall logs for perimeter security, and endpoint logs for monitoring devices within the on-premises network. This approach ensures comprehensive visibility across the entire network.

### Identifying Potential Threats and Attacks

Understanding the types of threats and attacks most relevant to the organization helps prioritize telemetry sources. Common threats include malware, phishing, insider threats, and distributed denial-of-service (DDoS) attacks. **Example:** For an organization concerned about DDoS attacks, it would be essential to monitor telemetry sources such as AWS Shield Advanced logs, which provide detailed information about DDoS attacks and mitigation actions. Additionally, monitoring web application logs can help identify patterns indicative of DDoS attacks targeting application layers.

### Key Telemetry Sources to Monitor

**VPC Flow Logs:** These logs capture information about IP traffic going to and from network interfaces in the VPC. They are crucial for monitoring network traffic, detecting unusual patterns, and investigating potential security incidents. **Example:** Enabling VPC Flow Logs on all subnets and network interfaces can help identify unexpected inbound or outbound traffic, which may indicate a compromised instance communicating with a command-and-control server.

**AWS CloudTrail:** CloudTrail provides a record of actions taken by a user, role, or AWS service in the AWS Management Console, AWS SDKs, command-line tools, and other AWS services. Monitoring these logs helps in detecting unauthorized access and changes to resources. **Example:** Setting up CloudTrail to log all API calls and management events can help detect unauthorized attempts to create, modify, or delete resources within the AWS environment.

**Amazon GuardDuty:** GuardDuty analyzes and processes data from multiple AWS data sources, including CloudTrail logs, VPC Flow Logs, and DNS logs. It uses threat intelligence and machine learning to detect malicious activity. **Example:** Using GuardDuty can help identify compromised instances, malicious IP addresses, and unusual API calls indicative of potential security breaches.

**AWS Config:** This service provides a detailed view of the configuration of AWS resources. It can be used to monitor changes and assess compliance with security policies. **Example:** AWS Config rules can be set up to alert on changes to security groups, such as allowing unrestricted SSH access, which may violate security policies.

**Amazon CloudWatch Logs:** CloudWatch Logs can collect and monitor log data from various AWS services and applications. It supports creating metrics from log data, which can trigger alarms based on predefined thresholds. **Example:** Configuring CloudWatch Alarms to monitor error rates in application logs can help detect potential issues before they escalate into significant incidents.

Selecting the appropriate telemetry sources for monitoring is vital for maintaining a secure network. By considering the network design, potential threats, and types of attacks, organizations can collect and analyze the right data to detect and respond to security incidents effectively.

## 11.3.10 Redundancy and Security for On-Premises Communication

When determining redundancy and security workload requirements for communication between on-premises environments and the AWS Cloud, it's essential to ensure that both high availability and robust security measures are in place. This involves evaluating the network architecture, selecting appropriate AWS services, and implementing best practices to meet these requirements.

### Redundancy Requirements

Redundancy is critical for maintaining uninterrupted communication and ensuring that services remain available even during failures. Key considerations include:

**Multiple VPN Connections:** Establish multiple VPN connections from on-premises data centers to AWS. This setup provides a failover path if one connection goes down.
Example: An organization might use AWS Site-to-Site VPN to set up two VPN tunnels from their data center to two different AWS regions or availability zones, ensuring continuous connectivity.

**AWS Direct Connect:** AWS Direct Connect can be used for higher bandwidth and more stable connectivity. Direct Connect provides a dedicated network connection between the on-premises environment and AWS.
Example: An organization can establish multiple Direct Connect connections to different AWS Direct Connect locations, ensuring redundancy and higher availability.

**AWS Transit Gateway:** Utilize AWS Transit Gateway to connect multiple VPCs and on-premises networks. Transit Gateway simplifies network management and allows for scalable and redundant connectivity.
Example: By connecting their on-premises environment to AWS Transit Gateway, an organization can ensure that traffic can still be routed through another available path if one VPN connection fails.

### Security Workload Requirements
Security is paramount when connecting on-premises environments to the cloud. Key security measures include:

**Encryption:** Ensure that all data transmitted between on-premises environments and AWS is encrypted. This includes using VPN tunnels with IPsec encryption and Direct Connect with MACsec (Media Access Control Security) encryption where available.
Example: Configuring AWS Site-to-Site VPN with AES-256 encryption for data in transit can protect sensitive information from interception.

**Access Controls:** Implement strict access controls and network segmentation to limit who can access resources both on-premises and in the cloud.
Example: AWS Identity and Access Management (IAM) policies and Network Access Control Lists (ACLs) are used to restrict access based on the principle of least privilege.

**Monitoring and Logging:** Enable comprehensive logging and monitoring to detect and respond to security incidents. Services like AWS CloudTrail, AWS Config, and Amazon CloudWatch can be used to track changes and monitor traffic.
Example: Setting up VPC Flow Logs and CloudTrail to log all API calls and network traffic, then using AWS CloudWatch Alarms to alert on suspicious activity.

### Example Scenario
Consider an organization that has critical workloads running both on-premises and in AWS. They need to ensure that their communication channels are redundant and secure.
- **Redundancy Setup:** The organization sets up two AWS Site-to-Site VPN connections to two different AWS regions. They also establish two AWS Direct Connect connections to different Direct Connect locations. These connections are integrated with AWS Transit Gateway for seamless failover and management.
- **Security Measures:** All data transmitted over the VPN and Direct Connect is encrypted using IPsec and MACsec. IAM policies restrict access to only those users who need it, and Network ACLs further segment the network to protect sensitive resources.
- **Monitoring:** The organization enables VPC Flow Logs, AWS CloudTrail, and CloudWatch Logs to monitor network traffic and API calls. They configure CloudWatch Alarms to notify their security team of any unusual activity, ensuring they can respond quickly to potential threats.

Determining redundancy and security workload requirements involves a comprehensive approach that includes multiple VPN connections, AWS Direct Connect, and AWS Transit Gateway for redundancy. Security measures like encryption, access controls, and monitoring are also essential to protect data and ensure compliance. By implementing these strategies, organizations can maintain secure and resilient communication between their on-premises environments and the AWS Cloud.

## 11.3.11 Identifying and Removing Unnecessary Access
Identifying and removing unnecessary network access is crucial for maintaining a secure and efficient AWS environment. Unnecessary access points can be potential security vulnerabilities, exposing your infrastructure to attacks and unauthorized access. Techniques for identifying and removing such access include regular audits, using AWS services, and implementing strict access controls.

### Techniques for Identifying Unnecessary Network Access
**Regular Network Audits:** Conducting regular audits of your network configurations can help identify open ports, security group rules, and network ACLs that are no longer needed.

Example: Use AWS Config to record and evaluate configurations of your AWS resources. AWS Config Rules can be used to automatically check for overly permissive security group rules and alert you to them.

**Flow Logs Analysis:** Analyze VPC Flow Logs to understand traffic patterns and identify unused network paths. VPC Flow Logs capture information about the IP traffic going to and from network interfaces in your VPC.
Example: Enable VPC Flow Logs for your VPC and use Amazon Athena to query these logs. This can help you identify security groups or network ACLs that are allowing traffic that is not needed.

**AWS Trusted Advisor:** Utilize AWS Trusted Advisor to get insights and recommendations on your AWS environment, including checks for security issues such as open ports on EC2 instances.
Example: AWS Trusted Advisor provides a Security category that includes checks for security groups with unrestricted access (e.g., 0.0.0.0/0 for inbound rules).

**Security Hub Findings:** AWS Security Hub aggregates and prioritizes security findings from multiple AWS services. It can provide insights into security group configurations and other network settings that may need to be tightened.
Example: Use AWS Security Hub to review and act on findings related to network security, such as overly permissive security group rules.

### Techniques for Removing Unnecessary Network Access

**Refine Security Group Rules:** Modify or delete security group rules that are too permissive or no longer necessary. This includes tightening CIDR ranges and removing rules that allow traffic from 0.0.0.0/0 unless absolutely necessary.
Example: Replace a rule that allows SSH access from any IP (0.0.0.0/0) with a rule that only allows access from your organization's IP range.

**Implement Network Segmentation:** Use network segmentation to restrict traffic between different parts of your network based on necessity. Network segmentation can limit the spread of attacks and reduce the attack surface.
Example: Create separate security groups for different tiers of your application (e.g., web, application, and database tiers) and only allow necessary traffic between them.

**Apply Principle of Least Privilege:** Ensure that all network access controls follow the principle of least privilege, granting only the minimum necessary permissions required for a particular task.
Example: If an application only needs to access a specific database port, configure the security group to allow traffic only on that port from specific IP ranges.

**Automated Remediation:** Use automated tools and scripts to identify and remediate unnecessary access. AWS Lambda can be used in conjunction with CloudWatch Events to automatically remove or modify security group rules based on specific criteria.
Example: Set up a CloudWatch Event rule to trigger a Lambda function that checks for security groups allowing inbound traffic from 0.0.0.0/0 and modifies or removes those rules.

### Example Scenario

Consider an organization that has multiple EC2 instances within a VPC. Over time, various security groups have been created, some of which have overly permissive rules. To secure their network, the organization performs the following steps:

- **Audit and Identify:** They use AWS Config to audit their security groups and identify rules that allow traffic from 0.0.0.0/0.

- **Analyze Traffic:** They enable VPC Flow Logs and analyze the logs using Amazon Athena to confirm which security groups are actually being used.
- **Refine Rules:** Based on the findings, they refine their security group rules to restrict access to only necessary IP ranges and ports.
- **Implement Segmentation:** They implement network segmentation by creating new security groups for different application tiers and configuring inter-tier traffic rules based on the principle of least privilege.
- **Automated Remediation:** They set up a Lambda function triggered by CloudWatch Events to automatically detect and remediate overly permissive security group rules in the future.

Regularly identifying and removing unnecessary network access is a critical aspect of maintaining a secure AWS environment. By conducting audits, analyzing traffic, refining access controls, and implementing automated remediation, organizations can significantly reduce their attack surface and improve overall security.

## 11.3.12 Managing Network Configurations

Managing network configurations as requirements change is essential for maintaining a secure and efficient network infrastructure in AWS environments. AWS Firewall Manager is a powerful tool that can help organizations manage and enforce network configurations, ensuring they adapt to evolving security and compliance requirements. This tool simplifies managing firewall rules, security groups, and other network security policies across multiple AWS accounts and resources.

**AWS Firewall Manager** enables administrators to centrally configure and manage firewall rules for AWS WAF, AWS Shield Advanced, security groups, and VPC security configurations. By using Firewall Manager, organizations can apply consistent security policies across their entire AWS environment, reducing the risk of misconfigurations and ensuring compliance with organizational standards.

### Example of Managing Network Configurations with AWS Firewall Manager

Imagine an organization that operates several AWS accounts and VPCs for different departments, each with specific security requirements. As the organization grows, it becomes challenging to maintain consistent security policies across all accounts and VPCs. This is where AWS Firewall Manager comes into play.

**Step-by-Step Process:**

- **Set Up AWS Organizations:** First, ensure that your AWS accounts are part of an AWS Organization. AWS Firewall Manager requires AWS Organizations to manage policies across multiple accounts.
  Example: The organization has three accounts: Development, Testing, and Production, all part of the same AWS Organization.

- **Configure AWS Firewall Manager:** Configure AWS Firewall Manager by setting up an administrative account that will manage the firewall policies. This account will have the necessary permissions to enforce security policies across all member accounts.
  Example: The Security Team account is designated as the administrative account for Firewall Manager.

- **Create Firewall Policies:** Define firewall policies that align with your organization's security requirements. These policies can include AWS WAF rules to protect web applications, AWS Shield Advanced protections against DDoS attacks, and security group policies to control inbound and outbound traffic.
  Example: The organization creates a WAF policy to block common web exploits, a Shield Advanced policy to mitigate DDoS attacks, and a security group policy to restrict SSH access to specific IP ranges.

- **Apply Policies Across Accounts:** Use AWS Firewall Manager to apply these policies across all relevant accounts and VPCs. Firewall Manager automatically enforces the policies and ensures that any new resources created in the member accounts adhere to the defined rules.
  Example: The WAF policy is applied to all web applications in the Development, Testing, and Production accounts, ensuring consistent protection against web exploits.

- **Monitor and Update Policies:** Continuously monitor the effectiveness of the policies using AWS Firewall Manager's reporting and alerting features. Policies must be updated to address new threats or compliance requirements as security requirements change.
  Example: The organization monitors the effectiveness of the WAF rules and updates them to address new vulnerabilities identified by its security team.

Managing network configurations in a dynamic environment requires tools that provide centralized control and automation. AWS Firewall Manager offers a robust solution for enforcing consistent security policies across multiple AWS accounts and VPCs. By using Firewall Manager, organizations can adapt to changing security requirements, ensure compliance, and maintain a strong security posture.

## 11.4 Security Controls for Compute Workloads

Ensuring robust security controls for compute workloads is crucial for protecting sensitive data and maintaining the integrity of applications in AWS environments. These controls encompass various strategies and tools designed to safeguard compute resources from threats and vulnerabilities. Implementing comprehensive security measures helps organizations meet compliance requirements, prevent unauthorized access, and mitigate potential risks.

## 11.4.1 Provisioning and Maintenance of EC2 Instances

Provisioning and maintaining EC2 instances are fundamental tasks in managing AWS environments effectively. Adhering to best practices ensures that instances are secure, reliable, and performant. Here are some key practices to follow:

- **Patching EC2 Instances:** Regularly patching your EC2 instances is crucial to protect them from known vulnerabilities. AWS Systems Manager Patch Manager can automate the process of patching managed instances with both security-related and other types of updates. This service allows you to define patch baselines, schedule patching during maintenance windows, and track the state of patches across your instances. For example, by setting up a patch baseline that includes critical and security updates, you can ensure that all instances are automatically updated without manual intervention.

- **Inspecting EC2 Instances:** Continuous monitoring and inspection of EC2 instances help identify potential security issues. AWS Inspector is a useful tool for assessing the security and compliance of applications deployed on EC2 instances. It performs automated security assessments, identifying vulnerabilities and deviations from best practices. For instance, running an assessment with AWS Inspector can reveal missing patches, insecure configurations, and common vulnerabilities, allowing you to take corrective actions promptly.

- **Creating Snapshots:** Regularly creating snapshots of your EC2 instances ensures that you have a reliable backup and recovery mechanism. Snapshots capture the state of an instance's EBS volumes at a specific point in time. These can be automated using AWS Backup or AWS Lambda functions to ensure consistent backups. For example, you might set up a daily Lambda function that triggers snapshots of critical instances, ensuring that recent backups are always available for recovery in case of data loss or instance failure.

**Example Implementation:**
Consider an organization that runs a web application on several EC2 instances. To maintain these instances, the organization implements the following strategy:
- **Patching:** They configure AWS Systems Manager Patch Manager to apply critical and security updates automatically during off-peak hours.
- **Inspecting:** AWS Inspector is scheduled to run weekly assessments, checking for vulnerabilities and compliance with security best practices.
- **Snapshots:** A Lambda function is set to create daily snapshots of the EC2 instances, ensuring that recent backups are always available.

By following these best practices, the organization can maintain secure and reliable EC2 instances, reducing the risk of vulnerabilities and ensuring quick recovery from potential failures.

## 11.4.2 IAM Instance Roles and Service Roles

IAM instance roles and service roles are crucial concepts in AWS for managing permissions and authorizations for compute workloads. Here's a detailed explanation of each, followed by a discussion on their application.

**IAM Instance Roles:**
IAM instance roles are IAM roles that you can assign to your Amazon EC2 instances. These roles provide temporary security credentials (access keys, secret keys, and session tokens) to applications running on the instances, enabling them to interact with other AWS services securely and without the need to store AWS credentials in the code. For example, an EC2 instance role might allow an application running on an EC2 instance to read from an S3 bucket without embedding the AWS credentials directly in the application.

**Example of an IAM Instance Role:**
Suppose you have an application running on an EC2 instance that needs to read files from an S3 bucket. You can create an IAM role with a policy that grants read access to the S3 bucket and then attach this role to your EC2 instance. When the application tries to access the S3 bucket, it uses the temporary credentials provided by the IAM role.

**IAM Service Roles:**
IAM service roles are similar to instance roles but are intended for use by AWS services on your behalf. These roles delegate permissions to AWS services to perform actions on your behalf. For instance, an IAM service role might allow AWS Lambda to log to CloudWatch Logs or allow Amazon RDS to access an S3 bucket for database backups.

**Example of an IAM Service Role:**
Consider an AWS Lambda function that needs to log execution details to CloudWatch Logs. You can create an IAM role with a policy that grants write access to CloudWatch Logs and assign this role to the Lambda function. This way, the Lambda function can log events without embedding AWS credentials.

### Applying IAM Instance Roles and Service Roles to Authorize Compute Workloads:
Applying IAM instance roles and service roles to authorize compute workloads involves a few steps. Here's how to do it effectively:

**Define the Required Permissions:**
Determine the specific actions that your compute workload needs to perform on other AWS services. For instance, if an EC2 instance needs to read from an S3 bucket, define a policy with the necessary S3 read permissions.

**Create an IAM Role:**
Create an IAM role with the defined policy. Ensure that the role type matches the use case: create an instance role for EC2 instances or a service role for other AWS services like Lambda, RDS, etc.

**Attach the Role to the Compute Workload:**

- For EC2 instances, you can attach the IAM instance role when launching the instance or to an existing instance using the AWS Management Console, CLI, or SDKs.
- For AWS services like Lambda or RDS, assign the IAM service role when configuring the service. For Lambda, this is done in the function configuration, and for RDS, during the database setup or configuration phase.

**Verify Role Assumption and Permissions:**
Ensure that the compute workload can successfully assume the IAM role and perform the required actions. This involves checking the AWS CloudTrail logs for role assumption events and validating that the workload can access the resources as intended.

## Example Implementation:
Suppose you have a data processing application running on an EC2 instance that needs to read data from an S3 bucket and write processing results to a DynamoDB table. Here's how you can set up the IAM roles:

**Create an IAM Role for the EC2 Instance:**

```
1.  {
2.    "Version": "2012-10-17",
3.    "Statement": [
4.      {
5.        "Effect": "Allow",
6.        "Action": [
7.          "s3:GetObject",
8.          "dynamodb:PutItem"
9.        ],
10.       "Resource": [
11.         "arn:aws:s3:::example-bucket/*",
12.         "arn:aws:dynamodb:us-east-1:123456789012:table/example-table"
13.       ]
14.     }
15.   ]
16. }
```

Attach this role to the EC2 instance.

**Create an IAM Role for AWS Lambda (if needed):**
If you also have a Lambda function that processes data and needs to log to CloudWatch:

```
1.  {
2.    "Version": "2012-10-17",
3.    "Statement": [
4.      {
5.        "Effect": "Allow",
6.        "Action": "logs:CreateLogStream",
7.        "Resource": "arn:aws:logs:us-east-1:123456789012:log-group:/aws/lambda/example-log-group:*"
8.      },
9.      {
10.       "Effect": "Allow",
11.       "Action": "logs:PutLogEvents",
```

```
12.        "Resource": "arn:aws:logs:us-east-1:123456789012:log-group:/aws/lambda/example-log-
group:log-stream:*"
13.      }
14.    ]
15. }
```

Assign this role to the Lambda function.

By following these steps, you ensure that your compute workloads are authorized to interact with other AWS services securely and efficiently, without the need for hardcoded credentials.

## 11.4.3 Vulnerability Scanning for Compute Workloads

Using services like Amazon Inspector and Amazon Elastic Container Registry (ECR) to scan compute workloads for vulnerabilities is crucial to maintaining security and compliance in AWS environments. These services help identify potential security risks and protect workloads against known vulnerabilities.

### Amazon Inspector

Amazon Inspector is an automated security assessment service that can improve the security and compliance of applications deployed on AWS. The service can automatically assess applications for vulnerabilities or deviations from best practices. Amazon Inspector produces a detailed list of security findings prioritized by severity level. These findings can be used to remediate issues and improve applications' security posture.

**Example Use Case for Amazon Inspector:** Consider a scenario where an organization has multiple EC2 instances running various applications. The organization can continuously monitor these instances for vulnerabilities by integrating Amazon Inspector. For instance, Amazon Inspector can identify instances with outdated software versions or misconfigurations that might expose the application to security risks. The findings from Amazon Inspector can then be reviewed and acted upon to ensure that all instances are compliant with security best practices.

### Amazon Elastic Container Registry (ECR)

Amazon ECR is a fully managed container registry that makes storing, managing, and deploying Docker container images easy. ECR integrates with Amazon Inspector to provide vulnerability scanning for container images, helping ensure that they are free from known vulnerabilities before they are deployed.

**Example Use Case for Amazon ECR:** Suppose an organization is using Docker containers to deploy applications. By pushing their container images to Amazon ECR, they can enable vulnerability scanning for these images. For example, if an image contains a version of a library with a known security flaw, Amazon ECR will detect this vulnerability and alert the development team. This allows the team to address the issue before the image is deployed to production, thereby reducing the risk of security breaches.

### Implementing Vulnerability Scanning

To implement vulnerability scanning using Amazon Inspector and Amazon ECR, follow these steps:

**Setup Amazon Inspector:**
- Navigate to the Amazon Inspector console.
- Create an assessment target by selecting the EC2 instances you want to scan.
- Configure an assessment template, specifying the rules packages and scheduling options.
- Run the assessment and review the findings in the console or set up notifications using Amazon SNS.

**Integrate Amazon ECR with Vulnerability Scanning:**
- Push your Docker images to Amazon ECR.

- Navigate to the ECR console, select the repository, and enable scan on push to enable image scanning on the repository.
- Monitor the scan results in the ECR console. Address any identified vulnerabilities by updating the base image or the dependencies used in your Dockerfile.

**Example Implementation**

For an application running on EC2 instances, you might use Amazon Inspector to perform a security assessment. Suppose the Inspector identifies that one of the instances is running an outdated version of OpenSSL with a known vulnerability. To mitigate the risk, the security team can then prioritize updating OpenSSL in this instance.

Similarly, push an image to Amazon ECR and enable scanning for containerized applications. Suppose the scan identifies a vulnerable version of a library in the image. In that case, the development team can update the Dockerfile to use a secure version of the library, rebuild the image, and push the updated image to ECR.

Using Amazon Inspector and Amazon ECR for vulnerability scanning helps ensure that your compute workloads are secure and compliant, reducing the risk of exploitation due to known vulnerabilities. Organizations can maintain a robust security posture and protect their applications and data by continuously monitoring and addressing security findings.

## 11.4.4 Host-Based Security Mechanisms

Implementing host-based security mechanisms such as firewalls and hardening is essential for securing individual hosts within an AWS environment. These mechanisms provide an additional layer of defense by protecting hosts from unauthorized access and reducing the attack surface.

### Host-Based Firewalls

A host-based firewall is a software application that controls incoming and outgoing network traffic based on an applied rule set. It acts as a barrier between the host and the network, filtering traffic to ensure that only authorized connections are allowed. In AWS, the most common host-based firewall used is the built-in firewall capabilities of the operating system, such as iptables for Linux or the Windows Firewall.

**Example Use Case for Host-Based Firewalls:**
Consider a scenario where an organization has a web server running on an EC2 instance. To secure this server, the organization can configure iptables rules on the Linux operating system to allow only necessary inbound traffic, such as HTTP (port 80) and HTTPS (port 443), and block all other ports. This ensures that only web traffic can reach the server, reducing the risk of unauthorized access.

### Host Hardening

Host hardening involves applying various security measures to strengthen the security posture of a host. This includes removing unnecessary software, disabling unused services, applying security patches, and configuring security settings to reduce vulnerabilities. Hardening makes it more difficult for attackers to exploit weaknesses in the host.

**Example Use Case for Host Hardening:** For an EC2 instance running a database server, the organization can perform the following hardening steps:
- Remove Unnecessary Software: Uninstall software that is not required for the database server's operation to reduce the potential attack surface.
- Disable Unused Services: Turn off services that are not in use, such as file sharing or remote desktop, to prevent unauthorized access points.

- Apply Security Patches: Regularly update the operating system and database software to the latest versions to mitigate known vulnerabilities.
- Configure Security Settings: Enforce strong password policies, enable encryption for data at rest and in transit, and configure audit logging to track access and changes to the database.

## Implementing Host-Based Security

To implement host-based security mechanisms in AWS, follow these steps:

### Configure Host-Based Firewalls

For Linux instances, use iptables or firewalld to define firewall rules.

```
1. # Example iptables rule to allow HTTP and HTTPS traffic
2. iptables -A INPUT -p tcp --dport 80 -j ACCEPT
3. iptables -A INPUT -p tcp --dport 443 -j ACCEPT
4. iptables -A INPUT -j DROP
```

For Windows instances, use Windows Firewall to configure inbound and outbound rules.

```
1. # Example PowerShell command to allow HTTP and HTTPS traffic
2. New-NetFirewallRule -DisplayName "Allow HTTP" -Direction Inbound -LocalPort 80 -Protocol TCP -Action Allow
3. New-NetFirewallRule -DisplayName "Allow HTTPS" -Direction Inbound -LocalPort 443 -Protocol TCP -Action Allow
```

### Perform Host Hardening

- **Remove Unnecessary Software:** Use package management tools like `yum`, `apt`, or Windows Add/Remove Programs to uninstall unneeded software.
- **Disable Unused Services:** Use `systemctl` or Windows Services Manager to disable unnecessary services.
- **Apply Security Patches:** Regularly run update commands like `yum update`, `apt update`, or use Windows Update.
- **Configure Security Settings:** Use tools like `chage` for password policies on Linux or Local Group Policy Editor on Windows for security configurations.

### Example Implementation

For a Linux-based web server, configure iptables to allow only web traffic and block all other traffic. Harden the server by uninstalling unused software like mail clients, disabling services like SSH if not needed, applying the latest security patches, and enforcing strong password policies.

Implementing host-based security mechanisms like firewalls and hardening enhances the overall security posture of individual hosts in an AWS environment. By controlling network traffic and reducing vulnerabilities, organizations can better protect their infrastructure from potential threats and attacks.

## 11.4.5 Creating Hardened EC2 AMIs

Creating hardened Amazon Machine Images (AMIs) is a crucial practice for ensuring the security and stability of EC2 instances in AWS environments. Hardening involves configuring an AMI to minimize vulnerabilities and comply with security policies before it is used to launch EC2 instances. Here are several techniques to create hardened AMIs:

### Base AMI Selection

Start by selecting a minimal base AMI. Using a lightweight, minimal operating system reduces the attack surface by including only the essential components. For example, Amazon Linux 2 or a minimal version of Ubuntu can serve as a good starting point.

## Patch Management

Ensure the base AMI is up-to-date with the latest security patches and updates. Regularly updating the operating system and installed software mitigates known vulnerabilities. Automated tools like AWS Systems Manager can help in keeping instances updated.

```
1. # For Linux
2. sudo yum update -y
3. sudo apt-get update && sudo apt-get upgrade -y
4.
5. # For Windows
6. Install-WindowsUpdate -AcceptAll -AutoReboot
```

## Remove Unnecessary Software

Uninstall software packages and services that are not required for the instance's intended function. This reduces the attack surface and potential entry points for attackers.

```
1. # For Linux
2. sudo yum remove -y <unnecessary-package>
3. sudo apt-get remove -y <unnecessary-package>
4.
5. # For Windows
6. Get-WindowsFeature | Where-Object {$_.Installed -eq $true} | Remove-WindowsFeature
```

## Disable Unnecessary Services

Disable services that are not needed. Services running on an instance can expose it to additional risks if they are not properly secured.

```
1. # For Linux
2. sudo systemctl disable <unnecessary-service>
3.
4. # For Windows
5. Get-Service | Where-Object {$_.Status -eq 'Running'} | Stop-Service -PassThru | Set-Service -StartupType Disabled
```

## Configure Security Settings

Apply security configurations such as strong password policies, user account restrictions, and firewall settings. Ensuring only authorized users have access and configuring the firewall to allow only necessary traffic are fundamental security measures.

```
1. # For Linux - example of firewall configuration
2. sudo iptables -A INPUT -p tcp --dport 22 -j ACCEPT
3. sudo iptables -A INPUT -j DROP
4.
5. # For Windows - example of configuring Local Group Policy
6. secedit /configure /db secedit.sdb /cfg C:\Windows\security\templates\hisecws.inf /overwrite
```

## Enable Logging and Monitoring

Enable logging to capture important system and security events. AWS CloudWatch and CloudTrail can be configured to monitor and log activity on your instances.

```
1. # For Linux - enabling auditd
2. sudo yum install audit
3. sudo systemctl enable auditd
```

```
4. sudo systemctl start auditd
5.
6. # For Windows - enabling Event Log forwarding
7. wecutil qc
```

### Implement Access Controls
Configure IAM roles and policies to manage access to the instances and resources. Ensuring that instances run with the minimum necessary privileges reduces the risk of exploitation.

```
1. # Example of attaching IAM role to EC2 instance
2. aws ec2 associate-iam-instance-profile --instance-id i-1234567890abcdef0 --iam-instance-profile Name=EC2InstanceRole
```

### Use Automated Tools for Hardening
Automated tools like AWS Inspector, CIS-CAT, or OpenSCAP can be used to scan instances for compliance with security benchmarks and automatically apply hardening measures.

```
1. # Running AWS Inspector
2. aws inspector start-assessment-run --assessment-template-arn arn:aws:inspector:us-west-2:123456789012:target/0-0kFIPusq/template/0-WEcUF8pF
3.
4. # Using CIS-CAT for hardening
5. sh cis-cat.sh -a
```

### Perform Security Testing
Regularly test the hardened AMIs using penetration testing and vulnerability assessments to ensure that all security controls are effective.

By following these techniques, organizations can create hardened AMIs that provide a secure foundation for their EC2 instances, helping to protect against various security threats and ensuring compliance with best practices and regulatory requirements.

## 11.4.6 Applying Patches Across EC2 Instances
Applying patches across a fleet of EC2 instances or container images is critical to ensure security and stability in an AWS environment. Here's a comprehensive discussion on how to approach this:

### Applying Patches to EC2 Instances
#### Using AWS Systems Manager
AWS Systems Manager (SSM) efficiently automates the patching process across EC2 instances.
- Systems Manager Patch Manager: Patch Manager automates patching managed instances with security-related and other types of updates. You can create patch baselines that include rules for auto-approving patches within days of their release, and a list of approved and rejected patches.
- Automation Documents: Use automation documents (runbooks) to create, manage, and run SSM automation workflows to patch your instances. For example, AWS provides a document named AWS-RunPatchBaseline that you can execute to apply patches.

#### Setting Maintenance Windows
Define maintenance windows to schedule patches and updates during off-peak hours to minimize disruption.

Maintenance Window Tasks: Create tasks in a maintenance window to perform patching operations, such as running the `AWS-RunPatchBaseline` document.

### Amazon EC2 Auto Scaling:
When using Auto Scaling groups, you can ensure new instances are launched with the latest AMIs (Amazon Machine Images) that include recent patches.
Update AMI: Regularly update the AMI with the latest patches and set Auto Scaling groups to use this updated AMI.

## Applying Patches to Container Images
### Using Amazon Elastic Container Registry (ECR)
Amazon ECR is a secure, scalable, and reliable managed AWS Docker registry service.

Image Scanning: ECR provides image scanning functionality to identify vulnerabilities in the container images. When a new image is pushed to the repository, it can be automatically scanned, and you can set up notifications to alert you to vulnerabilities.

### Continuous Integration/Continuous Deployment (CI/CD) Pipeline:
Implement a CI/CD pipeline to automate the process of building, scanning, and deploying container images.

- Jenkins, GitLab CI/CD, or AWS CodePipeline: Use these tools to automate the build process. Incorporate steps to pull the latest base images, apply patches, build the container image, scan it for vulnerabilities, and deploy it.
- AWS CodeBuild and CodePipeline: CodeBuild can compile your source code, run tests, and produce software packages that are ready to deploy. CodePipeline can orchestrate the end-to-end release process using CodeBuild and other services.

### Updating Running Containers
Ensure that the running containers are updated to the latest patched versions without downtime.

Amazon ECS or EKS: Amazon Elastic Container Service (ECS) or Amazon Elastic Kubernetes Service (EKS) can be used to orchestrate containerized application deployment. These services support rolling updates to update tasks and services without downtime.

## Example: Patching EC2 Instances Using AWS Systems Manager
**Set Up SSM Agent:** Ensure the SSM Agent is installed and running on all EC2 instances. This agent is pre-installed on Amazon Linux and Windows AMIs.

**Create a Patch Baseline:**
```
aws ssm create-patch-baseline --name "MyPatchBaseline" --operating-system "AMAZON_LINUX_2" --approved-patches-compliance-level "CRITICAL" --approval-rule-content file://path-to-json-file
```

**Create a Maintenance Window:**
```
aws ssm create-maintenance-window --name "MyMaintenanceWindow" --schedule "cron(0 3 ? * SUN *)" --duration 4 --cutoff 1
```

**Register Targets with the Maintenance Window:**
```
aws ssm register-target-with-maintenance-window --window-id "mw-0c50858d01EXAMPLE" --resource-type "INSTANCE" --targets Key=tag:Environment,Values=Production
```

**Register a Patch Task:**
```
aws ssm register-task-with-maintenance-window --window-id "mw-
0c50858d01EXAMPLE" --task-arn "AWS-RunPatchBaseline" --task-type
"AUTOMATION" --task-invocation-parameters
'{"Automation":{"DocumentVersion":"$LATEST","Parameters":{"Operation":
["Scan"]}}}'
```

By systematically applying patches using these techniques, organizations can ensure their EC2 instances and container images are secure and up-to-date, thus maintaining the integrity and security of their infrastructure.

## 11.4.7 Analyzing Amazon Inspector Findings

Amazon Inspector is a security assessment service that helps identify vulnerabilities and deviations from best practices in applications running on AWS. It generates detailed findings that are prioritized based on severity, enabling security teams to take appropriate actions to mitigate risks. Analyzing these findings and determining the right mitigation techniques is crucial for maintaining a secure environment.

### Analyzing Findings from Amazon Inspector

When Amazon Inspector completes an assessment run, it provides a detailed report with findings categorized by severity: High, Medium, Low, and Informational. Each finding includes a description of the issue, the affected resource, the potential impact, and recommended remediation steps.

### Example of Findings Analysis

**High Severity Finding**
- Description: A high severity finding might indicate a critical vulnerability, such as an unpatched software flaw that can be exploited remotely.
- Affected Resource: EC2 instance running a specific version of a web server software.
- Potential Impact: If exploited, this vulnerability could allow an attacker to execute arbitrary code, leading to a complete system compromise.
- Recommended Remediation: Apply the latest security patch provided by the software vendor to address this vulnerability.

**Medium Severity Finding:**
- Description: A medium severity finding could highlight a configuration issue, such as overly permissive security group rules.
- Affected Resource: A security group associated with multiple EC2 instances.
- Potential Impact: Overly permissive rules could allow unauthorized access to resources, increasing the risk of attacks.
- Recommended Remediation: Modify the security group rules to follow the principle of least privilege, allowing only necessary traffic.

**Low Severity Finding:**
- Description: A low severity finding might report an outdated software version that is not immediately exploitable but should be updated.
- Affected Resource: An application running on an EC2 instance.
- Potential Impact: While not currently exploitable, running outdated software can become a risk if vulnerabilities are later discovered.
- Recommended Remediation: Schedule an update to the latest software version during the next maintenance window.

## Determining Appropriate Mitigation Techniques

Once the findings are analyzed, appropriate mitigation techniques can be determined based on the severity and nature of the issues identified.

**Patching and Updates:**
- For findings related to unpatched vulnerabilities, the primary mitigation technique is to apply the relevant patches or updates. This involves downloading the latest security patches from the software vendor and deploying them across affected instances.
- Example: Applying a critical security patch to the web server software on an EC2 instance to fix a remote code execution vulnerability.

**Configuration Changes:**
- Configuration issues, such as overly permissive security group rules, can be mitigated by making appropriate changes to the configuration settings. This includes tightening security group rules, updating IAM policies, and adjusting other security settings.
- Example: Modifying a security group to restrict inbound SSH access to specific IP addresses rather than allowing access from anywhere.

**Monitoring and Alerts:**
- For findings that require continuous monitoring, setting up alerts and monitoring mechanisms is essential. Using AWS CloudWatch to set up alarms and log monitoring can help detect and respond to potential security incidents.
- Example: Configuring CloudWatch Alarms to monitor for unusual API activity that might indicate unauthorized access attempts.

**Best Practices Implementation:**
- Implementing AWS best practices, such as enabling multi-factor authentication (MFA), enforcing strong password policies, and using encryption for data at rest and in transit, can mitigate various findings.
- Example: Enabling MFA for all IAM users to enhance account security and prevent unauthorized access.

**Automated Remediation:**
- Leveraging AWS services like AWS Lambda to automate remediation tasks can help quickly address certain findings. For instance, Lambda functions can be triggered by CloudWatch Events to automatically remediate security group misconfigurations.
- Example: Using a Lambda function to automatically remove overly permissive rules from security groups when they are detected.

Analyzing findings from Amazon Inspector and determining appropriate mitigation techniques is a critical aspect of maintaining a secure AWS environment. By prioritizing findings based on severity and applying relevant mitigation strategies, organizations can effectively address vulnerabilities and configuration issues, thereby enhancing their overall security posture.

## 11.4.8 Passing Secrets and Credentials Securely

Passing secrets and credentials securely to compute workloads is a critical aspect of maintaining security in an AWS environment. Mismanagement of sensitive information can lead to significant security breaches. AWS offers several robust services and techniques to manage and securely distribute secrets and credentials, ensuring they are only accessible to authorized entities.

## AWS Secrets Manager

AWS Secrets Manager helps you protect access to your applications, services, and IT resources without the upfront cost and complexity of managing your own hardware security module (HSM) infrastructure. Secrets Manager enables you to rotate, manage, and retrieve database credentials, API keys, and other secrets throughout their lifecycle.

**Example:** Suppose you have an application running on an EC2 instance that needs to connect to a MySQL database. Instead of hardcoding the database credentials in the application code, you can store these credentials in AWS Secrets Manager. The application retrieves the credentials at runtime using the AWS SDK or CLI.

```
1. import boto3
2. from botocore.exceptions import NoCredentialsError, PartialCredentialsError
3.
4. def get_secret():
5.     secret_name = "my-database-secret"
6.     region_name = "us-west-2"
7.
8.     # Create a Secrets Manager client
9.     session = boto3.session.Session()
10.    client = session.client(service_name='secretsmanager', region_name=region_name)
11.
12.    try:
13.        get_secret_value_response = client.get_secret_value(SecretId=secret_name)
14.        secret = get_secret_value_response['SecretString']
15.        return secret
16.    except NoCredentialsError as e:
17.        print("Credentials not available", e)
18.    except PartialCredentialsError as e:
19.        print("Incomplete credentials", e)
```

## AWS Systems Manager Parameter Store

AWS Systems Manager Parameter Store provides a centralized store to manage configuration data and secrets across your AWS environment. Parameter Store is integrated with AWS Key Management Service (KMS), allowing you to store secrets using encryption keys that you manage.

**Example:** Store an API key in the Parameter Store and retrieve it securely in your application.

**Storing the Secret**

```
aws ssm put-parameter --name "api-key" --value "my-secret-api-key" --type "SecureString" --key-id "alias/aws/ssm"
```

**Retrieving the Secret**

```
1. import boto3
2.
3. ssm = boto3.client('ssm')
4. response = ssm.get_parameter(
5.     Name='api-key',
6.     WithDecryption=True
7. )
8. api_key = response['Parameter']['Value']
```

## IAM Roles and Policies

Using IAM roles and policies is another effective technique to pass secrets securely. IAM roles provide temporary security credentials for applications running on EC2 instances, Lambda functions, or other AWS services.

Example: Attach an IAM role to an EC2 instance that grants permission to retrieve secrets from AWS Secrets Manager.

**Create an IAM Role with Permissions**

```
1.  {
2.      "Version": "2012-10-17",
3.      "Statement": [
4.          {
5.              "Effect": "Allow",
6.              "Action": "secretsmanager:GetSecretValue",
7.              "Resource": "arn:aws:secretsmanager:us-west-2:123456789012:secret:my-database-secret"
8.          }
9.      ]
10. }
```

**Assign the Role to an EC2 Instance**

When launching the EC2 instance, assign the IAM role to it. The application running on this instance can then use the AWS SDK to retrieve the secret.

## Environment Variables

For containerized applications, environment variables are a common way to pass secrets. However, environment variables should be used cautiously as they can be exposed through various means such as logs or debugging tools. It's better to use environment variables to pass references to secrets stored in more secure services like AWS Secrets Manager or Parameter Store.

**Example:** Use AWS Secrets Manager in an ECS task definition to pass the secret as an environment variable.

```
1.  "containerDefinitions": [
2.      {
3.          "name": "my-container",
4.          "image": "my-image",
5.          "environment": [
6.              {
7.                  "name": "DB_CREDENTIALS",
8.                  "valueFrom": "arn:aws:secretsmanager:us-west-2:123456789012:secret:my-database-secret"
9.              }
10.         ]
11.     }
12. ]
```

Using services like AWS Secrets Manager, AWS Systems Manager Parameter Store, and IAM roles ensures that secrets and credentials are passed securely to compute workloads. These methods help prevent hardcoding sensitive information in code, reduce the risk of exposure, and provide centralized management and auditing capabilities.

# 11.5 Troubleshooting Network Security
## 11.5.1 Analyzing Reachability

Analyzing network reachability and security vulnerabilities in an AWS environment is crucial for ensuring the integrity and security of your infrastructure. AWS provides powerful tools such as VPC Reachability Analyzer and Amazon Inspector to assist in these tasks. These tools help identify potential network issues, misconfigurations, and security vulnerabilities, allowing you to take proactive measures to secure your environment.

## VPC Reachability Analyzer

VPC Reachability Analyzer is a network diagnostics tool that helps you analyze and debug network reachability between two endpoints in your VPC. It provides a comprehensive view of the path taken by network traffic, including all intermediary components such as security groups, network ACLs, route tables, and internet gateways. This tool is invaluable for troubleshooting connectivity issues and verifying that network configurations comply with security policies.

### Example Use Case

Suppose you have an EC2 instance that cannot reach a database instance in another subnet, and you need to determine the cause. You can use VPC Reachability Analyzer to analyze the path between the two instances.

**Configure Endpoints:** Specify the source and destination endpoints in the Reachability Analyzer. The source could be the ENI (Elastic Network Interface) of the EC2 instance, and the destination could be the ENI of the database instance.

**Run the Analysis:** VPC Reachability Analyzer will simulate the network traffic and provide a detailed report on the network path. It will highlight any misconfigurations or issues in the path, such as a missing route, incorrect security group rules, or blocked traffic by a network ACL.

**Example Analysis Result:** The analysis might reveal that the security group attached to the database instance does not allow inbound traffic from the EC2 instance's security group. By updating the security group rules to permit the required traffic, you can resolve the connectivity issue.

## Amazon Inspector

Amazon Inspector is an automated security assessment service that helps improve the security and compliance of applications deployed on AWS. It analyzes the network configurations of EC2 instances and identifies potential security vulnerabilities, misconfigurations, and deviations from best practices. Amazon Inspector provides a detailed list of findings, categorized by severity, and offers recommendations for remediation.

**Example Use Case:** You want to ensure that your EC2 instances are secure and compliant with best practices. By running Amazon Inspector, you can identify vulnerabilities and misconfigurations in your instances' network settings.

**Create an Assessment Target:** Define an assessment target by selecting the EC2 instances you want to analyze. Configure an assessment template that includes rules for network reachability and security best practices.

**Run the Assessment:** Amazon Inspector will evaluate the selected instances and provide a report with findings. The findings will include issues such as overly permissive security group rules, outdated software versions, and potential network vulnerabilities.

**Example Findings:** The assessment might reveal that an EC2 instance has a security group rule allowing inbound SSH traffic from any IP address (0.0.0.0/0), which poses a significant security risk. The recommended remediation would be to restrict SSH access to specific IP addresses or use a VPN.

## Integrating VPC Reachability Analyzer and Amazon Inspector

By integrating the insights from VPC Reachability Analyzer and Amazon Inspector, you can gain a comprehensive understanding of your network's security posture. VPC Reachability Analyzer helps you diagnose and resolve network reachability issues, while Amazon Inspector provides a deeper analysis of security vulnerabilities.

**Example Integration:** Use VPC Reachability Analyzer to ensure that your network paths are correctly configured and that there are no connectivity issues. Run Amazon Inspector to identify and remediate security vulnerabilities in your network configurations. For instance, if VPC Reachability Analyzer shows that a network path is blocked by a security group rule, and Amazon Inspector highlights that the same security group is overly permissive, you can adjust the security group rules to both enable connectivity and enhance security.

Using tools like VPC Reachability Analyzer and Amazon Inspector allows you to analyze network reachability and security vulnerabilities effectively. These tools provide detailed insights and recommendations, helping you maintain a secure and compliant AWS environment.

## 11.5.2 Understanding TCP/IP Networking Concepts

Understanding fundamental TCP/IP networking concepts is essential for managing and troubleshooting network operations. This includes grasping the differences between UDP and TCP, recognizing the role of ports, and understanding the OSI model.

**TCP vs. UDP:** TCP (Transmission Control Protocol) and UDP (User Datagram Protocol) are the two primary protocols used for data transmission over the internet.

**TCP:** TCP is a connection-oriented protocol that ensures reliable data transfer between devices. It establishes a connection before data is sent and ensures that all packets arrive in the correct order. TCP is used in applications where data integrity and order are crucial, such as web browsing (HTTP/HTTPS), email (SMTP), and file transfer (FTP).

Example: When you access a website, your browser uses TCP to ensure that all the web page data is received correctly and in order. If any packet is lost or corrupted, TCP will retransmit the packet.

**UDP:** UDP is a connectionless protocol that does not guarantee reliable delivery or order. It is faster and more efficient for applications that can tolerate some data loss or require real-time data transmission, such as video streaming, online gaming, and voice over IP (VoIP).

Example: When you watch a live video stream, UDP is often used because it allows the continuous flow of data with minimal delay, even if some packets are lost or arrive out of order.

**Ports:** Ports are numerical identifiers in TCP/IP networking that help distinguish different services or applications running on the same device. Ports range from 0 to 65535 and are categorized into well-known ports, registered ports, and dynamic or private ports.

- **Well-known Ports (0-1023):** Assigned to commonly used services (e.g., HTTP on port 80, HTTPS on port 443, FTP on port 21).
- **Registered Ports (1024-49151):** Assigned to specific services or applications by IANA.
- **Dynamic/Private Ports (49152-65535):** Used for temporary or private communication, typically for client-side applications.

For example, when you send an email using SMTP, the email client communicates with the SMTP server on port 25. Similarly, when you browse the web, your browser connects to web servers using port 80 for HTTP or port 443 for HTTPS.

**OSI Model:** The OSI (Open Systems Interconnection) model is a conceptual framework that standardizes the functions of a telecommunication or computing system into seven distinct layers. Each layer has specific responsibilities and interacts with the layers directly above and below it.

- Physical Layer: Handles the physical connection between devices, including cables, switches, and signal transmission.
- Data Link Layer: Manages data transfer between devices on the same network, providing error detection and correction (e.g., Ethernet, MAC addresses).
- Network Layer: Determines the best path for data to travel from source to destination, using logical addressing (e.g., IP addresses, routing).
- Transport Layer: Ensures reliable data transfer between devices, managing flow control, error checking, and retransmission (e.g., TCP, UDP).
- Session Layer: Manages sessions or connections between applications, handling establishment, maintenance, and termination of connections.
- Presentation Layer: Translates data between the application layer and the network, handling data encryption, compression, and formatting.
- Application Layer: Provides network services directly to user applications, such as web browsers and email clients (e.g., HTTP, FTP, SMTP).

**Example:**
When you visit a website, the data travels through the OSI model as follows:
- Physical Layer: The data is transmitted over the physical medium (e.g., Ethernet cable).
- Data Link Layer: The data is framed and transmitted to the next device on the network.
- Network Layer: The data is routed through various networks to reach the destination IP address.
- Transport Layer: TCP ensures that the data packets are delivered reliably and in order.
- Session Layer: A session is established between your browser and the web server.
- Presentation Layer: The data is encrypted/decrypted and formatted as needed.
- Application Layer: Your browser displays the web page content.

## 11.5.3 Reading Relevant Log Sources

Reading and interpreting relevant log sources such as Route 53 logs, AWS WAF logs, and VPC Flow Logs is crucial for monitoring and securing an AWS environment. These logs provide detailed information about network traffic, DNS queries, web application requests, and more. Understanding how to analyze these logs can help identify potential security issues, performance bottlenecks, and other operational concerns.

### Route 53 Logs

Amazon Route 53 is a scalable Domain Name System (DNS) web service. Route 53 logs can provide insights into DNS queries, helping administrators understand how users are accessing their services and identify potential DNS attacks.

**Reading Route 53 Logs:** Route 53 logs can be stored in Amazon S3 and typically include fields such as the request ID, query name, query type, response code, and more.

**Example:**
```
1c4a2b9f-9b00-4db5-a5d4-b084dcd3bede example.com. A NOERROR UDP
```
- Request ID: 1c4a2b9f-9b00-4db5-a5d4-b084dcd3bede
- Query Name: example.com
- Query Type: A (address record)
- Response Code: NOERROR (indicating successful resolution)
- Protocol: UDP (indicating the query was sent using the User Datagram Protocol)

**Interpreting Route 53 Logs:** This log entry shows a successful DNS query for "example.com" using an A record. By analyzing such logs, you can monitor DNS traffic patterns, detect abnormal query rates, and identify potential DNS abuse.

## AWS WAF Logs

AWS Web Application Firewall (WAF) helps protect web applications from common web exploits. AWS WAF logs capture detailed information about web requests that are monitored or blocked by the WAF rules.

**Reading AWS WAF Logs:** WAF logs can be stored in Amazon S3, Amazon CloudWatch Logs, or Amazon Kinesis Data Firehose. Each log entry typically includes the request details, such as the client IP address, request URI, action taken (allowed or blocked), and matched rule.

**Example:**

```
1.  {
2.      "timestamp": 1625097600,
3.      "formatVersion": 1,
4.      "webaclId": "arn:aws:wafv2:us-east-1:123456789012:regional/webacl/example-web-acl/12345678-1234-1234-1234-123456789012",
5.      "terminatingRuleId": "example-rule-id",
6.      "terminatingRuleType": "REGULAR",
7.      "action": "BLOCK",
8.      "httpRequest": {
9.          "clientIp": "192.0.2.44",
10.         "country": "US",
11.         "uri": "/example",
12.         "httpMethod": "GET",
13.         "httpVersion": "HTTP/1.1"
14.     }
15. }
```

- Timestamp: 1625097600
- WebACL ID: example-web-acl
- Terminating Rule ID: example-rule-id
- Action: BLOCK
- Client IP: 192.0.2.44
- URI: /example
- HTTP Method: GET

**Interpreting AWS WAF Logs:** This log entry indicates that a GET request to "/example" from IP address 192.0.2.44 was blocked by a specific rule. By analyzing WAF logs, you can identify attack patterns, such as SQL injection attempts or cross-site scripting (XSS) attacks, and adjust your WAF rules to enhance security.

## VPC Flow Logs

VPC Flow Logs capture information about the IP traffic going to and from network interfaces in a VPC. These logs help you monitor network traffic, troubleshoot connectivity issues, and detect potential security threats.

**Reading VPC Flow Logs:** VPC Flow Logs can be stored in Amazon S3, Amazon CloudWatch Logs, or Amazon Kinesis Data Firehose. Each log entry includes fields such as the source IP, destination IP, source port, destination port, protocol, and action.

**Example**

```
version account-id interface-id srcaddr dstaddr srcport dstport protocol packets bytes start end action log-status 2 123456789012 eni-12345678 192.0.2.1 198.51.100.1 12345 80 6 10 5000 1625097600 1625097660 ACCEPT OK
```

- Version: 2
- Account ID: 123456789012
- Interface ID: eni-12345678
- Source IP: 192.0.2.1

- Destination IP: 198.51.100.1
- Source Port: 12345
- Destination Port: 80
- Protocol: 6 (TCP)
- Packets: 10
- Bytes: 5000
- Start Time: 1625097600
- End Time: 1625097660
- Action: ACCEPT

**Interpreting VPC Flow Logs:** This log entry shows that TCP traffic from source IP 192.0.2.1 and port 12345 to destination IP 198.51.100.1 and port 80 was accepted. By analyzing flow logs, you can identify unauthorized access attempts, unusual traffic patterns, and potential data exfiltration.

Understanding and analyzing logs from Route 53, AWS WAF, and VPC Flow Logs is crucial for maintaining a secure and efficient AWS environment. These logs provide valuable insights into DNS queries, web application traffic, and network flows, helping you detect and respond to security threats and operational issues.

## 11.5.4 Identifying Network Connectivity Problems

Identifying, interpreting, and prioritizing problems in network connectivity are crucial for maintaining the reliability and performance of an AWS environment. Effective network troubleshooting involves a combination of monitoring tools, diagnostic techniques, and a systematic approach to addressing issues. Here are key techniques to achieve this:

### Identifying Network Connectivity Problems

**Monitoring Tools:** Using monitoring tools like Amazon CloudWatch, VPC Flow Logs, and AWS CloudTrail helps you track network performance and detect anomalies.
Example: Amazon CloudWatch can be set up to monitor metrics such as network traffic, latency, and error rates. If you notice a sudden spike in latency or a drop in network throughput, it may indicate a connectivity issue.

**Network Diagnostics Tools:** AWS provides tools like VPC Reachability Analyzer, AWS Direct Connect, and network performance metrics to diagnose connectivity problems.
Example: VPC Reachability Analyzer can help determine whether a network path between two endpoints is reachable and identify any configuration issues preventing connectivity.

**Logs and Alerts:** Analyzing logs from Route 53, AWS WAF, and VPC Flow Logs can provide insights into potential network problems. Setting up alerts for specific events can help in early detection.
Example: If VPC Flow Logs indicate repeated denied access attempts, it may point to a misconfiguration in security groups or network ACLs.

### Interpreting Network Connectivity Problems

**Analyzing Logs and Metrics:** Interpret logs and metrics to understand the nature of the connectivity issue. Look for patterns or anomalies that can indicate the root cause.
Example: If CloudWatch metrics show increased latency, correlating this with VPC Flow Logs might reveal that the traffic is being routed through an unexpected path, causing delays.

**Using Diagnostic Tools:** Tools like VPC Reachability Analyzer can provide detailed information about the network path and highlight where the connectivity is failing.

Example: Running VPC Reachability Analyzer between an EC2 instance and an RDS database can show if a security group rule or network ACL is blocking the traffic.

**Checking Configuration:** Review the configuration of network components such as security groups, route tables, network ACLs, and VPC peering connections to ensure they are correctly set up.
Example: If an instance cannot reach a subnet, verify that the route table associated with the subnet includes a route to the destination CIDR block.

### Prioritizing Network Connectivity Problems

**Assessing Impact:** Determine the impact of the connectivity issue on your applications and business operations. Issues affecting critical services or large numbers of users should be prioritized.
Example: A connectivity issue affecting the database of a production application should be prioritized over a similar issue in a development environment.

**Severity and Frequency:** Consider the severity and frequency of the connectivity problems. Frequent or severe issues that cause significant downtime or data loss should be addressed urgently.
Example: If users frequently experience timeouts when accessing a web application, this indicates a high-severity issue that requires immediate attention.

**Root Cause Analysis:** Prioritize problems based on the likelihood of recurring issues. Problems with identified root causes that can prevent future occurrences should be given high priority.
Example: If a misconfigured security group is identified as the root cause of repeated connectivity failures, fixing this should be a top priority to prevent similar issues.

### Example Scenario

Scenario: A company experiences intermittent connectivity issues between its web servers and a database hosted in another subnet.

#### Steps to Identify, Interpret, and Prioritize

**Identify:** Use CloudWatch to monitor network latency and throughput. Enable VPC Flow Logs to capture traffic information. Set up alerts for high latency or packet loss.

**Interpret:** Analyze CloudWatch metrics to identify periods of high latency. Check VPC Flow Logs to see if traffic is being dropped or rerouted. Use VPC Reachability Analyzer to ensure the network path is correctly configured.

**Prioritize:** Assess the impact: Since the issue affects the production environment, it is critical. Determine severity: Frequent timeouts indicate a high-severity issue. Conduct root cause analysis: If a security group misconfiguration is identified, prioritize fixing this to prevent recurrence.

By systematically identifying, interpreting, and prioritizing network connectivity problems, you can ensure that critical issues are addressed promptly, minimizing downtime and maintaining optimal network performance.

## 11.5.5 Determining Solutions for Desired Network Behavior

Determining solutions to achieve desired network behavior in an AWS environment involves understanding the current network configuration, identifying gaps or issues, and implementing best practices and appropriate AWS services to meet the requirements. Here's a detailed discussion on how to achieve this, including examples and references.

## Understanding Current Network Configuration

The first step in achieving desired network behavior is to thoroughly understand the current network setup. This includes mapping out all network components such as VPCs, subnets, route tables, security groups, network ACLs, and any peering connections or Direct Connect links. Tools like AWS Network Manager and AWS Config can be used to visualize and audit the network configuration.

**Example:** An organization has multiple VPCs for different departments, interconnected via VPC peering. They need to ensure that only specific subnets can communicate across VPCs while others remain isolated.

## Identifying Gaps or Issues

Next, identify any gaps or issues that may prevent the network from functioning as desired. This can be done by analyzing network traffic patterns using VPC Flow Logs, checking route tables for correct routes, reviewing security group and network ACL rules, and using AWS Trusted Advisor to identify any misconfigurations or security risks.

**Example:** The organization notices that some subnets in the development VPC can access resources in the production VPC, which is against their security policy. VPC Flow Logs reveal that traffic from development subnets is reaching production subnets.

## Implementing Best Practices and Appropriate AWS Services

After identifying gaps or issues, implement solutions and best practices to achieve the desired network behavior. This involves configuring AWS services and network settings correctly.

**Configuring Route Tables:** Ensure that route tables are correctly configured to control the flow of traffic within and between VPCs. For cross-VPC traffic, routes should be carefully set up to only allow necessary traffic.
Example: Update the route table in the development VPC to ensure that only specific subnets have routes to the production VPC subnets, and vice versa. This can be achieved by adding or modifying route entries.

**Using Security Groups and Network ACLs:** Security groups and network ACLs should be configured to enforce granular access controls, ensuring that only authorized traffic is allowed.
Example: Modify the security group rules to restrict access between the development and production VPCs. For instance, ensure that only the web server subnet in the development VPC can access the database subnet in the production VPC.

**Implementing AWS Transit Gateway:** For complex networks with multiple VPCs and on-premises connections, AWS Transit Gateway can simplify network management by acting as a hub for interconnecting VPCs and on-premises networks.
Example: The organization can use AWS Transit Gateway to centralize and manage connectivity between multiple VPCs. This allows for consistent and scalable routing policies and reduces the complexity of managing multiple peering connections.

**Utilizing Network Address Translation (NAT) and PrivateLink:** For secure access to the internet and AWS services, use NAT gateways or instances to enable outbound internet traffic for instances in private subnets. AWS PrivateLink can be used to securely access AWS services and third-party services without exposing traffic to the public internet.
Example: Deploy a NAT gateway in the public subnet to allow instances in private subnets to access the internet securely. Use AWS PrivateLink to connect to AWS services like S3 or third-party services directly within the VPC.

### Example Implementation: Achieving Desired Network Isolation

**Scenario:** The organization wants to ensure that the production environment is isolated from the development environment, except for specific communication needed for application development. The following are the steps:

**Review and Update Route Tables:** Identify and remove any unnecessary routes that allow development subnets to reach production subnets. Ensure that only the required routes are present for necessary communication.

**Configure Security Groups:** Define security group rules that only allow traffic from the web server subnet in the development VPC to the database subnet in the production VPC. Block all other traffic between the VPCs using appropriate security group rules.

**Implement AWS Transit Gateway (if applicable):** Create a Transit Gateway and attach both VPCs to it. Define route tables within the Transit Gateway to control the traffic flow between the VPCs.

**Use NAT Gateway and PrivateLink:** Set up a NAT gateway for outbound internet access for private subnets. Utilize AWS PrivateLink to access AWS services securely from the VPCs.

Determining solutions to achieve desired network behavior involves a combination of understanding the current setup, identifying gaps, and implementing AWS best practices and services. By carefully configuring route tables, security groups, network ACLs, and leveraging services like AWS Transit Gateway and PrivateLink, organizations can ensure their networks function securely and efficiently.

## 11.5.6 Analyzing Log Sources

Analyzing log sources is a critical task for identifying and troubleshooting network security problems in an AWS environment. Logs provide detailed information about network traffic, security events, and system behaviors, allowing administrators to detect anomalies, diagnose issues, and respond to threats. Key log sources include VPC Flow Logs, AWS CloudTrail, and AWS WAF logs. Here's how to analyze these log sources effectively.

### VPC Flow Logs

VPC Flow Logs capture information about IP traffic going to and from network interfaces in a VPC. They are essential for monitoring network traffic and troubleshooting connectivity issues. Each flow log record includes details such as source and destination IP addresses, ports, protocol, and action taken (ACCEPT or REJECT).

**Example:**
Suppose you notice unusual traffic patterns or suspect a network intrusion. By analyzing VPC Flow Logs, you can identify unauthorized access attempts or data exfiltration.

**Analysis Steps:**
**Enable VPC Flow Logs:** Ensure VPC Flow Logs are enabled for your VPCs and are being stored in Amazon S3 or CloudWatch Logs for analysis.

**Filter and Search Logs:** Use filters to search for specific IP addresses, ports, or protocols. For instance, you can filter logs to identify traffic from suspicious IP addresses.

**Identify Anomalies:** Look for unusual traffic patterns, such as high volumes of traffic from unexpected sources or attempts to access restricted ports.

**Example Log Entry:**

```
1. 2 123456789012 eni-12345678 192.0.2.1 198.51.100.1 12345 80 6 10 5000 1625097600 1625097660 ACCEPT
OK
```

- Source IP: 192.0.2.1
- Destination IP: 198.51.100.1
- Source Port: 12345
- Destination Port: 80
- Action: ACCEPT

In this example, if 192.0.2.1 is an unauthorized IP trying to access port 80, this could indicate a potential threat.

## AWS CloudTrail

AWS CloudTrail logs provide a record of API calls made within your AWS account, including actions taken through the AWS Management Console, AWS SDKs, command-line tools, and other AWS services. CloudTrail logs are crucial for auditing and monitoring user activities and identifying potential security issues.

**Example:** If you suspect unauthorized access or changes to your network configuration, CloudTrail logs can help you trace the actions performed by users or services.

**Analysis Steps:**

**Enable CloudTrail:** Ensure CloudTrail is enabled and configured to log all API calls and store the logs in Amazon S3 or CloudWatch Logs.

**Search for Specific Events:** Filter logs to search for specific API calls, such as changes to security group rules or the creation of new EC2 instances.

**Audit User Activities:** Review logs to audit user activities and identify any suspicious or unauthorized actions.

**Example Log Entry:**

```
1.  {
2.    "eventTime": "2021-07-01T12:00:00Z",
3.    "eventSource": "ec2.amazonaws.com",
4.    "eventName": "AuthorizeSecurityGroupIngress",
5.    "awsRegion": "us-west-2",
6.    "sourceIPAddress": "203.0.113.1",
7.    "userAgent": "aws-cli/2.1.29",
8.    "requestParameters": {
9.      "groupId": "sg-12345678",
10.     "ipPermissions": [{
11.       "ipProtocol": "tcp",
12.       "fromPort": 22,
13.       "toPort": 22,
14.       "ipRanges": [{"cidrIp": "0.0.0.0/0"}]
15.     }]
16.   },
17.   "responseElements": null,
18.   "requestID": "12345678-1234-1234-1234-123456789012"
19. }
```

- Event Name: AuthorizeSecurityGroupIngress
- Source IP Address: 203.0.113.1
- User Agent: aws-cli/2.1.29
- Action: Added a rule to allow SSH access from any IP address (0.0.0.0/0)

This log entry shows that an SSH access rule was added to a security group, which can be a security risk if not intended.

## AWS WAF Logs

AWS WAF logs provide information about web requests that are monitored or blocked by your Web Application Firewall rules. These logs are useful for detecting and analyzing web-based attacks, such as SQL injection or cross-site scripting (XSS).

**Example:** If your web application is experiencing suspicious or malicious traffic, AWS WAF logs can help you identify and block these threats.

**Analysis Steps:**
**Enable WAF Logging:** Ensure WAF logging is enabled and logs are being stored in Amazon S3, CloudWatch Logs, or Kinesis Data Firehose.

**Filter and Analyze Logs:** Filter logs based on request patterns, IP addresses, or specific WAF rules to identify malicious activities.

**Review Blocked Requests:** Analyze logs of blocked requests to understand the nature of the attacks and adjust WAF rules accordingly.

**Example Log Entry:**

```
1.  {
2.      "timestamp": 1625097600,
3.      "formatVersion": 1,
4.      "webaclId": "arn:aws:wafv2:us-east-1:123456789012:regional/webacl/example-web-acl/12345678-1234-1234-1234-123456789012",
5.      "terminatingRuleId": "example-rule-id",
6.      "terminatingRuleType": "REGULAR",
7.      "action": "BLOCK",
8.      "httpRequest": {
9.          "clientIp": "192.0.2.44",
10.         "country": "US",
11.         "uri": "/example",
12.         "httpMethod": "GET",
13.         "httpVersion": "HTTP/1.1"
14.     }
15. }
```

- Action: BLOCK
- Client IP: 192.0.2.44
- URI: /example
- HTTP Method: GET

This log entry indicates that a GET request to "/example" from IP 192.0.2.44 was blocked by a specific WAF rule, suggesting a potential attack attempt.

Analyzing log sources such as VPC Flow Logs, AWS CloudTrail, and AWS WAF logs is essential for identifying and troubleshooting network security problems in an AWS environment. These logs provide detailed insights into network traffic, user activities, and web requests, enabling you to detect anomalies, diagnose issues, and respond to threats effectively.

# 11.5.7 Capturing Traffic Samples

Capturing traffic samples for problem analysis is essential in diagnosing and resolving network issues, detecting anomalies, and enhancing security. AWS offers tools like VPC Traffic Mirroring that facilitate the collection and analysis of network traffic in real-time. Here's how to leverage these techniques effectively:

**Traffic Mirroring** in AWS allows you to capture and inspect network traffic from EC2 instances. This feature is useful for performing deep packet inspection, troubleshooting network issues, and analyzing traffic patterns to detect security threats.

**Example Use Case:** Suppose you are experiencing intermittent connectivity issues in your application hosted on EC2 instances. Using Traffic Mirroring, you can capture network traffic to diagnose the root cause of the problem.

## Setting Up Traffic Mirroring

**Create a Traffic Mirror Target:**
The target is where the mirrored traffic will be sent. This can be an ENI (Elastic Network Interface) of another EC2 instance that will analyze the traffic, or an AWS Network Load Balancer.

```
aws ec2 create-traffic-mirror-target --network-interface-id eni-12345678 --description "MyTrafficMirrorTarget"
```

**Create a Traffic Mirror Filter:**
Filters determine which traffic is mirrored. You can define rules based on protocol, port range, and CIDR blocks.

```
aws ec2 create-traffic-mirror-filter --description "MyTrafficMirrorFilter"
```

Add inbound and outbound rules to the filter:

```
aws ec2 create-traffic-mirror-filter-rule --traffic-mirror-filter-id tmf-12345678 --rule-number 1 --direction ingress --action accept --destination-cidr-block 0.0.0.0/0 --source-cidr-block 0.0.0.0/0 --protocol 6 --destination-port-range FromPort=80,ToPort=80
```

**Create a Traffic Mirror Session:**
The session ties the source (the instance where traffic will be mirrored from), target, and filter together.

```
aws ec2 create-traffic-mirror-session --network-interface-id eni-87654321 --traffic-mirror-target-id tmt-12345678 --traffic-mirror-filter-id tmf-12345678 --session-number 1
```

## Analyzing Captured Traffic

Once traffic mirroring is set up, the captured traffic can be analyzed using packet inspection tools like Wireshark, tcpdump, or managed services like AWS Traffic Mirroring with third-party solutions such as Suricata or Zeek.

**Example Analysis with Wireshark:**

**Capture Traffic:**
Use an EC2 instance with the mirrored traffic target and install Wireshark.

```
sudo yum install wireshark -y
```

**Analyze Traffic:**
Open Wireshark and start capturing on the interface associated with the Traffic Mirror Target. You can filter traffic by protocols, IP addresses, or ports to pinpoint issues.

```
tcpdump -i eth0 'tcp port 80'
```

## Benefits of Traffic Mirroring

**Deep Packet Inspection:** Traffic Mirroring allows for detailed inspection of packets, enabling you to diagnose complex network issues that are not detectable through logs alone.

**Security Analysis:** By mirroring traffic to an intrusion detection system (IDS) like Suricata or a network traffic analyzer like Zeek, you can identify malicious activity and potential security breaches.

**Troubleshooting Connectivity Issues:** Capturing traffic between application components can help identify bottlenecks, latency issues, or misconfigurations affecting connectivity.

## Best Practices

**Scope Your Mirroring Sessions:** Be selective about which traffic to mirror. Mirroring all traffic can be resource-intensive and may lead to performance issues. Use filters to capture only relevant traffic.

**Secure the Analysis Environment:** Ensure that the instances or systems receiving mirrored traffic are secure and have the necessary access controls in place to prevent unauthorized access to sensitive data.

**Compliance and Privacy:** Be mindful of compliance requirements and privacy concerns when capturing and analyzing network traffic. Ensure that traffic mirroring complies with organizational policies and regulatory standards.

Capturing traffic samples using tools like AWS Traffic Mirroring provides invaluable insights into network behavior, enabling you to diagnose and resolve issues effectively. By carefully setting up traffic mirroring sessions, using appropriate filters, and analyzing captured traffic with powerful tools, you can enhance the security, performance, and reliability of your AWS environment.

# 11.6 Lab Exercises
## 11.6.1 Implementing Edge Security Controls

Implementing security controls on edge services like AWS WAF, Amazon CloudFront, and Amazon Route 53 involves setting up protective measures to ensure your web applications are secure from common threats. Here is a step-by-step hands-on lab to achieve this.

### Part 1: Setting Up AWS WAF

**Objective:** Configure AWS WAF to protect your web applications from common web exploits.

#### Step 1: Create a Web ACL

**Navigate to the AWS WAF Console:** Go to the AWS WAF Console.

**Create a Web ACL:** Click on "Create web ACL." Enter a name for the Web ACL (e.g., "MyWebACL"). Choose the region where you want to create the Web ACL. For the CloudFront distribution, choose "CloudFront."

**Configure Metrics:** Enter a metric name (e.g., "MyWebACLMetric"). Set up sampling if needed for performance monitoring.

**Add Rules:** Add predefined AWS Managed Rules (e.g., "AWSManagedRulesCommonRuleSet"). Optionally, create custom rules to meet specific security requirements.

**Set Default Action:** Choose the default action for requests that don't match any rules (e.g., "Allow" or "Block").

**Review and Create:** Review the configuration and click "Create Web ACL."

### Step 2: Associate the Web ACL with a Resource
**Add AWS Resources:** Click on "Add AWS resources." Select the CloudFront distribution, API Gateway, or Application Load Balancer to associate with the Web ACL.

**Confirm Association:** Click "Add" to confirm the association.

## Part 2: Configuring Amazon CloudFront
**Objective:** Configure Amazon CloudFront to distribute your content securely.

### Step 1: Create a CloudFront Distribution
**Navigate to the CloudFront Console:** Go to the Amazon CloudFront Console.

**Create Distribution:** Click on "Create Distribution." Select "Web" as the delivery method.

**Configure Distribution Settings:** Enter the origin domain name (e.g., your S3 bucket or HTTP server). Configure default cache behavior settings (e.g., Viewer Protocol Policy set to "Redirect HTTP to HTTPS"). Set allowed HTTP methods (e.g., "GET, HEAD, OPTIONS" for static content or "GET, HEAD, OPTIONS, PUT, POST, PATCH, DELETE" for dynamic content).

**Enable Logging:** Enable logging to an S3 bucket for monitoring and troubleshooting.
**Enable AWS WAF:** In the "AWS WAF Web ACL" section, choose the Web ACL created in Part 1.
**Review and Create:** Review the settings and click "Create Distribution."

### Step 2: Configure Security Headers (Optional)
**Add Custom Headers:** Navigate to the "Behaviors" tab of your CloudFront distribution. Select the default behavior and click "Edit." Add custom headers (e.g., Content-Security-Policy, X-Content-Type-Options) for additional security.

## Part 3: Securing DNS with Amazon Route 53
**Objective:** Secure your DNS records and enable routing policies in Amazon Route 53.

### Step 1: Create a Hosted Zone
**Navigate to the Route 53 Console:** Go to the Amazon Route 53 Console.
**Create Hosted Zone:** Click on "Create hosted zone." Enter the domain name and optional description. Choose the type (e.g., "Public Hosted Zone") and click "Create."

### Step 2: Create DNS Records
**Add Records:** In the hosted zone, click on "Create Record Set." Enter the record name (e.g., "www") and select the type (e.g., "A" record). Enter the alias target or IP address. Configure routing policies (e.g., latency-based routing, geolocation routing).
**Enable DNSSEC (Optional):** Enable DNSSEC signing for the hosted zone to protect against DNS spoofing.

### Step 3: Implement Health Checks
**Create Health Check:** Click on "Health Checks" and then "Create Health Check." Configure the endpoint to be checked (e.g., a specific URL or IP address). Set up the protocol, port, and path to check.

Associate with DNS Records: Associate the health check with relevant DNS records to enable failover routing.

By following these steps, you can implement security controls on edge services like AWS WAF, Amazon CloudFront, and Amazon Route 53. These configurations will help protect your web applications from common web exploits, ensure secure content distribution, and secure your DNS infrastructure.

## 11.6.2 Designing Network Security Configurations
Network security in AWS VPCs can be managed using Security Groups and Network ACLs (Access Control Lists). These mechanisms help control the flow of traffic to and from your resources in the VPC. Here's a hands-on lab to design and configure these network security mechanisms.

### Part 1: Designing and Configuring Security Groups
**Objective:** Configure Security Groups to control inbound and outbound traffic for EC2 instances within a VPC.

### Step 1: Create a VPC
**Navigate to the VPC Console:** Go to the Amazon VPC Console.
**Create a VPC:** Click on "Your VPCs" in the navigation pane. Click "Create VPC." Enter a name for your VPC (e.g., "MyVPC"). Specify an IPv4 CIDR block (e.g., "10.0.0.0/16"). Leave other settings as default and click "Create VPC."

### Step 2: Create Security Groups
**Create a Security Group:** Click on "Security Groups" in the navigation pane. Click "Create security group." Enter a name for your security group (e.g., "WebServerSG"). Select the VPC you created earlier. Add a description (e.g., "Security group for web servers").

**Configure Inbound Rules:** Click "Add rule." Type: Select "HTTP" to allow web traffic. Protocol: Automatically set to "TCP." Port Range: Automatically set to "80." Source: Select "Anywhere" (0.0.0.0/0) to allow traffic from any IP address (for public access). Add another rule for HTTPS (port 443) similarly. Optionally, add a rule for SSH (port 22) but restrict it to your IP address for management purposes.

**Configure Outbound Rules:** By default, all outbound traffic is allowed. You can modify this as needed. Click "Create security group."

### Step 3: Attach Security Groups to EC2 Instances
**Launch an EC2 Instance:** Navigate to the EC2 Console. Click "Launch Instance." Follow the wizard to select an Amazon Machine Image (AMI) and instance type. In the "Configure Security Group" step, select the security group you created earlier (WebServerSG). Complete the wizard and launch the instance.

**Verify Security Group:** Once the instance is running, verify that it's accessible via HTTP/HTTPS by navigating to its public IP address in a web browser.

## Part 2: Designing and Configuring Network ACLs

**Objective:** Configure Network ACLs to provide an additional layer of security by controlling inbound and outbound traffic at the subnet level.

### Step 1: Create Subnets

**Create Subnets:** Navigate to the VPC Console. Click on "Subnets" in the navigation pane. Click "Create subnet." Enter a name for the subnet (e.g., "PublicSubnet"). Select the VPC you created earlier. Specify an IPv4 CIDR block (e.g., "10.0.1.0/24"). Click "Create."

### Step 2: Create Network ACLs

**Create a Network ACL:** Click on "Network ACLs" in the navigation pane. Click "Create network ACL." Enter a name for the Network ACL (e.g., "MyNetworkACL"). Select the VPC you created earlier. Click "Create."

**Configure Inbound Rules:** Select the Network ACL you created. Click on the "Inbound Rules" tab, then click "Edit inbound rules."

**Add the following rules:**
- Rule 100: Allow HTTP (Type: "HTTP", Protocol: "TCP", Port Range: "80", Source: "0.0.0.0/0", Allow/Deny: "ALLOW").
- Rule 110: Allow HTTPS (Type: "HTTPS", Protocol: "TCP", Port Range: "443", Source: "0.0.0.0/0", Allow/Deny: "ALLOW").
- Rule 120: Allow SSH (Type: "SSH", Protocol: "TCP", Port Range: "22", Source: "your IP address", Allow/Deny: "ALLOW").
- Rule 130: Allow all traffic from within the VPC (Type: "All Traffic", Protocol: "All", Port Range: "All", Source: "10.0.0.0/16", Allow/Deny: "ALLOW").
- Rule 140: Deny all other traffic (Type: "All Traffic", Protocol: "All", Port Range: "All", Source: "0.0.0.0/0", Allow/Deny: "DENY").

**Configure Outbound Rules:** Click on the "Outbound Rules" tab, then click "Edit outbound rules."
Add the following rules:
Rule 100: Allow all traffic (Type: "All Traffic", Protocol: "All", Port Range: "All", Destination: "0.0.0.0/0", Allow/Deny: "ALLOW").

**Associate Network ACL with Subnet:** Click on the "Subnet Associations" tab, then click "Edit subnet associations." Select the subnet you created earlier (PublicSubnet) and click "Save."

## Part 3: Verification and Testing

**Verify Security Groups:** Ensure that the EC2 instance is accessible via HTTP/HTTPS. Try accessing the instance via SSH to verify the SSH rule. Attempt to access the instance on other ports to ensure they are blocked.

**Verify Network ACLs:** Launch another instance in the same subnet or a different subnet within the VPC. Verify that the inbound and outbound rules are working as expected by testing connectivity between instances and from external sources.

By following these steps, you can design and configure network security mechanisms using VPC Security Groups and Network ACLs. Security Groups provide instance-level security, while Network ACLs offer subnet-level security, ensuring a robust defense against unauthorized access and potential threats.

## 11.6.3 Hardening EC2 Instances

Hardening EC2 instances and creating secure Amazon Machine Images (AMIs) are essential steps to ensure that your AWS environment is secure. This involves configuring the instances to reduce vulnerabilities, applying security patches, and creating an AMI for consistent deployments. Here is a hands-on lab to guide you through this process.

### Part 1: Hardening EC2 Instances

**Objective:** Apply security configurations and best practices to an EC2 instance to reduce vulnerabilities.

### Step 1: Launch an EC2 Instance

**Navigate to the EC2 Console:** Go to the Amazon EC2 Console.

**Launch Instance:** Click on "Launch Instance." Select an Amazon Machine Image (AMI) such as Amazon Linux 2. Choose an instance type (e.g., t2.micro for this lab). Configure instance details and click "Next."

**Configure Security Group:** Add rules to allow only necessary inbound traffic (e.g., SSH from your IP, HTTP/HTTPS if needed). Click "Review and Launch."

**Launch Instance:** Select or create a key pair for SSH access and launch the instance.

### Step 2: Update and Patch the Instance

**Connect to the Instance:** Use SSH to connect to your instance.

```
ssh -i your-key-pair.pem ec2-user@your-instance-public-dns
```

**Update Packages:** Update the instance with the latest security patches.

```
sudo yum update -y
```

**Install Security Tools:** Install common security tools such as fail2ban, auditd, and clamav.

```
sudo yum install -y fail2ban auditd clamav
```

### Step 3: Configure System Security

**Configure SSH:** Edit the SSH configuration file to enhance security.

```
sudo vim /etc/ssh/sshd_config
```

Disable root login: PermitRootLogin no
Disable password authentication: PasswordAuthentication no

Change the default SSH port (optional): Port 2222. Restart the SSH service.

```
sudo systemctl restart sshd
```

**Set Up Firewall:** Use iptables or firewalld to configure firewall rules.

```
1. sudo yum install firewalld -y
2. sudo systemctl start firewalld
3. sudo systemctl enable firewalld
4. sudo firewall-cmd --permanent --add-service=ssh
5. sudo firewall-cmd --permanent --add-service=http
6. sudo firewall-cmd --permanent --add-service=https
7. sudo firewall-cmd --reload
```

**Configure Fail2ban:** Edit the jail.local file to enable protection for SSH.

```
sudo vim /etc/fail2ban/jail.local
```

Add the following configuration:

```
1. [sshd]
2. enabled = true
3. port = 2222
4. filter = sshd
5. logpath = /var/log/secure
6. maxretry = 3
7. bantime = 600
```

Start and enable fail2ban.

```
1. sudo systemctl start fail2ban
2. sudo systemctl enable fail2ban
```

**Enable Auditing:** Start and enable the auditd service.

```
1. sudo systemctl start auditd
2. sudo systemctl enable auditd
```

**Configure ClamAV:** Update the virus database and perform a scan.

```
1. sudo freshclam
2. sudo clamscan -r /home
```

## Part 2: Creating Secure AMIs

**Objective:** Create an AMI from the hardened instance to use for future deployments.

### Step 1: Prepare the Instance

**Clean Up the Instance:** Remove temporary files and sensitive information.

```
1. sudo yum clean all
2. sudo rm -rf /tmp/*
```

```
3. sudo rm -rf /var/tmp/*
```

**Stop the Instance:** Stop the instance before creating an AMI.
```
sudo shutdown -h now
```

### Step 2: Create an AMI

**Navigate to the EC2 Console:** Go to the Amazon EC2 Console.

**Create Image:** Select the instance you hardened. Click on "Actions," then "Image," and "Create Image." Enter a name and description for the AMI (e.g., "Hardened-AMI"). Click "Create Image."

**Monitor Image Creation:** Navigate to the "AMIs" section to monitor the status of the image creation. Once the AMI is available, it can be used to launch new instances with the same hardened configuration.

### Part 3: Verifying the AMI

**Launch a New Instance from the AMI:** Select the newly created AMI and launch an instance. Verify that the security configurations are in place.

**Test Security Configurations:** Ensure SSH is configured correctly, and only allowed traffic can reach the instance. Verify that fail2ban, auditd, and other security services are running.

By following these steps, you can harden EC2 instances and create secure AMIs for consistent, secure deployments. This process includes updating and patching the instance, configuring system security, and using security tools. The resulting AMI can be reused to ensure all instances in your environment maintain the same level of security.

## 11.6.4 Troubleshooting Network Issues

Troubleshooting and resolving network security issues in AWS involves using various AWS tools to monitor, analyze, and secure your network environment. The primary tools include Amazon CloudWatch, VPC Flow Logs, AWS CloudTrail, and VPC Reachability Analyzer. Here is a hands-on lab to guide you through this process.

### Part 1: Setting Up and Monitoring with Amazon CloudWatch

**Objective:** Use Amazon CloudWatch to monitor network security metrics and set up alerts.

#### Step 1: Enable CloudWatch Metrics

**Navigate to the CloudWatch Console:** Go to the Amazon CloudWatch Console.
**Enable Detailed Monitoring:** Select your EC2 instances. Click "Actions" -> "Monitor and troubleshoot" -> "Manage detailed monitoring." Enable detailed monitoring for your instances.

**Create a CloudWatch Alarm:** Navigate to the "Alarms" section and click "Create Alarm." Select a metric (e.g., NetworkIn or NetworkOut) for your EC2 instance. Set the conditions (e.g., when NetworkIn exceeds a certain threshold). Configure the alarm actions to notify you via SNS (Simple Notification Service).

#### Step 2: Monitor CloudWatch Metrics

**View Metrics:** Go to the "Metrics" section in the CloudWatch console. Select the namespace (e.g., EC2) and view the metrics for network traffic.

**Analyze Metrics:** Analyze metrics to identify any unusual patterns or spikes in network traffic that could indicate a security issue.

## Part 2: Analyzing Network Traffic with VPC Flow Logs

**Objective:** Use VPC Flow Logs to capture and analyze network traffic in your VPC.

### Step 1: Enable VPC Flow Logs

**Navigate to the VPC Console:** Go to the Amazon VPC Console.
**Create a Flow Log:** Select your VPC and click "Create Flow Log."
**Configure the flow log settings:**
- Filter: "All" to capture all traffic.
- Destination: Choose "CloudWatch Logs" or "S3" for storing the logs.

Click "Create Flow Log."

### Step 2: Analyze Flow Logs

**View Flow Logs in CloudWatch:** Go to the CloudWatch console and navigate to "Logs." Select the log group created for your VPC Flow Logs. Use the log insights feature to query and analyze the logs.

**Example Query:** Use a query to filter traffic from a specific IP or to a specific port.

```
fields @timestamp, @message
| filter srcAddr = '192.0.2.1'
| sort @timestamp desc
```

**Identify Anomalies:** Look for unusual traffic patterns, such as high volumes of traffic from unknown IP addresses or repeated attempts to access restricted ports.

## Part 3: Auditing with AWS CloudTrail

**Objective:** Use AWS CloudTrail to audit API calls and detect unauthorized activities.

### Step 1: Enable CloudTrail

**Navigate to the CloudTrail Console:** Go to the AWS CloudTrail Console.
**Create a Trail:** Click "Create Trail." Enter a name for the trail and configure the settings. Specify an S3 bucket for log storage. Enable logging for all regions and management events.

### Step 2: Analyze CloudTrail Logs

- **View CloudTrail Logs:** Go to the S3 bucket specified for log storage or use CloudWatch Logs if configured.
- **Search for Specific Events:** Use CloudTrail Insights or AWS Athena to search for specific API calls, such as changes to security group rules or the creation of new EC2 instances.

```
SELECT *
FROM cloudtrail_logs
WHERE eventName = 'AuthorizeSecurityGroupIngress'
```

**Identify Unauthorized Activities:** Look for signs of unauthorized access or changes, such as API calls from unexpected IP addresses or by unusual IAM users.

### Part 4: Diagnosing with VPC Reachability Analyzer
**Objective:** Use VPC Reachability Analyzer to diagnose connectivity issues within your VPC.

#### Step 1: Run Reachability Analysis
**Navigate to the VPC Console:** Go to the Amazon VPC Console.
**Access Reachability Analyzer:** Click on "Reachability Analyzer" in the navigation pane. Click "Create and analyze path."
**Configure Path:** Specify the source and destination resources (e.g., EC2 instance and an RDS database). Click "Create path."

#### Step 2: Analyze Results
**View Analysis Results:** Once the analysis is complete, view the results to see if the path is reachable. The results will show any misconfigurations or issues preventing connectivity.

**Identify Issues:** Look for specific issues such as incorrect security group rules, network ACLs, or route table configurations. The tool will highlight the exact point of failure in the network path.

By following these steps, you can use AWS tools to troubleshoot and resolve network security issues effectively. Amazon CloudWatch provides monitoring and alerting, VPC Flow Logs capture and analyze network traffic, AWS CloudTrail audits API calls, and VPC Reachability Analyzer diagnoses connectivity issues. Combining these tools enables a comprehensive approach to maintaining and securing your AWS environment.

## 11.7 Key Exam Tips

### Master Security Controls for Edge Services
**Edge Security Fundamentals:** Be familiar with AWS services like Amazon CloudFront, AWS WAF, and AWS Shield that provide edge security. These services help mitigate Distributed Denial of Service (DDoS) attacks, web application threats, and unauthorized traffic at the edge.
**Common Attacks:** Understand common attack vectors such as SQL injection, cross-site scripting (XSS), DDoS attacks, and how AWS edge services prevent these threats.
**Layered Web Application Architecture:** You should be able to design a layered security architecture using services like CloudFront, WAF, Shield, and Route 53. Learn to combine these services for defense-in-depth strategies at the network edge.
**Monitoring Edge Services:** Ensure you know how to monitor and log events for edge services using CloudWatch and AWS WAF logs for real-time visibility into potential security incidents.

### Know VPC Security Mechanisms
**Network ACLs vs. Security Groups:** Be clear on the differences between Network ACLs (stateless, apply to subnets) and Security Groups (stateful, apply to instances). You'll need to design secure VPC architectures using these mechanisms.
**VPC Flow Logs:** Use VPC Flow Logs to capture information about IP traffic going to and from network interfaces in your VPC. Make sure you understand how to analyze flow logs for security issues such as unauthorized access attempts.
**Network Segmentation:** Implement network segmentation using private and public subnets within VPCs. Be able to design solutions that isolate sensitive resources and reduce attack surfaces by segmenting different workloads.

### Implement Secure Connectivity
**VPN Technology:** Know how to set up and manage VPN connections between AWS and on-premises environments. Understand when to use AWS Site-to-Site VPN or AWS Direct Connect to ensure secure data transfers.
**Inter-VPC Connectivity:** Study VPC peering, Transit Gateway, and PrivateLink to securely connect VPCs across regions or accounts. Ensure you know how to control traffic between VPCs using route tables, security groups, and network ACLs.

### Apply Layered Security for Workloads
**EC2 Instance Security:** Master security practices for EC2 instances, such as using IAM roles for instances to restrict access, deploying hardened AMIs, and applying security patches regularly.
**Host-Based Security:** Understand host-based security options, including Amazon Inspector for vulnerability scanning and AWS Systems Manager Patch Manager for patching EC2 instances.
**Secrets Management:** Be prepared to implement AWS Secrets Manager or Systems Manager Parameter Store for securely passing secrets, credentials, and sensitive data to your workloads.

### Understand Network Flow Design and Monitoring
**Designing Network Flows:** Be proficient in designing secure and efficient network flows within AWS environments. This includes routing traffic through NAT Gateways, VPNs, Transit Gateway, and Elastic Load Balancing to ensure both security and high availability.
**Monitoring Network Traffic:** Use CloudWatch metrics, VPC Flow Logs, and AWS Traffic Mirroring to capture and monitor traffic data for anomaly detection. Learn how to analyze network telemetry to detect unusual patterns that could signal a security breach.

### Vulnerability Scanning and Patch Management
**Amazon Inspector:** Be comfortable using Amazon Inspector to assess EC2 instances for vulnerabilities. You should know how to interpret and act on the findings from Inspector scans, including applying patches and mitigating risks.
**Patching EC2 Instances:** Regular patching is key for infrastructure security. Use AWS Systems Manager Patch Manager to automate patching across EC2 instances. Understand how to configure patch baselines and schedules for effective patch management.

### Use IAM Roles and Policies for Compute Security
**IAM Instance Roles:** Implement IAM roles to control what actions your EC2 instances or Lambda functions can perform. Make sure you're familiar with least privilege principles and how to use IAM policy conditions to further restrict access.
**Instance Metadata:** Be aware of the security implications of the EC2 Instance Metadata Service and best practices, such as using IMDSv2 to prevent unauthorized access to instance metadata.

### Troubleshooting Network Security
**Network Reachability:** Know how to use tools like VPC Reachability Analyzer to troubleshoot connectivity issues and identify misconfigurations that could lead to network vulnerabilities.
**Log Analysis:** Be familiar with analyzing relevant logs (VPC Flow Logs, CloudTrail, CloudWatch Logs) to investigate and troubleshoot security incidents. Use CloudWatch Logs Insights or Athena for in-depth analysis of log data.
**TCP/IP Concepts:** Have a solid understanding of TCP/IP networking concepts, such as how IP addresses, subnets, and routing affect connectivity and security within a VPC.

### Identify and Remove Unnecessary Access
**Review and Audit Security Groups:** Regularly review security group rules to eliminate any overly permissive inbound or outbound rules, such as rules allowing unrestricted access (e.g., 0.0.0.0/0 for all traffic).
**IAM Access Reviews:** Conduct regular IAM access reviews using tools like IAM Access Analyzer to identify and reduce excessive privileges or unnecessary permissions.
**Network ACLs:** Use network ACLs to create additional layers of security by restricting traffic at the subnet level. Ensure you review and audit ACL configurations regularly.

### Best Practices for Infrastructure Security
**Defense in Depth:** Implement a layered defense strategy using a combination of edge services, security groups, network ACLs, and IAM policies to minimize vulnerabilities.
**Secure Remote Access:** Use bastion hosts or Session Manager for secure remote access to instances. Avoid direct SSH access whenever possible and always require multi-factor authentication (MFA).
**Infrastructure as Code (IaC):** Implement IaC best practices to enforce security policies consistently across environments. Use services like AWS CloudFormation or Terraform to deploy secure infrastructure at scale.

### Summary
Mastering edge security services (WAF, Shield), VPC security controls, and EC2 instance hardening is essential for the AWS Certified Security Specialty Exam. You need to know how to design secure network architectures, manage security configurations for workloads, and monitor network flows. Being proficient in tools like Amazon Inspector, VPC Flow Logs, CloudWatch, and AWS Systems Manager will be critical to ensuring the security of AWS infrastructure, detecting vulnerabilities, and troubleshooting issues.

## 11.8 Chapter Review Questions

**Question 1:**
Which AWS service is commonly used to monitor and manage security at the edge of your infrastructure?
A. Amazon RDS
B. Amazon CloudFront
C. AWS Lambda
D. Amazon S3

**Question 2:**
What is the primary goal of applying security controls to edge services?
A. To reduce costs associated with data transfer
B. To protect web applications from DDoS and other attacks before they reach your origin servers
C. To accelerate application performance
D. To store data securely in Amazon S3

**Question 3:**
Which of the following is a key security measure used in VPC security?
A. Security groups and network access control lists (NACLs)
B. Route tables
C. AWS Elastic Beanstalk
D. S3 bucket policies

**Question 4:**
What is the primary function of Amazon Inspector in securing EC2 instances?
A. Monitoring network traffic
B. Scanning EC2 instances for vulnerabilities and security exposures
C. Enforcing IAM policies
D. Providing automated backups of instances

**Question 5:**
Which of the following is a critical security consideration for IAM roles on EC2 instances?
A. Creating custom security patches
B. Ensuring least privilege access is applied to the role
C. Using the same IAM role for all instances
D. Avoiding the use of temporary credentials

**Question 6:**
Which service can be used to manage secrets and credentials securely for EC2 workloads?
A. AWS Secrets Manager
B. Amazon DynamoDB
C. AWS Config
D. Amazon EC2 Auto Scaling

**Question 7:**
What is a best practice when implementing network segmentation in AWS?
A. Isolating critical workloads in separate VPCs or subnets
B. Using a single public subnet for all resources
C. Disabling VPC flow logs to reduce costs
D. Allowing unrestricted access to security groups

**Question 8:**
What is the role of host-based security mechanisms in securing compute workloads?
A. Controlling permissions to AWS Lambda functions
B. Encrypting data at rest on EC2 instances
C. Providing vulnerability management and intrusion detection at the instance level
D. Managing CloudWatch metrics for EC2 instances

**Question 9:**
Which AWS service can be used to monitor and capture network traffic for troubleshooting and security analysis?
A. Amazon Inspector
B. AWS CloudTrail
C. VPC Traffic Mirroring
D. AWS Systems Manager

**Question 10:**
What is the Layered Web Application Architecture strategy primarily used for in infrastructure security?
A. Reducing the cost of hosting web applications
B. Improving application redundancy
C. Providing multiple layers of defense against web-based attacks
D. Accelerating content delivery using edge locations

**Question 11:**
You are running a global web application that leverages Amazon CloudFront as a content delivery network (CDN) to serve content from edge locations. Recently, you have been facing distributed denial of service (DDoS) attacks targeting your application. What additional AWS service can you integrate with CloudFront to protect your application, and how would this service help mitigate these attacks?
A. AWS Lambda
B. AWS WAF (Web Application Firewall)
C. Amazon S3

D. AWS Config

**Question 12:**
Your organization has strict compliance requirements that dictate all EC2 instances must be hardened and regularly patched. You have a fleet of EC2 instances across multiple regions. How can you automate vulnerability scanning and ensure all instances are up to date with security patches across your infrastructure?
A. Manually patch each instance
B. Use AWS Systems Manager and Amazon Inspector
C. Create new AMIs and redeploy instances
D. Use CloudTrail to log EC2 instance actions

**Question 13:**
A team member accidentally opened SSH access to the entire internet by modifying the security group rules for a critical EC2 instance. How can you prevent similar misconfigurations in the future while ensuring proper security controls are enforced across the environment?
A. Enable VPC flow logs and analyze traffic
B. Implement AWS Config with managed rules to detect and automatically remediate insecure security group configurations
C. Disable IAM role usage on EC2 instances
D. Use Amazon CloudWatch to monitor security groups

**Question 14:**
You are setting up a hybrid cloud architecture where your on-premises data center is connected to your AWS environment using a VPN. What security measures should you implement to ensure secure communication between your on-premises network and AWS VPCs, and how can you monitor the VPN connection for security issues?
A. Use a public subnet for VPN communication and monitor with CloudTrail
B. Use VPN encryption (IPSec) and monitor VPN traffic with VPC flow logs
C. Enable default VPC for all communications
D. Use Lambda functions to handle all VPN traffic

**Question 15:**
You have a multi-VPC architecture with sensitive data hosted in one VPC. The other VPCs require access to this data for processing. To maintain strong security, how should you design the network to limit access while allowing necessary communication?
A. Enable unrestricted traffic between all VPCs
B. Implement VPC peering and restrict access using security groups and network ACLs
C. Allow all VPCs to access the sensitive data VPC via the internet
D. Use EC2 instance-based firewall rules to control access

## 11.9 Answers to Chapter Review Questions

1. B. Amazon CloudFront
Explanation: Amazon CloudFront is a content delivery network (CDN) that also provides security at the edge, helping to protect against DDoS attacks and other threats before they reach your origin servers.

2. B. To protect web applications from DDoS and other attacks before they reach your origin servers
Explanation: Applying security controls at the edge helps mitigate threats like DDoS attacks, providing an additional layer of protection for your web applications.

3. A. Security groups and network access control lists (NACLs)

Explanation: Security groups and NACLs are key security measures in VPC security that control inbound and outbound traffic to AWS resources within a VPC.

4. B. Scanning EC2 instances for vulnerabilities and security exposures
Explanation: Amazon Inspector automatically scans your EC2 instances for vulnerabilities and potential security exposures, helping you maintain a secure environment.

5. B. Ensuring least privilege access is applied to the role
Explanation: Applying least privilege access to IAM roles ensures that EC2 instances only have the permissions they need to perform their functions, minimizing security risks.

6. A. AWS Secrets Manager
Explanation: AWS Secrets Manager is designed to securely manage and rotate secrets and credentials for applications running on AWS, including EC2 workloads.

7. A. Isolating critical workloads in separate VPCs or subnets
Explanation: A best practice for network segmentation is to isolate critical workloads in different VPCs or subnets, ensuring a more secure and manageable environment.

8. C. Providing vulnerability management and intrusion detection at the instance level
Explanation: Host-based security mechanisms provide vulnerability management and intrusion detection on EC2 instances, offering an extra layer of protection at the operating system level.

9. C. VPC Traffic Mirroring
Explanation: VPC Traffic Mirroring allows you to capture and monitor network traffic for security analysis and troubleshooting in your VPC environment.

10. C. Providing multiple layers of defense against web-based attacks
Explanation: A Layered Web Application Architecture provides multiple layers of security controls to defend against various web-based attacks, enhancing the overall security posture.

11. B. AWS WAF (Web Application Firewall)
Explanation: AWS WAF can be integrated with Amazon CloudFront to help mitigate DDoS attacks by filtering and blocking malicious traffic before it reaches your application. AWS WAF provides rules to block common web attacks such as SQL injection and cross-site scripting (XSS).

12. B. Use AWS Systems Manager and Amazon Inspector
Explanation: You can use AWS Systems Manager to automate patch management across EC2 instances, and Amazon Inspector to scan instances for vulnerabilities. This ensures that your instances are hardened and regularly updated with security patches across regions.

13. B. Implement AWS Config with managed rules to detect and automatically remediate insecure security group configurations
Explanation: AWS Config can monitor security group configurations and enforce compliance with security best practices. You can set up managed rules to detect open SSH access and automatically remediate it, preventing misconfigurations in the future.

14. B. Use VPN encryption (IPSec) and monitor VPN traffic with VPC flow logs
Explanation: IPSec VPN encryption ensures secure communication between your on-premises network and AWS VPCs. VPC flow logs can be used to monitor the traffic passing through the VPN and detect any security issues.

15. B. Implement VPC peering and restrict access using security groups and network ACLs
Explanation: VPC peering allows secure communication between VPCs without using the public internet. By applying security groups and network ACLs, you can restrict access to only the necessary resources, ensuring that only authorized traffic can access sensitive data.

# Chapter 12. Data Protection

**This chapter addresses the following exam objectives:**
Domain 5: Data Protection
Task Statement 5.1: Design and implement controls that provide confidentiality and integrity for data in transit.
Knowledge of:
- TLS concepts
- VPN concepts (for example, IPsec)
- Secure remote access methods (for example, SSH, RDP over Systems Manager Session Manager)
- Systems Manager Session Manager concepts
- How TLS certificates work with various network services and resources (for example, CloudFront, load balancers)

Skills in:
- Designing secure connectivity between AWS and on-premises networks (for example, by using Direct Connect and VPN gateways)
- Designing mechanisms to require encryption when connecting to resources
- (for example, Amazon RDS, Amazon Redshift, CloudFront, Amazon S3,
- Amazon DynamoDB, load balancers, Amazon Elastic File System [Amazon EFS], Amazon API Gateway)
- Requiring TLS for AWS API calls (for example, with Amazon S3)
- Designing mechanisms to forward traffic over secure connections (for example, by using Systems Manager and EC2 Instance Connect)
- Designing cross-Region networking by using private VIFs and public VIFs

Task Statement 5.2: Design and implement controls that provide confidentiality and integrity for data at rest.
Knowledge of:
- Encryption technique selection (for example, client-side, server-side, symmetric, asymmetric)
- Integrity-checking techniques (for example, hashing algorithms, digital signatures)
- Resource policies (for example, for DynamoDB, Amazon S3, and AWS Key Management Service [AWS KMS])
- IAM roles and policies

Skills in:
- Designing resource policies to restrict access to authorized users (for example, S3 bucket policies, DynamoDB policies)
- Designing mechanisms to prevent unauthorized public access (for example, S3 Block Public Access, prevention of public snapshots and public AMIs)

- Configuring services to activate encryption of data at rest (for example,
- Amazon S3, Amazon RDS, DynamoDB, Amazon Simple Queue Service
- [Amazon SQS], Amazon EBS, Amazon EFS)
- Designing mechanisms to protect data integrity by preventing modifications (for example, by using S3 Object Lock, KMS key policies, S3
- Glacier Vault Lock, and AWS Backup Vault Lock)
- Designing encryption at rest by using AWS CloudHSM for relational databases (for example, Amazon RDS, RDS Custom, databases on EC2 instances)
- Choosing encryption techniques based on business requirements

Task Statement 5.3: Design and implement controls to manage the lifecycle of data at rest.
Knowledge of:
- Lifecycle policies
- Data retention standards

Skills in:
- Designing S3 Lifecycle mechanisms to retain data for required retention periods (for example, S3 Object Lock, S3 Glacier Vault Lock, S3 Lifecycle policy)
- Designing automatic lifecycle management for AWS services and resources
- (for example, Amazon S3, EBS volume snapshots, RDS volume snapshots,
- AMIs, container images, CloudWatch log groups, Amazon Data Lifecycle Manager)
- Establishing schedules and retention for AWS Backup across AWS services

Task Statement 5.4: Design and implement controls to protect credentials, secrets, and cryptographic key materials.
Knowledge of:
- Secrets Manager
- Systems Manager Parameter Store
- Usage and management of symmetric keys and asymmetric keys (for example, AWS KMS)

Skills in:
- Designing management and rotation of secrets for workloads (for example, database access credentials, API keys, IAM access keys, AWS KMS customer managed keys)
- Designing KMS key policies to limit key usage to authorized users
- Establishing mechanisms to import and remove customer-provided key material

◆◆◆◆◆◆

In the realm of cloud computing, protecting data is a fundamental requirement that spans various dimensions, from ensuring data integrity to safeguarding it from unauthorized access. This chapter offers a comprehensive guide to designing and implementing effective data protection strategies within AWS environments. The chapter delves into the principles and practices necessary to secure data both in transit and at rest, manage data lifecycle, and protect sensitive credentials and cryptographic materials.

We begin with an introduction to data protection, establishing the importance of safeguarding data against threats and ensuring compliance with regulatory standards. The chapter then explores designing and implementing controls for data in transit, covering concepts such as TLS, VPN, secure remote access methods, and the use of Systems Manager Session Manager for secure sessions. The role of TLS certificates and network services in protecting data during transmission is also discussed.

Implementing secure connectivity is a critical aspect of data protection. We examine methods for establishing secure connections between AWS and on-premises networks, encryption techniques for connecting to AWS resources, requiring TLS for AWS API calls, and forwarding traffic over secure connections. Cross-region networking with private and public virtual interfaces (VIFs) is also covered.

The chapter then focuses on designing and implementing controls for data at rest, including encryption techniques, methods for encrypting S3 objects, integrity-checking techniques, resource policies, and IAM roles and policies that enhance data protection. We further discuss implementing encryption for data at rest, activating encryption for AWS services, protecting data integrity, and using AWS CloudHSM for managing encryption keys.

Managing the lifecycle of data at rest is essential for maintaining data security and compliance. This section covers lifecycle policies, S3 lifecycle mechanisms, automatic lifecycle management for AWS services, and strategies for backup scheduling and retention.

Protecting credentials, secrets, and cryptographic key materials is another critical area. We explore the use of Systems Manager Parameter Store, symmetric and asymmetric key management, managing and rotating secrets, KMS key policies, and importing and removing customer-provided key material.

Best practices for data protection are emphasized throughout the chapter, including encryption best practices, data integrity best practices, managing data lifecycle best practices, and strategies for protecting credentials and secrets. These best practices provide a framework for implementing robust data protection measures in AWS environments.

To reinforce the theoretical knowledge, the chapter concludes with lab exercises that provide hands-on experience in configuring TLS for AWS services, implementing encryption for data at rest, managing secrets with AWS Secrets Manager, and designing S3 lifecycle policies. These exercises are designed to enhance your practical skills and confidence in securing data within AWS.

By the end of this chapter, readers will have a thorough understanding of data protection principles, techniques, and best practices, enabling them to design and implement comprehensive data protection strategies in their AWS environments.

# 12.1 Introduction to Data Protection

Data protection in AWS is critical to ensuring that information remains secure, reliable, and accessible. Understanding the core principles of data confidentiality, integrity, and availability is essential for effective data protection.

**Data Confidentiality** refers to data protection from unauthorized access and disclosure. It ensures that sensitive information is only accessible to those who have been granted permission. For example, using AWS Key Management Service (KMS) to encrypt data at rest and in transit ensures that only authorized users with the correct decryption keys can access the data.

**Data Integrity** involves maintaining data accuracy and completeness. It ensures that unauthorized individuals have not tampered with or altered data. For instance, AWS CloudTrail logs can be used to track and monitor changes to data, helping to detect and prevent unauthorized modifications.

**Data Availability** ensures that data is accessible when authorized users need it. It involves implementing redundancy and failover mechanisms (for example, single point of failure) to protect against data loss and downtime. AWS services like Amazon S3 and RDS provide high availability features, such as multi-AZ deployments, which ensure that data remains available even in the event of hardware failures or other disruptions.

The importance of data protection in AWS can be understood through these principles. Data confidentiality is paramount to protect sensitive information from unauthorized access. For instance, an organization storing customer personal information in AWS must use encryption and access controls to ensure that this data remains confidential.

Data integrity is crucial for maintaining trust in the data's accuracy. Consider a financial institution that relies on AWS to store transaction records; ensuring the integrity of these records is vital to prevent fraud and errors. Data availability is essential for operational continuity. An e-commerce platform hosted on AWS must ensure the high availability of its databases and applications to provide uninterrupted service to its customers.

By adhering to the principles of confidentiality, integrity, and availability (CIA), organizations can effectively protect their data in AWS, ensuring it remains secure, accurate, and accessible. This holistic approach to data protection helps mitigate risks and supports regulatory compliance, ultimately safeguarding the organization's most valuable asset: its data.

## 12.2 Designing and Implementing Controls for Data in Transit

Designing and implementing controls for data in transit is crucial for ensuring the confidentiality and integrity of data as it moves across networks. Effective controls, such as encryption and secure communication protocols, help protect data from interception and tampering during transmission. Implementing these controls is essential for safeguarding sensitive information and complying with regulatory requirements.

### 12.2.1 TLS Concepts

Transport Layer Security (TLS) is a cryptographic protocol designed to provide secure communication over a computer network. The main role of this protocol is to ensure the confidentiality, integrity, and authenticity (CIA) of data transmitted between parties. TLS achieves this by encrypting the data before it is sent and decrypting it upon receipt, thereby preventing eavesdropping, tampering, and message forgery.

TLS operates between the application layer and the transport layer in the Internet protocol suite. When a connection is initiated, the TLS handshake process begins, during which the client and server agree on encryption algorithms, exchange cryptographic keys, and authenticate each other using digital certificates. Once the handshake is complete, data can be transmitted securely over a secure communication channel that is established after the handshake is complete.

For example, when a user accesses their bank account online, TLS is used to secure the data exchanged between the user's browser and the bank's server. This secure communication ensures that sensitive information, such as login credentials and account details, cannot be intercepted or altered by malicious actors during transmission.

The use of TLS is ubiquitous in securing data in transit across various applications, including web browsing, email, instant messaging, and voice over IP (VoIP). By implementing TLS, organizations can protect sensitive data that helps maintain user trust, and comply with regulatory requirements.

### 12.2.2 VPN Concepts

A Virtual Private Network (VPN) creates a secure and encrypted connection over the Internet. VPNs are used to ensure privacy, data integrity, and secure communications for users and organizations. One of the most commonly used protocols for implementing VPNs is Internet Protocol Security (IPsec).

IPsec is a suite of protocols used to authenticate and encrypt each IP packet in a communication session to secure Internet Protocol (IP) communications. IPsec operates at the network layer and can be used to protect data flows between host-to-host, between network-to-network, or between network-to-host. It provides two main security services: Authentication Header (AH) for packet integrity and origin authentication, and Encapsulating Security Payload (ESP) for packet encryption, ensuring confidentiality and optional authentication.

**Use cases for VPNs include:**
- Remote Access: Employees can securely connect to their company's internal network from remote locations. For instance, a remote worker connecting to the corporate network via a VPN ensures that their communication is encrypted and secure, protecting sensitive business information from interception.
- Site-to-Site Connectivity: Organizations with multiple offices can use VPNs to securely connect their local networks over the internet. For example, a company with offices in different cities can use an IPsec VPN to establish a secure and encrypted link between the offices, enabling seamless and secure data sharing.
- Secure Communication: VPNs are often used to secure communications over public networks. For instance, a user accessing a public Wi-Fi network can use a VPN to encrypt their internet traffic, protecting against potential eavesdropping and data theft.

An example of VPN use is a financial institution that requires secure communication channels for its remote employees. By implementing an IPsec VPN, the institution ensures that its employees' communications, including sensitive financial data, are encrypted and protected from unauthorized access, maintaining the confidentiality and integrity of the information.

## 12.2.3 Secure Remote Access Methods

Secure remote access is crucial for maintaining the confidentiality and integrity of data and systems. Two common methods for secure remote access are Secure Shell (SSH) and Remote Desktop Protocol (RDP). Additionally, AWS Systems Manager Session Manager offers enhanced security for managing instances.

Secure Shell (SSH) is a cryptographic network protocol used for remote login securely and other secure network services over an insecure network. SSH provides strong authentication and secure encrypted communications between two untrusted hosts. It is commonly used to access Unix/Linux systems. For example, a system administrator can use SSH to connect to a remote server to perform administrative tasks securely. The use of key pairs for authentication instead of passwords enhances security by reducing the risk of brute-force attacks.

Remote Desktop Protocol (RDP) is a proprietary protocol developed by Microsoft that provides a user with a graphical interface to connect to another computer over a network connection. It is commonly used for remote administration of Windows servers and workstations. For instance, an IT support team can use RDP to troubleshoot and manage a user's desktop remotely. RDP sessions can be secured by enforcing strong authentication methods and using network-level authentication (NLA) to protect against unauthorized access.

AWS Systems Manager Session Manager further enhances security by providing a fully managed, auditable, and secure method for connecting to Amazon EC2 instances and on-premises servers. Session Manager eliminates the need to open inbound ports, manage SSH keys, or use bastion hosts. It allows administrators to establish secure shell connections to instances through the AWS Management Console, CLI, or SDKs without needing an SSH client.

For example, a company using AWS can use Session Manager to manage its EC2 instances securely. Administrators can start sessions from the AWS Management Console, ensuring all actions are logged and auditable in AWS CloudTrail. This approach (using Session Manager) enhances security by reducing the attack surface and providing robust auditing capabilities, ensuring compliance with security policies.

## 12.2.4 Systems Manager Session Manager Concepts

AWS Systems Manager Session Manager is a fully managed service that provides secure and auditable access to Amazon EC2 instances and on-premises servers without going through the efforts of opening inbound ports, managing SSH keys, or using bastion hosts. It facilitates secure remote access and session management, enabling administrators to connect to their instances using the AWS Management Console, AWS CLI, or AWS SDKs.

Session Manager is a robust security tool that enhances the safety of your operations. It allows administrators to establish shell or command prompt sessions to instances without requiring an SSH client or RDP, thereby minimizing the attack surface. With no inbound ports to be opened and no need for managing SSH keys or passwords, the risk of unauthorized access is significantly reduced. Sessions are encrypted, and all activity is logged and auditable through AWS CloudTrail, providing a secure and compliant way to manage instances.

For example, consider a development team that needs to troubleshoot an application running on an EC2 instance. Using Session Manager, a team member can start a secure session directly from the AWS Management Console. This session is established without the need for an open SSH port or managing SSH keys, reducing the risk of unauthorized access.

Furthermore, every command executed during the session is logged, ensuring that all actions are traceable and meet compliance requirements.

In summary, AWS Systems Manager Session Manager simplifies and secures the process of managing EC2 instances and on-premises servers. By providing encrypted, port-less access and comprehensive session logging, it significantly enhances the security posture and operational efficiency of managing remote instances.

## 12.2.5 TLS Certificates and Network Services

Transport Layer Security (TLS) certificates play a critical role in securing data in transit by enabling encrypted communication between clients and servers. In the context of AWS network services such as Amazon CloudFront and Elastic Load Balancing (ELB), TLS certificates ensure that data transmitted over the network is encrypted and secure.

Amazon CloudFront is a content delivery network (CDN) that uses TLS certificates to secure data as it travels from the origin server to end users. When a request is made to a CloudFront distribution, CloudFront negotiates a TLS connection with the client's browser using the TLS certificate associated with the distribution. This ensures that the data being delivered, such as web pages, images, or videos, is encrypted and cannot be intercepted by malicious actors. For example, an e-commerce website using CloudFront to deliver its content globally can secure all transactions and user data by deploying a TLS certificate on its CloudFront distribution, thereby protecting customer information during transmission.

Elastic Load Balancing (ELB) distributes incoming application traffic across multiple targets, such as Amazon EC2 instances. ELB supports both Application Load Balancers (ALB) and Network Load Balancers (NLB), both of which can use TLS certificates to secure data in transit. With an ALB, TLS termination occurs at the load balancer level, where the ALB decrypts the incoming traffic and then forwards it to the backend instances in plain text. This allows the backend instances to offload the resource-intensive task of decryption to the load balancer. For instance, a web application using an ALB can protect user data by configuring a TLS certificate on the load balancer, ensuring all user requests are encrypted while traveling over the internet.

Using TLS certificates with AWS network services is essential for securing data in transit, protecting sensitive information, and ensuring compliance with industry standards and regulations. AWS Certificate Manager

(ACM) simplifies the process by providing a service to easily provision, manage, and deploy public and private TLS certificates for use with AWS services.

## 12.3 Implementing Secure Connectivity

Implementing secure connectivity is essential for protecting data as it travels across networks and ensuring that only authorized users can access sensitive resources. It involves using technologies and protocols such as VPNs, TLS, and secure tunnels to create encrypted communication channels. These measures help prevent unauthorized access, data breaches, and ensure compliance with security standards.

### 12.3.1 Secure Connectivity between AWS and On-Premises Networks

Secure connectivity between AWS and on-premises networks is crucial for organizations that operate in hybrid cloud environments. This setup ensures that data can be securely transferred and accessed between on-premises data centers and AWS infrastructure, providing a seamless and secure extension of an organization's internal network into the cloud. Secure connectivity helps maintain data integrity, confidentiality, and availability while enabling businesses to leverage the scalability and flexibility of AWS services.

**AWS Direct Connect** and **VPN gateways are** two primary solutions for establishing secure connectivity between AWS and on-premises networks.

**AWS Direct Connect** provides a dedicated, private connection between an organization's on-premises data center and AWS. This dedicated connection offers consistent network performance, lower latency, and increased bandwidth compared to standard internet connections. Direct Connect is ideal for workloads that require a stable and high-performance connection, such as real-time data analytics, large-scale data transfers, and mission-critical applications. For example, a financial institution may use Direct Connect to ensure that its sensitive transaction data is transferred securely and reliably between its on-premises systems and AWS.

**VPN gateways,** on the other hand, provide a cost-effective solution for secure connectivity over the internet. AWS VPN gateways use IPsec tunnels to create encrypted connections between the on-premises network and AWS. This setup is suitable for use cases where lower data transfer volumes and flexible connectivity are required. For example, a company with multiple branch offices can use VPN gateways to securely connect its on-premises networks to AWS, enabling remote access to cloud-based applications and resources without the need for a dedicated connection.

When designing secure connectivity solutions, organizations can combine both Direct Connect and VPN gateways to achieve high availability and redundancy. For instance, an organization may use Direct Connect as its primary connection to AWS and configure a VPN gateway as a backup. This approach ensures continuous connectivity even if the primary connection fails, maintaining business continuity and data accessibility.

In summary, establishing secure connectivity between AWS and on-premises networks is essential for hybrid cloud environments. Solutions like AWS Direct Connect and VPN gateways offer robust options for secure, reliable, and scalable connectivity, enabling organizations to extend their on-premises infrastructure to the cloud securely.

### 12.3.2 Encryption for Connecting to AWS Resources

Encryption for connecting to AWS resources is a fundamental practice to ensure the confidentiality and integrity of data transmitted between clients and AWS services. Encryption protects sensitive information from unauthorized access and eavesdropping, thus securing data in transit. AWS provides several mechanisms to enforce encryption when accessing its resources, including database services, storage solutions, and managed database services.

For **Amazon RDS (Relational Database Service),** AWS supports encryption in transit using SSL/TLS. When connecting to an RDS instance, clients can be configured to use SSL/TLS to encrypt the connection, ensuring that data transmitted between the client application and the RDS instance is secure. For example, when connecting to a MySQL database on RDS, the client application can be configured to use an SSL certificate provided by AWS to establish an encrypted connection.

**Amazon Redshift**, a fully managed data warehouse service, also supports encryption in transit. Clients can use SSL to encrypt the connection to the Redshift cluster, ensuring that queries and data transfers are secure. To enforce encryption, administrators can configure Redshift to require SSL connections, thus preventing any unencrypted connections to the cluster.

**Amazon S3 (Simple Storage Service)** provides server-side encryption for data at rest and supports encryption in transit using SSL/TLS. When accessing S3 buckets, clients can use HTTPS to ensure that data transfers are encrypted. To enforce encryption, bucket policies can be configured to require that all requests to the bucket use HTTPS, thus ensuring that data is always encrypted during transit.

**Amazon DynamoDB**, a fully managed NoSQL database service, also supports encryption in transit using TLS. When connecting to DynamoDB, clients automatically use TLS to encrypt data transmitted between the client and the DynamoDB service. This encryption ensures that sensitive data, such as user information or application data, is protected during transmission.

For example, an e-commerce application that stores customer data in DynamoDB can rely on TLS to secure communications between the application and the database. Additionally, the application can use HTTPS to interact with S3 for storing product images, ensuring that all data transfers are encrypted and secure.

In summary, encryption for connecting to AWS resources is essential for protecting data in transit. AWS provides various mechanisms, such as SSL/TLS and HTTPS, to enforce encryption for services like RDS, Redshift, S3, and DynamoDB. These mechanisms ensure that sensitive data remains secure during transmission, preventing unauthorized access and maintaining data integrity.

## 12.3.3 Requiring TLS for AWS API Calls

Requiring TLS for AWS API calls is a crucial security measure to ensure that data transmitted between clients and AWS services remains encrypted and secure. Transport Layer Security (TLS) provides a secure channel by encrypting the data in transit, preventing unauthorized access and data breaches. TLS is mandatory for all AWS API endpoints, and using it ensures the confidentiality and integrity of the data being transmitted.

AWS services inherently require the use of HTTPS, which relies on TLS, for API calls. When interacting with AWS services, clients must use HTTPS endpoints, ensuring that all communications are encrypted. This practice helps protect sensitive data, such as API keys, access tokens, and request payloads, from interception and tampering.

To **configure services to enforce TLS for API calls**, users must ensure that their applications and services are set up to interact with AWS APIs over HTTPS. For example, when using the AWS SDKs or AWS Command Line Interface (CLI), the default configuration uses HTTPS to make API calls to AWS services.
For **Amazon API Gateway**, administrators can configure API Gateway to require TLS for client connections. By setting up custom domain names with SSL/TLS certificates through AWS Certificate Manager (ACM), API Gateway ensures that all incoming API requests are encrypted. Additionally, administrators can enforce specific TLS versions and ciphers to meet their security compliance requirements.

In the case of **AWS Lambda**, which often works in conjunction with API Gateway, it inherently supports HTTPS for secure invocation of functions. When configuring Lambda to receive API calls via API Gateway, ensuring that the API Gateway endpoint uses HTTPS will maintain secure communication between clients and Lambda functions.

**Amazon S3** can also enforce the use of TLS for API calls by configuring bucket policies to require HTTPS. By setting a bucket policy that denies requests not using secure transport (HTTPS), administrators can ensure that all data interactions with S3 are encrypted in transit. This is particularly important when sensitive data is being uploaded to or downloaded from S3 buckets.

For example, a company that processes financial transactions via an API hosted on API Gateway can configure the gateway to require HTTPS connections, ensuring that all transaction data is encrypted. By using a custom domain with an SSL certificate from ACM, they can provide additional assurance that the communications are secure and comply with industry standards.

In summary, requiring TLS for AWS API calls is essential for secure communication. Configuring services like API Gateway, Lambda, and S3 to enforce TLS ensures that all interactions with AWS APIs are encrypted, maintaining the confidentiality and integrity of the data. This practice is critical for protecting sensitive information and meeting compliance requirements.

## 12.3.4 Forwarding Traffic over Secure Connections

Forwarding traffic over secure connections is a critical aspect of network security, ensuring that data transmitted between clients and servers is protected from interception and tampering. Secure connections are typically established using protocols such as TLS/SSL, which encrypt the data in transit. This encryption ensures that sensitive information, such as login credentials, financial data, and personal details, is kept confidential and intact as it traverses the network.

One way to forward traffic securely within AWS is by using **AWS Systems Ma**nager and **EC2 Instance Connect.** AWS Systems Manager provides a unified user interface to manage and secure AWS resources. It includes features like Session Manager, which allows for secure, auditable connections to EC2 instances without the need to open inbound ports or manage SSH keys. This is particularly useful for system administrators who need to access instances securely for management and troubleshooting.

**EC2 Instance Connect** simplifies the process of securely connecting to EC2 instances by leveraging AWS IAM policies and SSH keys. It allows users to push a one-time SSH key to an instance for the duration of a session, ensuring that only authorized users can access the instance.

For example, consider a scenario where an administrator needs to securely connect to an EC2 instance for maintenance tasks. **Using AWS Systems Manager Session Manager**, the administrator can initiate a session directly from the AWS Management Console. This connection is established over HTTPS, and all session activity is logged in AWS CloudTrail, ensuring a secure and auditable process. The administrator can then perform necessary tasks without exposing the instance to potential security risks associated with open inbound ports.

Similarly, **EC2 Instance Connect** can be used to securely forward traffic to an EC2 instance. When an administrator needs to connect to an instance, they can use EC2 Instance Connect to push an SSH key to the instance. The key is valid only for the duration of the session, ensuring that access is tightly controlled and temporary. This method reduces the risks associated with long-term SSH key management and helps maintain a secure connection.

In summary, forwarding traffic over secure connections is essential for protecting data integrity and confidentiality. AWS Systems Manager and EC2 Instance Connect provide robust solutions for securely accessing and managing EC2 instances. By leveraging these tools, administrators can ensure secure and auditable connections, reducing the risk of unauthorized access and data breaches.

## 12.3.5 Cross-Region Networking with Private and Public VIFs

Cross-region networking in AWS involves connecting resources across different geographical regions to enhance availability, redundancy, and global reach. This can be achieved using AWS Direct Connect, which offers private and public Virtual Interfaces (VIFs) to establish secure, high-bandwidth connections between AWS regions and on-premises networks.

A **Private VIF (Virtual Interface) is** used to connect to an Amazon VPC using private IP addresses. This type of connection is ideal for accessing resources within a VPC, such as EC2 instances, RDS databases, and internal applications. Private VIFs ensure that traffic remains within the AWS network and does not traverse the public internet, providing enhanced security and consistent network performance.

A **Public VIF (Virtual Interface),** on the other hand, allows connections to AWS public services, such as Amazon S3, Amazon DynamoDB, and AWS Management Console endpoints, using public IP addresses. Public VIFs facilitate access to these services without needing to traverse the public internet, which can improve performance and security.

When designing secure cross-region networking using private and public VIFs, several best practices should be considered. For example, to connect an on-premises data center to AWS resources in multiple regions, an organization can set up a private VIF for secure access to VPCs in each region. This approach ensures that data transfers between the data center and AWS resources are encrypted and do not travel over the public internet.

For instance, a global enterprise with headquarters in North America and branch offices in Europe and Asia can use AWS Direct Connect with private VIFs to establish secure, high-speed connections to VPCs in different regions. By doing so, the enterprise can synchronize databases, replicate applications, and ensure consistent access to critical resources across all regions without exposing the data to the public internet.

In addition to private VIFs, the enterprise can use public VIFs to access AWS public services globally. For example, if the enterprise uses Amazon S3 for data storage, a public VIF can be set up to enable fast and secure access to S3 buckets from any region. This setup helps improve data transfer speeds and reduces latency, ensuring efficient and secure access to cloud storage.

In summary, cross-region networking with private and public VIFs in AWS provides secure, high-performance connections between regions and on-premises networks. By designing a network architecture that leverages private VIFs for VPC access and public VIFs for AWS public services, organizations can enhance their global connectivity, improve security, and ensure consistent access to their resources.

## 12.4 Designing and Implementing Controls for Data at Rest

Designing and implementing controls for data at rest is essential to protect stored information from unauthorized access and breaches. These controls typically involve encryption, access management, and monitoring to ensure the data remains secure while stored on physical or virtual storage devices. Implementing robust security measures for data at rest helps organizations comply with regulatory requirements and safeguard sensitive information.

## 12.4.1 Encryption Techniques

Encryption is a fundamental technique used to protect data at rest by converting plaintext information into an unreadable format, which can only be deciphered by someone with the correct decryption key. Various encryption techniques can be applied depending on the specific requirements and context of data protection. These include client-side encryption, server-side encryption, symmetric encryption, and asymmetric encryption.

**Client-side encryption** refers to the process where data is encrypted by the client before it is sent to the server. This ensures that the server only stores the encrypted version of the data, and the decryption key remains with the client. An example of client-side encryption is when a user encrypts files using a tool like GnuPG before uploading them to a cloud storage service. This approach provides a high level of security since the service provider does not have access to the encryption keys.

**Server-side encryption** involves the server handling the encryption and decryption processes. The data is encrypted as it is written to storage and decrypted when read. AWS services, such as Amazon S3, offer server-side encryption (SSE) where AWS manages the encryption keys. For instance, when using SSE with Amazon S3, users can opt for AWS Key Management Service (KMS) to manage the keys, ensuring that data is encrypted automatically before it is stored and decrypted when accessed by authorized users.

**Symmetric encryption** uses the same key for both encryption and decryption. This method is efficient and suitable for encrypting large volumes of data. Advanced Encryption Standard (AES) and Data Encryption Standard (DES) are examples of symmetric encryption algorithms. For instance, AES is widely used in securing data stored on hard drives and in database encryption solutions because of its strength and speed.

**Asymmetric encryption**, also known as public-key cryptography, uses a pair of keys: a public key for encryption and a private key for decryption. This technique is used in scenarios where secure key exchange is crucial. One common use case of asymmetric encryption is in Secure Sockets Layer (SSL) and Transport Layer Security (TLS) protocols, which secure data transmitted over the internet. For example, when a user accesses a secure website, their browser uses the website's public key to encrypt the data before sending it, and only the website's private key can decrypt this data, ensuring secure communication.

In summary, various encryption techniques—client-side, server-side, symmetric, and asymmetric—provide robust methods to secure data at rest and in transit. Each technique has its specific use cases and advantages, contributing to a comprehensive data security strategy that protects sensitive information from unauthorized access and breaches.

## 12.4.2 Encryption for S3 Objects at Rest

There are four methods of encrypting objects on S3:
- SSE-S3: encrypts S3 objects using keys handled & managed by AWS.
- SS3-KMS: leverages AWS Key Management Service (KMS) to manage encryption keys.
- SSE-C: you use it when you want to manage your own encryption keys.
- Client Side Encryption

## SSE-S3

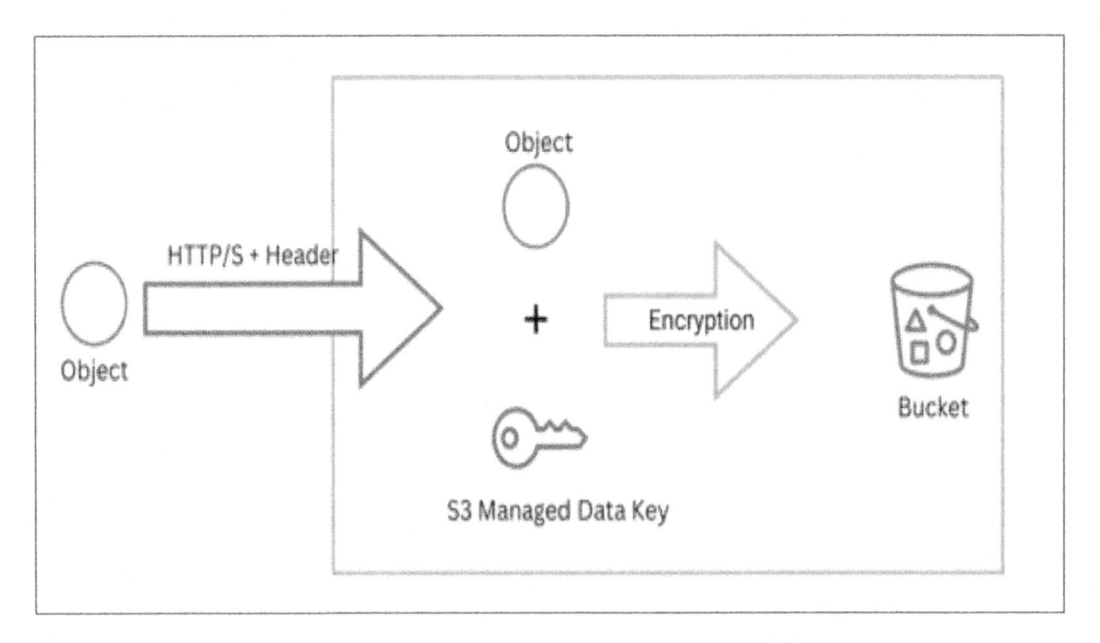

This encryption method of encrypting S3 objects uses keys handled and managed by Amazon S3. The object is encrypted on the server side using AES-256 symmetric encryption. The HTTP request must have custom HTTP Header field: "x-amz-server-side-encryption": "AES256"

## SSE-KMS

This encryption method of encrypting S3 objects uses keys handled and managed by KMS. AWS KMS offers you centralized control over the cryptographic keys to protect your data. The service is also integrated with AWS CloudTrail, which allows you to audit who used which keys, on which resources, and when.

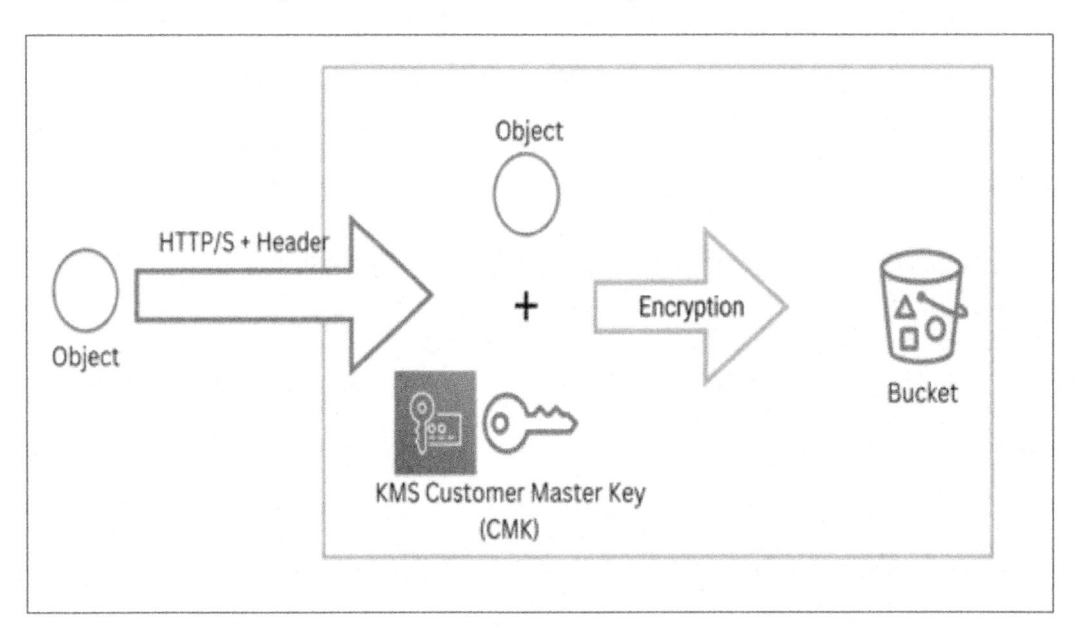

The object is encrypted on the server side using AES-256 symmetric encryption. The HTTP request must have custom HTTP Header field: "x-amz-server-side-encryption": "aws:kms"

## SSE-C

This method uses server-side encryption using data keys fully managed by the customer outside of AWS. Amazon S3 does not store the encryption key that you provide.

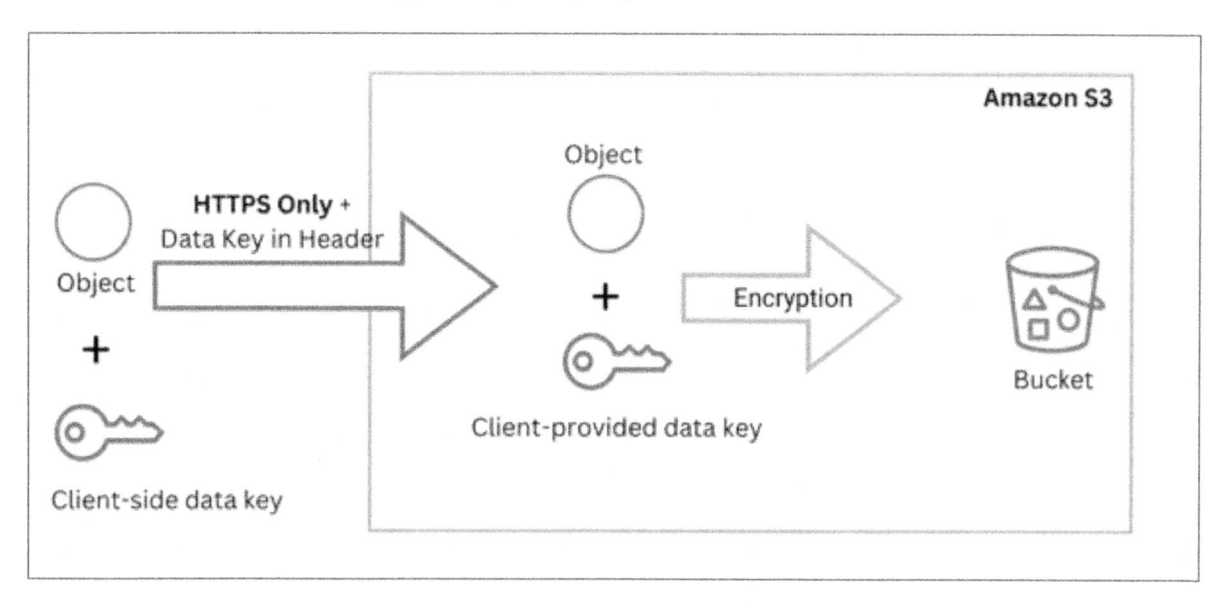

In this method, HTTPS must be used, and an encryption key must be provided in HTTP headers for every HTTP request.

## Client-Side Encryption

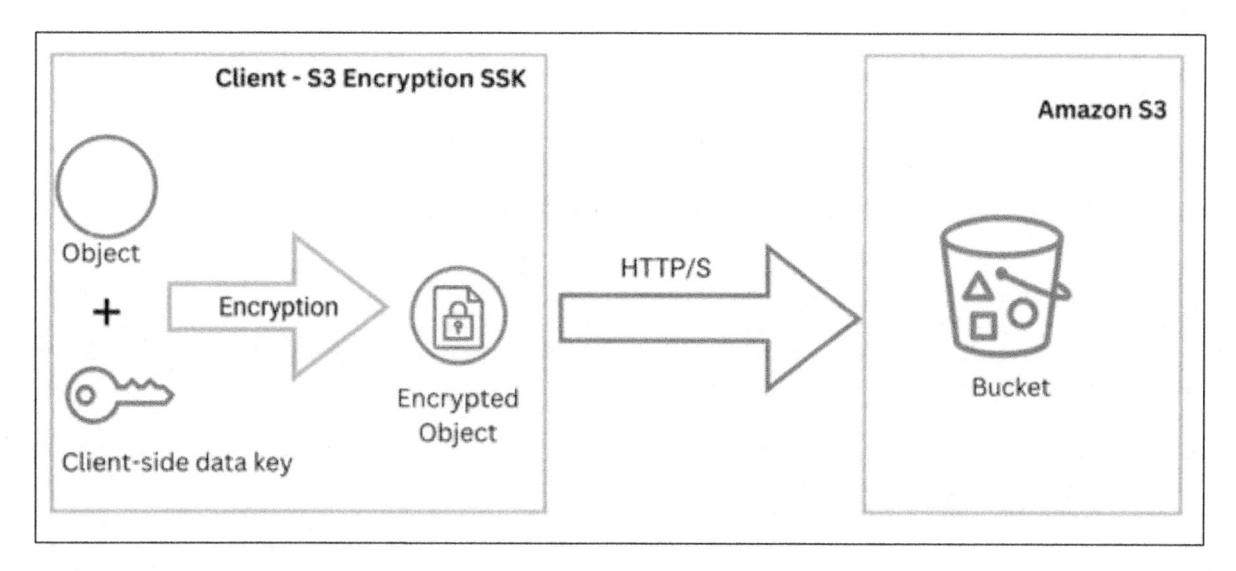

In this encryption method, clients must encrypt data themselves before sending it to S3, and clients must decrypt data themselves when retrieving from S3. The customer fully manages the keys and encryption cycle. Client library such as the Amazon S3 Encryption Client is used.

# 12.4.3 Integrity-Checking Techniques

Integrity-checking techniques are essential for ensuring that data remains accurate, consistent, and unaltered during storage or transmission. These techniques help detect accidental or malicious modifications, ensuring that the data received or retrieved is the same as the data originally sent or stored. Integrity-checking is crucial for maintaining trust in data across various applications, including financial transactions, software distribution, and secure communications.

**Hashing algorithms** are one of the primary methods for ensuring data integrity. A hashing algorithm takes an input (or message) and returns a fixed-size string of characters, which is typically a digest that appears random. The output, known as a hash, uniquely represents the input data. Common hashing algorithms include MD5 (Message Digest Algorithm 5), SHA-1 (Secure Hash Algorithm 1), and SHA-256 (part of the SHA-2 family).

For example, when downloading a file, the provider might offer a hash value generated from the file. The user can then generate a hash from the downloaded file using the same algorithm and compare it with the provided hash. If the two hashes match, the file integrity is confirmed.

**Digital signatures** are another robust technique for ensuring data integrity. They combine the use of hashing and asymmetric encryption to provide both integrity and authenticity. A digital signature is created by generating a hash of the data and then encrypting this hash with the sender's private key. The resulting signature is sent along with the data. Upon receiving the data, the recipient can decrypt the signature using the sender's public key to retrieve the hash. The recipient also generates a hash of the received data using the same hashing algorithm. If the decrypted hash matches the newly generated hash, the data integrity is confirmed, and the recipient is assured that the data has not been altered and is from the legitimate sender.

For example, in email communication, digital signatures ensure the integrity and authenticity of the messages. When a sender digitally signs an email, the recipient can verify that the message has not been altered during transmission and that it genuinely comes from the purported sender. This process is crucial for preventing tampering and spoofing in sensitive communications.

In summary, integrity-checking techniques such as hashing algorithms and digital signatures play a vital role in maintaining data integrity. Hashing algorithms provide a quick and efficient way to detect changes in data, while digital signatures offer additional assurances of data authenticity and integrity through the use of cryptographic methods. These techniques are essential for safeguarding data across various applications, ensuring that information remains trustworthy and secure.

## 12.4.4 Resource Policies for Data Protection

Resource policies for data protection are critical components in managing and controlling access to data within cloud environments. These policies define who can access specific resources and under what conditions, ensuring that only authorized users and applications can interact with sensitive data. Properly designed resource policies help enforce security best practices, comply with regulatory requirements, and protect data from unauthorized access and breaches.

When designing resource policies to control access to data at rest, AWS provides various services like Amazon S3, DynamoDB, and AWS Key Management Service (KMS) that offer robust policy management capabilities.

Amazon S3 uses bucket policies and Identity and Access Management (IAM) policies to manage access to objects stored in S3 buckets. Bucket policies are JSON-based access policy language statements that define the actions allowed or denied on the bucket and its objects. For example, a bucket policy can be configured to allow only specific IAM users or roles to read and write data to the bucket, or to restrict access to certain IP ranges.

For instance, an S3 bucket policy to allow access only from a specific VPC endpoint might look like this:

```
1.  {
2.      "Version": "2012-10-17",
3.      "Statement": [
4.          {
5.              "Effect": "Allow",
6.              "Principal": "*",
7.              "Action": "s3:*",
8.              "Resource": ["arn:aws:s3:::example-bucket/*"],
9.              "Condition": {
10.                 "StringEquals": {
11.                     "aws:sourceVpce": "vpce-1a2b3c4d"
12.                 }
13.             }
14.         }
15.     ]
16. }
```

This policy ensures that only requests coming from the specified VPC endpoint can access the bucket, adding an additional layer of security.

Amazon DynamoDB uses IAM policies to control access to tables and items. These policies can specify which users or roles can perform specific actions, such as reading or writing items. By using conditional statements, access can be further restricted based on attributes such as the user's IP address or the presence of certain item attributes.

For example, an IAM policy to allow only read access to a DynamoDB table for a specific user might look like this:

```
1.  {
2.      "Version": "2012-10-17",
3.      "Statement": [
4.          {
5.              "Effect": "Allow",
6.              "Action": ["dynamodb:GetItem", "dynamodb:Scan", "dynamodb:Query"],
7.              "Resource": "arn:aws:dynamodb:us-west-2:123456789012:table/ExampleTable"
8.          }
9.      ]
10. }
```

This policy ensures that the user can only read data from the specified table, preventing unauthorized write operations.

AWS Key Management Service (KMS) allows for the creation and management of encryption keys used to protect data at rest. KMS policies control access to these keys, specifying who can use them and for what actions. KMS policies can also include conditions to restrict access based on factors like the source IP address or the presence of specific AWS tags.

An example KMS policy that allows a specific role to use a key for encryption but not for decryption might look like this:

```
1.  {
2.      "Version": "2012-10-17",
3.      "Statement": [
4.          {
5.              "Effect": "Allow",
6.              "Principal": {"AWS": "arn:aws:iam::123456789012:role/ExampleRole"},
7.              "Action": ["kms:Encrypt", "kms:ReEncrypt*"],
8.              "Resource": "*"
```

```
 9.          },
10.          {
11.              "Effect": "Deny",
12.              "Principal": {"AWS": "arn:aws:iam::123456789012:role/ExampleRole"},
13.              "Action": ["kms:Decrypt"],
14.              "Resource": "*"
15.          }
16.      ]
17. }
```

This policy ensures that the role can encrypt data but cannot decrypt it, providing fine-grained control over key usage.

In summary, resource policies for data protection in AWS involve using services like S3, DynamoDB, and KMS to define and enforce access controls. Properly designed resource policies ensure that data at rest is accessed only by authorized users and applications, enhancing security and compliance. By leveraging bucket policies, IAM policies, and KMS policies, organizations can implement comprehensive data protection strategies tailored to their specific security requirements.

## 12.4.5 IAM Roles and Policies

IAM roles and policies in AWS are fundamental components for managing access to AWS resources. An IAM (Identity and Access Management) role is a set of permissions that define what actions are allowed or denied for an entity in AWS. Unlike users, roles do not have permanent credentials; instead, they are assumed by trusted entities such as IAM users, applications, or AWS services, which are granted temporary security credentials to perform actions defined by the role's permissions.

IAM policies are JSON documents that define permissions for actions on AWS resources. Policies can be attached to IAM roles, users, or groups, specifying the allowed or denied actions on specified resources under certain conditions. These policies ensure that only authorized users or services can perform specific actions, providing a secure way to control access to AWS resources.

Using IAM roles and policies to secure data at rest involves defining and enforcing permissions that control access to data storage services such as Amazon S3, DynamoDB, and AWS Key Management Service (KMS). By carefully crafting IAM roles and policies, organizations can ensure that only authorized entities can access or modify sensitive data.

For example, to secure data stored in an Amazon S3 bucket, an organization can create an IAM role with a policy that grants read and write access only to specific users or applications. Here is a sample IAM policy that allows an IAM role to read and write to an S3 bucket named "example-bucket":

```
 1. {
 2.     "Version": "2012-10-17",
 3.     "Statement": [
 4.         {
 5.             "Effect": "Allow",
 6.             "Action": ["s3:GetObject", "s3:PutObject"],
 7.             "Resource": "arn:aws:s3:::example-bucket/*"
 8.         }
 9.     ]
10. }
```

This policy ensures that only entities assuming the role can read from and write to the objects within the "example-bucket," providing controlled access to the data at rest in the bucket.

For securing data in Amazon DynamoDB, an organization can create an IAM role with a policy that allows only specific actions on a DynamoDB table. For instance, the following policy grants permissions to read items from a table named "ExampleTable" but denies write operations:

```
{
    "Version": "2012-10-17",
    "Statement": [
        {
            "Effect": "Allow",
            "Action": ["dynamodb:GetItem", "dynamodb:Scan", "dynamodb:Query"],
            "Resource": "arn:aws:dynamodb:us-west-2:123456789012:table/ExampleTable"
        },
        {
            "Effect": "Deny",
            "Action": ["dynamodb:PutItem", "dynamodb:UpdateItem", "dynamodb:DeleteItem"],
            "Resource": "arn:aws:dynamodb:us-west-2:123456789012:table/ExampleTable"
        }
    ]
}
```

This policy ensures that the role can only read data from the table, protecting the data at rest from unauthorized modifications.

In the context of AWS KMS, roles and policies can control access to encryption keys. By creating an IAM role with a policy that grants key usage permissions only to specific entities, an organization can ensure that sensitive data is encrypted and decrypted only by authorized users or services. Here is an example policy that allows an IAM role to use a KMS key for encryption but denies decryption:

```
{
    "Version": "2012-10-17",
    "Statement": [
        {
            "Effect": "Allow",
            "Action": ["kms:Encrypt", "kms:ReEncrypt*"],
            "Resource": "arn:aws:kms:us-west-2:123456789012:key/1234abcd-12ab-34cd-56ef-1234567890ab"
        },
        {
            "Effect": "Deny",
            "Action": ["kms:Decrypt"],
            "Resource": "arn:aws:kms:us-west-2:123456789012:key/1234abcd-12ab-34cd-56ef-1234567890ab"
        }
    ]
}
```

This policy ensures that the role can encrypt data with the KMS key but cannot decrypt it, providing an additional layer of security for data at rest.

In summary, IAM roles and policies are critical tools for securing data at rest in AWS. By defining precise permissions and attaching them to roles, organizations can ensure that only authorized users and services can access or modify sensitive data, thereby enhancing data security and compliance.

## 12.5 Implementing Encryption for Data at Rest

Implementing encryption for data at rest is a crucial security measure that ensures sensitive information stored on disks, databases, and backups remains protected from unauthorized access and breaches. By encrypting data at rest, organizations can safeguard their assets against threats and comply with regulatory requirements, ensuring that data remains secure even if physical or virtual storage media are compromised.

## 12.5.1 Activating Encryption for AWS Services

Activating encryption for AWS services is a critical step in securing data at rest. AWS provides robust encryption capabilities across its services, allowing users to protect sensitive information stored in databases, file systems, and message queues. Encryption can be enabled by default or configured manually, depending on the service, to ensure that data remains secure and compliant with regulatory standards.

To **configure encryption for Amazon S3,** users can enable server-side encryption (SSE) on S3 buckets. SSE can use AWS Key Management Service (KMS) keys, S3-managed keys (SSE-S3), or customer-provided keys (SSE-C). For example, enabling SSE with KMS for an S3 bucket ensures that objects stored in the bucket are encrypted with a key managed by AWS KMS. Users can specify encryption settings when creating a bucket or update existing bucket properties to enable encryption.

**Amazon RDS** (Relational Database Service) supports encryption for data at rest using AWS KMS. When creating a new RDS instance, users can select the "Enable Encryption" option, which encrypts the underlying storage and automated backups using the specified KMS key. For example, an RDS instance for a MySQL database can be encrypted to protect sensitive customer information stored in the database. Encryption settings must be specified at the time of instance creation, as encryption cannot be enabled for an existing unencrypted instance.

**Amazon DynamoDB** offers encryption at rest by default, using AWS-owned keys or AWS KMS customer-managed keys. This ensures that all data stored in DynamoDB tables is encrypted without additional configuration. For instance, an application that stores user data in DynamoDB can benefit from automatic encryption, ensuring data protection with minimal administrative overhead.

**Amazon SQS** (Simple Queue Service) can be configured to use server-side encryption to protect the contents of the message queues. By enabling encryption for an SQS queue, messages are encrypted using an AWS KMS key when they are stored in the queue. For example, sensitive messages containing transaction data can be securely stored in an SQS queue by enabling encryption with a KMS key, ensuring that the data is protected during processing and storage.

**Amazon EBS** (Elastic Block Store) allows users to enable encryption when creating EBS volumes. Encrypted EBS volumes use KMS keys to encrypt data at rest, including data at the volume, snapshot, and backup levels. For example, an EC2 instance with encrypted EBS volumes ensures that all data stored on the volumes is protected, including any snapshots or backups created from the volumes.

**Amazon EFS** (Elastic File System) supports encryption at rest using KMS keys. When creating a new EFS file system, users can enable encryption to ensure that all files stored in the file system are encrypted. For instance, an EFS file system used to store sensitive documents can be encrypted to protect the data from unauthorized access, providing an additional layer of security for shared file storage.

In summary, activating and configuring encryption for AWS services like S3, RDS, DynamoDB, SQS, EBS, and EFS is essential for protecting data at rest. By leveraging AWS's built-in encryption capabilities, users can ensure that their data remains secure and compliant with industry standards and regulations.

## 12.5.2 Protecting Data Integrity

Protecting data integrity is essential to ensure that data remains accurate, consistent, and trustworthy over its lifecycle. Data integrity involves safeguarding data from unauthorized modifications, corruption, or tampering, which can occur due to malicious activities, software bugs, or human errors. Ensuring data integrity is crucial for maintaining the reliability of data used in decision-making processes, financial transactions, and regulatory compliance.

One effective method for protecting data integrity in Amazon S3 is using S3 Object Lock. S3 Object Lock allows users to store objects using a write-once-read-many (WORM) model, which prevents objects from being deleted or overwritten for a specified retention period. This feature is particularly useful for compliance requirements that mandate data immutability, such as financial records or legal documents. For example, a financial institution can use S3 Object Lock to ensure that its transaction logs are protected from unauthorized modifications, thereby maintaining the integrity of the data for audit purposes.

To enable S3 Object Lock, users can configure a bucket with Object Lock enabled and then apply retention policies to individual objects or set default retention periods for the entire bucket. This mechanism ensures that once an object is written, it cannot be altered or deleted until the retention period expires, thereby protecting the data from accidental or intentional modifications.

Another powerful tool for protecting data integrity is AWS Key Management Service (KMS) key policies. KMS key policies define who can use and manage encryption keys and specify the actions that users and services can perform with these keys. By designing strict key policies, organizations can control access to encryption keys, thereby preventing unauthorized data modifications.

For example, a company can create a KMS key policy that restricts key usage to specific IAM roles or users and allows only certain actions, such as encryption and decryption, while denying key deletion or modification. Here is an example of a KMS key policy that grants an IAM role permission to use the key for encryption but not for decryption:

```
{
    "Version": "2012-10-17",
    "Statement": [
        {
            "Effect": "Allow",
            "Principal": {
                "AWS": "arn:aws:iam::123456789012:role/ExampleRole"
            },
            "Action": ["kms:Encrypt", "kms:ReEncrypt*"],
            "Resource": "*"
        },
        {
            "Effect": "Deny",
            "Principal": {
                "AWS": "arn:aws:iam::123456789012:role/ExampleRole"
            },
            "Action": ["kms:Decrypt"],
            "Resource": "*"
        }
    ]
}
```

This policy ensures that only authorized roles can encrypt data, thereby maintaining the integrity of the encrypted data by preventing unauthorized decryption.

In summary, protecting data integrity involves implementing mechanisms to prevent unauthorized modifications to data. Tools like S3 Object Lock and KMS key policies provide robust solutions to safeguard data from tampering and ensure that data remains accurate and trustworthy. By leveraging these tools, organizations can enhance their data integrity measures, comply with regulatory requirements, and maintain the reliability of their critical data assets.

## 12.5.3 Using AWS CloudHSM

Implementing encryption at rest using AWS CloudHSM for relational databases provides a highly secure method for protecting sensitive data stored within your database. AWS CloudHSM (Hardware Security Module) allows you to manage your own encryption keys using dedicated hardware appliances within the AWS cloud, providing enhanced security and control over key management. This is particularly important for applications with stringent compliance requirements, such as financial services and healthcare.

When using AWS CloudHSM for encrypting data at rest in relational databases, the process involves generating and storing encryption keys within the HSMs. These keys are used to encrypt the database files, ensuring that data is protected from unauthorized access, even if the physical storage is compromised. The encryption and decryption operations are performed by the HSMs, providing a high level of security since the keys never leave the secure hardware environment.

To implement encryption at rest using AWS CloudHSM with a relational database, such as Amazon RDS for MySQL, the following steps can be taken:

Provision AWS CloudHSM: Set up and configure an AWS CloudHSM cluster. This involves creating an HSM cluster, configuring security groups, and initializing the HSMs. AWS CloudHSM provides dedicated hardware security modules that you can manage and use to store encryption keys.

Create a Key in CloudHSM: Use the AWS CloudHSM client to create a key within the HSM. This key will be used to encrypt the data stored in the database. For example, you can use the AWS CloudHSM SDK or command line tools to generate a symmetric key.

Configure the Database to Use CloudHSM: Modify the database configuration to use the encryption key stored in CloudHSM. For Amazon RDS, you need to use AWS Key Management Service (KMS) to integrate with CloudHSM. You can create a customer master key (CMK) in AWS KMS backed by CloudHSM, and then use this CMK to encrypt the data in RDS.

Enable Encryption for the Database: When creating a new RDS instance, specify the CMK backed by CloudHSM for encryption. If you are encrypting an existing database, create a snapshot of the database, copy the snapshot with encryption enabled, and restore the database from the encrypted snapshot. This ensures that all data at rest in the database is encrypted using the key stored in CloudHSM.

For example, to create a new encrypted RDS instance using CloudHSM, you would specify the KMS key ID of the CMK backed by CloudHSM during the RDS instance creation process. Here is a sample configuration snippet for creating an encrypted RDS instance:

```
1.  {
2.      "DBInstanceIdentifier": "mydbinstance",
3.      "AllocatedStorage": 100,
4.      "DBInstanceClass": "db.m5.large",
5.      "Engine": "mysql",
6.      "MasterUsername": "admin",
7.      "MasterUserPassword": "password",
8.      "KmsKeyId": "arn:aws:kms:us-west-2:123456789012:key/abcd1234-5678-90ab-cdef-1234567890ab",
9.      "StorageEncrypted": true
10. }
```

In this configuration, the `KmsKeyId` parameter specifies the CMK backed by CloudHSM, and the `StorageEncrypted` parameter enables encryption at rest for the RDS instance.

Implementing encryption at rest using AWS CloudHSM provides robust security for relational databases by ensuring that encryption keys are managed in a secure hardware environment. This approach enhances the protection of sensitive data and helps meet compliance requirements for data security.

## 12.5.4 Choosing Encryption Techniques

Selecting appropriate encryption techniques based on business requirements is a critical aspect of ensuring data security and regulatory compliance. Different business scenarios necessitate specific encryption methods to protect sensitive information effectively. The choice of encryption technique depends on factors such as the type of data, compliance and regulatory requirements, performance (SLA) considerations, and the level of security needed.

For data in transit, **Transport Layer Security (TLS)** is widely used to secure communications over networks, such as web traffic, email, and other internet-based communications. TLS ensures that data sent between systems is encrypted, preventing eavesdropping and tampering. For instance, an e-commerce website processing credit card payments will use TLS to encrypt data between the customer's browser and the web server, ensuring that PI (personal information) related payment information is protected during transmission.

For data at rest, **symmetric encryption algorithms** like Advanced Encryption Standard (AES) are commonly employed due to their efficiency and strong security properties. AES is suitable for encrypting large volumes of data, such as databases and file systems. For example, a financial institution storing customer account details in a relational database might use AES-256 to encrypt the database files, ensuring that sensitive information remains secure even if the storage media is compromised.

**Asymmetric encryption**, or public-key cryptography, is typically used for scenarios requiring secure key exchange or digital signatures. Asymmetric algorithms like RSA or Elliptic Curve Cryptography (ECC) provide strong security but are computationally intensive compared to symmetric encryption. An example use case is securing email communications: a user can encrypt an email with the recipient's public key, ensuring that only the recipient, who holds the corresponding private key, can read the messag by decrypting it.

For environments requiring stringent compliance and high-security standards, **hardware security modules (HSMs)**, such as AWS CloudHSM, provide a higher level of protection for encryption keys. HSMs are dedicated hardware devices that generate, store, and manage cryptographic keys in a secure environment. For example, a healthcare provider handling patient records might use CloudHSM to manage encryption keys for encrypting patient data, ensuring compliance with regulations like HIPAA, which mandates stringent security controls for sensitive health information.

In summary, selecting the appropriate encryption technique depends on various factors, including the nature of the data, regulatory requirements, performance needs, and security considerations. By evaluating these factors, organizations can choose the most suitable encryption method to protect their sensitive information effectively.

# 12.6 Managing the Lifecycle of Data at Rest

Managing the lifecycle of data at rest is essential for ensuring data security, compliance, and efficient storage management. This process involves implementing policies and controls to govern data from creation and storage to archival and deletion. Effective lifecycle management helps organizations protect sensitive information, optimize storage costs, and comply with regulatory requirements.

## 12.6.1 Lifecycle Policies

Understanding and implementing lifecycle policies for data retention and management is crucial for organizations to maintain data integrity, ensure compliance with legal and regulatory requirements, and optimize storage costs. Lifecycle policies define the rules and processes for managing data from its creation to its eventual deletion, helping organizations systematically handle data throughout its lifespan.

**Data retention policies** determine how long different types of data should be kept. These policies are often driven by regulatory requirements, legal considerations, and business needs. For example, financial institutions may be required to retain transaction records for several years to comply with regulations like the Sarbanes-Oxley Act. Similarly, healthcare providers must retain patient records for a specified period to comply with HIPAA regulations. By defining retention periods for various data categories, organizations can ensure that they meet all legal and regulatory obligations while preventing unnecessary data accumulation.

**Data management policies** involve classifying data, applying appropriate security controls, and defining processes for data archiving and deletion. For example, an organization might classify data based on sensitivity levels (e.g., public, internal, confidential) and apply corresponding encryption and access controls. This ensures that sensitive data is adequately protected and only accessible to authorized personnel.

Implementing lifecycle policies in AWS can be facilitated using services like Amazon S3, which offers lifecycle management features to automate data retention and deletion. For instance, an organization can create a lifecycle policy for an S3 bucket to transition objects to lower-cost storage classes (e.g., S3 Glacier) after a certain period and permanently delete them after a specified retention period.

Here is an example of an S3 lifecycle policy that transitions objects to S3 Glacier after 30 days and deletes them after one year:

```
{
    "Rules": [
        {
            "ID": "Archive and Delete Rule",
            "Status": "Enabled",
            "Prefix": "",
            "Transitions": [
                {
                    "Days": 30,
                    "StorageClass": "GLACIER"
                }
            ],
            "Expiration": {
                "Days": 365
            }
        }
    ]
}
```

This policy helps reduce storage costs by moving older data to more cost-effective storage and ensures that obsolete data is deleted, maintaining compliance with data retention requirements.

In summary, understanding and implementing lifecycle policies for data retention and management is vital for organizations to handle their data efficiently and securely. By defining clear retention and management policies and leveraging tools like AWS S3 lifecycle management, organizations can ensure compliance, optimize storage costs, and protect sensitive information throughout its lifecycle.

## 12.6.2 S3 Lifecycle Mechanisms

S3 Lifecycle Mechanisms are features provided by Amazon S3 to automate the management of object storage, allowing users to define rules for transitioning objects between different storage classes and setting expiration for data deletion. These mechanisms help optimize storage costs and ensure that data retention policies are enforced consistently. S3 supports various storage classes such as Standard, Intelligent-Tiering, Standard-IA (Infrequent Access), One Zone-IA, Glacier, and Glacier Deep Archive. Lifecycle rules can be configured to automatically transition objects to more cost-effective storage classes based on their age or access patterns and to delete objects after a certain period.

**Designing S3 Lifecycle policies** involves creating rules that define how objects should be managed throughout their lifecycle. These rules specify when to transition objects to different storage classes and when to delete them. Designing effective lifecycle policies requires understanding the access patterns and retention requirements of the data stored in S3. By doing so, organizations can balance cost savings with data availability and compliance needs.

For example, consider an organization that stores large amounts of log data in S3. These logs are frequently accessed for the first month but are rarely needed afterward.

To optimize costs while ensuring the data remains available if needed, the organization can design a lifecycle policy with the following rules:
- Transition logs to the Standard-IA storage class 30 days after creation.
- Move logs to Glacier 90 days after creation.
- Delete logs 365 days after creation.

Here is how such a lifecycle policy might be defined in JSON:

```
{
    "Rules": [
        {
            "ID": "Log Management Policy",
            "Status": "Enabled",
            "Prefix": "logs/",
            "Transitions": [
                {
                    "Days": 30,
                    "StorageClass": "STANDARD_IA"
                },
                {
                    "Days": 90,
                    "StorageClass": "GLACIER"
                }
            ],
            "Expiration": {
                "Days": 365
            }
        }
    ]
}
```

In this policy:
- The "Prefix" specifies that the rules apply to objects stored under the "logs/" directory.
- The "Transitions" section defines when objects are moved to different storage classes. Objects are moved to Standard-IA after 30 days and to Glacier after 90 days.
- The "Expiration" section specifies that objects are permanently deleted 365 days after creation.

By implementing this policy, the organization can reduce storage costs by moving less frequently accessed data to cheaper storage classes while ensuring that logs are retained for a year to meet any regulatory or operational requirements.

In summary, S3 Lifecycle Mechanisms allow users to automate data management tasks, helping to reduce storage costs and enforce data retention policies. By designing effective lifecycle policies, organizations can manage data retention periods and transitions seamlessly, ensuring that data is stored in the most cost-effective manner while meeting access and compliance requirements.

## 12.6.3 Automatic Lifecycle Management for AWS Services

Automatic lifecycle management for AWS services refers to the automation of data and resource management tasks throughout their lifecycle. This includes transitioning data to different storage tiers, archiving, and deleting obsolete data, as well as managing compute resources and other AWS services. Automatic lifecycle management helps organizations optimize costs, improve operational efficiency, and ensure compliance with data retention policies without manual intervention.

### Implementing Automatic Lifecycle Management

Implementing automatic lifecycle management for various AWS services involves configuring specific rules and policies that govern the handling of data and resources over time. AWS provides several tools and services that support lifecycle management, enabling users to automate processes and maintain control over their infrastructure.

For example, in **Amazon S3,** lifecycle policies can be set up to automatically transition objects between storage classes or delete them after a specified period. This helps manage storage costs by moving infrequently accessed data to cheaper storage options and removing data that is no longer needed. A lifecycle policy might transition data to S3 Standard-IA after 30 days, then to Glacier after 90 days, and finally delete it after one year.

Similarly, **Amazon EC2** instances and **Elastic Block Store (EBS)** volumes can benefit from lifecycle management by automating snapshot creation and deletion. For example, AWS Data Lifecycle Manager (DLM) allows users to create policies that automatically take snapshots of EBS volumes at regular intervals and delete older snapshots that are no longer needed. This ensures that backups are up-to-date and that storage costs are minimized by removing obsolete snapshots.

**Amazon RDS** (Relational Database Service) supports automatic backups and the deletion of older backups. Users can configure RDS to automatically create backups of their databases and retain these backups for a specified number of days before deletion. This ensures that recent backups are available for recovery while controlling storage costs by eliminating outdated backups.

**AWS Config** provides automatic lifecycle management for compliance and resource management by monitoring resource configurations and comparing them against desired configurations. Users can set up AWS Config rules to automatically evaluate resources for compliance and take remediation actions if resources are non-compliant. For instance, AWS Config can automatically delete or stop non-compliant EC2 instances based on defined rules.

**For example**, a company may implement automatic lifecycle management for its data stored in S3 and its EC2 instances using the following approaches:

**S3 Lifecycle Policy:** Configure a policy to transition logs to Standard-IA after 30 days, to Glacier after 90 days, and delete them after one year.

```
1. {
2.     "Rules": [
3.         {
4.             "ID": "Log Management Policy",
```

```
5.            "Status": "Enabled",
6.            "Prefix": "logs/",
7.            "Transitions": [
8.                {
9.                    "Days": 30,
10.                   "StorageClass": "STANDARD_IA"
11.               },
12.               {
13.                   "Days": 90,
14.                   "StorageClass": "GLACIER"
15.               }
16.           ],
17.           "Expiration": {
18.               "Days": 365
19.           }
20.       }
21.   ]
22. }
23.
```

**EBS Snapshot Lifecycle Policy:** Use AWS Data Lifecycle Manager to create a policy that takes daily snapshots of critical EBS volumes and retains these snapshots for 30 days before deletion. This ensures that recent snapshots are available for disaster recovery while managing storage costs by removing older, unnecessary snapshots.

In summary, automatic lifecycle management for AWS services automates the process of managing data and resources over time, helping organizations optimize costs, improve efficiency, and ensure compliance. By leveraging tools like S3 lifecycle policies, AWS Data Lifecycle Manager, RDS automatic backups, and AWS Config, users can implement effective lifecycle management strategies tailored to their specific needs.

## 12.6.4 Backup Scheduling and Retention

Backup scheduling and retention are critical components of data protection strategies, ensuring that data can be restored in the event of loss, corruption, or disaster. Backup scheduling involves defining the frequency and timing of backup operations to capture the most recent data changes, while retention policies determine how long these backups are kept before they are deleted. Together, these practices help organizations maintain data integrity, comply with regulatory requirements, and optimize storage costs.

**Establishing schedules and retention policies for AWS Backup across services** involves creating backup plans that specify the timing, frequency, and duration of backups for various AWS resources, such as Amazon RDS, EC2 instances, DynamoDB tables, and Amazon EFS file systems. AWS Backup provides a centralized service to automate and manage backups across AWS services, offering flexibility and consistency in backup operations.

For example, to set up a comprehensive backup plan for a critical application, an organization might establish the following backup schedules and retention policies:

**Daily Backups:** Schedule daily backups at 2 AM for all critical databases hosted on Amazon RDS to capture daily data changes. These backups can be retained for 30 days to ensure that recent data is available for recovery.
**Weekly Backups:** Perform weekly full backups of Amazon EFS file systems every Sunday at midnight. These backups can be retained for 12 weeks to provide a longer recovery window for important files.
**Monthly Backups:** Conduct monthly backups of Amazon EC2 instances on the first day of each month at 1 AM. These backups can be retained for one year to comply with long-term data retention policies.

To implement these schedules and retention policies using AWS Backup, the organization can create a backup plan with multiple rules, each defining specific backup schedules and retention periods. Here is an example backup plan configuration:

```
{
    "BackupPlanName": "CriticalAppBackupPlan",
    "Rules": [
        {
            "RuleName": "DailyRDSBackups",
            "TargetBackupVaultName": "Default",
            "ScheduleExpression": "cron(0 2 * * ? *)",
            "StartWindowMinutes": 60,
            "CompletionWindowMinutes": 120,
            "Lifecycle": {
                "MoveToColdStorageAfterDays": 30,
                "DeleteAfterDays": 90
            },
            "RecoveryPointTags": {
                "Environment": "Production",
                "Frequency": "Daily"
            },
            "CopyActions": []
        },
        {
            "RuleName": "WeeklyEFSBackups",
            "TargetBackupVaultName": "Default",
            "ScheduleExpression": "cron(0 0 ? * SUN *)",
            "StartWindowMinutes": 60,
            "CompletionWindowMinutes": 240,
            "Lifecycle": {
                "MoveToColdStorageAfterDays": 84,
                "DeleteAfterDays": 365
            },
            "RecoveryPointTags": {
                "Environment": "Production",
                "Frequency": "Weekly"
            },
            "CopyActions": []
        },
        {
            "RuleName": "MonthlyEC2Backups",
            "TargetBackupVaultName": "Default",
            "ScheduleExpression": "cron(0 1 1 * ? *)",
            "StartWindowMinutes": 60,
            "CompletionWindowMinutes": 240,
            "Lifecycle": {
                "MoveToColdStorageAfterDays": 365,
                "DeleteAfterDays": 730
            },
            "RecoveryPointTags": {
                "Environment": "Production",
                "Frequency": "Monthly"
            },
            "CopyActions": []
        }
    ]
}
```

In this backup plan:
- The DailyRDSBackups rule schedules daily backups for RDS databases and retains them for 90 days.

- The WeeklyEFSBackups rule schedules weekly backups for EFS file systems and retains them for one year.
- The MonthlyEC2Backups rule schedules monthly backups for EC2 instances and retains them for two years.

By defining clear backup schedules and retention policies, organizations can ensure that their critical data is regularly backed up and retained for appropriate periods, balancing the need for data protection with storage cost management. AWS Backup simplifies this process by providing a centralized and automated solution for managing backups across various AWS services.

# 12.7 Protecting Credentials, Secrets, and Cryptographic Key Materials

Protecting credentials, secrets, and cryptographic key materials is essential for maintaining the security and integrity of systems and data. Effective management and safeguarding of these sensitive items help prevent unauthorized access and ensure that encryption processes remain robust. Techniques such as secure storage, access control, and regular rotation are critical components of a comprehensive security strategy.

## 12.7.1 AWS Secrets Manager

AWS Secrets Manager is a fully managed service that helps organizations securely manage access to secrets such as database credentials, API keys, and other sensitive information. It simplifies the process of secret management by enabling automatic rotation, secure storage, and fine-grained access control, thereby reducing the risk of unauthorized access and enhancing overall security. AWS Secrets Manager integrates seamlessly with other AWS services, making it easy to incorporate into existing workflows and applications.

**Using AWS Secrets Manager for managing and rotating secrets securely** involves storing secrets in a secure and centralized repository, where they can be accessed by authorized applications and users when needed. Secrets Manager encrypts secrets using AWS Key Management Service (KMS) keys, ensuring that they are protected both at rest and in transit. One of the key features of Secrets Manager is its ability to automatically rotate secrets, which helps mitigate the risk of credential exposure and unauthorized access.

For example, consider a scenario where an application needs to connect to a MySQL database. Instead of hardcoding the database credentials in the application code, the credentials can be stored in AWS Secrets Manager. Here's how it can be set up:

- **Store the secret:** Create a new secret in AWS Secrets Manager with the database credentials (username and password).
- **Grant access:** Use IAM policies to grant the application permission to access the secret.
- **Integrate with the application:** Modify the application code to retrieve the database credentials from Secrets Manager using the AWS SDK or CLI.

Here is an example of a Python script using the AWS SDK (Boto3) to retrieve a secret:

```
1.  import boto3
2.  import json
3.  from botocore.exceptions import ClientError
4.
5.  def get_secret():
6.      secret_name = "my-database-secret"
7.      region_name = "us-west-2"
8.
9.      # Create a Secrets Manager client
10.     client = boto3.client("secretsmanager", region_name=region_name)
```

```
11.
12.     try:
13.         get_secret_value_response = client.get_secret_value(SecretId=secret_name)
14.     except ClientError as e:
15.         raise e
16.
17.     # Decrypts secret using the associated KMS key.
18.     secret = get_secret_value_response["SecretString"]
19.     secret_dict = json.loads(secret)
20.     return secret_dict
21.
22. # Usage
23. credentials = get_secret()
24. db_username = credentials["username"]
25. db_password = credentials["password"]
```

Automatic rotation can be enabled for the secret, specifying the rotation interval (e.g., every 30 days) and providing a Lambda function to handle the rotation process. AWS Secrets Manager takes care of updating the secret value and ensuring that applications using the secret are not disrupted.

Here is how to enable automatic rotation:
- **Create a Lambda function:** Write a Lambda function that knows how to update the database password and update the secret in Secrets Manager.
- **Enable rotation:** In the Secrets Manager console, select the secret and enable rotation, specifying the Lambda function created for rotation.

By using AWS Secrets Manager, organizations can enhance the security of their applications by centrally managing and automatically rotating secrets, thereby reducing the risk of credential compromise and ensuring that sensitive information remains protected.

## 12.7.2 Systems Manager Parameter Store

AWS Systems Manager Parameter Store is a secure, scalable, and centralized service that allows users to manage configuration data, secrets, and parameters used by their applications and services. It provides a unified repository to store various types of data, such as plain text values, encrypted data, and hierarchical data structures, enabling easy management and retrieval of these parameters when needed. Parameter Store integrates seamlessly with other AWS services and supports features like versioning, access control, and notifications.

### Storing and Managing Configuration Data and Secrets

Storing and managing configuration data and secrets with Systems Manager Parameter Store involves defining parameters that can be securely accessed by applications and services. Parameter Store supports both plain text and encrypted parameters. Encrypted parameters are protected using AWS Key Management Service (KMS) keys, ensuring that sensitive information remains secure. For example, to store a database connection string in Parameter Store, follow these steps:

**Store the parameter:** Navigate to the AWS Systems Manager console. Select "Parameter Store" under the "Application Management" section. Click on "Create parameter." Enter a name for the parameter, such as /my-app/db-connection-string. Select the type (String, StringList, or SecureString). For sensitive data, choose "SecureString" and specify the KMS key to use for encryption. Enter the value (e.g., the database connection string) and save the parameter.

**Grant access:** Use IAM policies to grant applications and users permission to access the parameter. Create an IAM policy that allows the necessary actions (ssm:GetParameter, ssm:GetParameters, ssm:GetParametersByPath) on the parameter resource. Attach the policy to the IAM roles or users that require access.

**Integrate with the application:** Modify the application code to retrieve the parameter value from Parameter Store using the AWS SDK or CLI. For example, in a Python application, use the Boto3 library to fetch the parameter:

```python
import boto3
from botocore.exceptions import ClientError

def get_parameter(parameter_name):
    ssm_client = boto3.client('ssm')
    try:
        response = ssm_client.get_parameter(
            Name=parameter_name,
            WithDecryption=True
        )
        return response['Parameter']['Value']
    except ClientError as e:
        print(f"Error retrieving parameter: {e}")
        return None

# Usage
db_connection_string = get_parameter('/my-app/db-connection-string')
print(f"Database Connection String: {db_connection_string}")
```

In this example, the `get_parameter` function retrieves the encrypted parameter value from Parameter Store and decrypts it using the specified KMS key. The application can then use the retrieved value for its configuration or operational needs.

Versioning in Parameter Store allows users to maintain multiple versions of a parameter, making it easy to roll back to previous values if needed. This is particularly useful for managing changes to configuration data or secrets over time. Additionally, Parameter Store can be integrated with AWS CloudWatch to monitor and receive notifications about parameter changes, ensuring that any unauthorized modifications are detected promptly.

By leveraging AWS Systems Manager Parameter Store, organizations can securely store and manage configuration data and secrets, streamline application deployment and management, and enhance overall security and compliance.

## 12.7.3 Symmetric and Asymmetric Key Management

Managing symmetric and asymmetric keys with AWS Key Management Service (KMS) is a fundamental aspect of ensuring the security and integrity of encrypted data in the AWS ecosystem. AWS KMS is a managed service that simplifies the creation, management, and usage of cryptographic keys for encrypting data across various AWS services and applications. KMS supports both symmetric and asymmetric keys, catering to different encryption and decryption needs.

Symmetric keys in AWS KMS use the same key for both encryption and decryption operations. This type of key is suitable for encrypting large amounts of data efficiently. Symmetric keys in KMS are typically used with AWS services like Amazon S3, Amazon EBS, and Amazon RDS to encrypt data at rest. For example, when an object is uploaded to an S3 bucket with server-side encryption enabled, KMS can be used to manage the encryption keys, ensuring that the object is encrypted before it is stored.

To create and manage a symmetric key in AWS KMS, follow these steps:

**Create a symmetric key:** Navigate to the AWS KMS console. Click on "Create key." Select "Symmetric" for the key type. Provide key metadata such as an alias and description. Define key administrative and usage permissions using IAM roles and policies. Review and create the key.

**Use the symmetric key:** The created key can now be used to encrypt and decrypt data. For example, encrypting data with the AWS SDK (Python Boto3):

```
1.  import boto3
2.
3.  # Initialize a session using Amazon KMS
4.  kms_client = boto3.client('kms')
5.
6.  # Define the data to be encrypted
7.  plaintext = b'Sensitive data to encrypt'
8.
9.  # Encrypt the data
10. response = kms_client.encrypt(
11.     KeyId='arn:aws:kms:us-west-2:123456789012:key/abcd1234-5678-90ab-cdef-1234567890ab',
12.     Plaintext=plaintext
13. )
14.
15. # The encrypted data
16. ciphertext = response['CiphertextBlob']
17. print(f'Encrypted data: {ciphertext}')
```

Asymmetric keys in AWS KMS use a pair of related keys: a public key for encryption or signature verification, and a private key for decryption or signing. Asymmetric keys are typically used in scenarios where secure key distribution is crucial, such as digital signatures and public key encryption. KMS supports RSA and elliptic curve (ECC) key pairs, making it suitable for a wide range of cryptographic operations.

To create and manage an asymmetric key in AWS KMS, follow these steps:

**Create an asymmetric key:** Navigate to the AWS KMS console. Click on "Create key." Select "Asymmetric" for the key type and specify whether you need an RSA or ECC key pair. Provide key metadata such as an alias and description. Define key administrative and usage permissions using IAM roles and policies. Review and create the key.

**Use the asymmetric key:** The created key can now be used for encryption, decryption, signing, and verification operations. For example, encrypting data with the public key using the AWS SDK (Python Boto3):

```
1.  import boto3
2.
3.  # Initialize a session using Amazon KMS
4.  kms_client = boto3.client('kms')
5.
6.  # Define the data to be encrypted
7.  plaintext = b'Sensitive data to encrypt'
8.
9.  # Encrypt the data using the public key
10. response = kms_client.encrypt(
11.     KeyId='arn:aws:kms:us-west-2:123456789012:key/abcd1234-5678-90ab-cdef-1234567890ab',
12.     Plaintext=plaintext
13. )
14.
15. # The encrypted data
16. ciphertext = response['CiphertextBlob']
17. print(f'Encrypted data: {ciphertext}')
```

Managing symmetric and asymmetric keys with AWS KMS provides robust encryption capabilities, enhancing data security across AWS services. By leveraging KMS, organizations can ensure that their cryptographic keys are stored securely, rotated automatically, and used efficiently in compliance with security best practices and regulatory requirements.

## 12.7.4 Managing and Rotating Secrets

Designing and implementing mechanisms for managing and rotating secrets is essential for maintaining the security and integrity of various workloads. Secrets such as API keys, database credentials, and encryption keys need to be securely stored and regularly rotated to mitigate the risk of unauthorized access and credential compromise. AWS offers several tools, including AWS Secrets Manager and AWS Systems Manager Parameter Store, to help automate the management and rotation of secrets.

AWS Secrets Manager is a powerful service designed specifically for managing and rotating secrets. It provides built-in integrations with databases and other AWS services, allowing for seamless automatic rotation of credentials. When using AWS Secrets Manager, secrets are stored securely with encryption keys managed by AWS Key Management Service (KMS). This ensures that secrets are protected both at rest and in transit. Automatic rotation can be configured to rotate secrets on a predefined schedule without disrupting applications that rely on these secrets.

For example, consider a scenario where an application needs to connect to an Amazon RDS database. The database credentials can be stored in AWS Secrets Manager and rotated automatically. Here's how it can be done:

**Store the secret:** Navigate to the AWS Secrets Manager console. Click on "Store a new secret." Select "Credentials for RDS database" and enter the database username and password. Choose the RDS database instance. Provide a name for the secret (e.g., MyDatabaseSecret) and store it.

**Enable rotation:** In the Secrets Manager console, select the secret you just created. Click on "Rotate this secret." Configure the rotation schedule (e.g., every 30 days). Select or create a Lambda function that will handle the rotation. AWS provides templates for rotation Lambda functions for different database engines.

**Grant access:** Use IAM policies to grant the application permission to access the secret. Attach the policy to the IAM roles or users that require access.

**Integrate with the application:** Modify the application code to retrieve the database credentials from Secrets Manager using the AWS SDK.

```
1. import boto3
2. from botocore.exceptions import ClientError
3.
4. def get_secret():
5.     secret_name = "MyDatabaseSecret"
6.     region_name = "us-west-2"
7.
8.     # Create a Secrets Manager client
9.     client = boto3.client("secretsmanager", region_name=region_name)
10.
11.     try:
12.         get_secret_value_response = client.get_secret_value(SecretId=secret_name)
13.     except ClientError as e:
14.         raise e
15.
16.     secret = get_secret_value_response["SecretString"]
```

```
17.     secret_dict = json.loads(secret)
18.     return secret_dict
19.
20. # Usage
21. credentials = get_secret()
22. db_username = credentials["username"]
23. db_password = credentials["password"]
```

**AWS Systems Manager Parameter Store** can also be used to manage secrets, though it does not offer built-in automatic rotation. Secrets are stored as parameters with the "SecureString" type and are encrypted using KMS keys. While Parameter Store requires more manual management for rotation, it is well-suited for simpler use cases or where automatic rotation is not needed.

To rotate secrets with Parameter Store, a Lambda function can be scheduled using Amazon CloudWatch Events to periodically generate new secrets, update the parameters, and update the associated services with the new credentials. Here is an example of a Lambda function to rotate a database password:

```
1.  import boto3
2.  import string
3.  import random
4.  from botocore.exceptions import ClientError
5.
6.  def rotate_password():
7.      parameter_name = "/my-app/db-password"
8.      region_name = "us-west-2"
9.
10.     # Generate a new password
11.     new_password = ''.join(random.choices(string.ascii_letters + string.digits, k=16))
12.
13.     # Update the parameter in Parameter Store
14.     ssm_client = boto3.client("ssm", region_name=region_name)
15.     try:
16.         ssm_client.put_parameter(
17.             Name=parameter_name,
18.             Value=new_password,
19.             Type="SecureString",
20.             Overwrite=True
21.         )
22.     except ClientError as e:
23.         print(f"Error updating parameter: {e}")
24.
25.     # Update the database with the new password (example for RDS)
26.     rds_client = boto3.client("rds", region_name=region_name)
27.     try:
28.         rds_client.modify_db_instance(
29.             DBInstanceIdentifier="mydbinstance",
30.             MasterUserPassword=new_password
31.         )
32.     except ClientError as e:
33.         print(f"Error updating database password: {e}")
34.
35. # Schedule this function using CloudWatch Events
```

In summary, designing and implementing mechanisms for managing and rotating secrets involves securely storing secrets, configuring automatic rotation, granting appropriate access, and integrating with applications. AWS Secrets Manager offers robust features for automatic secret rotation, while AWS Systems Manager Parameter Store provides a flexible alternative for manual rotation. By leveraging these tools, organizations can enhance the security of their workloads and reduce the risk of credential compromise.

## 12.7.5 KMS Key Policies

Creating and managing KMS key policies to control access to cryptographic keys is a critical aspect of securing sensitive data within AWS. AWS Key Management Service (KMS) provides a flexible and robust mechanism for defining permissions and access controls through key policies. These policies are JSON-based documents that specify who can use and manage the KMS keys and what actions they can perform. Properly crafted key policies ensure that only authorized users and applications can access or modify encryption keys, thereby enhancing data security and compliance with regulatory requirements.

To create a KMS key policy, you start by defining the principal (user, role, or service) and the actions they are allowed to perform on the key. The actions can include key management tasks such as enabling, disabling, rotating, or deleting keys, as well as cryptographic operations like encrypting, decrypting, and generating data keys.

Here's an example of a KMS key policy that grants a specific IAM role the permissions to use the key for encryption and decryption, but restricts key management actions to administrators:

```
{
  "Version": "2012-10-17",
  "Id": "key-policy-example",
  "Statement": [
    {
      "Sid": "Enable IAM User Permissions",
      "Effect": "Allow",
      "Principal": {
        "AWS": "arn:aws:iam::123456789012:root"
      },
      "Action": "kms:*",
      "Resource": "*"
    },
    {
      "Sid": "Allow Administration of the Key",
      "Effect": "Allow",
      "Principal": {
        "AWS": "arn:aws:iam::123456789012:role/AdminRole"
      },
      "Action": [
        "kms:Create*",
        "kms:Describe*",
        "kms:Enable*",
        "kms:List*",
        "kms:Put*",
        "kms:Update*",
        "kms:Revoke*",
        "kms:Disable*",
        "kms:Get*",
        "kms:Delete*",
        "kms:ScheduleKeyDeletion",
        "kms:CancelKeyDeletion"
      ],
      "Resource": "*"
    },
    {
      "Sid": "Allow Use of the Key",
      "Effect": "Allow",
      "Principal": {
        "AWS": "arn:aws:iam::123456789012:role/ApplicationRole"
      },
      "Action": [
        "kms:Encrypt",
        "kms:Decrypt",
```

```
45.            "kms:ReEncrypt*",
46.            "kms:GenerateDataKey*",
47.            "kms:DescribeKey"
48.         ],
49.         "Resource": "*"
50.      }
51.   ]
52. }
53.
```

In this policy:

- The first statement (**Enable IAM User Permissions**) allows the root user of the AWS account to perform any KMS action on the key.
- The second statement (**Allow Administration of the Key**) grants an IAM role named **AdminRole** full administrative control over the key, including actions like creating, updating, and deleting the key.
- The third statement (**Allow Use of the Key**) grants an IAM role named **ApplicationRole** permissions to perform cryptographic operations such as encryption, decryption, and data key generation, but does not allow key management tasks.

**Managing KMS key policies** involves periodically reviewing and updating the policies to ensure they reflect the current security requirements and access controls. Key policy management best practices include:

- **Principle of Least Privilege:** Grant only the minimum necessary permissions required for users and applications to perform their tasks.
- **Separation of Duties:** Separate administrative and usage roles to reduce the risk of unauthorized key management activities.
- **Regular Audits:** Regularly audit key policies and access logs to identify and rectify any unauthorized access or policy misconfigurations.

For example, if an organization decides to add a new application that requires access to the KMS key for encryption, they can update the key policy to include permissions for the IAM role associated with the new application. Here's how to add a new statement to the existing policy to grant access to a new NewAppRole:

```
1.  {
2.    "Sid": "Allow Use of the Key for NewAppRole",
3.    "Effect": "Allow",
4.    "Principal": {
5.      "AWS": "arn:aws:iam::123456789012:role/NewAppRole"
6.    },
7.    "Action": [
8.      "kms:Encrypt",
9.      "kms:Decrypt",
10.     "kms:ReEncrypt*",
11.     "kms:GenerateDataKey*",
12.     "kms:DescribeKey"
13.    ],
14.    "Resource": "*"
15.  }
```

By following these best practices and regularly managing key policies, organizations can ensure that their cryptographic keys are securely managed and accessible only to authorized entities.

# 12.7.6 Importing and Removing Customer-Provided Key Material

Establishing mechanisms to import and remove customer-provided key material in AWS Key Management Service (KMS) allows organizations to maintain full control over their cryptographic keys. This process involves securely importing externally generated key material into AWS KMS and managing its lifecycle, including key deletion when it is no longer needed. By using customer-provided key material, organizations can meet stringent compliance and regulatory requirements that mandate full control over cryptographic keys.

**To import customer-provided key material into AWS KMS, follow these steps:**

**Create a CMK (Customer Master Key):** First, create a new CMK in AWS KMS with the External origin. This key will serve as a placeholder for the imported key material. Navigate to the AWS KMS console, select "Create key," and choose "Symmetric" or "Asymmetric," depending on the type of key you are importing. Select "External" as the key material origin. Configure the key's metadata and policies, then create the key.

**Download the wrapping key and import token:** After creating the CMK, download the public key (wrapping key) and the import token from AWS KMS. These items are used to securely import the key material. The wrapping key is used to encrypt your key material, and the import token authenticates the import process.

**Encrypt the key material:** Use the downloaded wrapping key to encrypt your key material. This can be done using cryptographic tools or libraries that support RSA encryption. The encrypted key material ensures that the key is securely transferred to AWS KMS.

**Import the key material:** Use the AWS CLI or SDK to import the encrypted key material into the CMK. Specify the expiration date for the key material if needed, which defines how long the key material will remain active.

For example, using the AWS CLI to import key material:

```
1. # Encrypt the key material with the wrapping key
2. openssl rsautl -encrypt -inkey wrapping_key.pem -pubin -in key_material.bin -out encrypted_key_material.bin
3.
4. # Import the encrypted key material into the CMK
5. aws kms import-key-material --key-id <key-id> --encrypted-key-material fileb://encrypted_key_material.bin --import-token fileb://import_token.bin --expiration-model KEY_MATERIAL_EXPIRES --valid-to 2024-12-31T12:00:00Z
6.
```

To remove customer-provided key material from AWS KMS, follow these steps:

**Delete the key material:** Use the AWS CLI or SDK to delete the key material from the CMK. This operation makes the key unusable until new key material is imported. When the key material is deleted, any cryptographic operations using the CMK will fail until new key material is imported.

For example, using the AWS CLI to delete key material:

```
aws kms delete-imported-key-material --key-id <key-id>
```

**Manage the CMK lifecycle:** If the CMK is no longer needed, you can schedule it for deletion. Use the AWS CLI or SDK to schedule key deletion, specifying a waiting period (7-30 days) before the key is permanently deleted.

For example, using the AWS CLI to schedule key deletion:

```
aws kms schedule-key-deletion --key-id <key-id> --pending-window-in-days 30
```

By establishing these mechanisms to import and remove customer-provided key material, organizations can maintain complete control over their cryptographic keys, ensuring that they meet regulatory and compliance requirements. AWS KMS provides the tools necessary to manage the key material lifecycle securely and efficiently.

## 12.8 Best Practices for Data Protection

Best practices for data protection are essential for safeguarding sensitive information from unauthorized access, breaches, and loss. These practices encompass a range of strategies, including encryption, access control, and regular audits, to ensure data integrity, confidentiality, and availability. Implementing robust data protection measures helps organizations comply with regulatory requirements and maintain the trust of their customers and stakeholders.

### 12.8.1 Encryption Best Practices

Best practices for encrypting data in transit and at rest are essential for ensuring that sensitive information is protected from unauthorized access and breaches during storage and transmission. By implementing robust encryption strategies, organizations can safeguard data integrity, confidentiality, and availability, meeting regulatory requirements and maintaining customer trust.

**Encrypting Data in Transit**

- **Use Strong Encryption Protocols:** Always use strong encryption protocols like TLS (Transport Layer Security) to protect data in transit. TLS ensures that data transmitted between clients and servers is encrypted, preventing eavesdropping and tampering. For example, when accessing a website, ensure that HTTPS is used instead of HTTP.

- **Enforce Secure Connections:** Configure services to enforce the use of secure connections. For instance, AWS services like S3, CloudFront, and API Gateway should be set to require HTTPS connections, ensuring that data is encrypted during transmission.

- **Regularly Update Certificates:** Keep TLS/SSL certificates up to date and use certificates from trusted Certificate Authorities (CAs). Regularly renew and manage certificates to avoid lapses in encryption coverage.

- **Implement Mutual TLS (mTLS):** For critical systems, consider implementing mutual TLS, which requires both the client and server to authenticate each other using certificates. This adds an extra layer of security by ensuring that both parties in the communication are verified.

**Encrypting Data at Rest**

- **Use Strong Encryption Algorithms:** Encrypt data at rest using strong algorithms like AES-256. AWS services such as S3, RDS, and EBS offer built-in encryption capabilities using AWS Key Management Service (KMS) for key management and AES-256 for encryption.

- **Enable Encryption by Default:** Configure services to enable encryption by default. For example, when creating new S3 buckets or RDS instances, ensure that encryption settings are enabled from the start.

- **Manage Encryption Keys Securely:** Use AWS KMS to manage encryption keys securely. KMS allows you to create, rotate, and manage keys centrally, ensuring that keys are stored securely and access is controlled.

- **Regularly Rotate Encryption Keys:** Implement a key rotation policy to regularly rotate encryption keys. AWS KMS supports automatic key rotation, which helps minimize the risk of key compromise and ensures that encryption keys remain secure.

- **Monitor and Audit Access to Encrypted Data:** Use logging and monitoring tools to track access to encrypted data. AWS CloudTrail and AWS Config can be used to audit access and changes to encryption keys and encrypted resources, ensuring that any unauthorized access attempts are detected and addressed promptly.

### Example Implementation

For example, to encrypt data in transit for an AWS S3 bucket, you can enforce the use of HTTPS by creating a bucket policy:

```
{
  "Version": "2012-10-17",
  "Statement": [
    {
      "Sid": "EnforceHTTPS",
      "Effect": "Deny",
      "Principal": "*",
      "Action": "s3:*",
      "Resource": [
        "arn:aws:s3:::your-bucket-name",
        "arn:aws:s3:::your-bucket-name/*"
      ],
      "Condition": {
        "Bool": {
          "aws:SecureTransport": "false"
        }
      }
    }
  ]
}
```

For encrypting data at rest in an RDS instance, ensure that encryption is enabled when creating the database:

```
aws rds create-db-instance \
    --db-instance-identifier mydbinstance \
    --allocated-storage 20 \
    --db-instance-class db.t2.micro \
    --engine mysql \
    --master-username admin \
    --master-user-password password \
    --storage-encrypted \
    --kms-key-id arn:aws:kms:us-west-2:123456789012:key/abcd1234-5678-90ab-cdef-1234567890ab
```

By following these best practices for encrypting data in transit and at rest, organizations can enhance their data protection measures, ensuring that sensitive information remains secure and compliant with industry standards.

## 12.8.2 Data Integrity Best Practices

Ensuring data integrity is essential for maintaining the accuracy, consistency, and trustworthiness of data throughout its lifecycle. Data integrity measures protect data from unauthorized modifications, corruption, and accidental alterations. AWS provides various tools and best practices to help organizations ensure data integrity across their services and applications.

### Best Practices for Ensuring Data Integrity

- Use Checksums and Hash Functions: Implement checksums and hash functions to verify data integrity during transmission and storage. Algorithms like SHA-256 can generate unique hash values for data, allowing verification by comparing the hash of the received data with the original hash. AWS services such as Amazon S3 automatically calculate and store MD5 checksums for objects, enabling users to validate data integrity.

- Enable Versioning: Enable versioning in storage services like Amazon S3 to maintain historical versions of objects. Versioning helps track changes and allows recovery of previous versions in case of data corruption or accidental deletion. This ensures that data integrity can be preserved by restoring known good versions of objects.

- Implement Data Replication: Use data replication across different regions and availability zones to protect against data corruption and loss. Services like Amazon RDS and DynamoDB support multi-AZ deployments and global tables, respectively, to replicate data and ensure consistency across geographically dispersed locations.

- Use IAM Policies and Access Controls: Define strict IAM policies and access controls to prevent unauthorized access and modifications to data. By limiting who can read, write, or delete data, organizations can reduce the risk of accidental or malicious alterations that compromise data integrity.

### AWS Tools for Ensuring Data Integrity

**AWS DataSync:** AWS DataSync simplifies the process of automating and accelerating data transfer between on-premises storage and AWS storage services. DataSync uses built-in integrity checks to verify that data is copied accurately during transfer, ensuring that the data integrity is maintained.

**AWS CloudTrail:** AWS CloudTrail records API calls and user activity across AWS services, providing a detailed audit trail for monitoring changes and detecting unauthorized actions. By analyzing CloudTrail logs, organizations can identify and respond to activities that might compromise data integrity.

**Amazon S3 Object Lock:** Amazon S3 Object Lock enables write-once-read-many (WORM) protection for objects, preventing them from being deleted or overwritten for a specified retention period. This feature ensures that data remains unaltered and is available for compliance and data integrity purposes.

### Example Implementation

For example, to ensure data integrity in an Amazon S3 bucket, you can enable versioning and configure an S3 bucket policy to enforce data integrity practices:

**Enable Versioning:** Navigate to the S3 console. Select the bucket and choose "Properties." Enable versioning for the bucket.

**Configure Bucket Policy:**
Use the following bucket policy to enforce read-only access, preventing unauthorized modifications:

```
1.  {
2.    "Version": "2012-10-17",
3.    "Statement": [
4.      {
5.        "Sid": "AllowReadOnlyAccess",
6.        "Effect": "Allow",
7.        "Principal": {
8.          "AWS": "arn:aws:iam::123456789012:user/ReadOnlyUser"
9.        },
10.       "Action": ["s3:GetObject", "s3:GetObjectVersion"],
```

```
11.         "Resource": "arn:aws:s3:::your-bucket-name/*"
12.       },
13.       {
14.         "Sid": "DenyWriteAccess",
15.         "Effect": "Deny",
16.         "Principal": "*",
17.         "Action": ["s3:PutObject", "s3:DeleteObject", "s3:DeleteObjectVersion"],
18.         "Resource": "arn:aws:s3:::your-bucket-name/*"
19.       }
20.     ]
21. }
```

By following these best practices and leveraging AWS tools, organizations can ensure data integrity, protecting their data from unauthorized modifications, corruption, and loss. These measures help maintain the accuracy, consistency, and trustworthiness of data across various AWS services.

## 12.8.3 Managing Data Lifecycle Best Practices

Best practices for managing the lifecycle of data are crucial for ensuring compliance with regulatory requirements and optimizing operational efficiency. Effective data lifecycle management involves establishing policies and processes for data creation, storage, usage, archiving, and deletion. By implementing these best practices, organizations can maintain data integrity, secure sensitive information, and reduce storage costs.

### Best Practices for Managing the Data Lifecycle

- Data Classification: Classify data based on its sensitivity and importance. Data classification helps determine appropriate handling, storage, and security measures. Categories can include public, internal, confidential, and restricted. This ensures that sensitive data receives the highest level of protection and is handled according to compliance requirements.

- Data Retention Policies: Establish clear data retention policies that define how long different types of data should be kept. Retention periods should be based on legal, regulatory, and business requirements. For example, financial records may need to be retained for seven years to comply with tax regulations. These policies ensure that data is retained for the appropriate duration and deleted when no longer needed.

- Automated Lifecycle Management: Use automated tools to manage data lifecycle processes. AWS offers services like Amazon S3 Lifecycle policies and AWS Backup to automate data transition and retention. Automated policies reduce the risk of human error and ensure consistent application of data management rules.

- Regular Audits and Reviews: Conduct regular audits and reviews of data lifecycle policies and practices to ensure compliance with regulations and internal policies. Audits help identify gaps and areas for improvement, ensuring that data management practices remain effective and compliant.

- Secure Deletion: Implement secure deletion practices to ensure that data is irretrievably erased when it is no longer needed. AWS services like AWS KMS provide mechanisms for securely deleting encryption keys, rendering the associated data unusable. This practice is crucial for protecting sensitive information and meeting data protection regulations.

### Example Implementation

Consider an organization that handles sensitive customer data and must comply with GDPR. The organization can implement the following best practices to manage the lifecycle of this data:

**Data Classification:** Classify customer data as confidential, requiring stringent access controls and encryption.

**Data Retention Policies:** Define a retention policy that retains customer data for five years, in line with legal requirements.
After five years, customer data should be securely deleted unless required for ongoing legal or business reasons.

**Automated Lifecycle Management:** Use Amazon S3 Lifecycle policies to transition data to cost-effective storage classes as it ages. For example, move data to S3 Standard-IA after 30 days and to S3 Glacier after 90 days.

```
{
  "Rules": [
    {
      "ID": "Transition and Expire Policy",
      "Status": "Enabled",
      "Prefix": "customer-data/",
      "Transitions": [
        {
          "Days": 30,
          "StorageClass": "STANDARD_IA"
        },
        {
          "Days": 90,
          "StorageClass": "GLACIER"
        }
      ],
      "Expiration": {
        "Days": 1825
      }
    }
  ]
}
```

**Regular Audits and Reviews:**
Schedule quarterly audits to review data management practices and ensure compliance with GDPR.

**Secure Deletion:**
Use AWS KMS to delete encryption keys for customer data that exceeds the retention period, ensuring that the data is irretrievably erased.

By following these best practices, the organization can effectively manage the lifecycle of customer data, ensuring compliance with GDPR and optimizing storage costs.

## 12.8.4 Protecting Credentials and Secrets

Best practices for managing and protecting credentials, secrets, and cryptographic keys are crucial for maintaining the security and integrity of systems and data. These practices help prevent unauthorized access, data breaches, and potential misuse of sensitive information. Effective management and protection of credentials, secrets, and cryptographic keys involve using secure storage solutions, implementing robust access controls, and automating secret rotation and management.

### Best Practices for Managing and Protecting Credentials and Secrets

- Use Secure Storage Solutions: Store credentials and secrets in secure, centralized repositories such as AWS Secrets Manager or AWS Systems Manager Parameter Store. These services provide built-in encryption and access control mechanisms to protect sensitive data.

- Implement Least Privilege Access: Grant the minimum necessary permissions required for users and applications to access credentials and secrets. Use IAM roles and policies to enforce least privilege access, ensuring that only authorized entities can access sensitive information.

- Automate Secret Rotation: Regularly rotate credentials and secrets to minimize the risk of exposure and unauthorized access. AWS Secrets Manager offers automatic rotation of secrets, which can be configured to update secrets at regular intervals without disrupting applications.

- Audit and Monitor Access: Use logging and monitoring tools such as AWS CloudTrail and Amazon CloudWatch to track access to credentials and secrets. Regularly review access logs to detect and respond to unauthorized access attempts.

## Best Practices for Managing and Protecting Cryptographic Keys

- Use a Managed Key Management Service: Utilize a managed key management service like AWS Key Management Service (KMS) to generate, store, and manage cryptographic keys. AWS KMS provides secure key storage, key rotation, and fine-grained access control.

- Encrypt Keys at Rest and in Transit: Ensure that cryptographic keys are encrypted both at rest and in transit. AWS KMS encrypts keys using hardware security modules (HSMs) and supports TLS for secure communication.

- Implement Key Rotation: Regularly rotate cryptographic keys to enhance security. AWS KMS supports automatic key rotation, which can be enabled for customer master keys (CMKs) to rotate keys annually.

- Define Key Policies and Access Controls: Create detailed key policies that specify who can use and manage cryptographic keys and what actions they can perform. Use IAM policies to enforce these access controls and ensure that only authorized users and applications can access keys.

## Example Implementation

Consider an organization that needs to manage and protect database credentials and encryption keys for an application:

**Store Credentials in AWS Secrets Manager:**
- Store the database credentials in AWS Secrets Manager for secure management.
- Enable automatic rotation for the database credentials to ensure they are updated regularly.

```
1.  import boto3
2.  from botocore.exceptions import ClientError
3.
4.  def get_secret():
5.      secret_name = "MyDatabaseSecret"
6.      region_name = "us-west-2"
7.
8.      client = boto3.client("secretsmanager", region_name=region_name)
9.
10.     try:
11.         get_secret_value_response = client.get_secret_value(SecretId=secret_name)
12.     except ClientError as e:
13.         raise e
14.
15.     secret = get_secret_value_response["SecretString"]
16.     return secret
17.
18. credentials = get_secret()
```

**Use AWS KMS for Key Management:**
- Create a customer master key (CMK) in AWS KMS to encrypt sensitive data.
- Enable automatic key rotation for the CMK.

```
1. aws kms create-key --description "My Application Key" --key-usage ENCRYPT_DECRYPT --origin AWS_KMS
3. aws kms enable-key-rotation --key-id <key-id>
```

**Implement Least Privilege Access:**
- Define IAM policies that grant the application role permission to access the database credentials and use the KMS key.
- Apply these policies to the relevant IAM roles and users.

```
1.  {
2.    "Version": "2012-10-17",
3.    "Statement": [
4.      {
5.        "Effect": "Allow",
6.        "Action": ["secretsmanager:GetSecretValue"],
7.        "Resource": "arn:aws:secretsmanager:us-west-2:123456789012:secret:MyDatabaseSecret"
8.      },
9.      {
10.       "Effect": "Allow",
11.       "Action": ["kms:Decrypt", "kms:GenerateDataKey"],
12.       "Resource": "arn:aws:kms:us-west-2:123456789012:key/<key-id>"
13.     }
14.   ]
15. }
```

By following these best practices, organizations can effectively manage and protect credentials, secrets, and cryptographic keys, ensuring the security of their applications and data.

# 12.9 Lab Exercises
## 12.9.1 Configuring TLS for AWS Services

Configuring TLS (Transport Layer Security) to secure data in transit is an essential practice to protect data from eavesdropping, tampering, and man-in-the-middle attacks. The following step-by-step hands-on lab instructions will guide you through configuring TLS for various AWS services, including Amazon S3, Amazon EC2, Amazon RDS, and Amazon CloudFront.

### Step 1: Configuring TLS for Amazon S3

**Create an S3 Bucket:** Open the Amazon S3 console at https://console.aws.amazon.com/s3/. Click on "Create bucket." Enter a unique bucket name and select the desired region. Click "Create bucket" at the bottom of the page.

**Enable Bucket Policy to Enforce HTTPS:** Select your newly created bucket and go to the "Permissions" tab. Click "Bucket Policy" and add the following policy to enforce HTTPS:

```
1.  {
2.    "Version": "2012-10-17",
3.    "Statement": [
4.      {
5.        "Sid": "EnforceHTTPS",
6.        "Effect": "Deny",
7.        "Principal": "*",
8.        "Action": "s3:*",
```

```
 9.        "Resource": [
10.          "arn:aws:s3:::your-bucket-name",
11.          "arn:aws:s3:::your-bucket-name/*"
12.        ],
13.        "Condition": {
14.          "Bool": {
15.            "aws:SecureTransport": "false"
16.          }
17.        }
18.      }
19.    ]
20. }
21.
```

**Save the Policy:** Replace your-bucket-name with the name of your bucket. Click "Save changes."

## Step 2: Configuring TLS for Amazon EC2

**Launch an EC2 Instance:** Open the Amazon EC2 console at https://console.aws.amazon.com/ec2/. Click "Launch Instance" and follow the wizard to configure your instance. Select an AMI (e.g., Amazon Linux 2) and instance type. Configure instance details, add storage, and add tags as needed.

**Configure Security Group to Allow HTTPS:** In the "Configure Security Group" step, create a new security group. Add rules to allow HTTP (port 80) and HTTPS (port 443) traffic.

**Install and Configure Apache with SSL:** SSH into your EC2 instance. Install Apache and mod_ssl:

```
1. sudo yum update -y
2. sudo yum install -y httpd mod_ssl
```

Start Apache:

```
1. sudo systemctl start httpd
2. sudo systemctl enable httpd
3.
```

Obtain an SSL certificate. For simplicity, you can use a self-signed certificate (not recommended for production):

```
1. sudo openssl req -newkey rsa:2048 -nodes -keyout /etc/pki/tls/private/selfsigned.key -x509 -days 365 -out /etc/pki/tls/certs/selfsigned.crt
2.
```

Configure Apache to use SSL by editing /etc/httpd/conf.d/ssl.conf to point to your certificate and key:

```
1. SSLCertificateFile /etc/pki/tls/certs/selfsigned.crt
2. SSLCertificateKeyFile /etc/pki/tls/private/selfsigned.key
```

Restart Apache:

```
sudo systemctl restart httpd
```

## Step 3: Configuring TLS for Amazon RDS

**Launch an RDS Instance:** Open the Amazon RDS console at https://console.aws.amazon.com/rds/. Click "Create database" and follow the wizard to configure your database. Choose a DB engine (e.g., MySQL) and configure instance settings.

**Download SSL Certificate:** Download the RDS SSL certificate from AWS documentation.

**Configure RDS to Require SSL:** Modify your DB instance to require SSL connections by setting the rds.force_ssl parameter to 1 in the DB parameter group.

**Connect to RDS Using SSL:** Use the downloaded SSL certificate to connect to your RDS instance via SSL. For example, with MySQL:

```
mysql -h your-db-endpoint.rds.amazonaws.com -u your-username -p --ssl-ca=/path/to/your/rds-combined-ca-bundle.pem
```

### Step 4: Configuring TLS for Amazon CloudFront

**Create a CloudFront Distribution:** Open the Amazon CloudFront console at https://console.aws.amazon.com/cloudfront/. Click "Create Distribution" and select "Web" as the delivery method. Configure the distribution settings, specifying your origin (e.g., S3 bucket or EC2 instance).

**Configure SSL/TLS Settings:** In the "Distribution Settings" section, under "SSL Certificate," choose "Custom SSL Certificate" if you have your own certificate, or use the default CloudFront certificate.

**Enforce HTTPS:** In the "Cache Behavior Settings" section, set "Viewer Protocol Policy" to "Redirect HTTP to HTTPS" to ensure all traffic uses HTTPS.

**Create the Distribution:** Review your settings and create the distribution. It may take a few minutes for the distribution to be deployed.

By following these step-by-step instructions, you can ensure that data in transit is securely encrypted using TLS across various AWS services, enhancing the security and compliance of your applications.

## 12.9.2 Implementing Encryption for Data at Rest

This hands-on lab provides detailed steps for implementing encryption on three AWS services: Amazon S3, Amazon RDS, and Amazon DynamoDB. These steps will help ensure that your data at rest is securely encrypted.

### Amazon S3 Encryption
### Step 1: Enable Default Encryption for an S3 Bucket

**Create or select an S3 bucket:** Open the Amazon S3 console at https://console.aws.amazon.com/s3/. Click on "Create bucket" or select an existing bucket.

**Enable default encryption:** Go to the "Properties" tab of your bucket. Scroll down to the "Default encryption" section. Click "Edit" and choose one of the following encryption options:
- Amazon S3-managed keys (SSE-S3): Amazon S3 manages the encryption keys.
- AWS KMS-managed keys (SSE-KMS): AWS Key Management Service (KMS) manages the keys.

If you choose SSE-KMS, select an existing KMS key or create a new one. Click "Save changes."

**Verify encryption:** Upload a file to the bucket and check the properties of the file to ensure it is encrypted.

### Step 2: Upload Files with Encryption

**Upload a file:** Click "Upload" in your S3 bucket. Select a file to upload.

**Set encryption (if not using default encryption):** In the "Properties" section during the upload process, under "Server-side encryption," choose the encryption method (SSE-S3 or SSE-KMS).

## Amazon RDS Encryption
### Step 1: Create an Encrypted RDS Instance

**Open the RDS console:** Go to https://console.aws.amazon.com/rds/.

**Create a new database:** Click "Create database." Select the database engine (e.g., MySQL, PostgreSQL).

**Configure instance details:** Choose an instance type and configure settings.

**Enable encryption:** In the "Additional configuration" section, under "Storage," check the "Enable encryption" box. Choose a KMS key. If you don't have a key, you can use the default KMS key.

**Create the database:** Click "Create database" and wait for the instance to be created.

### Step 2: Verify Encryption
Check the instance details: Go to the "Databases" section in the RDS console. Select your RDS instance and check the "Configuration" tab to verify that encryption is enabled.

## Amazon DynamoDB Encryption
### Step 1: Create an Encrypted DynamoDB Table

**Open the DynamoDB console:** Go to https://console.aws.amazon.com/dynamodb/.

**Create a new table:** Click "Create table." Enter the table name and primary key details.

**Enable encryption (default):** DynamoDB encrypts all tables by default using AWS owned keys. To use a customer-managed key (CMK), click "Advanced settings" during table creation. Under "Encryption," choose "AWS owned CMK" (default) or "AWS managed CMK" or "Customer managed CMK" and select or create a KMS key.

**Create the table:** Click "Create table" and wait for the table to be created.

### Step 2: Verify Encryption
**Check table details:** Select the table and go to the "Overview" tab. Verify that encryption is enabled and check the type of encryption key used.

By following these steps, you can ensure that your data at rest is encrypted for Amazon S3, Amazon RDS, and Amazon DynamoDB. Implementing encryption helps protect your data from unauthorized access and meets compliance requirements.

# 12.9.3 Managing Secrets with AWS Secrets Manager
AWS Secrets Manager is a service that helps you protect access to your applications, services, and IT resources without the upfront cost and complexity of managing your own hardware security modules (HSMs) and infrastructure. These instructions will guide you through the process of storing, managing, and rotating secrets using AWS Secrets Manager.

### Step 1: Storing a Secret
**Open the Secrets Manager Console:** Go to the AWS Management Console at https://console.aws.amazon.com/secretsmanager/.

**Store a New Secret:** Click on "Store a new secret." Select the secret type: Credentials for RDS database: For storing database credentials. Other type of secrets: For other types of secrets (e.g., API keys, passwords).

Enter the secret details:
- For database credentials, enter the username and password, and specify the database connection details (DB engine, instance, port, etc.).
- For other secrets, provide the key/value pairs of the secret.

**Configure Secret Encryption:** Secrets Manager encrypts secrets using AWS KMS keys. By default, it uses the default KMS key for your account. You can choose to use a different KMS key if needed.

**Specify the Secret Name and Description:** Enter a name for your secret (e.g., MyDatabaseSecret). Optionally, provide a description.

**Add Tags:** Optionally, add tags to your secret for better management and billing.

**Review and Store the Secret:** Review your settings and click "Next." Configure the automatic rotation settings if required (we'll cover this in the next section). Click "Store" to save the secret.

### Step 2: Managing Secrets
**View Stored Secrets:** In the Secrets Manager console, you can view a list of stored secrets.

**Access a Secret:** Click on the secret you want to access. In the "Secret details" section, you can view the secret's metadata and configuration. To retrieve the secret value, click on "Retrieve secret value."

**Edit or Delete a Secret:** To edit a secret, click on "Edit" and update the details as needed. To delete a secret, click on "Delete" and confirm the deletion.

**Monitor Secret Access:** Use AWS CloudTrail to monitor access to your secrets. CloudTrail logs provide a record of all API calls made to Secrets Manager.

### Step 3: Rotating Secrets Automatically
**Enable Automatic Rotation:** Go to the secret you want to enable rotation for and click on "Rotate secret." Enable the automatic rotation toggle.

**Set Rotation Interval:** Specify the rotation interval (e.g., every 30 days).

**Choose a Lambda Function for Rotation:** Secrets Manager uses AWS Lambda to handle the rotation of secrets. You can create a new Lambda function or use an existing one.

**To create a new Lambda function:** Click "Create a new Lambda function." Select a blueprint that matches your use case (e.g., for RDS databases, select the appropriate blueprint). Follow the prompts to create and configure the Lambda function.

To use an existing Lambda function: Select the Lambda function from the dropdown list.

**Configure Rotation Settings:** Specify any additional settings required by the Lambda function (e.g., database connection details).

**Review and Save:** Review your rotation configuration and click "Save."

### Example: Storing and Rotating RDS Database Credentials
**Store Database Credentials:** Follow the steps in Step 1 to store the database credentials for your RDS instance.

**Enable Automatic Rotation:** Go to the stored secret for your RDS credentials. Enable automatic rotation and set the interval to 30 days. Choose to create a new Lambda function using the RDS rotation template.

**Configure Lambda Function:** Provide the necessary permissions and settings for the Lambda function to access your RDS instance and update the credentials. Test the Lambda function to ensure it can successfully rotate the credentials.

**Monitor Rotation:** Use CloudWatch Logs to monitor the execution of the Lambda function and ensure that the rotation process is working as expected. Regularly check the Secrets Manager console to confirm that the secret's rotation status is up-to-date.

By following these steps, you can securely store, manage, and automatically rotate secrets using AWS Secrets Manager, thereby enhancing the security and management of your sensitive information.

## 12.9.4 Designing S3 Lifecycle Policies
Amazon S3 Lifecycle policies help you manage your objects so that they are stored cost-effectively throughout their lifecycle. These policies allow you to transition objects between different storage classes and to expire objects that are no longer needed. This hands-on lab will guide you through the process of designing and implementing S3 Lifecycle policies for efficient data management.

### Step 1: Create an S3 Bucket
**Open the Amazon S3 Console:** Navigate to the Amazon S3 console at https://console.aws.amazon.com/s3/.

**Create a Bucket:** Click "Create bucket." Enter a unique bucket name and select the desired AWS region. Configure any additional settings as needed, such as versioning, logging, and encryption. Click "Create bucket" to finalize.

### Step 2: Upload Sample Data
**Select Your Bucket:** In the S3 console, select the bucket you just created.

**Upload Files:** Click "Upload" and add some files to the bucket for testing lifecycle policies. Follow the prompts to upload the files.

### Step 3: Define Lifecycle Policies
**Navigate to Lifecycle Configuration:** In the bucket details page, go to the "Management" tab. Click "Create lifecycle rule."

**Create a Lifecycle Rule:** Enter a rule name (e.g., "Archive and Expire Old Data"). Define the scope of the rule by choosing whether it applies to the entire bucket or to a specific prefix (folder).

**Add Transition Actions:**

Click "Add transition."

**Define the first transition rule to move objects to the Standard-IA storage class after 30 days:** Transition current versions of objects. Select "Standard-IA" as the storage class. Enter "30" days after object creation.

**Click "Add transition" again to define a rule to move objects to the Glacier storage class after 90 days:** Transition current versions of objects. Select "Glacier" as the storage class. Enter "90" days after object creation.

**Add Expiration Actions:** Click "Add expiration." Define the expiration rule to permanently delete objects 365 days after creation: Set the expiration for current versions of objects to 365 days after creation.

**Configure Cleanup of Incomplete Multipart Uploads (Optional):** Click "Configure rule for incomplete multipart uploads." Specify the number of days after initiation to clean up incomplete multipart uploads (e.g., 7 days).

**Review and Create:** Review the configuration of your lifecycle rule. Click "Create rule" to apply the lifecycle policy to the bucket.

## Step 4: Verify Lifecycle Policies

**Check Lifecycle Rules:** Navigate to the "Management" tab of your bucket. Ensure that the lifecycle rule you created is listed and active.

**Monitor Object Transitions and Expirations:** Monitor the transitions and expirations as they occur. Note that these actions may take some time to reflect in the S3 console. Use Amazon S3 Inventory reports to track the storage class and status of objects over time.

## Example Lifecycle Policy JSON Configuration

If you prefer to use the AWS CLI or SDK, you can also define your lifecycle policy in JSON format and apply it to your bucket. Below is an example JSON configuration for the lifecycle policy we defined:

```
{
  "Rules": [
    {
      "ID": "ArchiveAndExpireOldData",
      "Status": "Enabled",
      "Prefix": "",
      "Transitions": [
        {
          "Days": 30,
          "StorageClass": "STANDARD_IA"
        },
        {
          "Days": 90,
          "StorageClass": "GLACIER"
        }
      ],
      "Expiration": {
        "Days": 365
      },
      "AbortIncompleteMultipartUpload": {
        "DaysAfterInitiation": 7
      }
    }
  ]
}
```

To apply this lifecycle policy using the AWS CLI, use the following command:

```
aws s3api put-bucket-lifecycle-configuration --bucket your-bucket-name --lifecycle-configuration file://lifecycle.json
```

Replace `your-bucket-name` with the name of your bucket and `lifecycle.json` with the path to your JSON file.

## 12.10 Key Exam Tips

### Understand Data in Transit Security
**TLS Concepts:** Be well-versed in Transport Layer Security (TLS), which ensures secure communication over networks. Know how to use AWS Certificate Manager (ACM) to manage and provision TLS certificates for encrypting data in transit.
**VPN Concepts:** Learn the basics of Virtual Private Network (VPN) technology, particularly Site-to-Site VPN and Client VPN, for secure communication between AWS and on-premises environments. Be ready to implement encryption for VPN connections.
**Secure Remote Access** Methods: Master the secure remote access options, such as AWS Systems Manager Session Manager, which allows you to access instances without needing SSH access or opening inbound ports. This is important for reducing the attack surface.

### Implementing Secure Connectivity
**Encryption for Data in Transit:** Know how to use TLS to encrypt data in transit between AWS services and external connections. Be sure you understand the importance of requiring TLS for AWS API calls and enforcing secure HTTPS endpoints.
**Cross-Region and VPC Connectivity:** Understand secure connectivity between AWS regions or VPCs using VPC Peering, AWS Transit Gateway, or Direct Connect with encryption to ensure data is securely transmitted.

### Master Data at Rest Encryption
**Encryption Techniques:** Be familiar with the encryption options provided by AWS, including server-side encryption (SSE) with SSE-S3, SSE-KMS, and SSE-C. Ensure you understand how to apply encryption to S3 objects, EBS volumes, and RDS databases.
**AWS KMS:** Master the use of AWS Key Management Service (KMS) for managing encryption keys. Know the difference between symmetric and asymmetric keys, and how to use KMS key policies to control key usage and permissions.
**CloudHSM:** Know when and how to use AWS CloudHSM for advanced use cases requiring dedicated hardware security modules for storing and managing cryptographic keys.

### Ensuring Data Integrity
**Integrity-Checking Techniques:** Learn how to maintain data integrity using mechanisms like S3 Object Lock, Versioning, and Checksums. Be prepared to use these features to ensure data has not been tampered with during transmission or storage.
**AWS Config and AWS CloudTrail:** These services can be used to monitor changes in configuration and access to sensitive data, helping to detect integrity issues.

### Best Practices for Encryption
**Automatic Encryption:** Ensure that encryption is enforced automatically for all data stored in AWS services (e.g., S3, RDS, EBS) by using AWS Service-Managed Keys (SSE) or Customer-Managed Keys (CMK) in KMS. This helps simplify the process of encrypting data at rest.

**Encryption Key Rotation:** Know the importance of regular encryption key rotation and how AWS KMS handles automatic rotation of keys. You should also understand how to set up manual rotation policies for customer-managed keys.

**Requiring Encryption for APIs:** Make sure you understand how to require TLS for API calls and how to enforce encryption for connections, especially when transmitting sensitive data.

## Managing Data Lifecycle and Retention

**S3 Lifecycle Policies:** Learn how to configure S3 lifecycle policies to automatically transition data to lower-cost storage classes (e.g., Glacier) or delete old data. Be able to design lifecycle policies that meet compliance and retention requirements.

**Backup Scheduling and Retention:** Know how to configure automatic backups using services like AWS Backup, RDS automated backups, and EBS snapshots. Familiarize yourself with retention policies and how to ensure backups meet organizational policies.

## Protecting Credentials and Secrets

**Secrets Management:** Be proficient in using AWS Secrets Manager and AWS Systems Manager Parameter Store for securely storing and managing credentials, API keys, and other sensitive information. Understand how to implement automatic secrets rotation to enhance security.

**IAM Policies for Secrets:** Know how to design IAM policies to control access to secrets and credentials, ensuring only authorized users and applications can retrieve sensitive information.

**KMS Key Policies:** Be able to configure KMS key policies to enforce strong access controls and limit the use of encryption keys to authorized services and users.

## Key Management Techniques

**Symmetric vs Asymmetric Key Management:** Understand the differences between symmetric (single key for encryption and decryption) and asymmetric (public/private key pairs) encryption and when to use each type.

**Customer-Provided Key Material:** Be prepared to manage customer-provided keys in KMS, including importing, using, and removing them for enhanced control over encryption processes.

## Compliance and Best Practices

**Encryption Best Practices:** Know the encryption best practices, such as enforcing encryption by default, using multi-region keys for resilience, and auditing key usage with AWS CloudTrail.

**Data Integrity Best Practices:** Ensure that all critical data is protected against unauthorized modification by implementing integrity checks, using S3 Object Lock, and enabling logging and versioning.

**Managing Data Lifecycle:** Understand the importance of optimizing data lifecycle management, including regular audits of lifecycle policies and backups to ensure data retention and disposal meet compliance requirements.

## Tools for Data Protection Auditing

**AWS Config and CloudTrail:** Use AWS Config to audit resource configurations and ensure compliance with encryption policies. CloudTrail can be used to log API calls and access to encryption keys, allowing you to monitor and investigate key usage.

**Compliance and Auditing with Security Hub:** Leverage AWS Security Hub for compliance auditing and to run automated checks against frameworks like PCI DSS, HIPAA, or CIS AWS Foundations Benchmark to ensure data protection compliance.

## Summary

To pass the AWS Certified Security Specialty Exam, you must understand how to protect data in transit and data at rest using encryption, secure connectivity, and robust key management practices. You should be familiar with using AWS KMS, CloudHSM, and Secrets Manager for managing encryption keys and sensitive data. Mastering lifecycle management, backup retention, and compliance with data protection regulations will also be critical. By implementing encryption best practices and ensuring the integrity of data, you will be equipped to design and secure AWS environments effectively.

By following these steps, you can design and implement effective S3 Lifecycle policies to manage your data efficiently. Lifecycle policies help you optimize storage costs by transitioning objects to lower-cost storage classes and expiring objects that are no longer needed.

## 12.11 Chapter Review Questions

**Question 1:**
What is the primary purpose of TLS in securing data in transit?
A. To encrypt data at rest
B. To encrypt data being transmitted between systems
C. To create backups of data
D. To generate cryptographic keys

**Question 2:**
Which AWS service is recommended for managing cryptographic keys for encryption in AWS?
A. Amazon S3
B. AWS KMS (Key Management Service)
C. Amazon CloudFront
D. AWS Lambda

**Question 3:**
When encrypting S3 objects at rest, which encryption method is managed entirely by AWS?
A. Client-side encryption
B. Server-Side Encryption with Customer-Provided Keys (SSE-C)
C. Server-Side Encryption with AWS KMS-Managed Keys (SSE-KMS)
D. Using CloudHSM

**Question 4:**
What is the purpose of AWS Secrets Manager?
A. To store S3 bucket policies
B. To rotate, manage, and retrieve database credentials, API keys, and other secrets
C. To monitor API calls made to AWS services
D. To manage EC2 instances

**Question 5:**
Which method is used to ensure data integrity when transferring or storing data?
A. Hashing algorithms
B. Data compression
C. Load balancing
D. Data partitioning

**Question 6:**
How can you enforce TLS for AWS API calls?
A. By configuring CloudTrail
B. By using IAM roles
C. By using AWS Systems Manager
D. By enabling the AWS API Gateway for requiring HTTPS

**Question 7:**
What is the best practice for managing encryption keys in AWS KMS?
A. Keeping keys in plaintext format
B. Using automated key rotation for sensitive data
C. Sharing key management credentials across accounts
D. Disabling key rotation for important keys

**Question 8:**
Which AWS service allows you to automate lifecycle policies for managing the lifecycle of objects in an S3 bucket?
A. AWS Config
B. Amazon CloudWatch
C. Amazon S3
D. AWS Secrets Manager

**Question 9:**
What is the purpose of using AWS CloudHSM?
A. To store high-availability backups of EC2 instances
B. To provide dedicated hardware security modules (HSMs) for managing encryption keys
C. To automate patch management on EC2 instances
D. To perform vulnerability assessments for your AWS infrastructure

**Question 10:**
What is the role of Systems Manager Parameter Store in data protection?
A. It stores and retrieves secrets and configuration data securely
B. It monitors network traffic across VPCs
C. It automates lifecycle management for Amazon S3 objects
D. It performs encryption for EBS volumes

**Question 11:**
You are tasked with encrypting sensitive financial data stored in an S3 bucket to meet regulatory compliance. Which encryption technique should you use, and how can you ensure that only specific IAM roles have access to the encryption keys?
A. Use SSE-S3 for server-side encryption and allow access to all users
B. Use SSE-KMS for server-side encryption and enforce key access through IAM policies
C. Use client-side encryption and store the keys in Amazon CloudFront
D. Use S3 default encryption with public access enabled

**Question 12:**
Your company is establishing a secure connection between an on-premises data center and AWS resources. What is the best method to ensure that all traffic is encrypted and securely transmitted over this connection?
A. Set up an Internet Gateway for communication
B. Use AWS Direct Connect without additional encryption
C. Configure a VPN connection with IPSec encryption
D. Use a public VIF for direct data transfer

**Question 13:**
You are implementing a solution to store secrets such as API keys and database credentials for a production environment. The solution should support automatic secret rotation and provide audit logs for access. Which AWS service should you choose, and how does it meet these requirements?
A. Use AWS Systems Manager Parameter Store with manual secret rotation

B. Use AWS Secrets Manager, which supports automatic secret rotation and integrates with CloudTrail for audit logging
C. Store secrets in an S3 bucket with bucket policies
D. Use IAM roles to store and rotate secrets

**Question 14:**
You need to ensure that all data transmitted to and from your AWS resources is encrypted, including API calls to AWS services. How would you implement this requirement, and which feature would you enable?
A. Enable HTTPS for API calls by requiring TLS encryption
B. Use IAM policies to enforce encryption
C. Set up S3 encryption for data at rest
D. Enable SSH for all API calls

**Question 15:**
A security audit reveals that some critical data in your S3 buckets is not encrypted. You want to automate encryption for all objects and ensure new uploads are encrypted without manual intervention. What approach should you take to enforce encryption across all objects?
A. Manually encrypt each S3 object using client-side encryption
B. Enable S3 bucket default encryption and configure bucket policies to reject unencrypted uploads
C. Use CloudWatch to monitor unencrypted objects
D. Rotate encryption keys manually for each object

## 12.12 Answers to Chapter Review Questions

1. B. To encrypt data being transmitted between systems
Explanation: TLS (Transport Layer Security) ensures that data in transit between systems is encrypted, preventing unauthorized access during transmission.

2. B. AWS KMS (Key Management Service)
Explanation: AWS KMS allows you to create and control encryption keys used to secure your data in AWS services.

3. C. Server-Side Encryption with AWS KMS-Managed Keys (SSE-KMS)
Explanation: With SSE-KMS, AWS manages encryption keys using KMS, ensuring security for S3 objects at rest without manual key management.

4. B. To rotate, manage, and retrieve database credentials, API keys, and other secrets
Explanation: AWS Secrets Manager securely stores, manages, and rotates secrets, such as database credentials and API keys.

5. A. Hashing algorithms
Explanation: Hashing algorithms ensure data integrity by generating unique hash values for data, allowing verification that the data has not been altered.

6. D. By enabling the AWS API Gateway for requiring HTTPS
Explanation: You can enforce TLS for AWS API calls by configuring AWS API Gateway to require HTTPS connections.

7. B. Using automated key rotation for sensitive data
Explanation: Automating key rotation in AWS KMS ensures that encryption keys are regularly updated, improving security and compliance.

8. C. Amazon S3
Explanation: Amazon S3 supports lifecycle policies, allowing you to automate the management of objects, such as transitioning objects to lower-cost storage or deleting them after a set period.

9. B. To provide dedicated hardware security modules (HSMs) for managing encryption keys
Explanation: AWS CloudHSM provides dedicated hardware security modules (HSMs) for securely managing and storing encryption keys.

10. A. It stores and retrieves secrets and configuration data securely
Explanation: AWS Systems Manager Parameter Store is used to securely store and retrieve parameters, such as secrets and configuration data, across AWS services.

11. B. Use SSE-KMS for server-side encryption and enforce key access through IAM policies
Explanation: SSE-KMS integrates with AWS KMS to manage encryption keys and allows fine-grained control over who can access the keys using IAM policies. This ensures that only authorized IAM roles can decrypt the data.

12. C. Configure a VPN connection with IPSec encryption
Explanation: An IPSec VPN provides a secure, encrypted connection between your on-premises data center and AWS, ensuring that all traffic is encrypted as it travels between the two environments.

13. B. Use AWS Secrets Manager, which supports automatic secret rotation and integrates with CloudTrail for audit logging
Explanation: AWS Secrets Manager supports automatic rotation of secrets, such as API keys and credentials, and integrates with CloudTrail to provide audit logs for access and actions taken on secrets.

14. A. Enable HTTPS for API calls by requiring TLS encryption
Explanation: You can enforce TLS encryption to ensure that all API calls are securely encrypted. HTTPS is required to provide secure, encrypted communication between clients and AWS services.

15. B. Enable S3 bucket default encryption and configure bucket policies to reject unencrypted uploads
Explanation: By enabling default encryption on the S3 bucket, you ensure that all new objects are automatically encrypted. You can also configure bucket policies to reject any upload that does not comply with the encryption requirements.

# Chapter 13. Management and Security Governance

**This chapter addresses the following exam objectives:**
Domain 6: Management and Security Governance
Task Statement 6.1: Develop a strategy to centrally deploy and manage AWS accounts.
Knowledge of:
- Multi-account strategies
- Managed services that allow delegated administration
- Policy-defined guardrails
- Root account best practices
- Cross-account roles

Skills in:
- Deploying and configuring AWS Organizations
- Determining when and how to deploy AWS Control Tower (for example, which services must be deactivated for successful deployment)
- Implementing SCPs as a technical solution to enforce a policy (for example, limitations on the use of a root account, implementation of controls in AWS Control Tower)
- Centrally managing security services and aggregating findings (for example, by using delegated administration and AWS Config aggregators)
- Securing AWS account root user credentials

Task Statement 6.2: Implement a secure and consistent deployment strategy for cloud resources.
Knowledge of:
- Deployment best practices with infrastructure as code (IaC) (for example, AWS CloudFormation template hardening and drift detection)
- Best practices for tagging
- Centralized management, deployment, and versioning of AWS services
- Visibility and control over AWS infrastructure

Skills in:
- Using CloudFormation to deploy cloud resources consistently and securely
- Implementing and enforcing multi-account tagging strategies
- Configuring and deploying portfolios of approved AWS services (for example, by using AWS Service Catalog)
- Organizing AWS resources into different groups for management

- Deploying Firewall Manager to enforce policies
- Securely sharing resources across AWS accounts (for example, by using AWS Resource Access Manager [AWS RAM])

Task Statement 6.3: Evaluate the compliance of AWS resources.
Knowledge of:
- Data classification by using AWS services
- How to assess, audit, and evaluate the configurations of AWS resources (for example, by using AWS Config)

Skills in:
- Identifying sensitive data by using Macie
- Creating AWS Config rules for detection of noncompliant AWS resources
- Collecting and organizing evidence by using Security Hub and AWS Audit Manager

Task Statement 6.4: Identify security gaps through architectural reviews and cost analysis.
Knowledge of:
- AWS cost and usage for anomaly identification
- Strategies to reduce attack surfaces
- AWS Well-Architected Framework

Skills in:
- Identifying anomalies based on resource utilization and trends
- Identifying unused resources by using AWS services and tools (for example, AWS Trusted Advisor, AWS Cost Explorer)
- Using the AWS Well-Architected Tool to identify security gaps

◆◆◆◆◆◆

Ensuring effective management and security governance in cloud environments is crucial for maintaining compliance, securing resources, and optimizing operations. The chapter on "Management and Security Governance" provides a comprehensive exploration of the strategies, tools, and best practices necessary to achieve robust governance within AWS environments. This chapter guides you through the principles of multi-account management, security policies, compliance evaluation, and secure deployment strategies, offering a detailed roadmap for managing AWS resources effectively and securely.

We begin with an introduction to management and security governance, emphasizing the importance of structured and proactive governance practices in cloud infrastructure. The chapter then delves into multi-account management with AWS Organizations, explaining the role of organizational units (OUs) and providing examples of their usage.

AWS Service Control Policies (SCPs) are examined in detail, including strategies for using SCPs as deny lists or allow lists, and the benefits of each approach. We explore IAM conditions, covering various restrictions based on source IP, region, tags, and MFA requirements, and discuss the differences between IAM roles and resource-based policies.

IAM permission boundaries and policy evaluation logic are critical components for managing permissions and ensuring secure access. The chapter outlines strategies for centrally deploying and managing AWS accounts, including multi-account strategies, managed services for delegated administration, policy-defined guardrails, and best practices for securing the AWS root account and implementing cross-account roles.

Central deployment and management techniques are covered extensively, including deploying and configuring AWS Organizations, AWS Control Tower, and implementing SCPs. We discuss methods for securing root user credentials and ensuring centralized management and aggregation of AWS resources.

Implementing secure and consistent deployment strategies is essential for maintaining a robust security posture. The chapter highlights Infrastructure as Code (IaC) best practices, tagging strategies, and techniques for centralized management, deployment, and versioning. Visibility and control are emphasized through monitoring with AWS CloudWatch, auditing with AWS CloudTrail, and configuration management with AWS Config and Systems Manager.

Secure deployment practices using CloudFormation, tagging strategies, deploying portfolios with AWS Service Catalog, organizing AWS resources, and using AWS Firewall Manager are detailed to ensure consistent and secure deployments. Sharing resources securely with AWS Resource Access Manager (RAM) is also covered.

Evaluating compliance of AWS resources involves data classification with AWS services like Amazon Macie, AWS Glue Data Catalog, and AWS Key Management Service (KMS). We discuss assessing and auditing configurations using AWS Config and its rules and aggregators, and the importance of continuous monitoring and alerts.

The chapter concludes with identifying security gaps through reviews and analysis, including anomaly identification based on cost and usage, resource utilization, and trends. We explore methods for reducing attack surfaces, identifying unused resources, and leveraging the AWS Well-Architected Framework and Tool.

Lab exercises provide hands-on experience in deploying AWS Organizations, creating and implementing SCPs, using CloudFormation for secure deployment, evaluating compliance with AWS Config, and identifying and addressing security gaps.

By the end of this chapter, readers will have a thorough understanding of management and security governance principles, best practices, and tools, enabling them to implement effective governance strategies in their AWS environments.

# 13.1 Introduction to Management and Security Governance

The principles of management and security governance in AWS are foundational for maintaining a secure, compliant, and efficient cloud environment. Centralized control, compliance adherence, and the implementation of security best practices are crucial elements in ensuring that organizational assets are protected and managed effectively.

Centralized control is vital for maintaining oversight and consistency across an organization's cloud infrastructure. AWS provides a range of tools and services, such as AWS Organizations and AWS Control Tower, to enable centralized management of multiple AWS accounts. These tools help enforce policies, manage permissions, and consolidate billing, thus providing a unified view and control over the cloud environment. Centralized control simplifies administration and enhances security by ensuring that all resources adhere to predefined policies and standards.

Compliance is critical to security governance, particularly for organizations operating in regulated industries such as healthcare, finance, and government. AWS offers comprehensive compliance programs and certifications, including ISO 27001, HIPAA, and GDPR, to help organizations meet regulatory requirements. AWS Config and AWS Audit Manager are among the services that assist in continuously monitoring and auditing resources to ensure compliance with internal and external standards. By leveraging these tools, organizations can automate compliance checks, generate audit reports, and maintain a secure posture that aligns with regulatory obligations.

Security best practices in AWS involve a multi-faceted approach to protecting data, applications, and infrastructure. AWS Well-Architected Framework outlines key security principles such as implementing strong identity and access management (IAM), enabling encryption for data at rest and in transit, and continuously monitoring and logging activities. IAM policies, AWS Key Management Service (KMS), and AWS CloudTrail are examples of services that facilitate the application of these principles. Organizations can mitigate risks, detect vulnerabilities, and respond promptly to security incidents by adopting a defense-in-depth strategy.

In summary, AWS's effective management and security governance are predicated on centralized control, compliance, and security best practices. These principles ensure that cloud environments are secure, compliant, and efficiently managed, providing a robust foundation for organizational operations in the cloud.

## 13.2 Multi-Account Management with AWS Organizations

AWS Organizations allows you to consolidate multiple AWS accounts into an organization -- that you create and manage centrally. That way, AWS organizations enable you to manage policies, permissions, and billing for multiple AWS accounts from a single location.

Suppose you have many AWS accounts, such as an AWS account for your marketing department, an AWS account for your sales department, an AWS account for your engineering department, and maybe many other AWS accounts. In that case, you can use AWS Organizations services to manage all of them in one place. For example, you can manage policies, apply policies at the organizational level to control access to resources, enforce security standards, and manage costs across all of your accounts.

Alternatively, with AWS Organizations, you can create separate accounts for different departments, teams, or applications within your organization and manage them as a single entity. That way, as we discussed in the above paragraph, you can manage policies, apply policies at the organizational level to control access to resources, enforce security standards, and manage costs across all of your accounts.

AWS Organizations enables you to simplify billing by consolidating all of your AWS accounts into a single payment method, which can help you track your spending and optimize your costs. AWS Organizations can also automate account provisioning by using the AWS Organizations APIs to add AWS accounts to their respective groups quickly.

Using AWS Organizations, you can group your AWS accounts into organizational units (OU) and attach Service Control Policies (SCPs) to limit permissions within those accounts. Organizational units allow you to group accounts and other organizational units hierarchically. This hierarchical structure allows you to mimic your organizational structure, break down the OUs into teams, and then apply SCPs to OUs to limit permissions/service usage per team.

AWS Organizations is a management service that consolidates multiple AWS accounts. The consolidation helps in the central management of accounts. As a result, AWS Organizations can help simplify account management – particularly for organizations with multiple AWS accounts.

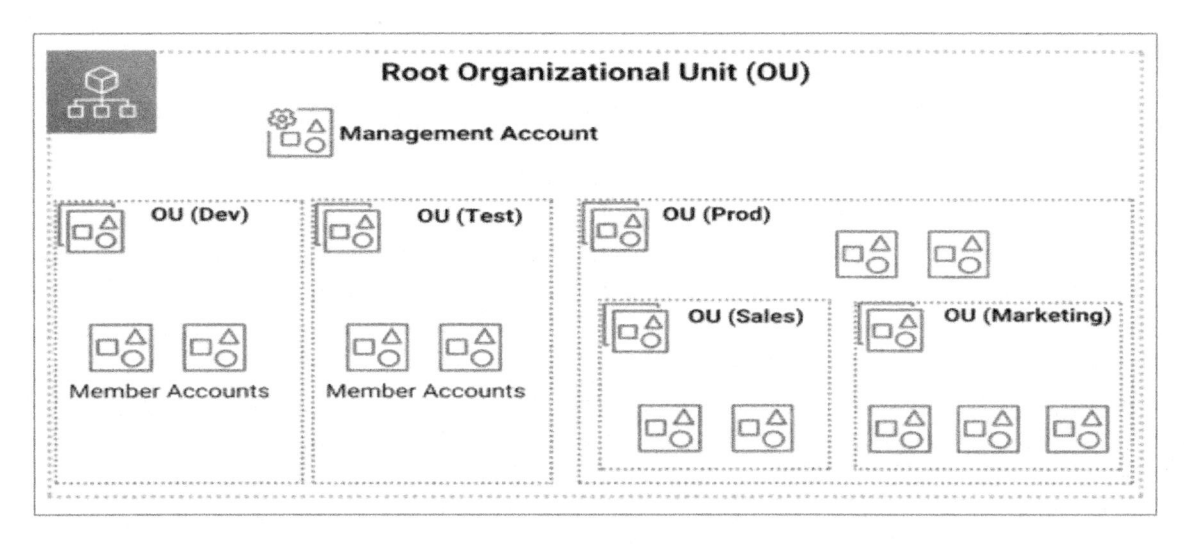

For example, AWS Organizations can help create automated account creation, apply policies to the group of accounts, and consolidate billing. Thus, AWS Organizations provides centralized account and billing management control for organizations and companies with multiple AWS accounts.

Many organizations have used multiple AWS accounts as they have scaled up their AWS usage for various reasons. For example, some customers have added AWS accounts incrementally as more users or departments started using AWS. Other customers have created separate AWS accounts for Dev, Test, and Prod environments to meet strict guidelines such as HIPPA, PCI, or other compliance. As these AWS accounts grow, these customers would like to add policies and manage billing across their accounts in a simple and more scalable way – without requiring manual processes or custom scripts. And they also would like to add or create new accounts with the policies applied.

AWS Organizations can help with account management. Organizations want policy-based management for multiple AWS accounts. You can create a group of accounts and then add policies to those accounts that centrally control the use of AWS services down to the API level across multiple accounts. For example, you can create a collection of production accounts and then apply policies about which AWS services, resources, and API calls those accounts can use. You can also use AWS Organizations API to help automate the creation of AWS accounts. With simple API calls, you can create new accounts programmatically and then apply policies to these new accounts automatically. With AWS Organizations, you can set up a single payment to all AWS accounts to get consolidated billing. AWS Organizations is free and available to all AWS customers at no additional charge.

## 13.2.1 Organization Units (OU) Examples

**Example 1:**

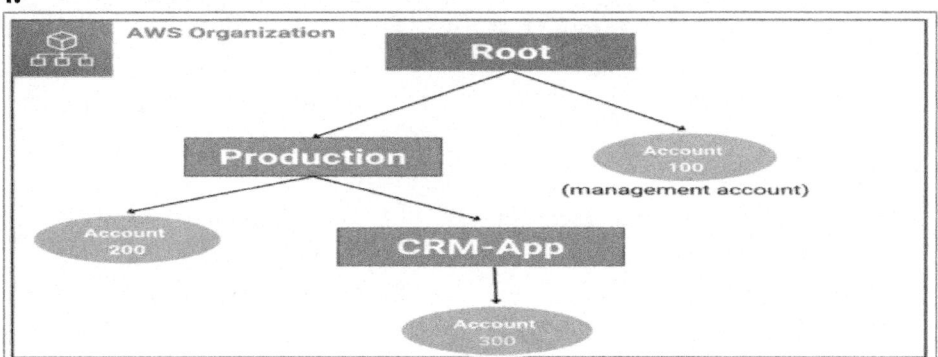

**Example 2:**

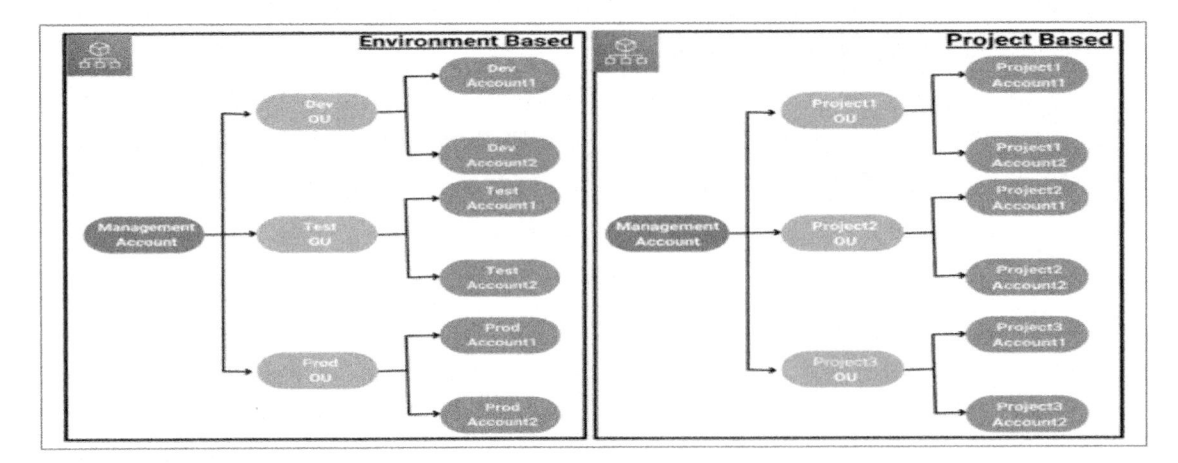

As you can notice in the diagram, we can organize AWS Organizations in different ways. For example, one is environment based, and the other is project-based. We could have AWS Organizations based on business functions (sales, HR, finance, etc.).

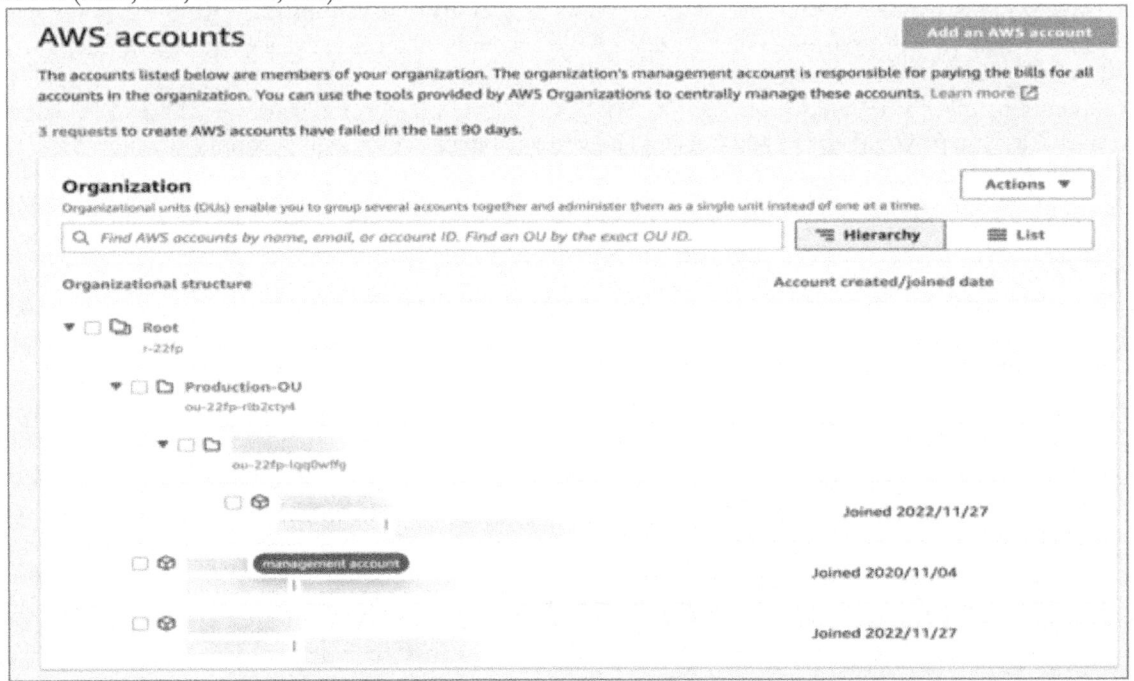

Screenshot of an AWS Organization

AWS Certified Security – Specialty Exam Guide    455

## KEY POINTS

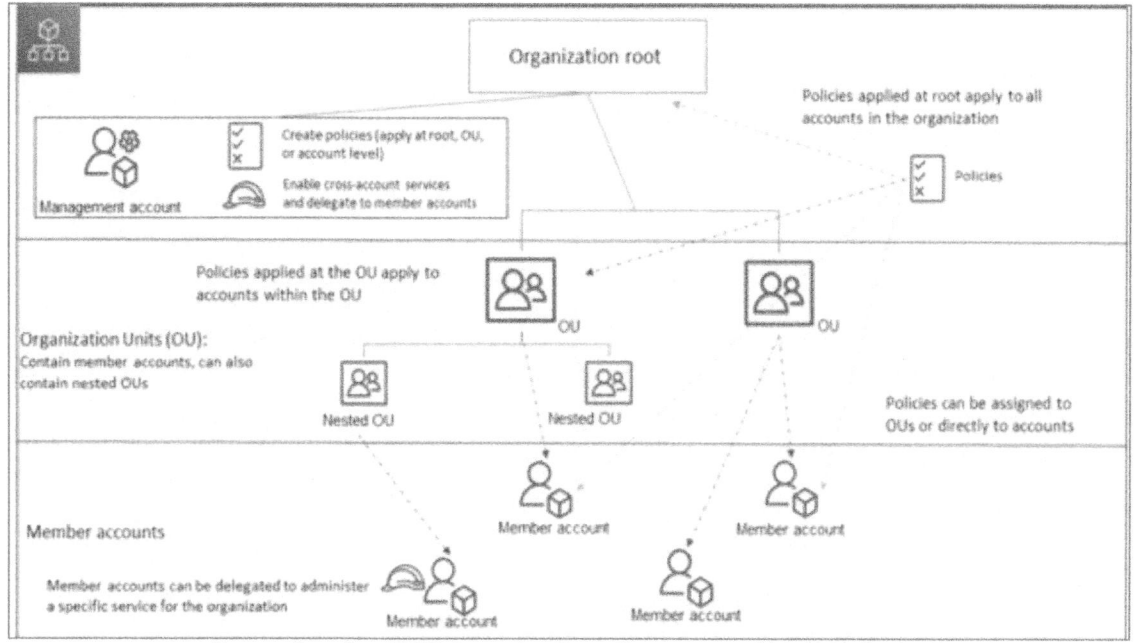

Screenshot for AWS Organizations Concepts and Terminologies
Reference: https://docs.aws.amazon.com/organizations/latest/userguide/orgs_getting-started_concepts.html

- It is a global service.
- It allows the managing of multiple AWS accounts, Multi VPC.
- The default maximum number of accounts allowed in an organization is 10.

**Management Account:** The main account is the management account. Management account has full admin power.

**Member Accounts:** An AWS account can be a member of only one organization at a time. Other accounts are member accounts. Member accounts can only be part of one organization. AWS account creation can be automated with API.

**Security:** Establish Cross Account Roles for Admin purposes IAM policies applied to OU or accounts to restrict users and roles It must have an explicit allow -- it does not allow anything by default – like IAM. SCP can be assigned to OUs or directly to accounts. In other words, you can apply SCPs to OUs and only member accounts in an organization. They do not affect users or roles in the management account.

**Logging:** Enable CloudTrail on all accounts Send CloudWatch Logs to the central logging account.

**Billing & Pricing:** Consolidated Billing across all accounts. Use tags for billing purposes. Pricing benefits from aggregated usage (such as volume discount for EC2, S3, etc.) Shared reserved instances and Savings Plans discounts across accounts.

# 13.3 AWS Service Control Policy (SCP)

AWS Service Control Policy is a tool if you would like to control policies organization-wide centrally. It is a type of organizational policy you can use to manage permissions in your organization. Service control policies (SCPs) offer central control over the maximum available permissions for all accounts in your organization.

SCPs help you ensure your accounts stay within your organization's access control guidelines. SCPs are available only in an organization that has all features enabled. For example, SCPs aren't available if your organization only enabled consolidated billing features.

SCP can be assigned to OUs or directly to accounts. In other words, you can apply SCPs to OUs and only member accounts in an organization. They do not affect users or roles in the management account.

SCPs alone are insufficient to grant permissions to the accounts in your organization. An SCP grants no permissions. Instead, an SCP defines a guardrail or sets limits on the actions that the account's administrator can delegate to the IAM users and roles in the affected accounts.

To grant permissions, the administrator must still attach identity-based or resource-based policies to IAM users, roles, or the resources in your accounts. Effective permissions are the logical intersection between what is allowed by the SCP and what is allowed by the IAM and resource-based policies.

### SCP Hierarchy

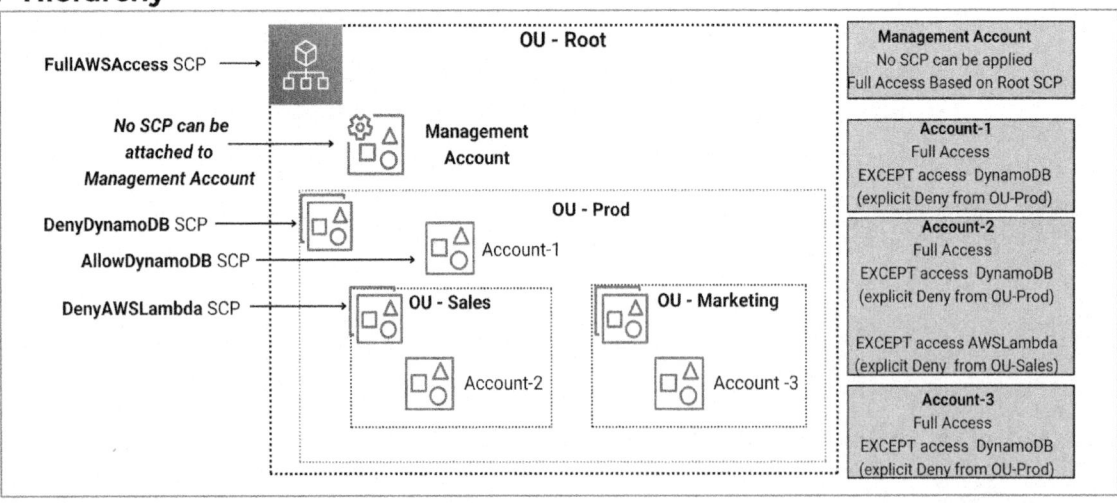

## 13.3.1 Strategies for Using SCP

To configure SCPs in an AWS Organization, you have two options: deny list and allow list.
deny list: by default, actions are allowed, and you specify the services and actions you want to restrict.
allow list – by default, actions are not allowed, and you specify what services and actions you want to allow.

### Using SCPs as a deny list

This is the default configuration of AWS Organizations. To support this, AWS Organizations attaches an AWS-managed SCP named FullAWSAccess to every root and OU when it's created. This policy allows all services and actions.

```
1. {
```

```
 2.      "Version": "2012-10-17",
 3.      "Statement": [
 4.          {
 5.              "Effect": "Allow",
 6.              "Action": "*",
 7.              "Resource": "*"
 8.          }
 9.      ]
10. }
11.
```

You can attach an SCP that explicitly restricts actions that you don't want users and roles in certain accounts to perform.

```
 1. {
 2.     "Version": "2012-10-17",
 3.     "Statement": [
 4.         {
 5.             "Sid": "AllowsAllActions",
 6.             "Effect": "Allow",
 7.             "Action": "*",
 8.             "Resource": "*"
 9.         },
10.         {
11.             "Sid": "DenyDynamoDB",
12.             "Effect": "Deny",
13.             "Action": "dynamodb:*",
14.             "Resource": "*"
15.         }
16.     ]
17. }
18.
```

The users in the affected accounts can't perform DynamoDB actions because the explicit "Deny" element in the second statement that overrides the explicit "Allow" in the first.

You could also configure this by leaving the `FullAWSAccess` policy in place and then attaching a second policy with only the Deny statement, as shown here.

```
 1. {
 2.     "Version": "2012-10-17",
 3.     "Statement": [
 4.         {
 5.             "Effect": "Deny",
 6.             "Action": "dynamodb:*",
 7.             "Resource": "*"
 8.         }
 9.     ]
10. }
11.
```

## Using SCPs as an allow list

To use SCPs as an allow list, you must replace the AWS-managed FullAWSAccess SCP with an SCP that explicitly permits only those services and actions that you want to allow. Your custom SCP then overrides the implicit Deny with an explicit Allow for only those actions that you want to allow. An allow list policy might look like the following example, which enables account users to perform operations for Amazon EC2 and Amazon CloudWatch, but no other service.

458

```
1.  {
2.      "Version": "2012-10-17",
3.      "Statement": [
4.          {
5.              "Effect": "Allow",
6.              "Action": [
7.                  "ec2:*",
8.                  "cloudwatch:*"
9.              ],
10.             "Resource": "*"
11.         }
12.     ]
13. }
14.
```

Reference: https://docs.aws.amazon.com/organizations/latest/userguide/orgs_manage_policies_scps_strategies.html

## 13.4 IAM Conditions

With IAM Conditions, you can grant principals access only if specified conditions are met. For example, you could grant temporary access to users so they can resolve a critical production issue, or you could grant access only if an API call is requested from a certain IP address. The Condition element (or Condition block) lets you specify conditions for when a policy is in effect. The Condition element is optional. Let's see some examples of IAM Policy having a Condition block.

### Restrict Based on Source IP

Condition block with `aws:SourceIp`. The example restricts the client IP from which the API calls are being made.

```
{
    "Version": "2012-10-17",
    "Statement": {
        "Effect": "Deny",
        "Action" "*",
        "Resource": "*",
        "Condition": {
            "NotIpAddress": {
                "aws:SourceIp": [
                    "192.0.2.2/24",
                    "204.0.113.1/24"
                ]
            }
        }
    }
}
```

Reference: https://aws.amazon.com/premiumsupport/knowledge-center/iam-restrict-calls-ip-addresses/

### Restrict Based on Region

Condition block with `aws:RequestedRegion`. The example restricts the Region the API calls are made to.

```json
{
    "Version": "2012-10-17",
    "Statement": {
        "Sid": "AllowFromOnlyInsideUS",
        "Effect": "Allow",
        "Action": [
            "ec2:*",
            "rds:*",
            "s3:*"
        ],
        "Resource": "*",
        "Condition": {
            "StringEquals": {
                "aws:RequestedRegion": [
                    "us-east-1",
                    "us-west-1"
                ]
            }
        }
    }
}
```

## Restrict Based on Tags

The example IAM policy restricts based on tags.

```json
{
    "Version": "2012-10-17",
    "Statement": {
        "Sid": "StartStopInstanceIfTag",
        "Effect": "Allow",
        "Action": [
            "ec2:StartInstances",
            "ec2:StopInstances",
            "ec2:DescribeTags"
        ],
        "Resource": "arn:aws:ec2:region:account-id:instance/*",
        "Condition": {
            "StringEquals": {
                "ec2:ResourceTag/Project": "ETL-Pipeline",
                "aws:PrincipalTag/Department": "Analytics"
            }
        }
    }
}
```

## Restrict Based on MFA (Force MFA)

The example IAM forces MFA to stop and terminate EC2 instances.

```json
{
    "Version": "2012-10-17",
    "Statement": [
        {
            "Sid": "AllActionsOnEC2",
            "Effect": "Allow",
            "Action": "ec2.*",
            "Resource":"*"
        },
        {
            "Sid": "DenyStopAndTerminateActionsIfNoMFA",
            "Effect": "Deny",
            "Action": [
                "ec2:StopInstances",
                "ec2:TerminateInstances"
            ],
            "Resource": "*",
            "Condition": {
                "StringEquals": {"aws:MultiFactorAuthPresent" : false}
            }
        }
    ]
}
```

**Reference:**
https://docs.aws.amazon.com/IAM/latest/UserGuide/reference_policies_elements_condition.html
https://docs.aws.amazon.com/eventbridge/latest/userguide/eb-use-conditions.html

### IAM for S3

```json
{
    "Version": "2012-10-17",
    "Statement": [
        {
            "Sid": "S3ListBucket",
            "Effect": "Allow",
            "Action": ["s3:ListBucket"],
            "Resource":["arn:aws:s3:::test"]
        },
        {
            "Sid": "GetPutObjectOnS3",
            "Effect": "Allow",
            "Action": [
                "s3:PutObject",
                "s3:GetObject"
            ],
            "Resource":["arn:aws:s3::::test/*"]
        }
    ]
}
```

The example IAM policy shows two IAM statements:
- Allowed ListBucket action on the bucket.
- Allowed GetObject, PutObject action on the bucket. This is object-level permission.

# 13.5 IAM Roles vs. Resource-Based Policies

Often, an IAM user may not have sufficient permissions to perform some operations, such as accessing a bucket in another account or accessing some resources in the same account on which the IAM user doesn't have the required permission. In these scenarios, instead of modifying the IAM policy associated with the IAM user, the IAM user can be assigned (or assumed) a role as a proxy to perform the operation, or a resource-based policy can also be used.

The question is when to use IAM Roles and when to use Resource-Based Policies.

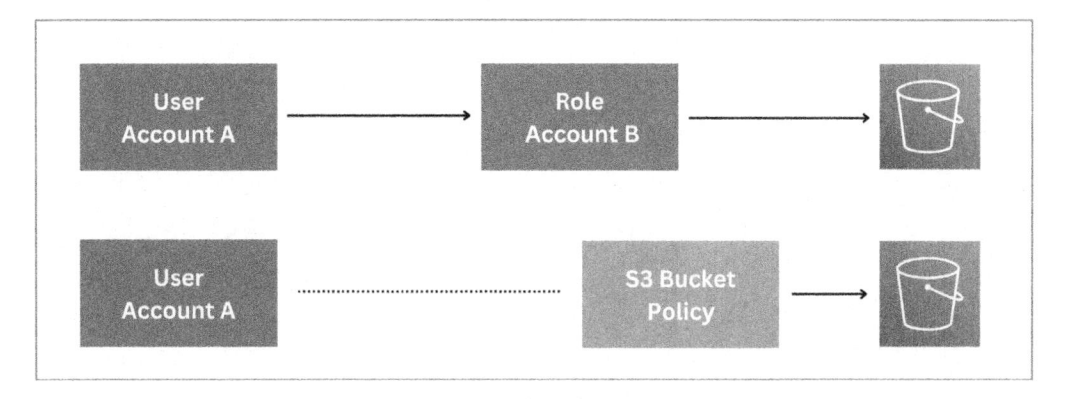

**Roles are the common way to grant cross-account access.** However, for some AWS services, you can attach a policy directly to a resource (instead of using a role as a proxy). These policies are called resource-based policies, and you can use them to grant principals in another AWS account access to the resource. Some of these resources are S3 buckets, S3 Glacier vaults, SNS topics, and SQS queues.

IAM roles and resource-based policies delegate access to accounts within a single partition. For example, assume that you have an account in us-west-1 in the standard aws partition. And, say you also have an account in China (Beijing) in the aws-cn partition. You can't use an Amazon S3 resource-based policy in your account in China (Beijing) to allow access for users in your standard AWS account.

When you assume a role (user, application, or service), you give up your original permissions and take the permissions assigned to the role. When using a resource-based policy, the principal doesn't have to give up his permission. That way, cross-account access with a resource-based policy has some advantages over cross-account access with a role. As the principal doesn't have to give up his permission, a resource-based policy is useful for tasks such as copying information to or from the shared resource in the other account.

Reference: https://docs.aws.amazon.com/IAM/latest/UserGuide/id_roles_compare-resource-policies.html

# 13.6 IAM Permission Boundaries

A permissions boundary is an advanced feature for using a managed policy to set the maximum permissions that an identity-based policy can grant to an IAM entity.

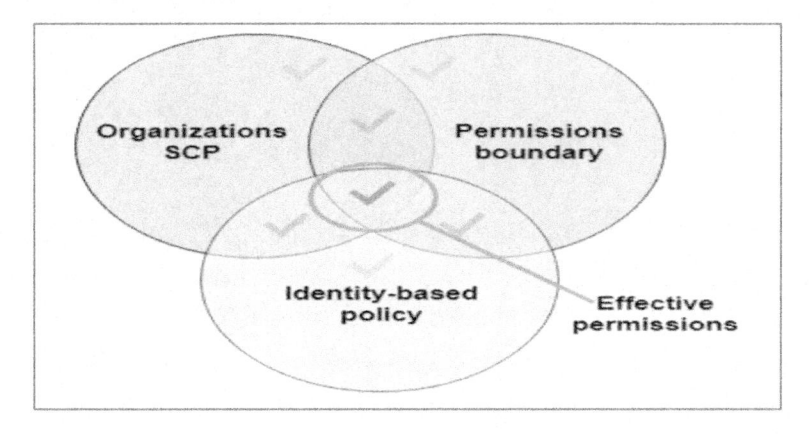

Reference: https://docs.aws.amazon.com/IAM/latest/UserGuide/access_policies_boundaries.html

An entity's permissions boundary allows it to perform only the actions that are allowed by both its identity-based policies and its permissions boundaries. IAM Permission Boundaries are supported for users and roles -- not groups

IAM Permission Boundaries can be used in combinations of AWS Organizations SCP

**Use Cases:** It can be used to delegate responsibilities to non-administrators within their permission boundaries, for example, to create new IAM users. It allows developers to self-assign policies and manages their own permissions while making sure they can't "escalate" their privileges (in other words, make themselves admin) It is useful to restrict one specific user -- instead of an entire account using Organizations & SCP.

## 13.7 IAM Policy Evaluation Logic

When a principal tries to use AWS, the principal sends a request to AWS. Before making the final decision about allowing or denying the request, AWS performs multiple steps: authentication, processing the request context, evaluating policies within a single account, and finally, determining whether a request is allowed or denied.

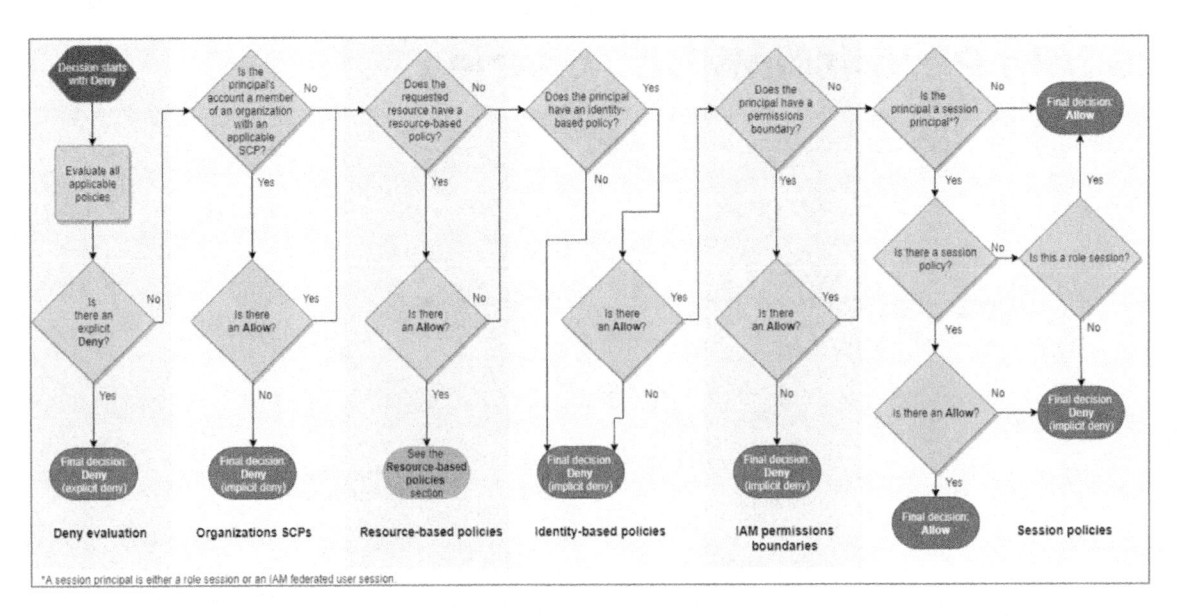

Reference: https://docs.aws.amazon.com/IAM/latest/UserGuide/reference_policies_evaluation-logic.html

# 13.8 Developing a Strategy to Centrally Deploy and Manage AWS Accounts

Developing a strategy to centrally deploy and manage AWS accounts is essential for organizations seeking to maintain control, security, and compliance across their cloud environment. Centralized account management allows for streamlined administration, consistent application of policies, and efficient resource allocation. By leveraging tools such as AWS Organizations and AWS Control Tower, organizations can automate account creation, enforce governance at scale, and ensure a cohesive approach to cloud management.

## 13.8.1 Multi-Account Strategies

Managing multiple AWS accounts is a critical strategy for improving security, compliance, and billing efficiency within an organization. By structuring AWS accounts to align with organizational needs, such as by department, project, or environment (e.g., development, staging, production), organizations can achieve better isolation, control, and governance. AWS offers several tools and best practices to facilitate the management of multiple accounts, ensuring streamlined operations and enhanced security.

One of the primary tools for managing multiple AWS accounts is **AWS Organizations**. AWS Organizations allows for the centralized management of multiple accounts, providing a single point of control to automate account creation, apply policies, and manage billing. With AWS Organizations, administrators can create organizational units (OUs) to group accounts and apply Service Control Policies (SCPs) that define the permissions for accounts within each OU. This hierarchical structure ensures consistent policy enforcement across the organization and simplifies compliance management.

For example, an enterprise might use AWS Organizations to create separate OUs for its Finance, Marketing, and IT departments. Each department's OU can have specific SCPs that restrict access to certain AWS services or regions, ensuring that only the necessary permissions are granted. This segregation of accounts enhances security by limiting the blast radius of potential security incidents to individual accounts rather than affecting the entire organization.

**AWS Control Tower** builds on AWS Organizations by providing a pre-configured landing zone with best practices for multi-account management. AWS Control Tower automates the setup of new accounts, configures baseline security controls, and establishes guardrails to enforce governance. These guardrails, which are implemented as SCPs and AWS Config rules, ensure that all accounts comply with organizational policies from the outset. AWS Control Tower also integrates with AWS Single Sign-On (SSO) to streamline user access management across multiple accounts.

In terms of billing, AWS Organizations offers consolidated billing, which aggregates usage across all member accounts into a single bill. This consolidation allows organizations to benefit from volume discounts and gain a comprehensive view of their AWS spending. By analyzing billing data across accounts, organizations can identify cost-saving opportunities and optimize resource usage.

For instance, a company might use consolidated billing to track and allocate costs to different business units. By examining usage patterns and identifying underutilized resources, the company can implement cost-saving measures such as rightsizing instances or leveraging reserved instances for predictable workloads.

In summary, managing multiple AWS accounts through AWS Organizations and AWS Control Tower provides a robust framework for enhancing security, ensuring compliance, and optimizing billing. These tools offer centralized control, automated policy enforcement, and visibility into resource usage, enabling organizations to effectively manage their AWS environments at scale.

## 13.8.2 Managed Services for Delegated Administration

Managed services like AWS Organizations and AWS Control Tower play a crucial role in enabling delegated administration and centralized management of AWS accounts, providing a robust framework for maintaining security, compliance, and operational efficiency at scale.

**AWS Organizations** allows organizations to manage multiple AWS accounts in a centralized manner. It provides a hierarchical structure where accounts can be grouped into organizational units (OUs), and policies can be applied to these units to enforce governance. AWS Organizations enables the use of Service Control Policies (SCPs) to define and control the actions that accounts and their users can perform. This capability is critical for maintaining security and compliance across all accounts by ensuring that only approved services and actions are allowed.

Delegated administration is facilitated through the creation of management accounts and member accounts. The management account has full control over the organization and can delegate administrative tasks to specific member accounts. For example, a central IT team could use the management account to set up SCPs that restrict access to certain AWS regions or services for all accounts within the organization, ensuring that compliance requirements are consistently enforced.

**AWS Control Tower** builds on the capabilities of AWS Organizations by providing a pre-configured, secure, multi-account AWS environment known as a landing zone. Control Tower automates the creation of new accounts and applies best-practice configurations, including baseline security controls and compliance guardrails. These guardrails, which include SCPs and AWS Config rules, help enforce organizational policies and monitor compliance.

With AWS Control Tower, delegated administration is streamlined through the use of shared accounts for logging, auditing, and security. For instance, the Audit account can be set up to centrally collect and monitor logs from all other accounts, ensuring that security teams have visibility into all activities across the organization. The Security account can manage AWS Security Hub and AWS Config, ensuring consistent security monitoring and compliance checks across all accounts.

For example, consider a large enterprise with multiple departments, each requiring its own AWS accounts for various projects. By using AWS Organizations, the enterprise can create a management account that oversees all departmental accounts. Each department's accounts can be organized into OUs, and SCPs can be applied to enforce policies such as restricting the use of non-compliant services. AWS Control Tower can then be used to set up a landing zone, automate account creation, and apply guardrails to ensure that all new accounts adhere to the organization's security and compliance standards.

This setup allows each department to manage its own AWS resources within the constraints defined by the central IT team, enabling both flexibility and control. The central IT team retains oversight and can quickly implement policy changes or respond to security incidents across all accounts, thanks to the centralized management capabilities provided by AWS Organizations and Control Tower.

In summary, managed services like AWS Organizations and AWS Control Tower enable delegated administration and centralized management by providing tools and frameworks for grouping accounts, enforcing policies, and automating account setup and governance. These services ensure that organizations can scale their AWS usage while maintaining security, compliance, and operational efficiency.

# 13.8.3 Policy-Defined Guardrails

Service Control Policies (SCPs) are a powerful feature of AWS Organizations that enable administrators to centrally control the maximum available permissions for accounts in their organization. SCPs are used to enforce organization-wide policies and guardrails, ensuring that individual accounts within the organization adhere to the desired security and compliance standards.

SCPs operate by specifying the services and actions that can be used by accounts within an AWS Organization. They do not grant permissions themselves but rather limit the permissions that can be granted by Identity and Access Management (IAM) policies. This means that even if an IAM policy in an account allows certain actions, those actions can be restricted or denied by an SCP applied to that account or its organizational unit (OU).

## Using SCPs to Enforce Organization-wide Policies

To implement SCPs effectively, an organization can define policies that reflect its security and compliance requirements. For example, an organization may want to prevent the use of certain high-risk services, restrict access to specific regions, or ensure that all data is encrypted in transit and at rest.

### Example SCP to Deny Use of Specific Services

Consider an organization that wants to prevent the use of AWS Lambda in its accounts due to specific compliance concerns. The following SCP denies access to AWS Lambda:

```
{
    "Version": "2012-10-17",
    "Statement": [
        {
            "Effect": "Deny",
            "Action": [
                "lambda:*"
            ],
            "Resource": "*"
        }
    ]
}
```

By applying this SCP to the root of the organization or specific OUs, the organization ensures that no account can use AWS Lambda, regardless of any IAM policies that might grant Lambda permissions.

### Example SCP to Enforce Data Encryption

An organization may also want to enforce data encryption for all S3 buckets. The following SCP ensures that any S3 bucket created must have default encryption enabled:

```
{
    "Version": "2012-10-17",
    "Statement": [
        {
            "Effect": "Deny",
            "Action": "s3:PutBucketPolicy",
            "Resource": "arn:aws:s3:::*",
            "Condition": {
                "StringNotEquals": {
                    "s3:x-amz-server-side-encryption": "AES256"
                }
            }
        }
    ]
}
```

This SCP denies the action of setting a bucket policy unless server-side encryption with AES256 is specified, ensuring that all data stored in S3 buckets is encrypted by default.

### Applying SCPs in AWS Organizations

To apply an SCP, follow these steps:

**Create the SCP:** Open the AWS Organizations console at https://console.aws.amazon.com/organizations/. Navigate to the "Policies" section and select "Service control policies." Click "Create policy" and define the policy using the JSON editor.

**Attach the SCP to an OU or Account:** After creating the SCP, select it from the list of policies. Click "Actions" and choose "Attach." Select the organizational unit or specific account to which you want to attach the SCP.

**Verify Policy Application:** Ensure that the SCP is active and properly attached to the desired OU or account. Test the policy by attempting to perform the restricted actions in an account within the scope of the SCP to confirm that the policy is enforced.

### Benefits of Using SCPs

- SCPs provide several benefits for organization-wide policy enforcement:
- Consistency: Ensures that security and compliance policies are consistently applied across all accounts in the organization.
- Control: Limits the permissions that can be granted, reducing the risk of over-permissioning and potential security vulnerabilities.
- Compliance: Helps meet regulatory requirements by enforcing specific actions and configurations, such as data encryption and region restrictions.

In summary, SCPs are a crucial tool for enforcing organization-wide policies and guardrails in AWS Organizations. They provide a centralized mechanism to limit the permissions of AWS accounts, ensuring adherence to security and compliance standards across the entire organization.

## 13.8.4 Root Account Best Practices

Securing the AWS root account is a critical step in maintaining the overall security posture of your AWS environment. The root account -- can do any operation on any resource in your AWS account -- has unrestricted access to all resources and services in your AWS account. Thus, it makes it a prime target for malicious actors. Implementing best practices for credential management and multi-factor authentication (MFA) can reduce the risk of unauthorized access and enhance the security of your AWS root account significantly.

### Best Practices for Securing the AWS Root Account

#### Enable Multi-Factor Authentication (MFA)

Enabling MFA for the AWS root account adds an additional layer of security because it requires a second form of authentication in addition to the password. This can be achieved through a virtual MFA device, such as a mobile app (e.g., Google Authenticator), or a hardware MFA device.

**To enable MFA:** Log in to the AWS Management Console using the root account. Navigate to the "IAM" service. Select "Dashboard" and click on "Activate MFA on your root account." Follow the prompts to configure the MFA device.

Example: Enabling MFA means that even if an attacker obtains the root account password, they would also need access to the MFA device to log in, thereby enhancing security.

## Use Strong, Unique Passwords
Ensure that the password for the AWS root account is strong and unique. A strong password are usually longer (>8 characters), includes a combination of uppercase and lowercase letters, numbers, and special characters. Avoid using easily guessable passwords or reusing passwords from other accounts.

Example: Use a password manager to generate and store a complex password for the root account, ensuring it is both strong and unique.

## Limit Use of the Root Account
Avoid using the root account for daily administrative tasks. Instead, IAM users should be created with the necessary permissions to perform routine operations. The root account should only be used for specific administrative activities that IAM users cannot perform.

Example: Create an IAM user with administrative privileges to manage your AWS environment and reserve the root account for tasks such as account setup, billing management, and support requests.

## Monitor Root Account Activity
Monitor the root account's activity regularly to detect unusual or unauthorized actions. AWS CloudTrail can be used to log and track API calls made by the root account, providing visibility into account activity.

Example: Set up CloudTrail to log all root account activity and configure Amazon CloudWatch Alarms to alert you of any unexpected root account usage.

## Lock Away Root Account Access Keys
If root account access keys (i.e., access key ID and secret access key) are not needed, delete them. If they are required for some reason, ensure they are stored securely and rotated regularly.

**To delete root access keys:** Log in to the AWS Management Console using the root account. Navigate to the "IAM" service. Select "Users" and then the root account. Delete any existing access keys or generate new ones as needed.

Example: If you must use root access keys, store them in a secure location such as an encrypted secrets manager and limit their use to specific, controlled scenarios.

## Use IAM Policies to Enforce Least Privilege
Apply the principle of least privilege by creating IAM policies that grant users and roles only the permissions they need to perform their tasks. Avoid assigning broad permissions to IAM users, especially those that allow full administrative access.

Example: Create specific IAM roles for different job functions (e.g., developers, auditors) with tailored policies that grant only the necessary permissions.

## Regularly Review Permissions and Access
Conduct periodic reviews of IAM users, roles, and policies to ensure that they adhere to the principle of least privilege and that no unnecessary permissions are granted. Remove any unused IAM users and roles to reduce the attack surface.

Example: Schedule regular audits of IAM policies and access permissions using AWS IAM Access Analyzer to identify and mitigate risks.

By implementing these best practices, organizations can significantly enhance the security of their AWS root account, reduce the risk of unauthorized access, and protect critical resources within their AWS environment.

## 13.8.5 Cross-Account Roles

Using cross-account roles to grant access to resources across AWS accounts securely is a powerful way to manage permissions and maintain control over your cloud environment. This method allows you to delegate access to resources in one AWS account (the resource account) to users or services in another AWS account (the trusted account) without sharing long-term credentials. This approach enhances security and operational efficiency by leveraging IAM roles and policies.

### Overview of Cross-Account Roles

Cross-account roles use AWS Identity and Access Management (IAM) to establish a trust relationship between the resource account and the trusted account. By creating an IAM role in the resource account and specifying the trusted account as a principal in the role's trust policy, users or services from the trusted account can assume the role and gain temporary access to the specified resources.

### Steps to Implement Cross-Account Roles

**Create an IAM Role in the Resource Account:** Open the AWS Management Console for the resource account. Navigate to the IAM service and click on "Roles." Click "Create role." Select "Another AWS account" as the type of trusted entity. Enter the AWS account ID of the trusted account. Click "Next: Permissions" and attach the necessary policies that define the permissions the role will grant. Review the role configuration and click "Create role."

**Example Trust Policy:**

```
1.  {
2.    "Version": "2012-10-17",
3.    "Statement": [
4.      {
5.        "Effect": "Allow",
6.        "Principal": {
7.          "AWS": "arn:aws:iam::123456789012:root"
8.        },
9.        "Action": "sts:AssumeRole"
10.     }
11.   ]
12. }
```

In this example, 123456789012 is the account ID of the trusted account.

**Example Permissions Policy:**

```
1.  {
2.    "Version": "2012-10-17",
3.    "Statement": [
4.      {
5.        "Effect": "Allow",
6.        "Action": [
7.          "s3:ListBucket",
8.          "s3:GetObject"
9.        ],
10.       "Resource": [
```

```
11.            "arn:aws:s3:::example-bucket",
12.            "arn:aws:s3:::example-bucket/*"
13.        ]
14.    }
15.  ]
16. }
```

This policy allows the role to list the contents of an S3 bucket and get objects from it.

**Allow Trusted Account to Assume the Role:** In the trusted account, configure an IAM user or service to assume the role. Create or modify an IAM policy for the user/service in the trusted account to include permissions to assume the role.

**Example IAM Policy for Trusted Account:**
```
1.  {
2.    "Version": "2012-10-17",
3.    "Statement": [
4.      {
5.        "Effect": "Allow",
6.        "Action": "sts:AssumeRole",
7.        "Resource": "arn:aws:iam::111122223333:role/ExampleCrossAccountRole"
8.      }
9.    ]
10. }
11.
```

In this example, `111122223333` is the account ID of the resource account, and `ExampleCrossAccountRole` is the name of the role created in the resource account.

**Assume the Role in the Trusted Account:** Use the AWS CLI, SDK, or AWS Management Console to assume the role and gain the necessary permissions to access the resources.

**Example CLI Command to Assume Role:**
```
aws sts assume-role --role-arn "arn:aws:iam::111122223333:role/ExampleCrossAccountRole" --role-session-name "ExampleSession"
```

The command returns temporary security credentials that can be used to access the resources in the resource account.

## Example Use Case

Consider an organization with multiple AWS accounts for different departments, such as development, testing, and production. The production account has an S3 bucket that contains shared resources needed by the development account. Instead of copying data or managing separate IAM users, the organization can use cross-account roles to grant the development account access to the S3 bucket.

**Create the IAM role in the production account:** Follow the steps outlined above to create a role that grants s3:ListBucket and s3:GetObject permissions on the specific S3 bucket. Configure the trust policy to allow the development account to assume the role.

**Configure the development account to assume the role:** Create or update an IAM policy in the development account to allow assuming the role. Use the AWS CLI or SDK in the development account to assume the role and access the S3 bucket.

By using cross-account roles, the organization ensures that access to resources is secure and managed centrally, without the need for sharing long-term credentials. This approach also simplifies the management of permissions and enhances security by adhering to the principle of least privilege.

## 13.9 Central Deployment and Management

Central deployment and management of AWS resources is essential for maintaining control, consistency, and efficiency across an organization's cloud environment. By leveraging tools such as AWS Organizations and AWS Control Tower, organizations can automate account creation, enforce security policies, and monitor compliance from a single control point. This centralized approach ensures that resources are deployed according to best practices, reducing the risk of misconfigurations and enhancing overall operational governance.

### 13.9.1 Deploying and Configuring AWS Organizations

Deploying and configuring AWS Organizations for centralized management involves several key steps that help streamline the control of multiple AWS accounts, enforce policies, and consolidate billing. Here's a step-by-step guide to getting started with AWS Organizations:

#### Step 1: Create an AWS Organization

**Access the AWS Management Console:** Log in to the AWS Management Console with the root account or an IAM user with the necessary permissions.

**Navigate to AWS Organizations:** In the AWS Management Console, navigate to the AWS Organizations service.

**Create an Organization:** If you are not already using AWS Organizations, you will see an option to create an organization. Click on "Create organization" to begin the setup. AWS will create an organization with a single account (the management account).

#### Step 2: Invite Existing Accounts or Create New Accounts

**Invite Existing Accounts:** Go to the "Accounts" section within AWS Organizations. Click on "Add account" and choose "Invite account." Enter the email address of the AWS account you want to invite and send the invitation. The invited account must accept the invitation from its AWS Organizations console to join the organization.

**Create New Accounts**: In the "Accounts" section, click on "Add account" and choose "Create account." Provide the necessary details such as the email address, account name, and optionally, an IAM role name that will be used for cross-account access. AWS will create a new account and add it to your organization automatically.

#### Step 3: Organize Accounts into Organizational Units (OUs)

**Create Organizational Units:** In the AWS Organizations console, navigate to the "Organizational units" section. Click on "Create organizational unit" and provide a name for the OU (e.g., "Development," "Production," "Finance"). Drag and drop the accounts into the appropriate OUs.

#### Step 4: Apply Service Control Policies (SCPs)

**Create a Service Control Policy:** Go to the "Policies" section in AWS Organizations and select "Service control policies." Click "Create policy" and define the policy using the JSON editor. For example, to deny access to certain services:

```
1. {
```

```
2.      "Version": "2012-10-17",
3.      "Statement": [
4.        {
5.          "Effect": "Deny",
6.          "Action": [
7.            "ec2:*",
8.            "s3:*"
9.          ],
10.         "Resource": "*"
11.       }
12.     ]
13.   }
```

**Attach SCP to Organizational Units:** After creating the SCP, select it from the list of policies. Click "Actions" and choose "Attach." Select the OUs or accounts to which you want to apply the SCP. This ensures that all accounts within these OUs adhere to the defined policies.

### Step 5: Set Up Consolidated Billing
**Enable Consolidated Billing:** Navigate to the "Billing and Cost Management" console from your management account. Ensure that all member accounts are linked to the management account for consolidated billing. This setup aggregates usage and charges across all accounts, providing a single bill and potential cost savings through volume discounts.

### Step 6: Monitor and Audit
**Use AWS CloudTrail:** Enable AWS CloudTrail in the management account to log all API calls made within the organization. This provides a comprehensive audit trail for security and compliance purposes.

**Implement AWS Config:** Use AWS Config to continuously monitor and record the configuration of your AWS resources. AWS Config rules can help ensure that resources comply with organizational policies.

### Example Scenario
Consider an organization with separate AWS accounts for development, testing, and production. By using AWS Organizations, the organization can:

- **Create OUs for each environment**: Development, Testing, Production.
- **Apply SCPs to enforce specific policies**: Restrict certain services in the development environment, enforce stringent security controls in the production environment.
- **Centralize billing**: Aggregate all charges to the management account for simplified billing and potential discounts.
- **Monitor compliance**: Use AWS Config and CloudTrail to ensure that all accounts comply with the organization's security and compliance standards.

In summary, AWS Organizations provides a powerful framework for centralized management of multiple AWS accounts. By creating OUs, applying SCPs, enabling consolidated billing, and monitoring activities, organizations can enforce consistent policies, enhance security, and simplify account management.

## 13.9.2 Deploying AWS Control Tower
AWS Control Tower is a managed service that provides a secure and compliant multi-account AWS environment, known as a landing zone. It offers automated account provisioning, centralized policy enforcement, and integrated monitoring to help organizations manage their AWS accounts at scale. AWS Control Tower leverages AWS Organizations to manage accounts, AWS Service Catalog for account provisioning, and AWS Config and AWS CloudTrail for governance and compliance.

## When to Deploy AWS Control Tower
Organizations should consider deploying AWS Control Tower when they need to:

- **Scale Cloud Operations**: Simplify the management of multiple AWS accounts by automating account creation and configuration.
- **Enforce Security and Compliance**: Ensure that all AWS accounts adhere to organizational policies and industry regulations using pre-configured guardrails.
- **Centralize Governance**: Maintain centralized control over security, compliance, and operational activities across multiple accounts.
- **Improve Operational Efficiency**: Reduce the manual effort involved in setting up and managing multiple AWS accounts by using automated workflows and best practices.

## How to Deploy on Deploying AWS Control Tower
**Prerequisites**

- **AWS Root Account Access**: You need root account access or an IAM user with the necessary permissions to set up AWS Control Tower.
- **AWS Organizations**: Ensure AWS Organizations is set up with all accounts you wish to include in your landing zone.
- **Service Quotas**: Verify that your account has sufficient service quotas for resources required by AWS Control Tower (e.g., AWS Config rules, AWS CloudTrail trails).

## Step-by-Step Deployment
**Enable AWS Control Tower**: Log in to the AWS Management Console using the root account or an IAM user with the necessary permissions. Navigate to AWS Control Tower at https://console.aws.amazon.com/controltower/. Click "Get started."

**Set Up Your Landing Zone**:
- **Region Selection**: Choose the AWS region where you want to deploy AWS Control Tower. Note that AWS Control Tower must be deployed in supported regions.
- **Pre-checks**: AWS Control Tower will perform pre-checks to ensure your environment is ready. Address any issues highlighted during these checks.

**Configure Organizational Units (OUs)**: AWS Control Tower requires at least two OUs: one for the management (or master) account and another for member accounts (e.g., Core OU for shared services like logging and security). Follow the prompts to create and configure these OUs.

**Define Guardrails**: Guardrails are pre-configured policies that enforce best practices. AWS Control Tower provides mandatory, strongly recommended, and elective guardrails. Review the default guardrails and customize them based on your organization's requirements.

**Set Up AWS Single Sign-On (SSO)**: AWS Control Tower integrates with AWS SSO to provide centralized access management. Configure AWS SSO by selecting or creating user groups and assigning permissions to those groups.

**Create Shared Accounts**: AWS Control Tower will automatically create shared accounts for logging and auditing, such as the Log Archive account and Audit account. These accounts help centralize and secure logs and audit information across your AWS environment.

**Launch Your Landing Zone**: Review the configuration settings and click "Set up landing zone" to begin the deployment process. AWS Control Tower will take approximately 1-2 hours to set up your landing zone, during which it will create necessary AWS resources and apply configurations.

**Provision New Accounts**: After the landing zone is set up, you can use AWS Control Tower to provision new AWS accounts. Navigate to the AWS Control Tower dashboard and click "Account Factory" to create new accounts. Follow the prompts to specify account details and select the appropriate OU for the new account.

**Monitor and Manage Your Landing Zone**: Use the AWS Control Tower dashboard to monitor the status of your landing zone, including compliance with guardrails and the status of member accounts. AWS Control Tower provides a centralized view of account activities and compliance, helping you maintain governance and security across your AWS environment.

## Example Configuration

Let's consider an example where you set up AWS Control Tower for a medium-sized enterprise with the following requirements:
- Centralized logging and auditing.
- Separate OUs for development, testing, and production environments.
- Mandatory encryption for all S3 buckets.

**Create OUs**: Core (for shared services), Development, Testing, and Production.
**Define Guardrails**: Enable mandatory guardrails such as "Enable S3 Bucket Encryption" and elective guardrails like "Disallow Unencrypted CloudTrail Logs."
**Set Up AWS SSO**: Create user groups for Developers, Testers, and Administrators, and assign appropriate permissions.
**Create Shared Accounts**: Automatically create Log Archive and Audit accounts during the landing zone setup.
**Launch Landing Zone**: Review and confirm the setup. AWS Control Tower will apply the configurations and set up the environment.

In summary, deploying AWS Control Tower involves configuring organizational units, defining guardrails, setting up AWS SSO, creating shared accounts, and provisioning new accounts. This setup ensures centralized management, security, and compliance across multiple AWS accounts, helping organizations maintain control and operational efficiency.

## 13.9.3 Implementing Service Control Policies (SCPs)

Service Control Policies (SCPs) are an essential feature of AWS Organizations that allow administrators to manage and enforce governance policies across multiple AWS accounts within an organization. SCPs are used to set permission guardrails, ensuring that all accounts within an organization adhere to specific security and compliance policies. Here's how to create and implement SCPs to enforce organization-wide policies.

### Step 1: Access AWS Organizations

**Log in to the AWS Management Console**: Use the root account or an IAM user with the necessary permissions.

**Navigate to AWS Organizations:** Open the AWS Organizations console at https://console.aws.amazon.com/organizations/.

### Step 2: Create a Service Control Policy (SCP)

**Go to Policies**: In the AWS Organizations console, click on the "Policies" tab. Select "Service control policies" from the list.

**Create a New SCP**: Click "Create policy." Enter a name and description for your SCP (e.g., "DenyS3PublicAccess"). Use the JSON editor to define the policy. For example, to deny all S3 public access settings:

```
1.  {
2.    "Version": "2012-10-17",
3.    "Statement": [
4.      {
5.        "Effect": "Deny",
6.        "Action": [
7.          "s3:PutBucketPublicAccessBlock",
8.          "s3:PutBucketAcl",
9.          "s3:PutObjectAcl"
10.       ],
11.       "Resource": "*",
12.       "Condition": {
13.         "Bool": {
14.           "aws:SecureTransport": "false"
15.         }
16.       }
17.     }
18.   ]
19. }
20.
```

**Review and Create**: Click "Review policy." Ensure the policy is correct and click "Create policy."

## Step 3: Attach SCP to Organizational Units (OUs) or Accounts

**Select the SCP**: In the "Service control policies" section, find the SCP you just created. Click on the SCP to open its details.

**Attach the SCP**: Click the "Actions" button and select "Attach." Choose the OUs or individual accounts you want to apply this SCP to. Click "Attach" to enforce the policy.

## Step 4: Verify the SCP Implementation

**Test the Policy**: Attempt to perform actions that are restricted by the SCP in an account within the OU to which the SCP is attached. For example, try to change the S3 bucket ACL to public. The action should be denied if the SCP is correctly implemented.

**Review Policy Effectiveness**: Use AWS CloudTrail to monitor API calls and ensure that the actions are being denied as specified by the SCP. Check the AWS Organizations console to verify that the SCP is properly attached and active.

# Example Scenario: Enforcing Multi-Factor Authentication (MFA)
## Step 1: Create an SCP to Enforce MFA

```
1.  {
2.    "Version": "2012-10-17",
3.    "Statement": [
4.      {
5.        "Effect": "Deny",
6.        "Action": "*",
7.        "Resource": "*",
8.        "Condition": {
9.          "BoolIfExists": {
10.           "aws:MultiFactorAuthPresent": "false"
11.         }
```

```
12.         }
13.      }
14.   ]
15. }
```

### Step 2: Attach the SCP to Relevant OUs
**Navigate to Policies**: Go to the "Service control policies" section in the AWS Organizations console. Select the "EnforceMFA" SCP.

**Attach to OUs**: Click "Actions" and select "Attach." Choose the OUs or accounts to which you want to enforce MFA. Click "Attach" to apply the policy.

### Step 3: Monitor and Verify
**Test MFA Requirement**: Log in to an account within the OU without using MFA. Attempts to perform any actions should be denied. Log in using MFA and verify that actions can be performed as expected.

**Audit with CloudTrail**: Use AWS CloudTrail to review logs and confirm that actions are being denied for users not authenticated with MFA.

## Benefits of Using SCPs
- **Centralized Control**: SCPs provide a way to enforce policies across all AWS accounts in an organization, ensuring consistent security and compliance.
- **Granular Permissions**: SCPs allow for fine-grained control over what actions can be performed within each account, minimizing the risk of accidental or malicious activity.
- **Compliance**: By enforcing mandatory policies such as data encryption, MFA, and restricted access, organizations can ensure compliance with industry standards and regulatory requirements.

Creating and implementing SCPs in AWS Organizations allows for robust governance and security across multiple AWS accounts. By following the steps outlined above, organizations can effectively enforce organization-wide policies, ensuring that all accounts adhere to best practices and compliance requirements. Regular monitoring and testing are essential to verify that SCPs are working as intended and to maintain a secure AWS environment.

## 13.9.4 Central Management and Aggregation
Centrally managing security services and aggregating findings are critical components of maintaining a secure and compliant AWS environment. AWS provides several tools, including AWS Config and delegated administration, that facilitate centralized management and provide comprehensive visibility into security and compliance status across multiple accounts.

### AWS Config
AWS Config is a service that enables you to assess, audit, and evaluate the configurations of your AWS resources. AWS Config continuously monitors and records your AWS resource configurations and allows you to automate the evaluation of recorded configurations against desired configurations. By enabling AWS Config across all accounts within an AWS Organization, administrators can centrally manage and monitor resource configurations to ensure compliance with organizational policies and regulatory requirements.

To implement AWS Config for centralized management:

- Enable AWS Config: Begin by enabling AWS Config in each account. This can be done manually via the AWS Management Console or programmatically using AWS CloudFormation StackSets, which allows you to deploy AWS Config rules across multiple accounts and regions in a single operation.
- Create Config Rules: Define AWS Config rules that represent your desired configurations and compliance policies. These rules can be AWS-managed or custom rules that you create to meet specific needs.
- Aggregate Findings: Use AWS Config Aggregator to consolidate configuration and compliance data from multiple accounts and regions into a single account. This provides a centralized view of your compliance status across your entire organization.

### Example of AWS Config Aggregator Setup

```
aws configservice put-configuration-aggregator --configuration-aggregator-name example-aggregator --account-sources AccountId=123456789012
```

In this example, replace 123456789012 with the account ID from which you want to aggregate data.

## Delegated Administration

Delegated Administration is a feature within AWS Organizations that allows you to designate member accounts as administrators for specific services, such as AWS Config, AWS Security Hub, and AWS IAM Access Analyzer. Delegated administrators can manage security services and aggregate findings across all accounts in the organization, providing a centralized approach to governance and compliance.

### Steps to Enable Delegated Administration

**Designate a Delegated Administrator:** In the AWS Organizations console, select the service (e.g., AWS Config) for which you want to delegate administration. Designate a member account as the delegated administrator for the service. This account will have the necessary permissions to manage the service across all accounts in the organization.

**Configure Service in Delegated Account:** In the delegated administrator account, configure the service to manage and monitor resources across the organization. For AWS Config, set up rules and aggregators to collect compliance data from all member accounts.

**Aggregate and Monitor Findings:** Use the delegated administrator account to review and aggregate findings. For example, with AWS Security Hub, you can consolidate security findings from multiple AWS accounts and services into a single dashboard, providing a comprehensive view of security issues and compliance status.

### Example of Setting Up Delegated Administration for AWS Security Hub

Enable AWS Security Hub in the management account and designate a member account as the delegated administrator.

Configure the Delegated Administrator Account: In the delegated administrator account, configure AWS Security Hub to aggregate findings from all member accounts. Use the Security Hub dashboard to review findings and take corrective actions as needed.

### Example Command to Enable Delegated Administration for AWS Config

```
aws organizations register-delegated-administrator --account-id 123456789012 --service-principal config.amazonaws.com
```

In this example, replace 123456789012 with the account ID you wish to designate as the delegated administrator for AWS Config.

By leveraging AWS Config, delegated administration, and other AWS security services, organizations can achieve centralized management of security and compliance across multiple accounts. This approach ensures that security policies are consistently applied, compliance is continuously monitored, and findings are aggregated for comprehensive oversight. Regular reviews and audits of configuration and compliance data further enhance the security posture and help maintain adherence to industry standards and regulatory requirements.

## 13.9.5 Securing Root User Credentials

Securing AWS root user credentials is a critical aspect of maintaining the security and integrity of your AWS environment. The root user has unrestricted access to all resources and services in an AWS account, making it a primary target for attackers. Implementing best practices for securing the root user involves using strong password policies, enabling multi-factor authentication (MFA), and minimizing the use of the root account. Here's a detailed discussion on these best practices:

### Enable Multi-Factor Authentication (MFA)

Enabling MFA for the root user significantly enhances security by adding an additional layer of protection beyond just the password. MFA requires the user to provide two forms of authentication: something they know (password) and something they have (MFA device). This makes it much more difficult for an unauthorized user to gain access to the root account.

**Steps to Enable MFA:**
- Log in to the AWS Management Console using the root account.
- Navigate to the IAM Service: Go to the IAM dashboard.
- Activate MFA: Click on "Activate MFA on your root account" and follow the prompts to configure either a virtual MFA device (like Google Authenticator) or a hardware MFA device.

**Example of Enabling MFA:**
Using a virtual MFA device, scan the QR code provided by AWS with an authenticator app, enter the generated codes, and complete the setup.

### Use Strong, Unique Passwords

Using strong, unique passwords for the root account is crucial to prevent unauthorized access. A strong password typically includes a mix of upper and lower-case letters, numbers, and special characters, and it should be at least 12 characters long. Avoid using easily guessable information, such as common words, phrases, or personal information.

**Best Practices for Passwords**
- **Complexity**: Ensure the password includes a mix of character types.
- **Length**: Use a minimum length of 12 characters.
- **Uniqueness**: Avoid reusing passwords from other accounts.
- **Regular Updates**: Change the root account password regularly and immediately if a breach is suspected.
- **Example of a Strong Password:** A$1dFg#4kL&7xZp

### Minimize Use of the Root Account

The root account should only be used for tasks that cannot be performed by other IAM users or roles. Instead, create IAM users with the necessary permissions for day-to-day operations. This minimizes the risk associated with the root account and provides better tracking and management of user activities.

**Steps to Minimize Root Account Usage:**
- **Create IAM Users**: Create IAM users for administrative tasks.
- **Assign Policies**: Grant these users the necessary permissions through IAM policies.
- **Monitor Activities**: Use CloudTrail to monitor API calls and activities performed by IAM users.

**Example of IAM User Creation:**
Create an IAM user named `AdminUser`, assign administrative permissions, and use this user for management tasks instead of the root account.

### Lock Away Root Account Access Keys
If root account access keys are not needed, they should be deleted to prevent misuse. If they are required, ensure they are stored securely and rotated regularly.

**Steps to Manage Access Keys:**
- **Delete Unnecessary Keys**: Log in as the root user, navigate to the IAM console, and delete any unnecessary access keys.
- **Secure Storage**: Store any necessary keys in a secure location, such as an encrypted secrets manager.
- **Regular Rotation**: Rotate access keys regularly to minimize the risk of key compromise.

**Example of Deleting Access Keys:**
In the IAM console, select the root account, view access keys, and delete keys that are not in use.

### Monitor and Audit Root Account Activity
Regularly monitor the activities of the root account to detect any unusual or unauthorized actions. AWS CloudTrail provides detailed logs of API calls and activities performed within your AWS account.

**Steps to Monitor Activity:**
- **Enable CloudTrail**: Set up CloudTrail to log all API calls.
- **Review Logs**: Regularly review CloudTrail logs to identify any suspicious activities.
- **Set Up Alerts**: Use Amazon CloudWatch to create alarms that notify you of root account usage.

**Example of CloudTrail Setup:**
Enable CloudTrail in all regions, configure it to log all management and data events, and store the logs in an S3 bucket for centralized monitoring.

By implementing these best practices, organizations can significantly enhance the security of their AWS root user credentials, reducing the risk of unauthorized access and ensuring a secure AWS environment.

# 13.10 Implementing Secure and Consistent Deployment Strategies

Implementing secure and consistent deployment strategies is crucial for maintaining the integrity, security, and reliability of applications in the cloud. By leveraging infrastructure as code (IaC) and automated deployment pipelines, organizations can ensure that their deployments are reproducible, traceable, and compliant with security best practices. This approach not only mitigates the risk of human error but also enhances the ability to quickly and safely deploy updates across multiple environments.

## 13.10.1 Infrastructure as Code (IaC) Best Practices

Using Infrastructure as Code (IaC) to deploy AWS resources securely and consistently is a cornerstone of modern cloud management. IaC allows organizations to define, provision, and manage their infrastructure using code, which enhances automation, repeatability, and compliance. To achieve secure and consistent deployments, it is essential to follow best practices such as template hardening and drift detection.

## Best Practices for Using IaC to Deploy AWS Resources
### Template Hardening

Template hardening involves securing IaC templates to ensure they adhere to security best practices and organizational policies. This includes:

- **Use of Parameterization:** Avoid hardcoding sensitive information, such as credentials and secrets, directly in templates. Instead, use parameters to pass these values securely at runtime. AWS CloudFormation and Terraform support parameterization.

- **Resource Policies and Permissions:** Define least privilege permissions in IAM roles and policies to ensure that resources can only perform necessary actions. Avoid using wildcard permissions (e.g., "Effect": "Allow", "Action": "*", "Resource": "*") and instead specify exact actions and resources.

- **Enable Encryption:** Ensure that all data storage services (e.g., S3, RDS, EBS) have encryption enabled by default. Use AWS KMS for managing encryption keys and specify the encryption configuration in your templates.

- **Network Security:** Configure security groups and network ACLs to restrict access to only necessary IP ranges and ports. Ensure that default security group rules are modified to enhance security.

**Example of a Hardened CloudFormation Template:**

```
1.  AWSTemplateFormatVersion: '2010-09-09'
2.  Parameters:
3.    InstanceType:
4.      Type: String
5.      Default: t2.micro
6.      AllowedValues:
7.        - t2.micro
8.        - t2.small
9.      Description: EC2 instance type
10.   KeyName:
11.     Description: Name of an existing EC2 KeyPair to enable SSH access to the instance
12.     Type: AWS::EC2::KeyPair::KeyName
13.  
14. Resources:
15.   MyInstance:
16.     Type: AWS::EC2::Instance
17.     Properties:
18.       InstanceType: !Ref InstanceType
19.       KeyName: !Ref KeyName
20.       ImageId: ami-0abcdef1234567890
21.       SecurityGroupIds:
22.         - !Ref InstanceSecurityGroup
23.   InstanceSecurityGroup:
24.     Type: AWS::EC2::SecurityGroup
25.     Properties:
26.       GroupDescription: Enable SSH access
27.       SecurityGroupIngress:
28.         - IpProtocol: tcp
29.           FromPort: 22
30.           ToPort: 22
31.           CidrIp: 0.0.0.0/0
32.       SecurityGroupEgress:
```

```
33.          - IpProtocol: -1
34.            FromPort: -1
35.            ToPort: -1
36.            CidrIp: 0.0.0.0/0
37.    MyS3Bucket:
38.      Type: AWS::S3::Bucket
39.      Properties:
40.        BucketName: my-secure-bucket
41.        BucketEncryption:
42.          ServerSideEncryptionConfiguration:
43.            - ServerSideEncryptionByDefault:
44.                SSEAlgorithm: AES256
45. Outputs:
46.   InstanceId:
47.     Description: The Instance ID
48.     Value: !Ref MyInstance
49.   BucketName:
50.     Description: The name of the S3 bucket
51.     Value: !Ref MyS3Bucket
52.
```

## Drift Detection

Drift detection involves monitoring and identifying deviations between the IaC-defined infrastructure and the actual deployed infrastructure. This helps ensure that any unauthorized or unintended changes are detected and addressed promptly.

**Enable Drift Detection:** Use AWS CloudFormation drift detection to identify changes in stack resources that differ from the expected template configurations. Regularly run drift detection checks to ensure that your infrastructure remains in the desired state.

**Automate Detection and Alerts:** Integrate drift detection with AWS CloudWatch and AWS Lambda to automate the detection process and send alerts when drift is detected. This allows for real-time monitoring and quick remediation.

**Example of Running Drift Detection in CloudFormation:**

```
aws cloudformation detect-stack-drift --stack-name my-stack
```

To view the drift status:

```
aws cloudformation describe-stack-drift-detection-status --stack-drift-detection-id <drift-detection-id>
```

## Version Control and CI/CD Integration

**Use Version Control:** Store IaC templates in a version control system (VCS) like Git. This allows for tracking changes, collaboration, and rollback to previous versions if needed.

**CI/CD Pipelines:** Integrate IaC with Continuous Integration/Continuous Deployment (CI/CD) pipelines to automate testing, validation, and deployment of infrastructure changes. Use tools like AWS CodePipeline, Jenkins, or GitLab CI/CD to streamline deployments.

**Example CI/CD Workflow for IaC with GitHub Actions:**

```
1. name: Deploy CloudFormation Stack
2.
3. on:
```

```
 4.  push:
 5.    branches:
 6.      - main
 7.
 8. jobs:
 9.   deploy:
10.     runs-on: ubuntu-latest
11.     steps:
12.       - name: Checkout code
13.         uses: actions/checkout@v2
14.       - name: Configure AWS credentials
15.         uses: aws-actions/configure-aws-credentials@v1
16.         with:
17.           aws-access-key-id: ${{ secrets.AWS_ACCESS_KEY_ID }}
18.           aws-secret-access-key: ${{ secrets.AWS_SECRET_ACCESS_KEY }}
19.           aws-region: us-west-2
20.       - name: Deploy CloudFormation stack
21.         run: |
22.           aws cloudformation deploy \
23.             --template-file template.yaml \
24.             --stack-name my-stack \
25.             --capabilities CAPABILITY_IAM CAPABILITY_NAMED_IAM
```

By following these best practices, organizations can ensure that their AWS resources are deployed securely and consistently using Infrastructure as Code. Template hardening helps enforce security policies, while drift detection ensures that infrastructure remains compliant with the desired state. Integrating IaC with version control and CI/CD pipelines further enhances the reliability and efficiency of deployments.

## 13.10.2 Tagging Best Practices

Tagging is a crucial practice in AWS resource management, providing a way to categorize resources for various purposes, such as cost allocation, automation, access control, and operational management. By assigning metadata to AWS resources in the form of tags, organizations can gain granular visibility and control over their cloud environment, streamline management processes, and ensure compliance with organizational policies.

### Importance of Tagging for Resource Management

**Cost Allocation and Optimization:** Tags can be used to allocate costs accurately across different departments, projects, or environments. By tagging resources with identifiers such as project names, business units, or cost centers, organizations can generate detailed cost reports and optimize spending. This enables more precise tracking and accountability for cloud expenditures.

**Automation: Tags facilitate the automation of resource management tasks.** Automation scripts and tools can use tags to identify and manage resources dynamically. For instance, tags can be used to start or stop instances during specific hours to save costs, enforce backup policies, or apply security configurations.

**Access Control and Security:** IAM policies can reference tags to control access to resources. This allows for more flexible and granular permissions management. For example, an IAM policy can restrict access to resources tagged with a specific project or environment, ensuring that users only have access to the resources they need.

**Operational Management:** Tags help organize and manage resources more effectively by providing contextual information. This is particularly useful in large environments where it can be challenging to keep track of numerous resources. Tags can indicate the resource owner, environment (e.g., development, staging, production), or criticality, aiding in resource tracking and incident management.

## Best Practices for Implementing a Tagging Strategy

**Define a Tagging Schema:** Establish a consistent tagging schema before applying tags to resources. This schema should be standardized across the organization to ensure uniformity and ease of management. The schema should include key-value pairs that are meaningful and relevant to the organization's needs.

**Use Standardized Tags:** Create a set of standardized tags that all teams and departments must use. Common tags include Environment (e.g., Dev, Test, Prod), Project (e.g., ProjectX, ProjectY), Owner (e.g., user@example.com), and CostCenter (e.g., CC1234).

**Enforce Tagging Policies:** Use AWS Config rules to enforce tagging policies and ensure compliance. AWS Config can continuously monitor resources and report on non-compliant resources that lack required tags or have incorrect tag values.

**Automate Tagging:** Implement automated tagging mechanisms to ensure that all resources are tagged consistently at creation. AWS CloudFormation, AWS Service Catalog, and infrastructure-as-code tools like Terraform can include tagging specifications in their templates.

**Monitor and Audit Tags:** Regularly review and audit tags to ensure they are up-to-date and accurately reflect the intended categorization. AWS Tag Editor and AWS Resource Groups can help manage and update tags across multiple resources.

Example Tagging Strategy:

```
1.  [
2.    {
3.      "Key": "Environment",
4.      "Value": "Production"
5.    },
6.    {
7.      "Key": "Project",
8.      "Value": "WebsiteRedesign"
9.    },
10.   {
11.     "Key": "Owner",
12.     "Value": "john.doe@example.com"
13.   },
14.   {
15.     "Key": "CostCenter",
16.     "Value": "CC1001"
17.   }
18. ]
19.
```

## Implementing this tagging strategy involves:

**Defining Tagging Policies:** Create policies that require the above tags for all resources.

**Automating Tagging:** Use CloudFormation templates to automatically apply these tags when creating resources:

```
1. Resources:
2.   MyInstance:
3.     Type: AWS::EC2::Instance
4.     Properties:
5.       InstanceType: t2.micro
6.       ImageId: ami-0abcdef1234567890
7.       Tags:
```

```
 8.       - Key: Environment
 9.         Value: Production
10.       - Key: Project
11.         Value: WebsiteRedesign
12.       - Key: Owner
13.         Value: john.doe@example.com
14.       - Key: CostCenter
15.         Value: CC1001
```

**Monitoring Compliance:** Set up AWS Config rules to ensure all resources have the required tags.

By following these best practices, organizations can implement a robust tagging strategy that enhances resource management, improves cost tracking, enables automation, and strengthens security. Consistent tagging leads to better-organized resources, streamlined operations, and more effective governance of the cloud environment.

## 13.10.3 Centralized Management and Deployment

Centralized management, deployment, and versioning of AWS services are critical for maintaining consistency, security, and efficiency in cloud operations. These techniques ensure that resources are deployed in a standardized manner, configurations are consistent across environments, and changes are tracked and controlled effectively. AWS provides several tools and services that facilitate these processes, including AWS CloudFormation, AWS Service Catalog, AWS Systems Manager, and version control systems like AWS CodeCommit.

### Centralized Management

Centralized management allows organizations to control and monitor their AWS resources from a single point of control. AWS Organizations is a foundational service for centralized management, enabling the creation of multiple AWS accounts and applying policies across the organization. Service Control Policies (SCPs) help enforce governance and compliance by restricting actions at the account or organizational unit level.

Example: Using AWS Organizations, an enterprise can create separate accounts for development, testing, and production, and apply SCPs to enforce security policies, such as restricting the use of specific services in production environments.

### Deployment

Automated deployment is key to maintaining consistency and reducing errors. AWS CloudFormation and AWS Service Catalog are powerful tools for this purpose. AWS CloudFormation allows you to define your infrastructure as code (IaC) using templates, which can be versioned and reused across different environments. AWS Service Catalog enables the central management of approved service offerings, ensuring that only compliant and pre-approved resources are deployed.

Example: A company can use AWS CloudFormation templates to deploy a multi-tier application, including an EC2 instance, an RDS database, and an S3 bucket. These templates can be stored in an S3 bucket or a version control system like AWS CodeCommit, ensuring that the infrastructure can be consistently deployed across multiple environments.

### Versioning

Version control is crucial for tracking changes to infrastructure and application code. AWS CodeCommit, a fully managed source control service, supports Git repositories, allowing teams to version their CloudFormation templates, configuration scripts, and application code. Combined with AWS CodePipeline, AWS CodeBuild, and AWS CodeDeploy, organizations can implement a complete CI/CD pipeline, automating the build, test, and deployment processes.

Example: A development team can use AWS CodeCommit to store their CloudFormation templates and application code. AWS CodePipeline can then automate the process of deploying these templates to different environments, ensuring that all changes are tracked and can be rolled back if necessary.

### Techniques for Centralized Management, Deployment, and Versioning

**Infrastructure as Code (IaC):** Define infrastructure using CloudFormation or Terraform templates. These templates ensure that infrastructure is deployed consistently and can be versioned for tracking changes.

**AWS Service Catalog:** Create portfolios of approved products and services that can be deployed by different teams. This ensures compliance and standardization across the organization.

**AWS Systems Manager:** Use Systems Manager to manage and automate operational tasks across your AWS resources. Features like State Manager, Patch Manager, and Automation allow for centralized control of configurations, patching, and routine maintenance tasks.

**CI/CD Pipelines:** Implement CI/CD (continuous integration and continuous deployment) pipelines using AWS CodePipeline, CodeBuild, and CodeDeploy. These AWS developer tools automate the process of building, testing, and deploying applications, ensuring that changes are consistently and reliably propagated across environments.

### Example CI/CD Pipeline with AWS CodePipeline

**Source**: The source stage retrieves the latest code from an AWS CodeCommit repository.
**Build**: AWS CodeBuild compiles the code and runs tests to ensure quality.
**Deploy**: AWS CodeDeploy deploys the built application to EC2 instances, Lambda functions, or other AWS services.

## 13.10.4 Visibility and Control

Ensuring visibility and control over AWS infrastructure is essential for maintaining security, performance, and compliance. AWS provides a comprehensive suite of monitoring and management tools that help organizations gain insights into their resources, track changes, and respond to incidents effectively. Key tools include AWS CloudWatch, AWS CloudTrail, AWS Config, and AWS Systems Manager, each offering distinct functionalities to enhance visibility and control.

### Monitoring with AWS CloudWatch

AWS CloudWatch is a powerful monitoring and observability service that provides data and actionable insights for AWS resources, applications, and services. It collects and tracks metrics, monitors log files, and sets alarms to help you stay informed about the health and performance of your infrastructure. CloudWatch allows you to create dashboards for real-time visualization of key metrics, set thresholds for alarms, and automate responses to specific conditions.

Example: Using CloudWatch, an organization can monitor the CPU utilization of its EC2 instances. If the CPU utilization exceeds a predefined threshold, CloudWatch can trigger an alarm and automatically scale out the EC2 instances to handle increased load, ensuring application performance remains optimal.

### Auditing with AWS CloudTrail

AWS CloudTrail provides visibility into API activity by recording API calls made on your account. It logs details such as the identity of the API caller, the time of the API call, the source IP address, and the request parameters. This audit trail helps ensure compliance, track changes, and troubleshoot operational issues by providing a comprehensive log of all actions taken within your AWS environment.

Example: An organization can use CloudTrail to detect unauthorized access attempts. By analyzing CloudTrail logs, security teams can identify suspicious activities, such as repeated failed login attempts, and take appropriate action to secure the environment.

## Configuration Management with AWS Config

AWS Config is a service that enables you to assess, audit, and evaluate the configurations of your AWS resources. It continuously monitors and records AWS resource configurations and allows you to automate the evaluation of recorded configurations against desired configurations. AWS Config provides a detailed view of resource configurations and relationships, making it easier to track configuration changes and ensure compliance with organizational policies.

Example: AWS Config can be used to ensure that all S3 buckets have versioning enabled. By creating a Config rule that checks for bucket versioning, the organization can receive notifications and take corrective actions if any bucket is found to be non-compliant.

## Management with AWS Systems Manager

AWS Systems Manager is an integrated management service that helps you automate operational tasks across your AWS resources. It provides a unified user interface to view operational data from multiple AWS services and automate tasks such as patch management, resource inventory, and configuration management. Systems Manager includes features like State Manager, Patch Manager, and Automation to enhance operational efficiency and control.

Example: An organization can use AWS Systems Manager Patch Manager to automate the patching of EC2 instances. By defining patch baselines and maintenance windows, Systems Manager ensures that instances are kept up-to-date with the latest security patches, reducing the risk of vulnerabilities.

## Ensuring Visibility and Control

Combining these tools provides a comprehensive strategy for ensuring visibility and control over your AWS infrastructure. CloudWatch and CloudTrail offer real-time monitoring and detailed logging, while AWS Config ensures compliance with configuration standards. AWS Systems Manager centralizes management tasks, automating routine operations and providing a holistic view of your resources.

### Example Scenario

Consider an e-commerce company running its application on AWS. To ensure high availability and security, the company uses:
- **AWS CloudWatch** to monitor application performance and set up alarms for resource metrics.
- **AWS CloudTrail** to audit API calls and track changes to critical resources.
- **AWS Config** to enforce configuration policies, such as ensuring all EC2 instances are within approved instance types.
- **AWS Systems Manager** to manage and automate patching, inventory, and compliance checks.

By leveraging these AWS tools, the company gains enhanced visibility into its infrastructure, maintains strict control over configurations, and automates operational tasks, thereby ensuring a robust and secure cloud environment.

## 13.11 Secure Deployment

Secure deployment is a critical aspect of modern cloud operations, ensuring that applications and infrastructure are protected against vulnerabilities and threats from the outset. By implementing security best practices throughout the deployment process, organizations can safeguard their environments, maintain compliance, and reduce the risk of security incidents. This involves using automated tools, rigorous testing, and robust configuration management to create a secure, consistent, and efficient deployment pipeline.

## 13.11.1 Using CloudFormation

AWS CloudFormation is a powerful service that allows you to define and provision AWS infrastructure as code. By using CloudFormation templates, you can deploy cloud resources consistently and securely, ensuring that infrastructure is configured in a standardized manner across different environments. This approach enhances reproducibility, reduces the risk of configuration errors, and enables automation of deployment processes.

### Consistent and Secure Deployment with CloudFormation

**Defining Infrastructure as Code:** CloudFormation templates are written in JSON or YAML and describe the resources you need, such as EC2 instances, S3 buckets, and VPC configurations. By defining your infrastructure as code, you can version control these templates, enabling consistent deployment across development, staging, and production environments.

**Security Best Practices:** To ensure security, CloudFormation templates should incorporate best practices such as parameterization, encryption, and IAM roles. Parameterization allows you to pass sensitive information, such as passwords and keys, at deployment time rather than hardcoding them in the template. Using AWS Key Management Service (KMS) for encryption ensures that data at rest and in transit is protected. Additionally, defining IAM roles and policies within the template ensures that resources have the least privilege necessary to perform their functions.

**Example CloudFormation Template:**

```
1.  AWSTemplateFormatVersion: '2010-09-09'
2.  Parameters:
3.    KeyName:
4.      Description: Name of an existing EC2 KeyPair to enable SSH access to the instance
5.      Type: AWS::EC2::KeyPair::KeyName
6.    InstanceType:
7.      Description: EC2 instance type
8.      Type: String
9.      Default: t2.micro
10.     AllowedValues:
11.       - t2.micro
12.       - t2.small
13.       - t2.medium
14. Resources:
15.   MyEC2Instance:
16.     Type: AWS::EC2::Instance
17.     Properties:
18.       InstanceType: !Ref InstanceType
19.       KeyName: !Ref KeyName
20.       ImageId: ami-0abcdef1234567890
21.       SecurityGroups:
22.         - !Ref InstanceSecurityGroup
23.   InstanceSecurityGroup:
24.     Type: AWS::EC2::SecurityGroup
25.     Properties:
26.       GroupDescription: Enable SSH access via port 22
```

```
27.        SecurityGroupIngress:
28.          - IpProtocol: tcp
29.            FromPort: 22
30.            ToPort: 22
31.            CidrIp: 0.0.0.0/0
32.    MyS3Bucket:
33.      Type: AWS::S3::Bucket
34.      Properties:
35.        BucketName: my-secure-bucket
36.        BucketEncryption:
37.          ServerSideEncryptionConfiguration:
38.            - ServerSideEncryptionByDefault:
39.                SSEAlgorithm: AES256
40. Outputs:
41.   InstanceId:
42.     Description: The Instance ID
43.     Value: !Ref MyEC2Instance
44.   BucketName:
45.     Description: The name of the S3 bucket
46.     Value: !Ref MyS3Bucket
47.
```

In this example, the template defines an EC2 instance and an S3 bucket with encryption enabled. The use of parameters allows for flexibility in specifying instance types and key pairs at deployment time.

## Deployment Process

**Create the Stack:** Use the AWS Management Console, AWS CLI, or SDKs to create a CloudFormation stack from the template. During stack creation, you can provide parameter values, such as the key name and instance type.

```
aws cloudformation create-stack --stack-name my-stack --template-body file://template.yaml --parameters ParameterKey=KeyName,ParameterValue=my-key ParameterKey=InstanceType,ParameterValue=t2.micro
```

**Monitor Stack Creation:** CloudFormation handles the provisioning and configuration of resources. You can monitor the stack creation process through the AWS Management Console or using the describe-stacks command.

```
aws cloudformation describe-stacks --stack-name my-stack
```

**Update and Manage Stacks:** If you need to update your infrastructure, modify the template and use the update-stack command to apply changes. CloudFormation ensures that updates are applied in a controlled manner, minimizing disruption.

```
aws cloudformation update-stack --stack-name my-stack --template-body file://updated-template.yaml
```

## Advantages of Using CloudFormation

**Consistency:** CloudFormation ensures that infrastructure is deployed consistently across different environments, reducing the risk of configuration drift and manual errors.

**Security:** By incorporating security best practices into templates, such as encryption and IAM roles, you can ensure that your infrastructure adheres to organizational security policies.

**Automation:** CloudFormation enables automation of deployment processes, allowing for continuous integration and continuous deployment (CI/CD) pipelines to automatically provision and update infrastructure.

In summary, AWS CloudFormation provides a robust framework for deploying cloud resources consistently and securely. By defining infrastructure as code, incorporating security best practices, and leveraging automation, organizations can enhance their cloud operations and maintain a high level of control over their AWS environments.

## 13.11.2 Implementing Tagging Strategies

Tagging is a fundamental practice in AWS resource management that enables organizations to categorize and organize their resources effectively. By assigning metadata to resources in the form of tags, administrators can enhance visibility, streamline management processes, and ensure compliance with organizational policies. Tags are key-value pairs that can be used for various purposes, including cost allocation, access control, automation, and operational efficiency.

### Importance of Tagging for Resource Management

**Cost Allocation and Optimization:** Tags play a crucial role in cost management by allowing organizations to allocate costs accurately across different departments, projects, or environments. By tagging resources with identifiers such as project names, business units, or cost centers, detailed cost reports can be generated, enabling better tracking and optimization of cloud spending. This practice ensures that each team or department is accountable for their cloud usage and can identify cost-saving opportunities.

**Access Control and Security:** Tags can be integrated with AWS Identity and Access Management (IAM) policies to control access to resources. By referencing tags in IAM policies, organizations can enforce granular access controls, ensuring that users and roles have permissions only to the resources they are supposed to manage. This approach enhances security by limiting access based on the resource's tags, thereby reducing the risk of unauthorized access.

**Automation and Operational Efficiency:** Tags facilitate automation by enabling the dynamic identification and management of resources. Automation scripts and tools can use tags to perform tasks such as starting or stopping instances, applying patches, or enforcing security policies. For example, a tag indicating the environment (e.g., "development" or "production") can be used to apply different operational rules or schedules, improving efficiency and consistency in resource management.

**Compliance and Governance:** Implementing a tagging strategy helps ensure that resources comply with organizational policies and regulatory requirements. Tags can be used to track compliance-related information, such as data classification, retention policies, or security levels. Regular audits of tags can help identify non-compliant resources and take corrective actions, ensuring adherence to standards and reducing the risk of regulatory penalties.

### Best Practices for Implementing a Tagging Strategy

**Define a Tagging Schema:** Establish a standardized tagging schema that includes key-value pairs relevant to your organization's needs. This schema should be consistent across all teams and departments to ensure uniformity. Common tags include Environment (e.g., Development, Production), Project (e.g., ProjectX, ProjectY), Owner (e.g., user@example.com), and CostCenter (e.g., CC1234).

**Use Standardized Tags:** Create a set of mandatory tags that must be applied to all resources. These tags should be enforced through policies and automated checks. Standardized tags help ensure consistency and make it easier to manage and report on resources.

**Enforce Tagging Policies:** Use AWS Config rules to enforce tagging policies and ensure compliance. AWS Config can continuously monitor resources and report on those that lack required tags or have incorrect tag values. This automated enforcement helps maintain the integrity of the tagging strategy.

**Automate Tagging:** Implement automation mechanisms to ensure that all resources are tagged at the time of creation. AWS CloudFormation, AWS Service Catalog, and infrastructure-as-code tools like Terraform can include tagging specifications in their templates, ensuring consistent application of tags.

**Monitor and Audit Tags:** Regularly review and audit tags to ensure they are up-to-date and accurately reflect the intended categorization. AWS Tag Editor and AWS Resource Groups can help manage and update tags across multiple resources. Regular audits help identify any discrepancies and ensure compliance with the tagging strategy.

**Example Tagging Strategy:**

```
[
  {
    "Key": "Environment",
    "Value": "Production"
  },
  {
    "Key": "Project",
    "Value": "WebsiteRedesign"
  },
  {
    "Key": "Owner",
    "Value": "john.doe@example.com"
  },
  {
    "Key": "CostCenter",
    "Value": "CC1001"
  }
]
```

Implementing this tagging strategy involves:
- Defining Tagging Policies: Create policies that require the above tags for all resources.
- Automating Tagging: Use CloudFormation templates to automatically apply these tags when creating resources.

```
Resources:
  MyInstance:
    Type: AWS::EC2::Instance
    Properties:
      InstanceType: t2.micro
      ImageId: ami-0abcdef1234567890
      Tags:
        - Key: Environment
          Value: Production
        - Key: Project
          Value: WebsiteRedesign
        - Key: Owner
          Value: john.doe@example.com
        - Key: CostCenter
          Value: CC1001
```

**Monitoring Compliance:** Set up AWS Config rules to ensure all resources have the required tags.

By following these best practices, organizations can implement a robust tagging strategy that enhances resource management, improves cost tracking, enables automation, and strengthens security. Consistent tagging leads to better-organized resources, streamlined operations, and more effective governance of the cloud environment.

## 13.11.3 Deploying Portfolios with AWS Service Catalog

Configuring and deploying portfolios of approved AWS services using AWS Service Catalog allows organizations to manage and govern their cloud resources efficiently. AWS Service Catalog enables the central management of commonly deployed IT services, helping organizations achieve consistent governance, compliance, and cost control. By defining and organizing a collection of approved services into portfolios, administrators can ensure that only compliant and pre-approved resources are deployed across the organization.

### Configuring AWS Service Catalog Portfolios

To begin with, administrators need to create and configure portfolios that contain a set of products (AWS resources) approved for deployment. These portfolios can be customized to meet the needs of different departments, projects, or compliance requirements.

**Create a Portfolio:** Navigate to the AWS Service Catalog in the AWS Management Console. Select "Create portfolio" and provide a name and description for the portfolio. Specify an owner for the portfolio, typically the team or individual responsible for managing the resources.

**Add Products to the Portfolio:** Products in AWS Service Catalog can be individual AWS resources or complex applications composed of multiple resources. These products are defined using AWS CloudFormation templates. Select "Upload a new product" to add a product to the portfolio. Provide a name and description, and upload the CloudFormation template that defines the product. Configure the product settings, including any parameters required by the template.

**Define Constraints:** Constraints are rules that restrict how products can be used. They can be used to enforce governance policies such as tagging requirements, usage limits, and IAM role restrictions. Add constraints to the products in the portfolio by selecting the product and defining the necessary constraints, such as specifying allowed instance types or required tags.

**Share the Portfolio:** Portfolios can be shared across multiple AWS accounts using AWS Organizations. This allows centralized control over approved services while enabling teams in different accounts to access and deploy the resources they need. To share a portfolio, select "Share" from the portfolio actions and specify the AWS accounts or organizational units (OUs) with which the portfolio should be shared.

### Deploying Products from AWS Service Catalog

Once the portfolios are configured, users can deploy the approved products within their AWS accounts. This ensures that all deployed resources adhere to organizational standards and policies.

**Access the Portfolio:** Users with access to the portfolio can browse the available products in the AWS Service Catalog. Select the desired portfolio and choose a product to deploy.

**Launch the Product:** Click "Launch product" and provide the necessary parameters as defined in the CloudFormation template. Review the configuration settings and confirm the deployment.

**Monitor and Manage Deployed Resources:** AWS Service Catalog provides a dashboard to monitor the status of deployed products. Users can view details such as product instances, parameters, and compliance status. Administrators can update or delete products as needed, ensuring that all deployed resources remain compliant with organizational policies.

**Example:** Consider an organization that needs to manage the deployment of a standardized web application stack, including an EC2 instance, RDS database, and S3 bucket. By using AWS Service Catalog, the organization can create a portfolio for the web application stack and enforce constraints to ensure compliance.

**CloudFormation Template Example:**

```
1.  AWSTemplateFormatVersion: '2010-09-09'
2.  Resources:
3.    MyEC2Instance:
4.      Type: AWS::EC2::Instance
5.      Properties:
6.        InstanceType: t2.micro
7.        ImageId: ami-0abcdef1234567890
8.        SecurityGroups:
9.          - !Ref InstanceSecurityGroup
10.   MyRDSInstance:
11.     Type: AWS::RDS::DBInstance
12.     Properties:
13.       DBInstanceClass: db.t2.micro
14.       Engine: MySQL
15.       MasterUsername: admin
16.       MasterUserPassword: password
17.   MyS3Bucket:
18.     Type: AWS::S3::Bucket
19.     Properties:
20.       BucketName: my-app-bucket
21.       BucketEncryption:
22.         ServerSideEncryptionConfiguration:
23.           - ServerSideEncryptionByDefault:
24.               SSEAlgorithm: AES256
25. Outputs:
26.   InstanceId:
27.     Description: The Instance ID
28.     Value: !Ref MyEC2Instance
29.   BucketName:
30.     Description: The name of the S3 bucket
31.     Value: !Ref MyS3Bucket
```

The following are the steps:

**Create the Portfolio:** In AWS Service Catalog, create a portfolio named "WebAppStack."
Add the Product: Upload the CloudFormation template as a product within the "WebAppStack" portfolio.
**Define Constraints:** Add constraints to enforce instance types and tagging requirements.
Share the Portfolio: Share the "WebAppStack" portfolio with development and production accounts within the organization.
**Deploy the Product:** Developers in the shared accounts can now deploy the standardized web application stack using the approved CloudFormation template.

By using AWS Service Catalog, organizations can manage and deploy portfolios of approved AWS services securely and consistently. This approach ensures compliance with organizational policies, optimizes resource utilization, and simplifies the management of AWS environments.

## 13.11.4 Organizing AWS Resources

Organizing AWS resources into different groups is essential for improving management, enhancing visibility, and enforcing policies across the cloud environment. Techniques such as tagging, using AWS Resource Groups, leveraging AWS Organizations, and employing AWS Control Tower can help achieve this. These methods allow administrators to categorize resources effectively, streamline operations, and maintain control over various AWS accounts and services.

## Tagging Resources

Tagging involves assigning metadata to AWS resources in the form of key-value pairs. Tags can represent information such as the environment, project, cost center, and owner. This helps in categorizing resources for various purposes, including cost allocation, access control, and automation.

Example: An organization can tag its resources with keys like `Environment` (Development, Production), `Project` (ProjectA, ProjectB), and `Owner` (user@example.com). This makes it easier to generate reports, allocate costs, and manage permissions based on these tags.

## Using AWS Resource Groups

AWS Resource Groups allow you to create logical groupings of resources based on tags. This provides a way to manage and automate tasks across a collection of resources that share common attributes. AWS Resource Groups integrate with AWS Systems Manager, enabling you to apply automation and monitoring tools to grouped resources.

Example: An organization can create a resource group for all resources tagged with Environment=Production. This group can then be used to apply consistent monitoring, patching, and compliance checks across all production resources using AWS Systems Manager.

## Leveraging AWS Organizations

AWS Organizations is a service that helps manage multiple AWS accounts. It enables centralized management of accounts, application of policies, and consolidation of billing. Organizational units (OUs) can be created to group accounts by function, department, or project, and Service Control Policies (SCPs) can be applied to enforce governance and compliance across these groups.

Example: An enterprise can create separate OUs for its development, testing, and production environments. Each OU can have specific SCPs that restrict the use of certain services or regions, ensuring that only approved actions are performed within those accounts. This helps maintain security and compliance across different environments.

## Employing AWS Control Tower

AWS Control Tower automates the setup of a secure, well-architected multi-account AWS environment. It uses AWS Organizations to set up and manage accounts, applying guardrails to ensure compliance with best practices. AWS Control Tower provides a landing zone with predefined blueprints and governance controls, simplifying the process of setting up and managing multi-account environments.

Example: By using AWS Control Tower, an organization can quickly establish a landing zone that includes accounts for development, testing, and production. Guardrails are applied to enforce security policies and compliance requirements, ensuring that each account adheres to organizational standards.

## Techniques Summary

**Tagging:** Apply tags to resources for categorization and management. Tags can be used for cost allocation, automation, and access control.
**AWS Resource Groups:** Create resource groups based on tags for easier management and automation. Integrate with AWS Systems Manager for operational tasks.
**AWS Organizations:** Manage multiple AWS accounts with centralized control. Create OUs and apply SCPs for governance and compliance.
**AWS Control Tower:** Automate the setup of multi-account environments with predefined governance controls and best practices.

By implementing these techniques, organizations can achieve better resource organization, improved management efficiency, and enhanced control over their AWS environments.

## 13.11.5 Using AWS Firewall Manager

AWS Firewall Manager is a security management service that allows you to centrally configure and manage firewall rules across your AWS organization. It helps enforce security policies for AWS WAF, AWS Shield Advanced, VPC security groups, and AWS Network Firewall. By using AWS Firewall Manager, organizations can ensure consistent and comprehensive protection for their resources across multiple accounts and applications.

### Deploying and Using AWS Firewall Manager

To deploy and use AWS Firewall Manager effectively, follow these steps:

**Prerequisites and Initial Setup**

Before you can use AWS Firewall Manager, you need to set up AWS Organizations and enable AWS Config for all accounts in your organization. AWS Firewall Manager requires that AWS Organizations is used to manage your accounts and that AWS Config is enabled to record configurations and changes.

**Step-by-Step Setup:**

**AWS Organizations** Setup: Ensure that your AWS accounts are part of an organization managed by AWS Organizations. If not, create an organization and invite your accounts to join.

**Enable AWS Config:** Enable AWS Config in all accounts to record resource configurations. This can be done via the AWS Management Console, AWS CLI, or AWS SDKs. AWS Config must also be recording for VPCs, subnets, and security groups.

```
1. aws configservice put-configuration-recorder --configuration-recorder name=default --role-arn arn:aws:iam::account-id:role/AWSConfigRole
2. aws configservice start-configuration-recorder --configuration-recorder-name default
```

**Enable AWS Firewall Manager**

Next, enable AWS Firewall Manager in the AWS Management Console: Go to the AWS Firewall Manager console. Click on "Get started" and follow the prompts to configure the service. Designate an AWS account as the Firewall Manager administrator account. This account will manage firewall policies across the organization.

**Create Security Policies**

With AWS Firewall Manager enabled, you can now create security policies. These policies define the firewall rules and their application across your AWS environment. AWS Firewall Manager supports multiple types of policies, including AWS WAF rules, AWS Shield Advanced protections, and VPC security group policies.

Example:
**Creating an AWS WAF Policy:** Navigate to the AWS Firewall Manager console and click on "Create policy." Choose "AWS WAF" as the policy type. Configure the policy settings, including the rule groups and any specific WAF rules you want to enforce. Specify the resource types and scope of the policy (e.g., which accounts or regions the policy applies to). Review and create the policy.

**Apply and Enforce Policies**

Once a policy is created, AWS Firewall Manager automatically applies the specified rules to the resources within the scope of the policy. This centralized enforcement ensures that all designated resources adhere to the defined security policies, helping to prevent misconfigurations and vulnerabilities.

Example:
**Enforcing VPC Security Group Policies:** Create a security group policy in the Firewall Manager console. Define the security group rules you want to enforce across your VPCs, such as allowing traffic only from specific IP ranges or blocking certain ports. Specify the resources to which the policy applies and any exceptions if needed. Save and activate the policy.

**Monitor and Manage Compliance:** AWS Firewall Manager provides comprehensive monitoring and reporting capabilities. You can use the console to view the compliance status of your policies, see which resources are compliant or non-compliant, and take action to address any issues.

Example:
**Monitoring Compliance:** In the AWS Firewall Manager console, navigate to the "Dashboard" or "Compliance" section. Review the compliance status of your policies and resources. Use AWS Config to investigate any non-compliant resources and take corrective actions.

### Benefits of AWS Firewall Manager
**Centralized Management:** AWS Firewall Manager allows you to manage firewall rules and security policies from a single console, simplifying the administration of security across multiple accounts and resources.
**Consistent Enforcement:** By applying policies centrally, you ensure that all resources comply with your organization's security standards, reducing the risk of misconfigurations and vulnerabilities.
**Automated Compliance:** AWS Firewall Manager continuously monitors resources for compliance with security policies, providing automated alerts and reports to help you maintain a secure environment.

### Example Use Case
Consider a large enterprise with multiple AWS accounts and numerous web applications. To protect against common web exploits, the enterprise uses AWS WAF. By deploying AWS Firewall Manager, the enterprise can create a central WAF policy that includes rules to block SQL injection and cross-site scripting attacks. This policy is then applied to all web applications across all AWS accounts, ensuring consistent protection without the need to configure WAF rules individually for each application.

By following these steps, organizations can deploy and use AWS Firewall Manager to enforce security policies consistently across their AWS environment, ensuring comprehensive protection and compliance.

## 13.11.6 Sharing Resources Securely
Securely sharing resources across AWS accounts using AWS Resource Access Manager (AWS RAM) enables organizations to utilize shared resources efficiently while maintaining security and control. AWS RAM allows you to share AWS resources, such as Amazon VPC subnets, transit gateways, license configurations, and more, without the need to create duplicate resources in each account. This centralized sharing model helps reduce costs, simplify resource management, and enforce security policies consistently across accounts.

### Using AWS RAM to Share Resources Securely

#### Setting Up AWS RAM
To begin sharing resources, you need to configure AWS RAM in your management account. This account will act as the administrator and manage resource shares across your organization or with specific AWS accounts.

**Steps to Set Up AWS RAM:** Log in to the AWS Management Console with the management account. Navigate to the AWS RAM console. Click on "Create resource share" to start the configuration process.

## Creating Resource Shares

When creating a resource share, you define which resources to share and specify the accounts or organizational units (OUs) that will have access to these resources. You can also apply tags to the resource share for better organization and management.

**Steps to Create a Resource Share:** In the AWS RAM console, click on "Create resource share." Select the resources you want to share, such as VPC subnets, Route 53 Resolver rules, or license configurations. Specify the principals (AWS accounts or OUs) that will have access to these resources. You can choose specific account IDs or select OUs if you are using AWS Organizations. Optionally, apply tags to the resource share to categorize and manage it easily. Review the configuration and create the resource share.

Example: Sharing a VPC Subnet:

```
1. aws ram create-resource-share --name "MyResourceShare" \
2. --resource-arns arn:aws:ec2:region:account-id:subnet/subnet-id \
3. --principals account-id1 account-id2
```

This command shares a VPC subnet with two specified AWS accounts.

## Accepting Resource Shares

The specified AWS accounts or OUs need to accept the resource share invitation to access the shared resources. This ensures that only authorized accounts can utilize the shared resources.

**Steps to Accept a Resource Share:** The recipient account logs in to the AWS Management Console. Navigate to the AWS RAM console. In the "Shared with me" section, find the resource share invitation and accept it.

## Using Shared Resources

Once the resource share is accepted, the shared resources become available to the recipient accounts. These resources can be used as if they were created in the recipient account, enabling seamless integration and operation.

**Example Use Case:**
Consider an organization with multiple AWS accounts for different business units. Each business unit requires access to a common VPC subnet for networking purposes. Instead of creating duplicate subnets in each account, the organization can use AWS RAM to share a single VPC subnet across all accounts. The management account creates a resource share for the VPC subnet and shares it with the relevant accounts. Each account then accepts the resource share and gains access to the subnet, allowing them to use the shared network infrastructure without duplication.

## Benefits of Using AWS RAM

**Cost Efficiency:** Sharing resources reduces the need to create and manage duplicate resources, leading to cost savings and simplified management.

**Centralized Control:** AWS RAM enables centralized management of resource shares, ensuring that sharing is controlled and monitored by the management account.

**Security and Compliance:** Resource sharing through AWS RAM adheres to AWS security best practices, ensuring that only authorized accounts can access shared resources. Tags and IAM policies can be used to enforce compliance and governance.

**Scalability:** AWS RAM supports sharing with multiple accounts or organizational units, making it easy to scale resource sharing across large organizations.

By leveraging AWS RAM, organizations can securely share resources across AWS accounts, enhancing efficiency, reducing costs, and maintaining robust security and compliance.

## 13.12 Evaluating Compliance of AWS Resources

Evaluating the compliance of AWS resources is crucial for maintaining security, governance, and adherence to regulatory standards. By continuously assessing the configurations and operations of cloud resources, organizations can ensure they meet internal policies and external requirements. AWS provides several tools and services, such as AWS Config, AWS Audit Manager, and AWS Security Hub, to help monitor and evaluate the compliance of AWS resources effectively.

## 13.12.1 Data Classification with AWS Services

Data classification is an essential practice for ensuring proper handling and compliance of sensitive information within an organization. It involves categorizing data based on its sensitivity and the level of protection it requires. AWS provides various services and tools that facilitate effective data classification, enabling organizations to manage their data securely and comply with regulatory requirements.

Techniques for Data Classification Using AWS Services

### AWS Macie

AWS Macie is a fully managed data security and data privacy service that uses machine learning and pattern matching to discover and protect sensitive data. Macie automatically identifies and classifies sensitive data such as personally identifiable information (PII), financial data, and intellectual property stored in Amazon S3. It provides dashboards and alerts for real-time visibility into data security and compliance risks.

**Example:** An organization can use AWS Macie to scan its S3 buckets for sensitive information. Macie will classify the data and generate alerts if it detects any PII, such as social security numbers or credit card information, helping the organization take immediate action to secure the data.

```
aws macie2 create-classification-job --name MyMacieJob --s3-job-definition
'{"bucketDefinitions":[{"accountId":"123456789012","buckets":["my-sensitive-data-bucket"]}]}' --
custom-data-identifier-ids <custom-data-identifier-ids> --client-token <client-token>
```

### AWS Glue Data Catalog

AWS Glue Data Catalog is a central repository to store metadata about data assets. By creating and managing data catalogs, organizations can classify data across various AWS services, making it easier to search, query, and analyze data while ensuring it is handled according to its classification level.

**Example:** An organization can use AWS Glue Data Catalog to tag datasets with classifications such as "Confidential," "Internal Use Only," and "Public." These tags can then be used to control access and enforce data handling policies across different AWS services.

```
1.  # Example of defining a table with classification in AWS Glue Data Catalog
2.  {
3.    "DatabaseName": "mydatabase",
4.    "TableInput": {
5.      "Name": "mytable",
6.      "StorageDescriptor": {
7.        "Columns": [
8.          {"Name": "id", "Type": "int"},
9.          {"Name": "name", "Type": "string"},
10.         {"Name": "ssn", "Type": "string"}
11.       ],
12.       "Location": "s3://my-data-bucket/",
13.       "InputFormat": "org.apache.hadoop.mapred.TextInputFormat",
14.       "OutputFormat": "org.apache.hadoop.hive.ql.io.HiveIgnoreKeyTextOutputFormat"
```

```
15.     },
16.     "TableType": "EXTERNAL_TABLE",
17.     "Parameters": {
18.       "classification": "confidential"
19.     }
20.   }
21. }
```

## AWS Key Management Service (KMS)

AWS KMS helps manage encryption keys used to protect classified data. By tagging keys with data classification levels, organizations can enforce encryption policies that align with the sensitivity of the data. KMS integrates with other AWS services, ensuring that data is encrypted at rest and in transit according to its classification.

**Example:** Encrypt sensitive data in an S3 bucket using a KMS key tagged as "Confidential." This ensures that only users with the appropriate permissions can decrypt and access the data.

```
aws s3api put-object --bucket my-data-bucket --key sensitive-data.txt --body sensitive-data.txt --server-side-encryption aws:kms --ssekms-key-id <kms-key-id>
```

## AWS Identity and Access Management (IAM)

IAM policies can enforce access controls based on data classification. By using tags and policies, organizations can ensure that only authorized users can access sensitive data, aligning access permissions with data classification levels.

**Example:** Create an IAM policy that allows access to S3 objects tagged as "Public" but denies access to objects tagged as "Confidential" unless the user has the appropriate role.

```
1.  {
2.    "Version": "2012-10-17",
3.    "Statement": [
4.      {
5.        "Effect": "Deny",
6.        "Action": "s3:GetObject",
7.        "Resource": "arn:aws:s3:::my-data-bucket/*",
8.        "Condition": {
9.          "StringEquals": {
10.           "aws:RequestTag/classification": "confidential"
11.         }
12.       }
13.     },
14.     {
15.       "Effect": "Allow",
16.       "Action": "s3:GetObject",
17.       "Resource": "arn:aws:s3:::my-data-bucket/*",
18.       "Condition": {
19.         "StringEquals": {
20.           "aws:RequestTag/classification": "public"
21.         }
22.       }
23.     }
24.   ]
25. }
```

By leveraging AWS services such as AWS Macie, AWS Glue Data Catalog, AWS KMS, and AWS IAM, organizations can effectively classify their data, enforce appropriate handling procedures, and ensure compliance with regulatory requirements. These tools provide comprehensive capabilities for discovering, tagging, encrypting, and controlling access to data based on its classification, thereby enhancing overall data security and governance.

## 13.12.2 Assessing and Auditing Configurations

Assessing, auditing, and evaluating the configurations of AWS resources is crucial for maintaining security, compliance, and operational efficiency. AWS Config is a powerful service that provides a detailed view of the configurations of AWS resources in your account, tracks changes, and evaluates resource configurations against desired settings. By using AWS Config, organizations can ensure that their resources remain compliant with internal policies and external regulations, detect configuration drift, and manage resource changes effectively.

### Using AWS Config for Configuration Assessment

AWS Config continuously monitors and records the configuration of your AWS resources. It provides a history of configuration changes and allows you to compare the current state of your resources with previous states or desired configurations.

**Example:** To enable AWS Config, you can use the AWS Management Console, AWS CLI, or AWS SDKs. Here's a CLI example to create a configuration recorder and start recording:

```
1. aws configservice put-configuration-recorder --configuration-recorder name=default --role-arn arn:aws:iam::account-id:role/AWSConfigRole
2. aws configservice start-configuration-recorder --configuration-recorder-name default
```

Once enabled, AWS Config records the configurations of supported resources, such as EC2 instances, S3 buckets, and IAM policies, and stores the configuration history in an S3 bucket.

### Auditing Configurations with AWS Config Rules

AWS Config rules allow you to define compliance policies for your AWS resources. These rules evaluate the configuration of resources continuously and provide a compliance status for each resource.

**Example:** Suppose you want to ensure that all S3 buckets are configured with server-side encryption. You can use an AWS Config managed rule called s3-bucket-server-side-encryption-enabled to achieve this:

```
aws configservice put-config-rule --config-rule '{"ConfigRuleName": "s3-bucket-encryption", "Source": {"Owner": "AWS", "SourceIdentifier": "S3_BUCKET_SERVER_SIDE_ENCRYPTION_ENABLED"}}'
```

This rule evaluates all S3 buckets and marks them as compliant or non-compliant based on their encryption settings. AWS Config provides a dashboard where you can view the compliance status of all resources and take corrective actions for non-compliant resources.

### Evaluating Resource Configurations with AWS Config Aggregators

AWS Config aggregators enable you to aggregate configuration data from multiple AWS accounts and regions into a single account. This provides a centralized view of resource configurations and compliance status across your entire organization.

**Example:** To create an aggregator that collects configuration data from multiple accounts, you can use the following CLI command:

```
aws configservice put-configuration-aggregator --configuration-aggregator-name MyAggregator --account-sources AccountId=123456789012,AllAwsRegions=true
```

Replace 123456789012 with the account ID from which you want to aggregate data. This command creates an aggregator that collects configuration and compliance data from all regions in the specified account, providing a unified view for auditing and evaluation.

### Continuous Monitoring and Alerts

AWS Config integrates with AWS CloudWatch to provide continuous monitoring and alerts for configuration changes and compliance violations. You can set up CloudWatch Alarms to receive notifications when resources become non-compliant or when significant configuration changes occur.

**Example:** To create a CloudWatch Alarm for a specific AWS Config rule, use the following CLI command:

```
aws cloudwatch put-metric-alarm --alarm-name S3BucketEncryptionAlarm --metric-name 
ComplianceResourceCount --namespace AWS/Config --statistic Average --period 300 --threshold 1 --
comparison-operator LessThanThreshold --dimensions Name=ConfigRuleName,Value=s3-bucket-encryption --
evaluation-periods 1 --alarm-actions arn:aws:sns:region:account-id:sns-topic
```

This command sets up an alarm that triggers when the number of compliant S3 buckets falls below the threshold, sending a notification to an SNS topic.

By leveraging AWS Config, organizations can continuously assess, audit, and evaluate the configurations of their AWS resources. AWS Config provides a comprehensive view of resource configurations, tracks changes, enforces compliance through rules, aggregates data across accounts and regions, and integrates with CloudWatch for continuous monitoring and alerts. These capabilities ensure that resources remain secure, compliant, and operationally efficient, helping organizations maintain control over their AWS environment.

## 13.13 Compliance Evaluation

Compliance evaluation is the process of assessing and verifying that cloud resources and configurations adhere to regulatory requirements, internal policies, and industry standards. By using tools like AWS Config, organizations can automate the evaluation of their resources, ensuring continuous compliance and the ability to quickly identify and remediate non-compliant configurations. Regular compliance evaluations help mitigate risks, maintain security, and ensure operational integrity.

## 13.13.1 Identifying Sensitive Data

Amazon Macie is a fully managed data security and data privacy service that uses machine learning and pattern matching to discover and protect sensitive data in your AWS environment. By continuously monitoring and analyzing data stored in Amazon S3, Macie helps identify personal data, financial information, and other types of sensitive content, providing valuable insights and actionable alerts to enhance data protection and compliance.

### Using Amazon Macie to Identify Sensitive Data

Amazon Macie automatically scans S3 buckets to detect and classify sensitive data. It identifies data such as personally identifiable information (PII), financial records, and credentials. Once Macie is enabled, it continuously monitors your S3 environment, providing a comprehensive view of your data security posture and alerting you to any risks.

Setup and Configuration: To start using Amazon Macie, you need to enable the service in your AWS account. This involves setting up a Macie administrator account and configuring it to scan your S3 buckets.

## Example:

**Enable Amazon Macie:** Navigate to the Amazon Macie console. Click "Enable Macie" to start the setup process. Macie will automatically begin scanning your S3 buckets for sensitive data.

**Create a Classification Job:** Go to the Macie console and select "Jobs." Click "Create job" to define the scope and criteria for your data classification job. Choose the S3 buckets you want Macie to scan. Specify the types of sensitive data you are interested in, such as PII or financial information.

```
1. aws macie2 create-classification-job --name "SensitiveDataScanJob" --s3-job-definition '{"bucketDefinitions":[{"accountId":"123456789012","buckets":["my-data-bucket"]}]}' --custom-data-identifier-ids <custom-data-identifier-ids> --client-token <client-token>
2.
```

In this example, replace "123456789012" with your account ID and specify your S3 bucket name.

## Analyzing Results

After the job is created and executed, Macie provides detailed findings about the sensitive data detected in your S3 buckets. These findings include information such as the type of sensitive data, the specific files where the data was found, and the severity of the findings. This allows you to take appropriate actions to secure the data and mitigate risks.

**Example Findings:** Macie may identify files containing social security numbers, credit card information, or API keys. For each finding, Macie provides the file path, the type of sensitive data detected, and a recommendation for remediation.

```
1. {
2.   "accountId": "123456789012",
3.   "bucketName": "my-data-bucket",
4.   "objectKey": "sensitive-data.txt",
5.   "findingType": "SensitiveData:S3Object/Personal",
6.   "severity": {
7.     "description": "High",
8.     "score": 8.5
9.   },
10.  "createdAt": "2024-07-24T12:00:00Z"
11. }
```

## Automating Actions

You can automate actions based on Macie findings using AWS Lambda and Amazon SNS. For instance, you can configure Macie to send alerts to an SNS topic when sensitive data is detected. An associated Lambda function can then take predefined actions, such as encrypting the detected files, moving them to a secure location, or notifying the security team.

### Example Automation:

Create an SNS Topic: In the SNS console, create a new topic to receive Macie alerts.
Set Up a Lambda Function: Create a Lambda function that subscribes to the SNS topic. Define the function to take actions based on Macie findings, such as logging the event, encrypting the file, or alerting the security team.

```
1. aws sns create-topic --name MacieFindingsTopic
2. aws lambda create-function --function-name ProcessMacieFindings --runtime python3.8 --role arn:aws:iam::123456789012:role/lambda-execution-role --handler lambda_function.lambda_handler --zip-file fileb://function.zip
```

By leveraging Amazon Macie, organizations can proactively identify and protect sensitive data within their AWS environment. This capability is crucial for maintaining data privacy, meeting regulatory compliance requirements, and enhancing overall data security.

## 13.13.2 Creating AWS Config Rules

Creating AWS Config rules to detect noncompliant AWS resources is an effective way to ensure that your AWS environment adheres to security, operational, and compliance standards. AWS Config rules continuously evaluate the configuration settings of your AWS resources against desired configurations and provide notifications when resources deviate from these standards. By automating compliance checks, AWS Config helps maintain a secure and well-managed cloud environment.

### Creating AWS Config Rules

AWS Config rules can be created using the AWS Management Console, AWS CLI, or AWS SDKs. There are two types of AWS Config rules: managed rules and custom rules. Managed rules are predefined by AWS and cover common compliance scenarios, while custom rules allow you to define your own compliance checks using AWS Lambda functions.

**Example: Creating a Managed Config Rule**

To ensure that all S3 buckets have server-side encryption enabled, you can use the managed rule S3_BUCKET_SERVER_SIDE_ENCRYPTION_ENABLED.

**Using the AWS Management Console:** Navigate to the AWS Config console. In the left navigation pane, choose "Rules." Click "Add rule." Search for S3_BUCKET_SERVER_SIDE_ENCRYPTION_ENABLED and select it. Configure the rule by specifying the scope (all resources or specific ones) and any additional parameters. Click "Add rule" to create the rule.

**Using the AWS CLI:**
```
aws configservice put-config-rule --config-rule '{"ConfigRuleName": "s3-bucket-encryption", "Source": {"Owner": "AWS", "SourceIdentifier": "S3_BUCKET_SERVER_SIDE_ENCRYPTION_ENABLED"}}'
```

This rule continuously evaluates all S3 buckets in your account to ensure they have server-side encryption enabled. If a bucket does not comply, AWS Config marks it as noncompliant and can trigger alerts or remediation actions.

Example:
**Creating a Custom Config Rule:** For scenarios not covered by managed rules, you can create custom rules using AWS Lambda. Custom rules allow you to write custom logic to evaluate resource configurations.

**Create a Lambda Function:** Write a Lambda function that checks for compliance. For instance, a function to ensure that EC2 instances are of a specific type:

```
1. import json
2. import boto3
3.
4. def lambda_handler(event, context):
5.     config = boto3.client('config')
6.     ec2 = boto3.client('ec2')
7.
8.     # Get the list of all EC2 instances
9.     response = ec2.describe_instances()
10.    non_compliant_instances = []
11.
```

```
12.        for reservation in response['Reservations']:
13.            for instance in reservation['Instances']:
14.                if instance['InstanceType'] != 't2.micro':
15.                    non_compliant_instances.append(instance['InstanceId'])
16.
17.        # Report the result to AWS Config
18.        config.put_evaluations(
19.            Evaluations=[
20.                {
21.                    'ComplianceResourceType': 'AWS::EC2::Instance',
22.                    'ComplianceResourceId': instance['InstanceId'],
23.                    'ComplianceType': 'NON_COMPLIANT' if instance['InstanceId'] in non_compliant_instances else 'COMPLIANT',
24.                    'OrderingTimestamp': instance['LaunchTime']
25.                },
26.            ],
27.            ResultToken=event['resultToken']
28.        )
29.
30.        return {
31.            'statusCode': 200,
32.            'body': json.dumps('Compliance check complete')
33.        }
34.
```

**Create the Custom Rule:** In the AWS Config console, go to "Rules" and click "Add rule." Choose "Add custom rule." Provide a name and description for the rule. Select the Lambda function created earlier. Specify the trigger type (e.g., configuration changes or periodic checks). Define the scope of the rule (all resources or specific types). Click "Add rule" to create the custom rule.

**Using the AWS CLI:**

```
aws configservice put-config-rule --config-rule '{"ConfigRuleName": "ec2-instance-type-check", "Source": {"Owner": "CUSTOM_LAMBDA", "SourceIdentifier": "arn:aws:lambda:region:account-id:function:function-name"}, "InputParameters": "{\"desiredInstanceType\":\"t2.micro\"}"}'
```

### Monitoring and Managing Compliance

After creating AWS Config rules, you can monitor the compliance status of your resources through the AWS Config console. AWS Config provides a dashboard that shows the compliance status of all resources and details of noncompliant resources. You can set up Amazon CloudWatch Alarms to receive notifications when resources become noncompliant, enabling you to take immediate corrective actions.

By creating AWS Config rules, organizations can automate the detection of noncompliant AWS resources and ensure continuous compliance with internal policies and external regulations. Managed rules simplify the process for common compliance checks, while custom rules provide flexibility for specific requirements. Regularly monitoring compliance status and responding to noncompliant findings help maintain a secure and well-managed AWS environment.

## 13.13.3 Collecting and Organizing Evidence

Using AWS Security Hub and AWS Audit Manager to collect and organize evidence for compliance audits streamlines the process of maintaining and demonstrating compliance with industry standards and regulations. These tools provide comprehensive security and compliance visibility, automate evidence collection, and help organize audit documentation, ensuring that your AWS environment adheres to best practices and regulatory requirements.

## Using AWS Security Hub for Compliance

AWS Security Hub is a security and compliance service that centralizes and prioritizes security findings from multiple AWS services, such as Amazon GuardDuty, Amazon Inspector, and AWS Config. Security Hub continuously monitors your AWS environment against security standards and best practices, providing a consolidated view of your security and compliance status.

### Key Features of AWS Security Hub:

**Security Standards:** Security Hub includes predefined security standards, such as the AWS Foundational Security Best Practices, CIS AWS Foundations Benchmark, and PCI DSS standards. These standards help evaluate the security configuration of your AWS resources.

**Centralized Findings:** Security Hub aggregates security findings from various AWS services and third-party tools, providing a single pane of glass for security and compliance monitoring.

**Automated Insights:** Security Hub uses machine learning and automation to analyze findings and provide actionable insights, helping you prioritize and remediate security issues.

### Example:

To enable Security Hub and evaluate your AWS environment against the CIS AWS Foundations Benchmark:

**Enable Security Hub:** Navigate to the AWS Security Hub console. Click "Enable Security Hub" to start the setup process.

**Enable Security Standards:** In the Security Hub console, go to "Standards" and select the CIS AWS Foundations Benchmark. Security Hub will begin evaluating your resources against the selected standard.

```
1. aws securityhub enable-security-hub
2.     aws    securityhub    batch-enable-standards    --standards-subscription-requests
StandardsArn=arn:aws:securityhub:us-west-2::standards/cis-aws-foundations-benchmark/v/1.2.0
```

## Using AWS Audit Manager for Compliance Audits

AWS Audit Manager automates the collection of evidence needed to prepare for audits, helping you continuously audit your AWS usage and simplify compliance with industry standards and regulations. Audit Manager enables you to map your AWS resources and configurations to specific control requirements, automating evidence collection and organizing audit documentation.

### Key Features of AWS Audit Manager:

**Predefined Frameworks:** Audit Manager includes predefined frameworks for common standards, such as GDPR, HIPAA, PCI DSS, and ISO 27001. These frameworks map AWS services and resources to control requirements.

**Automated Evidence Collection:** Audit Manager automatically collects evidence from AWS services based on your defined frameworks and control mappings.

**Custom Frameworks:** You can create custom frameworks to tailor evidence collection to your specific compliance requirements.

### Example:

To create an assessment for PCI DSS compliance using AWS Audit Manager:

**Enable Audit Manager:** Navigate to the AWS Audit Manager console. Click "Get started" to enable the service.

**Create an Assessment:** In the Audit Manager console, click "Create assessment." Provide a name and description for the assessment. Select the PCI DSS framework from the list of predefined frameworks. Choose the AWS accounts and services to include in the assessment. Configure the assessment settings and click "Create assessment."

```
aws auditmanager create-assessment --name "PCI DSS Assessment" --description "Assessment for PCI DSS compliance" --framework-id <framework-id> --roles arn:aws:iam::123456789012:role/AuditManagerRole
```

### Integrating Security Hub and Audit Manager

By integrating AWS Security Hub with AWS Audit Manager, you can enhance the efficiency of your compliance audits. Security Hub findings can be used as evidence in Audit Manager assessments, providing a seamless flow of security information into your audit documentation.

**Example Integration:**

**Export Security Hub Findings:** In the Security Hub console, go to "Findings." Select the findings relevant to your compliance requirements and export them as a CSV or JSON file.

**Import Findings into Audit Manager:** In the Audit Manager console, go to your assessment and click "Import evidence." Upload the exported Security Hub findings as evidence for the relevant control requirements.

Using AWS Security Hub and AWS Audit Manager together allows organizations to efficiently collect and organize evidence for compliance audits. Security Hub provides continuous security and compliance monitoring, while Audit Manager automates evidence collection and organizes audit documentation. This integration ensures that your AWS environment adheres to regulatory requirements and industry standards, simplifying the audit process and enhancing overall security posture.

## 13.14 Identifying Security Gaps through Reviews and Analysis

Identifying security gaps through reviews and analysis is essential for maintaining a robust and secure cloud environment. Regular security reviews and thorough analysis help detect vulnerabilities, misconfigurations, and compliance issues before they can be exploited. By systematically evaluating security postures, organizations can proactively address potential threats, ensuring that their AWS infrastructure remains resilient against attacks.

## 13.14.1 Anomaly Identification Based on Cost and Usage

Using AWS cost and usage data to identify anomalies is a powerful method for uncovering potential security issues in your cloud environment. By monitoring cost and usage patterns, you can detect unusual spikes or irregular activities that may indicate a security breach, misconfiguration, or unauthorized usage. AWS provides various tools and services, such as AWS Cost Explorer, AWS Budgets, and AWS CloudWatch, to help analyze cost and usage data and set up alerts for anomalies.

### Identifying Anomalies with AWS Cost Explorer

AWS Cost Explorer allows you to visualize and analyze your cost and usage data over time. It provides detailed insights into your AWS spending, enabling you to identify trends and detect anomalies.

Example: Suppose you notice a sudden increase in EC2 instance usage in a particular region where you don't typically operate. This could indicate unauthorized usage or a misconfigured auto-scaling policy.

### Steps to Use AWS Cost Explorer:
**Access Cost Explorer:** Navigate to the AWS Cost Management console and select "Cost Explorer." Enable Cost Explorer if it is not already enabled.

**Analyze Cost and Usage:** Use the Cost Explorer dashboard to visualize your cost and usage data. Filter and group data by service, region, or usage type to identify anomalies.

```
aws ce get-cost-and-usage --time-period Start=2024-07-01,End=2024-07-24 --granularity MONTHLY --metrics "BlendedCost" --group-by Type=DIMENSION,Key=SERVICE
```

## Setting Up AWS Budgets for Anomaly Detection
AWS Budgets allows you to set custom cost and usage budgets and receive alerts when your spending exceeds the defined thresholds. By setting up budgets, you can proactively monitor your costs and detect anomalies early.

Example: Create a budget to monitor monthly spending on EC2 instances. Set an alert to notify you if the spending exceeds a certain threshold, indicating potential unauthorized usage.

### Steps to Use AWS Budgets:

**Create a Budget:** Navigate to the AWS Budgets console. Click "Create budget" and select "Cost budget." Define the budget parameters, such as the amount and time period.

**Set Alerts:** Configure alerts to notify you when your spending exceeds the defined threshold. Specify the email addresses or SNS topics to receive notifications.

```
1. aws budgets create-budget --account-id 123456789012 --budget '{"BudgetName": "MonthlyEC2Budget", "BudgetLimit": {"Amount": "500", "Unit": "USD"}, "TimeUnit": "MONTHLY", "CostFilters": {"Service": ["Amazon Elastic Compute Cloud - Compute"]}}'
2. aws budgets create-notification --account-id 123456789012 --budget-name "MonthlyEC2Budget" --notification '{"NotificationType": "ACTUAL", "ComparisonOperator": "GREATER_THAN", "Threshold": 80.0, "ThresholdType": "PERCENTAGE"}' --subscribers '[{"SubscriptionType": "EMAIL", "Address": "user@example.com"}]'
```

## Monitoring with AWS CloudWatch
AWS CloudWatch provides monitoring and observability for your AWS resources and applications. By setting up CloudWatch Alarms, you can receive real-time alerts for unusual activity in your cost and usage patterns.

Example: Monitor the number of API calls to your AWS account. A sudden spike in API calls could indicate a security issue, such as a compromised access key.

### Steps to Use AWS CloudWatch:
**Create a CloudWatch Alarm:** Navigate to the CloudWatch console and select "Alarms." Click "Create Alarm" and choose the metric you want to monitor (e.g., API call count).

**Configure the Alarm:** Define the threshold for the alarm and set up notifications. Specify the actions to take when the alarm is triggered, such as sending an SNS notification.

```
aws cloudwatch put-metric-alarm --alarm-name "HighAPICallVolume" --metric-name "APICallCount" --namespace "AWS/Usage" --statistic "Sum" --period 300 --threshold 1000 --comparison-operator "GreaterThanThreshold" --evaluation-periods 1 --alarm-actions arn:aws:sns:us-west-2:123456789012:NotifyMe
```

By leveraging AWS cost and usage data, organizations can detect anomalies that may indicate security issues. AWS Cost Explorer, AWS Budgets, and AWS CloudWatch provide powerful tools to analyze cost patterns, set up budgets and alerts, and monitor resource usage in real-time. These tools enable proactive identification and response to potential security incidents, helping maintain a secure and well-managed AWS environment.

## 13.14.2 Anomaly Identification Based on Resource Util and Trends

Identifying anomalies based on resource utilization and trends is a critical practice for maintaining the security, performance, and cost-efficiency of your AWS environment. Techniques such as monitoring usage patterns, setting thresholds for alerts, employing machine learning models, and using AWS-native tools like AWS CloudWatch and Amazon Lookout for Metrics can help detect unusual activities that may indicate security issues, misconfigurations, or operational inefficiencies.

### Monitoring Usage Patterns

Monitoring the usage patterns of your AWS resources over time helps establish a baseline of normal behavior. By understanding what typical resource utilization looks like, you can more easily spot deviations that may signal anomalies. AWS CloudWatch provides metrics for various AWS services, enabling you to track and visualize resource usage trends.

**Example:** Use AWS CloudWatch to monitor the CPU utilization of EC2 instances. Create a CloudWatch dashboard to visualize CPU usage trends over the past month. If an instance shows an unexpected spike in CPU usage, it could indicate a security breach, such as a compromised instance being used for cryptocurrency mining.

```
aws cloudwatch get-metric-statistics --metric-name CPUUtilization --start-time 2024-06-01T00:00:00Z --end-time 2024-07-01T00:00:00Z --period 3600 --namespace AWS/EC2 --statistics Average --dimensions Name=InstanceId,Value=i-1234567890abcdef0
```

### Setting Thresholds for Alerts

Setting thresholds for resource usage metrics can help trigger alerts when utilization exceeds expected levels. AWS CloudWatch Alarms can be configured to notify you when specific metrics cross predefined thresholds, enabling you to take immediate action.

Example: Create a CloudWatch Alarm to monitor the read/write operations on an RDS database. If the number of read operations suddenly increases beyond a certain threshold, it could indicate a potential DDoS attack or an inefficient query causing high load.

```
aws cloudwatch put-metric-alarm --alarm-name "HighReadOpsOnRDS" --metric-name ReadIOPS --namespace AWS/RDS --statistic Average --period 300 --threshold 1000 --comparison-operator GreaterThanThreshold --evaluation-periods 1 --dimensions Name=DBInstanceIdentifier,Value=mydbinstance --alarm-actions arn:aws:sns:us-west-2:123456789012:NotifyMe
```

### Employing Machine Learning Models

Machine learning models can automatically detect anomalies by analyzing historical data and identifying patterns that deviate from the norm. Amazon Lookout for Metrics is an AWS service that uses machine learning to detect anomalies in your data without requiring you to build custom models.
Example: Use Amazon Lookout for Metrics to monitor billing data for unexpected spikes in costs. If the service detects an anomaly, such as a sudden increase in S3 storage costs, it can alert you to investigate further.

### Steps to Use Amazon Lookout for Metrics:
**Create a Dataset:** In the Amazon Lookout for Metrics console, create a new dataset by connecting to your billing data source.

**Configure the Anomaly Detector:** Set up the anomaly detector to analyze the dataset and specify the detection interval.

**Review and Act on Anomalies:** Amazon Lookout for Metrics will continuously analyze the data and alert you to any detected anomalies. Investigate these anomalies to determine if they indicate security issues or misconfigurations.

## Utilizing AWS Trusted Advisor
AWS Trusted Advisor provides real-time guidance to help you provision your resources following AWS best practices. It includes checks for cost optimization, security, fault tolerance, performance, and service limits. Trusted Advisor's checks can help identify anomalies in resource utilization that might indicate potential issues. Example: Use AWS Trusted Advisor to check for underutilized or idle EC2 instances. An unexpected increase in the number of idle instances might indicate that resources are being launched without proper planning or could signal automation issues.

## Example Scenario
Consider an organization that runs a fleet of EC2 instances for a web application. By setting up CloudWatch dashboards and alarms, they monitor CPU utilization, network traffic, and disk I/O metrics. Additionally, they employ Amazon Lookout for Metrics to analyze application usage patterns and billing data. One day, they receive an alert from CloudWatch indicating a sudden spike in network traffic for one of the instances. Simultaneously, Amazon Lookout for Metrics detects an anomaly in the billing data, showing a sharp increase in costs related to data transfer. Investigating these anomalies, the security team discovers that the instance was compromised and used for unauthorized data transfer. They take immediate action to mitigate the issue, shut down the compromised instance, and review security policies to prevent future incidents.

By leveraging techniques such as monitoring usage patterns, setting thresholds for alerts, employing machine learning models, and utilizing AWS tools like CloudWatch, Trusted Advisor, and Amazon Lookout for Metrics, organizations can effectively identify anomalies based on resource utilization and trends. These practices enhance the security, performance, and cost-efficiency of AWS environments, enabling proactive detection and mitigation of potential issues.

# 13.14.3 Reducing Attack Surfaces
Reducing attack surfaces in AWS environments is crucial for minimizing the risk of unauthorized access and potential security breaches. This involves implementing various strategies that limit the exposure of your resources and strengthen the security posture of your AWS infrastructure. Key strategies include network segmentation, enforcing least privilege access, using secure configurations, continuous monitoring, and implementing automated security practices.

## Network Segmentation
Network segmentation involves dividing your AWS environment into isolated networks to restrict access and control traffic flow between different segments. By using Amazon Virtual Private Cloud (VPC) to create separate subnets for different application tiers, you can ensure that only necessary communication is allowed, reducing the potential impact of a security breach.

**Example:** Create separate VPC subnets for web servers, application servers, and databases. Use security groups and network ACLs to restrict traffic between these subnets, allowing only specific, necessary traffic.

```
1.  Resources:
2.    MyVPC:
3.      Type: AWS::EC2::VPC
4.      Properties:
5.        CidrBlock: 10.0.0.0/16
6.        EnableDnsSupport: true
7.        EnableDnsHostnames: true
8.    WebSubnet:
9.      Type: AWS::EC2::Subnet
10.     Properties:
11.       VpcId: !Ref MyVPC
12.       CidrBlock: 10.0.1.0/24
13.       MapPublicIpOnLaunch: true
14.   AppSubnet:
15.     Type: AWS::EC2::Subnet
16.     Properties:
17.       VpcId: !Ref MyVPC
18.       CidrBlock: 10.0.2.0/24
19.   DBSubnet:
20.     Type: AWS::EC2::Subnet
21.     Properties:
22.       VpcId: !Ref MyVPC
23.       CidrBlock: 10.0.3.0/24
24.
```

## Enforcing Least Privilege Access

Implementing the principle of least privilege involves granting users and applications the minimum permissions necessary to perform their tasks. By using AWS Identity and Access Management (IAM) roles and policies, you can enforce granular access controls, ensuring that users and services have only the permissions they need to perform their functions.

Example: Create an IAM policy that grants read-only access to S3 buckets for a specific user group, ensuring that they cannot modify or delete data.

```
1.  {
2.    "Version": "2012-10-17",
3.    "Statement": [
4.      {
5.        "Effect": "Allow",
6.        "Action": ["s3:GetObject", "s3:ListBucket"],
7.        "Resource": ["arn:aws:s3:::my-bucket", "arn:aws:s3:::my-bucket/*"]
8.      }
9.    ]
10. }
```

## Using Secure Configurations

Ensuring that your AWS resources are securely configured helps reduce vulnerabilities. Use AWS Config to continuously monitor configurations and enforce compliance with security best practices. AWS Config rules can automatically check resource configurations and alert you to any deviations.

Example: Use AWS Config to ensure that all S3 buckets have server-side encryption enabled.

```
aws configservice put-config-rule --config-rule '{"ConfigRuleName": "s3-bucket-encryption", "Source": {"Owner": "AWS", "SourceIdentifier": "S3_BUCKET_SERVER_SIDE_ENCRYPTION_ENABLED"}}'
```

### Continuous Monitoring

Continuous monitoring of your AWS environment helps detect and respond to security incidents in real-time. Use services like Amazon GuardDuty, AWS CloudTrail, and Amazon CloudWatch to monitor for suspicious activity, unauthorized access, and configuration changes.

Example: Enable GuardDuty to monitor your AWS environment for malicious activity and unauthorized behavior.

```
aws guardduty create-detector --enable
```

### Implementing Automated Security Practices

Automating security measures ensures consistent application of security practices and reduces the risk of human error. Use AWS Lambda and AWS Config rules to automate security checks and remediation actions.

**Example:** Use AWS Lambda to automatically remediate non-compliant S3 buckets by enabling server-side encryption.

```python
import boto3

def lambda_handler(event, context):
    s3 = boto3.client('s3')
    bucket = event['detail']['requestParameters']['bucketName']

    response = s3.put_bucket_encryption(
        Bucket=bucket,
        ServerSideEncryptionConfiguration={
            'Rules': [{
                'ApplyServerSideEncryptionByDefault': {
                    'SSEAlgorithm': 'AES256'
                }
            }]
        }
    )
    return response
```

Reducing the attack surface in AWS environments involves a multi-faceted approach that includes network segmentation, enforcing least privilege access, using secure configurations, continuous monitoring, and implementing automated security measures. By applying these strategies, organizations can enhance their security posture, minimize vulnerabilities, and reduce the risk of security incidents, ensuring a secure and well-managed AWS infrastructure.

## 13.14.4 Identifying Unused Resources

Using AWS tools like Trusted Advisor and AWS Cost Explorer to identify and remove unused resources is essential for optimizing costs and improving the efficiency of your AWS environment. These tools provide insights into resource utilization and cost patterns, enabling you to detect and eliminate underutilized or idle resources that contribute to unnecessary expenses.

### AWS Trusted Advisor

AWS Trusted Advisor is a service that offers real-time guidance to help you optimize your AWS environment according to best practices. It provides recommendations in several categories, including cost optimization, performance, security, fault tolerance, and service limits. Trusted Advisor helps you identify unused or underutilized resources, such as idle EC2 instances, unattached EBS volumes, and low-utilization RDS instances.

**Example:** To identify and remove unused EC2 instances using AWS Trusted Advisor:

**Access Trusted Advisor:** Navigate to the AWS Trusted Advisor console. Ensure that you have the necessary permissions to access Trusted Advisor checks.

**Review Cost Optimization Recommendations:** Go to the "Cost Optimization" category. Review the "Underutilized Amazon EC2 Instances" check to identify EC2 instances that have low utilization.

**Take Action:** Stop or terminate the identified idle instances to reduce costs.

```
aws ec2 describe-instances --filters "Name=instance-state-name,Values=running" --query "Reservations[*].Instances[*].[InstanceId,InstanceType,State.Name,Monitoring.State]"
```

## AWS Cost Explorer

AWS Cost Explorer is a tool that allows you to visualize, understand, and manage your AWS costs and usage over time. It provides detailed insights into your spending patterns, helping you identify areas where you can optimize costs by removing or downsizing unused resources.

Example: To identify and remove unused resources using AWS Cost Explorer:

**Access Cost Explorer:** Navigate to the AWS Cost Management console and select "Cost Explorer." Enable Cost Explorer if it is not already enabled.

**Analyze Cost and Usage Data:** Use the Cost Explorer dashboard to visualize your cost and usage data. Filter and group data by service, region, or usage type to identify resources with low or no utilization.

**Identify Unused Resources:** Look for services with consistent low usage, such as S3 buckets with little to no data access or EC2 instances with low CPU utilization.

**Take Action:** Decommission or downsize the identified resources to optimize costs.

```
aws ce get-cost-and-usage --time-period Start=2024-06-01,End=2024-07-01 --granularity MONTHLY --metrics "BlendedCost" --group-by Type=DIMENSION,Key=SERVICE
```

## Example Scenario

Consider an organization that runs multiple AWS services, including EC2, RDS, and S3. By using AWS Trusted Advisor, they identify several underutilized EC2 instances and unattached EBS volumes. Additionally, using AWS Cost Explorer, they notice that certain S3 buckets have not been accessed in months and that their RDS instances are consistently running below 20% CPU utilization.

### Steps Taken:

**Using Trusted Advisor:** Trusted Advisor recommends stopping or terminating the idle EC2 instances and deleting the unattached EBS volumes. The organization stops the identified EC2 instances, monitors their impact, and then terminates them if they are no longer needed.

**Using Cost Explorer:** Cost Explorer highlights the underutilized S3 buckets and RDS instances. The organization transitions the inactive S3 buckets to cheaper storage classes, such as S3 Glacier, and right-sizes the RDS instances to smaller instance types.

By leveraging AWS Trusted Advisor and AWS Cost Explorer, the organization successfully identifies and removes unused resources, leading to significant cost savings and a more efficient AWS environment.

AWS Trusted Advisor and AWS Cost Explorer are powerful tools for identifying and removing unused resources in your AWS environment. Trusted Advisor provides actionable recommendations to optimize costs and improve performance, while Cost Explorer offers detailed insights into spending patterns and resource utilization. By regularly using these tools, organizations can enhance their cloud efficiency, reduce unnecessary expenses, and ensure that their AWS resources are being utilized effectively.

## 13.14.5 AWS Well-Architected Framework

The AWS Well-Architected Framework is a set of best practices designed to help cloud architects build secure, high-performing, resilient, and efficient infrastructure for their applications. It comprises five pillars: Operational Excellence, Security, Reliability, Performance Efficiency, and Cost Optimization. The Security pillar focuses specifically on protecting information, systems, and assets through risk assessment and mitigation strategies. By using the AWS Well-Architected Framework, organizations can systematically review and improve their security postures.

### Using the AWS Well-Architected Framework for Security

The Security pillar of the AWS Well-Architected Framework encompasses several key areas: Identity and Access Management (IAM), Detective Controls, Infrastructure Protection, Data Protection, and Incident Response. Each area provides guidelines and best practices to help organizations secure their AWS environments effectively.

#### Identity and Access Management

AWS recommends implementing the principle of least privilege and using roles instead of long-term credentials. This involves creating fine-grained IAM policies, using multi-factor authentication (MFA), and regularly reviewing and rotating credentials.

**Example:** Use IAM roles to provide temporary access to AWS services and resources, ensuring that permissions are limited to what is necessary for a specific task. Enforce MFA for all IAM users to add an extra layer of security.

```
{
   "Version": "2012-10-17",
   "Statement": [
      {
         "Effect": "Allow",
         "Action": "s3:ListBucket",
         "Resource": "arn:aws:s3:::example-bucket"
      }
   ]
}
```

#### Detective Controls

Implementing detective controls involves continuously monitoring and logging activities in your AWS environment to identify potential security threats. AWS CloudTrail, Amazon CloudWatch, and AWS Config are key services for achieving this.

Example: Enable AWS CloudTrail to log all API calls and account activity across your AWS environment. Use Amazon CloudWatch to set up alarms for specific events, such as changes to security groups or unauthorized access attempts.

```
1. aws cloudtrail create-trail --name myTrail --s3-bucket-name my-trail-bucket
2. aws cloudtrail start-logging --name myTrail
```

### Infrastructure Protection

Infrastructure protection focuses on securing the network and computing resources in your AWS environment. This includes using VPCs, security groups, network ACLs, and AWS Shield to protect against DDoS attacks.

Example: Use security groups to control inbound and outbound traffic to your EC2 instances. Define rules that allow only necessary traffic, such as allowing SSH access only from specific IP addresses.

```
1. {
2.   "GroupName": "my-security-group",
3.   "Description": "My security group",
4.   "IpPermissions": [
5.     {
6.       "IpProtocol": "tcp",
7.       "FromPort": 22,
8.       "ToPort": 22,
9.       "IpRanges": [{"CidrIp": "203.0.113.0/24"}]
10.    }
11.  ]
12. }
```

### Data Protection

AWS emphasizes the importance of encrypting data at rest and in transit. Use AWS Key Management Service (KMS) to manage encryption keys and enforce encryption policies for sensitive data.

Example: Encrypt an S3 bucket using AWS KMS to ensure that data at rest is protected. Use the following command to enable default encryption on an S3 bucket.

```
1. aws s3api put-bucket-encryption --bucket my-secure-bucket --server-side-encryption-configuration
'{
2.   "Rules": [{
3.     "ApplyServerSideEncryptionByDefault": {
4.       "SSEAlgorithm": "aws:kms"
5.     }
6.   }]
7. }'
```

### Incident Response

Preparing for security incidents involves creating and testing incident response plans. AWS recommends automating incident response where possible to quickly mitigate the impact of security events.

Example: Use AWS Lambda to automate incident response actions, such as isolating compromised instances or revoking compromised credentials.

```
1. import boto3
2.
3. def lambda_handler(event, context):
4.     ec2 = boto3.client('ec2')
5.     instance_id = event['detail']['instance-id']
6.
7.     response = ec2.terminate_instances(InstanceIds=[instance_id])
8.     return response
9.
```

By leveraging the AWS Well-Architected Framework, organizations can systematically review and enhance their security postures across various domains. The framework provides a comprehensive set of best practices for identity and access management, detective controls, infrastructure protection, data protection, and incident response. Regularly reviewing your AWS environment against these best practices helps ensure that your infrastructure remains secure, resilient, and compliant with industry standards.

## 13.14.6 Using AWS Well-Architected Tool

The AWS Well-Architected Tool is a service designed to help organizations review and improve their cloud architectures based on AWS best practices. By using the tool, you can identify security gaps, assess your current infrastructure against the AWS Well-Architected Framework, and receive actionable recommendations to enhance your security posture. The tool focuses on the five pillars of the Well-Architected Framework: Operational Excellence, Security, Reliability, Performance Efficiency, and Cost Optimization, with a dedicated section for Security.

### Using the AWS Well-Architected Tool to Identify and Address Security Gaps

The following is the step-by-step process.

**Access the Well-Architected Tool:** Navigate to the AWS Management Console and select the AWS Well-Architected Tool from the Services menu. If you haven't used the tool before, you may need to set it up for your account.

**Define a Workload:** Create a new workload by providing basic information such as the workload name, description, environment (production, development, etc.), and the AWS region. Specify the industry type and the criticality of the workload to your business.

**Review Questions:** The tool presents a series of questions based on the five pillars of the Well-Architected Framework. For the Security pillar, questions focus on identity and access management, detective controls, infrastructure protection, data protection, and incident response. Answer the questions to the best of your ability. The tool provides detailed guidance and examples to help you understand the best practices and assess your current implementations.

**Example:** One of the questions under the Security pillar might be, "How do you protect your data at rest?" You would assess your current data encryption methods and identify if there are any gaps, such as unencrypted S3 buckets or databases.

### Identify Risks and Improvement Plans

After completing the assessment, the tool generates a report highlighting the high-risk areas and providing specific recommendations to address the identified gaps.

The report includes actionable steps to mitigate risks. For example, if the tool identifies that some S3 buckets are not encrypted, it will recommend enabling server-side encryption.

```
1. aws s3api put-bucket-encryption --bucket my-secure-bucket --server-side-encryption-configuration
'{
2.    "Rules": [{
3.      "ApplyServerSideEncryptionByDefault": {
4.        "SSEAlgorithm": "aws:kms"
5.      }
6.    }]
7. }'
```

**Implement Recommendations:** Use the detailed guidance provided in the report to implement the recommended changes. This might involve configuring IAM policies, enabling logging and monitoring, setting up encryption, and automating incident response. Regularly review and update your security practices based on the latest AWS best practices and the changing needs of your organization.

**Example:** If the assessment reveals that IAM roles are overly permissive, you can create more granular IAM policies to enforce the principle of least privilege.

```
{
  "Version": "2012-10-17",
  "Statement": [
    {
      "Effect": "Allow",
      "Action": "s3:ListBucket",
      "Resource": "arn:aws:s3:::example-bucket"
    }
  ]
}
```

### Continuous Improvement
The AWS Well-Architected Tool is not a one-time assessment; it should be used regularly to review and improve your security posture continually. As your infrastructure evolves, new risks and vulnerabilities may arise, making it crucial to periodically reassess your workloads.

### Example Scenario
A company uses the Well-Architected Tool to assess their e-commerce application. The tool identifies that their current logging setup is insufficient, lacking detailed logs for API access. The tool recommends enabling AWS CloudTrail and integrating with Amazon CloudWatch for better visibility and alerting.

```
aws cloudtrail create-trail --name myTrail --s3-bucket-name my-trail-bucket
aws cloudtrail start-logging --name myTrail
```

By following the recommendations, the company enhances its monitoring capabilities, enabling it to detect and respond to suspicious activities more effectively.

The AWS Well-Architected Tool is a valuable resource for identifying and addressing security gaps in your AWS environment. By systematically reviewing your workloads against AWS best practices and implementing the tool's recommendations, you can enhance your security posture, ensure compliance with industry standards, and reduce the risk of security incidents. Regular use of the tool promotes a culture of continuous improvement and proactive security management.

## 13.15 Lab Exercises
## 13.15.1 Deploying AWS Organizations
Deploying and configuring AWS Organizations provides a unified way to manage and govern multiple AWS accounts. AWS Organizations simplifies the process of managing billing, access, and compliance across an organization. The following is a step-by-step instructions to setting up and configuring AWS Organizations.

### Step 1: Create an AWS Organization
**Sign in to the AWS Management Console:** Use your root account credentials to sign in.

**Access AWS Organizations:** From the AWS Management Console, navigate to the AWS Organizations service.

**Create an Organization:** Click on "Create organization." Choose the "Create organization" option, which will create an organization with all features enabled (enabling consolidated billing and full control over policies and access). AWS will create the organization, and you will be directed to the AWS Organizations console.

## Step 2: Add AWS Accounts to the Organization

**Create New Accounts:** In the AWS Organizations console, click on "Accounts." Select "Add account" and choose "Create account." Fill in the account name and email address. AWS will send an invitation to the provided email to join the organization.

**Invite Existing Accounts:** Click on "Add account" and select "Invite account." Enter the email address or the account ID of the existing AWS account. AWS will send an invitation to the existing account to join the organization.

## Step 3: Organize Accounts into Organizational Units (OUs)

**Create Organizational Units:** In the AWS Organizations console, click on "Organizational units" under the "Accounts" section. Click "Create organizational unit." Provide a name for the OU (e.g., "Development," "Production," "Finance") and click "Create."

**Move Accounts to OUs:** Go back to the "Accounts" section. Select the account you want to move, click "Move," and choose the destination OU.

## Step 4: Set Up Service Control Policies (SCPs)

**Create SCPs:** In the AWS Organizations console, click on "Policies" and then "Service control policies." Click "Create policy." Provide a name and description for the SCP. Define the policy in JSON format. For example, to deny the creation of IAM users, you can use the following policy:

```
1.  {
2.    "Version": "2012-10-17",
3.    "Statement": [
4.      {
5.        "Effect": "Deny",
6.        "Action": "iam:CreateUser",
7.        "Resource": "*"
8.      }
9.    ]
10. }
```

**Attach SCPs to OUs or Accounts:** After creating the SCP, navigate to the "Organizational units" section. Select the OU or account where you want to apply the policy. Click "Attach policy" and select the SCP you created.

## Step 5: Enable Consolidated Billing

**Set Up Billing Preferences:** In the AWS Organizations console, click on "Billing" in the navigation pane. Enable "Consolidated billing" to manage billing and payments for all accounts in your organization.

**Review Cost and Usage:** Use the AWS Cost Explorer and AWS Budgets to monitor and manage costs across all accounts. Set up budget alerts to notify you when spending approaches predefined thresholds.

### Step 6: Enable AWS Control Tower (Optional)
AWS Control Tower provides additional governance and automated setup for multi-account environments. To enable AWS Control Tower:

**Navigate to AWS Control Tower:** From the AWS Management Console, go to AWS Control Tower.

**Set Up the Landing Zone:** Follow the setup wizard to configure your landing zone, which includes setting up OUs, account factories, and guardrails. AWS Control Tower automates the creation of accounts and the application of security policies.

By following these steps, you can deploy and configure AWS Organizations to manage multiple AWS accounts efficiently. This setup allows you to centralize billing, enforce policies, and streamline account management, thereby enhancing security and compliance across your organization. Regularly review and update your organizational structure and policies to adapt to the evolving needs of your business.

## 13.15.2 Creating and Implementing SCPs
Creating and implementing Service Control Policies (SCPs) in AWS Organizations allows you to centrally manage permissions and enforce compliance across multiple AWS accounts. SCPs are JSON policies that specify the maximum permissions for accounts in your organization, helping ensure that accounts adhere to your organization's security and compliance requirements. Below is a step-by-step hands-on lab for creating and implementing SCPs.

### Step 1: Access AWS Organizations
**Sign in to the AWS Management Console:** Use your root account credentials or an IAM user with administrative privileges.

**Navigate to AWS Organizations:** From the AWS Management Console, go to the AWS Organizations service.

### Step 2: Enable All Features in AWS Organizations
**Enable All Features:** In the AWS Organizations console, if your organization is set up with consolidated billing only, click on the "Enable all features" button to use all AWS Organizations features, including SCPs.

### Step 3: Create a Service Control Policy (SCP)
**Access the Policies Section:** In the AWS Organizations console, select "Policies" from the left-hand navigation pane. Click on "Service control policies."

**Create a New SCP:** Click the "Create policy" button. Provide a name and description for the SCP. For example, you might name it "DenyEC2Termination" and describe it as "This policy denies the ability to terminate EC2 instances."

**Define the Policy:** Enter the policy in JSON format. For example, to deny the termination of EC2 instances, use the following policy:

```
1.  {
2.    "Version": "2012-10-17",
3.    "Statement": [
4.      {
5.        "Effect": "Deny",
6.        "Action": "ec2:TerminateInstances",
7.        "Resource": "*"
8.      }
9.    ]
```

```
10. }
```

**Create the Policy:** Click "Create policy" to save the SCP.

### Step 4: Attach the SCP to Organizational Units (OUs) or Accounts
**Navigate to Organizational Units:** In the AWS Organizations console, click on "Organizational units" under the "Accounts" section.

**Select an OU or Account:** Choose the OU or account where you want to apply the SCP. For example, select the "Development" OU to apply the policy to all accounts within this OU.

**Attach the SCP:** Click "Attach policy." Select the SCP you created ("DenyEC2Termination") from the list and click "Attach."

### Step 5: Verify the SCP Implementation
**Test the Policy:** Log in to an account within the OU to which the SCP is attached. Attempt to terminate an EC2 instance. You should receive an error message indicating that the action is denied due to the SCP.

**Review Logs:** Use AWS CloudTrail to review logs and ensure that the SCP is being enforced as expected. Navigate to the CloudTrail console and search for events related to EC2 instance termination attempts.

```
aws cloudtrail lookup-events --lookup-attributes
AttributeKey=EventName,AttributeValue=TerminateInstances
```

### Step 6: Update and Manage SCPs
**Modify SCPs:** If you need to update an existing SCP, go back to the "Service control policies" section in AWS Organizations. Select the policy you want to edit, make the necessary changes, and save the policy.

**Detach SCPs:** If you need to remove an SCP from an OU or account, go to the "Organizational units" section. Select the OU or account, click "Policies," choose the attached SCP, and click "Detach."

By following these steps, you can create and implement Service Control Policies in AWS Organizations to enforce security and compliance across multiple AWS accounts. SCPs help you manage permissions centrally, ensuring that accounts within your organization operate within predefined security boundaries. Regularly review and update SCPs to adapt to changing business and security requirements.

## 13.15.3 Using CloudFormation for Secure Deployment
AWS CloudFormation allows you to model, provision, and manage AWS resources through code. By using CloudFormation templates, you can deploy resources securely and consistently, ensuring that your infrastructure adheres to best practices and organizational standards. Below is a step-by-step hands-on lab for using AWS CloudFormation to deploy resources securely and consistently.

### Step 1: Prepare the CloudFormation Template
**Define Your Resources:** Create a YAML or JSON file that describes the AWS resources you want to deploy. For example, a simple template to create an S3 bucket and an EC2 instance might look like this:

```
1. AWSTemplateFormatVersion: '2010-09-09'
2. Description: Simple CloudFormation template to create an S3 bucket and an EC2 instance
3. Resources:
4.   MyS3Bucket:
5.     Type: 'AWS::S3::Bucket'
6.     Properties:
```

```
7.         BucketName: 'my-secure-bucket'
8.    MyEC2Instance:
9.      Type: 'AWS::EC2::Instance'
10.     Properties:
11.       InstanceType: 't2.micro'
12.       ImageId: 'ami-0c55b159cbfafe1f0'  # Amazon Linux 2 AMI
13.       KeyName: 'my-key-pair'
14.       SecurityGroups:
15.         - !Ref MySecurityGroup
16.   MySecurityGroup:
17.     Type: 'AWS::EC2::SecurityGroup'
18.     Properties:
19.       GroupDescription: 'Allow SSH access'
20.       SecurityGroupIngress:
21.         - IpProtocol: 'tcp'
22.           FromPort: '22'
23.           ToPort: '22'
24.           CidrIp: '0.0.0.0/0'
```

**Secure the Template:** Ensure that all resources are configured securely. For example, limit SSH access to specific IP addresses, enable encryption for S3 buckets, and use IAM roles instead of hardcoded credentials.

### Step 2: Validate the Template
**Use AWS CloudFormation Validator:** Validate the CloudFormation template to ensure it is syntactically correct and follows best practices.

```
aws cloudformation validate-template --template-body file://my-template.yaml
```

### Step 3: Deploy the CloudFormation Stack
**Create the Stack:** Use the AWS Management Console, AWS CLI, or AWS SDKs to create a CloudFormation stack based on your template.

**Using AWS Management Console:** Navigate to the AWS CloudFormation console. Click "Create stack" and select "With new resources (standard)." Upload your template file or specify an S3 URL where the template is stored. Click "Next" and follow the prompts to configure stack options, including stack name, parameters, and IAM roles. Review the configuration and click "Create stack" to deploy the resources.

**Using AWS CLI:** Run the following command to create the stack:

```
aws cloudformation create-stack --stack-name my-stack --template-body file://my-template.yaml
```

### Step 4: Monitor the Stack Deployment
**Check Stack Status:** Monitor the status of the stack creation in the AWS CloudFormation console or using the AWS CLI. The stack creation process may take a few minutes.

```
aws cloudformation describe-stacks --stack-name my-stack
```

**Troubleshoot Issues:** If the stack creation fails, review the events in the CloudFormation console or use the following CLI command to identify the cause:

```
aws cloudformation describe-stack-events --stack-name my-stack
```

### Step 5: Update the Stack
**Modify the Template:** Make necessary updates to your CloudFormation template to add new resources or modify existing ones.

**Apply Updates:** Use the AWS Management Console or AWS CLI to update the stack with the new template.

**Using AWS Management Console:** Navigate to the AWS CloudFormation console. Select your stack and click "Update." Upload the updated template file and follow the prompts to update the stack.

**Using AWS CLI:** Run the following command to update the stack:

```
aws cloudformation update-stack --stack-name my-stack --template-body file://my-updated-template.yaml
```

### Step 6: Secure and Manage Resources
**Implement Security Best Practices:** Ensure that resources deployed via CloudFormation adhere to security best practices. For example, enable logging for S3 buckets, enforce IAM policies, and configure security groups with least privilege access.

**Use Stack Policies:** Apply stack policies to prevent unintended updates or deletions of critical resources.

```
1.  {
2.    "Statement": [
3.      {
4.        "Effect": "Deny",
5.        "Action": "Update:*",
6.        "Principal": "*",
7.        "Resource": "*"
8.      }
9.    ]
10. }
```

**Monitor and Audit:** Use AWS Config, CloudTrail, and CloudWatch to continuously monitor and audit the resources deployed via CloudFormation.

**Example:**
Enable AWS Config to track changes to your resources.

```
1. aws configservice put-configuration-recorder --configuration-recorder name=default --role-arn arn:aws:iam::123456789012:role/AWSConfigRole
2. aws configservice start-configuration-recorder --configuration-recorder-name default
```

By following these steps, you can use AWS CloudFormation to deploy resources securely and consistently. CloudFormation templates ensure that your infrastructure is deployed according to best practices, while monitoring and auditing tools help maintain security and compliance. Regularly review and update your templates to adapt to evolving security requirements and organizational needs.

## 13.15.4 Evaluating Compliance with AWS Config
Creating AWS Config rules and evaluating the compliance of AWS resources helps ensure that your environment adheres to security, operational, and compliance standards. AWS Config continuously monitors and records your AWS resource configurations and allows you to automate compliance checks using rules. Below are step-by-step instructions for creating AWS Config rules and evaluating the compliance of AWS resources.

### Step 1: Enable AWS Config
**Access AWS Config:** Sign in to the AWS Management Console and navigate to the AWS Config service.

Set Up AWS Config: Click on "Get started" if you are using AWS Config for the first time. Choose the resources you want AWS Config to record. For example, select "Record all resources supported in this region." Specify an S3 bucket to store configuration snapshots and configuration history. Choose an IAM role that AWS Config can use to access your resources. You can create a new role or use an existing one. Configure AWS Config to deliver configuration snapshots to an Amazon SNS topic for notifications (optional). Click "Next" and then "Confirm" to enable AWS Config.

## Step 2: Create AWS Config Rules

**Navigate to Rules:** In the AWS Config console, click on "Rules" in the left-hand navigation pane.

**Add a New Rule:** Click "Add rule." AWS provides a list of managed rules that you can use. Managed rules are predefined rules that address common compliance requirements.

**Select a Managed Rule** Choose a rule from the list. For example, to ensure that all S3 buckets have server-side encryption enabled, select the rule named s3-bucket-server-side-encryption-enabled. Click "Next" to configure the rule.

**Configure the Rule:** Provide a name and description for the rule. Specify the scope of resources to evaluate. You can choose to evaluate all resources or filter by resource type. Configure any additional parameters required by the rule, such as specifying an AWS KMS key for encryption. Click "Next" and then "Add rule" to create the rule.

```
aws configservice put-config-rule --config-rule '{"ConfigRuleName": "s3-bucket-encryption", "Source": {"Owner": "AWS", "SourceIdentifier": "S3_BUCKET_SERVER_SIDE_ENCRYPTION_ENABLED"}}'
```

## Step 3: Create a Custom AWS Config Rule (Optional)

**Create a Lambda Function:** For scenarios not covered by managed rules, you can create custom rules using AWS Lambda. Write a Lambda function that checks for compliance. For example, a function to ensure that EC2 instances are of a specific type:

```python
1.  import json
2.  import boto3
3.
4.  def lambda_handler(event, context):
5.      ec2 = boto3.client('ec2')
6.      config = boto3.client('config')
7.
8.      compliance_type = 'COMPLIANT'
9.
10.     response = ec2.describe_instances(
11.         Filters=[{
12.             'Name': 'instance-type',
13.             'Values': ['t2.micro']
14.         }]
15.     )
16.
17.     if len(response['Reservations']) == 0:
18.         compliance_type = 'NON_COMPLIANT'
19.
20.     config.put_evaluations(
21.         Evaluations=[
22.             {
23.                 'ComplianceResourceType': 'AWS::EC2::Instance',
24.                 'ComplianceResourceId': event['resourceId'],
25.                 'ComplianceType': compliance_type,
26.                 'OrderingTimestamp': event['notificationCreationTime']
27.             },
```

```
28.         ],
29.         ResultToken=event['resultToken']
30.     )
31.
32.     return {
33.         'statusCode': 200,
34.         'body': json.dumps('Compliance check complete')
35.     }
36.
```

**Create the Custom Rule:** In the AWS Config console, go to "Rules" and click "Add rule." Choose "Add custom rule." Provide a name and description for the rule. Select the Lambda function created earlier. Specify the trigger type (e.g., configuration changes or periodic checks). Define the scope of the rule (all resources or specific types). Click "Next" and then "Add rule" to create the custom rule.

## Step 4: Evaluate Compliance

**View Compliance Results:** In the AWS Config console, click on "Rules" to see the compliance status of each rule. Click on a rule to view detailed information about non-compliant resources.

**Take Action on Non-Compliant Resources:** Use the information provided by AWS Config to investigate and remediate non-compliant resources. For example, if a rule identifies unencrypted S3 buckets, you can enable server-side encryption on those buckets.

```
1. aws s3api put-bucket-encryption --bucket my-bucket --server-side-encryption-configuration '{
2.     "Rules": [{
3.         "ApplyServerSideEncryptionByDefault": {
4.             "SSEAlgorithm": "AES256"
5.         }
6.     }]
7. }'
```

## Step 5: Automate Remediation (Optional)

**Create a Lambda Function for Remediation:** Write a Lambda function that automatically remediates non-compliant resources. For example, a function to enable encryption on S3 buckets:

```
1.  import json
2.  import boto3
3.
4.  def lambda_handler(event, context):
5.      s3 = boto3.client('s3')
6.      bucket = event['detail']['requestParameters']['bucketName']
7.
8.      response = s3.put_bucket_encryption(
9.          Bucket=bucket,
10.         ServerSideEncryptionConfiguration={
11.             'Rules': [{
12.                 'ApplyServerSideEncryptionByDefault': {
13.                     'SSEAlgorithm': 'AES256'
14.                 }
15.             }]
16.         }
17.     )
18.     return response
```

**Associate the Lambda Function with the Rule:** In the AWS Config console, go to "Rules" and select the rule. Click "Manage remediation actions." Select the Lambda function for remediation and configure the action.

### Step 6: Monitor and Manage Compliance
**Set Up Notifications:** Use Amazon SNS to receive notifications when resources become non-compliant. Configure AWS Config to send notifications to an SNS topic.

```
1. aws sns create-topic --name ConfigComplianceTopic
2. aws configservice put-configuration-recorder --configuration-recorder name=default --role-arn arn:aws:iam::123456789012:role/AWSConfigRole
3. aws configservice put-delivery-channel --delivery-channel name=default --s3-bucket-name my-config-bucket --sns-topic-arn arn:aws:sns:us-west-2:123456789012:ConfigComplianceTopic
```

**Regularly Review Compliance:** Regularly review the compliance status of your resources in the AWS Config console. Update and refine AWS Config rules as necessary to adapt to changing requirements and best practices.

By following these steps, you can create AWS Config rules and evaluate the compliance of AWS resources. AWS Config helps automate compliance checks, providing continuous monitoring and detailed insights into your resource configurations. This ensures that your AWS environment remains secure, compliant, and well-managed.

## 13.15.5 Identifying and Addressing Security Gaps

Identifying and addressing security gaps in your AWS environment is crucial for maintaining a strong security posture and compliance. AWS offers several tools to help you achieve this, including AWS Trusted Advisor, AWS Config, Amazon Inspector, AWS Security Hub, and Amazon GuardDuty. Below is a step-by-step hands-on lab for using these AWS tools to identify and address security gaps.

### Step 1: Use AWS Trusted Advisor
AWS Trusted Advisor provides real-time guidance to help you optimize your AWS environment according to AWS best practices. It offers checks in several categories, including cost optimization, performance, security, fault tolerance, and service limits.

**Access AWS Trusted Advisor:** Sign in to the AWS Management Console. Navigate to AWS Trusted Advisor from the Services menu.

**Review Security Checks:** In the Trusted Advisor console, click on "Security" to view the security-related checks. Review the findings, such as "Security Groups - Specific Ports Unrestricted" and "MFA on Root Account."

**Implement Recommendations:** Address any high-risk issues identified by Trusted Advisor. For example, if the check identifies security groups with open ports, you can restrict access to specific IP addresses.

```
1. aws ec2 revoke-security-group-ingress --group-id sg-12345678 --protocol tcp --port 22 --cidr 0.0.0.0/0
2. aws ec2 authorize-security-group-ingress --group-id sg-12345678 --protocol tcp --port 22 --cidr 203.0.113.0/24
```

### Step 2: Use AWS Config
AWS Config continuously monitors and records your AWS resource configurations and allows you to automate compliance checks using rules.

**Enable AWS Config:**
- In the AWS Management Console, navigate to AWS Config.

- Click "Get started" and follow the setup steps, including specifying an S3 bucket for storing configuration snapshots and selecting an IAM role.

**Create Config Rules:**
- In the AWS Config console, click on "Rules."
- Click "Add rule" and select a managed rule, such as s3-bucket-server-side-encryption-enabled, to ensure that all S3 buckets have server-side encryption enabled.
- Configure the rule and click "Add rule."

```
aws configservice put-config-rule --config-rule '{"ConfigRuleName": "s3-bucket-encryption", "Source": {"Owner": "AWS", "SourceIdentifier": "S3_BUCKET_SERVER_SIDE_ENCRYPTION_ENABLED"}}'
```

**Review Compliance:**
- Check the compliance status of your resources in the AWS Config console.
- Address any non-compliant resources by following the recommendations provided.

## Step 3: Use Amazon Inspector

Amazon Inspector is an automated security assessment service that helps improve the security and compliance of applications deployed on AWS.

**Run an Assessment:**
- In the AWS Management Console, navigate to Amazon Inspector.
- Set up an assessment target by selecting the EC2 instances to be assessed.
- Create an assessment template by specifying the rules packages to be used, such as "Common Vulnerabilities and Exposures" (CVEs) and "Security Best Practices."
- Run the assessment.

**Review Findings:**
- Once the assessment is complete, review the findings in the Inspector console.
- Address high-severity findings by following the remediation steps provided, such as patching vulnerable software or reconfiguring security settings.

```
aws inspector list-findings --assessment-run-arns arn:aws:inspector:us-west-2:123456789012:target/0-0kFIPusq/template/0-7sbz2d8v/run/0-JAt4d5Mx
```

## Step 4: Use AWS Security Hub

AWS Security Hub provides a comprehensive view of your high-priority security alerts and compliance status across AWS accounts.

**Enable Security Hub:**
- In the AWS Management Console, navigate to AWS Security Hub.
- Click "Get started" to enable Security Hub and integrate it with other AWS security services.

**Review Findings:**
- Security Hub aggregates findings from services like Amazon GuardDuty, AWS Config, and Amazon Inspector.
- Review the findings and prioritize them based on severity.

**Implement Remediations:**

Follow the remediation recommendations provided in Security Hub to address security gaps. For example, if Security Hub identifies unencrypted EBS volumes, enable encryption for those volumes.

```
aws ec2 create-snapshot --volume-id vol-049df61146c4d7901
aws ec2 create-volume --snapshot-id snap-1234567890abcdef0 --encrypted --availability-zone us-west-2a
aws ec2 attach-volume --volume-id vol-049df61146c4d7901 --instance-id i-1234567890abcdef0 --device /dev/sdf
```

### Step 5: Use Amazon GuardDuty
Amazon GuardDuty is a threat detection service that continuously monitors for malicious activity and unauthorized behavior.

**Enable GuardDuty:** In the AWS Management Console, navigate to Amazon GuardDuty. Click "Get started" to enable GuardDuty.

**Review Threat Findings:** GuardDuty generates findings based on the analysis of AWS CloudTrail event logs, VPC Flow Logs, and DNS logs. Review the findings in the GuardDuty console and prioritize them based on severity.

**Take Action:** Follow the recommended actions to mitigate threats. For example, if GuardDuty detects a compromised instance, isolate the instance and investigate further.

```
1. aws ec2 modify-instance-attribute --instance-id i-1234567890abcdef0 --no-disable-api-termination
2. aws ec2 stop-instances --instance-ids i-1234567890abcdef0
```

By following these steps, you can use AWS tools to identify and address security gaps in your environment. AWS Trusted Advisor helps with security best practices, AWS Config continuously monitors compliance, Amazon Inspector provides vulnerability assessments, AWS Security Hub offers a centralized view of security findings, and Amazon GuardDuty detects threats. Regularly using these tools ensures that your AWS environment remains secure, compliant, and well-managed.

## 13.16 Key Exam Tips

### Multi-Account Management with AWS Organizations
**Understand Organizational Units (OUs):** AWS Organizations allow you to group accounts using Organization Units (OUs) to apply policies. Know how to structure OUs based on business functions (e.g., development, production) and apply Service Control Policies (SCPs) for governance across accounts.

**Multi-Account Strategies:** Familiarize yourself with multi-account strategies to separate workloads, enhance security, and manage permissions effectively. AWS Organizations can enforce centralized management and security policies across multiple accounts.

### Service Control Policies (SCPs)
**SCP Basics:** Understand that SCPs are used to define the maximum permissions allowed for accounts in an organization. SCPs are enforced at the OU or account level and do not grant permissions themselves but act as guardrails.

**Strategies for Using SCPs:** Learn how to use deny-based SCPs to restrict certain actions and implement allow-based SCPs to enforce least-privilege access. SCPs can be combined with IAM policies for additional layers of control.

**Common SCP Use Cases:** Be prepared to implement SCPs for cases such as restricting regions, disabling root access, or preventing the use of specific AWS services.

## IAM Policies and Conditions
**IAM Conditions:** Ensure you're familiar with how IAM policy conditions are used to control access based on attributes such as IP addresses, MFA, or tags. Conditions enhance fine-grained control over access policies.
**IAM Roles vs. Resource-Based Policies:** Understand the differences between IAM roles (for assigning temporary permissions) and resource-based policies (for directly attaching permissions to resources like S3 buckets or Lambda functions). Each has its own use cases for cross-account access and delegation.

## IAM Permission Boundaries
**Permission Boundaries:** These are policies that set the maximum permissions an IAM entity (user or role) can receive. Be ready to implement permission boundaries to ensure users or roles cannot exceed specified permissions, even if more permissive IAM policies are applied.

## IAM Policy Evaluation Logic
**Policy Evaluation Process:** AWS IAM evaluates policies using an explicit deny followed by allow logic. Be familiar with how this logic works, especially in the context of SCPs, permission boundaries, and IAM policies to troubleshoot issues with access and permissions.

## Best Practices for Securing Root Account and Cross-Account Roles
**Root Account Best Practices:** The root account should only be used for critical operations. Ensure you enable MFA on the root account and store the credentials securely. Know how to disable unnecessary root privileges.
**Cross-Account Roles:** Learn how to use cross-account roles to allow secure access between different AWS accounts without sharing credentials. Understand how to implement role assumptions and enforce least-privilege access in cross-account scenarios.

## Deploying AWS Control Tower
**AWS Control Tower:** This service automates the setup of AWS Organizations, OUs, and SCPs, making it easier to enforce governance at scale. Be familiar with the benefits of AWS Control Tower for landing zone management and governance in multi-account environments.
**SCP Integration:** AWS Control Tower automatically applies SCPs that enforce security best practices, such as restricting root user access and enabling logging.

## Infrastructure as Code (IaC) and Tagging Best Practices
**IaC Best Practices:** When using tools like AWS CloudFormation or Terraform, implement infrastructure as code to ensure consistent, repeatable deployments. Be familiar with CloudFormation Guard for enforcing policies on CloudFormation templates.
**Tagging Best Practices:** Understand the importance of tagging resources for cost management, operational governance, and access control. Create a tagging strategy that defines required tags (e.g., environment, owner) and ensures consistent usage across accounts.

## Centralized Management and Aggregation
**Centralized Management:** Use AWS Organizations to centralize governance across multiple accounts, including enforcing policies, monitoring resources, and managing access. Be prepared to integrate AWS services such as CloudTrail and AWS Config for centralized auditing.
**Aggregating Findings:** Use AWS Security Hub and AWS Config to aggregate security and compliance findings from multiple accounts. Learn how to use these tools to prioritize risks and maintain compliance with security frameworks.

### Evaluating Compliance of AWS Resources
**Compliance Tools:** Be familiar with tools like AWS Config and AWS Security Hub to evaluate compliance against security standards such as CIS AWS Foundations and PCI DSS. Learn how to configure AWS Config Rules to check for compliance with specific policies, such as ensuring encryption is enabled.
**Creating AWS Config Rules:** Understand how to create custom rules in AWS Config to enforce security policies, such as requiring S3 buckets to be encrypted or ensuring that EC2 instances are not using default security groups.

### Reducing Attack Surfaces and Identifying Unused Resources
**Reducing Attack Surfaces:** Implement strategies to reduce your attack surface by identifying unnecessary resources, removing unused services, and limiting exposure to the internet (e.g., closing open security groups).
**AWS Well-Architected Framework:** Use the AWS Well-Architected Tool to review your architecture and ensure that your infrastructure follows best practices. Understand the five pillars (operational excellence, security, reliability, performance efficiency, and cost optimization) and their security implications.

### Securing Resource Sharing
**Using AWS Firewall Manager:** Learn how to use AWS Firewall Manager to enforce security policies, such as security group policies, across multiple accounts. This is essential for maintaining consistent security controls across AWS Organizations.
**Sharing Resources Securely:** When sharing resources such as S3 buckets or RDS databases across accounts, use resource-based policies and IAM roles to ensure secure access. Be ready to configure cross-account access in a secure, least-privilege manner.

### Identifying Security Gaps
**Cost and Usage Anomalies:** Use AWS tools to identify security gaps, such as unusual cost or resource usage, which could indicate potential security issues (e.g., an unintentional public S3 bucket leading to high data transfer costs).
**AWS Well-Architected Tool:** Leverage the Well-Architected Tool to identify security vulnerabilities and gaps in your current architecture. Implement recommended improvements to ensure alignment with AWS security best practices.

### Summary
For the AWS Certified Security Specialty exam, focus on mastering multi-account management through AWS Organizations, IAM policies, SCPs, and cross-account roles. Understand the importance of securing root accounts, implementing permission boundaries, and enforcing compliance using AWS Config and Security Hub. Use IaC and tagging strategies to maintain consistency and governance in your deployments. Prioritize continuous evaluation of security gaps, attack surface reduction, and compliance to ensure your AWS environment remains secure. Familiarity with tools like AWS Control Tower, CloudFormation, AWS Firewall Manager, and the Well-Architected Tool will help ensure centralized and secure governance across your cloud infrastructure.

## 13.17 Chapter Review Questions
**Question 1:**
What is the primary purpose of AWS Organizations?
A. To monitor application performance
B. To manage multiple AWS accounts centrally
C. To manage EC2 instances
D. To perform DDoS mitigation

**Question 2:**

Which of the following statements best describes an Organizational Unit (OU) in AWS Organizations?
A. A unit for managing resource groups
B. A container for accounts within an AWS Organization
C. A container for policies within an AWS account
D. A type of IAM role

**Question 3:**
What is the purpose of Service Control Policies (SCPs) in AWS Organizations?
A. To provide network monitoring
B. To enforce permissions across AWS accounts
C. To monitor costs and usage
D. To manage DNS settings

**Question 4:**
Which of the following AWS services provides the ability to enforce IAM permission boundaries?
A. AWS Shield
B. AWS IAM
C. AWS CloudWatch
D. AWS Trusted Advisor

**Question 5:**
What is a key benefit of using AWS Control Tower?
A. Automated database backups
B. Multi-account management and security guardrails
C. Data migration from on-premises to AWS
D. Monitoring server logs

**Question 6:**
What best practice is recommended for the AWS Root Account?
A. Use it for all IAM role creation
B. Enable MFA and use it only when necessary
C. Use it for day-to-day administrative tasks
D. Share root credentials with team members

**Question 7:**
Which AWS service helps centrally manage and apply tagging strategies for resources?
A. AWS Config
B. AWS Firewall Manager
C. AWS Resource Groups
D. AWS CloudFormation

**Question 8:**
Infrastructure as Code (IaC) is best implemented in AWS using which of the following services?
A. AWS CloudTrail
B. AWS CloudFormation
C. AWS EC2
D. Amazon RDS

**Question 9:**
Which of the following helps in data classification within AWS resources?
A. Amazon Macie
B. AWS CloudWatch

C. AWS Glue
D. AWS CodeDeploy

**Question 10:**
Which tool is used to evaluate AWS architectures based on best practices for operational excellence, security, reliability, performance efficiency, and cost optimization?
A. AWS Systems Manager
B. AWS Well-Architected Tool
C. AWS Trusted Advisor
D. AWS CloudFormation

**Question 11:**
Your organization uses AWS Organizations to manage multiple AWS accounts. You need to ensure that developers can only launch specific instance types in the development accounts but have no restrictions in the production accounts. How would you achieve this using Service Control Policies (SCPs)?

A. Create a resource-based policy to restrict instance types.
B. Apply an SCP at the organizational unit (OU) level that restricts specific instance types in development accounts.
C. Use IAM roles to manage permissions at the account level.
D. Manually configure each account with its own set of permissions.

**Question 12:**
An AWS administrator in your company has created several IAM roles with permission boundaries. However, some roles still seem to have more permissions than expected. What could be causing this?

A. The permission boundary is not applied correctly to the IAM role.
B. The roles are using resource-based policies that grant additional permissions.
C. The roles are not following the least privilege principle.
D. The IAM policies applied at the account level are overriding the boundaries.

**Question 13:**
Your company is implementing AWS Control Tower to manage a multi-account environment. The security team wants to enforce specific tagging policies across all AWS accounts. What would be the best way to implement this using AWS Control Tower?

A. Configure Service Control Policies (SCPs) to enforce tagging policies.
B. Use IAM roles to apply tag restrictions manually.
C. Set up AWS Config rules to monitor and enforce tagging compliance across accounts.
D. Apply a centralized firewall policy to ensure all resources are tagged.

**Question 14:**
You are tasked with improving security in a multi-account setup. The company uses cross-account roles to grant access between accounts. A recent security audit highlighted potential risks. What security measures can you take to ensure safe and compliant cross-account access?

A. Implement cross-account resource-based policies with least privilege.
B. Use IAM Conditions to limit cross-account roles.
C. Enable AWS CloudTrail logging for all cross-account activities.
D. Use all of the above strategies.

**Question 15:**

Your organization needs to manage AWS accounts for different departments while ensuring centralized billing and security compliance. The company is also concerned about protecting root account credentials. What best practices should you implement to secure the root accounts while maintaining centralized control?

A. Apply MFA to all root accounts and avoid using the root account for day-to-day activities.
B. Implement AWS Control Tower to manage security guardrails and centralize access control.
C. Use AWS Organizations with SCPs to restrict root account access across departments.
D. Implement all of the above practices.

## 13.18 Answers to Chapter Review Questions

1. B. To manage multiple AWS accounts centrally
Explanation: AWS Organizations is a service that allows users to manage and consolidate multiple AWS accounts under a single organization. This facilitates centralized management, including applying policies, monitoring, and cost control.

2. B. A container for accounts within an AWS Organization
Explanation: Organizational Units (OUs) are containers within AWS Organizations that help group accounts and apply policies like Service Control Policies (SCPs) to manage security and permissions at scale.

3. B. To enforce permissions across AWS accounts
Explanation: Service Control Policies (SCPs) help control the services and actions that users and roles in AWS accounts can access, enforcing permission boundaries across multiple accounts in AWS Organizations.

4. B. AWS IAM
Explanation: AWS IAM supports permission boundaries, which define the maximum permissions that an IAM role or user can have. This ensures that users and roles can perform only the actions within their defined boundaries.

5. B. Multi-account management and security guardrails
Explanation: AWS Control Tower provides an easy way to set up and govern a secure, multi-account AWS environment. It automates the creation of OUs and enforces security guardrails.

6. B. Enable MFA and use it only when necessary
Explanation: AWS recommends enabling multi-factor authentication (MFA) on the root account and using it only when absolutely necessary to protect sensitive administrative functions.

7. C. AWS Resource Groups
Explanation: AWS Resource Groups allow users to manage and apply tagging strategies, which help organize and control access to AWS resources more effectively.

8. B. AWS CloudFormation
Explanation: AWS CloudFormation is a service that allows users to define and provision AWS infrastructure using code, enabling consistent and automated resource management.

9. A. Amazon Macie
Explanation: Amazon Macie helps classify and protect sensitive data in AWS, such as personally identifiable information (PII) and intellectual property, by using machine learning to identify data patterns.

10. B. AWS Well-Architected Tool

Explanation: The AWS Well-Architected Tool helps evaluate AWS architectures and provides recommendations for improving security, reliability, performance efficiency, cost optimization, and operational excellence.

11. B. Apply an SCP at the organizational unit (OU) level that restricts specific instance types in development accounts.
Explanation: SCPs allow you to manage permissions across accounts in an AWS Organization. By applying an SCP to the development OU, you can restrict instance types while keeping the production environment unrestricted.

12. B. The roles are using resource-based policies that grant additional permissions.
Explanation: Permission boundaries control the maximum allowed permissions, but resource-based policies can still grant more permissions, depending on their configuration. Both must be considered when troubleshooting.

13. C. Set up AWS Config rules to monitor and enforce tagging compliance across accounts.
Explanation: AWS Config provides the ability to set compliance rules for tagging and resource configuration across multiple accounts, ensuring governance in a multi-account environment.

14. D. Use all of the above strategies.
Explanation: Implementing least privilege, using IAM Conditions, and enabling CloudTrail logging are all essential for securing cross-account access in a multi-account AWS setup.

15. D. Implement all of the above practices.
Explanation: Protecting root accounts with MFA, using Control Tower for centralized management, and SCPs for security restrictions are critical for ensuring root account security and governance in multi-account environments.

# Practice Test Set 1

**Question 1:**
Domain: Infrastructure Security
A company needs to inspect and log traffic that passes between instances in the same subnet. They have deployed a virtual security appliance in the subnet. What configuration is required to allow the virtual security appliance to inspect and log traffic?
   A. Attach an elastic network adapter (ENA) and configure it for monitoring mode.
   B. Disable the Network Source/Destination check on the virtual security appliance's elastic network interface.
   C. Place the security appliance in a different subnet and route the traffic through it.
   D. Enable VPC Flow Logs on the subnet and route traffic through the virtual security appliance.

**Question 2:**
Domain: Data Protection
A company is using AWS KMS to manage encryption keys for an application that stores sensitive data. The company wants to ensure that the keys are automatically rotated every 6 months. What steps should be taken to meet these requirements?
   A. Create a custom Lambda function to rotate the keys every 6 months.
   B. Enable the automatic key rotation option in the AWS KMS console.
   C. Set up a CloudWatch Event Rule to trigger key rotation every 6 months.
   D. Use an AWS managed KMS key to automatically rotate the keys.

**Question 3:**
Domain: Security Logging and Monitoring
A company uses AWS Security Hub and AWS Inspector to manage and monitor security events. The security team wants to receive notifications via email whenever a medium-priority finding is detected. What is the best way to set this up?
   A. Set up an Amazon SNS topic and configure Inspector to send medium-priority findings to the topic.
   B. Create a CloudWatch Alarm for Security Hub findings and have it trigger an email notification for medium-priority findings.
   C. Configure an EventBridge rule in Security Hub to detect medium-priority findings and route them to an SNS topic for email notifications.
   D. Enable Security Hub's auto-remediation feature to automatically resolve medium-priority findings and send an email summary.

**Question 4:**
Domain: Infrastructure Security
A company is deploying a web application on Amazon EC2 instances within a private subnet. The application needs to be accessible from the internet, but the company wants to ensure that the backend database, hosted on RDS in the same VPC, is not accessible from the internet. What is the best way to configure the security groups and network architecture to meet these requirements?
   A. Attach an Internet Gateway to the VPC and allow all inbound traffic to the private subnet where the EC2 instances are hosted.
   B. Place the EC2 instances in a public subnet and configure a security group that allows inbound traffic on the necessary ports, and place the RDS instance in a private subnet with a security group that allows inbound traffic only from the EC2 instances.
   C. Place both the EC2 instances and the RDS instance in the same public subnet and use a security group to restrict inbound access to the RDS instance.
   D. Use a NAT Gateway in a public subnet and allow outbound internet access from the private subnet, with security groups configured to allow inbound traffic only from the NAT Gateway.

**Question 5:**
Domain: Infrastructure Security
A company is concerned about potential vulnerabilities in its EC2 instances and wants to ensure compliance with security best practices. What AWS service can be used to scan the instances for known vulnerabilities and compliance with CIS benchmarks?
    A. AWS Config with custom compliance rules.
    B. AWS Inspector with a Common Vulnerabilities and Exposures (CVE) scan and CIS benchmark assessment.
    C. AWS CloudTrail with detailed monitoring enabled.
    D. AWS GuardDuty with anomaly detection enabled.

**Question 6:**
Domain: Data Protection
A company replicates encrypted objects from an S3 bucket in one region to another region. However, only unencrypted objects are successfully replicating. Which actions should be taken to ensure the encrypted objects replicate successfully?
    A. Modify the replication configuration to include the KMS key for the destination region.
    B. Grant the replication IAM role the kms:Encrypt permission for the key in the destination region.
    C. Add the s3:ReplicateObject permission to the bucket policy in the source region.
    D. Provide the replication IAM role the kms:Decrypt permission for the key in the source region.

**Question 7:**
Domain: Identity and Access Management
A global organization wants to delegate IAM role creation to regional teams while ensuring that roles cannot be misconfigured to grant excessive permissions. What is the best approach to achieve this?
    A. Implement a permissions boundary on all IAM roles created by regional teams.
    B. Use AWS Organizations to enforce SCPs that limit IAM role permissions.
    C. Establish a centralized IAM policy template that regional teams must use.
    D. Conduct quarterly audits of all IAM roles created by regional teams.

**Question 8:**
Domain: Infrastructure Security
A company is worried about DDoS attacks on its application hosted behind an Application Load Balancer (ALB). What steps can be taken to mitigate the impact of Layer 7 DDoS attacks?
    A. Enable Shield Advanced on the ALB for enhanced DDoS protection.
    B. Configure AWS WAF rate-based rules to limit excessive requests from the same IP.
    C. Use AWS GuardDuty to automatically block DDoS traffic.
    D. Set up a CloudFront distribution with AWS WAF and rate-limiting rules in front of the ALB.

**Question 9:**
Domain: Data Protection
A security engineer configured an S3 bucket policy to deny access to all users except for a specific set of IAM users. What will be the effect of this policy?
    A. The specified IAM users will have full access to the bucket and its objects.
    B. The specified IAM users will be denied access unless additional permissions are granted through IAM policies.
    C. The specified IAM users will be able to access the bucket only if they are in a specific IAM group.
    D. The bucket will be accessible only to the root user of the specified account.

**Question 10:**
Domain: Management and Security Governance

A company wants to enforce security best practices after an access key was accidentally exposed. What are the first steps that should be taken to mitigate the risk?

    A. Disable the exposed access key immediately.

    B. Rotate the access key and invalidate the old one.

    C. Attach an IAM policy that denies all actions using the exposed access key.

    D. Delete the IAM user associated with the exposed access key.

**Question 11:**

Domain: Infrastructure Security

A company needs to collect forensic data from an EC2 instance that has become unresponsive after a suspected attack. What steps should the security team take?

    A. Attach the EBS volumes to another instance and run the EC2Rescue CLI in offline mode.

    B. Reboot the instance and enable memory dump in safe mode.

    C. Use the AWS CLI to create an AMI of the affected instance for analysis.

    D. Take a snapshot of the EBS volumes and analyze them offline.

**Question 12:**

Domain: Infrastructure Security

A security architect needs to ensure secure, encrypted connections for a web application hosted on EC2 instances behind a Network Load Balancer (NLB). What actions should be taken?

    A. Use AWS Certificate Manager (ACM) to manage SSL/TLS certificates and apply them to the NLB.

    B. Enable HTTPS listeners on the NLB and configure EC2 instances to use self-signed certificates.

    C. Set up a CloudFront distribution in front of the NLB with an SSL certificate from ACM.

    D. Use a VPC endpoint to route all traffic through a secure, encrypted connection.

**Question 13:**

Domain: Data Protection

A company needs to rotate its KMS keys annually as part of its compliance requirements. The keys were originally created using imported key material. What is the most efficient process for rotating these keys?

    A. Import new key material into the existing KMS key.

    B. Create a new KMS key with new key material and update the alias to point to the new key.

    C. Enable automatic key rotation for the existing KMS key.

    D. Generate a new key using AWS KMS and manually rotate the keys in all applications.

**Question 14:**

Domain: Security Logging and Monitoring

A company wants to centralize log data from multiple AWS accounts into a single account for real-time processing and analysis. What is the most effective solution?

    A. Use Amazon Kinesis Data Streams to aggregate logs from all accounts into a central processing system.

    B. Set up AWS Config to monitor changes across accounts and aggregate data in a central account.

    C. Use Amazon CloudWatch Logs subscription filters to send log data to a central Kinesis Data Firehose stream.

    D. Write a custom Lambda function to collect logs from all accounts and send them to a central S3 bucket.

**Question 15:**

Domain: Infrastructure Security

An application is deployed on EC2 instances behind a Network Load Balancer (NLB), but the instances are failing health checks. What are possible reasons for this?

    A. The EC2 instance security group does not allow inbound traffic from the NLB's IP addresses.

    B. The NLB security group does not allow outbound traffic to the EC2 instances.

    C. The network ACL does not allow traffic on the health check port from the NLB.

    D. The NLB security group does not allow inbound traffic from the internet.

**Question 16:**
Domain: Management and Security Governance
A company wants to ensure all configuration changes and access activities in its AWS environment are logged for audit purposes. Which combination of services should be used?
    A. AWS Config for configuration changes and CloudTrail for access logs.
    B. CloudWatch for all logging and GuardDuty for monitoring.
    C. AWS Config for access monitoring and Macie for detailed activity tracking.
    D. GuardDuty for configuration changes and CloudTrail for API activity logs.

**Question 17:**
Domain: Data Protection
A company plans to store sensitive data in Amazon S3 and use KMS for encryption. The company's policies require the use of custom key material with specified expiration dates. What is the best way to configure KMS to meet these requirements?
    A. Create a custom key store in KMS and import the company's key material.
    B. Use the default KMS key store and set custom expiration dates for the key material.
    C. Set up a custom key store and configure automatic key expiration.
    D. Import the company's key material into an AWS-managed KMS key.

**Question 18:**
Domain: Infrastructure Security
A company is hosting a web application on EC2 instances in a private subnet. The application must be accessible through an Application Load Balancer (ALB) with secure, encrypted connections. What rules should be configured in the security groups?
    A. An inbound rule in ALB-SG allowing HTTPS traffic from the internet.
    B. An outbound rule in ALB-SG allowing traffic to the EC2 instances on port 443.
    C. An inbound rule in EC2-SG allowing traffic from ALB-SG on port 443.
    D. An outbound rule in EC2-SG allowing traffic to the ALB on port 443.

**Question 19:**
Domain: Data Protection
A company is storing sensitive customer data in an RDS database and wants to ensure the data is encrypted and the credentials are rotated automatically. What solutions should the security engineer implement?
    A. Use AWS Secrets Manager to store and automatically rotate the RDS credentials.
    B. Enable RDS encryption using AWS KMS and implement IAM database authentication.
    C. Store credentials in AWS Systems Manager Parameter Store with automatic rotation.
    D. Encrypt the RDS instance using AWS CloudHSM keys and configure automatic rotation.

**Question 20:**
Domain: Management and Security Governance
A university using AWS Organizations needs to enforce strict control over the root user accounts across all member accounts. What steps should be taken to achieve this?
    A. Apply a Service Control Policy (SCP) that limits the root user's access.
    B. Enable multi-factor authentication (MFA) on all root user accounts.
    C. Use CloudTrail to monitor root user activities and set up alerts for any unauthorized actions.
    D. Remove all access keys associated with the root user account.

**Question 21:**
Domain: Identity and Access Management
A security engineer needs to audit the creation of new AWS accounts in an organization where users authenticate through an on-premises IdP. What is the best way to determine who made the request?

A. Review AWS CloudTrail logs for the federated identity used.
B. Check the IAM Access Analyzer for recent account creation events.
C. Inspect the logs from the federated identity provider for the user details.
D. Use AWS Config to track the creation of new accounts and associated identities.

## Question 22:
Domain: Infrastructure Security
A security team needs to quickly identify any EC2 instances that are running a specific vulnerable version of software. What is the most efficient way to accomplish this?
  A. Use AWS Systems Manager to run a compliance check on the EC2 instances.
  B. Set up AWS Config rules to detect non-compliant instances and trigger an alert.
  C. Configure Amazon Inspector to scan instances for known vulnerabilities.
  D. Run a custom script on each instance to check for the vulnerable software version.

## Question 23:
Domain: Infrastructure Security
A company's security team is designing a distributed application that will operate across multiple AWS regions and on-premises servers. What are correct considerations for encryption in transit?
  A. Inter-region traffic is encrypted by default on the AWS global network.
  B. All traffic between Availability Zones is unencrypted unless configured otherwise.
  C. AWS Direct Connect traffic is automatically encrypted end-to-end.
  D. Intra-region traffic between EC2 instances is encrypted by default.

## Question 24:
Domain: Identity and Access Management
A developer has left a company, and the security team needs to ensure that the developer's code cannot be deployed to AWS Lambda functions. What is the best solution?
  A. Remove the developer's IAM permissions for accessing AWS Signer.
  B. Revoke the signing profile associated with the developer from all Lambda functions.
  C. Delete the developer's IAM account and any associated access keys.
  D. Rotate the encryption keys used for Lambda functions.

## Question 25:
Domain: Infrastructure Security
A company is using IPv6 in its VPC and needs to provide EC2 instances in a private subnet with internet access for updates. How can this be securely achieved?
  A. Deploy an egress-only internet gateway and update the route table for the private subnet.
  B. Set up a NAT gateway in a public subnet and route traffic from the private subnet through it.
  C. Use an internet gateway in the private subnet and create a custom route table for outbound traffic.
  D. Enable an internet gateway in a public subnet and route IPv6 traffic from the private subnet through it.

## Question 26:
Domain: Threat Detection and Incident Response
A company has detected that the credentials for one of its AWS IAM users have been compromised. The security team needs to immediately invalidate the compromised credentials and ensure that new, secure credentials are issued and rotated automatically moving forward. Which of the following actions should the security team take to meet these requirements? (Select TWO.)
  A. Revoke all active sessions for the compromised IAM user using the AWS Management Console or CLI.
  B. Delete the IAM user and create a new IAM user with a new set of credentials.
  C. Rotate the compromised credentials using AWS Secrets Manager and enable automatic rotation.
  D. Create a new access key for the IAM user, disable the old access key, and configure automatic rotation using AWS Secrets Manager.

E. Enable AWS CloudTrail to monitor the IAM user activities and automatically disable the credentials if suspicious activity is detected.

**Question 27:**
Domain: Threat Detection and Incident Response
A company's Amazon EC2 instance is suspected to be compromised. As part of the incident response process, the security team needs to isolate the instance from the rest of the network to prevent further damage. Which of the following steps should the security team take to effectively isolate the compromised instance?
    A. Change the instance's security group to one that denies all inbound and outbound traffic.
    B. Modify the Network ACL associated with the instance's subnet to block all traffic.
    C. Terminate the instance to ensure it no longer poses a threat.
    D. Move the instance to a separate VPC with no Internet Gateway or VPN connection.

**Question 28:**
Domain: Threat Detection and Incident Response
A company wants to streamline its incident response process for security threats detected in its AWS environment. The security team decides to create a set of playbooks and runbooks to standardize responses to specific incidents, such as unauthorized access to S3 buckets or compromised EC2 instances. Which of the following is the MOST effective approach to achieve this?
    A. Create a playbook that outlines the manual steps for responding to each type of incident and ensure all security team members are trained on it.
    B. Develop automated runbooks using AWS Systems Manager Automation to execute predefined steps in response to detected incidents, such as isolating compromised instances or revoking access to S3 buckets.
    C. Use AWS CloudTrail logs to manually investigate security incidents and update playbooks as new threats are discovered.
    D. Implement AWS Config rules to automatically remediate security incidents without the need for predefined playbooks or runbooks.

**Question 29:**
Domain: Threat Detection and Incident Response
Which AWS service provides a comprehensive view of your security alerts across multiple AWS services and helps to prioritize security findings?

    A. AWS Identity and Access Management (IAM) Access Analyzer
    B. Amazon GuardDuty
    C. AWS Security Hub
    D. Amazon Detective

**Question 30:**
Domain: Threat Detection and Incident Response
When configuring Amazon EventBridge to handle security findings from AWS Security Hub, which service or format is primarily used to standardize and centralize these findings?
    A. Amazon SNS (Simple Notification Service)
    B. ASFF (AWS Security Finding Format)
    C. Amazon S3
    D. AWS Config

**Question 31:**
Domain: Threat Detection and Incident Response
Your organization uses AWS Macie to monitor S3 buckets for sensitive data. Macie has generated a finding indicating the presence of PII in a publicly accessible S3 bucket. What should be your immediate action?
    A. Modify the bucket policy to restrict public access.
    B. Delete the S3 bucket to eliminate the risk.

C. Enable default encryption for the S3 bucket.
D. Create a CloudWatch alarm to monitor further public access.

**Question 32:**

Domain: Threat Detection and Incident Response

Which AWS service is best suited for investigating, analyzing, and visualizing security issues detected across multiple AWS accounts?

    A. AWS CloudTrail
    B. Amazon Detective
    C. Amazon GuardDuty
    D. AWS Security Hub

**Question 33:**

Domain: Threat Detection and Incident Response

A security engineer needs to validate suspicious API activities recorded in AWS CloudTrail logs. Which Amazon Athena SQL query should be used to identify all DeleteBucket operations performed by a specific IAM user within the last 24 hours?

    A.

```
1. SELECT * FROM cloudtrail_logs
2. WHERE eventName = 'DeleteBucket'
3. AND userIdentity.userName = 'specific-user'
4. AND eventTime > current_timestamp - interval '1' day;
```

    B.

```
1. SELECT * FROM cloudtrail_logs
2. WHERE requestParameters.bucketName = 'DeleteBucket'
3. AND userIdentity.userName = 'specific-user'
4. AND eventTime > current_timestamp - interval '1' day;
```

    C.

```
1. SELECT * FROM cloudtrail_logs
2. WHERE eventName = 'DeleteBucket'
3. AND userIdentity.sessionContext.sessionIssuer.userName = 'specific-user'
4. AND eventTime > current_date - interval '24' hour;
```

    D.

```
1. SELECT * FROM cloudtrail_logs
2. WHERE eventSource = 's3.amazonaws.com'
3. AND eventName = 'DeleteBucket'
4. AND userIdentity.principalId = 'specific-user'
5. AND eventTime > current_date - interval '1' day;
```

**Question 34:**

Domain: Threat Detection and Incident Response

A security engineer suspects that an Amazon EC2 instance in their VPC has been compromised. What is the quickest way to isolate this instance to prevent further damage while maintaining the ability to investigate?

    A. Terminate the instance immediately.
    B. Stop the instance to prevent further activity.
    C. Modify the security group associated with the instance to deny all inbound and outbound traffic.
    D. Move the instance to a private subnet with no internet access.

**Question 35:**

Domain: Threat Detection and Incident Response

When investigating a compromised Amazon EC2 instance, which AWS service allows you to capture a complete memory dump for forensic analysis?

A. AWS Systems Manager
B. AWS CloudTrail
C. AWS Elastic Beanstalk
D. EC2Rescue

**Question 36:**
Domain: Security Logging and Monitoring
A custom application running on an Amazon EC2 instance is designed to send operational metrics to Amazon CloudWatch. However, the application is not reporting any statistics as expected. What could be the possible cause of this issue?

A. The CloudWatch Logs agent is not installed on the EC2 instance.
B. The IAM role attached to the EC2 instance lacks the cloudwatch:PutMetricData permission.
C. The CloudWatch alarm associated with the application is not configured properly.
D. The EC2 instance is not in the same region as the CloudWatch service.

**Question 37:**
Domain: Security Logging and Monitoring
A financial services company needs to monitor AWS services for any unauthorized API calls or changes to critical resources. The monitoring solution must comply with stringent regulatory requirements for audit trails. Which AWS service should the company use to meet these security and compliance requirements?

A. AWS CloudTrail
B. Amazon CloudWatch
C. AWS GuardDuty
D. Amazon Macie

**Question 38:**
Domain: Security Logging and Monitoring
A security engineer needs to configure logging for an Amazon S3 bucket to capture and monitor access requests to the bucket, including requests that are denied due to permissions. Which actions should the security engineer take to enable and access the logs? (Select TWO.)

A. Enable server access logging for the S3 bucket.
B. Enable AWS CloudTrail Data Events for the S3 bucket.
C. Configure Amazon S3 Inventory to track object-level activities.
D. Use Amazon Athena to query the CloudTrail logs for S3 access.
E. Enable VPC Flow Logs for the VPC containing the S3 bucket.

**Question 39:**
Domain: Security Logging and Monitoring
An organization needs to ensure that its log data is retained for 7 years to comply with regulatory requirements. The log data is stored in Amazon S3. What should the organization do to implement this retention policy?

A. Use Amazon S3 Lifecycle policies to transition objects to Glacier after 7 years.
B. Use Amazon S3 Lifecycle policies to delete objects automatically after 7 years.
C. Enable versioning on the S3 bucket and configure a lifecycle policy to retain logs.
D. Move the logs to Amazon Glacier Deep Archive after 7 years for long-term storage.

**Question 40:**
Domain: Security Logging and Monitoring
A security engineer is setting up log ingestion for a new AWS environment. The engineer needs to ensure that logs from Amazon EC2 instances, Amazon S3, and Amazon RDS are captured and centralized for analysis. Which AWS services should the engineer configure to meet this requirement? (Select TWO.)

A. Amazon CloudWatch Logs for EC2 instance logs
B. AWS CloudTrail Data Events for S3 access logs
C. Amazon RDS Enhanced Monitoring for capturing database logs
D. AWS Config for tracking changes in resources
E. AWS X-Ray for tracing requests across services

## Question 41:
Domain: Security Logging and Monitoring
A security analyst notices that logs from an important application are missing from the centralized logging system. The application runs on Amazon EC2 instances, and the logs were previously being ingested into Amazon CloudWatch Logs. What should the analyst check first to determine the cause of the missing logs?
  A. Verify that the CloudWatch Logs agent is running on the EC2 instances.
  B. Ensure that the EC2 instances have network connectivity to the CloudWatch Logs endpoint.
  C. Check the CloudWatch Logs quota to ensure that it has not been exceeded.
  D. Review the IAM role associated with the EC2 instances to verify that it has the correct permissions for CloudWatch Logs.

## Question 42:
Domain: Security Logging and Monitoring
A security team is tasked with identifying suspicious activity by analyzing logs from various AWS services, including Amazon S3, AWS Lambda, and AWS CloudTrail. The team needs to correlate logs from these services to detect patterns indicative of potential threats. Which AWS service should the team use to normalize, parse, and correlate these logs?
  A. Amazon Athena
  B. AWS Security Hub
  C. Amazon Macie
  D. AWS Lambda

## Question 43:
Domain: Security Logging and Monitoring
A company is deploying a new web application on AWS, which includes an Amazon EC2 instance, an RDS database, and an Application Load Balancer (ALB). The security team needs to identify and monitor security-related events across all these components. Which combination of AWS services should the security team use to collect and monitor logs from all components?
  A. AWS CloudTrail for API activity, Amazon CloudWatch Logs for EC2 logs, and AWS Config for configuration changes
  B. AWS GuardDuty for threat detection, AWS Config for configuration changes, and Amazon Inspector for vulnerability assessments
  C. AWS CloudTrail for API activity, AWS X-Ray for request tracing, and Amazon CloudWatch for custom metrics
  D. AWS CloudTrail for API activity, AWS Config for configuration changes, and AWS Systems Manager for patch compliance

## Question 44:
Domain: Security Logging and Monitoring
A security engineer needs to configure the storage and lifecycle management of logs according to AWS best practices. What is the recommended solution for managing long-term log storage while optimizing cost?
  A. Store logs in Amazon S3 with Intelligent-Tiering enabled and set lifecycle policies for transition to Glacier
  B. Store logs in Amazon RDS with automated snapshots enabled
  C. Store logs in AWS CloudWatch Logs with perpetual retention
  D. Store logs in Amazon DynamoDB with global tables enabled

**Question 45:**
Domain: Infrastructure Security
A company has deployed a public-facing website on AWS using Amazon CloudFront as a Content Delivery Network (CDN) and Amazon S3 to host static assets. The company is concerned about potential threats like DDoS attacks and injection vulnerabilities. Which combination of AWS services should the security engineer use to enhance the edge security of the website?
   A. AWS WAF to protect against SQL injection and XSS attacks, and AWS Shield Standard to mitigate DDoS attacks.
   B. AWS Config to monitor configuration changes and AWS GuardDuty for threat detection.
   C. AWS Certificate Manager (ACM) for SSL/TLS certificates and Amazon Macie for sensitive data discovery.
   D. Amazon Inspector to assess vulnerabilities and AWS Secrets Manager to manage sensitive information.

**Question 46:**
Domain: Infrastructure Security
A mobile application backend is hosted on AWS using serverless architecture, including Amazon API Gateway and AWS Lambda. The application is experiencing an increase in API request volumes, potentially indicating a DDoS attack. What edge security strategies should the security engineer implement to protect the application?
   A. Enable AWS Shield Advanced for API Gateway and configure rate-based rules in AWS WAF to block malicious requests.
   B. Use Amazon CloudFront to cache API responses and AWS Macie to detect sensitive data.
   C. Deploy AWS Systems Manager to automate the blocking of IP addresses and Amazon Inspector for vulnerability scanning.
   D. Implement AWS Key Management Service (KMS) to encrypt API requests and AWS Config for configuration management.

**Question 47:**
Domain: Identity and Access Management
A company is configuring an application that needs to access AWS resources in another account temporarily. The application requires short-lived access credentials for this purpose. Which service should the company use to issue these credentials?
   A. AWS Identity and Access Management (IAM)
   B. AWS Security Token Service (AWS STS)
   C. AWS Directory Service
   D. AWS Single Sign-On (SSO)

**Question 48:**
Domain: Identity and Access Management
A security engineer needs to enforce multi-factor authentication (MFA) for users accessing sensitive data in an Amazon S3 bucket. The users already have permissions to access the bucket. What is the best approach to enforce MFA for this access?
   A. Update the IAM policy attached to the users to require MFA for the S3 actions.
   B. Create an S3 bucket policy that denies access unless MFA is used.
   C. Enable MFA on the root account.
   D. Attach a service control policy (SCP) requiring MFA to the organizational unit (OU) containing the users.

**Question 49:**
Domain: Identity and Access Management

An organization uses attribute-based access control (ABAC) to manage permissions for its users. The company wants to ensure that employees only have access to resources tagged with their department name. Which IAM policy condition key should be used to enforce this requirement?

    A. aws:PrincipalTag
    B. aws:RequestTag
    C. aws:ResourceTag
    D. aws:RequestRegion

**Question 50:**

Domain: Identity and Access Management

A security engineer is reviewing an IAM policy that allows a user to perform actions on an Amazon S3 bucket but denies actions if the request is not from a specific IP range. What will be the effect of this policy?

    A. The user can access the S3 bucket only from the specified IP range.
    B. The user can access the S3 bucket from any IP address.
    C. The user cannot access the S3 bucket at all.
    D. The policy will be ignored, and the default allow behavior will apply.

**Question 51:**

Domain: Identity and Access Management

A developer is troubleshooting a Lambda function that cannot access an Amazon DynamoDB table. The IAM role attached to the function has the necessary permissions. What should the developer check next?

    A. Whether the IAM policy is attached to the correct role.
    B. Whether the IAM role has an explicit deny statement for DynamoDB.
    C. Whether the DynamoDB table's resource policy allows access to the role.
    D. Whether the Lambda function's VPC configuration is correct.

**Question 52:**

Domain: Identity and Access Management

A company needs to enforce the principle of least privilege for its IAM users. The security team discovered that some users have permissions that are not necessary for their roles. What is the best approach to address this issue?

    A. Use IAM Access Analyzer to identify and remove unnecessary permissions.
    B. Manually review each user's permissions and adjust as needed.
    C. Enable service control policies (SCPs) to limit permissions across the organization.
    D. Require multi-factor authentication (MFA) for all actions performed by users.

**Question 53:**

Domain: Identity and Access Management

A company has implemented role-based access control (RBAC) for its AWS environment. A new project requires specific access to a subset of resources by users from different roles. How should the company grant these permissions while maintaining the principle of least privilege?

    A. Create a new IAM role with the necessary permissions and assign it to the users.
    B. Modify the existing IAM roles to include the new permissions.
    C. Use resource-based policies to grant access to the specific resources.
    D. Use service control policies (SCPs) to enforce the new permissions.

**Question 54:**

Domain: Data Protection

A company needs to establish secure connectivity between their on-premises data center and AWS using Direct Connect. They want to ensure that all traffic is encrypted while traversing the connection. Which approach should the company take?

A. Use AWS Direct Connect with a private VIF and enable encryption using an AWS Site-to-Site VPN over Direct Connect.
B. Use AWS Direct Connect with a public VIF and enable SSL/TLS encryption for application-level traffic.
C. Use AWS Direct Connect with a private VIF and rely on AWS Shield for encryption.
D. Use AWS Direct Connect with a public VIF and configure encryption in the Direct Connect settings.

**Question 55:**
Domain: Data Protection
A company wants to ensure that all connections to their Amazon S3 buckets require encryption. How can the company enforce this requirement?
A. Apply a bucket policy that requires the use of the x-amz-server-side-encryption header for all PUT requests.
B. Enable default encryption on the S3 bucket using AWS KMS keys.
C. Configure a VPC endpoint for S3 and require all connections to use HTTPS.
D. Use AWS WAF to block any non-encrypted requests to the S3 bucket.

**Question 56:**
Domain: Data Protection
Your organization is setting up an Amazon RDS instance for a critical application. The security team requires that all connections to the RDS instance be encrypted. What should you do to meet this requirement?
A. Enable encryption in the RDS settings and configure the application to use SSL/TLS for connections.
B. Set up a VPN between the application server and the RDS instance to ensure encrypted traffic.
C. Use IAM roles to enforce encrypted connections to the RDS instance.
D. Apply an S3 bucket policy to enforce encryption when accessing the RDS instance.

**Question 57:**
Domain: Data Protection
A company is designing a cross-Region networking solution using AWS Direct Connect. They want to ensure that traffic between Regions is secure and does not traverse the public internet. What solution should they implement?
A. Use AWS Direct Connect with private VIFs in each Region and configure VPNs over Direct Connect for encryption.
B. Use AWS Direct Connect with public VIFs and enable AWS Shield for secure connections.
C. Use AWS Direct Connect Gateway to route traffic between private VIFs in different Regions.
D. Use AWS Global Accelerator to route traffic securely between Regions over the public internet.

**Question 58:**
Domain: Data Protection
A company needs to establish a secure, cross-Region connection between its AWS environments in the US East (N. Virginia) and Europe (Frankfurt) Regions. The company wants to ensure that traffic does not traverse the public internet. Which configuration should the company implement?
A. Set up a VPN over AWS Direct Connect with private VIFs in both Regions and route traffic through a Direct Connect Gateway.
B. Use a public VIF on AWS Direct Connect in both Regions to ensure traffic does not traverse the public internet.
C. Configure VPC peering between the VPCs in both Regions to route traffic securely.
D. Use AWS Transit Gateway with VPC attachments in both Regions and enable AWS Global Accelerator for secure routing.

**Question 59:**
Domain: Management and Security Governance

A company is planning to implement AWS Control Tower to manage its multi-account environment. Which prerequisite must be considered before deployment?
- A. Deactivate AWS Config across all existing accounts
- B. Ensure AWS Organizations is enabled with all features
- C. Disable Amazon CloudWatch Logs in all existing accounts
- D. Remove all existing Service Control Policies (SCPs) from the organization

## Question 60:
Domain: Management and Security Governance
An organization wants to enforce strict limitations on the use of root accounts across its AWS accounts. Which strategy should the organization implement using AWS Organizations?
- A. Apply an SCP that denies all actions except billing for root users
- B. Enable AWS CloudTrail to log all actions performed by the root account
- C. Use IAM policies to restrict root account access
- D. Set up AWS Config to monitor root account activities and alert when used

## Question 61:
Domain: Management and Security Governance
An organization needs to securely share resources like Amazon S3 buckets and Amazon RDS instances across multiple AWS accounts. Which service provides a solution for securely sharing resources?
- A. AWS Resource Access Manager (RAM)
- B. AWS Control Tower
- C. AWS Organizations
- D. AWS Service Catalog

## Question 62:
Domain: Management and Security Governance
A security engineer needs to enforce a centralized security policy across multiple AWS accounts to manage network firewalls. Which service should they deploy to achieve this?
- A. AWS Firewall Manager
- B. AWS Security Hub
- C. AWS Control Tower
- D. AWS Config

## Question 63:
Domain: Management and Security Governance
A company needs to deploy a consistent and secure cloud environment across multiple AWS accounts, ensuring only approved services are available for use. Which service should be used to create and manage portfolios of approved services?
- A. AWS Service Catalog
- B. AWS Control Tower
- C. AWS Resource Access Manager (RAM)
- D. AWS Firewall Manager

## Question 64:
Domain: Management and Security Governance
A security team is tasked with ensuring that all AWS accounts in an organization are consistently managed and that security configurations are centralized. What AWS service should be used to aggregate findings and manage security configurations across accounts?
- A. AWS Control Tower
- B. AWS Config aggregators
- C. AWS Resource Access Manager (RAM)

D. AWS Service Catalog

**Question 65:**
Domain: Management and Security Governance
Your company has multiple AWS accounts and wants to enforce a tagging strategy across all resources. What method can be used to ensure compliance with the tagging strategy?
    A. Implement an SCP that denies resource creation without proper tags
    B. Use AWS Config to create rules that evaluate resource tags across accounts
    C. Apply a CloudFormation template that enforces tagging on all resources
    D. Utilize AWS Service Catalog to enforce tagging during resource provisioning

# Practice Test Set 1 – Answers

**Question 1:**
Correct Answer: B. Disable the Network Source/Destination check on the virtual security appliance's elastic network interface.
Brief Explanation: Disabling the source/destination check on the virtual security appliance allows it to inspect and log traffic between other instances in the subnet, as it can now receive and inspect packets not destined for its own IP address.

**Question 2:**
Correct Answer: B. Enable the automatic key rotation option in the AWS KMS console.
Brief Explanation: AWS KMS allows automatic key rotation for customer-managed CMKs. Enabling this option will rotate the key every 365 days (about 6 months).

**Question 3:**
Correct Answer: C. Configure an EventBridge rule in Security Hub to detect medium-priority findings and route them to an SNS topic for email notifications.
Brief Explanation: AWS EventBridge can be used to create rules that detect specific findings in Security Hub and send notifications via SNS for further processing or alerts, such as sending emails.

**Question 4:**
Correct Answer: B. Place the EC2 instances in a public subnet and configure a security group that allows inbound traffic on the necessary ports, and place the RDS instance in a private subnet with a security group that allows inbound traffic only from the EC2 instances.
Brief Explanation: In this scenario, the best approach is to place EC2 instances that need internet access in a public subnet and configure their security group to allow inbound traffic on necessary ports (e.g., HTTP/HTTPS). The RDS instance should be in a private subnet with a security group allowing inbound traffic only from the EC2 instances. This configuration ensures that the RDS instance is not exposed to the internet, following best practices for network security.

**Question 5:**
Correct Answer: B. AWS Inspector with a Common Vulnerabilities and Exposures (CVE) scan and CIS benchmark assessment.
Brief Explanation: Amazon Inspector is used to scan EC2 instances for vulnerabilities, including checking against CIS benchmarks and CVEs.

**Question 6:**
Correct Answer: D. Provide the replication IAM role the kms
permission for the key in the source region.

Brief Explanation: To replicate encrypted objects, the replication role needs kms:Decrypt permission on the source key to decrypt the objects before replication.

**Question 7:**
Correct Answer: A. Implement a permissions boundary on all IAM roles created by regional teams.
Brief Explanation: Permissions boundaries allow restricting the maximum permissions that can be assigned to roles, ensuring that regional teams do not assign excessive permissions.

**Question 8:**
Correct Answer: B. Configure AWS WAF rate-based rules to limit excessive requests from the same IP.
Brief Explanation: AWS WAF allows rate-based rules to limit the number of requests from a single IP, helping to mitigate Layer 7 DDoS attacks.

**Question 9:**
Correct Answer: B. The specified IAM users will be denied access unless additional permissions are granted through IAM policies.
Brief Explanation: A deny rule in an S3 bucket policy will take precedence over allow rules, so unless IAM policies explicitly allow access, users will be denied.

**Question 10:**
Correct Answer: A. Disable the exposed access key immediately.
Brief Explanation: The first step to mitigate risk after exposure is to disable the compromised access key to prevent further unauthorized use.

**Question 11:**
Correct Answer: D. Take a snapshot of the EBS volumes and analyze them offline.
Brief Explanation: Taking snapshots of the EBS volumes allows for forensic analysis without further modifying the potentially compromised instance.

**Question 12:**
Correct Answer: A. Use AWS Certificate Manager (ACM) to manage SSL/TLS certificates and apply them to the NLB.
Brief Explanation: ACM can manage SSL/TLS certificates, and these can be applied directly to the Network Load Balancer to ensure secure connections.

**Question 13:**
Correct Answer: B. Create a new KMS key with new key material and update the alias to point to the new key.
Brief Explanation: Since automatic key rotation isn't available for keys with imported material, the best approach is to create a new key and update the alias.

**Question 14:**
Correct Answer: C. Use Amazon CloudWatch Logs subscription filters to send log data to a central Kinesis Data Firehose stream.
Brief Explanation: CloudWatch Logs subscription filters can be used to continuously stream log data from multiple accounts to a central Kinesis Data Firehose for processing and analysis.

**Question 15:**
Correct Answer: A. The EC2 instance security group does not allow inbound traffic from the NLB's IP addresses.
Brief Explanation: If the EC2 instance's security group does not allow traffic from the NLB, health checks and traffic from the NLB will be blocked, causing health check failures.

**Question 16:**
Correct Answer: A. AWS Config for configuration changes and CloudTrail for access logs.
Brief Explanation: AWS Config tracks configuration changes, and CloudTrail logs API calls and activities for audit purposes, meeting comprehensive logging needs.

**Question 17:**
Correct Answer: A. Create a custom key store in KMS and import the company's key material.
Brief Explanation: A custom key store allows you to manage the lifecycle of key material, including setting expiration dates according to policy requirements.

**Question 18:**
Correct Answer: C. An inbound rule in EC2-SG allowing traffic from ALB-SG on port 443.
Brief Explanation: For the ALB to forward traffic to the EC2 instances securely, the EC2 security group must allow inbound HTTPS traffic from the ALB's security group on port 443.

**Question 19:**
Correct Answer: A. Use AWS Secrets Manager to store and automatically rotate the RDS credentials.
Brief Explanation: AWS Secrets Manager is designed for securely managing and automatically rotating database credentials, including for RDS.

**Question 20:**
Correct Answer: B. Enable multi-factor authentication (MFA) on all root user accounts.
Brief Explanation: Enabling MFA on root accounts adds an extra layer of security and is recommended to enforce strict control over these highly privileged accounts.

**Question 21:**
Correct Answer: A. Review AWS CloudTrail logs for the federated identity used.
Brief Explanation: CloudTrail logs all API actions, including account creation, and can be used to identify the federated identity that performed the action.

**Question 22:**
Correct Answer: C. Configure Amazon Inspector to scan instances for known vulnerabilities.
Brief Explanation: Amazon Inspector can be used to scan EC2 instances for vulnerabilities, quickly identifying instances running specific vulnerable software.

**Question 23:**
Correct Answer: A. Inter-region traffic is encrypted by default on the AWS global network.
Brief Explanation: AWS automatically encrypts all inter-region traffic using the AWS global network, ensuring encryption in transit.

**Question 24:**
Correct Answer: B. Revoke the signing profile associated with the developer from all Lambda functions.
Brief Explanation: Revoking the signing profile prevents any code signed by the developer from being deployed to Lambda functions.

**Question 25:**
Correct Answer: A. Deploy an egress-only internet gateway and update the route table for the private subnet.
Brief Explanation: An egress-only internet gateway allows outbound-only IPv6 traffic, providing secure internet access for instances in a private subnet.

**Question 26:**

Correct Answer: A. Revoke all active sessions for the compromised IAM user using the AWS Management Console or CLI.
Correct Answer: D. Create a new access key for the IAM user, disable the old access key, and configure automatic rotation using AWS Secrets Manager.
Brief Explanation: Revoking sessions immediately disconnects the compromised user, and rotating the access key ensures that the old, compromised key is no longer valid.

## Question 27:
Correct Answer: A. Change the instance's security group to one that denies all inbound and outbound traffic.
Brief Explanation: Modifying the security group to deny all traffic effectively isolates the instance from the network while keeping it available for forensic analysis.

## Question 28:
Correct Answer: B. Develop automated runbooks using AWS Systems Manager Automation to execute predefined steps in response to detected incidents, such as isolating compromised instances or revoking access to S3 buckets.
Brief Explanation: Automated runbooks streamline the incident response process by executing predefined actions, reducing manual intervention and response time.

## Question 29:
Correct Answer: C. AWS Security Hub
Brief Explanation: AWS Security Hub provides a comprehensive view of security alerts across multiple AWS services, helping prioritize and respond to security findings.

## Question 30:
Correct Answer: B. ASFF (AWS Security Finding Format)
Brief Explanation: The AWS Security Finding Format (ASFF) is used by Security Hub and EventBridge to standardize and centralize security findings across AWS services.

## Question 31:
Correct Answer: A. Modify the bucket policy to restrict public access.
Brief Explanation: The immediate action should be to restrict public access to the S3 bucket to protect sensitive data identified by Macie.

## Question 32:
Correct Answer: B. Amazon Detective
Brief Explanation: Amazon Detective is specifically designed for investigating and analyzing security issues across AWS accounts, making it ideal for this scenario.

## Question 33:
Correct Answer: A.
SELECT * FROM cloudtrail_logs
WHERE eventName = 'DeleteBucket'
AND userIdentity.userName = 'specific-user'
AND eventTime > current_timestamp - interval '1' day;
Brief Explanation: This query correctly identifies all DeleteBucket operations performed by a specific IAM user within the last 24 hours.

## Question 34:
Correct Answer: C. Modify the security group associated with the instance to deny all inbound and outbound traffic.

Brief Explanation: Modifying the security group effectively isolates the instance without terminating it, allowing for further investigation.

**Question 35:**
Correct Answer: D. EC2Rescue
Brief Explanation: EC2Rescue can be used to capture a complete memory dump of an EC2 instance for forensic analysis.

**Question 36:**
Correct Answer: B. The IAM role attached to the EC2 instance lacks the cloudwatch permission.
Brief Explanation: The application may not be able to report metrics to CloudWatch if the IAM role lacks the necessary permission to put metric data.

**Question 37:**
Correct Answer: A. AWS CloudTrail
Brief Explanation: AWS CloudTrail logs all API calls and changes to resources, making it suitable for meeting stringent audit trail requirements.

**Question 38:**
Correct Answer: A. Enable server access logging for the S3 bucket.
Correct Answer: B. Enable AWS CloudTrail Data Events for the S3 bucket.
Brief Explanation: Server access logging captures details of requests made to the bucket, and CloudTrail Data Events provides detailed logging for object-level operations.

**Question 39:**
Correct Answer: B. Use Amazon S3 Lifecycle policies to delete objects automatically after 7 years.
Brief Explanation: Amazon S3 Lifecycle policies can be used to automatically delete objects after a specified period, ensuring compliance with retention requirements.

**Question 40:**
Correct Answer: A. Amazon CloudWatch Logs for EC2 instance logs.
Correct Answer: B. AWS CloudTrail Data Events for S3 access logs.
Brief Explanation: CloudWatch Logs and CloudTrail Data Events capture and centralize logs from EC2, S3, and other services for analysis.

**Question 41:**
Correct Answer: A. Verify that the CloudWatch Logs agent is running on the EC2 instances.
Brief Explanation: If the CloudWatch Logs agent is not running, logs from the application will not be ingested into CloudWatch, leading to missing logs.

**Question 42:**
Correct Answer: B. AWS Security Hub
Brief Explanation: AWS Security Hub can aggregate, normalize, and correlate logs from multiple AWS services to identify suspicious activity.

**Question 43:**
Correct Answer: A. AWS CloudTrail for API activity, Amazon CloudWatch Logs for EC2 logs, and AWS Config for configuration changes.
Brief Explanation: This combination covers API logging, operational metrics, and configuration changes across all components.

**Question 44:**
Correct Answer: A. Store logs in Amazon S3 with Intelligent-Tiering enabled and set lifecycle policies for transition to Glacier.
Brief Explanation: Using S3 with Intelligent-Tiering and lifecycle policies optimizes cost by automatically transitioning logs to lower-cost storage like Glacier.

**Question 45:**
Correct Answer: A. AWS WAF to protect against SQL injection and XSS attacks, and AWS Shield Standard to mitigate DDoS attacks.
Brief Explanation: AWS WAF protects against common web application attacks, while AWS Shield Standard offers DDoS protection for public-facing websites.

**Question 46:**
Correct Answer: A. Enable AWS Shield Advanced for API Gateway and configure rate-based rules in AWS WAF to block malicious requests.
Brief Explanation: Shield Advanced and WAF rate-based rules protect the application from high volumes of potentially malicious API requests, such as during a DDoS attack.

**Question 47:**
Correct Answer: B. AWS Security Token Service (AWS STS)
Brief Explanation: AWS STS provides temporary security credentials that are ideal for granting short-lived access to resources in another account.

**Question 48:**
Correct Answer: B. Create an S3 bucket policy that denies access unless MFA is used.
Brief Explanation: An S3 bucket policy can enforce MFA for users accessing the bucket, adding an additional layer of security.

**Question 49:**
Correct Answer: C. aws
Brief Explanation: The aws:ResourceTag condition key ensures that access is granted only to resources tagged with specific department names.

**Question 50:**
Correct Answer: A. The user can access the S3 bucket only from the specified IP range.
Brief Explanation: The IAM policy will allow access to the S3 bucket only if the request originates from the specified IP range.

**Question 51:**
Correct Answer: C. Whether the DynamoDB table's resource policy allows access to the role.
Brief Explanation: The DynamoDB table's resource policy must allow access to the IAM role attached to the Lambda function.

**Question 52:**
Correct Answer: A. Use IAM Access Analyzer to identify and remove unnecessary permissions.
Brief Explanation: IAM Access Analyzer helps identify unnecessary permissions, allowing the security team to enforce the principle of least privilege.

**Question 53:**
Correct Answer: C. Use resource-based policies to grant access to the specific resources.
Brief Explanation: Resource-based policies allow specific access to the required resources without altering the existing roles, maintaining the principle of least privilege.

**Question 54:**
Correct Answer: A. Use AWS Direct Connect with a private VIF and enable encryption using an AWS Site-to-Site VPN over Direct Connect.
Brief Explanation: A private VIF with a VPN provides encrypted traffic over Direct Connect, ensuring secure connectivity between the on-premises data center and AWS.

**Question 55:**
Correct Answer: A. Apply a bucket policy that requires the use of the x-amz-server-side-encryption header for all PUT requests.
Brief Explanation: This bucket policy ensures that all data uploaded to the S3 bucket is encrypted, enforcing the use of server-side encryption.

**Question 56:**
Correct Answer: A. Enable encryption in the RDS settings and configure the application to use SSL/TLS for connections.
Brief Explanation: Enabling SSL/TLS ensures that all connections to the RDS instance are encrypted, meeting the security requirements.

**Question 57:**
Correct Answer: A. Use AWS Direct Connect with private VIFs in each Region and configure VPNs over Direct Connect for encryption.
Brief Explanation: Using private VIFs with VPNs ensures that traffic remains secure and does not traverse the public internet, even between Regions.

**Question 58:**
Correct Answer: A. Set up a VPN over AWS Direct Connect with private VIFs in both Regions and route traffic through a Direct Connect Gateway.
Brief Explanation: This configuration secures cross-region traffic using a Direct Connect Gateway, ensuring it does not traverse the public internet.

**Question 59:**
Correct Answer: B. Ensure AWS Organizations is enabled with all features.
Brief Explanation: AWS Control Tower requires that AWS Organizations is enabled with all features to manage and govern a multi-account environment effectively.

**Question 60:**
Correct Answer: A. Apply an SCP that denies all actions except billing for root users.
Brief Explanation: An SCP restricting root user actions to billing tasks only is an effective strategy to limit the use of root accounts across AWS accounts.

**Question 61:**
Correct Answer: A. AWS Resource Access Manager (RAM)
Brief Explanation: AWS RAM allows the secure sharing of AWS resources like S3 buckets and RDS instances across multiple AWS accounts.

**Question 62:**
Correct Answer: A. AWS Firewall Manager
Brief Explanation: AWS Firewall Manager centrally manages firewall rules across multiple AWS accounts, ensuring consistent security policy enforcement.

**Question 63:**

Correct Answer: A. AWS Service Catalog
Brief Explanation: AWS Service Catalog allows organizations to create and manage portfolios of approved services, ensuring a secure and consistent cloud environment.

**Question 64:**
Correct Answer: B. AWS Config aggregators
Brief Explanation: AWS Config aggregators enable the aggregation of compliance data from multiple accounts, centralizing security management and configuration compliance.

**Question 65:**
Correct Answer: B. Use AWS Config to create rules that evaluate resource tags across accounts.
Brief Explanation: AWS Config can evaluate resource tags and enforce compliance with tagging policies across all AWS accounts, ensuring consistency.

# Practice Test Set 2

**Question 1:**
Domain: Data Protection
A security engineer is tasked with ensuring that an organization's data is protected by an encryption method that allows for immediate cryptographic erasure. The engineer must implement a solution that provides the fastest possible removal of access to the encrypted data. Which option meets this requirement?
   A. Use an AWS KMS key with automatic key rotation enabled.
   B. Use an AWS managed KMS key.
   C. Use imported key material with an AWS KMS key and delete the key material when necessary.
   D. Use a customer-managed KMS key and enable the key deletion option.

**Question 2:**
Domain: Management and Security Governance
A company needs to ensure that CloudTrail logging is consistently enabled across all accounts within AWS Organizations. The logs should be stored in a centralized S3 bucket and protected against deletion or modification by account administrators. What is the most efficient solution?
   A. Create a new trail in each account and configure the S3 bucket with cross-account access.
   B. Use AWS Config to detect if CloudTrail is disabled and re-enable it.
   C. Create an organization trail in the management account and enforce the configuration using Service Control Policies (SCPs).
   D. Enable CloudTrail Insights and use a Lambda function to monitor for compliance.

**Question 3:**
Domain: Identity and Access Management
A security engineer needs to grant read-only access to a shared S3 bucket across multiple AWS accounts within an organization. The solution must ensure that the data is not publicly accessible and that permissions are managed centrally. Which approach should the security engineer take?
   A. Use S3 bucket policies with aws:PrincipalOrgId condition to restrict access to the organization.
   B. Configure a cross-account IAM role in each account and attach the role to the S3 bucket policy.
   C. Use AWS Organizations Service Control Policies (SCPs) to restrict bucket access.
   D. Use AWS Resource Access Manager (RAM) to share the bucket with the organization.

**Question 4:**
Domain: Infrastructure Security
A financial company has implemented an AWS Organizations structure with multiple accounts. To protect against accidental or intentional deletion of critical Amazon S3 data, the company wants to enforce the prevention of S3 object deletions across all accounts. Which strategy will achieve this goal most effectively?
   A. Implement S3 Object Lock with Compliance mode enabled.
   B. Apply Service Control Policies (SCPs) to deny s3:DeleteObject actions.
   C. Use S3 bucket policies with explicit deny statements for delete actions.
   D. Use IAM permissions boundaries to restrict delete operations.

**Question 5:**
Domain: Threat Detection and Incident Response
A company has set up an AWS Direct Connect connection to link its on-premises data center to AWS. The security team needs to ensure that data in transit between on-premises and AWS is encrypted. What is the best solution to implement this encryption?
   A. Set up an IPSec VPN over the Direct Connect connection.
   B. Enable TLS for the applications running on the instances using the Direct Connect.
   C. Use AWS KMS to encrypt data before it is transmitted over Direct Connect.

D. Use AWS Direct Connect Gateway to apply encryption at the transit level.

**Question 6:**
Domain: Identity and Access Management
After a recent security incident, a security engineer needs to revoke access to multiple Amazon EC2 instances for a developer who was recently terminated. The developer has access through SSH keys stored on their personal device. What is the most efficient way to revoke this access?
   A. Modify the SSH keys directly on the EC2 instances and replace them with new ones.
   B. Remove the developer's SSH keys from the instance metadata service.
   C. Disable the developer's access by updating the instance security groups to block SSH access.
   D. Use AWS Systems Manager to replace the SSH keys across all affected instances.

**Question 7:**
Domain: Infrastructure Security
A company uses an S3 bucket to store static content for its website. The website content is delivered using Amazon CloudFront. The security team wants to ensure that the S3 bucket can only be accessed through CloudFront and not directly from the internet. What steps should be taken to achieve this?
   A. Use an S3 bucket policy to allow access only from CloudFront's IP ranges.
   B. Configure a CloudFront origin access control (OAC) and update the bucket policy to restrict access to CloudFront.
   C. Enable S3 Block Public Access on the bucket and use a signed URL for CloudFront.
   D. Attach a VPC endpoint to the S3 bucket and restrict access to CloudFront's IP range.

**Question 8:**
Domain: Identity and Access Management
A company is planning to extend access to multiple AWS accounts to its employees. The solution needs to integrate with the company's existing Active Directory and provide scalable, centralized access management across all accounts. Which solution would best meet these requirements?
   A. Deploy AWS Control Tower and integrate AWS SSO with the existing Active Directory.
   B. Set up IAM roles in each account and use federated sign-in from Active Directory.
   C. Create IAM users in each AWS account and use IAM policies to manage permissions.
   D. Configure AWS Resource Access Manager (RAM) to share resources across accounts.

**Question 9:**
Domain: Data Protection
A security engineer is responsible for setting up and maintaining Amazon S3 Glacier vaults for a financial institution's data archival. The engineer has initiated a vault lock operation but realizes that the policy needs adjustment. What is the best course of action?
   A. Delete the existing vault and create a new one with the updated policy.
   B. Abort the vault lock process, update the policy, and restart the vault lock operation.
   C. Apply the policy changes and wait for the vault lock operation to complete.
   D. Update the policy during the vault lock in-progress state.

**Question 10:**
Domain: Security Logging and Monitoring
A security engineer needs to monitor Amazon S3 buckets for any changes to bucket policies. The engineer wants to receive alerts when a policy is modified. What is the most efficient way to achieve this?
   A. Set up an AWS Config rule to detect changes in bucket policies and trigger an SNS notification.
   B. Enable CloudTrail logs for S3 API events and create an EventBridge rule to send alerts via SNS.
   C. Use Amazon GuardDuty to monitor for changes to S3 bucket policies and trigger an SNS notification.
   D. Implement AWS Lambda to monitor CloudWatch logs and trigger alerts based on S3 policy changes.

**Question 11:**
Domain: Identity and Access Management
A company is using AWS Systems Manager Parameter Store to store secure string parameters. The parameters are encrypted using a customer-managed key in AWS KMS. Recently, the team encountered errors when attempting to retrieve parameters. What are the possible causes of this issue? (Select TWO.)
    A. The customer-managed key is set to 'Disabled' state.
    B. The IAM role lacks the kms:Decrypt permission for the customer-managed key.
    C. The customer-managed key has expired and is no longer valid.
    D. The secure string parameter limit has been exceeded for the specified KMS key.
    E. The IAM role is using a key alias instead of the key ID in its configuration.

**Question 12:**
Domain: Security Logging and Monitoring
A company uses Amazon API Gateway to provide APIs for their services. The security team needs to analyze usage patterns and detect anomalies without combing through log files manually. What actions should be taken to fulfill these requirements with minimal effort? (Select TWO.)
    A. Enable detailed CloudWatch Metrics for the API Gateway.
    B. Set up access logging in API Gateway and analyze the logs using CloudWatch Logs Insights.
    C. Create an AWS CloudTrail trail to log API Gateway requests and analyze using Athena.
    D. Use AWS Config to track changes in API Gateway and monitor anomalies.
    E. Enable data event logging for API Gateway in CloudTrail and analyze the logs with CloudWatch Logs Insights.

**Question 13:**
Domain: Infrastructure Security
A security engineer notices a high rate of suspicious HTTP requests to an Application Load Balancer (ALB) fronted by an Amazon CloudFront distribution. Users report performance degradation due to these requests. What is the most efficient way to mitigate these unwanted requests?
    A. Implement a rate-based rule in AWS WAF to block requests exceeding a threshold.
    B. Use AWS Shield Advanced to automatically mitigate DDoS attacks.
    C. Block the suspicious IP addresses using an IP set in AWS WAF.
    D. Configure an Amazon GuardDuty threat detection to block the IPs.

**Question 14:**
Domain: Threat Detection and Incident Response
A company has been notified of a potential security breach involving an IAM access key used in an automated process. The key was exposed on a public forum. What steps should the security engineer take to mitigate the exposure and improve security practices?
    A. Revoke the compromised IAM access key, create a new key, and update the automated process.
    B. Rotate the IAM access key and implement MFA on the associated IAM user.
    C. Disable the compromised IAM access key and switch to using IAM roles for the automation.
    D. Use AWS Secrets Manager to store the new access key securely and update the automation.

**Question 15:**
Domain: Infrastructure Security
A healthcare organization needs to establish secure connections to Amazon EC2 instances without managing SSH keys or opening inbound ports. Additionally, all session activity must be logged and stored securely. What is the best solution?
    A. Use AWS Systems Manager Session Manager for secure access and configure CloudWatch Logs for session logging.
    B. Use a bastion host for secure SSH access and log all session activity with Amazon CloudTrail.
    C. Implement AWS Inspector for secure access and configure CloudWatch Logs for logging.

D. Use AWS Systems Manager Run Command for access and store logs in an encrypted S3 bucket.

**Question 16:**
Domain: Security Logging and Monitoring
A security engineer has configured AWS Config to monitor changes to an Amazon S3 bucket and notify via SNS. However, notifications are not being sent when changes are made. What steps should the engineer take to resolve the issue? (Select THREE.)
A. Update the IAM role to allow sns:Publish action for config.amazonaws.com.
B. Add permissions for AWS Config to write to the S3 bucket.
C. Configure the SNS topic's access policy to allow publishing from AWS Config.
D. Enable bucket versioning to track changes more effectively.
E. Update the bucket ACLs to allow AWS Config to monitor the changes.
F. Ensure AWS Config is using the correct IAM role with necessary permissions.

**Question 17:**
Domain: Threat Detection and Incident Response
After locking down an Amazon S3 bucket with a restrictive policy, a security engineer tries to grant access to a forensic analyst but encounters access denied errors. What could be the reason for the denial?
A. The bucket is subject to eventual consistency, delaying policy changes.
B. The S3 Block Public Access feature is enabled, overriding the policy.
C. The IAM policy of the forensic analyst conflicts with the bucket policy.
D. The explicit deny in the bucket policy takes precedence over any allow statements.

**Question 18:**
Domain: Infrastructure Security
A company requires all traffic to a specific application hosted on Amazon EC2 to be inspected for anomalies. The application runs across several instances. What is the best approach to route traffic to an intrusion detection instance?
A. Set up VPC traffic mirroring to send traffic to the intrusion detection instance.
B. Disable source/destination checks and use VPC Flow Logs for inspection.
C. Use AWS Shield to detect and block anomalous traffic.
D. Deploy AWS Network Firewall and configure a rule to inspect the traffic.

**Question 19:**
Domain: Infrastructure Security
A security engineer is tasked with ensuring that the database subnets in a VPC do not have internet access, while the application subnets retain internet connectivity. What is the best way to achieve this?
A. Remove the NAT gateway from the route table of the database subnets.
B. Configure the database subnets' security groups to block outbound traffic.
C. Apply an inbound network ACL rule to deny traffic from the NAT gateway.
D. Create a separate route table for database subnets without the default route to the NAT gateway.

**Question 20:**
Domain: Infrastructure Security
A company is deploying a three-tier application in AWS and needs to configure security groups for the application and database tiers. The application uses port 1030, and the database uses port 3306. Which security group rules should be applied to follow best practices? (Select TWO.)
A. On the AppSG, allow inbound traffic on port 1030 from the WebSG.
B. On the DBSG, allow inbound traffic on port 3306 from the AppSG.
C. On the WebSG, allow inbound traffic on port 80 from the AppSG.
D. On the AppSG, allow inbound traffic on port 1030 from the DBSG.
E. On the DBSG, allow inbound traffic on port 3306 from the WebSG.

**Question 21:**
Domain: Data Protection
A company requires that encryption keys used for Amazon S3 data encryption are only usable by the Amazon S3 service. How can this be achieved?
    A. Configure the KMS key policy with a condition limiting the key to S3 service use only.
    B. Use an IAM policy to restrict the KMS key to Amazon S3 principals.
    C. Apply a Service Control Policy (SCP) to restrict key usage to S3 in the organization.
    D. Set up a KMS key policy that denies all services except S3.

**Question 22:**
Domain: Identity and Access Management
A company uses a mix of IAM users, federated users from Active Directory, and Amazon Cognito user pools for authentication. The security team requires that all users adhere to a strict password policy. Which settings should be configured to enforce this policy? (Select THREE.)
    A. Set up a password policy in IAM for IAM users.
    B. Enforce a password policy in the Active Directory for federated users.
    C. Implement a password policy in AWS Organizations for all users.
    D. Configure password policies in Amazon Cognito user pools.
    E. Use a Service Control Policy (SCP) to enforce password policies across the organization.
    F. Apply password policies in IAM roles used by federated users.

**Question 23:**
Domain: Security Logging and Monitoring
A company has deployed an application using Amazon ECS with the Fargate launch type. The logs need to be aggregated into a central CloudWatch log group. How should this be accomplished?
    A. Enable the awslogs log driver in the ECS task definition.
    B. Attach a CloudWatch Logs agent to the ECS tasks.
    C. Use FluentD to aggregate logs and send them to CloudWatch.
    D. Configure a Lambda function to pull logs from ECS and push to CloudWatch.

**Question 24:**
Domain: Infrastructure Security
A static website hosted on an Amazon EC2 instance needs protection from DDoS attacks. What are the two best methods to mitigate the risk?
    A. Use AWS WAF to filter and block malicious web traffic.
    B. Deploy Amazon CloudFront to cache content and shield the EC2 instance.
    C. Restrict inbound traffic to the EC2 instance using security groups.
    D. Monitor and analyze traffic using AWS X-Ray.
    E. Use an Application Load Balancer to distribute traffic and apply security settings.

**Question 25:**
Domain: Data Protection
A security engineer is responsible for ensuring that all Amazon RDS instances are encrypted at rest. The engineer needs to identify any unencrypted databases and apply encryption. What are the steps to achieve this? (Select TWO.)
    A. Use AWS Config to detect unencrypted RDS instances and notify the security team.
    B. Create encrypted snapshots of unencrypted databases and restore from these snapshots.
    C. Manually apply KMS encryption keys to the existing RDS databases.
    D. Enable encryption on existing databases directly in the RDS console.
    E. Configure CloudTrail to monitor changes to RDS encryption status and alert the security team.

**Question 26:**
Domain: Threat Detection and Incident Response
A security engineer wants to automate the discovery of Personally Identifiable Information (PII) in their S3 buckets. Which AWS service should they deploy?
 A. AWS Config
 B. Amazon Macie
 C. AWS Security Hub
 D. Amazon GuardDuty

**Question 27:**
Domain: Threat Detection and Incident Response
Which of the following is the MOST efficient way to integrate a third-party SIEM solution with AWS Security Hub findings?
 A. Use AWS Lambda to poll AWS Security Hub periodically.
 B. Use Amazon EventBridge to send findings to the third-party SIEM in real-time.
 C. Use an AWS Glue job to extract and transform findings data.
 D. Manually export findings from AWS Security Hub to the SIEM solution.

**Question 28:**
Domain: Threat Detection and Incident Response
AWS Config has flagged a security group that allows unrestricted access to port 22. What is the best course of action to address this finding?
 A. Update the security group to allow access only from known IP addresses.
 B. Create a new security group with tighter rules and apply it to the affected instances.
 C. Remove the rule allowing access to port 22 entirely.
 D. Add the security group to a VPC endpoint to limit its exposure.

**Question 29:**
Domain: Threat Detection and Incident Response
A security engineer needs to correlate VPC Flow Logs and AWS CloudTrail logs to identify potential threats within an AWS environment. Which service can assist in visualizing this data and performing threat correlation?
 A. Amazon Macie
 B. Amazon Detective
 C. AWS Config
 D. AWS X-Ray

**Question 30:**
Domain: Threat Detection and Incident Response
A company's security team needs to investigate potential unauthorized access to Amazon S3 objects. Which Amazon Athena SQL query should they use to identify any GetObject requests where the request IP address was from outside the company's allowed range?
 A.
SELECT * FROM s3_access_logs
WHERE operation = 'REST.GET.OBJECT'
AND requesterip NOT BETWEEN '192.168.0.1' AND '192.168.0.255';

 B.
SELECT * FROM s3_access_logs
WHERE requestOperation = 'GetObject'
AND sourceIPAddress NOT LIKE '192.168.%';

 C.

```
SELECT * FROM s3_access_logs
WHERE operation = 'GetObject'
AND requesterIpAddress NOT LIKE '192.168.%';
```

D.
```
SELECT * FROM s3_access_logs
WHERE operation = 'REST.GET.OBJECT'
AND requestIP NOT LIKE '192.168.%';
```

**Question 31:**
Domain: Threat Detection and Incident Response
During an incident response, you need to isolate a suspected compromised Amazon EC2 instance. Which AWS feature allows you to automate the isolation of this instance without manual intervention?

    A. AWS Config with a remediation action.
    B. AWS Systems Manager Automation.
    C. AWS Shield Advanced.
    D. AWS Trusted Advisor.

**Question 32:**
Domain: Threat Detection and Incident Response
Which of the following actions is necessary to capture a forensic snapshot of an Amazon EBS volume attached to a compromised instance without introducing further changes to the data?

    A. Stop the instance before taking a snapshot of the attached EBS volumes.
    B. Detach the EBS volume, attach it to a forensic instance, and then take a snapshot.
    C. Suspend the instance using EC2 Hibernate before taking a snapshot.
    D. Take an EBS snapshot while the instance is still running to capture the most recent data.

**Question 33:**
Domain: Threat Detection and Incident Response
Question: What is the primary advantage of using Amazon Detective in a root cause analysis process?

    A. It automatically mitigates detected security threats.
    B. It provides deep insights and visualizations for security incidents by linking and organizing data across multiple AWS sources.
    C. It offers real-time alerts for all types of security events.
    D. It can automatically quarantine compromised instances.

**Question 34:**
Domain: Security Logging and Monitoring
A security engineer notices that CloudTrail logs are not being delivered to the specified S3 bucket. Upon investigation, the engineer discovers that the S3 bucket policy is missing. Which of the following actions should the engineer take to restore logging functionality?

    A. Enable versioning on the S3 bucket to allow logging.
    B. Attach a bucket policy that grants CloudTrail write permissions to the S3 bucket.
    C. Modify the CloudTrail configuration to point to a different S3 bucket.
    D. Enable multi-factor authentication (MFA) for the S3 bucket.

**Question 35:**
Domain: Security Logging and Monitoring
An organization is not receiving VPC Flow Logs for a specific VPC. Upon investigation, it is found that the IAM role used by the VPC Flow Logs service does not have the correct permissions. What is the appropriate remediation step to resolve this issue?

A. Attach an IAM policy with logs:CreateLogGroup and logs:CreateLogStream permissions to the IAM role.
B. Enable server-side encryption on the S3 bucket receiving the logs.
C. Re-create the VPC Flow Logs with a different log format.
D. Modify the network ACLs to allow all traffic for the VPC.

## Question 36:
Domain: Security Logging and Monitoring
A security engineer is reviewing CloudWatch Logs and needs to normalize log data for easier analysis and correlation. Which of the following techniques would best achieve this?
A. Apply a CloudWatch Logs metric filter to aggregate data.
B. Use AWS Glue to convert the logs into a structured format.
C. Implement AWS Lambda to parse and normalize log data before storing it in CloudWatch Logs.
D. Use Athena to query the raw log data directly.

## Question 37:
Domain: Security Logging and Monitoring
While reviewing application logs, a security engineer identifies a pattern of repeated failed login attempts from the same IP address. Which AWS service can be used to automate a response to this threat?
A. AWS WAF to block the IP address.
B. AWS Config to monitor and alert on the activity.
C. AWS Trusted Advisor to recommend best practices.
D. Amazon Inspector to perform a vulnerability scan on the source IP address.

## Question 38:
Domain: Security Logging and Monitoring
A company requires monitoring for its critical workloads to detect security anomalies in near real-time. The solution should also help with compliance requirements. Which AWS service is BEST suited for this scenario?
A. AWS CloudWatch
B. AWS Config
C. AWS GuardDuty
D. Amazon Inspector

## Question 39:
Domain: Security Logging and Monitoring
A security engineer needs to enable logging for all API activity within an AWS environment to ensure compliance and audit requirements. Which AWS service should be configured to achieve this?
A. AWS CloudTrail
B. Amazon CloudWatch Logs
C. AWS Config
D. Amazon Kinesis Data Streams

## Question 40:
Domain: Security Logging and Monitoring
A security engineer needs to create a CloudWatch alarm that triggers when a specific metric exceeds a defined threshold. Which of the following is a required step to ensure the alarm functions correctly?
A. Configure a VPC flow log to capture all network traffic.
B. Create a CloudWatch log stream for the specific metric.
C. Define the threshold and period for the metric in the CloudWatch alarm configuration.
D. Set up an SNS topic to receive the alarm notifications.

## Question 41:

Domain: Security Logging and Monitoring
Which AWS service can be used to create custom insights and automate the discovery of security findings across multiple AWS accounts?

    A. AWS Systems Manager
    B. AWS Security Hub
    C. AWS Config
    D. Amazon Macie

**Question 42:**
Domain: Infrastructure Security
A company is hosting a web application using Amazon CloudFront and AWS WAF to protect against common web threats. The company is concerned about users from specific geographic locations accessing the application, as it has been noticed that these regions generate a significant amount of malicious traffic. How should the company apply restrictions based on geography to protect the application?

    A. Use AWS WAF to create a geo-match condition and block traffic from specific countries.
    B. Configure Amazon CloudFront to allow access only from specific IP ranges.
    C. Use AWS Shield Advanced to block traffic from unwanted geographic locations.
    D. Set up a rate-based rule in AWS WAF to limit the number of requests from specific regions.

**Question 43:**
Domain: Infrastructure Security
A company has implemented AWS WAF, Amazon CloudFront, and an Application Load Balancer (ALB) to secure its online services. To enhance the security posture, the security team wants to activate logging and metrics to monitor potential attack vectors. Which combination of actions should the team take?

    A. Enable AWS WAF logs and send them to Amazon S3 for storage and analysis.
    B. Configure Amazon CloudFront access logs and send them to AWS CloudTrail for detailed event tracking.
    C. Enable ALB access logs and send them to Amazon S3 for long-term storage and monitoring.
    D. Activate AWS Shield Advanced and use its metrics to monitor DDoS attacks.

**Question 44:**
Domain: Infrastructure Security
A security engineer is tasked with implementing network segmentation for a company's AWS environment. The company hosts both public-facing and internal applications within the same VPC. What is the most appropriate method to segment these applications based on security requirements?

    A. Create public subnets for public-facing applications and private subnets for internal applications, with appropriate security group rules.
    B. Deploy a NAT gateway for each subnet and restrict traffic between subnets using network ACLs.
    C. Use AWS WAF to control traffic between public and private subnets.
    D. Create separate VPCs for public and private applications and use VPC peering for communication.

**Question 45:**
Domain: Infrastructure Security
An application uses a third-party software library known to have vulnerabilities that could be exploited by attackers. The security team wants to implement protections at the edge to mitigate risks associated with these vulnerabilities. What is the most appropriate action?

    A. Use AWS WAF to create a rule that blocks requests containing patterns indicative of the known vulnerabilities.
    B. Implement AWS Shield Advanced to detect and block exploitation attempts of the vulnerabilities.
    C. Use AWS Secrets Manager to rotate keys and credentials to prevent unauthorized access.
    D. Enable CloudWatch alarms to monitor for potential exploits and notify the security team.

**Question 46:**
Domain: Infrastructure Security
A company uses Amazon CloudFront as a content delivery network (CDN) and wants to restrict access to its content based on the geographic location of the request. Additionally, the company wants to log all requests for future analysis. What steps should the company take to achieve these requirements?

    A. Configure a geo-restriction in CloudFront to deny access from specific countries and enable CloudFront logs to store all requests.
    B. Set up AWS WAF with a geo-match condition and configure CloudFront to cache the results for logging.
    C. Use AWS Shield Standard to block traffic from certain regions and enable logging in CloudTrail.
    D. Implement an ALB with geo-location based rules and send logs to Amazon S3.

**Question 47:**
Domain: Identity and Access Management
A security engineer is reviewing an IAM policy attached to an IAM role. The policy includes the following statements:

```
{
  "Version": "2012-10-17",
  "Statement": [
    {
      "Effect": "Allow",
      "Action": "s3:PutObject",
      "Resource": "arn:aws:s3:::example-bucket/*"
    },
    {
      "Effect": "Deny",
      "Action": "s3:DeleteObject",
      "Resource": "arn:aws:s3:::example-bucket/*"
    }
  ]
}
```

What will be the effect of this policy?

    A. The IAM role can only upload objects to the example-bucket but cannot delete them.
    B. The IAM role can neither upload nor delete objects in the example-bucket.
    C. The IAM role can delete objects in the example-bucket but cannot upload them.
    D. The IAM role can upload and delete objects in the example-bucket.

**Question 48:**
Domain: Identity and Access Management
A company has several teams that need access to different AWS services. The security team needs to ensure that each team can only access the resources required for their specific tasks. Which approach should the security team use to enforce this?

    A. Assign the same IAM policy to all teams, allowing access to all resources.
    B. Use Attribute-Based Access Control (ABAC) to grant permissions based on user attributes.
    C. Apply the principle of least privilege by creating specific IAM policies for each team.
    D. Grant full administrative access to all teams to simplify management.

**Question 49:**
Domain: Identity and Access Management
A developer is experiencing an "Access Denied" error when trying to access an S3 bucket. The IAM policy attached to the developer's role allows s3:ListBucket on the bucket. What could be the cause of the issue?

    A. The IAM policy does not explicitly allow s3:GetObject on the bucket.
    B. The IAM policy is missing the s3:PutObject permission.

C. The bucket policy is overriding the IAM policy and denying access.
D. The developer needs full S3 access to avoid errors.

**Question 50:**
Domain: Identity and Access Management
A company requires that different teams handle specific tasks within AWS, such as billing, security, and development. To enforce separation of duties, which strategy should be implemented?
   A. Assign full administrative access to one team and let them delegate tasks to others.
   B. Create distinct IAM roles for each team, limiting permissions to their respective tasks.
   C. Use a single IAM role for all teams but restrict access through a shared policy.
   D. Allow each team to create their own IAM policies without restrictions

**Question 51:**
Domain: Identity and Access Management
During a security audit, it was discovered that an IAM user has access to resources they should not. What is the most likely cause of this issue?
   A. The IAM user was granted unintended permissions through a misconfigured IAM policy.
   B. The user assumed a role with higher privileges temporarily.
   C. The user is part of a group that grants more permissions than needed.
   D. The user's permissions were escalated due to a policy evaluation error.

**Question 52:**
Domain: Data Protection
A company has a critical application that stores sensitive data in an Amazon S3 bucket. To comply with internal security policies, they need to ensure that no data in this bucket can be publicly accessible. Which configuration should the security team implement?
   A. Enable S3 Block Public Access at the bucket level and review bucket policies to prevent public access.
   B. Apply an IAM policy that denies s3:GetObject permissions to all users.
   C. Use S3 Object Lock in compliance mode to prevent public access.
   D. Configure the S3 bucket to only allow access from specific IP addresses.

**Question 53:**
Domain: Data Protection
An organization needs to prevent unauthorized public sharing of Amazon RDS snapshots. What action should the security team take to achieve this?
   A. Apply an RDS policy that prevents the creation of public snapshots.
   B. Enable AWS Config rules to detect and alert when a public snapshot is created.
   C. Use AWS Shield Advanced to protect against unauthorized access to RDS snapshots.
   D. Configure Amazon RDS to automatically encrypt all snapshots with an AWS KMS key.

**Question 54:**
Domain: Data Protection
A financial institution requires that data stored in Amazon S3 must be protected from unauthorized modifications. Which feature should the institution enable to meet this requirement?
   A. Enable S3 Object Lock in governance mode.
   B. Apply an S3 bucket policy that restricts delete operations to specific IAM roles.
   C. Use S3 Object Lock in compliance mode to prevent any changes.
   D. Enable AWS Config to monitor changes to objects in the S3 bucket.

**Question 55:**
Domain: Data Protection

A company is designing a solution to ensure that all data stored in Amazon S3 is encrypted at rest. They also want to manage their encryption keys using AWS CloudHSM. Which approach should they use?
   A. Enable server-side encryption with AWS KMS (SSE-KMS) and select a custom AWS CloudHSM key.
   B. Enable server-side encryption with Amazon S3-managed keys (SSE-S3) and store keys in CloudHSM.
   C. Use client-side encryption with AWS CloudHSM keys and upload encrypted data to S3.
   D. Enable server-side encryption with customer-provided keys (SSE-C) and store the keys in AWS CloudHSM.

## Question 56:
Domain: Data Protection
An e-commerce company needs to store customer data in DynamoDB. The security team has mandated that this data must be encrypted at rest. What should the company do to comply with this requirement?
   A. Enable encryption at rest in DynamoDB and use an AWS KMS key for encryption.
   B. Create a custom encryption mechanism within the application before storing data in DynamoDB.
   C. Use DynamoDB Streams to replicate data to an encrypted S3 bucket.
   D. Enable server-side encryption using customer-provided keys in DynamoDB.

## Question 57:
Domain: Data Protection
A media company needs to ensure that certain critical data is retained in Amazon S3 for at least 5 years and cannot be deleted during this period. What should they implement to meet this requirement?
   A. Use S3 Object Lock in compliance mode with a retention period of 5 years.
   B. Apply an S3 bucket policy that prevents deletions for 5 years.
   C. Use S3 Lifecycle policies to transition data to S3 Glacier after 5 years.
   D. Enable AWS Config rules to prevent deletions for the specified time.

## Question 58:
Domain: Data Protection
A healthcare provider is using Amazon RDS to store patient records. The organization must encrypt all patient data at rest using a custom encryption key generated by AWS CloudHSM. What is the most appropriate solution?
   A. Enable encryption at rest for the RDS instance using a custom AWS KMS key backed by AWS CloudHSM.
   B. Use AWS CloudHSM to create a client-side encryption library that encrypts data before storing it in RDS.
   C. Enable encryption at rest for the RDS instance using Amazon RDS-managed encryption keys.
   D. Use server-side encryption with customer-provided keys (SSE-C) and manage the keys in AWS CloudHSM.

## Question 59:
Domain: Management and Security Governance
A company wants to ensure that all AWS accounts in its organization adhere to a consistent tagging strategy across resources. Which service should be used to enforce this policy across multiple accounts?
   A. AWS Config
   B. AWS Service Catalog
   C. AWS CloudFormation
   D. AWS Control Tower

## Question 60:
Domain: Management and Security Governance

Your company wants to organize and manage AWS resources across multiple accounts based on different projects and environments (e.g., development, staging, production). What AWS feature can be used to group these resources effectively?
 A. AWS Organizations
 B. AWS Resource Access Manager (RAM)
 C. AWS CloudFormation StackSets
 D. AWS Resource Groups

**Question 61:**
Domain: Management and Security Governance
Your organization needs to regularly audit AWS resources for compliance with security policies. This includes detecting noncompliant resources and organizing evidence for security audits. Which combination of AWS services is most appropriate for this task?
 A. AWS Config and AWS CloudTrail
 B. AWS Security Hub and AWS Audit Manager
 C. AWS Macie and AWS Firewall Manager
 D. AWS Trusted Advisor and AWS Cost Explorer

**Question 62:**
Domain: Management and Security Governance
An organization wants to automatically detect and alert on the storage of sensitive data, such as personally identifiable information (PII), within Amazon S3 buckets across all AWS accounts. Which service should be used to identify this sensitive data?
 A. AWS Macie
 B. AWS Security Hub
 C. AWS Audit Manager
 D. AWS CloudTrail

**Question 63:**
Domain: Management and Security Governance
A company wants to securely share Amazon RDS databases and Amazon S3 buckets between AWS accounts within its organization. Which AWS service can facilitate this secure sharing?
 A. AWS Resource Access Manager (RAM)
 B. AWS Service Catalog
 C. AWS Organizations
 D. AWS CloudFormation

**Question 64:**
Domain: Management and Security Governance
An organization needs to deploy and manage a consistent portfolio of approved AWS services across several accounts. What is the best service to achieve this goal?
 A. AWS Resource Access Manager (RAM)
 B. AWS Service Catalog
 C. AWS CloudFormation
 D. AWS Firewall Manager

**Question 65:**
Domain: Management and Security Governance
A security engineer needs to enforce security policies, such as blocking public access to S3 buckets, across all AWS accounts in the organization. Which service is best suited for this task?
 A. AWS Control Tower
 B. AWS Firewall Manager

C. AWS Security Hub
D. AWS IAM Access Analyzer

# Practice Test Set 2 – Answers

**Question 1:**
Correct Answer: C. Use imported key material with an AWS KMS key and delete the key material when necessary.
Brief Explanation: Using imported key material with AWS KMS allows for immediate cryptographic erasure by deleting the key material, which ensures that the data encrypted with that key becomes irrecoverable.

**Question 2:**
Correct Answer: C. Create an organization trail in the management account and enforce the configuration using Service Control Policies (SCPs).
Brief Explanation: Creating an organization trail ensures that CloudTrail logging is enabled across all accounts in the organization, and SCPs enforce that this configuration cannot be modified by individual accounts.

**Question 3:**
Correct Answer: A. Use S3 bucket policies with aws
condition to restrict access to the organization.
Brief Explanation: Using aws:PrincipalOrgId in the S3 bucket policy restricts access to accounts within the organization, ensuring that data is not publicly accessible and is managed centrally.

**Question 4:**
Correct Answer: A. Implement S3 Object Lock with Compliance mode enabled.
Brief Explanation: S3 Object Lock in Compliance mode prevents object deletions and modifications, which is ideal for protecting critical data against accidental or intentional deletions.

**Question 5:**
Correct Answer: A. Set up an IPSec VPN over the Direct Connect connection.
Brief Explanation: An IPSec VPN provides encryption for data in transit over the Direct Connect connection, ensuring that the data is secure.

**Question 6:**
Correct Answer: D. Use AWS Systems Manager to replace the SSH keys across all affected instances.
Brief Explanation: AWS Systems Manager allows for the automated and centralized management of SSH keys across multiple instances, making it the most efficient method to revoke access.

**Question 7:**
Correct Answer: B. Configure a CloudFront origin access control (OAC) and update the bucket policy to restrict access to CloudFront.
Brief Explanation: Using an OAC ensures that the S3 bucket can only be accessed via CloudFront, preventing direct access from the internet.

**Question 8:**
Correct Answer: A. Deploy AWS Control Tower and integrate AWS SSO with the existing Active Directory.
Brief Explanation: AWS Control Tower with AWS SSO integration provides scalable and centralized access management across multiple accounts, integrated with the existing Active Directory.

**Question 9:**

Correct Answer: B. Abort the vault lock process, update the policy, and restart the vault lock operation.
Brief Explanation: If the vault lock policy needs adjustment, the best approach is to abort the process, update the policy, and restart the vault lock operation.

**Question 10:**
Correct Answer: A. Set up an AWS Config rule to detect changes in bucket policies and trigger an SNS notification.
Brief Explanation: AWS Config can monitor changes in S3 bucket policies, and when combined with SNS, it can send notifications whenever a policy is modified.

**Question 11:**
Correct Answer: A. The customer-managed key is set to 'Disabled' state.
Correct Answer: B. The IAM role lacks the kms
permission for the customer-managed key.
Brief Explanation: If the KMS key is disabled, it cannot be used to decrypt parameters. Additionally, the IAM role must have kms:Decrypt permission to access the secure string parameters.

**Question 12:**
Correct Answer: A. Enable detailed CloudWatch Metrics for the API Gateway.
Correct Answer: B. Set up access logging in API Gateway and analyze the logs using CloudWatch Logs Insights.
Brief Explanation: Detailed CloudWatch Metrics provide insights into API usage, and access logs can be analyzed using CloudWatch Logs Insights to detect anomalies without manual log inspection.

**Question 13:**
Correct Answer: A. Implement a rate-based rule in AWS WAF to block requests exceeding a threshold.
Brief Explanation: A rate-based rule in AWS WAF can block excessive requests from specific IPs, mitigating the impact of suspicious traffic on performance.

**Question 14:**
Correct Answer: C. Disable the compromised IAM access key and switch to using IAM roles for the automation.
Brief Explanation: Disabling the compromised key stops unauthorized use, and switching to IAM roles for automation is a more secure approach than using static access keys.

**Question 15:**
Correct Answer: A. Use AWS Systems Manager Session Manager for secure access and configure CloudWatch Logs for session logging.
Brief Explanation: AWS Systems Manager Session Manager provides secure, SSH-free access to EC2 instances, and it can log all session activity to CloudWatch Logs for auditing.

**Question 16:**
Correct Answer: A. Update the IAM role to allow sns
action for config.amazonaws.com.
Correct Answer: C. Configure the SNS topic's access policy to allow publishing from AWS Config.
Correct Answer: F. Ensure AWS Config is using the correct IAM role with necessary permissions.
Brief Explanation: Ensuring the correct permissions for SNS publishing and IAM roles is essential for AWS Config to function properly and send notifications.

**Question 17:**
Correct Answer: D. The explicit deny in the bucket policy takes precedence over any allow statements.
Brief Explanation: In AWS, explicit deny statements in a policy override any allow statements, which could be causing access denied errors for the forensic analyst.

**Question 18:**
Correct Answer: A. Set up VPC traffic mirroring to send traffic to the intrusion detection instance.
Brief Explanation: VPC traffic mirroring allows the inspection of network traffic by sending a copy to an intrusion detection system for analysis.

**Question 19:**
Correct Answer: D. Create a separate route table for database subnets without the default route to the NAT gateway.
Brief Explanation: By using a separate route table without a route to the NAT gateway, you can ensure that the database subnets do not have internet access.

**Question 20:**
Correct Answer: A. On the AppSG, allow inbound traffic on port 1030 from the WebSG.
Correct Answer: B. On the DBSG, allow inbound traffic on port 3306 from the AppSG.
Brief Explanation: These rules ensure that the application tier can communicate with the web tier on the correct port, and the database tier can communicate with the application tier securely.

**Question 21:**
Correct Answer: A. Configure the KMS key policy with a condition limiting the key to S3 service use only.
Brief Explanation: A KMS key policy can be configured to limit the use of the key to the S3 service, ensuring that the key is only used for encrypting/decrypting S3 data.

**Question 22:**
Correct Answer: A. Set up a password policy in IAM for IAM users.
Correct Answer: B. Enforce a password policy in the Active Directory for federated users.
Correct Answer: D. Configure password policies in Amazon Cognito user pools.
Brief Explanation: To enforce a strict password policy, you need to configure it for all types of users: IAM, federated, and Cognito users.

**Question 23:**
Correct Answer: A. Enable the awslogs log driver in the ECS task definition.
Brief Explanation: The awslogs log driver allows ECS tasks to send logs directly to CloudWatch Logs, facilitating centralized log management.

**Question 24:**
Correct Answer: A. Use AWS WAF to filter and block malicious web traffic.
Correct Answer: B. Deploy Amazon CloudFront to cache content and shield the EC2 instance.
Brief Explanation: AWS WAF helps protect against web-based threats, while CloudFront can offload traffic from the EC2 instance, providing additional DDoS protection.

**Question 25:**
Correct Answer: A. Use AWS Config to detect unencrypted RDS instances and notify the security team.
Correct Answer: B. Create encrypted snapshots of unencrypted databases and restore from these snapshots.
Brief Explanation: AWS Config can monitor and alert on unencrypted RDS instances, and creating encrypted snapshots allows you to transition to encryption without data loss.

**Question 26:**
Correct Answer: B. Amazon Macie
Brief Explanation: Amazon Macie is designed to discover and classify sensitive data, such as PII, in S3 buckets automatically.

**Question 27:**
Correct Answer: B. Use Amazon EventBridge to send findings to the third-party SIEM in real-time.
Brief Explanation: EventBridge allows real-time integration with third-party SIEM solutions, ensuring timely incident response.

**Question 28:**
Correct Answer: A. Update the security group to allow access only from known IP addresses.
Brief Explanation: Restricting access to port 22 (SSH) to known IP addresses mitigates the risk of unauthorized access while maintaining necessary functionality.

**Question 29:**
Correct Answer: B. Amazon Detective
Brief Explanation: Amazon Detective helps in visualizing and correlating VPC Flow Logs and CloudTrail logs to detect and investigate potential security threats.

**Question 30:**
Correct Answer: C.

```
1. SELECT * FROM s3_access_logs
2. WHERE operation = 'GetObject'
3. AND requesterIpAddress NOT LIKE '192.168.%';
4.
```

Brief Explanation: This query identifies GetObject requests where the IP address is outside the specified range, helping to detect unauthorized access.

**Question 31:**
Correct Answer: B. AWS Systems Manager Automation.
Brief Explanation: AWS Systems Manager Automation can be used to automate the isolation of an EC2 instance, such as detaching it from its security group or terminating it.

**Question 32:**
Correct Answer: A. Stop the instance before taking a snapshot of the attached EBS volumes.
Brief Explanation: Stopping the instance ensures that no additional changes are made to the EBS volumes before taking the forensic snapshot.

**Question 33:**
Correct Answer: B. It provides deep insights and visualizations for security incidents by linking and organizing data across multiple AWS sources.
Brief Explanation: Amazon Detective helps in the root cause analysis process by providing organized, linked, and visualized data from multiple sources.

**Question 34:**
Correct Answer: B. Attach a bucket policy that grants CloudTrail write permissions to the S3 bucket.
Brief Explanation: For CloudTrail to deliver logs to an S3 bucket, the bucket must have a policy that allows CloudTrail to write to it.

**Question 35:**
Correct Answer: A. Attach an IAM policy with logs:CreateLogGroup and logs:CreateLogStream permissions to the IAM role.
Brief Explanation: The IAM role used by VPC Flow Logs needs permissions to create log groups and streams to ensure logs are delivered.

**Question 36:**
Correct Answer: C. Implement AWS Lambda to parse and normalize log data before storing it in CloudWatch Logs.
Brief Explanation: AWS Lambda can be used to preprocess and normalize log data, making it easier to analyze and correlate within CloudWatch Logs.

**Question 37:**
Correct Answer: A. AWS WAF to block the IP address.
Brief Explanation: AWS WAF can be configured to block IP addresses after detecting patterns of malicious activity, such as repeated failed login attempts.

**Question 38:**
Correct Answer: C. AWS GuardDuty
Brief Explanation: AWS GuardDuty provides continuous monitoring for malicious or unauthorized behavior and helps detect security anomalies in near real-time.

**Question 39:**
Correct Answer: A. AWS CloudTrail
Brief Explanation: AWS CloudTrail captures all API activity within an AWS environment, making it essential for compliance and audit requirements.

**Question 40:**
Correct Answer: C. Define the threshold and period for the metric in the CloudWatch alarm configuration.
Brief Explanation: Defining the threshold and period is necessary for a CloudWatch alarm to function correctly and trigger based on specific metric values.

**Question 41:**
Correct Answer: B. AWS Security Hub
Brief Explanation: AWS Security Hub allows you to create custom insights and automate the discovery of security findings across multiple AWS accounts.

**Question 42:**
Correct Answer: A. Use AWS WAF to create a geo-match condition and block traffic from specific countries.
Brief Explanation: AWS WAF can be used to block traffic from specific geographic locations, helping protect the application from malicious regions.

**Question 43:**
Correct Answer: A. Enable AWS WAF logs and send them to Amazon S3 for storage and analysis.
Correct Answer: C. Enable ALB access logs and send them to Amazon S3 for long-term storage and monitoring.
Brief Explanation: Enabling logs for AWS WAF and ALB and sending them to S3 ensures that attack vectors and traffic patterns can be monitored and analyzed.

**Question 44:**
Correct Answer: A. Create public subnets for public-facing applications and private subnets for internal applications, with appropriate security group rules.
Brief Explanation: Segregating public-facing and internal applications into separate subnets with appropriate security controls ensures better security management and network segmentation.

**Question 45:**

Correct Answer: A. Use AWS WAF to create a rule that blocks requests containing patterns indicative of the known vulnerabilities.
Brief Explanation: AWS WAF can be configured to block traffic that matches patterns associated with known vulnerabilities, providing protection at the edge.

**Question 46:**
Correct Answer: A. Configure a geo-restriction in CloudFront to deny access from specific countries and enable CloudFront logs to store all requests.
Brief Explanation: CloudFront can restrict content delivery based on geographic location, and enabling logs ensures that all requests are recorded for future analysis.

**Question 47:**
Correct Answer: A. The IAM role can only upload objects to the example-bucket but cannot delete them.
Brief Explanation: The policy explicitly allows s3:PutObject (upload) and denies s3:DeleteObject, so the IAM role can upload but not delete objects.

**Question 48:**
Correct Answer: C. Apply the principle of least privilege by creating specific IAM policies for each team.
Brief Explanation: Creating specific IAM policies tailored to each team's needs ensures that they have only the permissions required to perform their tasks.

**Question 49:**
Correct Answer: C. The bucket policy is overriding the IAM policy and denying access.
Brief Explanation: Even if the IAM policy allows access, a bucket policy can override it by explicitly denying access, leading to an "Access Denied" error.

**Question 50:**
Correct Answer: B. Create distinct IAM roles for each team, limiting permissions to their respective tasks.
Brief Explanation: Using distinct IAM roles with limited permissions ensures separation of duties, allowing each team to perform only their designated tasks.

**Question 51:**
Correct Answer: A. The IAM user was granted unintended permissions through a misconfigured IAM policy.
Brief Explanation: Misconfigured IAM policies can unintentionally grant more permissions than intended, leading to security issues.

**Question 52:**
Correct Answer: A. Enable S3 Block Public Access at the bucket level and review bucket policies to prevent public access.
Brief Explanation: Enabling S3 Block Public Access and reviewing bucket policies ensures that the data in the S3 bucket cannot be accessed publicly.

**Question 53:**
Correct Answer: B. Enable AWS Config rules to detect and alert when a public snapshot is created.
Brief Explanation: AWS Config can be used to detect and alert on the creation of public RDS snapshots, preventing unauthorized sharing.

**Question 54:**
Correct Answer: C. Use S3 Object Lock in compliance mode to prevent any changes.
Brief Explanation: S3 Object Lock in compliance mode ensures that objects cannot be modified or deleted, protecting against unauthorized modifications.

**Question 55:**
Correct Answer: A. Enable server-side encryption with AWS KMS (SSE-KMS) and select a custom AWS CloudHSM key.
Brief Explanation: Using SSE-KMS with a custom CloudHSM key allows for encryption at rest in S3 while managing the encryption keys using CloudHSM.

**Question 56:**
Correct Answer: A. Enable encryption at rest in DynamoDB and use an AWS KMS key for encryption.
Brief Explanation: Enabling encryption at rest in DynamoDB using an AWS KMS key ensures that all customer data is encrypted in compliance with the security requirement.

**Question 57:**
Correct Answer: A. Use S3 Object Lock in compliance mode with a retention period of 5 years.
Brief Explanation: S3 Object Lock in compliance mode with a 5-year retention period ensures that the data is retained and cannot be deleted during this period.

**Question 58:**
Correct Answer: A. Enable encryption at rest for the RDS instance using a custom AWS KMS key backed by AWS CloudHSM.
Brief Explanation: Enabling encryption at rest with a custom KMS key backed by CloudHSM meets the requirement for encrypting patient records with a custom encryption key.

**Question 59:**
Correct Answer: A. AWS Config
Brief Explanation: AWS Config can be used to enforce a consistent tagging strategy across multiple AWS accounts, ensuring compliance with the policy.

**Question 60:**
Correct Answer: D. AWS Resource Groups
Brief Explanation: AWS Resource Groups allow you to organize and manage AWS resources across multiple accounts based on different projects and environments.

**Question 61:**
Correct Answer: B. AWS Security Hub and AWS Audit Manager
Brief Explanation: AWS Security Hub provides centralized security findings, while AWS Audit Manager helps gather and organize evidence for security audits.

**Question 62:**
Correct Answer: A. AWS Macie
Brief Explanation: AWS Macie is designed to automatically detect and alert on the storage of sensitive data, such as PII, in S3 buckets.

**Question 63:**
Correct Answer: A. AWS Resource Access Manager (RAM)
Brief Explanation: AWS RAM facilitates secure sharing of resources like RDS databases and S3 buckets between AWS accounts.

**Question 64:**
Correct Answer: B. AWS Service Catalog
Brief Explanation: AWS Service Catalog allows organizations to manage and deploy a consistent portfolio of approved AWS services across multiple accounts.

**Question 65:**
Correct Answer: B. AWS Firewall Manager
Brief Explanation: AWS Firewall Manager is best suited for enforcing security policies, such as blocking public access to S3 buckets, across all AWS accounts in an organization.

# Final Thoughts

As we reach the end of this comprehensive guide on AWS security, it's essential to reflect on the breadth and depth of the topics we've covered. The journey began with an introduction to AWS security fundamentals, emphasizing the critical nature of securing cloud environments and understanding the core principles of cybersecurity.

Throughout the chapters, we delved into various facets of AWS security, from foundational concepts to advanced strategies and best practices. We explored the intricacies of authentication and authorization, the importance of detective controls, and the steps to design and implement robust incident response plans. Our discussions on threat detection, anomaly identification, and securing AWS resources highlighted the dynamic nature of cloud security and the need for continuous vigilance and adaptation.

Hands-on exercises and practical examples provided throughout the book aimed to reinforce theoretical knowledge, ensuring that readers not only understand the concepts but also gain the skills necessary to implement them in real-world scenarios. Whether it was configuring AWS IAM, setting up AWS Config rules, or deploying security services like AWS Security Hub and Amazon GuardDuty, these exercises were designed to equip you with practical expertise.

The concluding chapters on management and security governance underscored the importance of a holistic approach to cloud security. By leveraging AWS tools and services, implementing multi-account strategies, and adhering to best practices for governance, organizations can achieve a secure and compliant AWS environment.

## Next Steps

- **Mock Practice Tests:** Take mock practice tests to feel comfortable passing the exam in the first attempt. You can go through: https://www.amazon.com/dp/B0CCLP4TF3 book. The book contains 700+ practice questions (11 practice tests) covering all the exam domains with answers and mix of brief and detailed explanations.

- **Hands-On Experience:** Utilize the AWS Free Tier to get hands-on experience with the services covered in this guide. Practical experience is crucial for solidifying your knowledge.

- **AWS Documentation and Whitepapers:** Regularly refer to AWS documentation and whitepapers to stay updated on new features, best practices, and architectural patterns.

- **Schedule the Exam:** Once you feel confident in your preparation, schedule your AWS Certified Security - Specialty (SCS-C02) exam and review the exam guide and blueprint provided by AWS.

By following these steps and leveraging the knowledge gained from this guide, you will be well-prepared to achieve your AWS Certified Security - Specialty (SCS-C02) Exam certification.

As you move forward in your career or continue to enhance your organization's security posture, remember that cloud security is an ongoing process. Stay informed about the latest developments, continuously evaluate and improve your security measures, and leverage the power of AWS's robust security tools and services.

Thank you for embarking on this journey with us. We hope this book has been a valuable resource in your quest to master AWS security. Armed with the knowledge and skills acquired here, you are well-prepared to tackle the challenges of securing cloud environments and achieving AWS Certified Security - Specialty (SCS-C02) certification.

# References

1. Aggregating AWS Config Data: https://docs.aws.amazon.com/config/latest/developerguide/aggregate-data.html
2. Amazon API Gateway Custom Domain Names: https://docs.aws.amazon.com/apigateway/latest/developerguide/how-to-custom-domains.html
3. Amazon API Gateway documentation: https://aws.amazon.com/api-gateway/
4. Amazon API Gateway Security:https://docs.aws.amazon.com/apigateway/latest/developerguide/apigateway-best-practices.html
5. Amazon Athena documentation: Available at: https://docs.aws.amazon.com/athena/latest/ug/what-is.html
6. Amazon Athena: https://docs.aws.amazon.com/athena/index.html
7. Amazon CloudFront: https://docs.aws.amazon.com/AmazonCloudFront/latest/DeveloperGuide/Introduction.html
8. Amazon CloudFront documentation: https://aws.amazon.com/cloudfront/
9. Amazon CloudFront Geo-Restriction: https://docs.aws.amazon.com/AmazonCloudFront/latest/DeveloperGuide/georestrictions.html
10. Amazon CloudFront: https://aws.amazon.com/cloudfront/
11. Amazon CloudWatch Documentation: https://docs.aws.amazon.com/cloudwatch/
12. Amazon CloudWatch Logs Documentation: https://docs.aws.amazon.com/AmazonCloudWatch/latest/logs
13. Amazon CloudWatch Logs User Guide: https://docs.aws.amazon.com/AmazonCloudWatch/latest/logs/WhatIsCloudWatchLogs.html
14. Amazon Cognito documentation - https://docs.aws.amazon.com/cognito/latest/developerguide/
15. Amazon Detective: https://docs.aws.amazon.com/detective/index.html
16. Amazon DynamoDB Encryption: https://docs.aws.amazon.com/amazondynamodb/latest/developerguide/encryption.tls.html
17. Amazon EBS Encryption: https://docs.aws.amazon.com/AWSEC2/latest/UserGuide/EBSEncryption.html
18. Amazon EC2 Documentation: https://docs.aws.amazon.com/ec2/index.html
19. Amazon EC2 Instance Connect: https://docs.aws.amazon.com/AWSEC2/latest/UserGuide/ec2-instance-connect-methods.html
20. Amazon EC2 User Guide: https://docs.aws.amazon.com/AWSEC2/latest/UserGuide/ec2-security-groups.html
21. Amazon EC2Rescue: https://docs.aws.amazon.com/AWSEC2/latest/UserGuide/ec2-instance-recovery.html
22. Amazon ECR Image Scanning: https://docs.aws.amazon.com/AmazonECR/latest/userguide/image-scanning.html
23. Amazon ECR: https://aws.amazon.com/ecr/
24. Amazon EventBridge: https://aws.amazon.com/eventbridge/
25. Amazon GuardDuty Documentation: https://docs.aws.amazon.com/guardduty/latest/ug/what-is-guardduty.html
26. Amazon GuardDuty Findings: https://docs.aws.amazon.com/guardduty/latest/ug/guardduty_findings.html
27. Amazon Inspector Documentation: https://docs.aws.amazon.com/inspector/latest/userguide/inspector_introduction.html
28. Amazon Inspector User Guide: https://docs.aws.amazon.com/inspector/latest/userguide/inspector_introduction.html
29. Amazon Inspector: https://aws.amazon.com/inspector/
30. Amazon Lookout for Metrics: https://docs.aws.amazon.com/lookoutmetrics/latest/dev/what-is.html
31. Amazon Machine Images (AMIs): https://docs.aws.amazon.com/AWSEC2/latest/UserGuide/AMIs.html
32. Amazon Macie: https://docs.aws.amazon.com/macie/latest/userguide/what-is-macie.html
33. Amazon RDS Multi-AZ: https://docs.aws.amazon.com/AmazonRDS/latest/UserGuide/Concepts.MultiAZ.html
34. Amazon RDS Security: https://docs.aws.amazon.com/AmazonRDS/latest/UserGuide/UsingWithRDS.SSL.html
35. Amazon RDS: https://aws.amazon.com/rds/
36. Amazon Redshift Security: https://docs.aws.amazon.com/redshift/latest/mgmt/security-server-side-encryption.html
37. Amazon Route 53 Documentation: https://docs.aws.amazon.com/Route53/latest/DeveloperGuide/
38. Amazon Route 53 Health Checks: https://docs.aws.amazon.com/Route53/latest/DeveloperGuide/dns-failover.html
39. Amazon Route 53 Logging: https://docs.aws.amazon.com/Route53/latest/DeveloperGuide/query-logs.html
40. Amazon S3 Bucket Policies: https://docs.aws.amazon.com/AmazonS3/latest/dev/example-bucket-policies.html
41. Amazon S3 Default Encryption for S3 Buckets: https://docs.aws.amazon.com/AmazonS3/latest/userguide/default-bucket-encryption.html

42. Amazon S3 Encryption: https://docs.aws.amazon.com/AmazonS3/latest/dev/UsingEncryption.html
43. Amazon S3 Lifecycle Configuration: https://docs.aws.amazon.com/AmazonS3/latest/dev/object-lifecycle-mgmt.html
44. Amazon S3 Lifecycle Policies: https://docs.aws.amazon.com/AmazonS3/latest/dev/object-lifecycle-mgmt.html
45. Amazon S3 Object Lock: https://docs.aws.amazon.com/AmazonS3/latest/dev/object-lock.html
46. Amazon S3 Security Best Practices: https://docs.aws.amazon.com/AmazonS3/latest/dev/security-best-practices.html
47. Amazon S3 Storage Classes: https://docs.aws.amazon.com/AmazonS3/latest/dev/storage-class-intro.html
48. Amazon S3 Versioning: https://docs.aws.amazon.com/AmazonS3/latest/dev/Versioning.html
49. Amazon S3: https://docs.aws.amazon.com/s3/index.html
50. Amazon SNS: https://docs.aws.amazon.com/sns/index.html
51. Amazon SQS Server-Side Encryption (SSE): https://docs.aws.amazon.com/AWSSimpleQueueService/latest/SQSDeveloperGuide/sqs-server-side-encryption.html
52. Amazon Virtual Private Cloud (VPC): https://docs.aws.amazon.com/vpc/latest/userguide/what-is-amazon-vpc.html
53. Amazon VPC Documentation: https://docs.aws.amazon.com/vpc/latest/userguide/what-is-amazon-vpc.html
54. Amazon VPC Flow Logs: https://docs.aws.amazon.com/vpc/latest/userguide/flow-logs.html
55. Analyzing AWS CloudTrail logs using CloudWatch Logs Insights: https://aws.amazon.com/blogs/mt/analyzing-aws-cloudtrail-logs-using-amazon-cloudwatch-logs-insights/
56. Analyzing Security Logs on AWS: https://aws.amazon.com/blogs/security/analyzing-security-logs-on-aws/
57. Apache HTTP Server Documentation: https://httpd.apache.org/docs/current/logs.html
58. Auto Scaling: https://docs.aws.amazon.com/autoscaling/ec2/userguide/what-is-amazon-ec2-auto-scaling.html
59. Automated Backups with Amazon RDS: https://docs.aws.amazon.com/AmazonRDS/latest/UserGuide/USER_WorkingWithAutomatedBackups.html
60. AWS Audit Manager: https://docs.aws.amazon.com/audit-manager/latest/userguide/what-is.html
61. AWS Backup: https://docs.aws.amazon.com/aws-backup/latest/devguide/whatisbackup.html
62. AWS Budgets: https://docs.aws.amazon.com/cost-management/latest/userguide/budgets-managing-costs.html
63. AWS Certificate Manager: https://docs.aws.amazon.com/acm/latest/userguide/acm-overview.html
64. AWS CloudFormation Best Practices: https://docs.aws.amazon.com/AWSCloudFormation/latest/UserGuide/best-practices.html
65. AWS CloudFormation: https://docs.aws.amazon.com/AWSCloudFormation/latest/UserGuide/Welcome.html
66. AWS CloudHSM: https://docs.aws.amazon.com/cloudhsm/latest/userguide/what-is-cloudhsm.html
67. AWS CloudTrail Best Practices: https://docs.aws.amazon.com/awscloudtrail/latest/userguide/cloudtrail-best-practices.html
68. AWS CloudTrail Documentation: https://docs.aws.amazon.com/awscloudtrail/latest/userguide/cloudtrail-user-guide.html
69. AWS CloudTrail Insights: Automating Detection of Unusual API Activities. Available at: https://aws.amazon.com/blogs/security/aws-cloudtrail-insights-automating-detection-of-unusual-api-activities/
70. AWS CloudTrail Insights: https://docs.aws.amazon.com/awscloudtrail/latest/userguide/cloudtrail-insights.html
71. AWS CloudTrail Log File Management: https://docs.aws.amazon.com/awscloudtrail/latest/userguide/cloudtrail-log-file-management.html
72. AWS CloudTrail Use Cases. Available at: https://aws.amazon.com/cloudtrail/use-cases/
73. AWS CloudTrail User Guide: https://docs.aws.amazon.com/awscloudtrail/latest/userguide/cloudtrail-user-guide.html
74. AWS CloudTrail: https://docs.aws.amazon.com/awscloudtrail/latest/userguide/cloudtrail-user-guide.html
75. AWS CloudWatch Agent Configuration: https://docs.aws.amazon.com/AmazonCloudWatch/latest/monitoring/CloudWatch-Agent-Configuration-File-Details.html
76. AWS CloudWatch and Athena integration. Available at: https://aws.amazon.com/blogs/big-data/analyze-aws-cloudtrail-logs-using-amazon-athena-and-amazon-quicksight/
77. AWS CloudWatch Documentation: https://docs.aws.amazon.com/cloudwatch/index.html
78. AWS CloudWatch Events: https://docs.aws.amazon.com/AmazonCloudWatch/latest/events/WhatIsCloudWatchEvents.html
79. AWS CloudWatch Logs Documentation: https://docs.aws.amazon.com/AmazonCloudWatch/latest/logs/WhatIsCloudWatchLogs.html
80. AWS CloudWatch Logs Insights Documentation: https://docs.aws.amazon.com/AmazonCloudWatch/latest/logs/AnalyzingLogData.html
81. AWS CloudWatch Logs Insights: https://docs.aws.amazon.com/AmazonCloudWatch/latest/logs/AnalyzingLogData.htm
82. AWS CodeCommit: https://docs.aws.amazon.com/codecommit/latest/userguide/welcome.html
83. AWS CodePipeline: https://docs.aws.amazon.com/codepipeline/latest/userguide/welcome.html
84. AWS Compliance Programs: https://aws.amazon.com/compliance/programs/
85. AWS Config Documentation: https://docs.aws.amazon.com/config/latest/developerguide/WhatIsConfig.html
86. AWS Config Managed Rules: https://docs.aws.amazon.com/config/latest/developerguide/managed-rules-by-aws-config.html
87. AWS Config Rules: https://docs.aws.amazon.com/config/latest/developerguide/evaluate-config.html
88. AWS Config: https://docs.aws.amazon.com/config/index.html
89. AWS Config: https://docs.aws.amazon.com/config/latest/developerguide/what-is-config.html
90. AWS Control Tower: https://docs.aws.amazon.com/controltower/latest/userguide/what-is-control-tower.html
91. AWS Cost Explorer: https://docs.aws.amazon.com/cost-management/latest/userguide/ce-what-is.html
92. AWS Data Lifecycle Manager: https://docs.aws.amazon.com/AWSEC2/latest/UserGuide/snapshot-lifecycle.html
93. AWS DataSync: https://docs.aws.amazon.com/datasync/latest/userguide/what-is-datasync.html
94. AWS Direct Connect Documentation: https://docs.aws.amazon.com/directconnect/latest/UserGuide/Welcome.html
95. AWS DNS Logs Documentation: https://docs.aws.amazon.com/Route53/latest/DeveloperGuide/logging.html

96. AWS EC2 Documentation: https://docs.aws.amazon.com/ec2/
97. AWS Elastic Block Store (EBS): https://docs.aws.amazon.com/AWSEC2/latest/UserGuide/AmazonEBS.html
98. AWS Encryption Documentation: https://docs.aws.amazon.com/general/latest/gr/aws-sec-credtypes.html#aws-securing-data
99. AWS Firewall Manager: https://docs.aws.amazon.com/waf/latest/developerguide/fms-chapter.html
100. AWS Glue Data Catalog: https://docs.aws.amazon.com/glue/latest/dg/populate-data-catalog.html
101. AWS Identity and Access Management (IAM): https://docs.aws.amazon.com/IAM/latest/UserGuide/introduction.html
102. AWS Identity and Access Management (IAM). Available at: https://aws.amazon.com/iam/
103. AWS Incident Response Whitepaper: https://aws.amazon.com/whitepapers/incident-response/
104. AWS Inspector Documentation: https://docs.aws.amazon.com/inspector/latest/userguide/inspector_introduction.html
105. AWS Key Management Service (KMS) - Key Policies: https://docs.aws.amazon.com/kms/latest/developerguide/key-policies.html
106. AWS Key Management Service (KMS): https://docs.aws.amazon.com/kms/latest/developerguide/key-policies.html
107. AWS Key Management Service (KMS): https://docs.aws.amazon.com/kms/latest/developerguide/overview.html
108. AWS Lambda in VPC Documentation: https://docs.aws.amazon.com/lambda/latest/dg/configuration-vpc.html
109. AWS Lambda Security Best Practices - https://docs.aws.amazon.com/lambda/latest/dg/best-practices.html
110. AWS Lambda: https://docs.aws.amazon.com/lambda/index.html
111. AWS Lambda@Edge: https://docs.aws.amazon.com/lambda/latest/dg/lambda-edge.html
112. AWS Logging Best Practices: https://aws.amazon.com/answers/logging/logging-best-practices/
113. AWS Macie Documentation: https://docs.aws.amazon.com/macie/latest/userguide/what-is-macie.html
114. AWS Network ACLs: https://docs.aws.amazon.com/vpc/latest/userguide/vpc-network-acls.html
115. AWS Network Firewall: https://aws.amazon.com/network-firewall/
116. AWS Network Manager: https://aws.amazon.com/vpc/network-manager/
117. AWS Organizations Documentation: https://docs.aws.amazon.com/organizations/latest/userguide/orgs_introduction.html
118. AWS Organizations: https://aws.amazon.com/organizations/
119. AWS Organizations: https://docs.aws.amazon.com/organizations/latest/userguide/orgs_introduction.html
120. AWS PrivateLink: https://aws.amazon.com/privatelink/
121. AWS Resource Access Manager: https://docs.aws.amazon.com/ram/latest/userguide/what-is.html
122. AWS Resource Groups: https://docs.aws.amazon.com/ARG/latest/userguide/welcome.html
123. AWS S3 Documentation: https://docs.aws.amazon.com/s3/
124. AWS SDK for JavaScript: https://docs.aws.amazon.com/AWSJavaScriptSDK/latest/
125. AWS Secrets Manager Documentation: https://docs.aws.amazon.com/secretsmanager/latest/userguide/intro.html
126. AWS Secrets Manager: https://aws.amazon.com/secrets-manager/
127. AWS Secrets Manager: https://docs.aws.amazon.com/secretsmanager/latest/userguide/intro.html
128. AWS Security Best Practices: https://docs.aws.amazon.com/whitepapers/latest/aws-security-best-practices/aws-security-best-practices.pdf
129. AWS Security Best Practices: https://docs.aws.amazon.com/whitepapers/latest/security-best-practices/security-best-practices.html
130. AWS Security Groups Overview: https://docs.aws.amazon.com/vpc/latest/userguide/VPC_SecurityGroups.html
131. AWS Security Groups: https://docs.aws.amazon.com/vpc/latest/userguide/VPC_SecurityGroups.html
132. AWS Security Hub Documentation: https://docs.aws.amazon.com/securityhub/index.html
133. AWS Security Hub: https://aws.amazon.com/blogs/security/aws-security-hub-a-comprehensive-view-of-security-alerts-and-compliance-status/
134. AWS Security Incident Response Guide: https://aws.amazon.com/whitepapers/incident-response/
135. AWS Service Catalog: https://docs.aws.amazon.com/servicecatalog/latest/adminguide/introduction.html
136. AWS Shared Responsibility Model: https://aws.amazon.com/compliance/shared-responsibility-model/
137. AWS Shield: https://docs.aws.amazon.com/shield/latest/dg/what-is.html
138. AWS Site-to-Site VPN: https://docs.aws.amazon.com/vpn/latest/s2svpn/VPC_VPN.html
139. AWS Step Functions: https://docs.aws.amazon.com/step-functions/index.html
140. AWS Systems Manager Automation: https://docs.aws.amazon.com/systems-manager/latest/userguide/systems-manager-automation.html
141. AWS Systems Manager Parameter Store: https://docs.aws.amazon.com/systems-manager/latest/userguide/systems-manager-parameter-store.html
142. AWS Systems Manager Patch Manager: https://docs.aws.amazon.com/systems-manager/latest/userguide/systems-manager-patch.html
143. AWS Systems Manager Session Manager: https://docs.aws.amazon.com/systems-manager/latest/userguide/session-manager.html
144. AWS Systems Manager: https://docs.aws.amazon.com/systems-manager/latest/userguide/what-is-systems-manager.html
145. AWS Tagging Strategies: https://aws.amazon.com/answers/account-management/aws-tagging-strategies/
146. AWS Traffic Mirroring Documentation: https://docs.aws.amazon.com/vpc/latest/mirroring/what-is-traffic-mirroring.html
147. AWS Transit Gateway Documentation: https://docs.aws.amazon.com/vpc/latest/tgw/what-is-transit-gateway.html
148. AWS Transit Gateway: https://aws.amazon.com/transit-gateway/
149. AWS Trusted Advisor: https://docs.aws.amazon.com/awssupport/latest/user/getting-started-advisor.html
150. AWS VPC Flow Logs: https://docs.aws.amazon.com/vpc/latest/userguide/flow-logs.html
151. AWS VPN: https://aws.amazon.com/vpn/

152. AWS WAF documentation: https://docs.aws.amazon.com/waf/latest/developerguide/what-is-aws-waf.html
153. AWS WAF Logging: https://docs.aws.amazon.com/waf/latest/developerguide/logging.html
154. AWS WAF Rate-Based Rules: https://docs.aws.amazon.com/waf/latest/developerguide/waf-rule-statement-type-rate-based.html
155. AWS Well-Architected Framework: https://docs.aws.amazon.com/wellarchitected/latest/framework/welcome.html
156. Backup Lifecycle Policies: https://docs.aws.amazon.com/aws-backup/latest/devguide/creating-backup-plan.html#backup-plan-lifecycle
157. Best practices for Amazon Athena: https://aws.amazon.com/big-data/athena/best-practices/
158. Best Practices for AWS Key Management Service: https://docs.aws.amazon.com/kms/latest/developerguide/best-practices.html
159. Bucket Policy Examples: https://docs.aws.amazon.com/AmazonS3/latest/userguide/example-bucket-policies.html
160. CloudWatch Logs documentation: https://docs.aws.amazon.com/AmazonCloudWatch/latest/logs/FilterAndPatternSyntax.html
161. Consolidated Billing for AWS Organizations: https://docs.aws.amazon.com/awsaccountbilling/latest/aboutv2/consolidated-billing.html
162. Creating a Distribution: https://docs.aws.amazon.com/AmazonCloudFront/latest/DeveloperGuide/distribution-web-creating.html
163. Creating Amazon EBS snapshots: https://docs.aws.amazon.com/AWSEC2/latest/UserGuide/ebs-creating-snapshot.html
164. Creating and Managing Amazon Macie Resources: https://docs.aws.amazon.com/macie/latest/userguide/macie-creating-resources.html
165. Creating Assessments in AWS Audit Manager: https://docs.aws.amazon.com/audit-manager/latest/userguide/getting-started.html
166. Creating Custom AWS Config Rules: https://docs.aws.amazon.com/config/latest/developerguide/evaluate-config_develop-rules.html
167. Cross-Account Access: https://docs.aws.amazon.com/IAM/latest/UserGuide/tutorial_cross-account-with-roles.html
168. Data Classification Guide: https://aws.amazon.com/whitepapers/data-classification/
169. Data Protection in Amazon S3: https://docs.aws.amazon.com/AmazonS3/latest/dev/DataProtection.html
170. Data Protection in Amazon Web Services: https://docs.aws.amazon.com/wellarchitected/latest/security-pillar/data-protection.html
171. DDoS Attacks: https://www.cloudflare.com/learning/ddos/what-is-a-ddos-attack/
172. Delegated Administration in AWS Organizations: https://docs.aws.amazon.com/organizations/latest/userguide/orgs_delegated_admin.html
173. Deleting Imported Key Material: https://docs.aws.amazon.com/kms/latest/developerguide/importing-keys-delete-key-material.html
174. Detecting CloudFormation Drift: https://docs.aws.amazon.com/AWSCloudFormation/latest/UserGuide/using-cfn-stack-drift.html
175. EBS Snapshots: https://docs.aws.amazon.com/AWSEC2/latest/UserGuide/EBSSnapshots.html
176. Elastic Load Balancing: https://docs.aws.amazon.com/elasticloadbalancing/latest/userguide/what-is-load-balancing.html
177. ELK Stack Documentation: https://www.elastic.co/what-is/elk-stack
178. Enabling and Configuring AWS Security Hub: https://docs.aws.amazon.com/securityhub/latest/userguide/securityhub-settingup.html
179. Enabling MFA on the AWS Root Account: https://docs.aws.amazon.com/IAM/latest/UserGuide/id_credentials_mfa_enable_virtual.html
180. Encrypting Amazon RDS Resources: https://docs.aws.amazon.com/AmazonRDS/latest/UserGuide/Overview.Encryption.html
181. Encrypting Data at Rest in Amazon EFS: https://docs.aws.amazon.com/efs/latest/ug/encryption-at-rest.html
182. Encryption at Rest: https://docs.aws.amazon.com/AmazonS3/latest/dev/UsingEncryption.html
183. Enforcing AWS Account Security Best Practices Using AWS Organizations Service Control Policies: https://aws.amazon.com/blogs/security/enforcing-aws-account-security-best-practices-using-aws-organizations-service-control-policies/
184. Example Lifecycle Configuration: https://docs.aws.amazon.com/AmazonS3/latest/userguide/lifecycle-configuration-examples.html
185. General Data Protection Regulation (GDPR): https://gdpr.eu/
186. Getting Started with AWS Firewall Manager: https://docs.aws.amazon.com/waf/latest/developerguide/getting-started-fms.html
187. Getting Started with AWS RAM: https://docs.aws.amazon.com/ram/latest/userguide/getting-started.html
188. Getting Started with AWS Service Catalog: https://docs.aws.amazon.com/servicecatalog/latest/adminguide/getting-started.html
189. Guardrails in AWS Control Tower: https://docs.aws.amazon.com/controltower/latest/userguide/guardrails.html
190. Host-Based Firewalls: https://en.wikipedia.org/wiki/Host-based_firewall
191. How AWS Systems Manager Session Manager Works: https://docs.aws.amazon.com/systems-manager/latest/userguide/session-manager-how-it-works.html
192. Hybrid Cloud Architectures: https://docs.aws.amazon.com/whitepapers/latest/hybrid-cloud-architecture/hybrid-cloud-architecture.html
193. IAM Best Practices: https://docs.aws.amazon.com/IAM/latest/UserGuide/best-practices.html
194. IAM Policies and Permissions: https://docs.aws.amazon.com/IAM/latest/UserGuide/access_policies.html

195. IAM Roles for Amazon EC2: https://docs.aws.amazon.com/IAM/latest/UserGuide/id_roles_use_switch-role-ec2.html
196. IAM Roles for AWS Lambda: https://docs.aws.amazon.com/lambda/latest/dg/lambda-permissions.html
197. IAM Roles: https://docs.aws.amazon.com/IAM/latest/UserGuide/id_roles.html
198. Importing Key Material in AWS KMS: https://docs.aws.amazon.com/kms/latest/developerguide/importing-keys.html
199. Infrastructure as Code (IaC) for AWS: https://aws.amazon.com/architecture/infrastructure-as-code/
200. Integrating Amazon Inspector with Amazon ECR: https://docs.aws.amazon.com/AmazonECR/latest/userguide/image-scanning.html
201. Internet Engineering Task Force: https://tools.ietf.org/html/rfc4301
202. Key Policies in AWS KMS: https://docs.aws.amazon.com/kms/latest/developerguide/key-policies.html
203. Load Balancing: https://aws.amazon.com/elasticloadbalancing/
204. Managing Amazon Macie Findings: https://docs.aws.amazon.com/macie/latest/userguide/macie-view-findings.html
205. Managing Delegated Administrators: https://docs.aws.amazon.com/organizations/latest/userguide/orgs_delegate_policies.html
206. Managing your storage lifecycle: https://docs.aws.amazon.com/AmazonS3/latest/userguide/object-lifecycle-mgmt.html
207. Monitoring AWS Config Rules with Amazon CloudWatch: https://docs.aws.amazon.com/config/latest/developerguide/monitor-config-with-cloudwatch.html
208. NAT Gateways: https://docs.aws.amazon.com/vpc/latest/userguide/vpc-nat-gateway.html
209. National Institute of Standards and Technology (NIST): https://nvlpubs.nist.gov/nistpubs/SpecialPublications/NIST.SP.800-88r1.pdf
210. Network ACLs: https://docs.aws.amazon.com/vpc/latest/userguide/vpc-network-acls.html
211. NIST Computer Security Incident Handling Guide: https://nvlpubs.nist.gov/nistpubs/SpecialPublications/NIST.SP.800-61r2.pdf
212. Object Lifecycle Management: https://docs.aws.amazon.com/AmazonS3/latest/dev/object-lifecycle-mgmt.html
213. OpenSCAP: https://www.open-scap.org/
214. OWASP Top 10: https://owasp.org/www-project-top-ten/
215. Patching Amazon EC2 Instances: https://aws.amazon.com/blogs/mt/patching-amazon-ec2-instances-using-aws-systems-manager/
216. Private Virtual Interface: https://docs.aws.amazon.com/directconnect/latest/UserGuide/WorkingWithVirtualInterfaces.html#private-virtual-interface
217. Public Virtual Interface: https://docs.aws.amazon.com/directconnect/latest/UserGuide/WorkingWithVirtualInterfaces.html#public-virtual-interface
218. RDS Point-in-Time Recovery: https://docs.aws.amazon.com/AmazonRDS/latest/UserGuide/USER_WorkingWithAutomatedBackups.html
219. Remote Desktop Protocol (RDP): https://docs.microsoft.com/en-us/windows-server/remote/remote-desktop-services/clients/remote-desktop-protocol
220. Retention and Disposal of Health Information: https://www.hhs.gov/hipaa/for-professionals/privacy/guidance/retention-and-disposal-of-health-information/index.html
221. Rotate AWS Secrets Manager Secrets: https://docs.aws.amazon.com/secretsmanager/latest/userguide/rotating-secrets.html
222. Rotating AWS Secrets Manager Secrets: https://docs.aws.amazon.com/secretsmanager/latest/userguide/rotating-secrets.html
223. S3 Lifecycle Policies: https://docs.aws.amazon.com/AmazonS3/latest/dev/object-lifecycle-mgmt.html
224. S3 Object Lock Overview: https://docs.aws.amazon.com/AmazonS3/latest/dev/object-lock-overview.html
225. S3 Versioning: https://docs.aws.amazon.com/AmazonS3/latest/dev/Versioning.html
226. Scheduling Key Deletion: https://docs.aws.amazon.com/kms/latest/developerguide/deleting-keys.html
227. Securely Connect to Linux Instances Running in a Private VPC: https://aws.amazon.com/blogs/security/securely-connect-to-linux-instances-running-in-a-private-vpc/
228. Securing Data in Transit with TLS: https://docs.aws.amazon.com/whitepapers/latest/security-pillar/securing-data-in-transit.html
229. Security Best Practices for AWS Key Management Service (KMS): https://docs.aws.amazon.com/kms/latest/developerguide/best-practices.html
230. Security Best Practices in IAM: https://docs.aws.amazon.com/IAM/latest/UserGuide/best-practices.html
231. Security in Parameter Store: https://docs.aws.amazon.com/systems-manager/latest/userguide/systems-manager-parameter-store-security.html
232. Security Pillar - AWS Well-Architected Framework: https://docs.aws.amazon.com/wellarchitected/latest/security-pillar/welcome.html
233. Service Control Policies: https://docs.aws.amazon.com/organizations/latest/userguide/orgs_manage_policies_scp.html
234. Setting Up Your Landing Zone: https://docs.aws.amazon.com/controltower/latest/userguide/setting-up.html
235. Sharing Resources with AWS RAM: https://docs.aws.amazon.com/ram/latest/userguide/sharing-resources.html
236. SQL Reference for Amazon Athena: https://docs.aws.amazon.com/athena/latest/ug/athena-sql-reference.html
237. Suricata IDS/IPS/NSM Engine: https://suricata-ids.org/
238. Tagging AWS Resources: https://docs.aws.amazon.com/general/latest/gr/aws_tagging.html
239. The Transport Layer Security (TLS) Protocol Version 1.2: https://tools.ietf.org/html/rfc5246
240. Transitioning Objects Using Amazon S3 Lifecycle: https://docs.aws.amazon.com/AmazonS3/latest/dev/lifecycle-transition-general-considerations.html
241. Transport Layer Security (TLS): https://docs.aws.amazon.com/general/latest/gr/aws-security.html#tls-certificate

242. Troubleshoot network reachability issues: https://docs.aws.amazon.com/vpc/latest/reachability/how-to-use-reachability-analyzer.html
243. Understanding AWS CloudTrail Log Events: https://aws.amazon.com/blogs/security/understanding-aws-cloudtrail-log-event-format/
244. Understanding CloudTrail Log File Structure: https://docs.aws.amazon.com/awscloudtrail/latest/userguide/cloudtrail-log-file-examples.html
245. Using Amazon CloudWatch Alarms: https://docs.aws.amazon.com/AmazonCloudWatch/latest/monitoring/AlarmThatSendsEmail.html
246. Using AWS CloudHSM with AWS Services: https://docs.aws.amazon.com/cloudhsm/latest/userguide/aws-services.html
247. Using AWS CloudTrail to Monitor Root Account Activity: https://docs.aws.amazon.com/awscloudtrail/latest/userguide/cloudtrail-user-guide.html
248. Using AWS Config to Manage Resource Tags: https://docs.aws.amazon.com/config/latest/developerguide/manage-resource-tags.html
249. Using AWS Lambda with AWS Secrets Manager: https://docs.aws.amazon.com/secretsmanager/latest/userguide/integrating_cloudwatch_logs.html
250. Using Checksums with Amazon S3: https://docs.aws.amazon.com/AmazonS3/latest/dev/UsingMD5.html
251. Using Identity-Based Policies (IAM Policies) for DynamoDB: https://docs.aws.amazon.com/amazondynamodb/latest/developerguide/using-identity-based-policies.html
252. Using Key Policies in AWS KMS: https://docs.aws.amazon.com/kms/latest/developerguide/using-policies.html
253. Using Multi-Factor Authentication (MFA) in AWS: https://docs.aws.amazon.com/IAM/latest/UserGuide/id_credentials_mfa.html
254. Using Secrets in AWS ECS: https://docs.aws.amazon.com/AmazonECS/latest/developerguide/specifying-sensitive-data-tasks.html
255. Using SSL/TLS to Encrypt a Connection to a DB Instance: https://docs.aws.amazon.com/AmazonRDS/latest/UserGuide/UsingWithRDS.SSL.html
256. Versioning in Amazon S3: https://docs.aws.amazon.com/AmazonS3/latest/dev/Versioning.html
257. VPC Endpoints Documentation: https://docs.aws.amazon.com/vpc/latest/userguide/vpc-endpoints.html
258. VPC Endpoints: https://docs.aws.amazon.com/vpc/latest/userguide/vpc-endpoints.html
259. VPC Flow Logs: https://docs.aws.amazon.com/vpc/latest/userguide/flow-logs.html
260. VPC Reachability Analyzer: https://docs.aws.amazon.com/vpc/latest/reachability/what-is-reachability-analyzer.html
261. VPN Technology: https://www.cisco.com/c/en/us/products/security/vpn-endpoint-security-clients/what-is-vpn.html
262. What Is Amazon CloudFront?: https://docs.aws.amazon.com/AmazonCloudFront/latest/DeveloperGuide/Introduction.html
263. What is AWS CloudTrail: https://docs.aws.amazon.com/awscloudtrail/latest/userguide/cloudtrail-user-guide.html.
264. What is AWS Control Tower?: https://docs.aws.amazon.com/controltower/latest/userguide/what-is-control-tower.html
265. What is IAM: https://docs.aws.amazon.com/IAM/latest/UserGuide/introduction.html
266. Windows Hardening: https://docs.microsoft.com/en-us/windows/security/threat-protection/windows-security-configuration-framework/windows-10-security-checklist
267. Working with Backup Plans: https://docs.aws.amazon.com/aws-backup/latest/devguide/creating-backup-plan.html
268. Working with Parameters: https://docs.aws.amazon.com/systems-manager/latest/userguide/param-create-cli.html
269. Zeek Network Security Monitor :https://zeek.org/

Thank you for choosing this book; your decision to invest your time and effort into this comprehensive guide reflects your commitment to achieving one of the most sought-after certifications.

I hope this book has provided you with valuable insights, clear explanations, and the confidence you need to successfully pass the AWS Certified Security - Specialty exam. Each chapter, practice question, and exam tip has been carefully crafted with your success in mind, and I trust that it has helped deepen your understanding about AWS security.

Remember, this journey doesn't end here. AWS technologies are ever-evolving, and staying updated is key to remaining a top-tier professional in cloud computing. Keep building on the knowledge you've gained, continue exploring AWS solutions, and leverage the skills you've acquired to make an impact in the cloud ecosystem.

If this guide helped you on your certification journey, I would be grateful if you could share your feedback, review the book, or recommend it to others preparing for the AWS Certified Security - Specialty exam. Your success is my greatest reward.

Best of luck with your certification, and I hope to see you thrive in your AWS career!

Thank you again for your trust in this guide.

Printed in Great Britain
by Amazon